THE GLOBAL SECURITIES MARKET

D1524449

The Global Securities Market

A History

RANALD C. MICHIE

OXFORD

UNIVERSITY PRESS

OXFORD

UNIVERSITY PRESS

Great Clarendon Street, Oxford OX2 6DP

Oxford University Press is a department of the University of Oxford.
It furthers the University's objective of excellence in research, scholarship,
and education by publishing worldwide in

Oxford New York

Auckland Cape Town Dar es Salaam Hong Kong Karachi
Kuala Lumpur Madrid Melbourne Mexico City Nairobi
New Delhi Shanghai Taipei Toronto

With offices in

Argentina Austria Brazil Chile Czech Republic France Greece
Guatemala Hungary Italy Japan Poland Portugal Singapore
South Korea Switzerland Thailand Turkey Ukraine Vietnam

Oxford is a registered trade mark of Oxford University Press
in the UK and in certain other countries

Published in the United States
by Oxford University Press Inc., New York

British Library Cataloguing in Publication Data

Data available

Library of Congress Cataloguing-in-Publication Data

Typeset by SPI Publisher Services, Pondicherry, India
Printed in Great Britain
on acid-free paper by
Antony Rowe Ltd, Chippenham, Wiltshire

ISBN 978–0–19–928061–2 (Hbk.)   978–0–19–928062–9 (Pbk.)
1 3 5 7 9 10 8 6 4 2

Contents

Preface   vi
List of Tables   xi

Introduction   1

1. Origins, Trends, and Reversals: 1100–1720   17

2. Advances and Setbacks: 1720–1815   38

3. New Beginnings and New Developments: 1815–50   60

4. Exchanges and Networks: 1850–1900   83

5. The Triumph of the Market: 1900–14   119

6. Crisis, Crash, and Control: 1914–39   155

7. Suppression, Regulation, and Evasion: 1939–70   205

8. A Transatlantic Revolution: 1970–90   253

9. A Worldwide Revolution: Securities Markets from 1990   297

Conclusion   333

Notes   341
Bibliography   376
Index   389

Preface

This book is the culmination of reading, writing, and researching financial history for over thirty years. This process started at Aberdeen University in 1971 when I began a Ph.D. on the Scottish stock exchanges in the nineteenth century. It then continued at Durham University from 1974 when I began to teach a course on International Economic History. This first taught me the practical importance of securities markets within financial systems whilst the second made me aware of the forces of globalization. Instead of looking at the Scottish stock exchanges in isolation, taking a particularly institutional and national approach, I started to employ the analytical tools of comparative economic history and to search for interactions between markets and financial systems, between institutions and markets, and between different markets. In turn that made clear the importance of the City of London as a financial centre both within Britain and internationally. The outcome was a twin-track approach to the study of financial history. The first was to pursue the comparative aspect leading to an in-depth study of the London and New York stock exchanges using the archives of both institutions. That was a major turning point in my research and led to the book I am most proud of. The second was to investigate the history of the City of London as a way into an understanding of the international financial system. That led to a book on the City of London as a financial centre. Two of these aspects came together with my next big project, which was a history of the London Stock Exchange. At the same time I became increasingly aware of the European dimension to financial history through the conferences hosted by the European Association of Banking History, and the edited volumes that arose from these meetings. These brought to my attention the major differences between the Anglo-American financial system and that of continental Europe, where banking took a different form in many countries. In addition, location within a Department of History from 1985 forced me to recognize the significance of government as an influence over financial markets, and how legislation and other forms of intervention could mould the way securities markets evolved and performed in different countries and at different times. The consequence of all this is this present book.

As I was writing up the research into both stock exchanges and the City of London I yearned for a book that would give me a deeper understanding of the global context and provide the longer term background. None was available though some of the studies on securities markets and stock exchanges undertaken at the end of the nineteenth and the early twentieth century in the United States did provide invaluable insights. Consequently, I decided to produce a book myself on the history of the global securities market, connecting the medieval to the present and covering the entire world. This turned out to be a task beyond my capabilities, as I came to recognize in the course of writing the present book. Slowly I became aware that such a history required the expertise of both an accomplished historian and an economist, the practical knowledge of a banker and a broker, and a command of the literature of financial, business, and economic history. The more I wrote, the more I noticed my own ignorance and the limitations of my analytical skill. However, I was unwilling to compromise by restricting the time period covered, the countries included, or the type of securities discussed. My aim was to include both stocks and bonds, to begin at the beginning and reach the present, and to discuss the world as a whole, and that is what I have tried to do throughout. I am only too well aware that the result is imperfect, and that this will be obviously so to anyone with an expertise in the different branches of the subject. I can only hope that the errors are not too serious and the argument reasonably convincing. Certainly, over the years I have felt that there is a serious deficiency in the understanding of the role played by the global securities market in the development of the world economy over the last millenium. It seems to have been written out of the account and its place supplanted by banks and governments. I can only hope that this book will awaken a recognition that securities markets are much less about headline catching events such as crises, manipulation, speculation, and fraud and much more about the mobilization of savings for investment and the ability to move money around the world in such a way as to produce equilibrium. Events such as the South Sea Bubble and the Wall Street Crash may catch the public's attention, as do the activities of people such as John Law or J. P. Morgan, but the stuff of history is the collective deeds of millions of people over hundreds of years, and that is more true in the world of finance than anywhere else. The history of financial centres such as Wall Street and the City of London is about the dull routine of work and the impersonal forces of technology and legislation rather than about panics, manias, and corruption, though that is what attracts the headlines. We need to understand the former as well as the latter if we are to be aware of how the financial world of today came into being, what has been achieved, what has been lost, and how we can ensure that the disasters of the past can be avoided. In doing so we need to accept that there is no stable vantage point from which we can observe the past for everything is constantly in flux.

Finally, this is a curious book in terms of sources. As it is based heavily on work of my own which is already published or in the process of appearing,

I have not normally included direct references to those books and articles. This affects particularly what I have included on the British, European, and north American stock exchanges in the nineteenth century, as well as the London Stock Exchange and the City of London since 1700. Where I have included material on these areas that does not appear in my published work I have fully referenced the sources used. This is especially the case with European securities markets in the nineteenth century and the US securities market before 1850. In addition, the pre-1700 portions of this book are almost entirely new as is the non-European/non-north American discussion for both the nineteenth and twentieth centuries. Finally, the post-1914 non-British portions of the book are also largely new, especially that dealing with developments in the United States, whilst I have relied on reports in the *Financial Times* for recent developments. Consequently, the reader should assume that where no footnotes occur the material is derived from my published work and should turn to that for further information and original sources. Otherwise, I have tried to be meticulous in referencing the work upon which I have based my evidence and conclusions. It goes without saying that a book of this kind rests upon the scholarship of generations of writers and without their efforts it could not have been produced. I only hope that I have fully acknowledged what they have done and not misrepresented their conclusions. Evidence not assertion has been a key element of what I have tried to do and that relies heavily in producing a paper trail so that the disbelieving can check for accuracy of detail and interpretation.

Of my own work the ones listed below are those most relevant to this study, both in terms of the information they contain and the analysis they develop.

'The Social Web of Investment in the Nineteenth Century', *Revue Internationale d'Histoire de la Banque*, 18 (1979).

Money, Mania and Markets: Investment, Company Formation and the Stock Exchange in Nineteenth-Century Scotland (Edinburgh, 1981).

'Options, Concessions, Syndicates, and the Provision of Venture Capital, 1880–1913', *Business History*, 23 (1981).

'The London Stock Exchange and the British Securities Market, 1850–1914', *Economic History Review*, 38 (1985).

'The London and New York Stock Exchanges, 1850–1914', *Journal of Economic History*, 46 (1986).

The London and New York Stock Exchanges 1850–1914 (London, 1987).

'Different in Name Only? The London Stock Exchange and Foreign Bourses c.1850–1914', *Business History*, 30 (1988).

'Dunn Fisher & Co. in the City of London, 1906–1914', *Business History*, 30 (1988).

'The Finance of Innovation in Late Victorian and Edwardian Britain: Possibilities and Constraints', *Journal of European Economic History*, 17 (1988).

'The Canadian Securities Market, 1850–1914', *Business History Review*, 62 (1988).

'The London Stock Exchange and the British Economy, 1870–1930', in J. J. Van Helten and Y. Cassis (eds.), *Capitalism in a Mature Economy* (London, 1989).

The City of London: Continuity and Change Since 1850 (London, 1992).

'The Development of the Stock Market', in *Palgrave Dictionary of Money and Finance* (London, 1992).

Financial and Commercial Services (Oxford, 1994).

'The London and Provincial Stock Exchanges, 1799–1973: Separation, Integration, Rivalry, Unity', in D. H. Aldcroft and A. Slavin (eds.), *Enterprise and Management* (Aldershot, 1995).

'The City of London: Functional and Spatial Unity in the Nineteenth Century', in H. A. Diedericks and D. Reader (eds.), *Cities of Finance* (North Holland: Amsterdam, 1996).

'Friend or Foe: Information Technology and the London Stock Exchange Since 1850', *Journal of Historical Geography*, 23 (1997).

'The Invisible Stabiliser: Asset Arbitrage and the International Monetary System Since 1700', *Financial History Review*, 15 (1998).

'Anglo-American Financial Systems, *c.*1800–1939', in P. Cottrell and J. Reis (eds.), *Finance and the Making of the Modern Capitalist World, 1750–1931* (Madrid, 1998).

'Insiders, Outsiders and the Dynamics of Change in the City of London Since 1900', *Journal of Contemporary History*, 33 (1998).

The London Stock Exchange: A History (Oxford, 1999, reprinted with an Epilogue, 2001).

'One World or Many Worlds? Markets, Banks, and Communications, 1850s–1990s', in T. de Graaf, J. Jonker, and J. J. Mabron (eds.), *European Banking Overseas, 19th–20th centuries* (Amsterdam, 2002).

'Banks and Securities Markets, 1870–1914', in D. J. Forsyth and D. Verdier (eds.), *The Origins of National Financial Systems: Gershenkron Revisited* (London, 2003).

'The City of London and British Banking, 1900–1939', in C. Wrigley (ed.), *A Companion to Early Twentieth-Century Britain* (Oxford, 2003).

'The City of London and the British Government: The Changing Relationship', in R. C. Michie and P. A. Williamson (eds.), *The British Government and the City of London in the Twentieth Century* (Oxford, 2004).

'A Financial Phoenix: The City of London in the Twentieth Century', in Y. Cassis and E. Bussierre (eds.), *London and Paris as International Financial Centres* (Oxford, 2005).

'Der Aufsteig der City of London als Finanzplatz: Vom Inlandsgeschaft zum Offshore-Centrum?', in C. M. Merki (hg.), *Europas Finanzzentren: Geschichte und Bedeutung im 20. Jahrhundert* (Frankfurt, 2005), 23–51.

'The City of London as a European Financial Centre in the Twentieth Century', in *Europaische Finanzplatze im Wettbewerb* (Stuttgart, 2006).

'The City of London as a Global Financial Centre, 1880–1939: Finance, Foreign Exchange and the First World War', in P. L. Cottrell, E. Lange, and U. Olsson (eds.), *Centres and Peripheries in Banking* (forthcoming).

'The City of London and the British Regions: From medieval to modern', in W. Lancaster *et al. Regional History* (forthcoming).

'The London Stock Exchange and the British Government in the Twentieth Century' in S. Battilossi and J. Reis, *The State and Financial Services: Regulation, Ownership and Deregulation* (forthcoming).

'Stock Exchanges and the Finance of Economic Growth, 1830–1939', in P. Cottrell, G. Feldman, and J. Reis (eds.), *Finance and the Making of Modern Capitalism* (forthcoming).

In the preparation of this book, I would also like to thank Christine Woodhead for her editorial skills and for forcing me to make clear what I was trying to say. Finally, I would like to thank my family for the forbearance shown to me during the time it took me to write this book. Writing is a lonely and selfish act as it occupies both time and the mind to the exclusion of all else. In particular I would like to dedicate this book to my eldest son, Alexander Uisdean Michie, as his sporting priorities were never mine, but led to achievements I was proud of.

List of Tables

I.1. Global Securities Outstanding: Market Value 1990–2003   4

I.2. Stock Market Capitalisation as a Percentage of GDP   7

I.3. Total Value of Equity Trading on Regulated Stock Exchanges, 2004 7

4.1. World railway mileage (km)   87

4.2. Securities as a proportion of national assets, 1850–1900   89

5.1. Securities as a proportion of national assets, 1912–14(2)   126

5.2. The leading stock exchanges in the world (*c.*1914)   136

5.3. Composition of corporate stock outstanding:
     United States, 1860–1912   149

6.1. Inter-allied war debts in 1919: Lending and borrowing (£ million) 168

6.2. Securities as a proportion of national assets, 1927–30   174

6.3. Securities as a proportion of national assets, 1937–40   200

7.1. Securities as a proportion of national assets, 1939–70   215

List of Tables

Introduction

JUSTIFICATION

The study of the development of securities markets was long neglected, beyond histories of individual stock exchanges or studies of particular events that caught the public's attention. The state of financial history as a whole was very similar until the 1960s, when it began to attract attention in academic circles, with the pioneering work of Rondo Cameron and his associates. However, that was almost exclusively focused on banking. As banks were regarded as the central elements in a financial system it was perfectly acceptable to confine the study of such systems to that of banking alone. Hence the focus on comparisons between Germany's universal banks, Britain's branch banks, and US unitary banks, and these formed the basis of the conclusions drawn about the superiority or inferiority of entire financial systems. To many observers, whether from the left or the right of the political spectrum, securities markets were considered little more than centres of gambling, where speculators bet on the rise and fall of prices, and were exposed to the fraudulent practices of unscrupulous intermediaries. As Raines recently noted '[i]n popular imagery, stock markets represent the most exciting aspect of capitalism...where soaring bull markets bring sudden wealth only to subsequently wipe it out during spectacular crashes with the bursting of speculative bubbles'.[1] Even to most economists securities markets were not worthy of serious study, being more symbols of popular capitalism than the substance of complex and sophisticated financial systems. What mattered was the process of capital formation, which involved consideration of the collection, mobilization, and use of savings for productive purposes rather than financial market activity that produced no obvious or measurable gain for society. As the function of the securities market was only to provide a forum for trading securities once they had been issued, it was the issue of those securities that attracted what interest there was, rather than what happened afterwards. At best securities markets were seen as rather marginal to the whole process.[2]

This verdict of marginality stemmed from the recognition that business across the world raised very little of the finance required for growth and development through the issue of stocks and bonds. Instead, the principal sources of finance were reinvested earnings and bank borrowing, whilst securities were issued to capitalize an existing earnings stream rather than contribute to the creation of new ones. It was recognized that securities markets did perform a number of specific functions but these were more in the realm of transmitting signals through their pricing mechanism or facilitating the transfer of control in a dynamic corporate economy rather than making a serious contribution to the finance of economic growth. There appeared to many almost an inverse relationship between the size and importance of the securities market and a successful economic perform-ance, as in the case of comparisons involving Britain and Germany or the United States and Japan. The ability of banks to mobilize, direct, and manage savings appeared to economists to make a much more obvious contribution to individual and collective prosperity that the often random nature of buying and selling stocks and bonds on securities markets. This again made banks the centrepieces of any financial system rather than securities markets.[3]

To others securities markets were more than marginal, being positively harmful. Trading in the secondary markets was often seen as having a rather negative impact on economic growth through its destruction of savings in wasteful speculation, its destabilizing effect on the pattern of investment over time, and the distortions it created in the flow of funds. The eminent American economist Robert Schiller recently encapsulated the dangers inher-ent in securities markets in a book entitled *Irrational exuberance*. Securities markets were prone to speculative outbursts, of which the Mississippi bubble in Paris, the railway mania in London, the Wall Street crash in New York, and the worldwide dotcom boom were the most prominent examples. These speculative bubbles were characterized by temporarily high prices for securities, sustained by investor enthusiasm rather than fundamentals. There was always some event to trigger this enthusiasm, such as new discoveries or technological change, but at their root was a combination of unrealistic expectations at a time of easy money. These bubbles were then followed by inevitable collapse as prices reached unsupportable levels and selling began to outweigh buying. In turn that had enormous consequences for the regular supply of credit and capital as banks collapsed because borrowers defaulted on loans taken out to buy securities and savers withdrew their deposits, leaving the entire financial system in a highly weakened state for years to come. Not only was there little to show for the investments made but what had been achieved was only at some considerable cost to the smooth operation of the economy. It was the steady reinvestment of the savings made out of income that produced the real long-term gains both to individuals and the economy. Though it is recognized that securities markets as a whole do make a contribution to economic growth, especially in the ability to mobilize funds for new developments, there clearly exist serious doubts among economists over this contribution.[4] Kay sought to explain and defend the importance of markets, arguing for their superiority over central planning by governments, despite imperfections. However, the securities market is the exception.

Most transactions in securities markets are not about sharing or spreading risks: they are like transactions in the betting shop.... Securities markets are better described as arenas for sophisticated professional gambling than as institutions which minimize the costs of risk bearing and allocate capital efficiently among different lines of business.

Finally, in referring to the recent dot.com or TMT (Technology, Media, and Telecommunications) boom his verdict was equally scathing. 'It is impossible to have lived through that period and believe that the securities markets allocate capital efficiently.'[5]

Consequently, from the standpoint of many academic economists as well as the public at large, securities markets were of rather dubious value and certainly could not be ranked along with governments and banks as making an important contribution to the progress of mankind. In fact, they could be seen as having the exactly opposite effect in many instances. However, this view assesses securities markets solely in relation to the needs of business in its quest for capital. If an alternative perspective is followed that recognizes both the needs of the lender and the investor and the importance of the link to money, then the central role played by securities markets becomes readily apparent. At all times those accumulating savings needed an outlet that suited their purposes, which ranged from small amounts invested for short periods to large amounts over long periods. The more complex and sophisticated the economy the greater the need there was for a financial system that continually responded to the ebb and flow of credit and capital both over time and space and between individuals, institutions, and businesses. By providing a flexible interface between borrowers and lenders and between credit and capital the securities market ensured that the needs of all could be met in a way that maximized the returns on savings and minimized the risks involved. This revisionist view has led to a reinterpretation of the role played by securities markets. Certainly, among the more recent work of economists there has been an attempt to emphasize the importance of securities markets within financial systems and the positive contribution they make to economic growth.[6] Inevitably in any market economy mismatches occur within the financial system, leading to speculative peaks and troughs. However, the most pronounced of these were often due to the actions of government rather than inherent flaws within the market. What may have appeared superficially as irrational exuberance or gamblers' folly was actually the product of market manipulation engineered by governments for their own ends or flawed policy decisions that produced short-term benefits but serious long-term problems. Before dismissing securities markets as flawed, and the most obvious weakness within a market economy, and thus justifying measures to curb or control it both nationally and internationally, its history needs to be understood from all angles and in the context of change over time and between countries. Certainly by the end of the 20th century and the beginning of the 21st securities were rapidly expanding in terms of amount and importance, with bonds rather than stocks dominant (see Table 1.1).

The actions of government clearly contributed to the environment within which financial systems operated, including securities markets, especially when the consequences of war are considered. The total cost of the First World War is put at $80 billion and that of Second at $400 billion, excluding the effects on Russia. In addition, governments over the ages intervened actively in the financial system whether it was the coinage of medieval Europe or the monetary policies operated after the Second World War. The number of central banks rose from 18 in 1900 to 59 in 1950 and then to 172 in 1999. The peak of peacetime intervention was probably reached around 1970 considering the role played by governments both domestically and their involvement in managing the international financial system. One indication of that power which is of particular importance to the securities markets was the rise, fall, and rise again of international investment. Governments the world over actively intervened to prevent such flows when it was seen to run contrary to national interests, as they perceived them to be. Foreign assets as a percentage of GDP rose from 6.9% in 1870 to 17.5% in 1913 and then fell

Table I.1 Global securities outstanding: market value 1990–2003 US$ trillion

Year	Total	Stocks	Bonds
1990	US$ 27.2 trillion	US$9.4 trillion (34.6%)	US$17.8 trillion (65.4%)
2003	US$ 82.0 trillion	US$31.2 trillion (38.0%)	US$50.8 trillion (62.0%)

Source: Bank for International Settlements, *Statistics*, 2006; *World Federation of Exchanges, The Significance of the Exchange Industry, July 2004*.

back, being only 8.4% in 1930 and 4.9% in 1945, after two world wars and a world depression. In an era of managed economies post-war recovery was slow, only reaching 17.7%, the pre-World War I level, in 1980. However, after that there was a rapid acceleration, reaching 56.8% in 1995, reflecting the dismantling of barriers by national governments.[7] It is thus essential to take account of the direct and indirect role played by governments in the development of securities markets.

Certainly, since the 1970s there has been a growing recognition that it is essential to study whole financial systems, rather than limit attention to one single component, and to be aware of the context within which they operated. This includes the study of the development and role of securities markets, if any real understanding of the way financial systems operate is to be achieved. Securities markets have played different roles in individual countries at different times, reflecting the way they are organized, their relationship to other parts of the financial system, and the effects of government intervention. One has only to consider here the long-term consequences for the US securities market of the Glass–Steagall Act passed in the 1930s. Only then can we reach conclusions about not only the role of securities markets in promoting or facilitating economic growth in general but also the consequences for national economies of the particular characteristics of that securities market. Also, the boundaries of such a study can no longer be confined to national borders for the increasing globalization of the world economy, and the recognition of the influence that external forces have upon determining national exchange rates and national interest rates makes it essential to place national securities markets in an international context. The characteristics and role of any national securities market were partly determined by the position they occupied within the worldwide movements of credit and capital. In this respect the long nineteenth century, 1815–1914, may provide more valuable pointers for the future than the more immediate past, conditioned as that was by restrictions and controls. A full understanding of the past can inform present and future decisions, through the ability to identify those features that were most important and their consequences.[8]

To achieve that end it is vital to place the development of securities markets in their appropriate historical setting and use comparisons as an analytical tool in order to produce conclusions of value today. Comparisons are immensely valuable in trying to understand why financial systems differ and to assess what the implications of these differences were for economic performance. However, care must be taken to ensure that like is being compared with like. The more complex the systems being compared the greater the risk that this is not so. It is essential to distinguish between those securities markets that served corporate equity and those for government debt, whilst recognizing that some catered for both stocks and bonds. There is also the need to recognize the difference between the role and importance of a securities market located in a major financial centre and those serving the interests of local investors in local companies. A securities market located in a major financial centre of international importance was as much part of the money market as the capital market, and this exerted a major influence on the functions that it performed. It is thus essential to identify these financial centres, recognize how they have developed, and assess the position they occupied within the global economy.[9] There must be constant recognition of such situations and circumstances because they help to explain why differences exist between countries and over time, and the relative importance of securities markets. This can be seen from the experience of the twentieth century where the importance of securities markets was very varied both chronologically and spatially. Though no comparisons are ever ideal, because there are so many variables at work, the very attempt to compare and contrast can be especially revealing about the causes and consequences of particular organizational traits (see Table I.2.)

Once securities markets moved beyond informal and irregular markets their organizational form becomes significant. The unique circumstantial features of each securities market interact with other components of the financial system so contributing to its further development. Superficially, securities markets can be seen as constant over time and common across countries because they simply provided places where stocks and bonds were bought and sold. However, to adopt that view would be akin to confining medicine to the study of the skeleton and ignoring all the other features of the human body, including the functioning of the brain. The way the trading of stocks and bonds was organized differed enormously over the centuries and between countries. We need to understand why stock exchanges were set up, what they did, how they operated, and why they changed. Why did different institutional arrangements arise for what was essentially the same purpose market? Why were restrictions placed on access to the market and what consequences did they have? What was the relationship between stock exchanges and the securities market as a whole? Why did governments impose controls and restrictions on the operation of the securities market? What were the results of the rules and regulations under which stock exchanges operated for the efficiency of the securities market as a whole? These are major questions of continuing significance as stock exchanges around the world search for a mode of ownership and control that satisfies all. Clearly there is a world of difference between the likes of the New York Stock Exchange on the

Table I.2 Stock market capitalization as a percentage of GDP

Country	1913	1938	1970	1999
World	56%	65%	55%	97%
UK	109%	192%	199%	225%
France	78%	19%	16%	117%
Germany	45%	18%	16%	67%
USA	41%	56%	66%	152%
Japan	49%	181%	23%	95%
India	2%	7%	6%	46%

Source: R. G. Rajan and L. Zingales, *The Great Reversals: The politics of financial development in the 20th century* [Paris 2000] pp 36, 39.

Table I.3 Total value of equity trading on regulated stock exchanges, 2004

Region/Exchange	Total (US$ Trillion)	Percentage
North America	21.6	51.3
(NYSE)	(11.6)	(27.6)
(NASDAQ)	(8.8)	(20.9)
Europe	13.2	31.4
(LSE)	(5.2)	(12.4)
(EURONEXT)	(2.5)	(5.9)
(DEUTSCHE BORSE)	(1.5)	(3.6)
Asia (excl. Middle East)	6.2	14.5
(TSE)	(3.2)	(7.6)
Australia/NZ	0.5	1.2
Africa/Middle East	0.4	1.0
South/Central America	0.2	0.5
WORLD	42.1	100

Source: World Federation of Exchanges: *Annual Report and Statistics*, 2004.

one hand and a stock exchange located in an emerging market on the other, even if only in coping with a hugely different turnover (see Table 1.3).

There is also the wider question of whether securities markets actually promote economic growth over time, within particular countries or globally. Undoubtedly, there is a link between a developed financial system and the level and pace of economic progress. Relatively sophisticated financial systems are necessary for the process of indigenously financed economic growth but do they actually initiate the process? It is not surprising to find a developed securities market within an advanced economy but was its presence there one of cause or effect? Particularly interesting is the variation in development of securities markets between different countries at a similar level of economic development. Why these differences exist and what were their consequences need examination. Only through that process can cause be distinguished from effect in the role played by the securities market in the process of economic growth. Is a well-developed securities market the product of a more sophisticated financial system or was that found within a highly developed banking system, incorporating the use of securities? Such a question lies at the heart of any comparison between the Anglo-American financial system, where securities markets play a central role, and that in continental Europe and Japan, where banks have been dominant. The assumption of superiority for either banks or securities markets cannot be justified without cross-country comparisons over a lengthy time period. Was either of these the product of the successes or failures of the other, and what role did government play in the process? These are questions of some importance considering the convergence of banking and broking worldwide and the existence of financial businesses operating on a global basis in a multitude of different activities and markets.[10]

ORIENTATION[11]

Transferable securities first existed in Italian city-states in medieval times. Repeated wars waged by relatively stable nation states provided ample need for governments to seek new means of financing their requirements, and one of the methods used was the creation of a permanent funded debt. This debt was attractive to investors as its yield was guaranteed by the state, but its indefinite duration meant that only a few could afford to purchase it with no date of redemption. A similar situation existed with joint-stock enterprise where the holder of the stock was guaranteed a share of the year's earnings, in the form of the annual dividend. The solution adopted for both govern-ment bonds and corporate stock was to make them transferable. A government could borrow in perpetuity, committed only to pay a fixed rate of interest, whilst the holder was at liberty to sell to another, at the prevailing market price. Similarly, a company obtained the capital it required whilst agreeing only to share any profits generated. However, these stocks and bonds were issued in relatively small amounts, were held by a very few people, and generated sporadic and limited trading. This did not provide the conditions necessary for the appearance of specialized intermediaries, let alone specific markets. Instead, what transfers were required could be perfectly well handled by private negotiation or as one of the many items bought and sold in the mercantile exchanges. It was only from the seventeenth century onwards, with the growing volume of negotiable instruments representing national indebtedness and transferable stocks, that the amount of trading generated justified the beginnings of professional mediation and organized markets. What was being established were markets in claims to future income whether this represented governments shifting the costs of current warfare onto generations of unborn citizens or commercial ventures spreading the costs of financing an expensive and risky undertaking among a wide body of investors. Both these types of securities generated extensive market activity. The very size of national debts created problems of matching buyers and sellers that could only be solved through organized markets. Whilst the size of the capital required by the joint-stock companies was tiny in comparison to the needs of government, turnover in their securities was often high as each rumour about current or future prospects produced speculative trading.

By the seventeenth century Amsterdam had become the principal centre for securities trading, with considerable activity in both domestic and foreign stocks. This volume of activity generated a group of specialist intermediaries who developed many of the modern techniques of stock exchange dealing, such as time bargains, price lists, and dealing for the account. These were then copied in other stock markets, especially London in the eighteenth century, aided by the migration there of a number of Amsterdam brokers. However, what Amsterdam lacked was any formal organization of this stock market. The brokers and their clients congregated around one of the forty-six pillars of Amsterdam's general exchange building, which inhibited the development of the rules and regulations necessary for the orderly conduct of business and left them exposed to the menace of defaults, which undermined the trust element crucial to the conduct of business. Instead it was in Paris in 1724 that a formal stock exchange was first established, in the wake of the speculative boom inspired by John Law's financial schemes. This stock exchange allowed entry only to specialist intermediaries, called *agents de change*, and had a code of conduct. However, due to government limitations on its membership a large alternative market continued to flourish in the streets outside the stock exchange building, representing the first fragmentation of the securities market because of institutional developments.

During the French Revolution and Napoleonic Wars, securities markets were seriously disrupted by warfare and inflation, with the international trading of securities almost non-existent. Nevertheless, the London Stock Exchange emerged at this time whilst securities markets took root in the newly independent United States. The nineteenth century saw a great expansion in issues of transferable securities both by governments and by corporate enterprise. Altogether, it has been estimated that there were £32.6 billion (nominal value) of securities outstanding in the world by

1910, owned by around 20 million investors. There was thus an increasing need for a securities market where stocks and bonds could be traded both in established financial centres and around the world. However, the distribution of both securities and investors was little related to either geography or population. Without organized markets there was little incentive to issue or hold securities, rather than the assets which they represented but, without the existence of such securities, there could be no markets. It took time to acquaint both investors and borrowers with the benefits of securities, especially their ease of transfer without the need to disturb underlying operations. Consequently, it tended to be the most developed countries that possessed organized exchanges, educated investors, and experienced borrowers, and so it was there that securities were most frequently both issued and bought. In turn, the securities owned by investors in the richest nations not only represented assets of their own countries but also those of other places to a growing extent.

Within this global securities market there existed a wide diversity of stock exchanges by the First World War. At the simplest level were those meeting a largely local need, providing a market for investors from a limited area in a restricted range of securities. Numerous local stock exchanges were formed during the second-half of the nineteenth century and each of these provided a convenient forum for the securities of the growing numbers of local joint-stock companies. However, investors were interested in a far wider range of securities than just those issued by local enterprise. The result was that these local stock exchanges both lost and gained business as orders were sent to markets offering a different choice whilst others were received for their specialities. Increasingly, local exchanges were integrated into national markets so that they catered less and less for the general needs of their local investors but offered more and more an active forum in the securities of a limited number of companies operating in one or a few particular areas. They could even become internationally important as in the case of the South African and Australian stock exchanges with their gold-mining stocks, for these were held extensively across the world. Incorporating the functions of a local exchange for the vicinity within which they operated, but offering far more than that, were the national exchanges. These national stock exchanges attracted orders from throughout the country, and concentrated upon securities that commanded a wide following and were actively traded. Initially this meant government bonds as these were held generally and required a central market, where they could be bought and sold. Without rapid communications this meant one place, frequently the capital city such as Berlin, London, Madrid, Paris, or Vienna, though it could also be the major commercial and financial centre where that was not the capital, as with

Johannesburg, Melbourne, Montreal, New York, and St Petersburg. In the course of the nineteenth century the development of large-scale joint-stock enterprise with a national appeal and widespread ownership, such as the railways, considerably increased the volume and variety of securities traded on a national basis. At the same time improvements in communications, especially the telegraph and the telephone, allowed them to attract orders more easily from all over the country, which could result in business for their markets or be distributed to the most appropriate local exchange. The membership of the principal stock exchange in each country came to act as central coordinators of the securities market, as with Berlin in Germany and Milan in Italy after unification. As well as providing a central exchange and clearing-house, the principal exchange also acted as the main link with the banks and the money market, for it possessed the most actively traded securities with the greatest appeal, ideal for either temporary holding or for collateral purposes. Thus, the difference between the local and national exchanges was not just one of the volume and variety of business, but a fundamental difference in the uses to which the securities traded were put. The national exchange provided the most liquid market in which money could be readily employed or securities quickly sold, and so it attracted that kind of business from all over the country. In north America, Canadian banks did business in New York, rather than Montreal or Toronto, for that very reason.

This specialization was also carried a stage further with the development of exchanges with an importance far beyond their national boundaries. With the revolution in communications that came with the international telegraph from the mid-nineteenth century onwards, the barriers that had preserved the independence and isolation of national exchanges were progressively removed, leading slowly to the creation of a world market for securities. Although many securities were of interest to only a small and localized group others came to attract a following from investors throughout the world, especially the major issues made by governments and railways. Securities quoted on each stock exchange became of interest to foreign investors, and so attracted external buying and selling. Increasingly, buying and selling between different stock exchanges, or arbitrage, ensured that the same security commanded an equivalent price on whatever market it was traded. Although most of the major stock exchanges of Western Europe developed a trade in foreign securities, often with particular special-ities by activity or country, it was London and Paris that became the major international markets, attracting business worldwide in an enormous variety of issues. Paris tended to specialize in government bonds and fulfill the role of the central securities market for continental Europe and the Mediterranean area, whilst London emerged as the major market for corporate stocks and bonds covering not only the securities of its extensive empire but also issues made by the United States, Argentina, and Japan. In north America, New York became the dominant securities market.

Consequently, though markets traded different securities and met the needs of different investors, their trading was increasingly conditioned by forces beyond the confines of their own locality, or even country or continent. Some became specialist markets commanding a region or activity, whilst others gained a position as international centres, but all responded to world developments and, in turn, influenced trends. By 1914 a reordering had taken place in which the old stock exchanges continued to flourish but the functions they performed had been altered, whilst new stock exchanges had been established which both competed with the established institutions and supplemented the market they provided, reflecting the rapid growth in importance of securities in finance and investment. With international portfolio investment on a rising tide, governments finding new uses for funded debt, and business increasingly converting to the joint-stock form and the issue of securities, there was every sign that the fundamental forces underlying the growth of stock exchanges would continue into the twentieth century. From humble beginnings the global securities market had emerged as central to the dynamic expansion of a global economy. Without their existence governments and railroads would have been deprived of finance, and the integration of the world economy through trade, migration, and investment would have been considerably slowed down, if not stopped. By the beginning of the twentieth century the influence of stock exchanges was becoming ever more pervasive as all types of business reorganized themselves into the joint-stock form and appealed to investors for support.

However, after 1914 there was a progressive undermining of the role of the securities market within the economic system, both in individual economies and internationally. With the outbreak of the First World War all major stock exchanges closed temporarily as financial markets tried to cope with the consequences of the disruption caused by such major military conflict. When the stock exchanges did reopen it was often under government supervision, as each country attempted to control the financial system in order to maximize finance for the war effort. Consequently, when the war ended in 1918 not only had a number of stock exchanges disappeared, as with those in Russia with the October revolution of 1917, but the climate of economic liberalism, within which the global securities market had developed and flourished, had begun to fade. Nevertheless most stock exchanges soon recovered their pre-war position aided by the needs of governments to fund massive debts and business to finance itself, along with the resumption of international lending and borrowing. The crash of 1929 and the end of the gold standard in 1931 did more than bring this general recovery to an end. Stock exchanges were blamed for the ensuing economic depression of the 1930s, rather than being seen as the victims of underlying economic instability, with the result that there was a flurry of legislation aimed at controlling their operations. In 1933–4 the US government established a Securities and Exchange Commission, to police new issues and secondary trading and, with the Glass–Steagall Act, prohibited the direct involvement of commercial banks in the securities market, which had grown as a result of the government's own wartime need for finance through bond sales. In Germany economic collapse was followed by a prolonged period of stock exchange closure, and then a complete reorganization of the system by the government in 1934, when the stock exchange was reduced to minor importance. Elsewhere wars and revolutions led to the temporary or permanent closure of stock exchanges. Internationally, the imposition and enforcement of exchange controls, with the collapse of the world monetary system, created major barriers between countries and severely impeded the operation of a global securities market. Although most stock exchanges continued to provide an important service as a market for government and corporate securities, political and economic nationalism severed the free flow of funds internationally upon which many stock exchanges had thrived, whilst domestically there was a growing preference for state provision or bank financing.

This setback was then compounded by the Second World War. Following on from the 1930s depression, when capitalism itself was blamed for the world's economic problems, the era after 1945 saw a greatly enhanced role for the state. In socialist countries the securities market simply ceased to exist with central planning replacing financial markets. Even in market economies, governments became much more involved in overall planning, which included the direction of financial resources. Many industries, like entire railway systems, were nationalized and their securities ceased to be traded on stock exchanges. At the same time the financial intermediation that was required was dominated by banks rather than markets. Only banks possessed the manpower and structure to cope with the huge increase in government regulation, both domestically with complex taxation and internationally with exchange controls. Thus, it was banks that dominated global financial flows and the domestic financing of business. For some twenty-five years after the Second World War securities markets appear to have settled for a minor role in the world's financial systems, whether at the national or international level. However, beginning in the 1960s, and gathering pace thereafter, government control over both national financial systems and global money and capital flows began to collapse. Market forces began to revive, bringing opportunities for the global securities market. At the very least a search by investors for securities that could cope with the effects of prolonged inflation directed their attention to corporate stocks rather than government bonds. The gradual abandonment of exchange controls also led to revival of an international market in securities, as financial institutions began to search for attractive investments beyond national boundaries. Finally, the recognition that nationalized industries had failed to deliver their promised benefits led to a programme of disposals from the 1980s onwards, creating many new securities in the process. With the collapse of Communist economies around the world this was given a further boost as the new regimes sold off underperforming state assets for whatever they would bring. This produced greatly increased activity on a number of long-established stock exchanges and the creation of numerous new ones, whether formally organized or comprising electronic networks. By the beginning of the twenty-first century the global securities market had reclaimed its position within national and international financial systems.

Nevertheless, the conditions within which the global securities market operated were now radically different. The continuing development of communications and computing technology had made possible the creation of electronic marketplaces linking participants around the world. No longer was a physical trading-floor a necessity, endangering the position occupied by many of the world's major stock exchanges, and leading to the closure of numerous local securities markets. The electronic revolution also combined with the active intervention of governments around the world to remove any restraints to trade, including the rules and regulations of many of these long-established exchanges. Since 1914, and especially since 1945, stock exchanges had become much more bureaucratic organizations occupying quasi-official status in the regulation of financial systems. As this was not compatible with the more open economies of the late twentieth century, formally organized stock exchanges lost out to informal markets and electronic trading, and had to fight not only to recover their position but also to retain what they still had. Consequently, though the last two decades of the twentieth century witnessed a dramatic revival in the fortunes of world securities markets, they also created serious challenges for existing stock exchanges. The outcome was a fundamental change in the composition and structure of the global securities market. No longer were stock exchanges the key components as they had been a century before. There now existed banks and brokers with a global network of operations capable of internalizing many of the functions of not only the securities market but also those for money, capital, and foreign exchange. This posed a serious threat to the power of both national stock exchanges and also national governments. The response of securities markets was to internationalize their operations and for stock exchanges to internationalize their institutional structure. In contrast, governments were much less willing to abandon national controls in favour of international regulations.

Over the long history of the global securities markets there has been a constant tension between them and governments. Government actions underpinned the very development of securities markets and also subjected them to suppression, regulation, and control. This intervention was driven by a variety of motives ranging from simple self-interest, when the interests of the market clashed with those of government, and better regulation, in the interests of investor protection and financial stability. The results of this intervention were to change the nature of national financial systems and both assist and impede the creation of a global securities market. This complex and ever-changing relationship between securities markets and governments continues to be an important element today. As Oxelheim concluded, 'Although some elements in the liberalization may be seen as irreversible, others may still lend themselves to re-regulation, thus engendering a great leap downwards in global welfare'.[12] Equally important was the role of the securities market within the financial system, especially the relationship between it and banks. Banks and securities markets competed with each other, as they both served investors and borrowers, and complemented each other, as banks needed the flexibility that markets gave to assets whilst markets needed the business of the banks. As the financial system became ever larger and more complex further tensions developed, through financial institutions that were large enough to internalize some transactions but not others. Another area of tension was between securities markets and stock exchanges. Again the relationship was complex, as stock exchanges contributed much to the creation of an orderly market, and thus its appeal and importance, whilst at the same time maintaining barriers to entry and other restrictions. At no time were markets and exchanges identical. There were always both securities and participants excluded from the stock exchanges which had major implications for the securities market as a whole. Finally, there was always the tension between national securities markets and the global marketplace. On the one hand trading between separate securities markets generated much activity, so benefiting those participating and contributing to the creation of wider and deeper markets. This made securities markets central to the whole process of global financial integration. Conversely, the very mobility of securities trading threatened the independence, and occasionally the existence, of national securities markets and even the economic sovereignty of nations. From the broad sweep of the history of the global securities markets, it is likely that few, if any of the problems found now or in the future, will turn out to be novel. All have occurred and been dealt with in the past, though the lessons learnt were usually not understood or, if they had been, were soon forgotten under pressure of more immediate considerations by some or all of the parties involved.

1

Origins, Trends, and Reversals: 1100–1720

MEDIEVAL FOUNDATIONS

The origins of the modern global securities market lie in medieval Italy where in the city states of Venice, Genoa, and Florence new financial arrangements emerged out of a growing trade between East and West. Advances included such developments as deposit banking, marine insurance, bills of exchange, joint stock companies, and transferable securities. An embryonic market in securities was created that extended beyond any specific location, in response to the financial requirements of both borrowers and investors, and to the need to make and receive payments over long distances. If a particular event can be taken to represent the beginnings of the global securities market it was the forced loan that Venice imposed on its inhabitants in 1171–2. Faced with a desperate need for money due to the exigencies of war, and unable to raise additional amounts from the normal sources of revenue such as taxation, the Venetian authorities extracted what they required from their own wealthy citizens. In return they promised to pay interest on the amount compulsorily borrowed until they were in a position to repay what they owed. These promises, in the form of interest-bearing bonds with no definite repayment date, then acquired a life of their own, being sold by those holders in need of money and bought by others seeking a regular income from their savings. Though initially regarded as of dubious worth, these transferable securities gradually gained acceptance as a secure form of investment that not only paid interest but also could be purchased and sold whenever the necessity for either action arose.

Between 1262 and 1379 Venice never failed to pay the promised interest at 5% per annum. As a result these bonds—known as *prestiti*—spread widely among long-term investors not only in Venice but also throughout Europe due to the financial network maintained by Italian merchant bankers. Other Italian city states such as Genoa, Florence, and Sienna followed the example of Venice and created debts in the form of interest-bearing transferable bonds. In the 1340s, for example, Florence consolidated its outstanding debts into one interest-bearing and negotiable stock. These city states all had wars to finance, which added an element of uncertainty to the value of the bonds created. There was always the possibility that military reverses and unexpected additional expenditures would mean that they would be unable to service their debts or would default upon them if the burden of repayment became too great. Hence an active market developed, attracting not only cautious investors but also those buying and selling for immediate gain. The resulting sustained turnover meant that there was sufficient business to make it worthwhile for bankers and others to act as brokers and so offer an intermediary service to investors. In turn, the existence of these intermediaries and the market they maintained meant that investors and speculators could be reasonably confident that they could resell the bonds they had purchased, so encouraging them to invest in the first place.

These bonds served a number of useful purposes. They allowed city states to finance wars without crippling their own populations through high taxes and other impositions, which would have been very damaging to the local economy. They also served two important functions within the financial system. The first was to bridge time, as there was a growing need for an investment that could be both short and long term. The practice of deposit banking, in particular, meant that bankers had to try and match the requirements of savers, who might want to withdraw their money at short notice, to those of borrowers, who wanted loans for a sufficient length of time so that the money could be productively used. Assets that both earned a rate of return and could be bought and sold quickly were thus ideal investments for bankers operating on the money deposited by others. Bonds were also useful for those offering marine insurance, who needed to invest the premiums paid in such a way that money was readily available if payment had to be made on a lost ship, but that it could also earn a return in the meantime. Large merchants who from time to time had spare funds as the volume of trade fluctuated both seasonally and annually were also attracted to these government bonds as a temporary home for their capital. The second use was to bridge space. Italian merchants traded widely to specific locations at specific times. Instead of paying for goods with gold and silver coins, which involved both high transport costs and a great risk of robbery, increasing use was made of bills of exchange issued by the merchant to the seller as a promise to pay a stated amount at a future date. In the meantime, the merchant would sell the goods bought and so be in a position to honour the bill when it became due. This greatly expanded the amount of money available to finance international trade so contributing enormously to the growth of the medieval European economy.

The use of bills of exchange and the development of a mercantile network across Europe increasingly allowed buying and selling to take place without the need to attend annual trade fairs. Instead, merchants could operate from counting-houses located in major commercial centres, working through a network of correspondents with whom they maintained regular contact, and between whom debits and credits existed representing the balance of trade at any one time. This greatly facilitated the conduct of trade by reducing the costs involved in transporting manufactures and commodities to and from central collection points. However, it was not always possible to make payments on these bills when and where required. The goods might remain unsold for longer than expected and the money not be available to clear the debt. Even if sold, payment could be received in one place whilst the money was owed in another, and the transaction could not be completed until bills of exchange became available that allowed the original deal to be reversed. Transferable securities were of great value in such cases, as they could be used to bridge both time and place in the payments system. It made no difference whether the bill of exchange was a product of a commercial or financial transaction, only that it represented a promise to pay a specific amount at a specific time, and thus securities could be used as substitutes.

As the bonds of the Italian city states possessed a market where they could be bought and sold, and the interest payments were regularly made, they acquired some of the attributes of money itself, being both a store of value and a means of payment. Bonds provided a temporary home for money until it was absorbed by the needs of trade with the constant need to buy and sell securities in order to absorb and release money generating a steady turnover. Considering the risks involved in medieval trade, merchant bankers had to maintain large reserves so that they could carry large stocks when required and make payments when bills became due. In contrast, wealthy individual investors traded little as they had little need to realize capital. Widows, orphans, and religious foundations, for example, looked to their investments, including securities, for the income they produced and were much less concerned by the existence of a market where investments could be easily sold if money was required for other purposes. Nevertheless, these investments came to include securities because of the ease of purchase and disposal.

The growth of a securities market was therefore an integral component of the financial developments taking place in later medieval Europe. However, the growth of this market was limited because of the lack of sufficient transferable securities. Though many public authorities wished to borrow by issuing long-dated or perpetual securities, few were in a position to do so. Such borrowing required the investor to have a high degree of confidence in the ability, willingness, and commitment of the issuer of the securities to pay the promised interest and to accept the binding nature of the contract made. Investors were aware of the potential sources of revenue that cities possessed, in the shape of their inhabitants and businesses, and the value of the tangible property located there, and they also knew that cities were not above the law and so could be pressurized into paying. In contrast, kings and princes were both above the law and could be deposed, so making their borrowings much riskier for those who lent them money, even though their needs were greater. That meant that investors were loath to lend to them other than for short periods and at high rates of interest. There were too many instances of wealthy bankers being ruined when kings and princes defaulted on their borrowings for this possibility not to be taken seriously. In 1399 the Italian merchant bankers, the Mannini, were forced to liquidate their business when the king of England, Richard II, to whom they had lent heavily, fell from power. Thus, the amount of long-term government debt traded in the market remained low as so many potential borrowers excluded themselves by a failure to gain the trust of potential investors. Even city states sometimes defaulted on payments of interest. The securities issued between 1275 and 1290 by Ghent were practically worthless by the 1330s as the town did not keep up the interest payments.

An alternative existed outside the realm of government, in the form of the securities issued by joint-stock companies. Also appearing initially in thirteenth-century Italy, these could be either bonds (*sopracorpo*) paying a fixed rate of interest or stocks (*corpo*) claiming a share of the profits as an annual dividend. However, this alternative was limited as medieval companies were generally small-scale enterprises owned by a few people often closely related through blood and marriage. Only in areas of business such as mining and long-distance trade were larger companies formed, as these were high-risk enterprises and required a significant amount of capital that few individuals possessed or were willing to risk losing. Even in these areas the companies formed were of a closed nature with the result that their securities did not command a market. Transfers were private affairs with only known and trusted individuals permitted to participate.

Consequently, the emerging securities market remained largely confined to the bonds of Italian city states, which were held mainly by investors located in northern Italy, and probably remained marginal investments for most. Merchants and bankers continued to keep large sums of money idle in the form of cash or to make loans that could not easily be reclaimed when required by depositors or other borrowers. Wealthy individuals invested mainly in their own business or in land and property, and kept large amounts of cash ready for any eventuality. Potential borrowers were often forced to accept loans for much shorter periods than they wished and to pay high rates of interest. The medieval European financial system evolved without a large and sophisticated market for securities. Although well on the way to solving problems associated with the supply and use of short-term credit and the creation of an international payments system, the system was unable to provide long-term capital or to structure assets and liabilities so as to reduce risk.

Therefore, though the origins of the global securities market can be traced to medieval Italy, developments in this period were limited. No stock exchange came into existence with its own specialist intermediaries housed in their own building and employing techniques appropriate to a market in both debt and claims to future profits. All the elements required to create such a market were there but it failed to develop because of a shortage of suitable securities. This shortage was due to the absence of large public or corporate bodies that could command the confidence of investors. Any default, however temporary, had serious consequences for the value and appeal of securities. The securities market remained poorly developed in comparison to the progress made in other areas of the financial system.

The progress that had been made in the development of a securities market suffered a major setback in the late fourteenth century. Between 1378 and 1381 Venice suspended interest payments during a war with Genoa. When payment was resumed the rate of interest paid was reduced to either 3% or 4% without consultation, so devaluing the securities. Though confidence did slowly return it vanished again in the fifteenth century as defaults became more common. Foreigners, in particular, were less well informed about conditions in Venice, and whether interest would be paid or not, and so did not want to hold the bonds. By the end of the fifteenth century Italian city state bonds had ceased to have wide appeal. Activity in the market became heavily dependent upon bouts of local speculation fuelled by the prospect of redemption or the payment of interest. By the 1480s the securities issued by Florence seemed to have degenerated into gambling counters whilst Venice was reduced to making new issues of securities such as the Monte Novo in 1482 and the Monte Novissimo in 1509, because the original loans were no longer being serviced. However, many investors held onto their original securities in the hope that they would be redeemed eventually, and avoided purchasing the new issues.[1]

EARLY MODERN ADVANCES

The limitations of the securities market in fifteenth-century Italy were compensated for by advances in other parts of Europe. By 1500 the momentum for financial innovation in Europe was already switching to the north, reflecting the growing importance of Atlantic shipping routes offering cheaper access not only to the East via the Cape of Good Hope but also to the new world of the Americas that came after the discoveries of Columbus in 1492. In the Low Countries, Bruges had emerged as the principal interface between the trade of the Mediterranean and that of the Baltic, and so it was there that the Italian merchants and bankers transposed their advances in financial technique. Much of their trading took place in the Place de la Bourse, named after the Beurse family who had an inn there; in continental Europe the term 'Bourse' subsequently became synonymous with that of Stock Exchange. However, what was traded on the Bruges Bourse was primarily money and bills. As in the Italian city states, there was no development of an actual stock exchange, nor the appearance of specialist intermediaries skilled in the techniques of trading securities. Thus, Bruges' contribution to the growth of the global securities market was as a carrier to northern Europe of the developments begun in northern Italy.[2]

By 1500 Bruges had already lost its position as the principal north European financial centre, being badly affected by the Flemish wars and the migration of the majority of its Italian merchants to its near neighbour Antwerp after 1488. For a time in the early sixteenth century both Bruges and Antwerp vied for financial leadership in Europe, along with the French city of Lyons and the Italian city state of Genoa. However, by the 1520s Antwerp's command of the Atlantic trades had given it the commercial base from which to emerge as the new financial centre of Europe. By the mid-sixteenth century Antwerp had also become a centre for public finance, with a variety of state, provincial, and city authorities raising loans there. Foreign governments also came to Antwerp to raise money, particularly England, France, Portugal, and above all Spain. In the 1550s Philip II of Spain forced his banking creditors to accept the conversion of their loans into long-term obligations paying a lower rate of interest. As long as payment of the promised interest was maintained these bonds (*juros*) were popular investments.

From the opening of a new Bourse in Antwerp in 1531 there were regular transactions in public funds. Though all types of commercial and financial transactions were accommodated, a division appeared to be emerging between those who frequented the Exchange to buy and sell manufactures and commodities and those who were there to trade bills and securities. This development in securities was allied to the growth during the sixteenth century of a discount market in Antwerp. Though the technique of discounting bills was known from the thirteenth century onwards, it had been little used and bills of exchange remained internalized as methods of payment within merchant networks. However, by selling a bill of exchange the holder could obtain immediate payment, at a small discount to the face value, rather than have to wait until the date when full payment was promised. In turn, the bill of exchange could be sold many times before redemption so making it attractive to those with funds temporarily at their disposal. A three-month bill of exchange could be sold at a discount to its face value, with the purchaser gaining the difference between the price paid and that obtained on maturity. Discounting was thus convenient to both parties to a commercial transaction. Those selling goods did not have to wait for payment, whilst the bill of exchange could serve the interests of many masters before its final demise through redemption. The growth of discounting was, in turn, related to the market in securities because one was the alternative to the other as both provided a temporary home for spare cash.

The securities market continued to expand during the sixteenth century. French government securities (*rentes*) were first issued in 1522, whilst the perpetual bonds (*luoghi*) issued by Genoa were actively traded at home and abroad throughout the period. Dutch cities issued securities which were popular among local investors because of their high interest, their ease of transfer, and the relative security of payment. Permanent markets within which securities could be traded appeared across Europe, with Bourses or exchanges built in Cologne in 1553, Paris in 1563, London in 1571, Seville in 1583, and Frankfurt in 1585. Catering mainly for merchants and bankers, these buildings provided a home for all kinds of financial and commercial transactions and a forum for business in commodities and bills rather than securities. Despite the revival of the bond market most financial transactions remained short term, including the borrowings of government, whilst joint-stock companies remained far too small and closely held to warrant a market in any stocks they might create. Investors were justified in their continuing distrust of governments, especially those led by kings and princes. In the crisis of 1557 both the king of Spain and the king of France suspended payments, with further defaults to follow and unfavourable changes in the terms of the loans. Spain reneged on its debts again in 1575 and 1596, whilst in 1597 the French government forcibly reduced the rate of return on its bonds from 8% to 4%.

The continuing growth in European trade and banking was creating an ever greater demand for the type of flexible investments represented by transferable securities. This demand was concentrated in financial and commercial centres like Antwerp, where there was a build up of funds that were temporarily idle at any one time. However, due to the failure of governments of all kinds to honour the commitments they had made, the market was restricted to smaller issues of bonds by towns or to short-term loans that were self-liquidating. Circumstances were little better with corporate securities. Though the scale and longevity of joint-stock enterprise did increase during the fifteenth and sixteenth centuries, the number of shareholders remained small and little trading took place in the securities issued. As in Bruges during the fifteenth century, the emerging market in sixteenth-century Antwerp remained short of securities that could be actively and regularly traded.[3]

Though governments had discovered a new way of financing abnormal levels of expenditure, such as that incurred in military campaigns, through short-term borrowings and long-term interest payments, they had yet to recognize that the success of such a system required them to honour the debts and payments created not just in principle but in practice, every single time without exception. It took time to build up trust among investors and governments were too ready too squander what they had achieved when faced with new demands upon their budgets, by deferring interest payments or reneging on debts. Kings and princes continued to regard borrowing as something to be imposed upon vulnerable groups, such as town dwellers, religious minorities, and resident foreigners rather than as a means to attract willing investors looking for good security and a reasonable rate of return. Government actions jeopardized financial developments across Europe, with bankers from Italy to Germany being ruined by failures to repay loans. More specifically, the bankruptcy of the Spanish government of the Low Countries destroyed Antwerp as the financial centre of Europe, by depriving it of the liquid funds necessary to undertake new lending. Antwerp itself defaulted on its borrowings in 1570. During the revolt of the Netherlands, Spanish troops sacked the city in 1576 and besieged it in 1584–5; thereafter access to the sea was blocked by the Dutch. Events such as these made Antwerp unsustainable as a major financial and commercial centre. From the 1580s it suffered an exodus of bankers to its rival Amsterdam, which was already replacing it as the pre-eminent commercial centre in Europe.[4]

Amsterdam became the payments centre for the seventeenth-century European economy. Increasingly it was only in Amsterdam that merchants and bankers could obtain the bills of exchange they required to settle transactions across Europe. In turn, that meant that they maintained credit balances in Amsterdam because it was there that they received or made payment. Contributing to Amsterdam's emerging position as the centre of a European-wide credit network was the founding of the Bank of Amsterdam (Wisselbank) in 1609, which provided the facility for bankers and merchants to transfer money between each other simply through debits and credits at the Wisselbank. As Europe's premier trading and shipping centre, Amsterdam also developed as the major supplier of marine insurance. By 1635 shipping valued at 15 million guilders was insured there, generating a large revenue by way of premium income as well as creating risks that had to be covered if losses took place. As in the past, these developments in trade, banking and insurance combined to spark an interest in transferable securities as a way of employing temporarily idle funds.

Though the Dutch national debt had been placed on a permanent basis in 1596 it was relatively small, and the provincial debts were largely of a short-term nature. This meant that there were no securities that served the needs of the short-term money market. Out of this situation emerged in 1602 the Verenigde Oostindische Compagnie (VOC) or the Dutch East India Company. This was a well-capitalized joint-stock company formed to send a fleet of ships regularly to the Far East for trading purposes, returning with goods for resale in Europe. It was thus a high-risk venture that employed the joint-stock form both to obtain the level of capital required and to minimize the possible losses incurred by any single individual. Whereas short-distance trade could be financed by small groups of merchants pooling their capital and sharing the risks, the development of long-distance trade to Asia posed an altogether different problem because of the increased size of the ship, the greater amount of cargo, and the longer journey time. All this greatly increased the costs involved. Companies formed in the past to undertake long-distance trade had generally been owned by small groups of merchants and shipowners and their shares were rarely traded. They did however generate large profits, making this business attractive to outside investors if a way could be devised to allow their participation, whilst spreading the investment as widely as possible to cover the risks involved. The result in 1602 was a company with a large fixed capital obtained through issuing a large number of shares to the public. From the outset the shares attracted Dutch investors, with at least 1,000 subscribing. Each share was for 500 guilders and had an equal claim to the profits of the company. They appealed to both speculators and investors. The results of each voyage were uncertain, dependent on the survival of the ships on both the outward and homeward journey and the sale of goods both in Asia and Europe. Until each trip was completed the level of profit or loss was a complete unknown, and thus the value of the shares was like a lottery ticket, but one that had a residual value as it could be resold at any time at a price reflecting current expectations. The shares also appealed to the investor as they possessed an active market, and so could be easily bought and sold. Turnover rose from around 100,000 a year between 1603 and 1607 to 400,000 per annum over the 1608–12 period. If shares were bought for immediate delivery and simultaneously sold for future delivery (spot and forward) or if an option was purchased, money could be profitably employed in holding these shares with little risk. Though the government attempted to ban such practices as early as 1610, on the grounds that they encouraged speculation, it proved unable to do so because of the role they played in assisting short-term investors against any sudden drop in value. Such devices also made the shares excellent collateral for loans as they could be quickly sold if repayment was required or they could be held on borrowed funds in the expectation that the profits would cover the interest paid.

As a result even the securities in an intrinsically risky trading venture like the VOC could serve the interests of those who had temporarily idle funds at their disposal. Consequently, an active securities market developed in Amsterdam as much in response to the needs of investors for a liquid asset as to provide the capital for long-distance trade and shipping. Traditional methods of finance could and did provide the capital required but the VOC moved the whole operation onto a much higher plain. In turn, the shares issued fostered the development of an active securities market in terms of technique of operation and specialist intermediaries as buying and selling was driven by both speculators and investors. Consequently, it was out of the private initiative of the Dutch East India Company that the global securities market began to take on its modern form. Other heavily capitalized joint stock companies followed, notably the Dutch West India Company in 1621. There was a growing realization among the various government bodies in the Netherlands that borrowing could be both cheaper and easier if similar methods were employed. Transferable bonds issued by Dutch public authorities thus became more numerous, with annual borrowing rising from 2.1 million guilders in the 1600–19 period to 7.8 million between 1672 and 1677. One estimate suggests that there were around 65,000 investors in the Netherlands by 1620 which would be more than sufficient to support a far more specialized market in securities than had ever existed in the past. However, most of these held government debt that was generally short term, not divided into standard units, dependent on specific conditions and spread throughout numerous separate issues. This made trading both less necessary, as the bonds were regularly repaid, and difficult, because of the lack of standardization. Thus, developments in the securities market continued to be driven long into the seventeenth century by activity in the shares of a few trading companies. This meant that securities still remained a minor business compared to the trading of commodities and bills or the short-term borrowing of governments.

Elsewhere in Europe the traditional problems of a lack of trust in the borrowings of governments continued to hamper the growth of the securities market. Governments continued to borrow, especially to meet the voracious demands of wars, but then reneged on these debts when they found themselves overwhelmed by the repayments and the prospect of levying unpopular taxes on their populations. It always seemed easier for kings to antagonize bankers and investors than subjects when the choice had to be made. The Spanish crown, the largest borrower in Europe at the time, went bankrupt three times in the first half of the seventeenth century. France declared insolvency in 1648, ruining many of the bankers who had lent to it, especially the Italians. Despite this, the debts created by national, provincial, and urban authorities continued to be traded in the various bourses and exchanges across Europe, suggesting a general widening of the market for the fixed interest securities issued by various governments and towns from Italy, Spain, France, Austria, and Russia. However, governments still failed to organize their finances in such a way as to make the issue of long-term securities attractive to investors. Even in Amsterdam the number of investors actively involved in buying and selling securities was probably quite low, being possibly around 1,000, apart from periodic bouts of speculation caused largely by the uncertainties of wars.[5]

Nevertheless, by the end of the seventeenth century a small but relatively sophisticated securities market existed in Amsterdam. A description by Joseph de la Vega in 1688 suggests that the main stock traded remained the shares of the Dutch East India Company but the techniques in use included spot and future contracts; call, put, and straddle options; margin trading, hedging, and short-selling; and the ability to defer both payment and delivery. Such was the level of trust that existed in this market that buying and selling was done for a monthly settlement when the outstanding differences in the money owed were cleared through the debiting and crediting of accounts at the Bank of Amsterdam. There also existed specialist intermediaries (*rescounters*) who could meet any deficiency in the supply of shares either from their own holdings or by anticipating purchase in the market before the settlement date. Finally, most though not all trading took place through a small group of largely Jewish brokers, who both acted for investors and dealt on their own account, so helping to ensure that the market was a highly liquid one. The market remained undeveloped in that it lacked any specific location, with trading taking place not only in the exchange itself but also outdoors in various parts of the city. This in turn created a major weakness in the market as anyone could participate and there was no way of excluding those who did not make good their promises, as de la Vega himself notes with some concern. De la Vega's securities market was still a minor adjunct to a business that remained dominated by the needs of trade and the provision of short-term credit. It also remained largely confined to Amsterdam and the interests of Dutch investors and Dutch issuers of securities, whether corporate or government. Though a number of governments did borrow in Amsterdam during the century, beginning with the Principality of Brandenburg in 1613, loans remained short term in nature because of the risks associated with sovereign debt.[6]

The real innovation that Amsterdam brought to the securities market was not the invention of either permanent government debt, for that had long existed, or even the creation of large and well-capitalized joint-stock companies, because these were already emerging in northern Europe in the sixteenth century. Instead it was the design of trading methods which permitted investors to buy and sell securities in such a way as allowed them to employ short-term funds remuneratively, without exposing themselves to undue risk of either absolute loss or inability to realize their investment when required. The existence of a securities market where exit and entry was virtually guaranteed and where simultaneous but reverse spot and future sales could be made represented a huge advance. This was only possible in a location such as Amsterdam where there was such a concentration of short-term money due to its position as the clearing centre for international payments. The English East India Company formed in 1600 had predated the Dutch VOC but its shares tended to be little traded. For most of the seventeenth century the shares of the limited number of English joint-stock companies remained closely held by small and interconnected groups of wealthy investors. The Hudson's Bay Company formed in 1670 had a capital of only £10,500 provided by a mere 32 investors. The East India Company was the only joint-stock enterprise of any size and the annual transactions in its shares averaged only 57 per annum in the 1660s or £25,000, rising to 136 or £52,000 in the 1670s, before leaping to 525 or £190,000 in the 1680s. Even this amounts to only ten trades a week. The position with government debt was little different. The British government continued to borrow short-term from London bankers as it did not command the trust of investors to do otherwise. Whereas the Dutch government could obtain loans at 4% in the 1670s the British government paid 12%, due partly to the fact that in 1672 Charles II reneged on his debts. There was little incentive in London to adopt the techniques of Amsterdam because the same level of interest and activity were absent. A similar position prevailed in France where neither the government nor joint-stock companies succeeded in issuing long-term securities that were attractive to investors. At this stage the growth of a large-scale securities market was little more than a Dutch experiment.[7]

The flight of James II from England and his replacement as king by William of Orange brought to the British throne a monarch who understood the financial techniques employed in the Dutch Republic. William III first issued a long-term loan in 1693 although this was not very successful. Investors were only too well aware of the promises of payment made in the past by English monarchs to be easily persuaded by the simple transplanting of Dutch methods of government borrowing to England. They knew the difficulties experienced in obtaining repayment by those whose loans to the government had been reneged on in 1672, despite the fact that they were numbered among the richest and most powerful bankers in the land. It took them until 1701 before they obtained the money owed. William III's masterstroke came with the formation of the Bank of England in 1694. It was not the formation of the bank was that was novel, but its purpose. It was the intention of the Bank of England to lend its entire capital of £1.2 million to the British government in perpetuity in return for a guaranteed interest of 8% per annum. Investors were presented with the opportunity of participating in an enterprise that would not only enter the potentially profitable world of banking, with guaranteed business from the government, but also a return of 8% on their money, with some reduction for the expenses of running the company. As individual investors they would have little bargaining power with the government if a default threatened or took place but, collectively, as an institution, their power was immense. In essence, the creation of the Bank of England combined in one institution the attractions of the Dutch East India Company and Dutch government borrowing, which had done so much to foster the development of the Amsterdam securities market.

The result was a great success, with the Bank of England attracting all the capital it required from numerous investors largely located in London. Whereas the Bank of England had 1,509 shareholders in the early 1690s the East India Company had only 449 and the Royal African Company only 213. What the Bank of England had done was quickly copied by others. The New East India Company was formed in 1698 to lend £2 million to the government, also at 8%. It eventually merged with the original East India Company in 1709, when a further £1.2 million was lent. In 1711 the South Sea Company lent the government another £9 million, to be used to replace a large amount of short-term borrowing with one large loan paying only 6%. Altogether, the Bank of England, the East India Company, and the South Sea Company had lent £15.8 million to the government by 1712. The London securities market was transformed. Between 1694 and 1709 the number of investors doubled from around 5,000 to 10,000 and this drove up the number of transactions. It was estimated that in 1704 turnover in the shares of the East India Company and the Bank of England totalled £1.8 million, or 85% of their combined capital. As neither short-term government debt nor the shares of the early joint-stock companies had been much traded, the effect on the London securities market was enormous. There now existed a large and permanent mass of securities held by numerous investors who regularly bought and sold for both short- and long-term purposes as well as speculation for a rise or fall in prices. Registered transfers in Bank of England, East India Company, and Government Stock fluctuated between 1,000 and 6,000 per annum over the 1694–1717 period whilst many transactions never reached the stage of actual change of ownership. Clearly there now existed in London the makings of an organized and established securities market.[8]

There was no specific location in London for the buying and selling of securities. Transactions were carried out not only in the Royal Exchange but also in adjacent streets and coffee houses. Nevertheless, a small number of stockbrokers were soon active in the market, arranging trades on behalf of investors among the general business they continued to conduct. Practices in use in Amsterdam were also quickly introduced, such as options and dealing for time. Illustrative of the rapid progress being made in London was the fact that as early as 1697 the government tried to restrict the number of brokers and time bargains, but to no avail. Driving this increasing sophistication in the market was not only the underlying growth of turnover but also the arrival of Dutch Jews and French Huguenots who brought with them continental practices. Dealers or jobbers also appeared who bought and sold securities on their own account, and not for clients. By being willing to either purchase or sell securities, without the prospect of immediate repurchase or resale, jobbers were instrumental in creating a ready market for both securities and money. Consequently, actively traded securities were more akin to short-term investments like bank deposits or bills of exchange rather than property investment or mortgages. Yet, the London securities market remained relatively small. There were possibly fewer than 50 active traders in 1712, only three stocks commanded a regular market, and international interest was confined to the Dutch.[9]

Despite the successful transfer of the practice and personnel of the securities market from Amsterdam to London from the 1690s, the diffusion was not a European wide phenomenon. France did not prove a receptive location despite the government's need for extensive borrowing due to wars and the possibilities of forming large trading and banking ventures in Paris, an important financial centre in other respects. The perpetual *rentes* issued by the French government, on which annual interest was paid, could have constituted an ideal security for trading purposes as repayment could not be demanded. They were traded in the Paris Bourse from 1639 onwards but no established market developed. An absence of trust in the administration of Louis XIV meant that investors were reluctant to buy and hold these securities, preferring instead to confine themselves to short-term self-liquidating loans. Rather than improve its credibility among investors the French government raised the money it required through selling rights to collect taxes and by borrowing from a few favoured financiers and their extensive network of contacts. Unlike either the Dutch or the English, the French East India Company, which was formed in 1604, was not a success and its shares did not generate even the level of activity to be found in London.

Furthermore, the French government hindered progress in the securities market by outlawing Protestants in 1685. Many of the most prominent French merchants and financiers were of that faith, especially in Lyon and Paris. Relocating to London and Amsterdam, they became successful bankers and major investors in securities. The outlawing and expulsion of religious minorities were hardly conducive to making Paris an important financial centre at a time when the conduct of international financial business required the existence of European-wide personal trust networks, as with the Jews. Instead, the dispersal of Huguenots across Europe contributed to the success of networks operating from rival centres in Amsterdam, Geneva, or London.[10]

THE FIRST SPECULATIVE BUBBLE

What brought the securities market to prominence was the speculative boom that infected Western Europe as a whole between 1717 and 1720, engulfing both Paris and London. Though the formation of joint-stock companies played a prominent role in this, as did the fevered buying and selling of shares, at the heart of the bubble were the actions of governments in France and then Britain. After the death of Louis XIV in 1715 it was clear that action had to be taken to put French government finances on a sounder footing, to prevent further defaults. In contrast, the British government was able to borrow and progressively lower rates of interest as the value of the outstanding debt rose and the yield fell, whilst the price of Bank of England stock grew.[11] John Law, a Scotsman well acquainted with the transformation of British government finances since the formation of the Bank of England in 1694, proposed to the French government a variation of that model and, impressed by what appeared to be a simple and quick solution to their financial difficulties, they instructed him to proceed. He first established a note-issuing General Bank in 1716. Shares in this bank were offered to investors in exchange for government debt, which was accepted at face value even though it could be bought at a discount of 60%. This made the shares very attractive to investors and demand was further stimulated by the payment of generous dividends to shareholders. At the same time the ability to buy shares was increased by a great expansion in the money supply through the issuing of a large volume of new bank notes. Such conditions whetted the appetite of investors for securities.

This demand was met by transforming a number of existing French joint-stock companies into attractive investment vehicles. This was done by exchanging government debt for shares and then using those shares in the master company to take over other companies. None of these companies had attracted investor interest in the past or enjoyed much in the way of trading success, unlike their counterparts in Amsterdam or London. The first to be given the 'Law treatment' was the Mississippi Company. This had begun as a chartered company with a trading monopoly in French Louisiana, the entire area of North America accessible via the Mississippi/Missouri river systems. Law then proceeded to merge the Mississippi Company, renamed the Compagnie des Indes, with a series of other French companies through a series of leveraged buyouts. The result was the creation of a huge joint-stock company that not only had monopoly rights over much of French trade with Asia, Africa, and North America but also to sell tobacco and mint coins within France. This convinced investors that it was capable of generating huge profits, a belief fuelled by a proposed dividend of 12% for 1720. By November 1719 the company had a market value of 5 billion livres. However, it was not simply expectation about the company's prospects that generated investor enthusiasm. This enthusiasm was also cleverly manipulated by the actions of John Law. In 1719 the General Bank was converted into the Royal Bank which extended almost unlimited credit to those wishing to buy shares in the Mississippi Company. These shares were available in a partly paid form so they could be bought by investors of limited means in the expectation that they would be paid up over time or, hopefully, sold at a great profit before further instalments were required. This was not all. It was stipulated that only holders of existing shares could subscribe to new issues, which were expected to offer even better returns. This caused a scramble for the existing shares which drove up their price, as those holding them were reluctant to sell in the hope of even greater gains in the future.

Shares in the Mississippi Company rose from around 500 livres each in mid-May 1719 to around 5,000 by the end of August, with hopes that they would rise even higher as the company was to refinance the entire French national debt. By then a speculative mania was in full swing, sustained not by any realistic prospects of future profits but by the money to be made through buying and selling the shares as the price rose. This sucked in more and more investors throughout France and even Europe. By December 1719 the price of the shares had reached around 10,000 livres, by which time a collective investment of 221.5 million livres possessed a market value of 4.6 billion livres. Attempts by Law to restrain speculation by limiting bank lending, proved unsuccessful and the boom continued into 1720. By then the Mississippi Company itself was supporting the market by buying in shares and guaranteeing a minimum price of 9,000 livres, so simultaneously reducing supply and limiting the risk of loss. A price of 12,500 was reached in March 1720, with many confidently expecting it to go much higher still. This confidence was based on the supposed prospects of a giant joint-stock company formed through the merger between the Mississippi Company and the Royal Bank. However, the bubble was on the point of collapse. Fearing that the situation was out of hand the French government attempted to reduce the amount of paper money in circulation, as that was leading to rampant inflation, and to dampen speculation by removing the guaranteed price for Mississippi shares. Investors were now faced with tighter credit and a falling share price, and so sought to sell rather than buy. In the course of two weeks in May the share price halved, reaching 4,200 livres by the end of the month. The speculative boom was over, with panic ensuing as investors attempted to sell so that they could pocket their profits or simply repay their borrowings. Law, who was possibly the richest commoner in the world in January 1720, had to abandon most of his wealth and flee the country in December for his own protection.[12]

Developments elsewhere in Europe contributed to the collapse as governments and financiers promoted their own schemes to attract investors. In 1717 the British government produced a proposal to consolidate some of its short-term debt paying 6% into long-term debt with a 5% rate of interest. This took place in 1718. In 1719 an even grander scheme was devised, intending to combine all outstanding government debt not already capitalized into one large loan which would then be exchanged for shares in the South Sea Company. The government would pay a lower rate of interest whilst investors would gain access to an attractive investment. The only losers would be the bankers and financiers of the City of London who had previously provided the government with short-term loans at high interest. In essence this was the same as previous schemes though on a grander scale, being essentially another debt for equity swap. The scheme began on 1 January 1720 when South Sea Stock stood at £128 and peaked in July of the same year at £950. Investor enthusiasm was stimulated by the ability to convert government debt of uncertain value into transferable securities with what appeared to be a certain if not rising value. Further, the new shares were issued in a part-paid form and loans were freely available, with the shares as collateral, which could be used to finance further purchases. The Bank of England lent £1 million whilst the South Sea Company itself lent out the money it received from its own investors to shareholders who then bought more shares in the expectation of rising prices and larger profits. Such actions then drove up prices, encouraging shareholders not to sell but to make additional purchases whilst new investors were attracted to the prospect of gain. Investors came not only from within Britain, with British investors selling Mississippi stock in Paris to purchase South Sea stock in London, but also from across Europe, including the Netherlands and Switzerland. French investors were also switching from Paris to London, so weakening the demand for Mississippi stock. The speculative boom spilled over into other investments with a wave of new joint-stock company promotions. During 1719–20 around 190 new joint-stock companies were proposed, expecting to raise £220 million. Apart from London Assurance and Royal Exchange Assurance, most came to nothing. Nevertheless, before they disappeared there was great activity in the securities market as shares changed hands at greatly inflated prices. Registered transfers in Bank of England, East India Company, and Government Stock reached 21,811 in 1720. To protect its own position within the securities market, as well as dampen down speculation, an Act of Parliament was passed in May 1720 banning joint-stock companies, so concentrating investor attention on the South Sea Company. However, as the number of investors converting government debt into South Sea Company shares began to falter, so did the rising price of these shares. With the Paris market already weakening from May 1720, London followed suit in July. Investors recognized that the only asset possessed by the South Sea Company was an income from the government of around £2 million per annum, resulting from the debts that had been exchanged for shares, and that this was not going to generate large returns on a capital of £14.5 million once all running expenses were met. Investors began to realize their gains and by September the boom was over. Share prices which had more than doubled in 1719 and 1720 were two-thirds less by 1722. Recriminations and blame took the place of optimism and self-confidence among the investing public.[13]

Though Paris and London were the main centres of speculation in 1720 they were joined by Amsterdam, Geneva, Hamburg, Lisbon, and Vienna. However, these speculative booms elsewhere in Europe were both short-lived and limited in scope, with collapse following shortly upon the ending of the boom in London. In Amsterdam, where investors and operators were much more experienced in financial matters, the mania was confined to the second-half of 1720 and focused on joint-stock companies, with around 40 being promoted. Many of these were in insurance and turned out successfully. Insurance was also the focus in Hamburg.[14] In Paris and London, steps had to be taken to stabilize the financial markets. In France the government liquidated the Mississippi Company, dissolved the Royal Bank, cancelled the paper currency and converted that part of the outstanding government debt it accepted continuing responsibility for into perpetual *rentes* yielding 2%–2.5%. This brought the level and servicing of the French national debt down to a manageable level, principally because the price inflation of the bubble years had significantly reduced its real value. However, in the process investor confidence in both government debt and corporate finance had been destroyed. In contrast, although many investors in Britain had lost money in the collapse of the speculative boom, especially those who had bought at the peak of the market, the government honoured its obligations to the South Sea Company, so that holdings were not worthless. Both the Bank of England and the East India Company survived, and London retained the basis of a functioning securities market.[15]

With the speculative mania of 1719–20 the world experienced its first global stock market boom and collapse. Though located in Paris and later London it spread to other financial centres and involved investors throughout Europe who bought and sold extensively its main stocks, namely those of the Mississippi Company and the South Sea Company. Despite the focus on corporate stocks this was not a speculative boom driven by company prospects. Instead, it was a product of the desire of governments, particularly that of France, to rescue themselves from war-induced financial chaos. It also arose from a failure to understand the consequences of the methods chosen to replace short-term debt with long-term but marketable securities, and the adverse results that came from a too rapid expansion in the money supply and the liberal lending policies adopted. The outcome was a situation where too much money was chasing too few securities, convincing investors that shares could go on rising if not for ever then certainly long enough for them to buy and sell repeatedly at a profit. Collapse was inevitable once those investors who wanted to exit were not replaced by new entrants. It had disastrous consequences for those investors operating on borrowed money who could not pay what they owed. The late involvement of Amsterdam, and the limited amount of speculation that took place there, indicates that the boom was not a product of normal market conditions nor of the activities of fraudulent company promoters, though they were quick to take advantage of the euphoria among investors. What does emerge from this speculative boom is the fact that a European-wide securities market linking the main financial centres was in existence by the beginning of the eighteenth century.

CONCLUSION

What is most remarkable about the early development of the securities market is the role played by governments and their need for finance due to the turbulent nature of medieval and early modern Europe. Through the creation of transferable long-term debt upon which interest was paid governments could access funds that would, in all probability, otherwise lie idle. Whatever the use to which long-term loans were put their existence in an easily transferable form made them attractive to investors. Obviously there were those who were always willing to speculate by buying for a rise or selling for a fall. However large-scale activities of this kind were of a spasmodic nature, and it took a set of very peculiar conditions to create the type of bubble experienced in 1719–20. Occasional speculative booms were hardly the basis upon which a permanent and sophisticated market with specialist intermediaries could develop. Other investors saw in transferable securities not some form of permanent investment but a temporary home for idle funds. Merchants and bankers, in particular, were eager to employ such funds by either buying securities for their yield or lending to those that did, knowing that the securities could be sold when funds were required. To do so, however, required the existence of a market where such transactions could be quickly and cheaply carried out, with specialist intermediaries ready not only to execute orders but to take risks by providing a willing counter-party for every deal. By buying for cash and selling for time a merchant or banker could employ their spare funds profitably on a relatively risk free basis, and receive a modest profit as a result.

Though the origins of the market lay with governments and their need to borrow, their failure to ensure that these debts were honoured and serviced constantly undermined further development. Hence the creation of a significant securities market constantly faltered over the centuries. There did not exist that mass of securities in which investors had confidence which could be moved around the major financial centres of Europe in response to the constantly changing conditions of supply and demand in the markets for credit and capital. This was one of the major weaknesses in the emerging financial system of a Europe where flows of commodities, manufactures, and money were increasingly important. It was not until the seventeenth century, with the growth in Amsterdam of a market in corporate securities, that specialist intermediaries devised methods of operation to cater for the needs of those who were searching for a convenient and profitable means of employing the abundant short-term funds constantly released and absorbed in the normal course of trade and banking. This market lacked a large mass of transferable securities sufficient to absorb such funds, as governments continued to renege on their debts and interest payments, so introducing a high level of uncertainty into their borrowing. With the privatization of government borrowing in London in 1694, through the establishment of the Bank of England, a beginning was made in converting illiquid public debt into liquid private debt in such a way that investors could have confidence that commitments would be honoured. This process had disastrous consequences when it was carried too far in Paris and London between 1717 and 1720.

Consequently, the growth of a global securities market owed much more to the needs of a particular group of investors looking for a short-term home for their money than to the long-term needs of either government or business. It required securities in which investors had confidence and which could be easily bought and sold. Government schemes were unreliable, and even when a market developed of itself, governments were keen to either police it by outlawing practices they little understood but disapproved of, or by manipulating it for their own ends. The global securities market of the early eighteenth century was not the product of governments and it did not serve political masters. It was the product of a need within the financial system to create a type of investment that could be bought and sold to provide a temporary home for funds and a means of transfer from one location to another. It transcended the needs of any particular regime for its master was international trade and finance.[16]

2

Advances and Setbacks: 1720–1815

PROGRESS IN THE EIGHTEENTH CENTURY, 1720–89

During the eighteenth century the global securities market grew in size and importance, with stock exchanges being established in several major European financial centres and in the 1780s extending overseas to the newly independent United States. The basis of this market remained government debt created for military purposes, whether for the incessant conflicts within Europe or the expenses incurred in gaining independence from colonial masters, as in the case of the United States. These debts were increasingly organized in a transferable form suitable for trading in the securities markets. Governments were also more conscious of the need to maintain the confidence of investors and mostly refrained from cancelling their borrowings unilaterally or failing to make interest payments when they fell due. Such was the growing belief in the guaranteed nature of government debt that it also attracted more distant investors. Amsterdam emerged as the centre of a global market for government debt used by both borrowers and investors from across Europe and later the United States. In contrast, the eighteenth century was not a period when joint-stock companies flourished once the excesses of the speculative bubble of 1719–20 was over. Only a small nucleus of companies existed whose shares were actively traded and these were more proxies for government debt, such as the Bank of England and the English East India Company. Even in Amsterdam activity centred increasingly on government debt rather than on shares in such as the VOC. Promotion of joint-stock companies was on a local or small scale, generating little by way of a market beyond the confines of a restricted group of investors. After 1720 the fortunes of the eighteenth-century global securities market rose and fell in line with government borrowing and their commitment to servicing their debts.

The speculative bubble of 1719–20 had few long-term implications for Amsterdam, then the world's largest securities market, as it had remained on the fringes of the frenzied buying and selling. That was not the case with Paris, the epicentre of speculation. Once the French government had unravelled the financial legacy bequeathed by Law, steps were taken to bring the nascent securities market under control. One of the consequences of the speculative boom and collapse had been the creation of a large volume of long-term French government debt. This could not be redeemed but did pay interest and could be bought and sold. It needed a better market than the intermittent trading in government debt which had previously taken place in the general Bourse in Paris. During the speculative boom in Paris the securities market had moved from place to place indicating that, unlike Amsterdam and London, it had failed to take root. The market had grown up rapidly as Law's schemes developed. Brokers, dealers, and investors first crowded into the Rue de Quincampoix where Law himself lived and other bankers were located. They then followed Law when he moved into the Place Louis-le-Grande (or Place Vendome). Tents and booths were set up in the square for the conduct of business, accompanied by others offering refreshments and providing entertainment. Finally, the market moved to the Hotel de Soissons, due to objections from those disturbed by the noise and inconvenience created by their presence in the Place Vendome. The Hotel de Soissons was officially designated as the only place in Paris where securities trading could take place; among the trees in the hotel garden brokers and dealers erected numerous small trading tents and pavilions. This still retained the appearance of a carnival or an annual fair that would be packed away and moved to a different location once the excitement was over. It certainly did not give the impression of being embedded into the general financial and commercial activities of Paris. Indeed, the market moved on again to the Rue St. Martin once the speculation had died away.

The French government was reluctant to allow a settled location to develop naturally out of the actions and interests of brokers and dealers, as had happened in Amsterdam and London. After the excesses of the Mississippi Bubble it was anxious to establish control over the Paris securities market rather than leave its development in the hands of those held responsible for the speculative boom in the first place. In 1724 a royal decree established an official stock exchange, to be regulated by the French government and located in a special room in the Rue Vivienne. The right to buy and sell securities in this room, called the Parquet, was restricted to a small number of official brokers called *agents de change*. The result was an official securities market handling transactions in government debt on behalf of investors. Considering the small number of agents permitted to trade and the restrictions under which they had to operate, an unofficial market known as the Coulisse quickly developed outside in the nearby Palais Royal. Members of the Paris Bourse were not permitted to deal in this market, or anywhere other than the Bourse, nor could they be in partnership with those who did.[1]

The consequence for Paris was to split the securities market in two with the main business being conducted by the *agents de change* who operated on a commission-only basis, could not trade on their own account, and did not utilize the whole range of beneficial trading practices pioneered in Amsterdam. The Paris Bourse provided a market for routine investment business under the watchful eye of a government that wanted to avoid any repetition of the events of 1720. Thus, though Paris was the first place in the world to establish a separate stock exchange, as distinct from the commercial exchanges to be found in most major European cities, the reason why it did so was to control not encourage trading. Those excluded from the stock exchange could respond to the needs of other users with access only to part of the trading. This deprived Paris of the deep and broad market essential if substantial amounts of securities were to be bought and sold quickly without causing major price fluctuations, as required by investors with short-term funds. Rather than a major step forward in the creation of a global securities market, the action of the French state in establishing a stock exchange in 1724 was a restrictive measure aimed at preventing further speculative outbursts.

However, the methods that had contributed to the speculative excesses and the participation of specialist dealers and brokers were both vital to the health of an active securities market. It could only exist with a large and steady turnover of business, for which buying and selling by a limited number of long-term investors was insufficient. The securities market in Paris was thus fractured and its development restricted compared to either Amsterdam or London. During the eighteenth century the Paris Bourse experienced long periods of only moderate activity. Trading was in the hands of 60 *agents de change* who possessed a royal monopoly and operated only as brokers, with business taking place for one hour a day in a room in the Hotel de Nevers. When the market was particularly active it spilled over into the street where a parallel market continued to exist dealing in the business neglected by the Bourse itself. However, it was not only the way the market was organized that hampered Paris's position. Investors continued to mistrust French government debt, because of the government's poor reputation for paying interest and honouring its financial commitments. Hence the government had difficulty borrowing long term and the Paris Bourse lacked the large mass of securities that would have underpinned its growth. Not only were there defaults in 1759 and 1770 but the French government failed to convert its outstanding debt into a single bond issue that would possess a deep and broad market. Nevertheless, trading in Paris did become more sophisticated. Securities were both bought on margin and sold short as well as being used as collateral for loans. Paris came to be ranked with Amsterdam, London, Hamburg, Geneva, and Genoa as one of the main financial centres in Europe.

Within France it consolidated its position as the dominant financial centre, rather than Lyon.

A major contribution to Paris' position as a financial centre appeared to have been made in the 1770s, with a renewed attempt to place French government finances on a more stable, long-term basis. In 1776 the Caisse d'Escompte was founded, modelled on the Bank of England. It was to lend its capital to the government as well as issue loans. In effect, however, it expanded vastly the supply of credit through a policy of generous lending on 90-day bills of exchange. This sparked a period of easy money that not only encouraged the government to borrow but also fuelled a speculative boom in which securities were chased higher and higher in price and new joint-stock companies were floated in such areas as insurance and water supply. This speculative boom had started to unravel by 1786 but was overtaken by the events of the French Revolution. Thus the French repeated the events of the Mississippi Bubble, though in a milder version, some 60 years later despite the creation of a formal securities market designed to limit such excesses. The failure to stabilize government finances and attempts to inflate the money supply so as to make borrowing easier, undermined the financial system and created the conditions that would support a speculative mania.[2] Speculation itself was not the problem, as that was an inevitable occurrence within any active market, but rather the excesses it was driven to and the failure to develop a sufficiently robust market mechanism and financial system that could cope with the progress and aftermath of bubbles. Governments were not passive bystanders in either the development of eighteenth-century securities markets or the events that influenced them, for they operated to their own agenda. The French example illustrated that a government-created securities market was not capable of developing mechanisms for coping with speculative booms and crashes if the government itself failed to learn either the lessons of past bubbles or the necessity of stabilizing its own finances.[3]

However, the French government was increasingly isolated in this respect. Most other European governments strove hard to place state finances on a permanent and sustainable basis and were able to borrow larger amounts at lower rates of interest. Few involved themselves in the organization of their securities market as the French government had done. An exception was the Austrian government. Borrowing heavily in the 1760s and 1770s to finance a series of wars, it not only committed itself to service its debts but also tried to improve the market for these securities. In 1771 the government set up a formal stock exchange in Vienna, modelled on the one in Paris. The Vienna Bourse similarly aimed to provide an orderly market under the supervision of the government. However, little trading took place despite the fact that it was open to all and included bills of exchange as well as securities. Instead, what trading there was in Vienna in the late eighteenth century continued to take place on the street and in cafes, despite attempts by the government to prohibit such activities.[4]

In England the consequences of the South Sea Bubble were much less profound than those of the Mississippi Bubble in France. Though many investors did lose money with the collapse in the price of South Sea stock, the government committed itself to pay interest on the loans it had obtained from the South Sea Company so that it, in turn, could pay those holding South Sea stock. The amount of stock was then scaled down to reflect these payments with each investor receiving £100 in stock for each £300 in cash paid. As many investors had acquired their holdings in South Sea stock by way of conversions of existing government debt, such as annuities, at highly inflated prices this deal was much less unfavourable that it might appear. In consequence, the cost to the government of servicing its debts remained much the same as before but the nature of that debt had been transformed. A large part was now in the form of a single loan from the South Sea Company instead of a large number of separate and complex borrowing arrangements. This South Sea stock was held by numerous investors and was easily transferable, contributing greatly to turnover in the London securities market. Whereas in 1719 the funded debt of the British government was £37 million, by 1720 it had reached £50 million. This compromise was deemed generally acceptable to all parties and helped boost investor confidence in the National debt. Eventually, in 1749 the government consolidated most of its remaining borrowings into one single loan, known as consols, paying a fixed fate of interest of 3% per annum. Thus, by 1750, 93% of the British government's debt of £78 million was in a form that could be easily bought and sold in the securities market, being either in consols or the stock of the Bank of England, the East India Company, and the South Sea Company. Thereafter British government borrowing became a routine matter as the risk of default receded. This left the London securities market to refine its techniques and operation, concerned only with the yield on long-term debt in comparison with the returns elsewhere and the general state of the money market.[5]

Though both the Bank of England and the East India Company continued to conduct trading operations, giving their shares a small but extra element of uncertainty, the South Sea Company abandoned its relatively small-scale activities in the South Atlantic and tied its fortunes wholly to the payments it received from the British government. By mid-century the Bank of England, the East India Company, and the South Sea Company had lent some £42.8 million to the government. Once the South Sea Bubble had died away registered transfers in Bank of England, East India Company, and government stock averaged between 4,000 and 7,000 per annum until 1749–50 when they rose to 25,000 in the wake of the conversion. Thereafter 20,000 transfers a year became standard, suggesting a solid underlying volume of trading in the London securities market. By 1760, when the National debt stood at £102 million there were an estimated 60,400 holders; by 1790 this debt had risen to £244 million, driven by the costs of wars and the failed attempt to retain the American colonies. With the British government consistently honouring its debts and interest payments, investors were attracted to transferable securities whose value was directly or indirectly dependent on government payments. British insurance companies preferred to hold the transferable securities issued by the government or the shares of the Bank of England and the East India Company, rather than invest in land or mortgages, which were more difficult to dispose of quickly if need be. As Fairman, the accountant for Royal Exchange Assurance, explained in the 1790s,

The regular payment of the interest on the government funds, and the number of persons in this country preferring the interest they afford to the hazardous profits of trade, occasion continual purchasers for those shares in them which are brought to market for sale. The facility, also, and trifling expense, with which transfers are made in these funds, are inducements to prefer vesting money in them to laying it out on mortgages or other private security, which, though probably yielding a greater interest, is frequently attended with trouble and uncertainty.[6]

In contrast to the increasing popularity of British government securities among investors, the formation and promotion of joint-stock companies were little in evidence. The Bubble Act of 1720, not repealed until 1825, outlawed joint-stock companies unless specifically permitted by Parliament. However, it is most unlikely that this was the explanation for their unpopularity. In Scotland, where the Bubble Act was considered not to apply, the joint-stock company was also little in evidence outside banking and trade. The reason was probably that investor demand for liquid securities was fully satisfied by government borrowing, increasingly in the shape of long-term transferable securities. As such borrowing rose consistently there was little opportunity to attract investor interest into alternative securities issued by joint-stock companies. Only in the second-half of the 1780s, when there was a lull in government borrowing, did interest in joint-stock enterprise revive in Britain. A speculative boom in Paris in this period also involved the formation of joint-stock companies, indicating the cross-currents existing within the global securities market. In Britain investor interest focused on the promotion of canal companies, which required a large initial investment but promised safe and steady dividends from the tolls paid by users. As with existing government securities or the shares of the Bank of England, it was income rather than capital gain that was the attraction. Speculators were attracted to canal shares because of the unknown prospects of profit once in operation due to the potential traffic they could carry, but this speculation was largely located away from the established securities market in London, in such provincial centres as Birmingham which was a hub for canal construction. Speculation quickly died away once government borrowing resumed its upward trajectory in the mid-1790s. Demands from investors rather than the needs of borrowers drove the growth of the British securities market.

The eighteenth-century securities market in Britain became increasingly sophisticated. Partly this was a response to its size and complexity and the uses to which it was put, but it also owed much to a continuing influx of Dutch Jews and French Huguenots who introduced continental practices. The use of a fixed date in the future, by which all stock had to be delivered and paid for, became standard practice, encouraged by a government attempt in 1734 to reduce speculation by banning the use of options. Techniques such as continuation and backwardation also became commonplace. By such means the London securities market became better able to meet the varied needs of investors, ranging from those who simply wanted to buy or sell for cash or immediate delivery to those who sought to profit from a cycle of rising or falling prices. Within this market dealers assumed growing importance. Willing to purchase or sell securities in response to demand, dealers were instrumental in creating a ready market for both securities and money. They operated in the largest and most actively traded securities, as it was only here that they had the prospect of reversing the deal at a profit within the settlement period. Consols and the shares of the Bank of England, East India Company, and South Sea Company were ideal for that purpose, as they existed in large amounts, were widely held, and were always being traded. Unlike many other types of investment, such as property or mortgages, securities were more akin to short-term investments like bank deposits or bills of exchange, where they possessed an active secondary market serviced by jobbers. This was not the case for most joint-stock enterprise, as even an established company like London Assurance had only a few hundred shareholders and thus a limited market.[7]

The London securities market served the needs not only of the long-term investor but also of merchants and banks with spare money to employ.[8] The rising number of banks contributed enormously to activity. Either by investing their idle balances directly in government or allied debt or by lending to those that did, banks increasingly provided the funds that underpinned the growth of the securities market. Provincial banks deposited part of their idle balances at short notice with a London private banker, who paid interest upon it. In turn the London banker employed part of those funds in the securities market, through broking connections there. Without such a market and its increasingly sophisticated operations, the risk involved in holding permanent debt with near liquid funds would not have been sustainable. The London securities market was thus an integral part of the evolving financial system, contributing particularly to the growth of a national money market and to the development of banking. Those depositing their savings in a bank expected to be able to withdraw them at their own convenience but banks could not force the repayment of loans as these could be tied up in unsold stocks of goods or raw materials. Consequently, banks had to maintain a substantial margin between the amount they had in deposits and the amount lent out by way of loans. This margin, or idle balance, generated no income, making it necessary to either pay depositors a lower rate of interest and charge borrowers a higher one or accept a greater degree of risk that deposits could not be repaid, so bringing the bank into financial crisis. If the idle balance could be remuneratively employed, whilst at the same time remaining readily available to repay depositors, not only could banks pay depositors higher rates of interest and charge borrowers lower ones but the level of risk would be manageable. Fewer banks would collapse, due to bad debts and panic withdrawals by depositors, and more savings would be placed in the hands of bankers, greatly expanding the supply of credit available. Such flexible and remunerative investment was increasingly important as a supply of abundant credit was of vital importance for developments in manufacturing and trade. In contrast, the direct contribution of the securities market to the financing of economic growth was very limited, being confined to canal shares in the 1780s. Instead, the direct contribution of the securities market was political, for it allowed the British government to finance the American and French revolutionary wars.

One area where the London securities market failed to develop satisfactory mechanisms was in providing some certainty to participants that purchases would be paid for and sales result in delivery. This could not be done in law as Barnard's Act of 1734 made time bargains illegal, classifying them as gambling. It was thus left to the market participants themselves to create an appropriate code of conduct. Specialist intermediaries wanted a means of restricting participation to those with a large business to transact and with a reputation for honouring their bargains. Filtering out those who did not fit these criteria would require the exclusive use of a room which had to be paid for as would the costs of the staff necessary to both bar entry to those excluded and police those inside. Attempts to achieve this failed repeatedly. Those to be excluded were openly hostile and many of them, as active investors, were also customers whose views could not be easily ignored. There was also reluctance to pay for participation in the market, which had been free in the past. Even when a building called a stock exchange was opened in 1773 it failed to capture the market as trading in securities continued to take place in various locations throughout the city of London.[9]

Despite the growth and sophistication of the London securities market during the eighteenth century, Amsterdam remained the most important centre and the most international. Whereas Paris and London traded exclusively in their own government's debts and the shares issued by their own joint-stock companies, Amsterdam increasingly provided a market for securities from around the world. The city provided the fulcrum of the global securities market. By 1750 its market traded not only 25 Dutch public funds and the shares of three Dutch companies but also thirteen foreign loans and three English companies. In 1772 this had risen to 57 Dutch and 39 foreign securities. Although the various Dutch governments did borrow they tried to restrain their expenditure and did not issue large amounts of securities on the Amsterdam market. The outstanding debt of the province of Holland, for example, rose quite modestly. It was 343 million guilders in 1713 and 350 million in 1794. As elsewhere, there was no great expansion in the number of highly capitalized large joint-stock companies attracting significant numbers of investors, despite the fact that there were few obstacles to the formation of such companies. Instead, there was a modest expansion of relatively small companies operating in such tried and tested areas as insurance, and even they appeared only towards the end of the century, as in France and Britain. This suggests that the excesses of the bubble years 1719 and 1720 had made investors across Europe suspicious of joint-stock enterprise for most areas of the economy, especially those requiring day-to-day management such as agriculture and manufacturing. Although the issued capital of Danish joint-stock companies rose in mid-century, it fell back in the 1770s and 1780s and was confined to small, closely held companies in the traditional areas of banking, insurance, and overseas trade. There appeared little need in Europe to utilize the joint-stock form of enterprise, as the scale of financial requirements for most ventures remained low and within the reach of individuals operating alone or in small groups. In the eighteenth century Western Europe probably enjoyed the highest per capita income in the world, which generated a high level of individual savings sufficient for most forms of enterprise.

Faced with a lack of domestic securities generated by either government or business, but with an abundance of short- and long-term money seeking a home, Dutch investors increasingly switched to foreign issues. Whereas Dutch public loans yielded between 2% and 3% per annum for most of the century foreign governments were paying from 4% to 6% on their borrowings. As confidence grew in the commitment of European governments to service their debts, Dutch investors were increasingly attracted by the higher yields on offer, and either subscribed to foreign loans floated in Amsterdam or bought securities issued elsewhere. By 1775 around one-third of the loans issued in Amsterdam was on behalf of foreign governments. Initially, Dutch investors focused heavily on British government debt and corporate securities as being most like the domestic securities with which they were familiar. Large holdings were built up in Bank of England shares, East India Company stock, and later consols. These holdings then created an active market in British securities both within the Amsterdam securities market and between Amsterdam and London. This was driven by Dutch Jews who established cadet branches of their firms in London and then traded extensively between the two centres. They operated both for the profits to be made from any price differences that emerged, mindful of the risks caused by delays in transmitting information by ship, and the money market opportunities created by the need of merchants to make or receive payments in the twin commercial centres of northern Europe. The result was to create a single securities market spanning Amsterdam and London though confined to a small group of British securities and limited by the transport difficulties of the day.

As other European governments copied the Dutch and British examples in putting their finances on a permanent and sustainable basis, their securities became increasingly attractive to Dutch investors, producing noticeable shifts in the distribution of Dutch foreign investment during the century. Whilst total investment in foreign securities more than doubled between 1770 and 1790, rising from 250 million guilders to 575 million, the amount that was British rose only moderately from 205 million to 265 million, and this took place before the outbreak of war with England in 1780. Dutch investors switched to French government debt attracted by the prospects of large capital gains in the belief that *rentes* were now much safer securities. Short-term loans in Amsterdam stood at 4–5% whereas French government debt yielded 8–10%. As long as the French government maintained interest payments Dutch investors would do well. In contrast, British government finances were seen to be deteriorating, especially after the disastrous war of American independence, despite attempts by the British government to bolster its credit rating by establishing a sinking fund in 1786 to buy back debt in the market. By the 1780s the Amsterdam securities market traded not only Dutch, British, and French securities but also those issued by the governments of Austria, Denmark, Poland, Russia, Spain, Sweden, and the United States as well as various German States. This placed Amsterdam at the very centre of the network of international finance as ownership of securities ebbed and flowed between the major European financial centres, reflecting not only the preferences of long-term investors but also the continually changing conditions of the money markets. Though still largely confined to Europe, a fully functioning international securities market now existed.[10]

Inevitably, however, the dominance of the Amsterdam securities market was gradually eroded. Financial crises in the Netherlands in 1763 and 1772–3 disrupted the operation of the securities market and led to the loss of business whilst the Bank of Amsterdam was in financial difficulties by 1781. Political instability and civil war in the mid-1780s was not conducive to a stable financial environment. At the same time London provided stronger competition to Amsterdam as an international financial centre, having overtaken it to become the leading commercial centre in Europe. This had implications for the securities market though the employment of the temporarily idle funds of merchants. Nevertheless, despite the rising import-ance of London during the eighteenth century, and the repatriation of much of the activity in its own stocks, it was not yet in a position to overtake Amsterdam as a financial centre. Though now dominating trade in British securities, most notably the National debt and the shares of the Bank of England and the East India Company, London did not provide a market for foreign securities. Rather, England remained a net debtor with investors across Europe holding not only the National debt but also Bank of England and East India Company stock. These were not only Dutch investors but other wealthy Europeans, such as the Landgrave of Hesse-Kassel, who in 1785 had a large part of his fortune invested in British government bonds.[11] London's participation in the global securities market was thus through the activities of foreign investors and foreign brokers, especially the international networks maintained by European Jews such as the Raphaels from Amsterdam and the Rothschilds from Frankfurt. Important as London was, in this respect it still remained an offshoot of Amsterdam.[12] London, like Paris and Vienna, was a national centre, whilst political divisions ensured that other markets served even more of a regional function. In Germany securities markets existed in Berlin, Frankfurt, and Hamburg but each traded their own securities and were more linked to Amsterdam than to each other.

Despite Amsterdam's leading role in the eighteenth-century international securities market, few advances in organization took place there. The buying and selling of securities still occurred in a variety of locations where any interested person might attend. Under such conditions it was difficult to develop rules and regulations controlling conduct within the market. The greatest risk remained the perennial one of the failure of the counter-party to pay for or deliver securities if there were no enforceable penalties for default. Even where legal enforcement was possible the whole process was simply too slow to cope with the needs of a market where prices changed quickly and deals had to be made on the basis of trust. As in London it proved impossible in Amsterdam to devise a compromise that would satisfy all participants in the market, and persuade brokers and dealers that it was worth paying for an exclusive and regulated marketplace. The business of buying and selling securities therefore remained fraught. Eventually, by 1789, brokers in Amsterdam did succeed in forming an organization designed to give its members some protection against those who defaulted on deals, whether it was non-payment or non-delivery. However, this achieved little without the creation of a separate securities market to provide an exclusive and orderly marketplace governed by an appropriate code of conduct. Instead, trading continued to take place in such places as the general merchants' exchange in Amsterdam, where those interested in the securities business congregated around one of the pillars. The building within which this exchange operated was owned by the Amsterdam City Council, who made it a condition that the building remain open to the public. As long as the securities market was located there, access to all and sundry could not be denied.[13]

These developments in Amsterdam were part of a general move within Europe where market participants tried to create more orderly trading conditions. Attempts by the authorities in France and later Austria to create more regulated markets had failed as they were more concerned with restriction and control rather than meeting the needs of an evolving marketplace. The result merely restricted official business and left the rest unregulated as it was undertaken elsewhere. Conversely, attempts in both Amsterdam and London to introduce self-regulation also proved ineffective. Though trading in securities had grown in importance it had yet to rival the markets in either property or commodities, and remained marginal to both trade and finance. Many who bought and sold securities did so only on an occasional basis, such as individual investors, or as part of a more general financial or commercial business. Bankers wanted the flexibility of being able to conduct their own buying and selling or to employ brokers but be able to observe what was happening. Consequently, they were little interested in either paying for the upkeep of a specialist market or abiding by any rules it might impose. Conversely, they were unwilling to be excluded from any market that might be created as they had business to be done, and they wanted direct access to those who could do it and the place where it took place. As these people were both numerous and powerful, and a group on which the intermediaries in the market were dependent, an impasse developed in which progress towards a specialist securities market was impossible. In Copenhagen, where trading in Danish joint-stock company shares dated from the early eighteenth century, it was again not until the 1780s that a more formally organized securities market began to take shape.[14] In Switzerland attempts were made to impose rules and regulations, with prominence given to the elimination of counter-party risk by restricting all trading to recognized brokers, but this was resisted and all attempts failed.[15] Thus, although enormous strides had been made in the development of eighteenth-century securities markets, they stopped short of providing the organized form required for the system to reach its potential.

From the 1780s new securities markets began to develop outside Europe. Under British influence there was some limited trading in government securities and bank shares in India. More significant were developments in the newly independent United States. Before independence the little borrowing undertaken by the individual states was of a short-term nature, whilst businesses did not issue transferable shares in order to obtain the finance required. Wealthy Americans who did invest in securities bought the issues traded in London. A domestic securities market appeared only in the 1780s in the wake of the large increase in state borrowing needed to finance the war of independence. Although trading in the securities issued both by governments and by companies grew, the number of specialized brokers was few and market organization remained almost non-existent. Most of the borrowing undertaken was largely short term and generated little market activity. Even after independence the US government chose to float a loan in Amsterdam to refinance war-related costs, and the resulting securities were traded there. A domestic securities market of any significance appeared only in the early 1790s.[16]

The financial systems developing in the economies of individual countries on both sides of the North Atlantic facilitated the growing economic relations existing through trade. Though the transferable securities traded on these markets made little direct contribution to economic growth, being used to finance wars rather than development, they did play a vital role in providing the domestic and international liquidity that contributed enormously to the provision of credit within and between countries. At the same time slow progress was being made in the creation of organized markets. However, the prospects of both national and international securities markets were suddenly transformed by the political, military, and economic disruption that followed the French Revolution in 1789. When stability of a kind finally returned over twenty-five years later the landscape of global securities was quite different.

REVOLUTION AND WAR 1789–1815

During the French Revolutionary and Napoleonic wars Amsterdam lost its position as the world's leading financial centre and the emerging global securities market was shattered. Whereas previous wars had encouraged government borrowing and the development of the securities market, the length and severity of the extensive political and military conflict between 1789 and 1815 produced far-reaching consequences for both the integrity of nation-states and for their international relations. Some foretaste of this had occurred in 1788 when the French government announced a partial suspension of the payment of interest on its debts. Investors assumed that suspension was temporary and foreign investors even bought French securities under that assumption, hoping to profit from temporarily depressed prices. This mood of optimism began to change, but only slowly, with the removal of the French monarchy and the government on whose authority loans had been negotiated. In 1793, faced with the outbreak of a European war and the collapse of the domestic monetary and financial system, the new French government simply cancelled its outstanding liabilities, and in 1797 reduced the outstanding debts by two-thirds. These actions destroyed investor confidence in French government securities. It was not until Napoleon came to power that some order began to be restored to the Paris securities market. Interest payments were resumed in 1800, the Banque de France was established in that year, and joint-stock companies with transferable shares were allowed in 1808. The Paris Bourse was re-opened in 1802 as a quasi-official institution and its 60 *agents-de-change* given a monopoly over the trading in securities.

As war and revolution spread throughout Europe other governments also ceased to pay interest on their debts and even refused to recognize their existence in certain cases. Faced with the prospect of either meeting payments on their outstanding debts or alienating their own people at a time of war and political upheaval, it was easier for governments to ignore the commitments made to investors, especially if they were foreign, than face the ire of their own population. The Austrian government suspended payments on its Dutch loans in 1795/6, having already switched its borrowing to London in 1794 as French troops threatened Amsterdam. It then reneged on its London loans in 1797, claiming that they were subsidies paid in return for Austrian military support, and thus were the responsibility of the British government. Though the Austrian government resumed the payment of interest on its Dutch loans in 1805 it did so in its own paper currency and not in Dutch guilders. Only in 1818 was a satisfactory settlement reached with the holders of these loans and the Austrian government could again return to tap foreign capital markets. As other regimes fell to revolutionary opponents, defaults on interest payments and repudiation of debts became widespread in Europe. Denmark, Russia, Spain, and Sweden all stopped servicing their debts. Holland itself stopped paying interest on its loans, arbitrarily reducing the amount owed in

1810, and then going bankrupt in 1813. Some governments reached a full settlement with their Dutch bondholders towards the end or shortly after the Napoleonic wars, as was the case with Russia. Others, such as Sweden, did not, which made it difficult for them to issue new securities in Amsterdam. The Danish government started to tap its own population for funds with issues of bonds from 1806 onwards. When governments returned to foreign borrowing after 1815 they sought alternative markets to Amsterdam. London, Frankfurt, and Hamburg then emerged as rival centres for international lending though local markets remained important, as was the case of the individual German states. As all these defaults, suspensions, and repudiations were not isolated occurrences confined to one country at one time, but a European-wide phenomenon, they combined to destroy the basis of trust upon which governments had been able to raise loans at home and abroad during the eighteenth century.[17]

War and revolution destroyed both international finance and financial centres. In the chaos following the overthrow of the established order in France, rampant inflation destroyed the money supply and the financial system. The government viewed the problem as one belonging to the financial systems, rather than of its own making, and so closed down the Paris Bourse in 1791 and banned all joint-stock companies. By then Paris had ceased to operate as part of the global securities market. Foreign business had become virtually impossible because of government controls and the uncertain degree of risk. The largest merchant bank in Paris, Thelluson, Necker, and Company, which was at the centre of an extensive Huguenot network across Europe, collapsed, breaking links to other financial centres such as Geneva as a result. As the French armies then waged destruction on the rest of Continental Europe, other financial centres suffered a similar fate. Frankfurt, for example, was occupied by French troops in 1792, freed, and the re-occupied in 1796 after a siege. The most severe blow for the global securities market was the eventual occupation of Amsterdam by French troops in 1795. Prominent bankers and brokers from across Europe fled to London, as the one financial centre still operating relatively normally. These included Walter Boyd from Paris, Henry Hope from Amsterdam, Johan Schroeder from Hamburg, and Nathan Rothschild from Frankfurt.[18] As the ravages of war and revolution in the 1790s destroyed, simultaneously, both the securities that underpinned the global securities market and the financial centres within which trading took place, the slow progress made since 1720 was undone in one dramatic decade.

Military defeat and the French occupation of Amsterdam in 1795 destroyed many of the international links through which flowed the currents of credit, such as that to London. The impetus behind the Amsterdam securities market was also lost as there was no longer the constant ebb and flow of short-term money seeking employment. In combination with the collapse of the international bond market because of the widespread defaults, Amsterdam's position as a financial centre was thus seriously undermined. Much of the financial infrastructure in Amsterdam was destroyed, with the disappearance of numerous specialist bankers and brokers. Though still a major financial centre after 1815 Amsterdam was no longer at the centre of the global securities market.[19]

In contrast, Britain's island location and command of the seas prevented invasion and London as a financial centre was able to profit from the demise of European rivals. International trade continued unabated but now fell more and more into the hands of British merchants. The implications for London were threefold: the removal of rival financial centres, principally Paris and Amsterdam; an influx of wealth and talent in the shape of foreign bankers and merchants; and a continuing need for international financial services. In consequence London was thrust into a position of financial leadership, particularly after 1795. As in the past the leading financial centre, Amsterdam, was displaced not by a relative newcomer but by a close contender, London, and only then as a result of military and political upheaval rather than a slow gravitational shift.

This shift in the fortunes of rival financial centres nevertheless had serious implications for the London securities market. The European political and military instability alone created a very volatile environment within which securities trading had to take place. The price of consols fell from 97 in 1792 to 47 in 1798, recovered to 71 by 1810, fell back to 54 in 1813, and then reached 84 in 1817. Rumour and counter-rumour about military successes and reverses produced a fevered atmosphere which drove prices up and down from minute to minute, making fortunes for some and losses for others. At the same time the amount of securities to be traded expanded enormously as the government sought to fund its greatly enlarged army and navy expenditure. By 1815 the British national debt stood at £745 million, having tripled in size since 1790. This massive expansion of government debt sucked in investors from all over the country, ending the provincial flirtation with canal shares. In 1815 there were an estimated 250,000 holders of the National debt. These included many from continental Europe who saw British government securities as a safe haven at a time of almost universal default. In consequence the London securities market was placed under ever greater strain as the volume and volatility of business increased. Ever more participants were attracted from home and abroad as they saw the daily fluctuations in prices as an ideal opportunity to make a quick fortune. Inevitably, this left the market professionals very exposed as it was difficult to know whom to trust. One solution appeared in Dublin in 1799 when a stock exchange was formed attracting thirteen brokers as members. Though the public were admitted to the stock exchange they were not permitted to buy or sell, for that privilege was given only to the members.

By the late 1790s a crisis had been reached in the London securities market. Those with some authority in the market were pressing for greatly increased powers to enforce discipline and exclude from the building where business was done those who had defaulted on deals. They were being overwhelmed by the disputes brought before them for adjudication, considering that they were unpaid and had to earn their own living as brokers and dealers. This crisis broke the impasse that had long prevented the creation of a separate and exclusive securities market. Faced with the impossibility of resolving the problems in any other way it was decided to restrict entry into the stock exchange building in London to those who paid an annual subscription and agreed to abide by the rules governing the conduct of business. Failure to pay this fee and the breaking of the rules meant exclusion. With this one decision those dealing in securities in London acquired the money to pay for an administrative structure and the power to enforce discipline. On 3 March 1801 the London Stock Exchange formally came into existence providing not only a market for securities but also enforceable regulations on how business was to be conducted. By this act the trading of securities in London had moved, decisively, from an open to a closed market. With 363 members by February 1802, the move appeared a successful one.

The emergence of this closed market in securities represented both an end to one evolutionary process, related to the mechanisms and techniques whereby stocks and shares were bought and sold, and the beginning of another that now included the control, distribution, and exercise of power and authority. What made it different from the establishment of the Paris Bourse some 80 years before was that it grew out of a requirement for self-regulation by those in the market rather than a government attempt to control and restrict. As such the rules and regulations framed for the conduct of business reflected the needs of those in the market not those in government. This made a fundamental difference to the way the market was organized and how it developed. For example, the London Stock Exchange sought to control access to the market not in terms of numbers as in Paris but with regard to type and character. It aimed to exclude those regarded as untrustworthy or who created acceptable risks for other members. From 1812 all new members had to confine their business to the buying and selling of securities because of the fear that a large loss made in business elsewhere would jeopardize the financial stability of the whole stock exchange. This exclusion of other members of the London financial community, such as bankers, could have had serious repercussions for the operation of the market, had the stock exchange introduced, and enforced a fixed scale for the fees that brokers charged their clients. That had been done in the Dublin Stock Exchange when it was formed in 1799 and was the case in Paris. However, such was the diversity of the securities market business in London, with so much being driven by money-market activity that it was not possible to agree on any common scale of charges. This left members of the London Stock Exchange free to make whatever arrangements they liked, so placating those excluded from entry. Bankers could employ brokers on a simple retainer rather than pay commission on each transaction, as was the custom adopted by the Bank of England. With this combination of easy entry, no fixed scale of charges, and close working relationships, the stock exchange increasingly dominated the London securities market, though did not monopolize it. Generally, the rules of the London Stock Exchange were solely concerned with policing the conduct of business between members so that buying and selling could take place quickly on the basis of trust. There was no attempt to interfere with the relationship existing between the member and his client or the way that members conducted their business. Members, for example, were free to deal for immediate delivery or for time, give or take option contracts, buy or sell on their own account or for clients, and trade on their own capital or on funds borrowed from banks.[20]

The remodelling of the London securities market was mirrored by developments elsewhere in the world though not on the same scale or to the same extent. In the United States the securities market was free to develop far removed from the political and military troubles of Europe. In 1790 the Federal government made three bond issues that redeemed and consolidated the various national and state debts resulting from the war of independence. A total of $65 million in transferable securities held by US investors was created, plus another $12 million held abroad. In addition to this national debt there were a growing number of joint-stock banks, insurance companies, and turnpike roads, whose shares generated significant investor interest. In 1791 the Bank of the United States was formed, modelled on the Bank of England. These developments laid the foundations of a more organized and specialist securities market. Activity in the various securities markets located in the major cities of the eastern United States grew apace. A growing number of people set themselves up as brokers to cater for the needs of these investors; this, in turn, produced the same kind of problems experienced earlier in the Amsterdam and London securities markets. There was an emerging need for some agreement on the rules under which business would be conducted. In 1790 in Philadelphia brokers agreed to a set of rules under which buying and selling would be conducted. This was followed by similar moves in New York in 1791, which were then strengthened and formalized in May 1792, in the face of a collapse in the speculation. These rules included a fixed scale of charges for customers, reflecting the competition between an expanding number of brokers for a contracting volume of business. However, as participation in the market was open to all there existed no mechanism for enforcing these rules or policing the market, a problem not resolved until later in the nineteenth century.

Though Philadelphia was the financial centre of the country in the 1790s, where the Bank of the United States was located, it was closely challenged by New York. As the first port of call for ships from Europe, and marginally better access to the information that was most likely to move the markets, New York gradually became the more important financial centre. Its securities market became more active than that in Philadelphia, which counteracted the early lead established by Philadelphia in both banking and market organization. Despite this growing importance of New York, trading in securities was widely diffused among the major cities located along the eastern seaboard. However, under the centralizing influence of the national debt, a growing integration was taking place, with a relatively high degree of price integration, especially between physically adjacent markets, such as Philadelphia and Baltimore as compared to Philadelphia and Boston. The national debt, which had fallen from $75.5 million in 1780 to $45.2 million in 1811, swelled to $127.3 during the war with Britain between 1812 and 1815, though much was held abroad. However, other securities were mainly regional or even local favourites. This was especially true of corporate stocks issued by the numerous banks, insurance companies, and turnpikes as well as some state and local authority bonds. Much of this was little traded, being held solely for the regular income produced. Overall, one estimate suggests that total US securities had reached $300 million by 1818. In that year the total funded debt of the United Kingdom was £780 million, or thirteen times greater, and all that was traded on the London Stock Exchange, whereas much of the US total was not traded in New York. Clearly, there was a different order of magnitude between the relative sizes of the London and New York markets at that time.[21]

CONCLUSION

Curiously, the turmoil and disruption introduced by the French Revolution in 1789 had both negative and positive consequences for the global securities market. The negative outcome was easy to see in terms of the eclipse of Amsterdam as the premier financial centre and the collapse of the international market because of widespread defaults. As a product of Dutch investment abroad, Amsterdam had emerged as the one centre where securities from around Europe and the United States were actively bought and sold. This trading in Amsterdam had wide significance for the operation of the international economy as it was through Amsterdam that flowed the currents of the world's payments system. The European economy was continuously moving away from a system where international payments were only in gold and silver currency and goods had all to be taken to and from specific trading locations. Instead, a multilateral system of payments and the use of credit became standard practice. This required a means of achieving continuous adjustment of balances between countries. A market thus developed in the credits and debits arising from international commerce, and the securities market became an increasingly important part of it during the eighteenth century. The ability to make payments between countries became easier and cheaper when bills of exchange created in the course of trade were supplemented by the international credits and debits resulting from the sales and purchases of securities in different markets. Inevitably this generated much activity in the securities market as prices of stocks rose and fell not only due to domestic monetary conditions but also those abroad. Thus, the existence of active securities markets in different centres was of major importance in achieving a high degree of monetary integration first within Europe and then across the Atlantic. It was this integration that was so damaged by the collapse of the global securities market after 1789.

Though by 1815 London replaced Amsterdam as the most active centre within the global securities market, the London market served the needs of Britain or, more specifically, the needs of the British government as the national debt ballooned due to the costs of maintaining not only a global naval presence but also armies operating in continental Europe. It was through the British government's national debt that the London securities market played what international role it did. This debt was held not only by a vastly expanded British investing public but also by numerous investors across Europe, as the only remaining government security that was not likely to suffer a default. The British government expanded its own debt in order to subsidize its European allies in the war against France, rather than those countries issuing loans at home and in London. Generally, in this period there was a far greater importance given to the national nature of securities markets. For example, whereas domestic investors subscribed to only half the securities issued by the US government to finance the war of independence between 1776 and 1783, the rest coming via Amsterdam and Paris, during the next war with Britain between 1812 and 1815, domestic investors absorbed most of the securities issued.[22] Securities markets thus lost the international dimension that had been so important before 1789. The switch was detrimental to the world economy as it removed an essential element of international liquidity that had been important in covering temporary imbalances between national economies, and so had contributed to expanding international trade. It was no surprise that the years following the end of the Napoleonic wars were ones of government-imposed trading restrictions and currency instability. Until the global securities market could be re-established the world economy lacked the means for maintaining international equilibrium.[23]

Though the securities market was nowhere directly involved in the provision of finance for economic growth in the eighteenth century, its ability to provide a large and remunerative outlet for short-term funds, for which it would be difficult to find an alternative use, did contribute to the maintenance of relatively low interest rates and gave some partial stability to the emerging banking system. It also meant that governments could obtain the finance they required to wage war without putting such a strain on their domestic capital market that productive areas of the economy would be disadvantaged. In the course of the eighteenth century securities markets became an integral part of national capital markets, through the finance of the government debt, and the money market, with the home it provided for the idle balances of merchants and bankers. By expanding the supply of credit and capital, and facilitating financial integration, securities markets made a significant contribution to eighteenth-century economic growth, though they were never central to the process. This was not only true nationally but also internationally as transferable securities were increasingly used as a means of transferring capital from where it was abundant, most notably the Netherlands, to where it faced growing demand as in the case of England and later the United States. Unfortunately that also included countries such as France which had yet to create a financial system sufficiently stable to cope with fluctuations in money and capital market activity.

Consequently, what drove the growth of the global securities market before 1789 was much less the general rise in the number of investors and the volume of stock, important as that was, but the constant need to buy and sell as money market conditions altered at home and abroad. The requirements of those closely involved with the money market were also different from those acting on behalf of private investors. In particular, the brokers acting for private investors usually had ample time to arrange payment or delivery. In contrast, those acting on behalf of domestic banks or foreign clients were required to act quickly before the opportunity was lost. This necessitated a much greater degree of understanding and trust among the participants in the market, as they had to be certain that payment would be made and stock delivered. The clearest difference between the two types of market participant was that those using the market for long-term investment tended to buy and sell for cash, having the money or securities to hand, whilst the professionals, buying and selling for themselves or for money market clients, dealt for time and did so frequently. The risk for them was that one default in the chain of operations could endanger their ability to pay or deliver in turn, and thus undermine the market itself. That then created a requirement for a market-place where speed of execution and speed of transaction were of paramount importance. Though moves in that direction were made in the eighteenth century, they had made little real advance by the 1780s. The formal stock exchanges that had been formed, as in Paris, did not have these twin concerns as a priority and so had not addressed them. In contrast, the most active markets in Amsterdam and London had yet to create these organized and dedicated markets. That was the positive outcome that came from the pro-longed period of war and revolution between 1789 and 1815. Such were the pressures exerted on London, the one fully functioning major market still operating at this time, that a solution had to be found. It came in the form of the London Stock Exchange, established in 1801 as a closed market, with control over entry and power to enforce rules of orderly behaviour. This produced a model that was then copied, though in a variety of different ways, by other securities markets, in the years after 1815. In the aftermath of the French Revolutionary and Napoleonic wars governments gradually reorgan-ized their finances, reaching agreement with investors regarding arrears on interest payments so that they could raise new loans. However, it took many years before the trust and stability of the pre-revolutionary years could be restored. Only the debts of Britain and the United States had been serviced regularly through the war years. The confidence that had been established before 1790 in the commitment of governments to servicing their debts, especially those held abroad, had been lost by 1815. It was confidence in the value of the securities being traded that was as much a key to the successful operation of a global securities market as was the ability to buy and sell easily, quickly, and cheaply under conditions of certainty and transparency.[24]

3

New Beginnings and New Developments: 1815–50

Twenty-five years of revolution and war between 1789 and 1815 shattered the global securities market. Amsterdam lost its primacy as a financial centre, numerous government loans were in default, and the confidence of investors in state guarantees was again very low. However, between the end of the Napoleonic wars and the middle of the nineteenth century not only was the global securities market restored to its former position but it was also extended and deepened. The securities market became firmly established across western Europe, in London and Paris especially, and across the eastern United States with organized markets becoming integral elements within emerging financial systems. The increasing use of the joint-stock form for business began to make transferable securities important in their own right. For the first time securities became an essential part of the capital market within which business raised the finance it required, rather than being an adjunct to the money market. By the mid-nineteenth century securities were being used directly to finance economic growth for the first time, so contributing to the material prosperity of all.

In 1815, however, serious questions hung over the global securities market. Would such a market revive and what role was to be played by Amsterdam? The years of war and revolution had forced financial markets to look inward with the needs of national governments being met from domestic sources, either taxation or loans. Even when the wars were over there was a legacy of outstanding debts and disruption that was hardly conducive to the rapid resumption of international borrowing and lending. It was several years before conditions existed where the issue and trading of securities could recover the international dimension of the 1780s. When that did happen would Amsterdam resume the position it had occupied then? For 200 years Amsterdam had been the most important securities market in the world, emerging as the one location where government bonds from around Europe and later North America could command a market. Subsequent defaults on these bonds, the flight of key players, and the disruption of established links all seriously undermined Amsterdam as an international financial centre but no alternative had emerged by 1815. Both London and Paris were fully occupied with domestic finance between 1790 and 1815 and had not developed much of an international presence. The French financial system had to be rebuilt after the chaos of the revolutionary years, and that was a slow process from 1815 onwards. The London securities market's early involvement with foreign government finance, in the shape of the Austrian loan, was not a success and this discouraged further attempts to overtake Amsterdam. What British purchases there were of foreign securities focused on those of the United States, despite the strained relations after independence. By 1803 British investors were the largest external holders of US securities though the Dutch still remained very significant. However, Anglo–American financial relations were strained again with the outbreak of war in 1812 and there appears to have been some disposal of US government securities by British investors as a result.[1] Consequently, the opportunity existed in 1815 for Amsterdam to recapture its traditional role. The city still retained a core of experienced bankers and brokers whilst others either returned from abroad or flowed in from elsewhere in Europe.

However, Amsterdam faced a number of serious problems in these post-war years. One stemmed from the fact that the Netherlands was a small country compared to both France and Britain. Though the Dutch national debt had more than doubled between 1796 and in 1814 it remained small in comparison to those of Britain and France. Instead, the Amsterdam market was heavily dependent on international business, which could be financed through the large amount of short-term money available there. This had served Amsterdam well before 1789, as it attracted an international business because Dutch investors were both keen and sufficiently wealthy to buy foreign government issues as substitutes. It was a disadvantage in the years after 1815 as the Dutch were no longer as wealthy as they had been and other centres were able to benefit from trading a large domestic national debt. In the balance between financial centres there had been a gravitational shift away from Amsterdam. In order to attract business from abroad Amsterdam had to offer more attractive terms and a better trading organization. Though the short-term money market revived after 1815, it was not nearly as important in the past. London had captured not only international trade but also the finance of it. Nevertheless, Amsterdam did recover as an international securities market, with the number of securities listed there increasing from 98 in 1815 to 108 in 1820. Those of foreign governments were the most numerous. As governments reached agreement with their creditors regarding lapsed interest payments, loans were issued representing the new amount outstanding. Sovereign borrowers in good standing, such as Russia, also returned to the Amsterdam market to raise fresh loans. However, Amsterdam was now just one of the components of a global securities market, rather than its principal co-coordinator. A significant proportion of the Dutch national debt itself was held abroad at this time and was traded between Amsterdam and other financial centres. War and revolution had not destroyed Amsterdam's securities market completely, but had seriously diminished its relative importance.

This exposed Amsterdam's inherent deficiencies of organization. As long as the market was small and stable the informal methods of the eighteenth century could cope with counter-party risk by restricting buying and selling to a small group of bankers and brokers who knew each other well and trusted each other as a result. However, the post-war market was much bigger, with the vastly expanded size of national debts, and was more volatile, given the difficult economic and political conditions at the time. It had also become a more anonymous marketplace where the informal arrangements of the past no longer sufficed. Unfortunately for Amsterdam its securities market had not made the advances necessary to cope with these changed circumstances. Attempts to create a specialized securities market, which could maintain discipline and enforce delivery and payment, had failed repeatedly in the past and remained unattainable after 1815. The result was that the Amsterdam securities market could offer little to compensate for its weakened state, and so relied upon inertia and the problems of its rivals to maintain its position.[2]

Strangely, despite France's eventual defeat in 1815, following three decades of financial and monetary chaos, Paris emerged as a key component of the global securities market. Under Napoleon the financial system had been put on a much more stable footing and improvements. In 1816 a national savings bank was established, the Caisse des Depots et Consignations, that invested its funds in government securities on which it received interest. A number of other banks and insurance companies were also formed between 1815 and 1820, so giving more depth and breadth to the financial system. The government was now able to borrow through the issue of long-term debt as opposed to the short-term devices in use under the *ancien regime*. This was especially necessary as the victorious allies imposed a large indemnity on France that could only be met through extensive borrowing. Three loans for around 300 million francs were issued in 1817, for example, to meet the terms of this indemnity. The result was a massive expansion in the issue of French *rentes* as the government borrowed to meet its internal and external obligations. As French investors could not absorb all these issues, capital markets across

Europe were tapped, particularly Amsterdam, Antwerp, Berlin, Frankfurt, London, and Vienna. As a result French *rentes* came to command the broadest and deepest market of any security at this time.

The constant ebb and flow of *rentes* between these financial centres reflected fluctuations in the domestic and international money markets. Some of the major players on the European financial scene, such as the Rothschilds, the Ricardos, and the Raphaels who had connections in different centres, were constantly buying and selling in these different markets. Though there was considerable activity in both Amsterdam and London, Paris was the main market, and remained central to the operation of global securities until the early 1820s. It was Paris rather than London that supplanted Amsterdam immediately after 1815, due partly to the existence of an organized securities market. Despite government control and operational restrictions, the very existence of the Paris Bourse was crucial, in that any organized exchange was better than none, given the need to impose discipline in a large, volatile market. Though the number of members was fixed at only 60 *agents de change*, they could cope with much of the business as they, in turn, employed a further 420 clerks to aid them. The Paris Bourse also provided a market that was not exclusively devoted to French government debt. By 1820 it had added a number of insurance companies and municipal stocks to the banks and canals it had traditionally quoted. It even traded one foreign security by then, namely the bonds of the State of Naples. Consequently, unlike Amsterdam, Paris gained from the post-war situation as it found itself the central market for the most important international security, and possessed of an institution which provided the necessary discipline and confidence for trading in securities generally. That combination pushed Paris to the forefront of the global securities market whilst the lack of it undermined Amsterdam.[3]

In many ways it was London that had appeared best placed to replace Amsterdam. Britain had the most advanced economy in the world, with its population poised to overtake the Dutch as the recipients of the highest per capita income. London was the world's leading commercial centre and the centre for international trade credit. Through the national debt in its various forms, London was home to securities that commanded a large and very active market. The establishment of the formal stock exchange in 1801 provided an institution better able to deal with the problems of risk inherent in a volatile, rapidly changing anonymous marketplace. However, these strengths also hindered London's progress towards primacy in the global securities market. The funded (and thus traded) part of the British national debt continued to grow until 1821, by which time an additional £120 million had been borrowed by the government compared to 1815. Not only was all this obtained from domestic investors but there was also a steady repatriation back to Britain of that portion held abroad. Foreign investors found more attractive investments elsewhere, such as French *rentes*, for example, which also attracted many British investors. Consequently, the main securities traded in London did not have an international appeal. The interest of foreign governments in the London market was slow to develop and remained limited before 1820.

Further, the London Stock Exchange remained an exclusive market reserved for British government debt and associated stocks, like those of the Bank of England and the East India Company, traded principally between British investors whether wealthy individuals or institutions such as banks and insurance companies. However, the stock exchange did not command even the whole British market, for its terrain was simply the direct and indirect issues of the British government. Trading in other securities, whether issued by foreign governments or domestic joint-stock enterprise, took place outside the stock exchange. For example, securities issued by the English canals or Scottish banks were traded in and between those provincial cities where their shareholders were clustered. Also outside the stock exchange, but in London, was the market in international securities, especially French *rentes* but also other foreign government issues such as those of the United States. London therefore possessed a fragmented securities market of which that located in the Stock Exchange was but one component.

In the United States the various securities markets were slowly moving towards a more formal organization. In Philadelphia brokers agreed to specific times when they would meet to do business, to trade under an agreed set of regulations, and to exclude those who were not brokers and who did not accept the conditions laid down. These rules were then copied in New York in 1817 when twenty-seven brokers rented a room to which entry was restricted and within which a strict code of conduct prevailed. Thus, the United States followed the British pattern in that the growth of organized markets came from the initiative of the broking community rather than as a response by government to speculative activity that threatened to destabilize the financial system. However, the US stock exchanges were unlike the London Stock Exchange as their rules included a fixed scale of charges. New York gradually emerged as the most important centre for the US securities market, consolidating its international position in trade and finance with improved access to the interior through the development of the Erie Canal from 1817. By the 1830s, turnover on the Philadelphia Stock Exchange was only around 15% of that in New York, where half of all trading in securities in the United States took place. However, New York's command over the US securities market was undermined by the absence of nationally held securities. From the end of the war with Britain in 1815 the US government took steps to repay the national debt, which fell from \$127 million to \$90 million between 1815 and 1820. In its place appeared the securities issued by banks, insurance companies, canals, and municipal and state bonds. The number of securities quoted in New York rose from 23 in 1815 to 35 in 1820. However, not only were these corporate securities insufficient to compensate for the decline in the size of the national debt, as many were closely held and little traded, but they also tended to be held on a local not a national basis, so contributing to the spatial fragmentation of the US market. As a result, the emerging US securities market remained small and localized. Nevertheless, it did help to provide both the liquidity that banks and merchants required and acted as a means of remittance between the United States and Europe as US securities were held internationally.[4]

Consequently, in the five years after Napoleon's defeat at Waterloo a fully functioning global securities market was once again in operation. In certain ways this market was stronger than the one that had been destroyed by war and revolution. It was not dependent on only one market but was multi-centred. There existed a large mass of securities that were traded between these centres, in the form of the French national debt. The level of organization had been greatly improved with formal stock exchanges operating not only in Paris but also in London and various cities in the United States. Nevertheless, this global securities market retained most of the characteristics of the old. Though there had been a reshuffling among the main players they were still mainly confined to the European triumvirate of Amsterdam, London, and Paris and communications between these financial centres remained restricted to whatever modes of land and sea travel were available. The result was that integration was limited and inter-market activity took place through trust networks. The market was also still one for government debt with corporate securities having made little impact. In many ways what had been achieved was a reconstruction of the market rather than any significant advance or remodelling.

GROWTH IN PEACETIME, 1820–40

Development continued along the same lines between 1820 and 1840. The market was expanded and the level of organization improved without any real advance or transformation being achieved. Nevertheless, some change did take place. Until the 1820s the key player in the global securities market was Paris.[5] Though London was probably the biggest single securities market it was much more domestically focused. Thereafter the relative standing of Paris and London changed, with Amsterdam continuing to play a residual role. The role of Paris in the global securities market was undermined by the very factors that had led to its prominence. As had happened earlier with the British national debt, there was a steady flow back to France of the *rentes* held abroad as French investors grew in numbers and wealth. Prosperity rose after the end of the Napoleonic wars, as reflected in the incomes enjoyed by its population and the growing sophistication of the financial system, with the formation of a number of new banks. As the country grew in wealth, and the government regularly serviced its large debts, individual French investors and French banks and insurance companies chose to hold *rentes* as a safe and remunerative asset. *Rentes* were backed by their own government, were denominated in their own currency, and gave a higher yield than the British national debt. Increasingly in the 1820s *rentes* were held only in France and so commanded an active market only in Paris. No longer did they circulate freely in Europe and act as the common security that linked activity on all main markets, with Paris at the centre. French investors even started to buy and trade the government issues of neighbouring states, such as Spain, Portugal, and Austria in the mid-1820s. By 1830 seven foreign securities were quoted on the Paris Bourse.[6]

However, developments taking place in London in the 1820s were to propel that market to the forefront for the first time. Since 1819 there had been little growth in the size of the British national debt and this freed up British savings for alternative investments. British investors were beginning to look at investments that offered the same flexibility as a holding in the National Debt but a better rate of return. The yield on 3% consols which had stood at 5% in 1816 had fallen to 3.8% in 1822 and declined further to 3.3% in 1824. The government itself took advantage of this steady fall to convert that part of its debt paying 5% per annum to a 4% basis in 1822. Holders unhappy with the new terms were repaid, with a total of £2.8m being returned to investors. With French *rentes* increasingly unavailable and less attractive because yields were also falling there, British merchant banks started issuing a series of foreign loans in London for a wider range of borrowers. Between 1822 and 1825 twenty foreign loans worth £40 million were issued. These were not only on behalf of other European countries but also, in particular, for the newly independent Latin American republics. They were responsible for twelve of the loans and half the amount as they offered very attractive rates of return. Though these loans were largely taken up in London, the merchant banks handling them were frequently part of a European-wide consortium. They recognized the need to appeal to as wide an investing public as possible if they were to get the securities fully taken up at close to the issue price. Accordingly, ownership of these securities became fairly widespread in Europe, and was not confined to Britain. The issues made by the Mexican government were quoted in most European securities markets, for example. Nevertheless, particular securities were preferred by investors in particular countries, and so their trading gravitated to those centres. Paris was the main market for the bonds of the Spanish government, Frankfurt for Austrian government loans whilst Amsterdam hung on to Russia. The Latin American issues were a British speciality, generating a great deal of speculative activity because so little was known about the countries. One country, Poyais, was entirely fictitious. Prices fluctuated wildly as rumours and expectations abounded.[7]

The growth of this market in foreign government bonds posed a serious challenge to the London Stock Exchange, as it did not permit dealings in these securities on its trading floor. Faced with growing pressure from many of its members, and the threat to establish a rival market where foreign government securities could be traded, the London Stock Exchange formed a separate market of its own to cater for these. Opened in January 1823, the Foreign Funds market was a great success with some 200 people attending. The London Stock Exchange was not in the privileged position of the Paris Bourse, which had a monopoly in the market for government debt, and so was less susceptible to competitive pressures. The tension between the those who owned the London Stock Exchange and those who used it produced a dynamic institution which could respond both to the threats of competition and to the needs of new securities. Another challenge appeared in London as speculation spilled over into the shares of joint-stock companies. Beginning with the shares belonging to the few companies in existence, this quickly gained momentum with a large number of new companies. An estimated 624 joint-stock companies were promoted in 1824–5 with a nominal capital of £372.2m, or four times the number and eight times the capital of those already in existence at the end of 1823. They covered a wide range of activities, ranging from domestic canal and railway projects to financial concerns aiming to channel British savings abroad. Among those attracting the greatest interest from speculators were foreign and domestic metal mining companies. As the London Stock Exchange did not provide a market for corporate stocks, apart from the likes of the Bank of England, the solution adopted in 1825 was to permit the buying and selling of shares within this Foreign Funds market. However, the speculative boom in London collapsed towards the end of 1825. A tightening of credit and rising interest rates, due to a poor harvest, caused a flurry of selling in which prices collapsed, leaving investors with large losses. This then brought down a number of banks, who had lent extensively to customers providing speculative stocks and shares as collateral, as they could not repay their borrowings. Investors began to recognize that many of the joint-stock schemes were illusory, impractical, or simply fraudulent, whilst many foreign states found themselves unable to raise sufficient money out of taxes to pay interest on their loans. Of the joint-stock companies 80% had disappeared by the end of 1826. Among the loans raised by Latin American republics only Brazil was still paying interest by December 1828, whilst among the European borrowers, Greece, Portugal, and Spain all defaulted. Nevertheless, out of this debacle came a permanent extension of the London securities market into both foreign government and corporate stocks and bonds. The absorption of the Foreign Funds market into the stock exchange during the 1830s produced a single securities market in London. In contrast, though the Paris Bourse did list a growing number of French corporate securities, with canals being especially popular, most of the new companies formed in the 1820s were not quoted and their shares were traded in the outside market.[8]

After the defaults of the late 1820s, British purchases of foreign government securities slowly revived as interest payments resumed and governments reached agreement with investors on refinancing their debts. In a new spate of borrowing in London, eleven foreign government loans totalling £23 million were issued between 1833 and 1837. In particular, London became the main European market for securities issued in the United States with British investors being large holders of both government debt and corporate securities, especially those of the banks, canals, and the early railroads. One estimate suggests that British holdings of US corporate stocks and bonds had reached some $20 million by 1838. Also held by investors across Europe and North America, these securities were actively traded between all the major markets on both sides of the Atlantic.[9] The number of securities traded in Amsterdam grew from 98 in 1815 to 126 in 1840 with foreign government issues, including Russian and US securities, comprising some two-thirds of the total throughout. As the Dutch national debt was also held extensively abroad, Amsterdam remained a major component of the global securities market in the 1820s and 1830s. However, Amsterdam was no longer able to challenge either London or Paris, given the small size of the Dutch economy, its greatly diminished international importance, and the rise in both taxation and the national debt, which absorbed domestic savings. The Amsterdam securities market remained poorly organized. Attempts in 1833 to create a more disciplined market organization again achieved little, other than the publication of more reliable closing prices.[10]

In addition to being the home market for French *rentes*, Paris also became the principal location for buying and selling the government debt of Spain and the various Italian city-states. Again, these were traded both in Paris and between it and other financial centres such as Madrid and Milan.[11] By the 1820s Frankfurt had also emerged as a securities market of international importance commanding the market for Austrian government bonds. In contrast, Vienna was of limited significance before 1840. Across the Atlantic the New York, Philadelphia, and Boston markets remained active, but small. There were only around fifty-five stockbrokers in New York in 1837, for example. Like Germany, the United States was a fragmented market in terms of securities, with trading divided up between the different centres. This limited the ability of one market either to absorb the largest issues, such as those of the Federal government, or to provide the deep markets needed by financial institutions and merchants, who employed short-term money in long-term debt. As the United States continued to look abroad for certain financial services, such as liquid securities markets, it turned particularly to London, which gradually emerged as the principal market where securities from throughout Europe and the Americas were traded.[12] However, London was by no means dominant. The Paris Bourse in the 1830s provided a market for Austrian, Belgian, Dutch, Greek, Portuguese, and Spanish government bonds as well those issued by individual German, Italian, and US states.[13]

The focus of this global securities market prior to 1840 continued to be government debt. The speculative boom in London in the mid-1820s had produced a large number of joint-stock companies whose shares were widely held and actively traded, but only for a brief period. Most collapsed within a few years, or even months, of their formation whilst even those that remained became closely held and little traded. In the 1830s there was another smaller flurry of joint-stock company formation, resulting in some additions to the number in operation. However, neither the number of companies nor their fields of enterprise had been much extended. The British economy remained mostly untouched by joint-stock enterprise. Those companies that did become well established before 1840 largely provided such services as banking, insurance, gas, and water supply, and transport by canal or railway on a local basis. Owned by the inhabitants of the areas within which they operated, they generated only localized buying and selling.

This was also the situation elsewhere. French investors focused on land and *rentes,* showing only limited demand for corporate stocks and bonds until after 1840. Though numerous joint-stock companies were formed most were little more than extended partnerships, being owned by relatively few investors. As elsewhere, the government's own borrowing needs, supplemented by those of neighbouring countries, were sufficient to meet what demand there was for securities. There were 130,000 individual holders of French government debt in 1830 whilst it was also popular with banks and insurance companies. As in Britain, many of the larger French companies formed in the speculative booms of the 1820s and 1830s collapsed in the subsequent financial crises leaving little trace in the market. An exception was banking, with the number of French joint-stock banks rising from four in the 1820s to twenty one in 1840. There also appeared a number of local gas lighting companies and in the late 1830s a few well-capitalized iron manufacturing companies. Although the total number of securities in the Paris market rose from 38 in 1830 to 260 in 1841, few of these were actively traded corporate stocks. The shares of foreign companies were even rarer with the first of these, the shares of the Banca Romana, being quoted on the Paris Bourse only in 1834. Although joint-stock companies were few and investors preferred land, mortgages, and government bonds, the very existence throughout Europe of joint-stock companies in a wide variety of activities, including manufacturing, do indicate recognition of this corporate form as a means of pooling funds and sharing risks in order to finance particular economic activities. In Germany joint-stock companies developed in such areas as banking, insurance, and textile production as well as the provision of roads and theatres, from the 1820s onwards.[14]

In the United States joint-stock company formation was more advanced. By the mid-1830s, the level of the US national debt had become almost negligible, which meant that there was considerable interest in alternative securities. This was only partially satisfied by the issues of individual states. Nevertheless, the issues of corporate securities were again largely restricted to the usual areas of banking, insurance, turnpike roads, canals, and the provision of such local services as gas supply. One of the few novelties was the appearance of railroad companies in the 1830s. The number of railroad stocks being regularly traded rose from three in 1835 to ten by 1840, by which time they were challenging banks as the most popular corporate security. However, important as these developments were, the size of the joint-stock corporate sector in the United States remained very small. Compared to Federal and State government borrowing or the capital needs of business as a whole, the issue of corporate securities was tiny. Most forms of enterprise could be financed from the savings of a few individuals supplemented by bank credit, and thus had no need to issue stocks and bonds that would appeal to the public at large. Even among the joint-stock companies that did appear only a few were large enough to attract more than a few hundred investors. Only an institution like the Second Bank of the United States had widespread investor appeal. It numbered 4,145 domestic shareholders in 1831, with many others from abroad. As the size of the Federal government debt shrank the US securities market was deprived of that critical mass of securities necessary for generating an active securities market other than during speculative booms. Trading on the New York Stock Exchange rose from $10,209 a day in 1820 to $67,976 in 1824 and then collapsed to $17, 244 in 1828. Similarly, in the 1830s trading rose from $26,156 in 1830 to $423, 763 in 1835 before halving to $214,876 in 1840. Though New York had become the largest securities market in the United Sates by the 1830s, with a turnover far in excess of Philadelphia, it was not nearly as dominant within its own domestic market as was London for Britain or Paris for France. The US securities markets were dependent on volatile corporate stocks or the smaller issues of individual states whereas London and Paris could rely upon the constant trading of their huge national debts, often driven by domestic and international money market conditions.[15]

The slow spread of organized markets remained confined to Europe and North America, being still informal and unspecialized in most countries. An organizational group of 58 bankers operating in Frankfurt from 1825 did not achieve a formal existence until 1836.[16] Even in Amsterdam it was difficult to implement the rules and regulations required to police conduct within the market. Where abuses and manipulation were seen to occur during speculative outbursts, one solution was for the government to intervene, particularly in countries where French influence was strong. In Belgium government-controlled stock exchanges operated in both Antwerp and Brussels in the 1820s, formed under the French Napoleonic code.[17] In Spain the Madrid stock exchange was established in 1831. The model followed was that of the Paris Bourse, with a maximum number of eighteen *agentos de cambios de la Bolsa* being permitted to trade government debt. They had no permanent home and either rented a room or met in the open.[18]

The problem with markets formed and controlled by governments was the regulations imposed. As French securities trading expanded in the 1820s and 1830s, the Paris Bourse faced growing capacity constraints. The cost of membership of the Bourse rose from 30,000 francs in 1816 to 850,000 in 1830 as a result. Inevitably, a large outside market in securities began to develop. For most brokers the cost of joining the Bourse was prohibitive whilst for others the strictures on the conduct of business made membership unattractive. Consequently, the Paris securities market remained fractured. The Bourse met the needs of those who invested in French government debt, were willing to pay the commission charged, and accepted the methods of business imposed. The outside market catered for the expanding market in other securities and catered for those whose business did not fit either the standard charges or standard conditions.[19] Generally, wherever stock exchange regulations were the product of government initiative the result was the existence of large and unregulated alternative markets.

In contrast, there was the slow evolution of securities markets organized from within. The London Stock Exchange provided a minimum set of regulations required for the orderly conduct of business, and no minimum charges, despite considerable support for this from among the membership.

As it catered for all types of securities trading and met the needs of those excluded, such as bankers, no significant outside market in securities arose in London. Outside London, in areas where there was a growing volume of localized transactions in the shares of joint-stock companies, local stock exchanges appeared, including two in Lancashire in the 1830s. This area was experiencing an economic boom linked to the expanding cotton textile industry. Provincial stock exchanges were fundamentally different from the London Stock Exchange as they traded only corporate securities and had a fixed scale of charges reflecting that. The London Stock Exchange continued to monopolize transactions in the national debt and investments in securities on a temporary basis for domestic and international money market purposes.

A similar evolution was taking place in the United States. Major American cities such as New York, Philadelphia, Baltimore, and Boston all had stock exchanges in the 1820s and 1830s. They were very similar to the British provincial stock exchanges, which they pre-dated, as they all regulated the conduct of business and imposed a minimum scale of charges. These charges did drive some business away, particularly the trading in government debt, where the volumes were large and the margins small. Whilst such deals were often done at no charge, with the broker being remunerated through the difference between the buying and selling price, this conflicted with the rules on minimum commissions, which were introduced so as to prevent members undercutting each other, especially in the aftermath of a speculative bubble. As long as the policing of the market was lax, as in the early years of these exchanges, the different types of trading activity were tolerated. However, as supervision of trading practices was gradually tightened and greater control obtained with a dedicated trading room, coexistence of commission and non-commission practices became impossible.

In Britain the clear division between the London Stock Exchange, where no scale of charges was imposed, and the provincial exchanges where it was, reflected the fact that the London Stock Exchange was the market for high volume business, especially on behalf of bankers, whereas the brokers on the provincial exchanges bought and sold corporate stocks on behalf of individual investors. What developed in the United States was a split in the securities market. The debt reduction carried out by the Federal government saw its entire borrowings repaid by 1835, so removing the one security held by all. Loans issued by individual states still tended to be held on a local basis. Localized company formation also created regional clusters of investors. In turn, the buying and selling of these investors provided much of the activity in the various US securities markets. Standard commission charges were acceptable for securities issued by individual companies as brokers had to be knowledgeable on the terms and conditions applying in each case and to work harder in matching sales and purchases in what were often thin markets. This made the whole process much more complex than trading in government debt on behalf of bankers. In contrast, that was much less true of bonds and so trading in these was increasingly located outside the stock exchanges. The New York Stock Exchange developed instead as a market for corporate securities, especially stocks. During the 1830s these constituted almost its entire business. The number of listed stocks rose from 28 in 1820 to 112 in 1840. In turn, the existence of specialized and orderly markets for corporate securities encouraged the formation and growth of companies whose shares were relatively widely held.[20]

The different ways in which securities markets were organized before 1840 had implications for the way national financial systems and business organizations evolved. A division was emerging both between those countries with stock exchanges and those without, and between those with stock exchanges created and controlled by governments and those arising from the needs of market participants. However, securities markets had not yet become central elements of national and international financial systems. The securities traded remained, overwhelmingly, the product of wars and indebtedness rather than the finance of economic growth and the creation of prosperity. As such, securities remained of tangential importance within a world where self-finance and bank credit were central. The growth in the volume of corporate stocks and bonds in circulation was largely confined to Britain and the United States, where securities markets were more responsive to the needs of brokers. Nevertheless, the huge size of national debts continued to dominate the major markets of London and Paris.

CAPITAL AND SECURITIES, 1840–50

Prior to 1840 almost all of the securities in existence had been issued by governments for the finance of wars.[21] Whilst this continued to comprise an important element of the securities market, in the 1840s there was also a significant expansion in the sales of securities for productive uses. However, this advance did not develop in all countries, nor did it encompass all areas of an economy. From the mid-nineteenth century especially, what characterized advanced economies were infrastructure developments, particularly the growth of urban areas and permanent transport links. Though being capital-intensive in nature many of these infrastructure developments could continue to be financed on an individual or incremental basis. The urban housing stock, for instance, could be gradually built up in response to demand without the need for a large initial investment. Thus, it had no need to tap securities markets for finance. However, others could not be provided in this way, such as gas and water supply and, especially, canal and railway networks. In these cases a relatively complete system was required if sufficient customers were to be carried and profits made. A large initial investment was essential, with only a promise of future payment of a regular income as an attraction. Infrastructure projects of this kind were beyond the capabilities of individuals operating alone or in small groups. Equally, the long-term nature of the investment, with no repayment possible for many years, placed such projects outside the scope of banks operating on short-term deposits and credit.

Here was a demand for capital that securities could meet. Companies providing canal transport and supplying water had already appeared before 1800, whilst a growing number of gas companies were promoted in the 1820s and 1830s. All had the classic characteristics of projects requiring a large initial investment but which then paid a steady return on shares cover the years. The corporate form had even been extended in a very small way to capital-intensive manufacturing in continental Europe, as with Belgium iron companies in the 1830s. However, the financial needs of railways was of an entirely different order of magnitude as this involved equipping an entire economy with a completely new transport system within a relatively few years. Only the use of the securities markets on a large scale could provide the amount of finance required, given the absence of any centrally managed transport policy financed by central government.

Developments in railway finance began in Britain. From a mere £0.2 million invested in Britain's railways in 1825, rising to £7.5 million in 1835, by 1840 capital investment had reached £48.1 million. Within the space of the next five years it almost doubled, with £88.5 million invested by 1845. Numerous railway companies were promoted, some of whose shares rose to a large premium, only to collapse subsequently with the schemes being abandoned. From 1843 to 1845 there was a railway mania in Britain as investors became ever more enthusiastic about the prospects of each line proposed. As previously, this speculative boom originated in a temporary mismatch between the growth of savings and the existence of remunerative openings. During the mid-1820s and mid-1830s, overseas investment had provided a major outlet, so moderating the level of domestic joint-stock company formation in Britain. In the mid-1830s, for example, individual states or even municipalities in the United States borrowed on the London market. However, many of these borrowers then defaulted between 1841 and 1843, discouraging British investors from taking up new loans as well as encouraging them to sell those they had. These defaults had a much greater impact on the British investor than the European. Of the $34.5 million in bonds issued by Pennsylvania, over $20 million was held in Britain compared to only $1.8 million in the Netherlands and $0.6 million in France. This was typical of the overall position.[22] With the debts of the major European governments being largely held by their own population, and the Latin American republics discredited after the defaults of the late 1820s, British investors turned towards corporate securities.

Even there the choice was restricted to the domestic economy. Investors were reluctant to extend their investments overseas as so many past ventures briefly flourished only to disappear without a trace, as with the mining companies in the speculative boom of the 1820s. Among the few attractive domestic alternatives the British government itself curtailed one obvious area, that of banking. With the passage of the Bank Charter Act the privilege of note issue was removed from new banks, which placed them at a disadvantage with respect to existing banks, and so forestalled those planning to bring new banking companies to the market. As gas and water companies already existed, and mining and manufacturing were both able to finance themselves and had a poor track record when it came to public companies, the choice was limited. Under these circumstances investors turned eagerly to railway company securities. These appeared to offer an almost guaranteed return as, once built, a railway line had a near monopoly of transport between the towns that it served. In addition, as more railway lines that were built, more traffic would be generated within an integrated railway network. Each line fed on others as the railway became the preferred route for freight and passengers rather than the more expensive roads or the slower waterways. Only the railway could offer the combination of speed, price, regularity, accessibility, and certainty that was required of transport in an advanced economy. In addition railway securities provided an ideal means whereby short-term funds could finance long-term projects, because their earnings were relatively predictable whilst the large size of individual issues made them easy to buy and sell in formally organized markets. This made available a vast supply of additional savings at low interest rates for infrastructure projects that could not have been easily financed otherwise.

As in past speculative bubbles, growing enthusiasm among investors developed a momentum of its own that eventually became a mania. The stocks and shares issued by railway companies, usually in a part-paid form, became speculative counters held for future gain rather than intrinsic worth. Though all recognized the contribution that railways would make to the improvement of transport within Britain, these expectations became increasingly unrealistic and prices were driven upwards. This situation was fuelled by generous bank lending using inflated share values as collateral. It spilled over into the securities of foreign railways with British investors buying those issued in

France and the United States, in particular. Eventually the boom came to an end towards the end of 1845. Triggering the collapse was a poor harvest as this led to a tightening of credit as prices rose and people drew on their savings. A wave of selling overwhelmed the market, bringing the boom to an abrupt end, bankrupting those who had borrowed too extensively, and bringing down the most exposed banks.

Nevertheless, corporate securities in Britain had been permanently expanded, not just in absolute terms but also in relation to the national debt. By 1853 the paid-up capital of the securities quoted on the London Stock Exchange amounted to £1.2 billion. Of this the British national debt had shrunk to 70% of quoted securities, as it was no longer growing, whilst 5% were securities issued by other governments. However, 25% had now been issued by companies. Of this British railways were by far the biggest component, and at £194m represented 16% of the overall total. Membership of the London Stock Exchange rose by 50%, reaching 906 in 1851 compared to 617 in 1844, whilst the securities market was extended to centres throughout Britain. The very vitality of local investment by local investors in local securities, combined with the excitement of speculation in the 1840s, drove the formation of organized markets outside London. The appearance of numerous well-capitalized railway companies, whose shares were actively traded among new and enthusiastic groups of provincial investors, represented a major challenge to the provincial securities market. Membership of existing provincial stock exchanges shot up, with Liverpool reaching 220 in 1846, whilst a rash of new stock exchanges appeared all over the country. By the end of 1845 there were some eighteen provincial stock exchanges in Britain compared to three at the beginning of the decade. Most major towns possessed at least one. In Dublin, there were at one time four separate rival stock exchanges, as the established Dublin Stock Exchange, controlled by its membership, limited entry, and enforced high commission changes.

Once the speculative boom passed, several of these provincial stock exchanges faded away, as with Huddersfield and Nottingham, or merged into one, as in Dublin, whilst the number of provincial stockbrokers slumped by around 20%, from *c.*500 in 1846 to *c.*400 in 1850. Nevertheless, there now existed a multi-centred British securities market with cities like Glasgow, Edinburgh, Manchester, Liverpool, Leeds, Birmingham, and Bristol all possessing established and active stock exchanges providing a local forum for the trading of locally held securities. A decisive shift had taken place. The securities market was now firmly placed within the national capital market, helping to meet the financial requirements of the British economy, particularly the transport infrastructure, rather than simply the needs of government, determined by military spending during wars.

Though the railway mania of the 1840s was very much a British affair it was mirrored to some extent in a number of other countries. France most nearly paralleled the British experience. As in Britain, there was an abundance of savings in France; this underpinned a speculative boom from 1843 to 1846 followed by a crisis in 1847. Unlike Britain this boom was not focused solely on railways but was more general. By 1848 around twenty-five quasi-banks and thirty joint-stock insurance companies, with a combined capital of around 300 million francs, had been established. These new banking facilities led to a large expansion in the supply of credit that stimulated further company promotions as there was considerable lending on the collateral of securities. In the wake of this France experienced its own railway mania. Numerous railway companies were promoted, issuing shares in a partly paid form, which fuelled speculative interest as they were repeatedly bought and sold in the expectation of large gains. The 400,000 shares issued by the Railway du Nord generated a turnover of 571,741 shares between 28 October 1845 and 1 January 1846. Altogether, shares with an estimated value of 1 billion francs were issued by French railway companies during the 1840s and were taken up by numerous investors across France. By 1847–8 railway shares had become as popular as government *rentes* with around 200,000 French investors holding both. This represented the first major breakthrough for corporate securities in France. Not confined to railway shares, the boom encompassed iron manufacturing companies and coal and iron mining, as railway construction created a huge need for increased capacity to produce rails. However, it was the railways that generated the mass appeal and underpinned the growth of the securities market. Whereas the Compagnie des Mines de Loire attracted 1,916 investors in 1845–6 the Bordeaux to Cette Railway found itself with 10,800.

As a result, the French securities market was transformed not only in terms of the level of activity but also the range of securities traded and the geographical extension beyond Paris. In sectors such as banking, transport, mining, and metallurgy businesses were now issuing transferable securities in order to finance their activities. Many new companies were located in the provinces where they attracted local investors and stimulated the creation of local securities markets. Towns such as Bordeaux, Lille, Marseilles, and Toulouse all developed active securities markets in the 1840s with Lyons emerging as the most important centre outside Paris. Despite the crisis following the collapse of the speculative boom many of these companies and the markets that served their securities survived. By 1850 there existed in France three distinct components of the securities market. The Paris Bourse continued to provide a market for government debt. Over 90% of this was French but a significant proportion was now foreign. The outside market in

Paris catered for much of the corporate securities created, especially the new banks, insurance companies, railways, and industrial concerns. Finally, the emerging provincial exchanges provided a market for the locally owned corporate stocks. Paris was now an international market not because French government debt was held abroad but because French investors themselves had extensive foreign holdings. This had happened simultaneously with the growth of provincial markets.[23]

Elsewhere in Europe the speculative boom was much less in evidence. Apart from in Belgium joint-stock enterprise had made little progress before 1840, with some governments restricting the formation of large joint-stock companies because of risks they might pose if they collapsed. However, the 1840s did witness some spread of joint-stock enterprise across Europe. In Spain numerous banks and mining companies, and a few railways, were promoted during a speculative outburst in the mid-1840s. In Germany railway companies were promoted following the building of some early lines in the 1830s. Much of the finance was obtained from local investors. However, the number of companies formed was low and most of the securities were traded in Berlin and failed to stimulate the growth of local markets. In 1846–7 Berlin provided a market for fifty-one different railway issues compared to only nine in Frankfurt, which remained a market for state debt rather than corporate securities. Nevertheless, there was sufficient business in Frankfurt to justify a building being dedicated to securities trading in 1843. Much the same situation prevailed in Austria with the Vienna Bourse trading railway securities from 1842. In Belgium activity in the securities market was largely in the shares of the leading financial institutions, the Societe Generale de Belgique and the Banque de Belgique. These acted as holding companies for industrial and railway securities as well as being major lenders to business in general. The railway mania passed Amsterdam by. Amsterdam remained a market for government bonds issued either by the Netherlands itself or by Russia. It had not yet moved into corporate securities to any extent.[24]

Railway securities appear to have been particularly attractive to investors as they so closely resembled government debt in terms of the volume of issue and the stability of income. Railway projects absorbed vast amounts of capital provided by numerous investors and, when built, produced regular payments as their income and expenditure varied little, making them much less risky compared to other forms of joint-stock enterprise. The popularity of railways inaugurated the extension of securities markets into the corporate arena.

Despite the early development of railways in the United States it was a rather late participant in the railway mania. The defaults of so many individual states in the early 1840s had seriously damaged investor confidence, already weakened by market abuses in the 1830s. The result was that in the United States the speculative boom centring on railways was both limited and came late. In the 1840s there was no great expansion in the number of securities traded on the main markets. Between 1840 and 1850 the total number of securities quoted on New York, Philadelphia, Boston, and Baltimore rose from 321 in 1840 to 329 in 1845 and then reached 390 by 1850. The volume of trading grew and the main US securities markets experienced an expansion in both locally held railway securities and those from a distance. Though Philadelphia and Boston were quick to develop a market for the railroad securities, including those from outside their regions, it was New York that dominated. Deprived of the debt of the national government, and shaken by state defaults, banks shifted in the 1840s to lending money using railroad stocks and bonds as collateral. As this became more common New York gradually became the leading market for railroad securities as those holding them could more easily and cheaply finance their positions there than elsewhere. There thus developed in New York a strong relationship between the call money market and the trading in railroad stocks, whereas in other financial centres such as London, Paris, and Amsterdam the links were more with the market in government debt.

In the United States the organized markets increasingly dominated trading in these corporate stocks, encouraged by various states' attempts to outlaw such speculative market practices as time bargains. This gave greater control of the securities market in the United States to the stock exchanges. Though missing out on the railway mania of the 1840s, the United States acquired in this decade a system of securities markets somewhat akin to the spread of provincial stock exchanges in Britain. These were markets controlled by their membership operating under rules free from government interference and utilizing a scale of fixed charges and tight control over admission. These markets largely traded corporate stocks. What the United States lacked at this stage was a market like London, Paris, or Amsterdam that specialized in meeting the needs of the government debt market and was closely connected to national and international money market activity. Instead, much of the money market transactions generated by the US's large trade was conducted in London, where not only was the country's extensive exports and imports financed but also internal commerce through the strong merchant banking links that existed between the two countries.[25]

Lagging behind developments in the United States but following a similar pattern was the gradual appearance of embryonic securities markets in those parts of the world also influenced by British practice and customs. In Australia securities trading in the major cities developed from the 1820s onwards. As the various Australian governments borrowed in London not locally, there was no market in these securities in Australia. That was also the case with the shares of many of the largest Australian joint-stock companies as they had been formed in Britain and that was where their investors were located. Instead, a market appeared in the shares issued by a growing number of Australian joint-stock companies operating in such areas as banking, insurance, and steam shipping. There was a flurry of these in the mid-1830s leading to a severe crash in the early 1840s, but the level of trading prior to 1850 did not reach that necessary to support specialized brokers let alone an organized market.[26] A similar situation existed in India where government debt was again held in London not in India. Thus, the securities that did circulate there were those of the small number of local joint-stock companies that were formed, copying British practice, and drawing in investors both from the resident British population and from among wealthy and entrepreneurial Indians. The Bank of Bombay, established in 1840, had 387 shareholders of whom a third were Indian. However, the great majority of the investors were British merchants operating in India, plus a few army officers and doctors. This confined the investing public to a very small number spread across the major Indian cities. Nevertheless, these investors and the securities that they held were sufficient to support a small stock broking community. Bombay and Calcutta had about six stockbrokers each in the mid-1840s but this was too low to justify the establishment of organized markets.[27]

CONCLUSION

Most of these developments in the global securities market were isolated responses to local conditions, though often sharing common characteristics in terms of timing and the nature of the securities traded. The mid-1840s witnessed a number of speculative booms around the world in which corporate securities, especially railways, were very much to the fore. However, unlike previous booms a degree of market integration was possible in the 1840s because of a transformation in communications. Important as the railway was in providing faster transport the greatest influence on the operation of the securities market was the telegraph. Significant construction of national telegraph systems took place in the 1840s. These linked major cities in countries such as Britain, France, and the United States. Telegraph lines even provided a unity to Germany that was absent politically at this time. The result was the creation of a national securities market as the telegraph allowed prices to be quickly disseminated among the various centres. By the late 1840s all the major securities markets in Britain had access to the national telegraph system. Prices could be quickly equalized by redistributing the ownership of securities in line with national supply and demand. Trading in the national debt and related securities remained located on the London Stock Exchange, as it was driven by money market considerations. In contrast the market for railway securities was widely dispersed, though there were local concentrations, and so there was considerable trading between separate stock exchanges. Depending on the strength of the market the telegraph contributed to both a centralization and decentralization of the British securities market in the 1840s.

The telegraph was also widely introduced into the United States in the 1840s with significant consequences for the securities markets there. It contributed to making a single market out of the stock exchanges located in the north-eastern seaboard, especially the twin centres of New York and Philadelphia. Those securities that were held in common, and in which active markets existed in both centres, were actively traded between the two by means of information and orders transmitted via the telegraph.[28] Similar developments were taking place in continental Europe in the late 1840s with the construction of national telegraph networks in the economically more advanced countries of the north and west. Amsterdam and Rotterdam were connected by telegraph in 1847, for example. Berlin and Frankfurt linked in 1849, though the transmission time took one hour as there were five intermediate stations for the message to pass through. These developments in continental Europe not only created more integrated national securities markets but, through links between telegraph systems, constituted the beginning of a more integrated global securities market. By the late 1840s Paris and Brussels were connected.[29] However, the use of the telegraph by the securities market was still in its infancy in the 1840s, even within individual countries. There was no link between London and other European centres, for example, let alone a connection across the Atlantic to the United States. Individual components of the global securities market still traded largely in ignorance of each other with only delayed corrections on the receipt of information that could be days or weeks old, accompanied by high-risk buying and selling orders based on hopelessly out-of-date prices.

What the global securities market experienced in the 1840s was a simultaneous deepening and broadening. There came into existence a class of corporate securities that could rival government debt in its attractiveness to investors. Though this had only really begun in a few countries, principally Britain followed by France and the United States, it introduced a means whereby securities markets could be tapped by business in their search for finance. At the same time securities trading, if not markets, had begun to appear beyond Western Europe and the United States. Though the level of activity was low and few specialist intermediaries existed, this was a significant new departure. Furthermore, the introduction and tentative use of the telegraph had the potential to break the spatial boundaries that had always limited the development of a truly global securities market. By 1850 the global securities market was on the edge of two major breakthroughs. One was in the realm of the securities traded. Railway development created a class of securities that had the properties of government debt but financed a major improvement in the provision of land transport instead of war. The other was in the realm of communications. The coming of the telegraph divorced communication from transport and so permitted a degree of market integration that had never before been possible.

4

Exchanges and Networks: 1850–1900

1850 marks a crucial stage in the development of a truly global securities market. Securities moved out of the realm of government debt and entered the mainstream of economic activity, becoming increasingly central to the processes whereby business obtained finance, banks balanced risk and return, and investors employed their savings. Not confined to national boundaries, this transformation became a worldwide phenomenon. By 1900 no continent was immune from the reach of securities and the markets that served them. National securities markets became integrated into an international network that was far deeper and broader than anything previously achieved. The revolution in communications conquered the problem of distance that had always existed when the only mode of contact was physical transport. With the development of the telegraph distant financial centres could be linked through messages that flowed back and forth in minutes rather than days and weeks, or even months. This period also experienced an enormous expansion in the number and spread of stock exchanges around the world. Advanced economies in western Europe and North America came to possess not one but several stock exchanges serving particular regions or specific types of stocks. In addition, stock exchanges were formed in every continent of the world, spreading across Australia and New Zealand, Latin America, Asia, and Africa as well as invading Eastern Europe and the Mediterranean area. Though part of this expansion was simply a by-product of the European diaspora of the nineteenth century, part was also the implantation of an alien organizational form into different cultures, as in the case of Japan. By 1900 the world possessed an integrated and functioning global securities market benefiting from an international communication network, a mass of easily transferable stocks and bonds, the existence of organized markets, and a minimum of government-imposed barriers at home or abroad.

There was a massive expansion in the amount and importance of securities in existence between 1850 and 1900. One estimate for 1880 put the aggregate value of quoted securities in Europe at £6.8 billion and this had trebled to

£20 billion by 1906, with a further £9 billion in the rest of the world, at least half of which was in the United States. In France the amount of securities owned by French investors rose from 9.1 billion francs in 1850 to 86.9 billion in 1899, an almost tenfold increase. Within that it was the foreign component which rose most rapidly, growing from 2.5 billion francs or 27% of the total to 27 billion or 31%.[1] Similarly, the value of the securities quoted on the London Stock Exchange, the world's largest and most international throughout the period, rose almost sixfold, from £1.2 billion in 1853 to £7 billion in 1903. This excludes the foreign bonds payable abroad, which would have added a further £1.9 billion to the 1903 figure. During a period of deflation and relative international peace the value of transferable securities grew strongly.[2] In relation to national assets securities also grew steadily in importance. Though biased towards the more developed economies a sample of countries for which data is available suggest that securities rose from 9.1% of national assets in the 1850s to 12.9% around 1880 and reached 15.7% by 1900. At a time of rapidly growing global wealth a rising proportion was in the form of securities compared to other types of assets (see Table 4.2).

SECURITIES AND NATIONAL ECONOMIES

Within this rapid expansion of the value of securities, those issued by governments continued to be of major importance. Between 1848 and 1895 global public debt rose from £1.7 billion to £6.2 billion, or over fourfold, and that figure excluded Asian, African, and Latin American countries. As always, governments borrowed to meet military expenditure. The debts associated with major conflicts ranged from £474 million for the US Civil war (1861–5) and £382 million for the Franco-German war (1870–1) to £305 million for the Crimean war (1854–6) and £211 million for the Russo-Ottoman war (1876–7).[3] By 1850 the French government had repaid the large debts incurred during and after the Napoleonic wars, including indemnity payments, only to incur new debt over the next 25 years. France ended up issuing 2.2 billion francs in bonds between 1855 (during the Crimean War) and 1874 (after the disastrous campaign of 1870–1 against Germany) and only redeeming 1.8 billion. The imposition of a war indemnity of 5 billion francs in 1871 created a major expansion in the securities issued. Only thereafter did the French government reduce its dependence on the securities market for finance. Though the French public debt grew from 24.3 billion francs in 1880 to 30.1 billion in 1900 this did not keep pace with the rise in national income, a feature common through Europe.[4] After 1871 a long period of peace in continental Europe reduced the pressure on government finances.

In consequence there were even a few countries in which the national debt actually fell both absolutely and relatively, the most marked being Britain. The British national debt fell by £225 million between 1850 and 1900 despite a series of wars fought largely in the Empire. Successive British governments so managed their finances that they were not only able to fund short or limited military engagements without resorting to massive borrowing, but were also able to repay outstanding debts.[5] More typical of what was happening in western Europe was the Dutch experience where the amount of the national debt remained roughly stable but shrank relative to rising national income.[6] Elsewhere in Europe and the Mediterranean area government indebtedness either grew strongly or remained high as governments embarked on imperial expansion and nation-building projects or were simply unable to raise sufficient money through taxation. In order to finance eastward expansion the Russian public debt climbed to 6.2 billion roubles by 1900. The Ottoman government resorted to frequent issues of securities in the late nineteenth century largely due to an inability to manage its finances and the costs of military campaigns. On top of already chaotic public finances the war with Russia between 1876 and 1878 led the Ottoman government to ignore or postpone its financial obligations and tap every possible source of funds in order to meet pressing military expenditures. Default was inevitable, followed by protracted negotiations with the bondholders.[7]

For the United States the Civil War dealt a massive blow to attempts to reduce the national debt. Whereas in 1861 the outstanding debt of the US Federal government was a mere $90.5 million, by 1866 this had escalated to $2.8 billion. Borrowing by the Confederate States, which was never recognized by the Union government, amounted to a further $303 million. Thereafter, however, the Federal government repaid debt and restrained borrowing. By 1900 the debt was down to $1.3 billion or only around 7% of US national income.[8] Other governments increasingly copied European/American practice and tapped the securities markets for funds. However, it was mainly in countries with a strong European influence, such as Australia and Canada, Argentina and Brazil, that governments used securities to supplement other sources of revenue such as customs duties and direct taxes. Their populations were familiar with European financing techniques, including the issue of interest-paying government bonds that could be traded on securities markets, and were able to exploit that knowledge. Other governments around the world also saw that borrowing in this way could both stabilize their finances and lower the interest payable. In the 1870s the Japanese government capitalized its pension obligations through the issue of transferable bonds to the 307,451 *samurai* to whom it had made commitments. These securities were then traded as many *samurai* wished to dispose of them whilst merchants, bankers, and landowners were ready to purchase.[9] In 1899, faced with the escalating costs of the Sino-Japanese war and deteriorating public finances the Japanese government borrowed £10 million through the issue of securities.[10]

Despite the growing popularity of government financing by means of security issues, the relatively peaceful nature of the post-1870 era restrained the level of government borrowing. A major improvement in state finances came through additional taxation. Government borrowing was also increasingly directed towards assisting economic development as with the construction of railways and other infrastructure projects or towards purchasing and running revenue-generating assets. Of the total public debt in Europe, North America, and Australia by 1894 around £1.4 billion (22%) had resulted from railway construction. Governments had either assumed direct responsibility for the construction of specific lines or taken into public ownership existing railway companies. Across Europe railway systems were nationalized in whole or part, with investors swapping holdings of stocks and bonds for issues of public debt. Instead of borrowing for unproductive military purposes, governments were bequeathing to later generations ownership of profitable assets like railways, docks, and public utilities and contributing to the means of paying these debts through rising national income. As government debt was less of a crippling burden the risk of default receded. As Mulhall observed in 1896, '... the debts of some countries in 1895 are largely made up of sums spent on state railways, the net proceeds of which considerably swell the public revenues'.[11]

Defaults continued to occur, as with the Ottoman government and even Argentina, when borrowing grew faster than increased revenue generated by the investments made. Generally, though, government debt was increasingly regarded as one of the safest investments of the late nineteenth century. A detailed examination into British investments conducted by Nash in 1881 concluded that

after deducting the losses incurred upon defaulting securities in 1874, 1875, and 1876, not only had Foreign Government stocks been a profitable holding to our investors taken as a whole, but ... they had during the past ten years been more profitable to us than Colonial Government Debentures, in spite, too, of the fact that no colonial securities were, or had been, in default.[12]

Despite occasional defaults and moratoriums governments were seen to honour their obligations after 1850. One consequence of this was a decline in the yield on government debt. In 1887 the French government converted its *rentes* from a 4.5/4% basis to 3% whilst the British government switched the longstanding 3% consols to 2.75% from 1889 with a reduction to 2.5% promised after 1903.[13] This encouraged investors to search for alternative securities carrying the same level of certainty of income but paying a somewhat better rate of return. As a result, despite the huge growth in the amount of government securities in existence, their importance declined relative to national assets, falling marginally from 5.1% in the 1850s to 4.6% in 1900.[14]

Alternative securities increased considerably in popularity after 1850, and especially after 1870. Already well established in several countries in Western Europe and in the United States before 1850, railway stocks and bonds were the first and the largest group of securities to fill this void. Their position was greatly strengthened as the early railways moved from being speculative counters to become dependable generators of revenue capable of not only servicing their bonds but also paying regular dividends on their stocks. Investor confidence, and investments, rose. In Britain the total track in operation rose from 6,447 miles in 1850 to 21,863 in 1900. Countries such as France and Germany constructed even larger railway networks, as did Russia, with its vast distances to be covered. Even more spectacular was the situation around the world. Argentina, Brazil, and Mexico all had extensive networks by 1900, with that of Argentina being by far the largest. Whereas Asia, Africa, and Australasia had no railways in 1850, collectively they had almost 100,000 km in operation by the end of the century. Even though the United States already had an extensive railroad system in 1850, at 14,518 km, this only served the eastern seaboard area. By 1900 operational track had grown to 311,160 km, reaching every corner of the country. Over the same period the Canadian railway network expanded from a mere 106 kilometres in 1850 to 29,531 kilometres and now stretched from the Atlantic to the Pacific. Overall, the length of the world's railway lines grew from 38,152 km in 1850 to 765,222 in 1900, a 20-fold increase. In terms of speed and extent this was a massive and unparalleled achievement. No wonder the railway was the symbol of the age[15] (see Table 4.1).

Table 4.1. World railway mileage (km)

Year	Total	Europe	North America	South/Central America	Asia	Africa	Australia/ New Zealand
1850	38,152	23,026	14,624	502	—	—	—
1900	765,222	265,574	340,868	60,843	56,624	16,319	24,994

Source: B. R. Mitchell, *International Historical Statistics* (London, 1998), vol 1–3, table F1.

To achieve such worldwide expansion so rapidly required vast investment. Though governments were involved, especially in mid-century, financing was largely left to individual companies and their ability to issue stocks and bonds to the investing public. No other means of finance was possible given the scale and timing of the financial requirements, as entire systems had to be constructed if individual components were to be viable. The capital cost of the world's railway system grew from £465 million in 1850 to £6.7 billion in 1894, by which time Mulhall claimed it was 'much greater than the aggregate of public debts, and equal to 10% of the total wealth of mankind'.[16] Certainly, the total value of the securities issued to fund the British railway system rose from £245.8 million in 1850 to £1,176 million in 1900 by which time it was over twice the size of the country's national debt. In the United States the stocks and bonds issued to finance the vast railroad network grew from $318million in 1850 to $11.5 billion by 1900, by then almost nine times the national debt.[17] Across the world the period 1850–1900 witnessed the displacement of government debt with railway stocks and bonds in the portfolios of major investors whilst securities as a whole were of growing importance as a share of national assets. Using the US data of securities issued for each kilometre of track by 1900 it can be estimated that the creation of the world's railway system had generated $1.4 billion in securities as early as 1850 but a massive $28.3 billion in 1900.[18]

The consequence for the global securities market was enormous as railway securities challenged and in some cases supplanted government debt as the investment of choice for many. As Caron has noted for France, 'there can be no doubt that massive issues of railway securities over the second half of the nineteenth century dominated and widened the market for paper securities in France right up to 1900'.[19] Whereas in 1851 only 12% of French securities were issued by railways, the figure for 1902 was 33%. Over the same period the proportion of government debt fell from 75% to 48%. In 1900 railway stocks and bonds accounted for 43% of the nominal value of all securities quoted on the Paris Bourse, 44% on the London Stock Exchange, and dominated trading on the New York Stock Exchange. In the United States the proportion of securities issued by companies rather than Federal, state, and other government bodies expanded from an already high 70% in the 1850s to 85% in 1900, due primarily to the finance of railway construction[20] (see Table 4.2). Where railways led other sectors of the economy followed, though with some delay. In France the proportion of securities not issued either by governments or railways grew from 13.1% in 1851 to 19.2% in 1902, and a similar pattern was observable for Britain.[21] In 1853 only 5% of the securities quoted on the London Stock Exchange had been issued by joint-stock companies other than railways. By 1903 that proportion had risen to 20%.

Table 4.2. Securities as a proportion of national assets, 1850–1900

Category	Belgium	France	Germany	India	Italy	UK	US	Average
1850/60								
Government Domestic Debt(%)	5.1	4.4	2.3	2.6	5.4	12.8	3.2	5.1
Corporate Bonds(%)	—	0.9	0.9	0.15	1.6	3.0	2.8	1.6
Corporate Stocks(%)	6.5	1.0	0.5	0.15	1.8	3.0	5.5	2.3
Foreign Assets (gross) (%)	—	1.7	—	—	—	—	0.5	
Foreign Assets (net) (%)	—	0.5	—	-2.2	-0.5	3.1	-2.1	1.7
Total(%)	11.6	7.8	3.7	0.7	8.3	21.9	9.4	9.1

Category	Belgium	Denmark	France	Germany	India	Italy	Japan	Norway	Switzerland	UK	US	Average
1875/85												
Government Debt(%)	4.3	2.7	7.8	2.1	1.8	13.6	3.7	2.2	2.2	7.2	4.9	4.8
Corporate Bonds(%)	1.5	0.4	4.5	1.0	0.2	1.1	—	—	2.8	4.0	4.2	2.2
Corporate Stocks(%)	6.5	9.2	2.7	1.7	0.2	0.9	0.5	1.7	4.7	4.0	9.2	3.8
Foreign Assets (gross) (%)	—	—	5.1	2.7	—	—	—	—	9.2	—	0.8	
Foreign Assets (net) (%)	—	2.6	4.9	—	-5.1	-2.4	-3.7	—	4.7	9.7	-2.5	4.3
Total(%)	12.3	14.9	19.9	7.5	—	13.2	0.5	3.9	14.4	24.9	17.8	12.9

(*Continued*)

Table 4.2. (*Continued*)

1875/85 Category	Belgium	Denmark	Germany	India	Italy	Japan	Norway	Switzerland	UK	US	Average
Government Domestic Debt(%)	6.7	2.5	5.2	1.9	13.1	2.3	3.7	2.3	5.9	2.2	4.6
Corporate Bonds(%)	1.6	0.3	0.4	0.3	1.0	—	—	3.5	6.2	3.4	2.1
Corporate Stocks(%)	5.1	8.8	2.7	0.3	1.2	3.8	3.1	6.2	16.1	9.2	5.7
Foreign Assets (gross)(%)	—	—	4.7	—	—	—	—	12.7	—	0.7	
Foreign Assets (net)(%)	4.7	−2.3	—	−6.1	−2.6	−1.2	—	8.4	14.6	−1.5	5.1
Total(%)	18.1	9.3	13.0	−3.6	12.7	4.9	6.8	20.4	42.8	13.3	15.7

Note: Method of calculation

This data is very crude and can only give a rough indication of the relative importance of securities across different countries at different times. In the use of Goldsmith's data the following assumptions are made:

1. All government debt, corporate stocks and bonds, and net foreign assets are transferable securities (cf. Goldsmith pp. 83, 95, 151, 175–6).
2. Where no net figure for foreign assets is given the gross is used.
3. Where corporate stocks and bonds are grouped together, the assumption is made that they divide equally.

Source: R. W. Goldsmith, *Comparative National Balance Sheets* (Chicago, 1985), tables 34, 35 and appendix A.

However, most of the expansion in corporate securities remained in areas already popular before 1850, especially banking, insurance, and basic public services such as water and gas. Similar economic activities developing in the late nineteenth century were also funded through securities issues. These included urban tramways, underground systems, telephone networks, and electricity generation and distribution. Once in full operation these each generated a steady revenue and possessed relative immunity from competition. As a result not only could they issue and service bonds but their shares were also attractive in offering both the prospect of income and the opportunity to share in the rising prosperity of the enterprise. There was a rapid growth in the number and variety of banking and insurance companies. Banks appeared specializing in mortgage finance whilst insurance companies extended beyond the traditional areas of fire, life, and marine into such areas as accident or reinsurance. New investment trusts pooled the savings of individual investors and then invested extensively in a portfolio of securities. However, prior to 1900 there was no massive extension of the joint-stock principle in spite of the fact that governments across the world abandoned attempts to control joint-stock company formation.[22] Only in particular sectors of the economy did a need to obtain external funding coincide with an ability to appeal to the investing public through the issue of transferable securities. Even then the issue of securities was only one option available within increasingly sophisticated financial systems, and often not the most appropriate one. Most businesses required mainly short-term credit which banks were ideal at providing because they could increasingly operate upon the short-term savings generated within developed economies. By 1880 deposits in European banks had reached around $4.6 billion with another $3.1 billion in North America, and this was in addition to the capital raised from the partners or shareholders.[23]

Outside western Europe and North America, there was a greater need to issue securities beyond the traditional areas of infrastructure development and financial services. In newly settled or less advanced economies the demand for finance often proved greater than the savings possessed by those directly involved and their informal networks and outran the resources of a nascent banking system, especially if the speed of expansion was rapid. This was especially true where a new industry was developing using a technology or product introduced from abroad, which involved considerable risk for investors. The adoption elsewhere of mass production techniques for textiles and iron manufacture developed in Western Europe made the prospects of individual enterprises highly uncertain. The use of the joint-stock company form and the issue of shares offered a way of both sharing risk and raising capital, and so was adopted in many countries. In Russia the cotton textile industry and the iron and steel industry were developed through joint-stock companies and the issue of stocks and shares. By 1900 the nominal capital of Russian companies in these two sectors totalled around £120 million and though dwarfed by that of the railways and government borrowing, which collectively came to over £1 billion, this represented a major investment for the Russian economy.[24] Similarly in Japan, though securities were used mainly to finance the government and the railway system, early industrialization was aided by share issues of the cotton spinning companies. By 1896 there were 76 quoted Japanese cotton spinning companies with a paid-up capital of ¥28.8 million, beginning with the Osaka Spinning Company in 1883.[25] In India the development of tea planting, textile production, and coal mining industries depended heavily on joint-stock companies and the issue of shares.[26]

The most prominent area of economic activity where securities were issued was in mining. Throughout the Americas, Australia, Asia, and Africa, and even in Europe, and ranging from gold and silver to copper and oil, joint-stock companies were formed to explore and develop mineral resources. Mining was an industry that delivered large gains to a fortunate few accompanied by total loss for the great majority, especially in the early development phase. Consequently, mining did not attract the support of the careful investor or the banker unless it was a well-established business as with coal and iron-ore production in a mature economy. Instead, the lure of incalculable gain attracted prospectors, using their own savings to search for a discovery that would bring vast wealth, and speculators hoping to gain a fortune from a small stake. Thus, mining companies both appealed to the gambling instincts of investors and also required their financial support if output was to move beyond individual effort. The capital requirements of mining companies were not particularly large compared to the voracious needs of governments and railway systems. The entire paid-up capital of the mining companies quoted on the London Stock Exchange, an important market for mining company securities, was only £7 million in 1853 and rose to only £41 million by 1903. In contrast, railway companies had a paid-up capital of £225 million and £3.1 billion on these dates.

In the second-half of the nineteenth century securities therefore grew in importance as a proportion of national assets around the world, and the uses to which these securities were put contributed significantly to economic growth. In some developed economies such as Germany, Austria-Hungary, and adjoining countries securities were largely confined to the finance of government, railways, and banks, with their direct role in railways actually declining in the late nineteenth century due to state ownership. In Britain, its Empire, and the US securities played a more general role slowly moving out of the traditional areas of government, infrastructure, and financial services. In many less developed economies such as Russia, Japan, and India securities played a more dynamic role making up for a shortage of personal savings and bank lending to finance large new economic activities. Throughout the world, including many poorly developed regions, securities—though still relatively few—were vital in providing the finance for the extraction of previously hidden natural resources, especially minerals. Above all, the principal achievement of the growing use of securities between 1850 and 1900 was the ability to finance a transformation in the world's transport system that both opened up the interior of entire continents for economic development and permitted a global economy to operate in terms of the mobility of people, capital, manufactures, commodities, and services.[27]

THE GROWTH OF STOCK EXCHANGES: EUROPE

With this huge increase in the amount and distribution of securities world-wide there was a corresponding need for organized trading markets. The nature of these securities markets differed markedly. In countries where formally organized stock exchanges already existed before 1850 the pattern thereafter was both the multiplication of the number in operation and a division according to regional or sectoral specialization. A hierarchy resulted in which each stock exchange played a particular role within an increasingly integrated yet complex national securities market. This was observable throughout Western Europe and the United States before 1900. Where stock exchanges were small or non-existent before 1850 the pace, progress, and pattern of development before 1900 were strongly influenced by the nature of existing informal trading arrangements, the role of government, competition from banks, the growth of joint-stock enterprise, and the ownership of national assets. A diverse range of organized securities markets emerged that varied enormously in operation and in their role within national economies. Of paramount importance was the nature and degree of state control; whether banks were accepted as members; and the imposition or not of a fixed scale of charges for any business conducted. Despite this diversity each stock exchange was increasingly drawn into a worldwide network that integrated them all into a single global securities market.

Within western Europe there were emerging securities markets before 1850. Even where no formal securities market had been set up stocks and bonds had long been traded in the commercial bourses, where custom over time determined the arrangements made. As these bourses in continental Europe owed much to municipal enterprise and were part of the general commercial and financial fabric of the community, it was inevitable that the stock exchanges that emerged were subjected to government control and dependent on the involvement of the banks. The state-controlled Paris Bourse remained at the heart of the French securities market, its main purpose being to provide a market for French government debt. It continued to have a restricted number of members who, as civil servants, had their methods of business and associated charges strictly regulated. In 1896 an English observer described the operation of the Paris Bourse.

In the centre of the Bourse there is a small enclosure especially reserved for the Agents de Change. This is called the 'Parquet'. The business carried on in the 'Parquet' is in French funds, a few foreign stocks and shares quoted in the official list.[28]

Though only authorized *agents de change* could buy and sell securities on the Paris Bourse, the major French banks were permitted to establish offices around the Parquet, so giving them direct access to the brokers. With direct access to the French investor through their branch networks, these banks were able to bring business to the Paris Bourse from throughout France, creating a highly integrated financial system.

The ability of *agents de change* to form partnerships from 1862 onwards, and the growing number of clerks they employed, created some extra capacity. However, as the number of *agents de change* only expanded from 60 to 70 in 1898, much of the increased demands on the French securities market were met outside the Paris Bourse. Only a minority of all corporate securities and stocks and bonds issued in France, whether domestic or foreign, were quoted on the Bourse. Instead, these securities were traded either on the Coulisse in Paris or on the provincial exchanges. The continued growth of provincial markets provided a convenient market for local investors holding the securities of local joint-stock companies. Of more national and even international importance was the outside market in Paris. Bolstered by its official status but restricted in what it could do, the Paris Bourse remained a market for little other than *rentes* and French railway securities until the 1890s. Even in *rentes* the Bourse provided a spot market whilst buying and selling for future delivery took place on the Coulisse, where the banks could participate in their own right unhindered by government regulations. Increasingly most transactions in government debt and railway stocks and bonds were for time not for cash. Of the total transactions in *rentes* in 1894–5 the proportion for time was 95% because much of the activity was driven by money market considerations and took place on borrowed money. Faced with growing competition from the Coulisse the Paris Bourse attempted to restrict all business in *rentes* and railway securities to itself, whilst extending the range of securities traded. This led to increasing tension between the Parquet and the Coulisse. In 1898 a compromise was reached whereby the Coulisse was partially recognized as the principal market for foreign securities and new corporate issues.

Elsewhere in France many regional stock exchanges developed out of the local commercial exchanges where stockbrokers had long bought and sold shares in local companies for local investors. Lille formed a stock exchange in 1861 to provide a formal market for local coal mining companies, with twenty-eight companies quoted along with the usual range of local stocks such as banks, utilities, and industrial concerns plus municipal bonds. Local stockbrokers had been pressing for the creation of a trading floor on the Lille commercial exchange for some time but the council only agreed to the request when it wanted a market for its own bonds. Between 1860 and 1890 the municipal authority in Lille raised 61 million francs through seven separate issues to finance civic improvement. However, these bonds were also popular with most distant investors and were traded in Paris and Brussels. The Lille Bourse developed primarily as a principal for coal mining stocks, which by 1900 comprised 93% of the market value of the securities quoted. The success of these French regional markets was heavily dependent on trading in the stocks and bonds issued by local companies and mainly held by local investors. Even though there was growing outside investment in these securities, as they became established and paid regular and high dividends, the most active market was often the local stock exchange, though they might also be quoted in Paris. This was not the case with railways, especially after the mania of the 1840s had abated, or in municipal debt. These were much more widely held and also attractive to institutional investors in money market centres.[29]

By 1900 France possessed three distinct components to its securities market. At provincial level were markets for local specialities where ownership was heavily concentrated among investors resident in particular towns. In Paris there existed two markets roughly divided along functional lines, the product not of specialization but of government intervention. Government control hampered the expansion of the regulated market, the Paris Bourse, into both foreign government bonds and domestic and foreign corporate securities. Much was left to the unofficial market where the degree of self-regulation and control was less certain. More generally, the French government took an active role in deciding which foreign securities, especially government bonds, were given a market in Paris. It also imposed a turnover tax in 1893 designed to restrict the activities of the Coulisse and to favour the official market on the Bourse. Between 1893 and 1897 this tax raised 36 million francs, of which two-thirds was paid by those operating on the

Coulisse. As the Bourse monopolized the market for French government debt and French railway securities it faced less competition from abroad than the Coulisse which traded more heavily in foreign securities where it faced the rivalry of London. The tax therefore harmed the role of Paris in the global securities market, diverting to London business in foreign government bonds and in the 1890s in South African mining shares. Although international securities that had a choice of markets tended to find a home elsewhere, the Paris securities market remained the largest in continental Europe before 1900, with the Coulisse playing a vital role in focusing national and international transactions there.[30]

The French securities market was replicated in those European countries that looked to Paris for financial leadership. In Spain the establishment of stock exchanges was subject to various legal controls. Liberalized in 1869, these were made more restrictive in 1885 due to speculative excesses. This limited the development of the Spanish securities market before 1900 and restricted the Madrid Stock Exchange to trading the national debt. Newly formed stock exchanges like Barcelona emerged as the main markets for corporate securities, especially railways and banks.[31] In Switzerland increasing government intervention in the securities market was at the level of each Canton. The Zurich Stock Exchange was forced to accept banks as members in 1896.[32] Until government control was ended in 1867 the Belgian securities market was also heavily influenced by the French model. Following a law of 1873 liberalizing joint-stock company formation, there was a general expansion in the issue of corporate securities and a growth in market activity. In contrast, the Netherlands had never adopted the French model. In 1876 brokers themselves established the Amsterdam Stock Exchange, whilst Rotterdam followed in 1898. What emerged was a uniquely Dutch solution which suited the small and intimate nature of the Dutch financial system. It was largely modelled on the London Stock Exchange but was much more inclusive, with bankers participating directly despite the opposition of some members. Reflecting its longstanding international importance, the Amsterdam Stock Exchange was a major market in foreign stocks and bonds, increasingly specializing in those issued by US railroads, which became particularly popular among Dutch investors.[33]

In central and eastern Europe the securities market also evolved in a distinct way in the half-century after 1850. Propelled by both government borrowing and, especially, the expansion of railway stocks and bonds, the German securities market not only expanded after 1850 but also took on a much more organized form. Stock exchanges emerged in all the major German urban centres such as Dresden in 1857, Stuttgart in 1860, and Dusseldorf in 1874, in addition to those already in existence. However, there was no obvious centre to the German securities market, in the way that Paris was for France and London was for Britain. Instead there was a series of stock exchanges of greater or lesser importance. This did not change until after German unification in 1871. The Berlin Stock Exchange then emerged as the dominant force in the German securities market, especially after currency unification in 1873 and the founding of the Berlin-based Reichsbank in 1875. Both these developments helped to foster financial integration in Germany and promoted the Berlin Stock Exchange over its rivals, particularly as a market for corporate securities including railway stocks and bonds. Frankfurt gradually lost its government bond market with Vienna taking the Austro-Hungarian business and Berlin that of the German states. By the 1881–93 period turnover on the Frankfurt Stock Exchange had dropped to 10% of the German total, and continued to fall as Berlin became the largest German market for both domestic and international transactions.

Nevertheless, stock exchanges continued to proliferate in the major German cities, catering for the growing number of local investors and the needs of local companies. Frankfurt not only provided a market for local stocks and bonds but also those the Austro-Hungarian Empire, because of traditional economic links, whilst Hamburg was an important market for the securities of German shipping and commercial companies and Scandinavian issues, by virtue of being a major port and its location. As banks were all members of these stock exchanges, reflecting the early participation of bankers in the commercial exchanges, the creation of an integrated market was largely due to the links they maintained to each other.[34] In addition, the development of the German securities market was seriously affected by various aspects of government taxation and legislation. Either at a municipal or state level German securities markets had long faced regulation and restriction. With unification this control became increasingly national. As early as 1881 a turnover tax was introduced, which was doubled in 1894. A law of 1896 then gave the imperial government supervision over all stock exchanges whilst, at the same time, buying and selling for future delivery were banned as being tantamount to speculation.

The law prohibiting speculation was not revised until 1908, by which time much German trading in securities had migrated abroad, especially to London which had already attracted much German international business, away from Paris, at the time of the Franco-German war of 1870–1. Of the securities business that could not be channelled abroad, part became internalized within or between the large banks. Such links help explain the development of integrated commercial and investment banking in Germany, as that shielded activity in securities from both taxation and external scrutiny. The combination of taxation and legislation, the direct participation of the banks in the stock exchanges, and the nationalization of the railway system impeded the development of the German securities market. Instead, German banks were forced to play a greater role in meeting the financial needs of the economy through extending long-term loans to their business customers whilst banks elsewhere were retreating from such practices because of the risks involved if depositors rushed to withdraw their savings during a financial crisis.

A similar pattern appeared in the Austro-Hungarian empire, for much the same reasons. In the 1850s and 1860s the Austrian government adopted a liberal policy towards joint-stock company formation and the development of securities markets. The result was a speculative boom fuelled by cheap and abundant credit from the numerous new banks and inflated prospects regarding the new companies, especially the railways. This culminated in a financial crash in 1873 followed by government restrictions on stock exchanges as early as 1875. The Austrian government then copied Germany in 1893 by imposing a turnover tax. The growth in the number of joint-stock companies stalled and the use of securities to finance economic development declined between 1875 and 1900. Instead, the Austrian securities market became heavily dependent on the trading of government debt. As in Germany banks developed in particular ways to meet the financing shortfall whilst the government stepped in to take control of the railway system.[35] The result for much of central and eastern Europe was to hamper the development of the securities market and to drive much of the business either abroad or out of the formal exchanges, so fragmenting the market.[36] In Italy, the government was also driven to intervene in 1873 in the wake of the speculative boom and collapse, with similar consequences for its securities market.[37]

For much of continental Europe, with the major exception of the Netherlands, national governments played a central role in shaping the securities market. In complete contrast, developments in Britain took place without government intervention of any kind. The London Stock Exchange remained the biggest and most important of its kind in the world but there also existed numerous local stock exchanges, reflecting the vitality of local joint-stock enterprise. This type of activity was not simply a product of the local market for sales and purchases as each local exchange was increasingly driven by national investments transmitted through a network of brokers and dealers using the telegraph system and from the 1880s the telephone. The specialities of each exchange gradually became available to investors throughout the British Isles, generating an increasing volume of inter-market activity. Within this network the London Stock Exchange emerged as the dominant market for most actively traded securities in Britain, whether they were domestic or foreign.

However, the principal feature of the London Stock Exchange between 1850 and 1900 was the increasing importance of foreign securities, principally foreign government bonds and foreign railway stocks and shares. Of the securities quoted on the London Stock Exchange the proportion representing foreign assets had risen to at least half by 1903 compared to less than 10% in 1853. With the British investor being responsible for around 40% of all international investment, this made the London Stock Exchange the most international in the world. With almost no restrictions on membership either in terms of numbers or costs, a willingness to provide a market for virtually any type of security, almost no limitations on the business methods employed by its members, and the absence of a fixed scale of charges, the London Stock Exchange provided an orderly market at low cost and with the minimum of regulation. The result was a period of virtually uninterrupted expansion during which membership rose from 864 in 1850 to 5,567 in 1905 or a more than sixfold growth.

Generally, Europe experienced a rapid expansion in the formation and growth of stock exchanges between 1850 and 1900, as this often required little more than the transformation of existing securities markets into distinct organizations once the level of business would support the costs involved. This was true across Italy where numerous mercantile exchanges had long existed and securities traded. Similarly in Switzerland three stock exchanges were created serving Geneva (1850), Zurich (1875), and Basle (1876), each trading a mixture of state and municipal debts along with the stocks and bonds issued by Swiss railways and banks.[38] In Denmark, the long-established Copenhagen Stock Exchange took on a formal existence in the 1870s, whilst Stockholm gained a stock exchange in 1863 and Oslo in 1881. Developments were slower in Russia where the principal securities market was in the commercial exchange in St Petersburg. As both the Russian government and Russian railways continued to rely heavily on foreign finance, before 1900 the main activity was trading in the shares of Russian joint-stock banks and industrial and mining companies as these were largely in the hands of local investors.[39] Given that European stock exchanges evolved out of existing securities markets that reflected national and local peculiarities, no single model predominated. The French model was influential in neighbouring countries but even there it was adapted to suit local conditions, as in Switzerland, or even abandoned, as in the case of Belgium. The German model held sway in central Europe but was not copied elsewhere. The British model was even less popular, being adopted only by the Dutch but in a heavily amended form as bankers, though not banks, could become members of the stock exchange. There thus existed enormous differences in the forms adopted by European stock exchanges. This had major implications for the role each played within their national financial system.

THE GROWTH OF STOCK EXCHANGES
IN THE WIDER WORLD

In contrast, of those stock exchanges established outside Europe by 1900, most though not all resembled those operating in Britain, indicating the apparent triumph of the London model as opposed to that of Paris or Berlin. However, none were the same as the London Stock Exchange, being akin instead to the British provincial stock exchanges but with features adopted from the United States. Though often regarded as the model for stock exchange development over the world it was not possible to transplant the complete package that constituted the London Stock Exchange. Certainly the exclusion of banks from membership was commonplace, as was a set of rules and regulations that imposed market discipline on members by expelling those who transgressed. However, in one crucial area there was a fundamental difference between the London Stock Exchange and its counterparts outside Europe. That was in the imposition of a fixed scale of charges on the membership. Before 1900 London did not publish or enforce such a scale, whereas stock exchanges elsewhere did. As a result those stock exchanges were confined to largely corporate stocks and bonds whereas London retained its market in government debt whilst also developing one in corporate securities.

One reason for this difference was the fact that most stock exchanges established around the world between 1850 and 1900 provided a local market for a restricted range of corporate securities. These securities reflected both local and regional specialities and the interests of local investors. In the large cities joint-stock enterprise took a variety of forms ranging from banking and insurance companies through local utilities providing gas, water, electricity, railways, and urban transport to the growing number of industrial, commercial, and mining concerns. Stock exchanges formed outside large cities were much more specialized, providing a forum for the trading of particular types of securities. Mining stocks in boomtowns were the commonest of these. Europeans took the stock exchange tradition with them to the continents in which they settled and so, when the need and opportunity arose, stock exchanges were quickly established there, whether in mining camps across the Americas, Australia, and Africa, or in the largest cities of India and China, where they were soon copied, modified, and developed by the local population of these and neighbouring countries.[40]

Government debt and often railway stocks and bonds were absent from the securities markets outside Western Europe and the United States, as such securities were not held by investors in these countries. Despite high and rising *per capita* incomes there was a shortage of finance in many of the rapidly developing economies of the late nineteenth century. Faced with rapid economic growth requiring prodigious amounts of capital, the newly settled countries of the world concentrated their savings and investment on those areas of most immediate use, such as the development of agriculture, the establishment of manufacturing, and the construction of houses. Little of this was undertaken through the use of securities, with self-finance, mortgages, and bank loans being the commonest methods employed. What remained of locally available savings was then invested in the shares of small joint-stock companies providing all manner of local products and services, with the usual ones of banking and urban utilities being the most prominent. This left the governments of those countries to seek the funds they required for national development from other sources. That was also the case with railway construction which demanded levels of funding far beyond that possessed by the populations through which the lines ran. Even the United States was a net debtor nation, with an average of 25% of its railroad securities held abroad in the late nineteenth century. Elsewhere outside western Europe a combination of low *per capita* incomes and a poorly developed financial system meant that many countries were unable to provide their own governments with the funds they sought to borrow, especially at a time of war, and certainly could not finance either public or private railway expansion.

In contrast, investors in Western Europe enjoyed both rising *per capita* incomes and a shortage of investment opportunities, given the relatively low level of government borrowing and the increasing maturity of the railway system and urban infrastructure. Such was the relative security and good returns provided by the debts of their own governments and the stocks and bonds of their own railways that investors in western Europe were increasingly attracted to similar securities from elsewhere. This was especially so when they faced falling yields from domestic securities compared to the combination of low risk and high returns offered by those issued to finance governments and railways further afield. Investors in Western Europe therefore purchased most of the government debt and the railway stocks and bonds issued to finance activities elsewhere. British investors emerged as the largest holders of the government and railway securities issued throughout its vast empire whether originating in Canada or India. In addition the British were also major holders of such securities from outside the empire, being the main holders of Japanese government debt and Argentinian railway stocks and bonds by 1900. One example of this development was the fact that between 1870 and 1900 foreign governments borrowed £1.9 billion in London.[41] Such government debts and railway securities were traded on the London Stock

Exchange, not in their country of origin. They were bought not just by British investors but by those in France, Germany, Belgium, the Netherlands, and Switzerland. The amount of foreign securities held in the Netherlands rose from 0.7 billion guilders in 1865 to 2.4 billion in 1895, for example. Second only to Britain as a major purchaser of foreign securities was France. Total French holdings of securities rose from around 9.1 billion francs in 1850 to 104.4 billion in 1908, and within that the proportion that was foreign grew from 27% to 36%, with the debts of other European countries being especially popular. Among corporate securities French investors were the major holders of Spanish and Russian railway stocks. Following on from railways European investors also purchased the securities issued elsewhere in the world by the largest utilities like gas and electricity supply, docks and harbours, and tramway and telephone lines as well as the major industrial and commercial companies. In consequence the most active markets in many securities from around the world were located in Western Europe, not in their own countries. The markets that catered for securities followed the investor not the issuer.[42]

This hampered the development of securities markets in those countries that relied heavily on overseas borrowing to fund their government debt or railway development.[43] Least affected was the United States despite its position as a major international borrower. Europeans were major holders of US railroad securities and also bought the national debt extensively, especially during and immediately after the Civil War when the price was depressed and the exchange rate favourable. Nevertheless, the rapidly growing wealth of the United States, the advanced level of its financial system, and the existence of such large cities as New York, Boston, and Philadelphia, meant that it was able to finance a very high proportion of the domestic investment required even in such areas as railroad construction. The United States before 1900 possessed a mini international economy with the wealthy investors of the east financing the rapid expansion of the west. As a consequence the development of stock exchanges in the United States was a mixture of the patterns observable in both Europe and the rest of the world. Established securities markets continued to develop in places like New York, Boston, and Philadelphia, whilst new exchanges were formed across the country in the wake of both the growth of established urban communities and the speculation engendered by mining booms. Once a sufficient level of business was reached that would support a more formal organization local brokers set up a local stock exchange. In Cincinnati, Ohio a stock exchange eventually appeared in 1885 once it possessed a range of locally owned securities issued by local joint-stock enterprise. It had become established over some thirty years during which the number of investors and brokers and the volume and variety of securities had all grown. In contrast a stock exchange was set up quickly in Los Angeles in California in 1899 following the speculative activity produced by the discovery of oil there. All these newly formed stock exchanges across the United States took their lead from the New York Stock Exchange. There thus emerged before 1900 a common type of US stock exchange. This was also adopted in Canada, despite that country being part of the British empire, whilst certain aspects of the US model were also followed in other countries.[44]

The New York Stock Exchange changed considerably in the aftermath of the Civil War and due to the huge expansion of the railroad network financed largely through the issue of corporate stocks and bonds. A speculative boom occurred during the Civil War when the rapid increase in government debt became the main focus of interest among investors and precipitated a large increase in the number of brokers handling the necessary buying and selling. This was especially the case in New York as war-related government debt commanded a national and even international market, unlike most of the previous state and corporate securities. However, the New York Stock Exchange, as a member-controlled institution, was reluctant to admit many of these additional brokers, wishing to preserve the market for itself. Lacking access to the trading floor of the New York Stock Exchange those refused admission established an alternative market called the 'Open Board'. Furthermore, those whose business was exclusively in the buying and selling of government bonds formed a separate market called the Government Bond Department, which operated under its own methods and rules. Thus, when the Civil War ended there existed three major securities markets in New York. In 1869 they merged to form one exchange combining the 533 members of the New York Stock Exchange with 354 from the Open Board and 173 from the Bond Room. The result was a stock exchange with 1,060 members, which was increased to 1,100 in 1879, when forty additional seats were sold to fund development.

Membership of the New York Stock Exchange was only possible through the purchase of the place or seat of an existing member. The cost involved fluctuated with the level of activity on the market and could be prohibitive. Such an artificial limit on the number of participants in an expanding market, along with the rules on the way business was conducted, was bound to stimulate the appearance of rivals in some form. There were always those who could not afford membership, especially during a speculative boom, and those whose business could not be made compatible with the fixed scale of charges. In addition, faced with a growing need to focus on particular securities, as it did not have the capacity to cater for the whole market, there emerged whole categories of stocks and bonds that were not traded on the New York Stock Exchange even if quoted there. As early as 1870 one observer noted that:

Government securities are not sold at the regular stock board. The demand for these securities requires a continuous sale. At the stock board they would have to take their place in the regular list and be called for when they were reached.[45]

Even after the call-over system of trading was abandoned in 1871, to be replaced with specialists operating as dealers in particular stocks, it proved impossible to meet the needs of those trading government debt. What the government debt market required was the ability to trade large amounts with no broker's commission but with profits generated from the differential between the buying and selling price. As this was not compatible with the minimum commission rules, such business ceased to be conducted on the New York Stock Exchange and instead was done directly between the main banks on an OTC (over-the-counter) market. At the other end of the scale the New York Stock Exchange also abandoned many securities that had been important in its formative years, such as bank and insurance stocks as well as state debts. These did not generate sufficient turnover to justify space on the trading floor and the attention of members, and so were also traded outside on the street or curb market. Increasingly the New York Stock Exchange became a specialist market for the stocks and bonds of US railroads plus the securities of a few of the largest industrial, commercial, mining and urban utility companies. As the volume of securities issued by US railroads expanded enormously, and the size of the Federal debt tended to shrink after the end of the Civil War, this focus did produce a huge increase in the business done on the New York Stock Exchange.[46]

Though the development of the US securities market was undertaken in the almost total absence of government intervention before 1900, the institutional form taken for the creation of an orderly market was a product of the way the stock exchanges themselves were organized, especially that of New York after 1850.[47] One long-standing member of the New York Stock exchange, Henry Clews, summed up what this meant.

A sale and purchase is the work of a moment in the Board Rooms, and no voucher is exchanged to prove it till comparisons are made at brokers' offices, usually after the Exchange closes. But no contract thus made in an instant of time is ever repudiated, no matter how heavy a loss it may Involve to buyer or seller, for the penalty of such a repudiation would be immediate suspension from the stock exchange, followed by expulsion when proved.[48]

Under circumstances such as these there was no need for government intervention to police the market, because the stock exchanges themselves possessed the power to do so. However, this self-regulation also gave the members the power to introduce both rules and charges that suited and benefited themselves but did not suit all, thus stimulating the creation of alternative markets. Hence the US securities market was driven by the restrictive practices employed by the existing stock exchanges, especially with regard to admission of new members, the fixed commissions charged, and the rules governing the conduct of business. These restrictions became particularly acute at the height of speculative booms when business expanded to such a degree that new brokers were attracted who, when refused membership of the established stock exchanges simply formed another exchange. In contrast, such a pattern had not appeared in London because ownership of the stock exchange and access to the trading floor remained separate. The London Stock Exchange was owned by a joint-stock company whose shares could be bought and held for the return they promised. As such it had a vested interest in increasing membership, as that produced both additional revenue from the fees paid, and limited potential competition from a rival market established by those refused admission.

However, it was the US pattern of stock exchange development that appeared in Canada in the second half of the nineteenth century. The first stock exchange appeared in Toronto in 1861 but collapsed some years later when the speculative bubble ended that had propelled its formation. Meanwhile a stock exchange was established in 1863 in Montreal, which was the financial centre of Canada in this period, and it was not until 1871 that a new and permanent stock exchange was founded in Toronto. As British investors largely monopolized holdings of Canadian government and railroad securities, what was left to trade on these local Canadian exchanges were the locally held stocks and bonds of the usual range of local joint-stock companies, most of which were unique to each market. Despite the presence of many British nationals among the membership, both the Montreal and Toronto Stock Exchanges, which initially resembled British provincial exchanges, were quick to adopt US practice, such as controls over membership and the sale and purchase of seats. Along with fixed commissions and an unwillingness to trade securities that could be deemed too speculative, this left the Montreal and Toronto stock exchanges vulnerable to competition. The Canadian mining boom of the 1890s resulted in the formation of a separate stock exchange in Toronto in 1897 to cater for those brokers, and the mining securities they traded, who had been excluded from the existing Toronto Stock Exchange.

In contrast, the establishment of all the Australian stock exchanges was due to mining booms, including those in the major centres of population. The gradual development of joint-stock companies had led to the growth of a stock broking community in places like Melbourne, Sydney, and Brisbane by the 1850s. These brokers provided a means through which the locally held shares of local companies could be traded, as with banks, insurance, gas, and water supply.

However, it was not until speculation in mining shares became rife that sufficient business was generated to propel the creation of organized markets. Following a gold mining boom in the State of Victoria brokers in Melbourne formed a stock exchange in 1861. In contrast the Sydney Stock Exchange was not established until 1871 when the State of New South Wales experienced its mining boom. After a number of false starts, all associated with mining booms and then collapses in Queensland, the Brisbane Stock Exchange was eventually formed in 1884. The problem was that the most numerous securities, namely those issued by the State governments, did not generate a local market as they were largely held in Britain and so traded in London. Australian government borrowing in Britain peaked in the 1880s, when £94 million was raised and then fell away in the 1890s, after the financial crisis of 1893. Even then a total of £43 million was raised in London in the 1890s indicating the continuing reliance placed upon external investors. In contrast the shares of the early mining companies were not only held locally, but also generated considerable buying and selling because of the prospects of enormous gain if successful. Between 1865 and 1884 the main business of the Melbourne Stock Exchange was in mining securities even though the main location of the gold fields was some distance away. Stock exchanges were also formed in the mining towns such as Ballarat and Bendigo in Victoria and Gympie and Charters Towers in Queensland, but these tended to fade away unless sustained by a sequence of subsequent discoveries. Adelaide developed as a major market for gold mining shares as many of the exchanges located in mining towns themselves disappeared when the gold ran out and the miners drifted away.

Once the mining industry moved from its initial speculative phase to one where large amounts of capital were required to generate a steady output, outside investors became more involved as the original pioneers moved on, selling their holdings in the process. These new investors were drawn from the main centres of population such as Melbourne and Sydney or from abroad, and the market moved to those centres. The Broken Hill Proprietary Mining Company was initially wholly owned in Australia whereas by the 1890s it was half owned by British investors, and much of the trading in its shares had moved to London. However, a stock exchange like Melbourne, Sydney, or Brisbane had the shares of a wide range of local joint-stock companies to fall back on whilst its pool of investors also moved on to hold and trade securities issued by mining companies operating elsewhere in Australia. The very existence of these organized and established markets for securities also encouraged local companies to adopt the joint-stock form and issue shares, and mining companies to be floated there. Finally, the growing wealth of the local community manifested itself in the eventual repatriation of government and related debt that had been originally issued in London and traded there.

However, in the 1890s the Australian stock exchanges were still largely dependent on the stocks and shares of local companies and mining securities for business. On the Melbourne Stock Exchange in 1900, of the corporate securities quoted £26.4 million came from mining companies operating throughout Australia and another £21.2 million had been issued by mainly local companies especially banks and other financial concerns. Initially, these Australian stock exchanges were organized in a very similar way to the provincial stock exchanges in Britain with fixed commissions, call-over trading, and no dealers. However, they also began to adopt US practices as with the introduction of the seat system in Sydney in 1888. The restrictive practices adopted and the control on membership encouraged the formation of rival stock exchanges during every speculative boom, which then disappeared once it was over. Gradually with the growing integration of the Australian economy and a degree of common ownership of the main securities the various Australian stock exchanges began to list the same securities. By 1900 there appeared a single Australian market for securities produced not through the domination of one single exchange but through inter-market dealing relying on the telegraph. This took in the main markets in Adelaide, Brisbane, Melbourne, and Sydney.[49]

A similar picture emerges for New Zealand. Though joint-stock companies had appeared there in the 1840s their shares were too closely held to generate much trading. Even with the growth of government borrowing and the development of railways the securities market failed to develop until the late 1860s, as the stocks and bonds issued were, again, largely held and traded in Britain. Only a few stockbrokers emerged to handle what business there was. The real beginnings of the New Zealand securities market came after the discovery of gold in 1861, which led to the formation of a growing number of mining companies whose shares attracted the speculative interest of local investors. The result was a considerable growth in the buying and selling of shares, the appearance of a numerous body of brokers, and the creation of a stock exchange in Otago in 1868. This pattern was then repeated time and again across the country as mining booms sprang up through chance discoveries. Not surprisingly, when stock exchanges were formed they were largely modelled on the pattern that of British provincial stock exchanges where minimum commission rules operated rather than London. Many of these mining markets had only a brief existence and fell into disuse as the discoveries became exhausted. Only where a substantial community developed did they survive, providing a market for local joint-stock companies providing gas and shipping, insurance, and a variety of industrial and commercial products and services. Nevertheless, mining shares continued to dominate the New Zealand share market before 1900, for it was only this type of securities that could generate a large turnover.[50]

The same story was repeated in South Africa with the development of the securities market coming late in the nineteenth century with diamond and gold mining discoveries. A stock exchange was established at Kimberley on the diamond fields but the real expansion came with the discovery of gold in the Transvaal in 1884. This led to the formation of a number of stock exchanges in the 1880s beginning with Barberton, which was in the centre of the early developments. However, with the slump in output from that area and the switch to the Witwatersrand area, activity switched to Johannesburg. When the Johannesburg Stock Exchange opened for business in January 1888, having been established the previous year, it attracted around 600 members. It was a highly speculative market trading the locally held shares issued by locally formed gold mining companies. Its success spelled the end for the Barberton securities market, which closed down in 1890. The Johannesburg Stock Exchange then secured its domination of the South African mining securities market with the second mining boom of 1894–5. This established Witwatersrand as one of the premier mining districts of the world capable of producing a regular output of gold at low cost, fuelled by both new discoveries and more efficient means for crushing ores and extracting gold. Substantial outside investment was attracted and a number of large and highly capitalized mining groups were created. At the height of the boom in July 1895 the market value of the mining companies quoted on the Johannesburg Stock Exchange was £103 million. The Johannesburg Stock Exchange became an integral part of a worldwide network of mining markets with trading in the same companies taking place as far apart as Austria, Britain, Egypt, France, Russia, Spain, and the Ottoman empire in the 1890s. Thus, instead of the South African securities market eventually gravitating to such established urban centres as Cape Town, where a local securities market was gradually developing, Johannesburg emerged as the dominant stock exchange. Mining securities were traded in Cape Town but activity was dwarfed by that in Johannesburg, where the stock exchange even moved into non-mining securities, as with the quotation of South African Breweries in 1897. Such was the volume of business being generated in Johannesburg, even after the end of the second mining boom, that a rival stock exchange was formed there in 1897 but it did not survive. However, the growth of the Johannesburg Stock Exchange came to an abrupt end in 1899 with the outbreak of the war between the British and the Boer governments in the Transvaal and the Orange Free State. The Johannesburg Stock Exchange closed in October 1899 and business transferred either abroad or to the smaller South African markets.[51]

In Latin America the development of securities markets and the eventual formation of stock exchanges did not conform to a single pattern. In Mexico a mining boom in the 1880s led to the formation of a short-lived stock exchange in 1894. Where mining booms were absent the development of a securities market took place more gradually, as in Buenos Aires where it evolved out of the trading in bank shares in the general merchants' exchange. In Brazil, after a number of failed attempts by local brokers to organize a market, the government established one in Rio de Janeiro in 1876. This, however, closed in 1891 after the imposition of a turnover tax during a speculative boom. When new stock exchanges were opened in 1895 in Rio and São Paulo they were modelled on that of Paris. In Chile a securities market developed in the commercial centre of Valparaiso from the 1870s, driven by the needs of local brokers, and a stock exchange was eventually formed there in 1898. However, it was the stock exchange established in Santiago that became the main market under the influence of the government. Though a securities exchange was established in Lima, Peru in 1860, on the basis of government legislation, it was not until 1898 that it really emerged as a proper securities market rather than a focus for general commercial and financial transactions. A major reason for the lack of activity was the absence of locally financed joint-stock companies in Peru. In 1900 there were only 46 companies quoted, including the usual local utilities, insurance, banks, a few manufacturing concerns, and a sugar plantation, and most of their shares were closely held. Generally, unlike the English speaking world the development of stock exchanges in Spanish America was both much more limited and subject to much greater government intervention and control. Though Buenos Aires did possess a securities market it largely traded local mortgage bonds rather than the shares of locally established joint-stock companies, as was the case in such comparable cities as Montreal or Melbourne. In other respects it was similar, for across Latin America the main issues made by either the government or the railways were largely held and traded abroad.[52]

Across the Far East securities markets appeared first in India and then spread to Japan and China before 1900. The influence of the British in India led to the development of both joint-stock companies and stock exchanges where their securities were traded. As government borrowing was largely undertaken in London, where the Indian railway companies also raised finance, the development of an Indian securities market was dependent on the growth of these local joint-stock companies. This took place first in Calcutta, where there was a large British community, and then spread to Bombay, where many Indians began to participate both in the establishment of joint-stock companies and as investors. However, whether involving British or Indian investors the level of activity was hardly sufficient to support a stock exchange as the shares were closely held among small groups of people. There was also the additional problem that the British investors tended to return home taking their securities with them, so depriving the Indian market of any buying and selling they undertook. It was not really until speculative booms such as that of 1864–6, driven by world demand for Indian cotton during the US Civil War, and gold mining manias in the 1880s and 1890s, that the Indian securities market came alive. One indicator of its small size was the fact that as late as 1901 paid-up capital of all Indian companies denominated in rupees amounted to only £25 million. The most numerous securities were denominated in £sterling and held externally. Nevertheless, a small but growing market in locally held securities of all kinds supported active securities markets in both Calcutta and Bombay. In Calcutta some kind of formal stock exchange had existed from 1858 but until the twentieth century was confined to European members whilst Indian brokers conducted business on the street without any real organization. In Bombay, where Indian brokers were dominant, trading also took place on the street and only moved into a rented hall in 1875. At the same time a Bombay stockbrokers' organization was formed to police the trading taking place among the 300 or so local brokers.[53]

In China the Shanghai stock exchange listed sixty-eight companies in 1900 covering a wide range of local enterprise, such as banking and insurance, mining and industry. However, an organized market did not originate with these companies, which produced only limited trading activity, or with Chinese government debt and railway securities, which were all held abroad. Again, it was a mining boom in the late 1880s and 1890s that led to the formation of a stock exchange in Shanghai in 1889, with the initiative coming from foreign residents.[54] However, in Japan the development of both a securities market and then formally organized markets was due to the Japanese themselves. Between 1874 and 1896 Japan did not draw upon foreign capital markets. Instead, internal sources of finance were tapped, including the issue of securities by both government and companies. Stock exchanges were established in both Tokyo and Osaka in 1878 to handle transactions resulting from the securitization of government debt obligations. From the early 1880s these markets then traded corporate securities, especially shares issued by railway companies. As the number of companies listed on the Tokyo Stock Exchange rose from 26 in 1885 to 130 in 1900, these markets became quite active, with over 90% of transactions being conducted for time and much of the activity supported by bank lending.[55] Securities markets were also appearing in the Middle East, with two in Egypt before 1900. The one in Alexandria in 1883 was largely the creation of the French speaking community, many of whom were merchants in the eastern Mediterranean. The one in Cairo in 1890 was the product of British expatriates. Both exchanges provided an active market for the increasingly numerous Egyptian joint-stock companies. In contrast, the Constantinople Stock Exchange of 1866 operated only intermittently.[56]

In the half-century before 1900 stock exchanges spread across the globe. This was largely driven by European migrants or people of European origin but the growth of markets in both India and Japan indicates that non-Europeans were quick to exploit this form of finance when opportunities arose. Conversely, the ownership by western Europeans of such a large proportion of world securities both hindered the formation of stock exchanges and altered the nature of the markets formed. Whereas the major stock exchanges of Western Europe combined trading in both government debt and corporate securities, markets elsewhere in the world really dealt only in the stocks and bonds of joint-stock companies. Some only traded shares, such as the numerous mining markets and the many stock exchanges, located in the smaller cities of the world. There was thus a fundamental division between those markets and exchanges trading fixed interest securities, especially those issued by governments, and those confining themselves exclusively to equities.

There also existed two major types of stock exchange. In continental Europe and a number of Latin American republics stock exchanges were, on the whole, subjected to considerable government intervention even leading to control. This was often driven by the desire to eradicate market abuses and limit speculative outbursts but resulted in the creation of alternative and unregulated markets by those seeking to avoid government controls, restrictions, and taxes. Encouragement was also given to trade securities abroad rather than domestically, wherever possible. Finally, such government action suppressed the use of securities as a means of financing economic activity, so stimulating alternative means, such as bank lending. In contrast, in most of the rest of the world, and especially in Britain, its empire, and the United States, the development of organized securities markets was largely free of government intervention, being driven by the needs of the market participants. The resulting stock exchanges were 'controlled by no special legislation, and they make their own rules and carry on dealings subject only to the laws which regulate such transactions everywhere'.[57] Exceptions were the Dutch and Belgian stock exchanges, which operated largely free of central government control, whilst in Japan the reorganization of the stock exchanges after the crisis of 1893 resulted in the government acquiring an element of control.[58] Nevertheless, government intervention produced a fundamental divide between the securities markets of continental Europe and those of the Anglo-Saxon world. This intervention then had wider implications for national financial systems, as manifested by the somewhat different roles played by banks and securities markets.

THE CONQUEST OF DISTANCE

Between 1850 and 1900 these securities markets and stock exchanges became increasingly integrated into national networks through the transformation of communication systems. During the 1850s telegraph systems were established throughout Western Europe and the eastern United States and were quickly extended to the rest of the world. By the 1870s all financial centres of any significance were connected either through land-lines or undersea cables, creating integrated national markets where prices and orders could be constantly transmitted between the different exchanges. Internationally, the London–Paris telegraph link of 1851 and the London–New York submarine cable of 1866 were milestones in the creation of a global network as they linked the main stock exchanges of Europe and North America. By 1900 there were some 350,000 km of submarine cables in existence, connecting all major financial centres and reducing communication delays to minutes. The introduction of the telephone from the late 1870s onwards eliminated even this delay. Throughout Western Europe and the north-eastern US stock exchange members were among the earliest and most numerous users of the telephone. The main subscribers to the Berlin telephone exchange opened in 1881 were stockbrokers and bankers quick to make use of the telephone links established to Hamburg and Frankfurt by the end of that year. In 1885 a long -distance telephone line opened between New York and Philadelphia provided instant and continuous communication between the two exchanges. By 1890 telephone connections between Montreal and Toronto had helped to make these stock exchanges into the twin locations of an emerging national market. The telephone intensified contact within national securities markets whereas the telegraph made possible the operation of a global market. However, the telephone even contributed to global integration before 1900 in north America, with Canada–US links and in Western Europe. A Paris–London telephone connection opened in the 1890s was extensively used by those operating in both securities markets.

Due to this revolution in communications, trading on separate stock exchanges was increasingly integrated into a national and then a global securities market. In Italy, the cost of sending a telegram fell from 20 lire in 1860 to 1 lire in 1871, bringing an increasing convergence of prices between the eight Italian stock exchanges, especially of government bonds which were common to all.[59] The long-term impact of this transformation of communications is seen in the Amsterdam Stock Exchange. A telegraph office opened in 1852 to serve the Amsterdam securities market was quickly resorted to by brokers because of the information regarding other markets relayed through

it. By the 1860s trading in Amsterdam had become dependent on the telegraph to transmit prices and orders between Amsterdam and Rotterdam and
to foreign centres such as Paris and London. These foreign connections were
vital for all business in Russian and US securities. By 1900 the Amsterdam
Stock Exchange was generating a vast telegraphic traffic. Between 1881 and
1889 the annual average traffic was 165,000 telegrams a year, approximately
500 a day, of which 27% were with Rotterdam. However, most of the
remainder was abroad with London (28%), Berlin (22%), Brussels (13%),
and Paris (7%) being especially important. By then the telephone was also
supplementing the telegraph for short-distance communication within the
Netherlands, so integrating trading in Amsterdam and Rotterdam.[60]

Though telegraph and telephone links between London, Paris, Berlin, and
New York were major conduits in the global securities market, from the 1870s
other centres and other connections were also of growing importance, including links with Sydney and Johannesburg, and Asian centres such as
Shanghai, Bombay, and Tokyo. Local stock exchanges acquired more than
simply local importance for the telegraph, and later the telephone, ensured
that anyone could be interested in the securities they traded. Mining markets,
for example, responded to the outside interests of distant investors. This made
the gold mining boom of the 1890s a truly global phenomenon as investors
across the continents were drawn into the speculation, either because mining
companies operated there, as in Africa, Australia, and India, or because
investors were located there as was the case with Europe, or both as happened
in North America. Conversely, the telegraph and the telephone permitted
local investors to purchase securities other than those available through
their local stock exchange. Whether directly for large investors, or indirectly
via local brokers for small investors, investors everywhere could purchase the
securities of their choice rather than those that happened to be available at any
one place and at any one time.

As part of this process particular stock exchanges grew to occupy positions
of national importance. These were usually located in the largest centres of
population, and were thus most convenient for the greatest concentration
of investors, whether individuals or institutions like banks and insurance
companies. In Spain, for instance, though both Bilbao and Barcelona
possessed important stock exchanges, being major industrial centres, 75%
of the total turnover in the Spanish securities market in 1902 took place on
the Madrid Stock Exchange, where the principal banks and insurance
companies were located and where government debt was traded.[61] Large
stock exchanges located in cities such as London, Paris, or New York filled a
national role as the market to which all others looked for prices and trends
and through which orders were sent and received. The members of these

central stock exchanges, by maintaining constant contact with brokers and dealers on local stock exchanges, created a national securities market. There even existed specialist intermediaries called *arbitrageurs*, who made a living by buying or selling on one exchange and immediately reversing the deal on another, when any price difference appeared in a security traded in two or more centres. Given the existence of these intermediaries and the rapid connections between them made possible by the communication revolution, prices of securities quickly moved in line within the various separate components of national markets. This was immediately true of those securities that commanded a national market and was rapidly transmitted to stocks and bonds that were only locally held.

This process took place both nationally and internationally. The half-century before 1900 was also a time of growing currency stability, especially from the 1870s onwards as one country after another joined the gold standard. By tying each unit of a national currency to a precise amount of gold governments effectively maintained a fixed rate monetary regime. Currency volatility and exchange risk were thereby removed from international investment whether it involved short- or long-term buying or selling, and the supply of globally mobile securities increased enormously. Initially it was the securities issued by indebted governments that possessed this international market as with those issued by Russia, Spain, the Latin American republics, or the United States as a result of the Civil War and France because of the indemnity payment. However, increasingly those securities issued by governments in western Europe and the United States that were held abroad in the middle of the century were held at home by the end, having been purchased by their own nationals as incomes and savings rose in those countries. This was true of both Italy and the Austro-Hungarian Empire whilst US investors had largely absorbed their own Federal, state, and local debts by 1900. As early as 1875 most of the French *rentes* issued abroad to fund the indemnity were held in France. One estimate for 1895 suggested that at least 90% of the French national debt was held by French investors.[62] This left only the likes of Russian government bonds and those of emerging borrowers elsewhere in the world, such as Japan, which were widely held abroad. Instead, the great expansion was in corporate stocks and bonds. Foreign holdings of US railroad securities grew from 20% in 1873 to 33% in 1890, before falling back in that decade.[63] Consequently, not only did modern communications permit almost instantaneous contact between the principal stock exchanges of the world, but trading in mutually quoted securities was also possible, with even tiny price differences prompting buying and selling by the *arbitrageurs*. Where government or railroad stocks did not exist other securities served the same function, as with the gold mining stocks of Australia and South Africa.[64]

The operations of numerous national securities markets were strongly influenced both by the general activities of the financial centre within which they were located and by fluctuations and developments within the global securities market. There evolved a hierarchy of stock exchanges reflecting not only size but also position with the global network. These ranged from London, which was heavily international, through St Petersburg, which was national, to the growing number of stock exchanges serving specific localities and industries. With this large mass of mobile stocks and bonds and the existence of international networks of contacts, facilitated by rapid communications, there now existed a truly global securities market. This, in turn, required particular centres from which business flowed or towards which it was directed. The London Stock Exchange in particular, and the Paris and later New York stock exchanges to a lesser degree, fulfilled this role. Their position is reflected in a description of the Vienna Bourse in 1892, as Vienna itself was an important securities market not only for the Austro-Hungarian Empire but also internationally.

The Vienna Bourse has on its active list numerous securities . . . for which there is an international market, but it deals in very few issues not entirely domestic. Its state debt is large, and its home securities numerous, and these absorb nearly all the capital and attention of Viennese operators. . . . Austrian capitalists who are venturesome go to London, Berlin or Paris when they desire to trade in foreign securities. What little operations such dealers may make in American stocks and bonds are generally conducted through London on account of its greater proximity and the closer financial relations of their brokerage and arbitrage houses. This will apply to all continental markets and localities. London is their common resort for any possible investments or speculations they may wish to make in the United States.[65]

Already established as major financial centres before 1850, London and Paris consolidated their position in the next half-century. Whilst the position of Paris was damaged by the Franco-German war, the successful funding of the indemnity largely restored its position though it was never again able to challenge London as the premier global financial centre. Nevertheless, Paris remained the most important financial centre in continental Europe, particularly for all countries bordering the Mediterranean. Both the Madrid and Milan stock exchanges looked at the Paris market for direction. This was despite the growing competition from Berlin, which emerged as Germany's most important financial centre with an important international dimension. In addition, the Amsterdam and Brussels stock exchanges were also important internationally, as was Geneva, reflecting the large holdings of foreign securities possessed by their residents. In contrast, all other European stock exchanges tended to play a largely domestic role before 1900 or, in the case of St Petersburg, an international role by virtue of the large foreign holdings of Russian securities. That was also true for New York as US government debt and then corporate securities were extensively held in western Europe, and so were traded in a transatlantic marketplace.

However, activity in these central securities markets, whether domestic or international, was not driven solely by the changing investment preferences of investors and the reactions of *arbitrageurs*. The marketability and mobility that stock exchanges gave to the largest and most widely held securities made these as much instruments of the money market as of the capital market. Though governments and companies issued securities that were either irredeemable or only matured at a distinct date in the future, the ease of transfer in organized markets meant that they were also attractive short-term investments. Consequently, financial intermediaries like banks and insurance companies could employ temporarily idle funds in such securities, because of the return they offered, in confidence that a sale could be made when required. In turn, the constant demand by those responding to money market conditions drove turnover on the principal stock exchange of each country, and in the main money market centres such as London, Paris, and New York which attracted idle funds on a global scale. In these centres lending short-term to those holding long-term securities became a common practice among bankers as a way of keeping funds liquid and ready for repayment or use whilst still earning some kind of return.

London was the natural centre for the employment of short-term funds not only from the countries of the empire, like India and Australia, but also from Germany, France, Japan, and the United States. The short-term money at the disposal of British commercial banks doubled from an estimated £43.5 million in 1880 to £97.6 million in 1900, for example, and much of this was lent out to borrowers using securities as collateral. Though much money was used to finance international trade a great deal was also invested, directly or indirectly, in securities commanding an active market and offering a stability of income, such as government debt and railway bonds.[66] As Sir Robert Giffen noted in the late 1890s, 'one of the chief parts of the business of banks is to lend to the leading members of the Stock Exchange for short terms on securities'.[67] The New York money market occupied a similar position within north America. Not only did thousands of separate banks in the United States employ their idle balances in New York, where they were lent on the call loan market with securities as collateral, but also the large Canadian banks did likewise.[68] There was thus a world of difference between the activity of stock exchanges driven by international money market conditions, like London,

Paris, and New York, and those where it was less in evidence, such as most of the other stock exchanges of the world.

Each stock exchange thus not only served its own specialist securities and local investors but also formed a constituent part of a worldwide network through which it responded to rises and falls in the prices of those securities it shared with others. The system was never at rest for as each stock exchange adjusted it provoked a response in return. Securities markets were also very responsive to changing conditions within the money markets. If money market conditions tightened, for instance, banks called in loans and lent less, leading to sales of securities which forced alterations in prices not only in the local market but internationally, depending on the severity of the squeeze.

CONCLUSION

In the years between 1850 and 1900 stock exchanges evolved into central institutions of the capitalist world, providing an essential interface between money and capital markets at the national and international levels. In the process they facilitated the mobilization of the vast sums of money required to finance the world's railway systems and contributed significantly to the stability of the world monetary system, normally associated with the gold standard. No longer did trading in individual markets take place in isolation as the communication revolution ensured that every sale or purchase was informed by the position prevailing elsewhere with only a minimal delay. A degree of integration between markets was now possible because of the availability of information that previously had been denied to even the most active and well-informed participant. Consequently, the global securities market achieved an unprecedented degree of sophistication, coverage, and intensity. Also during this half-century joint-stock companies became increasingly common as railway systems spread across the globe whilst they also appeared in other areas of economic life such as mining, manufacturing, and financial services. In ever more numerous areas of business the use of transferable securities to finance economic development or to share risks became commonplace, and this was no longer confined to Western Europe and the eastern United States. Securities were also an integral part of the money market, as their ease of purchase and sale gave them the characteristics of short-term financial instruments. They comprised a huge mass of mobile assets that flowed constantly between financial centres and helped to preserve equilibrium in an increasingly integrated world economy. Finally, it was in these years that specialized markets in securities, in the form of stock exchanges, began to spread around the world, giving a form and organization to the global trading of securities that it had never before possessed. The global securities market of 1900 was fundamentally different from what had existed in the past. This was revolution not evolution.

5

The Triumph of the Market: 1900–14

THE VICTORY OF SECURITIES

Between 1900 and the outbreak of the First World War the global securities market went from strength to strength. By 1914 securities markets played a key role in the financial systems of most advanced economies and had established a niche position within less developed countries. Though far from being the universal means through which government and business raised funds or people employed their savings, securities had achieved a high level of penetration among the most sophisticated borrowers and investors. Internationally, securities markets were instrumental in the worldwide movement of funds that provided the finance for major infrastructure projects and the development of the earth's minerals and oil. The operation of both money and capital markets, and the smooth functioning of banking systems, had become heavily dependent on the liquidity that securities markets provided. It was only through the constant buying and selling on securities markets around the world that an overall balance was achieved in the innumerable transactions taking place within an increasingly complex world economy. Finally, in the shape of stock exchanges these securities markets had established a presence for themselves in all the major financial centres of the world and most of the minor ones. Through these stock exchanges the global securities market possessed the stability, organization, and order that made the trading of stocks and bonds a fast, cheap, easy, reliable, and routine experience the world over. There was an immediacy and a certainty attached to the buying and selling of securities that other assets did not possess, and this gave them a power akin to money itself.

Nevertheless, what securities markets had achieved by the early twentieth century was not recognized by most people, including those in government. The reasons behind the constant buying and selling of stocks and bonds were little understood, and regarded as nothing more than speculation to be curbed and controlled. As Van Antwerp, of the New York Stock Exchange, noted in 1913

Singing the praises of stock exchanges is a thankless task, and one that falls upon deaf ears. The very nature of its functions makes dull reading. It cannot hope to enlist the lively enthusiasm of the casual observer, nor has it picturesqueness to brighten the pages of history. The layman visits the great exchanges as a matter of course; the scene is animate and diverting; he sees the outward manifestations of energy and movement, but too often he misses the great silent forces at work. The eye has a fine time of it, but the intellect comes away empty.[1]

As a result governments faced pressure from the public and the press to intervene when problems emerged, as in the aftermath of a speculative boom. Some responded to this but most left stock exchanges to police the securities market within a liberal economic environment. Although the role played by national governments had implications for the global securities market, the degree of state intervention at international level remained very low before 1914.

SECURITIES AND NATIONAL ECONOMIES

By 1900 the global securities market possessed a strong forward momentum. By 1912–3 securities averaged around 16.4% of national assets, ranging from 2% in Russia through 6% in Japan, 11% in Germany, 19% in the United States, and 26% in France to 41% in Britain.[2] Governments remained major participants in this process with a continuing rise in most national debts. However, the level of borrowing stayed relatively modest, though there were marked differences between individual countries. Absolute increases were quite large when driven by the costs of military conflict, as was the case in Russia and Japan due to the war of 1904–5. By 1913 the Russian national debt had reached 9.9 billion rubles, with much held in France, whilst the Japanese national debt was 2.7 billion Yen, with much held in Britain. However, the relative lack of military conflict before 1914 acted to restrain the growth of public debt. France was very restricted in the issue of securities over this period. Its national debt increased by only 2.8 billion francs, from 30.1 billion in 1900 to 32.9 billion in 1913. Even those countries experiencing major economic development, such as Argentina, Australia, Canada, and New Zealand, made relatively modest calls on securities markets. The borrowings of the Argentinian government were only slightly greater in 1913 than in 1900 whilst the public debt of the Dominion of Canada, which had grown from $72.8 million in 1867 to $236.5 million in 1900, only increased to $303.5 million by 1913. This was despite massive immigration, agricultural settlement, infrastructure development, and urbanization in both countries.

Additionally, Britain was joined by Spain, Italy, and the United States as countries where before 1914 the absolute size of the national debt was falling. Government debt continued to decline as a share of national assets, being only 4.3% of the total for a sample of relatively advanced economies in 1912–14. This ranged from a mere 1.9% of US national assets, through 3.4% for Japan, 4.2% for Germany, 5.3% for Britain, 7.8% for France to 10.1% for Italy.[3]

Even where government borrowing grew substantially it was rarely due to war and more to the finance of infrastructure development. It became increasingly fashionable for governments to nationalize their railway systems, with investors exchanging corporate securities for national debt, and then to finance further development by issuing more bonds. This helps explain the growth in the German national debt from 12.4 billion marks in 1900 to 20.2 billion in 1913. As the radical writer, Chiozza Money reported with approval in 1910

In Europe, Austria-Hungary, Belgium, Denmark, France, the various states of the German Empire, Italy, Norway, Portugal, Russia, Sweden, Switzerland, and even Turkey, have in whole or part state railways. Elsewhere Japan has recently followed what is the almost universal plan. Britain and America apart, the chief countries of the world, give a clear verdict for nationalization.[4]

In addition to railways, various levels of state authority were increasingly involved in the ownership and provision of public services, ranging from the supply of water, gas, and electricity to the running of urban tramways. As many of these were income-generating activities, and were often profitable, the additional securities issued by governments to finance them were matched by an additional revenue stream. The resulting burden of debt due to financing such projects was thus readily serviced from the income produced, and governments were able to borrow by issuing securities with very low yields. Investors seeking reasonably attractive returns from their savings had to look beyond government debt, particularly that issued by the countries of Western Europe, their empires, and the United States. Italian government debt, for example, was largely absorbed by Italian investors from the 1890s onwards, leaving foreigners who had previously been major holders, such as the French, to look elsewhere.[5] Consequently, even a relative newcomer to government borrowing such as Japan, which had found it difficult and expensive to borrow in the 1870s, faced no such difficulty by the early twentieth century.[6]

Railways continued to be a major beneficiary of funds looking for safe and remunerative investment, whether investors purchased the securities issued directly by companies or those by governments. Globally, the length of railway track in existence grew by 291,329 km, or roughly one-third between 1900 and 1913, reaching 1,056,551 km by 1913. In the United States, where the world's largest railway network was financed entirely through corporate stocks and bonds, the securities issued by US railroad companies almost doubled from $11.5 billion in 1900 to $20.3 billion in 1914. Even Britain's mature railway system, which was also privately financed, issued an additional £200 million in securities between 1900 and 1913.[7] The ability of investors to finance other types of economic activity continued to grow, extending beyond the needs of other capital-intensive infrastructure projects such as telephone systems and electricity generation and distribution. In the high-income/high-saving economies of Western Europe and the United States an increasingly sophisticated financial system effectively mobilized savings for investment. Investors seeking securities with the same characteristics as those issued by governments, railways, and urban utilities but offering a higher yield became more adventurous in terms of the securities they would consider purchasing.

In manufacturing industry numerous large and established businesses were ready for conversion into joint-stock companies. They were able to offer investors the type of returns that they were familiar with from railways and urban utilities, but with more generous dividends and interest payments. The largest joint-stock manufacturing company in the United States in 1912 was US Steel, capitalized at $757 million, which had a semi-monopolistic position in the supply of a basic material. Similarly, in 1912 the largest British manufacturing company was J. and P. Coats, capitalized at $300 million, and dominating the worldwide production of cotton thread, an essential ingredient in clothing manufacture. Firms such as these appealed most to investors before 1914, with breweries being an especial favourite given the relatively stable demand for their product. A business offering a combination of low risk and reasonable return was more attractive to investors than either government debt or railway stocks and bonds. Such businesses also had the greatest incentive to convert to the joint-stock form as they could use additional capital to invest in new capacity or expand their operations through mergers and acquisitions, so stabilizing their earning capacity even more.

Another category of enterprise that continued to appeal to investors was mining companies, because of their traditional combination of high risk and high return. During this period mining companies appeared which, through the size and spread of their operations, offered some immunity from sudden collapse when the deposits ran out. In the United States both Standard Oil, capitalized at $390 million in 1912, and Anaconda Copper ($178 million) attracted investors because of their strong position in each of those industries. For Britain in 1912 companies like Rio Tinto ($143 million), with its lucrative copper mines in Spain, and Shell Transport and Trading ($91 million), with its Far East oil distribution business, caught the attention of investors.[8] South African mining companies were similar as they could rely on the depth and extent of the gold-bearing rocks in the Witwatersrand to produce a regular output of a mineral which, uniquely, enjoyed a fixed price because of the operation of the gold standard. Though some of these businesses, such as mining, did issue securities in order to finance the initial stages of development, most did not. Instead, they were often capitalizing an income stream that gave the founding entrepreneurs a partial exit whilst also providing a foundation for future expansion through professional management. A growing number of industrial, commercial, and mining enterprises in western Europe and North America thus found it attractive to convert into public joint-stock companies. Nevertheless, the result was only a limited broadening of the range of corporate securities available before 1914 as those issued by railways remained dominant. On the London Stock Exchange the securities issued by all industrial and commercial companies were less than 10% of the total between 1900 and 1913, whilst those operating in mining and oil were generally less than 1%. On the New York Stock Exchange, 90% of the listed stocks and bonds in 1910 had been issued by railroad companies, despite the rise of the giant corporation in other avenues of US corporate life.[9]

Outside Western Europe and North America, the use of corporate securities remained very selective. Assets such as land, mortgages, and bank deposits were of far greater importance to investors whilst self-finance, informal networks, reinvested profits, and bank loans remained crucial for business. However, the use of securities to raise finance was of strategic importance in certain sectors of an economy, particularly those requiring a substantial injection of capital beyond the resources of a small group of individuals or which involved significant risk, as was the case with any new industry. In Russia by 1914 the development of such new industries as coal mining, iron and steel production, and engineering was largely undertaken by joint-stock companies that raised capital through the issue of securities. Even the commercial banks that increasingly dominated the provision of loans to Russian business before the First World War were organized on a joint-stock basis. Nevertheless, the great bulk of Russian economic activity was self-financed or relied on the support of social networks whilst most investors preferred the familiarity and flexibility of bank deposits to corporate securities.[10]

There were clear differences in the importance of securities even between apparently similar countries settled by Europeans. This is most marked between those that largely received migrants from northern Europe, especially Britain, and those that drew upon the populations of southern Europe, most notably Italy and the Iberian peninsula. In northern Europe joint-stock enterprise, corporate stocks and bonds, and securities markets had become well established during the nineteenth century, whereas such developments remained in their infancy in southern Europe, especially in the poorer areas such as southern Italy that produced so many migrants. Thus, though Europeans were responsible for spreading the concepts of joint-stock companies and markets for transferable securities, the degree to which they were used to overcome a shortage of finance in rapidly growing economies reflected the national origins of these Europeans. South American residents, whose immigrant origins lay predominantly in southern Europe, made relatively little use of securities before 1914, in contrast to the resident population of Australia, Canada, New Zealand, and South Africa, whose immigrant origins lay predominantly in northern Europe. It was not that the external ownership of the major securities generated in these South American republics robbed them of the incentive to develop local markets, for that was also the case elsewhere. More significant was the continuing preference among South American investors for bank deposits and mortgage bonds and a reluctance to deal in corporate stocks and bonds. Even local utilities in South America, like those providing electricity, tramways, and the telephone, were owned by joint-stock companies financed by foreign investors, which was not the case in Australia, Canada, New Zealand, and South Africa. Latin American investors did purchase some stocks and bonds, and entrepreneurs there used the joint-stock company to organize their business affairs, but before 1914 there was a far greater willingness in countries settled by northern Europeans to hold securities and to finance local enterprises that way.[11]

The Latin American experience was in many ways an exception, for the use of securities was becoming well established in diverse societies around the world, driven by the presence of expatriate Europeans. Although most Indian securities were held by investors resident in Britain, increasingly, investors resident in India held shares in a wide spectrum of local joint-stock enterprise. By 1911 there were some twenty-nine jute milling companies registered in India, which had raised £7 million from local investors compared to the £2.8 million raised by the eight companies registered in Britain. Similarly, tea planting companies drew their funds from investors in both India and Britain. The stocks and bonds of companies operating Indian cotton textile mills and coal mines were largely taken by local investors, mainly Indians rather than the expatriate population.[12] Though in India securities constituted only 2.7% of national assets in 1914, and most were held externally, local joint-stock companies supported by Indian investors had made a major contribution to a number of key areas in the economy. The situation in China was much less advanced by 1914. Both government debt and railway securities were largely held abroad and most Chinese joint-stock companies had been formed by foreigners and were owned by investors from the expatriate community.[13] One exception to the Asian pattern where securities markets owed most to an expatriate community was Japan. By 1905 the Japanese cotton textile industry had a paid-up capital of 34.3 million yen compared to outstanding loans of 5.6 million, its principal source of finance being securities rather than bank loans. Generally, securities provided an important source of finance for the Japanese economy, though much of this was government borrowing undertaken abroad. Nevertheless, a significant proportion consisted of the issue of stocks and bonds by Japanese companies, including banks and industrial concerns.[14]

In general, by 1914 corporate stocks and bonds had overtaken government debt in importance, with around 60% of the securities in existence having been issued by companies, compared to only 40% by government. Most corporate securities remained those issued by railway campanies. However, there was great variation in the relative importance of securities across the world that was not simply a product of relative economic progress. Whereas securities represented 41.4% of national assets in Britain in 1912–14, the figure for France was 26.0%, for the United States 18.5%, and for Germany only 11.1%. These were similar economies where it would be expected that the importance of securities would be roughly equal. However, that was not the case. Differences might be due to the state ownership of railways. In 1910 it was estimated that 63% of all securities in circulation in the United States and Britain had been issued by railways and manufacturing companies whilst the proportion was 29% in Germany, 20% in Italy, 16% in France, and as low as 2% in Austro-Hungary.[15] However, differences between state and corporate ownership of railway systems cannot explain the wide variation in the relative importance of securities, given the heavy use made of bond issues to finance infrastructure development whether in the public or private sphere. This leads to another simple explanation, which was the degree of foreign invest-ment in securities. However, even when this external element is removed the differences still remain, though less markedly. In 1912–14 domestic securities as a proportion of national assets still ranged from 23.6% in the UK through 19.2% in the United States and 18.4% in France to 8% in Germany (see Table 5.1).

This variation in the use of securities and the fact that most economic activities made little use of them has led to prominence being given to the importance of banks rather than securities markets within world financial systems. The German-style universal banks operating throughout central, eastern, and southern Europe appear to have been more significant in financing economic development than securities markets. Such banks were seen to possess close, wide-ranging, and long-term financial relationships

Table 5.1. Securities as a proportion of national assets, 1912–14(2)

Country	Government debt (%)	Corporate bonds (%)	Corporate stocks (%)	Domestic securities (%)	Foreign assets (%)	Total (%)
Belgium	6.9	2.2	8.3	17.4	7.7	25.1
Denmark	3.3	0.3	8.8	12.4	−3.3	9.1
France	7.8	5.5	5.1	18.4	7.6	26.0
Germany	4.2	0.6	3.2	8.0	3.1	11.1
India	1.7	0.5	0.5	2.7	−7.0	−4.3
Italy	10.1	0.6	0.8	11.5	−1.0	10.5
Japan	3.4	0.2	4.7	8.3	−2.5	5.8
Norway	3.4	0.4	4.5	8.3	—	8.3
Russia	2.2	0.2	2.1	4.5	−2.5	2.0
South Africa	1.2	—	16.4	17.6	—	17.6
Switzerland	4.5	1.1	7.5	13.1	8.5	21.6
UK	5.3	4.3	14.0	23.6	17.8	41.4
US	1.9	4.8	12.5	19.2	−0.7	18.5

Source: R. W. Goldsmith, *Comparative National Balance Sheets* (Chicago, 1985), national tables.

with their business customers, providing them with all necessary finance ranging from short-term credit to long-term capital. In contrast, where business relied on the issue of securities for finance no such relationship was seen to exist between investor and borrower, with banks in those countries confining themselves to the provision of credit, making the supply of long-term finance more difficult to obtain.

Certainly differences did exist between national banking systems, as these were especially prone to national legislation, with particular types of banks being favoured by the state at different times. This is evident in a comparison between Germany, Britain, and the United States, all of which possessed large and sophisticated banking systems by 1914. In Germany, despite the activities of the Universal banks it was the network of local savings banks that dominated the collection of deposits, taking 61% of the total in 1913. This occurred because Germany was a recent amalgam of separate states and provincial authorities wished to control savings. In contrast, savings banks were of minor importance in Britain and the United States, attracting only 19% and 21% respectively of bank deposits. However, the banking systems of Britain and the United States were in themselves fundamentally different. In Britain a branch banking system developed, where a small number of banks possessed numerous branches spread throughout the country. By 1913 there were only 104 banks with 8,260 branches. In contrast, the United States developed a unitary banking system due to legislation that gave the individual states a great deal of control over banking. This made the creation of a nationwide banking system impossible. By 1913 there were 24,514 separate banks in the

United States and only 548 branches, or the exact opposite to the situation in Britain.

These different systems had important implications for the role played by banks in each country. With such a large proportion of savings in Germany absorbed by the savings banks and then lent to the government, commercial banks were left to operate on capital rather than deposits. They could therefore make a higher proportion of long-term loans to business customers than for banks operating largely on the deposits of customers. The unitary nature of the US banking system had similar implications. Each bank had to ensure that it could meet any and every withdrawal, creating a need for a larger capital and thus the ability to make a higher proportion of long-term loans. Conversely, the branch banking system, found not only in Britain but also in Australia, Canada, New Zealand, and South Africa, was very effective at matching deposits and loans nationally. This minimized the capital and reserves that a bank needed even in a crisis, as funds could be easily, quickly, and secretly circulated around its branch network, as directed by head office. It also created a strong preference for short-term lending to counter the ever-present fear that panic withdrawals would lead to the closure of the bank. The difference between banking systems can be seen in the key ratio between a bank's permanent capital and the floating supply of funds it had access to through savings deposits. Whereas the British banking system could operate safely on a ratio of capital to deposits in 1913 of 1:9, banks in the United States required a ratio of 1:4 and those in Germany 1:3.[16]

However, bankers were learning how to operate within the parameters imposed by the amount and type of funds available, and the demands of their business customers. Recurring bouts of prosperity and optimism when funds were abundant, remunerative short-term openings few, and the prospect of default remote, conspired to encourage banks to make long-term loans. The less advanced the economy, the more pressing were the demands upon banks for long-term loans, as the initial capital requirements of a business could prove to be beyond the traditional informal networks through which funds were mobilized. Such lending was profitable for the bank, remunerative for the borrower, and productive for the economy as it financed long-term development. Nevertheless, it did involve a degree of risk greater than the provision of short-term credit, as no bank was ever in a position to liquidate all its loans and investments quickly enough if a large number of depositors decided to withdraw all their savings at once. Such circumstances had occurred frequently during the nineteenth century. The classic universal bank, the Credit Mobilier in France, formed in 1853, collapsed in 1867, having discovered that a policy of making long-term loans to customers on the basis of short-term deposits had disastrous consequences during a financial crisis. Similarly, overextended banks collapsed in Germany in the crisis of the 1870s, whilst in Russia and Japan extensive bank lending to a few favoured customers endangered the solvency of the entire financial system during financial crises in the 1890s. As a result, an orthodoxy was gradually established in banking circles that long-term loans to finance the permanent expansion of business were to be avoided if they were based on short-term deposits. Banks that learned this lesson survived whilst those that did not collapsed.[17]

This orthodoxy did not mean that banks no longer provided long-term finance. The rolling-over of short-term loans to major business customers was commonplace. This occurred even within the British banking system, where a virtue was made of the fact that banks did not provide long-term finance. Banks structured their assets to range from the cash always available to meet normal withdrawals, which earned nothing, through those loans that could be relied upon to be repaid at short notice, which earned a low rate of return, to those lent for longer periods for which repayment by the borrower was difficult and which earned much higher rates of interest. A bank could thus afford to allocate part of its funds for longer-term loans to businesses offering the most promising prospects. Finally, competitive pressures encouraged banks to develop the most efficient mix of assets to combine profit with prudence. A well-managed bank adjusted either its capital or its lending to maintain a match between assets and liabilities. For example, whilst the National City Bank of New York made more long-term loans to business customers from the 1890s, it also increased its operating capital from $3.4 m in 1891 to $49.3 m in 1907, so avoiding difficulties during the 1907 financial crisis.[18]

For a number of countries, especially in central and eastern Europe, highly capitalized banks used funds raised from the issue of stocks and bonds to lend to local business. This was often the outcome of government restrictions on either the development of securities markets or the formation of joint-stock companies. Unfortunate experiences in the past, especially during speculative manias, led governments to restrict the ability of securities markets to operate and the freedom of business to adopt the joint-stock form. Consequently, banks responded to the needs of business by making long-term loans. In the Austro-Hungarian Empire, for example, even when government restrictions on joint-stock company formation were relaxed after 1899 an unfavourable tax regime limited their popularity. Faced with a growing demand from business for long-term funding and from investors for corporate securities, Austrian banks satisfied both by issuing stocks and bonds to the public, and financing the expansion of their business customers by taking up equity stakes.[19] Similarly, German banks raised capital through the issue of securities, which they then lent to business customers, who might have issued securities themselves had the securities market been less restricted by government controls. This was especially so because the businesses receiving these loans were usually the largest industrial enterprises and the very type that were issuing stocks and bonds in the United States and Britain.[20]

Consequently, by the early twentieth century there existed a variety of banks and banking systems around the world with some more involved in providing long-term finance than others.[21] Whatever the banking system, though, securities came to play a role of increasing importance. Banks simply did not have sufficient funds to finance all economic activities, especially those requiring large amounts for the long term. By 1913 there existed an estimated $158 billion in securities. In contrast, the total deposits held by commercial and savings banks across the world came to $43 billion. Even if all these deposits had been applied to the investments represented by securities they would have covered only a quarter of the total.[22] Thus, there was no alternative to securities for governments, railways, and utilities and for a growing range of other economic activities. Banks themselves were among the most prominent businesses to raise the finance they required through the issue of stocks and bonds. Furthermore, an ever-closer relationship was growing between banks and securities markets, whatever the type of bank in existence. Instead of banks providing business with long-term capital, and risking collapse if there were sudden withdrawals by depositors, they could lend to investors, using securities as collateral. If these loans had to be recalled, as in a financial crisis, this could be easily done through the investor either obtaining alternative funds by borrowing elsewhere or by selling the securities in the marketplace to another with funds available. By 1910 35% of loans made by Swedish commercial banks used stocks and bonds as collateral. In Japan by 1914 22.8% of the collateral provided for bank loans was securities, though property and personal guarantees remained more important. By 1910 Tokyo had surpassed Osaka to become the largest component of the Japanese securities market, driven by the better availability of bank loans.[23]

Banks combining investment and commercial banking, such as Deutsche Bank and Citibank, often lent to corporate clients in return for unissued securities, in the expectation that these securities would be eventually sold to individual investors. These banks were anticipating the existence of a market for the stocks and bonds that they held, and hoping to profit from the premium they would eventually receive for these securities compared to the price originally paid. Obviously this involved risk as the securities could remain unmarketable or be only capable of sale at a loss. However, the banks operating in this way could limit their risks by concentrating on those sectors and companies whose securities were most likely to be well received by investors. German universal banks, for example, focused their long-term lending on a small number of firms in a few sectors, such as the major producers of steel and electrical products, rather than spreading themselves across the whole range of German industrial and commercial enterprises. Similarly, those American banks that were heavily involved in investment banking concentrated their attention on particular companies and particular activities. Citibank lent extensively to local utilities taking their bonds as collateral.[24] Therefore, whatever the banking system the existence of active markets for securities became increasingly important as they encouraged banks to be reasonably certain that the securities they held either in their own right or as collateral for loans could be sold to meet the needs of both those who wanted to lend short and those who wanted to borrow long.[25] The result was an increasing dovetailing of banks and securities markets providing finance to those requiring it in the most appropriate and cheapest way, and providing savers and investors with remunerative, safe, and flexible outlets for their money. This integration contributed enormously to the mobilisation of funds for productive investment and preserving the stability of national financial systems. This was only possible because of the major contribution made by securities markets at the national level, even in those economies where banks appeared dominant.

SECURITIES AND THE GLOBAL ECONOMY

National securities markets in the years before the First World War were not confined by national boundaries. Markets for money and capital were daily becoming more integrated as the capacity and reach of the global telegraph network continue to expand, especially through the number of submarine cables, and the service provided became cheaper and faster. Communication between London and New York was down to thirty seconds each way by 1911, and the cost was a mere 0.5% of the 1866 level. In addition the telephone became more useful for long-distance communications with the invention of the thermionic valve in 1906. In consequence the world possessed a means of rapid, instant, and continuous communication extending from the local to the national and international. With an open telephone line it was possible to have continuous two-way communication between London and Paris or New York and Montreal so even the small delays incurred in the use of the telegraph were eliminated. A telephone connection was established between Madrid and Barcelona in 1909 and one between Madrid and Paris in the same year.[26] By 1909 members of the London Stock Exchange were sending or receiving a telegram every second of the working day from or to continental Europe, with members of the Amsterdam, Berlin, Brussels, Frankfurt, and Paris stock exchanges being the main communicants. Between London and New York the exchange of telegrams was running at around one every six seconds during the working day, mostly concentrated into the time when trading was taking place in both centres simultaneously.

Such communications were fundamental to the operation of a global securities market, enabling a constant process of adjustment as information and orders flowed continuously between trading markets. In 1910 Huebner reported that

We are informed that the entire process of collecting quotations on the New York Stock Exchange, cabling them across the ocean, and transacting a purchase or sale on the London Stock Exchange takes only a few minutes, and that some days no fewer than 5,000 messages are cabled by the large arbitrage houses for this purpose.[27]

Though simultaneous buying and selling of securities took place within the United States, between New York and Boston, Chicago or Philadelphia, this was very small in volume compared to that between New York and London, where business was handled by a small group of highly skilled German Jewish brokers on either side of the Atlantic. Few securities moved as a result but constant buying and selling ensured that each market was always aware of what was happening elsewhere and forced to respond to it.[28]

However, this speed of communication and coordination of buying and selling was but one factor, and would have been of little value if other conditions had also not been present. One of these was the worldwide monetary stability existing in the years between 1900 and 1914. Though the depreciation of those Asian currencies on silver was a problem, as was the instability of Latin American exchange rates, most of the world had adopted the gold standard by this time. As a result exchange rates between the main currencies, such as the £, $, franc, and mark, hardly fluctuated and these currencies, especially the £, were widely used for trading and investment purposes throughout the world whatever the country involved. This gave a high degree of stability to international financial flows and removed many of the risks involved in the purchase and sale of securities on a global basis. Investors could buy and sell stocks and bonds in the secure knowledge that their value would not be destroyed through adverse currency movements. This was the case either with those securities denominated in currencies other than the investor's own, as with the US$ stocks and bonds, or with those using an international currency like the UK£ but dependent on the receipt of funds from abroad to pay interest and dividends or repay loans. Investors were left to ponder only the risks involved in the underlying investment. Equally, borrowers could be reasonably certain that no adverse movement in exchange rates would make it difficult for them to service or repay externally held securities. Under those circumstances issuing securities abroad posed no greater risks than doing so domestically, whilst offering access to a greater pool of finance at lower rates of interest.[29]

Greatly contributing to this situation was the role played by governments, both what they did not do as much as what they did do. The era between 1900 and the outbreak of the First World War was one of unrivalled economic liberalism both domestically and internationally. This manifested itself in the absence of exchange controls and the lack of other impediments to the free movement of money. Investors and savers were given relatively free rein to place their funds wherever they wished. More positively, the adoption of the gold standard and the maintenance of fixed exchange rates encouraged international financial flows, especially as the rights of foreign investors were generally respected. The existence of extensive European empires also created a situation where money could flow abroad as easily as domestically, as the same currency and the same laws often prevailed. However, empire was not an essential ingredient in this situation as political, economic, and financial stability were the key factors. The single largest destinations for international financial flows were the United States and Russia, of which neither were part of an empire and each had their own currency. Even within the British Empire the largest flow of funds was to Canada, which operated on the $ not the £, whilst Australia was no more favoured than a non-member like Argentina. Clearly, political arrangements contributed to the creation of a global securities market but they were by no means as central to it as the confidence that came from financial and monetary stability. The United States, for example, did not attract foreign investment in the 1890s, because of doubts over the value of its currency, due to the possible adoption of silver, and concerns about corporate governance, because of financial scandals in the railroads. Once these were resolved after 1900 foreign investors returned.

Generally the years before the First World War witnessed a huge expansion in international investment. By 1914 the total stock of internationally held assets was estimated to be around £9 billion or $45 billion, consisting largely of transferable securities issued by governments and companies. Approximately 90% of these securities continued to be held by investors in Western Europe, with British (40%) and French (20%) being the most prominent, though the practice was fairly widespread, including Belgians (3%), Dutch (4%), Germans (16%), and Swiss (3%). Falling returns from investments in western Europe, especially on domestic government debt and railway stocks and bonds, prompted a search for similar but higher yielding securities, taking investors increasingly abroad. Whereas the yield on the British and French national debts was around 3.5% in 1913 that on the Russian national debt was 4.5% whilst that of Argentina and Brazil was nearer 5%.[30] Even within Western Europe it was investors in these few countries who dominated international investment, with most others being net debtors, such as Denmark and Norway. The Norwegian government raised funds by issuing bonds in London and Paris.

Throughout the world the major classes of securities issued by governments and railways were largely or entirely held in Western Europe. Only the United States was a significant investor outside its own borders with 8% of the total. However, the United States was also the largest international borrower, with 16% of the total, making it a net debtor despite enjoying a level of per capita income in excess of almost any in the world at this time. Of funds borrowed by 1914, 60% had come from Britain, 16% Germany, 9% from the Netherlands, and 7% from France. Most of this investment had gone into the expansion of the railway network with approximately one-third of all US railroad securities owned in Europe. In addition to the United States the other major borrowers were Russia (8%), Canada (8%), Argentina (7%), Austro–Hungary (6%), Spain (6%), Brazil (5%), Mexico (4%), India (4%), South Africa (4%), Australia (4%), and China (4%). Thus, the source of international investment before 1914 was overwhelmingly a few countries in western Europe whilst the destinations were spread throughout the world. The nature of this international investment became increasingly diversified, expanding beyond government debt, railway stocks and bonds, and mining shares. In Norway foreign investors were large holders of the stocks and bonds issued by companies developing the country's mining and hydroelectric power.[31] However, foreign investors were not confined to purchasing those securities issued in the hope of appealing to them specifically. Such was the growing integration between national securities markets that investors were able to purchase securities issued domestically and denominated in currencies other than their own. For the United States foreign investors held $122 million of the common stock of US Steel by 1914. In Japan foreign investors began buying government debt issued domestically after the country had stabilized the external exchange rate for the yen by joining the gold standard in the 1890s. By 1910 these holdings had reached £18 million and were in addition to the Japanese securities valued at £173 million that had been issued abroad, mainly by the government (£145.4 million). However, a new stage had also been reached as foreign investors were now purchasing Japanese industrial securities previously confined to local investors. According to a handbook produced for foreign investors by the stockbrokers Nomura Shoten, '[t]he number of foreign shareholders in the leading gas, electric lighting, railways, brewery, shipping and spinning companies is rapidly increasing, and especially at present hydro-electric enterprises'.[32]

This internationalization of investment created a large mass of securities whose ownership was highly mobile. Within Europe, around 25% of the Austrian state debt was held abroad before the First World War, and was actively traded in Berlin, Frankfurt, Amsterdam, and Paris as well as Vienna. Internationally, US and Canadian railroad stocks and bonds were widely held on both sides of the Atlantic, and possessed active markets across north America and western Europe, particularly New York, London, Paris, Amsterdam, and Berlin. Consequently, not only did modern communications permit almost instantaneous contact between the principal securities markets, but trading in mutually quoted securities was also possible, with even tiny price differences prompting buying and selling by the arbitrageurs. Where government or railroad stocks did not exist other securities appeared serving the same function, as with the gold mining stocks of Australia and South Africa, or the rubber plantation company shares of Malaya.[33] As the French economist, Neymarck, observed in 1910, after reviewing his own country's vast holdings of foreign government bonds

We possess 30 billion in foreign bonds and securities, of which 20–25 billion in international bonds are negotiable on our markets and upon the exchanges of those foreign countries which are our debtors. This is a great advantage to us, for these debts, as long as they are regularly settled, guarantee us favourable conditions of exchange.[34]

By then the holdings of French investors in foreign securities, at 30 billion francs, were larger than that of their holdings in French government *rentes* at 26 billion. This indicated how the balance within world securities markets had shifted decisively towards the global and away from the national in the years before the First World War.

Consequently, by 1914 there existed a mass of securities, primarily government debt, and railway stocks and bonds, that commanded an international market highly responsive to the tiniest variations in prices. In turn the prices of these securities on national markets were highly responsive to national fluctuations in interest rates, as many of these international securities were held on a temporary basis, using money borrowed from banks. In 1913 the proportion of European bank funds lent to those using securities as collateral ranged from around 11% for Germany to 21% in the Netherlands, whilst in the United States an estimated $3.9 billion of bank loans were secured by holdings of stocks and bonds.[35] Thus, any change in the interest charged by banks and the expansion or contraction in the supply of credit would lead to an increase in the sales or purchases of securities, as investors sought to profit either from the low cost of financing holdings of securities or unloaded those they held on borrowed money. This would produce price changes on national markets that would be immediately exploited by those who bought and sold internationally. As an inflow or outflow of securities due to international sales and purchases had to be matched by a reverse flow of money, as purchases were paid for and receipts from sales received, the first response to any expansion or contraction in a country's money supply would be experienced in the securities market. The result was an automatic adjustment as the ownership of internationally held securities was redistributed worldwide.

It was not outflows and inflows of gold, as might be expected under the operation of the gold standard, that produced the international equilibrium that the world enjoyed before 1914, or the intervention of central bankers, but the routine operation of securities markets responding to national and international money market conditions. The movement of gold was costly and time consuming, making it a rather inadequate response in an integrated global economy, whereas the buying and selling of securities was routine and instantaneous. The combination of rapid international communications, a mass of mobile securities, and the development of sophisticated markets before the First World War provided a system for constantly adjusting imbalances between economies at a time when exchange rates were increasingly fixed under the gold standard. The British economist Hirst noted in 1910 that 'the debt of any important government can usually be bought on all the leading stock exchanges at pretty much the same price'.[36]

THE DIVERSITY OF STOCK EXCHANGES

On the eve of the First World War there existed stock exchanges not only in all the major financial centres of the world but also in virtually all the major cities as well (see Table 5.2). As the American economist Huebner noted in 1910

The enormous mass of corporate stocks and bonds, the wide distribution of their ownership among hundreds of thousands of persons of all classes, together with the increasing tendency to use such securities as collateral for loans, has necessitated the creation of a large number of stock exchanges in every important commercial country, where securities can be marketed with the greatest convenience and promptness.[37]

Thus, the securities market in Spain was to be found not only in Madrid, where government debt and railway stocks and bonds were traded, but also in Bilbao and Barcelona, as these existed to meet the needs of local investors in local securities issued by local banking, mining, and manufacturing companies. Similarly in France important stock exchanges were found outside Paris, in such cities as Lille, Lyons, and Marseilles, or in Germany with Hamburg, Essen, and Dusseldorf as well as Berlin and Frankfurt.[38]

Table 5.2. The leading stock exchanges in the world: (*c.*1914)

Country/Continent	Number	Examples	Country/Continent	Number	Examples
Europe	55	—	North America	16	—
Austria/Hungary	4	Vienna, Budapest, Prague	Canada	3	Montreal, Toronto
Belgium	2	Brussels	USA	13	New York. Boston, Chicago, San Francisco, Philadelphia
Bulgaria	1	Sofia	Latin America	10	—
Denmark	1	Copenhagen	Argentina	1	Buenos Aires
France	5	Paris, Lyons, Marseilles	Brazil	2	Rio de Janeiro
Germany	6	Berlin, Frankfurt	Chile	2	Santiago
Greece	1	Athens	Cuba	1	Havana
Italy	5	Milan, Genoa	Mexico	1	Mexico City
Netherlands	2	Amsterdam	Peru	1	Lima
Norway	1	Oslo	Uruguay	1	Montevideo
Portugal	1	Lisbon	Venezuela	1	Caracas
Rumania	1	Bucharest	Asia	14	—
Russia	5	St. Petersburg, Warsaw, Moscow	Burma	1	Rangoon
Serbia	1	Belgrade	Ceylon	1	Colombo
Spain	2	Madrid, Barcelona	China	2	Shanghai
Sweden	1	Stockholm	India	3	Bombay, Calcutta
Switzerland	4	Geneva, Zurich	Indonesia	1	Batavia
United Kingdom	10	London, Liverpool, Manchester, Glasgow	Japan	3	Tokyo, Osaka, Yokohama
Africa	11	—	Malaya	2	Singapore
Egypt	2	Alexandria	Turkey	1	Istanbul
Morocco	1	Casablanca	Australasia	15	—
Mozambique	1	Beira	Australia	12	Melbourne, Sydney
Rhodesia	2	Bulawayo	New Zealand	3	Wellington
S. Africa	5	Johannesburg	Total	106	—

Sources: H. Lowenfeld, 'The World's Stock Markets', *Financial Review of Reviews* October 1907, pp. 12–13; S. S. Huebner, 'The Scope and Functions of the Stock Market', in *Annals of the American Academy of Political and Social Science*, 35 (1910), p. 20; J. E. Meeker, *The Work of the Stock Exchange* (rev. edn) (New York, 1930), pp. 540–1.

However, unlike developments in the second half of the nineteenth century, the pace of stock exchange formation slowed greatly after 1900. Numerous stock exchanges had already appeared before 1900 and what happened thereafter was to fill in the gaps, often through the conversion of an informal securities market with a stock exchange, as happened in Calcutta in 1908.[39] Speculative activity associated with mining and oil discoveries also continued to spur the formation of many new stock exchanges, as in Canada where the Winnipeg Stock Exchange appeared in 1903, Vancouver in 1907, and Calgary in 1913.[40] It was also activity in mining and oil that led to a stock exchange being formed in Mexico City in 1907 to replace the one that had collapsed in the 1890s.[41] Similarly, a boom in oil shares led to the formation of the Taranaki Stock Exchange in New Zealand in 1906.[42] Elsewhere, the growth of new towns and cities in those parts of the world settled and developed by Europeans continued to throw up fresh stock exchanges once wealth and economic activity justified their existence. In the United States the Detroit Stock Exchange was organized in 1907 in response to the growth of a market in the stocks issued by the local automobile companies.[43]

These stock exchanges continued to exhibit a variety of different forms with the role of governments and of banks being crucial determining factors. Within Europe a clear divide remained between those stock exchanges controlled by the state and those left free to determine their own rules. In Britain stock exchanges remained totally unregulated, whereas in Germany government supervision and regulation were very much in evidence. In between there existed a number of different practices. These included relative freedom from government intervention in Belgium and the Netherlands, government control over only the main stock exchanges as in France and Spain, and the use of regional legislation in Switzerland. Located in a French-speaking canton the Geneva Bourse was subject to government control from 1856 onwards whereas Basle and Zurich, in German-speaking cantons, escaped until 1896–7. In 1912 the securities market in Zurich had almost became a function of government.[44] In Russia, when in 1900 the St Petersburg Exchange opened a specific department to provide a market in securities, an official of the State Credit Office was made a member of its governing council, indicating the degree of official involvement.[45]

Continuing government control affected the way national securities market developed. In Germany legislation attempting to outlaw speculation became law on 1 January 1897. Previously German stock exchanges had been essentially self-regulating though with a degree of public intervention in their affairs, usually at a local level. In 1908 there was a revision of the Bourse law in recognition of the damage it had done to the German securities market, given that much international business had drifted abroad whilst domestic business had become internalized within the large banks, so as to avoid external scrutiny and the turnover tax. Even after the 1908 revision, the Bourse law continued to restrict the ability to buy and sell securities freely, making it very difficult for the German stock exchanges to flourish as open markets in competition with the closed networks of the banks. One well-informed British investor, the investment banker Robert Benson, observed that one consequence of the German Bourse law was that 'the more adventurous of Germans came to speculate in London, and lost their money in gold mining and other shares along with the Briton'.[46] Generally, governments were increasingly interested in the introduction of some form of tax on transactions in the securities market, considered a lucrative source of revenue from a source that attracted little sympathy, namely the speculator who bought and sold repeatedly for gain. Such taxes first appeared in the late nineteenth century in Germany and Austria and spread to countries like France and Sweden before the First World War. The Swedish government introduced its tax in 1909 and raised it in 1913 whilst the French government introduced a 2% stamp duty on foreign stocks in April 1914.[47]

Nevertheless, it is important not to overstate the role played by governments in moulding the shape of national securities markets before 1914. The French government, for example, placed restrictive tax and legal requirements over the securities market which discouraged its use by foreign borrowers.[48] In 1905 it used these to stop Japan issuing a loan in Paris as it was at war with France's ally Russia. However, that did not prevent Paris being the main market for both Russian and Japanese government debt by the First World War.[49] As Vidal observed in 1910:

It is understood, however, that securities which have not been explicitly admitted on the official quotation list, either because the stockbrokers did not care to adopt them, or because the securities did not fulfil the required statutory conditions, may, nevertheless, be dealt in outside the Bourse.[50]

Though officially the *agents de change* of the Paris Bourse held a monopoly over all trading in the securities quoted there, in reality that was not the case with even government *rentes* being extensively traded by the curb brokers of the Coulisse. In addition to the Paris markets active stock exchanges continued to operated in all the important towns in France. Thus, the power exerted by the French government over the national securities market was limited to the Paris Bourse itself. Paris was regarded as the second most important securities market after London on the eve of the First World War.[51] What mattered was the nature and extent of government intervention in determining its effect upon the operation of stock exchanges, and that was clearly detrimental in the German case and of limited consequence for France.

Differences between stock exchanges in Western Europe were also influenced by the relationship existing between a stock exchange and the other major component of a national financial system, namely banks. In Germany, where banks were members of the stock exchanges, a number developed into universal banks spanning the entire range of financial activities from the collection of savings and the making of loans to the issue and trading of stocks and bonds. This combination suited German conditions given the continuing control exercised over the securities market by the government.[52] In many European countries banks were largely responsible for trading in stocks and bonds, and where denied membership of the stock exchange succeeded in gaining admittance with government backing, as in Sweden in 1911.[53] In the Netherlands the Amsterdam Stock Exchange excluded banks from membership when it finally acquired a separate trading floor for securities in 1903, within the merchants' exchange. However, in 1905 it was forced to offer favourable terms to Dutch provincial brokers, or risk losing business to the Rotterdam Stock Exchange. In 1913 Dutch banks forced their acceptance as members.[54] As a result the Amsterdam Stock Exchange adopted some of the features of the German stock exchanges, where banks were major players, but were also similar to the Anglo-Saxon position, being self-regulating organizations.

In contrast, British stock exchanges refused to accept banks as members. Provincial stock exchanges had maintained minimum commission rules since their formation, whereas the London Stock Exchange did not introduce them until shortly before the First World War. The result was to centralize in London the business banks conducted in the buying and selling of securities. By negotiating special terms with particular brokers banks could get their transactions handled at little cost, so making London a very attractive market. Even after the introduction of minimum commission rates the existence of numerous discounts, exemptions, and evasions ensured that this position remained relatively unchanged before 1914. This fostered a process of specialization within the British financial system. Thus, the division between commercial banking, investment banking, and stock broking was partly a product of the rules imposed by the London Stock Exchange as much as the unification of these activities in Germany was a product of government legislation and bank membership of the stock exchange. Something of a middle position existed in France, where the government would not permit banks to own an *agent de change* but did allow them to have an office within the Paris Bourse. In that sense there existed a similar but closer relationship than in Britain but a less integrated one than in Germany. However, French banks also operated extensively and directly in the large, unregulated outside market in Paris. French joint-stock banks, such as Société Generale, built up extensive branch networks that not only collected savings and made loans nationwide, as in the British pattern, but also handled new issues of securities and subsequent trading, as in the German pattern. Nevertheless, there also remained separate brokers and dealers in Paris, in addition to the *agents de change*, as well as specialist investment banks, indicating the diverse requirements of a sophisticated financial system in the early twentieth century.[55]

In the United States the New York Stock Exchange remained 'a lawfully constituted association with absolute power to make and enforce its own rules and regulations upon its members'. One rule was the exclusion of all corporate members on the grounds that '[t]ransactions between members are in most instances verbal, and as they amount to millions of dollars in value daily, confidence in each other is imperative.'[56] Commercial banks were therefore excluded though investment bankers could become members. This was standard practice throughout the United States. In order to maximize the benefits of membership of the New York Stock Exchange, which could be costly because of the need to buy a seat in order to gain membership, only one person in a firm needed to be a member. This meant that integrated finance houses developed in the major financial centres, spanning both the issue and retailing of securities and subsequent trading on the stock exchange, but not deposit banking and commercial lending. Consequently, in Germany, Britain, France, and the United States a combination of legislation and stock exchange rules had important repercussions for the structure and organization of the entire financial system. Outside Western Europe and the United States the pattern of stock exchange development was some variation of that found in these countries. The German pattern prevailed in Central Europe whilst that of France was found in Spain and in parts of Latin America. The US model prevailed in Canada and was also influential in Australia and New Zealand, where it was grafted on to a British style of stock exchange. In turn, these stock exchanges were adapted to suit local conditions as in mining camps or expatriate communities. In China, there existed one formal stock exchange, in Shanghai, which adopted the British provincial model, as most of the members were British, though other nationalities were also present, especially German. In addition there were a number of loose organizations in other cities, most notably Hankow, Hong Kong, and Tientsin.[57]

Linking all stock exchanges together was their role within the global securities market. None existed in isolation, even those in the most remote mining camp, for the telegraph and the network of brokers, ensured that buying and selling was conducted under the eyes of the international investment community. A high degree of differentiation and specialization developed. Some stock exchanges played a purely local role responding to the needs of local investors in local businesses. However, investors were not restricted to the securities traded on their local stock exchanges, and the securities they traded were not confined to local investors. Through banking and broking networks investors could access whatever securities were traded on the exchanges the world over. Certain stock exchanges developed particular specialities so that, as well as providing a market for local investors and locally issued securities, they also provided a market for investors interested in a particular range of securities wherever they were located. A hierarchy was also created, in which certain stock exchanges became central elements within the global securities market, both receiving and despatching orders on a worldwide basis and responding to the constant ebb and flow of the international money and capital markets. Stock exchanges of this kind existed only in major financial centres.

With such a large proportion of the bonds issued by both governments and companies around the world held by investors in Western Europe, most of the stock exchanges that existed before 1914 traded stocks and shares. In Norway 75% of the bonds issued were held abroad by 1914. These were not only the main issues of government debt but also corporate bonds. This left the emerging Oslo Stock Exchange dependent on the business generated by the issues made by Norwegian banks and industrial companies, as these were held by Norwegian investors and so traded on a local basis.[58] Though two-thirds of the Russian securities issued by 1914 were held domestically, foreign investors held a high proportion of government debt and of the stocks and bonds issued by railways, urban utilities and the major banks, and industrial and mining companies. As a result these possessed better markets abroad than in either St Petersburg or Moscow.[59] Such a position was typical of most stock exchanges before 1914.

This can be seen in Canada, where British investors absorbed 75% of the bonds issued between 1896 and 1914 whilst Canadian investors took 75% of the stocks. This was not simply government debt but extended to the main corporate issues. Of the bonds issued by the Canadian Pacific and Canadian Northern railroads around two-thirds were taken in London. Additionally, as these railways became better known to British investors, their shares were also increasingly held there. As a result the main Canadian stock exchanges in Montreal and Toronto were largely reduced to trading the securities issued by either municipal authorities or the smaller joint-stock companies such as tramways and local manufacturing concerns. In consequence, it was trading in stocks that dominated the Canadian stock exchanges, with a succession of mining booms fuelling speculative activity.[60]

A similar position prevailed in Australia. Although between 1900 and 1914 Australian governments did raise a growing share of funds from within Australia, this remained limited. In 1904 Australian governments raised £40 million in Australia, or 17% of their total requirements, and though the absolute amount had risen to £90 million in 1913 this was still only 31% of the total. Trading activity on the various Australian stock exchanges was underpinned by the securities issued by local companies, especially those involved in mining. What changed was the growth of a pan-Australian market in these local stocks, driven by the growing involvement of investors through-out eastern Australia in the gold mining developments taking place in the west. The result was an agreement in 1903 between the Australian stock exchanges to adopt comparable practices such as on listing requirements. Nevertheless, the Australian stock exchanges remained primarily local in focus, with the added speciality of mining stocks which attracted not only nationwide interest but also international. On the Brisbane Stock Exchange much of the trading activity was in the shares of eighty copper mining companies formed between 1901 and 1913 following large new discoveries. When trading in these was low so was the overall turnover despite the existence of a range of local companies providing such services as banking and insurance, operating in such areas as brewing and manufacturing, and undertaking the provision of gas or property development. Important as these were, their shares were tightly held and little traded compared to mining securities.[61]

Such was the worldwide interest in mining securities, especially when gold was involved, that certain stock exchanges played a major international role simply because of the importance of their local mineral deposits. Such was the case not only throughout north America and Australasia but also southern Africa. When the Johannesburg Stock Exchange reopened in December 1901, on the conclusion of the Anglo-Boer war, it resumed its position as not only the leading exchange in South Africa but also one of the world's most important mining markets with a speciality in gold mining stocks. Its fortunes were very much tied to the South African gold mining industry, which proved particularly resilient at this time. The costs of extraction and processing were kept low with advances in technology and chemistry whilst the price of gold remained fixed under the gold standard.[62] Other resource booms around the world resulted in a rise to international prominence of those stock exchanges located where the activity was centred. Though most of these related to discoveries of oil or minerals of any kind, ranging from gold and silver to tin and copper, other products were also involved. One such speculative mania concerned rubber as the boom in bicycles and then car ownership drove up the price and led to the development of plantation companies in such places as Malaya. These attracted great speculative interest that not only led to the formation of a securities market in Kuala Lumpur but also spilled over into markets around the world. Almost half of the 113 stocks quoted on the Shanghai Stock Exchange in 1910, for example, were plantation companies operating in Malaya. An additional exchange even made a brief appearance, such was the speculative interest among the expatriate community in Shanghai in a development taking place in a neighbouring region of the Far East. Investors even further away were similarly infected, with the formation of a separate rubber exchange in London in 1909 to cater for the huge number of individual companies formed and the speculative interest in their shares. Such was the global nature of the securities business in the years before the First World War that the shares of plantation companies operating in Malaya but formed in London were actively traded in Shanghai. When the boom collapsed business on the Shanghai Stock Exchange was paralyzed for a number of years.[63]

In western Europe stock exchange specialization was driven much less by external interest in the securities quoted and much more by the activities of national investors. This was unsurprising, given that this was the region of the world in which was located the overwhelming bulk of international investment. Though there remained local stock exchanges mainly serving as markets for the securities issued by local companies and held by local investors, a growing number also developed an international speciality. In turn this reflected the volume and variety of investments made by their national populations in securities created to finance economic activity elsewhere in the world.[64] By 1914 the three Swiss stock exchanges of Basle, Geneva, and Zurich provided a market for Swiss securities, which were largely held by Swiss investors. These were mainly government bonds following the nationalization of the railway system, supplemented by the stocks issued by banks and the large engineering and textile companies. In addition these stock exchanges provided a market for the foreign securities favoured by Swiss investors, particularly north American railroads, foreign government bonds, and a number of gold mining companies. The stocks and bonds issued by the Baltimore and Ohio and Pennsylvania Central railroads were especial favourites among Swiss investors before 1914. However, Swiss investors had also been attracted to foreign equivalents of securities that had done well for them domestically. Thus, there was a market in the stocks issued by banks and textile companies operating in neighbouring European countries. Even more pronounced was the fact that Swiss success in electrical engineering led investors to purchase the securities issued by electric supply utilities operating elsewhere, including Austria, France, Germany, Italy, Russia, Spain, and South America. These Swiss stock exchanges became a central market for the securities of many companies generating and supplying electricity in diverse parts of the world.[65]

This was not an isolated occurrence. It was most noticeable in the smaller stock exchanges where specialist activities stood out in comparison to the normal range of national securities. Supported by Belgian success in the construction of electric tramways, the Brussels Stock Exchange became the principal market for the securities issued by similar companies operating in Russia, Spain, and Latin America. Though Belgian investors were heavily involved so were American company promoters, Canadian financiers, and European bankers.[66] Even in Spain, despite heavy reliance upon imported capital in such areas as railways and mining, certain international specialities also developed, reflecting either geographic connections with north Africa or historic ones with Latin America. There was, for example, an active market in the issues of various banks such as the Oriental Bank of Mexico, the Banco Central Mexico, and the Banco Espanol del Rio de la Plata.[67]

Beyond even these, however, were a small number of stock exchanges that occupied a commanding position at the apex of the global hierarchy. Davies, commenting in 1920 on the pre-1914 situation, concluded that '[t]he capital of every fifth-rate country has its stock exchange, but the only ones of real international importance are those of New York, Paris, Berlin, Vienna, Frankfort-on-Maine, Brussels, and Amsterdam.'[68] He ranked London above all these and stressed the international nature of the securities traded between these exchanges, especially government debts, US railroads, and South African mining shares. These stock exchanges were of international importance because they provided a market for securities of interest to investors worldwide, whether driven by the export of capital in the Western European case or its import, as in the case of the United States. In addition, their importance rested on the fact that they operated at the interface between the money and capital markets. These were all stock exchanges located in the major financial centres of the world, namely London, Paris and New York, with Amsterdam, Berlin, Frankfurt, and Vienna playing subsidiary roles. The idle balances of the banks of the world were increasingly to be found in these centres. With the worldwide growth in banking operations funds of this kind had reached very large proportions by the First World War and banks were eager to employ them on a temporary basis. Given the stability of exchange rates the employment of this money was not confined to national centres but gravitated to the international ones where it could be more easily and remuneratively used.

London was central to this process, attracting funds not only from British and imperial banks but also from Europe, Latin America, Japan, and the United States. One estimate suggests that the supply of such funds in London had risen to £1.9 billion by 1914. Such funds could be employed in London due to the demand from those who borrowed using securities as collateral. This required securities commanding an active market and offering a stability of income, such as government debt and railway bonds. These could be held using borrowed funds, with profit derived from the differential between the interest paid and the interest or dividend received. Such was the depth and breadth of the London Stock Exchange market that if securities had to be sold following the recalling of a loan, this could be easily and quickly done without disturbing the market. Consequently, much of the trading in London was a product of the constant ebb and flow of the money market both domestically and internationally.

However, important as the London Stock Exchange was as the world's largest and most international securities market, it was not supreme in all areas before 1914. Domestically it faced competition from numerous provincial stock exchanges, with those in Glasgow and Liverpool being among the most important. These continued to cater for both the stocks and bonds of local companies and the securities that attracted local investors, even when these were also quoted on the London Stock Exchange. The Glasgow Stock Exchange provided both a market for Scottish securities and an active market in those overseas mining stocks that were extensively held locally. Internationally, the London Stock Exchange was becoming less important as a market for government debt though that issued within the Empire remained important, such as that of Australia and Canada. However, the repatriation of much European government debt and competition from Paris for that issued by countries such as Russia, Japan, and the Latin American republics greatly diminished their importance. Instead, the London Stock Exchange provided a vast market for the stocks and bonds issued by railways operating all over the world, especially those from the United States, Canada, Argentina, and India. A manual of 1910 described the American market on the London Stock Exchange as 'the most constantly active of all departments'. This market catered not only for the US railroad securities issued in both London and the United States, but also the major Canadian railroads such as the stocks and bonds of the Canadian Pacific. Of the $374 million raised by Canadian railways by 1914, $277 million had come from Britain compared to $51 million from the United States and $46 million from within Canada. London also functioned as an international market for securities issued by companies operating worldwide in the exploration, production, and distribution of minerals and oil. By 1914 it provided a market for twenty-four companies operating in the Russian oilfields, as well as others throughout eastern and central Europe, the Middle East, and the Far East.[69]

Money market activities also helped make the Paris securities market so important, in addition to the huge holdings of foreign securities amassed by the French population over the years. In 1906 the value of transferable securities marketed in Paris was 150 billion francs compared to only 5 billion in the provincial markets. The major French banks such as Credit Lyonaise and Société Generale, with their extensive branch networks, both collected orders for and lent extensively to those operating on the securities market. For July 1911, it was estimated that $300m was lent out on the Paris Bourse, whose operations depended heavily on such loans.[70] More than half the securities quoted on the Paris Bourse were foreign. Those issued by governments came to 57 billion francs, with foreign railroads far behind at 6 billion.[71] Whether on the Parquet of the Bourse or outside in the Coulisse, Paris was the leading market for Russian government bonds, having displaced Amsterdam, as well as for the national debts of most Mediterranean and Balkan countries including Spain, Portugal, the Ottoman empire, Greece, Egypt, Algeria, Tunisia, Rumania, and Serbia. By 1914 French investors held 60% of the public debt of the Ottoman Empire, compared to 14% for Britain and 10% for Germany, and a similar position prevailed for Egypt with 61% held in France. Paris also occupied an important position for debts of many South American republics as well as those of China and Japan. This made Paris the most important government bond market in the world with much of the activity driven by the ease of obtaining fortnightly and monthly loans via the *agents de change.*[72]

Between 1898 and 1913, 72% of the capital raised in Paris went abroad, establishing that city at the very centre of international finance. Not only was Paris one of the world's leading bond markets, it was also one of the most liquid. Such a market was ideal for French banks, providing them with a huge market in some of the safest securities of the day, namely public debt, and one in which there was constant buying and selling both in Paris and with other major financial centres. French banks were awash with the savings of the French people and so were well positioned to employ a significant proportion of their deposits through lending to those buying, selling, and holding these bonds in full knowledge that they would be able to reclaim their money at very short notice. Though operations of this kind were reputed to be six to seven times greater in London, operations in Paris made a vital contribution both to the mobilization of funds for impoverished governments and to the ability to adjust imbalances between these countries and the rest of the world on a continuous and instantaneous basis.[73]

The London Stock Exchange and the Paris Bourse both competed with and complemented each other in terms of the regions of the world they covered and the activities they financed. Paris had very much a European and Mediterranean focus, with government debt being of major importance, whilst London catered for the rest of the world and concentrated on corporate securities. Consequently the main links of the Paris Bourse were to other stock exchanges in continental Europe, between which flowed buying and selling orders for government debt, whereas London was strongly integrated with

New York, as they were the main markets for North American railroad stocks and bonds. In turn, each was connected to the other through mutually quoted securities, such as Asian and Latin American government bonds and international mining securities, as well as to a host of other stock exchanges. London was connected to Amsterdam through US railroads, to Brussels through Latin American tramways, and to Johannesburg through South African mining stocks. In contrast, Paris was linked to Madrid, Milan, and St Petersburg through their national debts and to Brussels through Russian corporate stocks.

In addition to London and Paris, the Amsterdam Stock Exchange continued to play an important role in international securities and money market activities. This reflected a position where Dutch holdings of securities were equally divided between foreign and domestic issues. Of the securities quoted on the Amsterdam Stock Exchange by 1914 half were foreign, including 194 different US railroad issues. In contrast, the securities issued by many Dutch joint-stock companies, such as the brewers Heineken and the insurance companies, had their market outside the stock exchange. Behind this lay the importance of the short-term *prolongatie* market through which Dutch investors borrowed extensively to invest directly in securities. As these loans could be recalled, investors focused on high-yielding securities possessing a good market, which tended to be US railroad stocks and bonds that were also traded in London and New York. In July 1914, 325 million guilders were lent out on the *prolongatie* market.[74]

Generally, stock exchanges in the capital-exporting countries of western Europe catered for both stocks and bonds, reflecting the sophisticated nature of their financial systems, and were heavily involved in providing a market for securities from all over the world, reflecting the high incomes of their investors. Though this was also true of Germany, its position differed from that not only in Britain and even France but also in neighbouring countries like Belgium, Switzerland, and the Netherlands. By 1913 there were twenty-four stock exchanges spread throughout Germany but many were of little importance beyond their own locality. The share of national turnover of one of the largest regional stock exchanges, Frankfurt, was only 5% between 1901 and 1913. This left Berlin as the dominant stock exchange within Germany. A similar picture prevailed in other large nation states in Western Europe, with a hierarchy of exchanges at the top of which was that located in the financial capital. Between 1900 and 1913 securities with a value of 35.5 billion marks were issued on the Berlin Stock Exchange, indicating its importance within the German securities market. However, of these 83% were domestic whilst only 17% were foreign, making Berlin a much less important international market than either London or Paris or even Amsterdam. In fact Berlin was in decline as an international market from 1897 onwards, the year the Bourse law came into force. Whereas foreign issues as a proportion of total issues had been 35% of the total between 1883 and 1897, they fell to 11% between 1897 and 1913, though increasingly slightly in absolute terms. Though Berlin had supplanted Frankfurt as the main foreign centre for trading Austrian government debt it had lost the position it held for Russian securities to Paris in the 1890s. Instead, Berlin was increasingly a market for German securities. Activity on the Berlin Stock Exchange was much less driven by the money market with the major German banks increasingly employing their short-term funds in London, where a significant proportion was lent to those operating on the London Stock Exchange. Essentially, Germany lacked an exchange that was responsive to ever-changing money market conditions and instead channelled that business to London, Paris, and Amsterdam. The German securities market was therefore not directly comparable to that of Britain and France as it lacked an exchange performing money market functions. In 1912, whereas 55% of the securities quoted in Paris and 48% of those in London were foreign bonds, the proportion for Berlin was only 6%. That made it more like Vienna where the proportion was 1%.[75]

Outside western Europe the only stock exchange to perform a combined role in both international securities and money market operations was the New York Stock Exchange. However, this position was not achieved by New York's emergence as a great centre for international securities. Between 1900 and 1913 foreign securities with a value of $1.1 billion were issued in the United States, but over 50% were on behalf of companies operating in Latin America and Canada, such as Mexican Railways and the Canadian Pacific. In many ways these were extensions of the vast railway network operating within the United States and so attractive to US investors. The same was true of developments in mining and oil in neighbouring countries, especially Mexico and Canada. Until the opening of a securities market in Vancouver in 1907 the Spokane Stock Exchange in neighbouring Washington State was the main market for gold mining companies operating in British Columbia.

Though foreign government debt was issued in New York before 1914, including British, Russian, and Japanese bonds, they were largely taken up in Europe either immediately or soon afterwards. The Japanese Government loan of 1904 for £10 million was issued half in London and half in New York. By 1907 87% was held in the UK with the rest distributed throughout Europe and 1% in Japan. The proportion held in the United States was negligible with the result that the bonds were not traded in New York. In fact New York experienced only a brief period as a market for foreign government bonds coinciding with the Russo-Japanese war, when their governments sought alternatives to Paris and London because of political complications.[76] Instead, the US stock exchanges remained markets for US securities, especially those issued by railroads and urban utilities plus a growing number of manufacturing, mining, and oil companies. It was estimated that a quarter of the stock of US Steel was held abroad in 1914, and was extensively traded between New York and London. Eastman Kodak and General Electric stock was similarly held, reflecting the international appeal of the securities issued by the largest US corporations whatever their field of operation.[77]

The New York Stock Exchange comprised only one component of the US securities market, though it was the part most integrated into the global securities market. Such was the size and dispersion of the US securities market, and the vigour of joint-stock company formation, that numerous securities were traded only on the local stock exchanges. The value of stocks listed on the New York Stock Exchange did rise from $5 billion to $13.5 billion between 1900 and 1912, but this was only one-third of all stocks outstanding in the United States.[78] (see Table 5.3).

Although over half of all US stocks before 1914 had been issued by mining and manufacturing companies, with another 15% by banks and insurance companies, few of these were actually traded on the New York Stock Exchange, which only catered for the largest companies and then mainly railroads. Instead, the bulk of US securities were traded on the numerous local stock exchanges and the curb and OTC markets in New York. A number of these did fulfil more specialized roles, as with the mining exchanges that mushroomed with every discovery and provided an opportunity for investors from a distance to speculate on the results of a new oil well or mineral lode. Others, notably in the major eastern cities, were akin to those found in Western Europe, as the securities for which they provided a market also included those issued by companies operating elsewhere in the United States. Following a similar pattern to the relationship between Western Europe and the rest of the world, as the income and wealth of the population resident in

Table 5.3. Composition of corporate stock outstanding: United States, 1860–1912

Category	1860	1900	1912
Railroads (%)	15	39	26
Public utilities (%)	13	7	7
Banking/Insurance (%)	39	20	15
Manufacturing/Mining (%)	33	34	52
Total stocks	$0.7 billion	$11.2 billion	$32.0 billion
Total bonds	$0.5 billion	$7.1 billion	$18.1 billion

Note: The percentages are based on the total corporate stocks outstanding whilst the total for both stocks and bonds only include those issued by non-financial corporations.

Source: R. W. Goldsmith (ed.), *Institutional Investors and Corporate Stock* (NBER, 1973), pp. 38, 45.

the north-eastern United States built up from the late nineteenth century onwards, part of the available savings flowed into the attractive investment opportunities appearing in the west of the country. Investors in Massachusetts, for example, participated extensively in railroad and mining developments in the western United States, attracted by the mixture of higher returns and speculative gain that was on offer. The result was to make the Boston Stock Exchange the main market for the Atchison, Topeka, and Santa Fe railway, which provided a railway network for the south-west United States. However, when the stocks and bonds of that company became increasingly attractive to foreign investors, the main market moved to New York, leading to the relative decline of the Boston Stock Exchange. This pattern was followed with the other specialities found on US stock exchanges.

What made New York the centre of the US securities market was much less the density of investors located in and around the city and more the fact that it was the fulcrum of the country's domestic and international communications network, giving it unrivalled access to information and orders, and its position within the national money market, making it the depository of the idle balances accumulated by banks. As US external trade was largely financed through London before 1914, the main employment of the enormous supply of short-term funds available in the New York call market was through loans to brokers holding easily marketable securities. These were largely the stocks and bonds issued by the major US corporations such as the railroads. These commanded both a national and an international market and so could be easily and quickly bought and sold at close to current prices, making them ideal as collateral. It was estimated for 1909 that two-thirds of the total amount of stock issued by US Steel was in play because it possessed such a deep and broad market spanning both sides of the Atlantic.[79] Much of the activity on the New York Stock Exchange was driven by international buying and selling and the employment of short-term funds accumulating in New York banks. It was this that gave it the appearance of being a highly speculative market compared to other major US exchanges.

Contributing to this appearance, and adding to the volatility of turnover experienced on the New York Stock Exchange in these years, was the particular nature of the business undertaken there. Unlike either the London Stock Exchange or the Paris Bourse, the New York Stock Exchange was predominantly a market for stocks not bonds. Turnover was largely focused on the buying and selling of corporate stocks, especially those of the major US railroads. An estimate made in 1911 suggested that whereas the annual turnover in stocks on the New York Stock Exchange was $15.5 billion that for bonds was considerably less at $0.8 billion, or 5% of the total. By their very nature stocks were more speculative securities than bonds. Though influenced

by market conditions and individual circumstances, bonds promised investors a certain and guaranteed payment at regular intervals with the prospect
of repayment at a specified date in the future. In contrast, stocks offered an
uncertain payment dependent on the performance of the company, which
could be good, and so leading to a large payout, or poor, with the result that
no dividend was declared. Consequently, company-specific information and
rumours had much more effect on the market for stocks than for bonds,
which were driven much more by interest rate considerations, and could
produce significant variations in turnover from day to day and even year to
year. Turnover in stocks on the New York Stock Exchange ranged from lows of
$83 million in 1913 and $127 million in 1911 to highs of $282 million in 1906
and $265 million in 1901.[80]

Though part of the explanation for this lies in the small size of the US
government debt and the external ownership of such a large proportion of
US corporate bonds, the main reason lay in the rules and regulations adopted
by the New York Stock Exchange and copied by all other US stock exchanges.
Of the turnover in bonds in New York before 1914, only around one-third
took place on the New York Stock Exchange. Two-thirds took place outside
either in the form of direct deals between the main participants in the bond
market, mainly banks, or the trading undertaken by a few specialized bond
houses. This was especially true for government bonds, whether issued by
Federal or State governments or by municipal authorities. In this category an
estimated 90% of all trading took place outside the New York Stock Exchange
even if its own members were involved, rendering its market in these securities virtually non-existent and the prices quoted purely nominal.[81] This arose
because the capacity of the New York Stock Exchange could not be expanded
due to the cap on the membership as the number of seats was fixed, and the
enforcement of a fixed scale of charges, which discouraged certain types of
business. Trading in bonds, for example, could not be easily accommodated
within the fixed commission structure. Much of it was conducted commission
free on behalf of banks and other financial institutions, with the return
coming through the profit to be made from the difference between the buying
and selling price. As a consequence bonds were traded on an OTC basis rather
than on the floor of the New York Stock Exchange. Also, by making
membership expensive, because of the cost of acquiring a seat, those brokers
who did join the New York Stock Exchange concentrated on high-volume
business, such as that generated by trading in the stocks of major
corporations. Consequently, the New York Stock Exchange did not provide
a market for either smaller companies whose shares were less actively traded or
the more volatile mining stocks. Instead, these stocks were also traded
outside, including on the street outside the Exchange itself. By 1906–7 there

were around 400 brokers and dealers operating in this curb market, trading in over 500 different stocks. Such was the level of business that a curb market was formally created in 1908. It provided a feeder market for the New York Stock Exchange. Once buying and selling in a particular corporate stock reached a level which justified a listing on the New York Stock Exchange, its market moved there from the curb.[82] The other components of the US securities market were catered for either by the OTC market for bonds, the curb market for smaller companies, or the regional exchanges for local stocks. However, excellent telegraph and telephone communications and the nationwide operation of brokers ensured that all operated within an integrated national securities market and were active participants in the global market, largely through the role played by the New York Stock Exchange. Though the actions of this Exchange did distort the structure of the US securities market, the consequences were relatively minor compared to the provision of a large and efficient trading platform for the most actively traded US securities, namely the stocks of the largest US corporations.

However, a focus on the stock exchanges located in the main financial centres of the world presents a distorted picture of the global securities market before 1914. What was so impressive about the market was its strength in depth due to the fact that organized stock exchanges could be found in almost any sizeable city. Even in Latin America stock exchanges were of growing importance as reflected in the rising number of joint-stock companies, investors, and securities. Though still adrift of the position in other parts of the European-settled world, an embryonic securities market had been firmly established in places such as Lima by 1914.[83] Even more impressive was the thriving securities market in Egypt where the Alexandria and Cairo stock exchanges were of major importance. The shares of numerous joint-stock companies formed by British and French expatriates were actively traded on these stock exchanges, attracting the interest of the resident population, especially those involved in trade and finance. By 1906 the Cairo Stock Exchange quoted 328 companies with a capital of 91 million Egyptian pounds.[84] Nothing can better represent the extent of the global securities market on the eve of the First World War than the importance it had assumed in economies like Egypt, where the ability to raise finance and share risk through the issue of shares by joint-stock companies was making an important contribution to the growth of the economy.

In contrast, the global nature of the securities market can be highlighted by considering the position occupied by Russian and US stocks and bonds, for these were the most widely traded of all securities. Russia was the second largest debtor nation in the world by 1914. The Paris Bourse made a market in Russian Government debt and the securities of the major railways and the largest coal mining and metallurgical companies. London specialized in Russian companies producing minerals and oil. Amsterdam handled Russian government debt as a legacy from its past. Brussels had a practical monopoly of dealings in Russian tramway companies along with metallurgical companies. Berlin was important for Russian electrical and chemical companies. Though many of these securities were unique to each market many were also shared, whilst others were traded in the St Petersburg and Moscow stock exchanges. Russian government bonds were found as far away as the Madrid Stock Exchange. The market for Russian securities had become so widespread that they acted as a common currency across Europe, with their sale and purchase acting as an instant correction to any national imbalances.[85]

As the largest debtor in the world on the eve of the First World War, US corporate securities had an even wider circulation than those from Russia. US railroad stocks and bonds were almost ubiquitous across Europe and north America. Consequently, they acted to correct transatlantic imbalances through buying and selling in London and New York and then cascading down to other markets. Thus, the major debtor nations did a great service to the world economy by providing it with a pool of securities shared by the main markets and capable of moving easily, quickly, and cheaply between the different financial centres in response to minute variation in price, as seen in the increasing price convergence between all the main markets before 1914. These securities constituted a form of international money but one that was not an idle product like gold, to be stored away in bank vaults, but one that also served a valuable function by providing the capital required for economic development throughout the world.[86]

CONCLUSION

By 1914 a world existed within which individual stock exchanges competed, cooperated, and complemented each other so as to produce a fully functioning global securities market without the need for central direction or control, whether emanating from government, financial institutions, or international agencies. Though government intervention did exist and created distortions, the level of interference was so low as to produce few barriers, and allowed markets to operate relatively freely at both the national and the international levels. At the same time, the existence of formal organizations in the shape of stock exchanges meant that trading could take place within an ordered environment, so creating the confidence necessary for investors to invest and borrowers to issue securities. As a result, between 1900 and 1914 the global securities market finally became one of the central institutions of the capitalist world, providing an essential interface between money and capital markets at both the national and international levels. In the process this global market facilitated the mobilization of the vast sums of money required for the finance of the world's railway systems and contributed significantly to the stability of the world monetary system.

Despite the diversity between national financial systems, the existence of this global securities market ensured that each was relatively stable. Even the 1907 financial crisis that began in the United States was surmounted with relative ease through the existence of a global market that dissipated its most extreme consequences. This left the US authorities time to plan an improvement in their own financial structure, itself a product of past interventions at federal and state government level. The result was the creation of the Federal Reserve System in 1913. Generally, in each country bankers and brokers learned what could be done both safely and profitably and devised their strategies accordingly. Individual failures occurred as particular bankers or brokers took risks and were caught out by unexpected events, but there was little sign that any of the financial systems were prone to sudden collapse. Each system rested upon the accumulated experience of its practitioners and their confidence in predicting the outcome of their activities within the known parameters within which they operated. In turn, that national financial system was heavily integrated into the global financial system and, though suffering the minor consequences of problems elsewhere, could avoid major upsets by drawing upon the strength of the international marketplace. Such was the mobility that securities possessed by this period that Patron, a French expert on international money markets writing in 1910, claimed that 'securities nowadays are money'.[87] Another French financial expert, Vidal, claimed in the same year that foreign securities held in France 'are in constant movement on account of their offerings of great inducements of arbitrage'.[88] The global securities market had finally triumphed.

6

Crisis, Crash, and Control: 1914–39

SECURITIES MARKETS DURING THE FIRST WORLD WAR

Despite the possibility that a major European war could have broken out at any time in the 10 years before 1914, neither national governments nor financial markets had made any provisions for such an eventuality.[1] Governments had no plans to deal with a financial crisis resulting from the imminent threat of war or with the complex international transactions that linked national securities markets together on a minute-by-minute basis.[2] They had certainly not consulted those running the stock exchanges even though they could not have been unaware of how integrated such markets had become, as exhibited by the global nature of speculative booms, collapses, and crises. Consequently the approach to war and its actual outbreak came as an enormous shock to those dealing on the securities markets, and one for which all involved were totally unprepared. An expert on stock exchange law, Schwabe, writing in 1915, recounted what had happened from the perspective of an observer in London.

During July, owing to the European crisis and the great demand for money, enormous selling orders were received on the stock exchange, prices fell heavily, and many persons, including a large number of foreign clients of London, brokers with large accounts open, defaulted. On July 28th war was declared between Austria and Serbia. In the last three days of the month several foreign exchanges were closed, and there were several failures on the London Stock Exchange. Unless steps had been taken to prevent it, there would have been a number of further failures among the members of the stock exchange, and a large number of other persons would have been inevitably ruined. The stock exchange met the situation by closing its doors on July 31st and keeping them closed, and by passing emergency regulations and rules. On August 3rd there was passed the Postponement of Payments Act, giving power to His Majesty by Proclamation to declare a moratorium. On August 4th Great Britain notified the German Government that a state of war existed between the two countries. Since that date the moratorium has been extended, the Courts (Emergency Powers) Act has been passed, trading with the enemy has been dealt with by statutes and proclamation, and the Government has propounded a scheme for the assistance of both lenders and borrowers of money on the stock exchange. The Committee of the stock exchange has postponed settlement, has inaugurated a new method of dealing with members unable to meet their engagements, and has taken steps to prevent speculation, forced sales, and undue depreciation of prices, and generally has made effective arrangements to alleviate the position of members and non-members alike who find themselves owing to the war involved in unexpected difficulties by reason of their stock exchange engagements.[3]

Behind this rather bland account the outbreak of the First World War meant a rapidly unfolding drama for the global securities market and especially the main players in it, as they tried to cope with a crisis that threatened to destroy both their institutions and members. This was done against a background where little support was received from their respective governments. This is clear from the diary of Sir R. W. Inglis, Chairman of the London Stock Exchange.

> Thursday 30 July 1914
> Dealings in the House practically nil and markets all flat. About 7 p.m. Mr Satterthwaite [Edward Satterthwaite, Secretary of the London Stock Exchange] called and said war was certain and that to prevent a panic and widespread failures we ought to close the House at 10 a.m. tomorrow for which hour the Committee was summoned. He also outlined the proposal for postponing the impending settlements. We got a motor, drove to Town and saw Mr Koch [William M. Koch, member of the Committee] (arranged by telephone before we left) and heard such news that I agreed with Mr Satterthwaite's suggestion and drove back home.
> Friday 31st July 1914.
>   Went up by 8.15 [train] and was with Mr Satterthwaite by 9.15 and agreed his Resolutions. Committee met at 10 and passed and confirmed them. It is believed this action will save the House from great disaster but whatever happens I wish to place on record that Mr Satterthwaite is entitled to the credit. He thought out the idea from first to last and drew up the Resolutions before he came to see me on Thursday night and I agreed that at once as I saw what would be the result of taking no action at all.[4]

Prior to that decision being taken there had been no consultations between the authorities at the London Stock Exchange, the officials at the Bank of England or those in government. The London Stock Exchange was left to fend for itself. The decision to close the market was taken in the face of collapsing prices and problems of payment for and delivery of securities, especially on international account. The enforcement of deals to buy or sell securities would bankrupt many members operating on credit provided by the banks and would have serious implications for the entire financial system. Such a crisis was not confined to the belligerent nations in Europe but was worldwide in scope. In New York a similar situation produced a similar response, judging from the views expressed by Noble, the President of the New York Stock

Exchange, in 1915: '[t]he crisis had developed so suddenly, and the conditions were so utterly without historic parallel, that the best informed men found themselves at a loss for guidance.' When the news reached New York that the London Stock Exchange was not to open on 31 July 1914, an emergency meeting was held in New York. The Governing Committee of the exchange were called to meet at nine o'clock (the earliest hour at which they could all be reached, for it was summer and many were out of town), and at that hour they assembled in the Secretary's office ready to consider what action should be taken. In addition to the Committee many members of prominent firms appeared in the room to report that orders to sell stocks at ruinous prices were pouring in upon them from all over the world and that security holders throughout the country were in a state of panic.

Though some members saw this as an opportunity 'to make New York the financial centre of the world', most felt that any gain would be purely temporary and not worth the risk that the members of the New York Stock Exchange would be exposed to if it stayed open when all others had closed. Many members were holding securities on borrowed money or had made purchases on behalf of foreign clients and so were very exposed to the sudden and dramatic collapse in prices. As in London there was no confidence that the banks would support them by not calling in their loans. Under these circumstances closure appeared the only option. The brokerage house of Merrill Lynch was close to failure at this time. According to Noble, 'the Exchange closed itself on its own responsibility and without either assistance or compulsion from any outside influence'.[5]

All over the world there was a financial crisis caused by the realization that a major European war was imminent. This caused panic conditions on securities markets from Japan to Italy as well as in Europe and north America. Banks recalled loans and brokers were bankrupted because they were unable to deliver or pay for securities, or meet their borrowings because of the collapse in prices. The universal response was the closure of stock exchanges in order to avert a crisis which threatened to engulf the entire market and all those who bought and sold securities. Each stock exchange was forced to respond in this way to the wave of selling that had begun in the epicentre of the crisis in Europe. Such were the interconnections that news and orders were transmitted almost instantaneously around the world, forcing down prices and leaving brokers and bankers highly exposed. The Madrid, Montreal, and Toronto stock exchanges closed on 28 July 1914; Amsterdam, Antwerp, Berlin, Brussels, Budapest, Rome, and Vienna on the 29th; St Petersburg and all the South American stock exchanges on the 30th; and on the 31st the London and New York stock exchanges closed. The Paris

Bourse had suspended all forward transactions as early as 25 July and was followed in that by the Coulisse on the 27th. That left only a nominal cash market, which was closed on 3 September. Within seven days the world's stock exchanges had ceased to function, such was the power and integration of the global securities market. Even minor stock exchanges, such as those in Barcelona, Shanghai, Vancouver, and Zurich had closed by 31 July. The Johannesburg Stock Exchange closed on 1 August, faced with an avalanche of foreign selling of South African mining stocks, which threatened to ruin their members as prices fell precipitously.[6]

These closures would not be brief, considering the worldwide nature of this intense conflict. Modern warfare required the mobilization of all resources available to each nation state, with implications for the domestic and international operations of securities markets. Consequently, there was a general reluctance among governments to condone a quick reopening. The securities market could provide rival attractions to investors for the use of savings, which belligerent governments wanted to monopolize for their own use. Moreover, speculative trading on the stock exchanges, with prices responding to military success or defeat, was considered a potential threat to both national morale and the stability of the national financial system and the foreign exchange rate. Conversely, the existence of a functioning securities market could be of advantage to those governments seeking to finance their war effort through successful bond issues. Governments thus had to weigh up the advantages and disadvantages of allowing stock exchanges to reopen in the months after the outbreak of war. In the meantime, stock exchanges themselves had to find ways of resuming trading that would avoid bankrupting members holding on borrowed money securities that had greatly depreciated in price, or who had agreed such purchases.

However, though stock exchanges were closed, buying and selling still took place elsewhere, on the street, in offices, or via the telephone. The longer the exchanges were closed the more active this unregulated market became. In New York the existence of a long-established and active curb market forced the New York Stock Exchange to create a limited market in stocks operating under minimum prices. By 28 November 1914 a cash market in bonds was re-established on the floor of the New York Stock Exchange. Stocks were added on 12 December, and the New York Stock Exchange formally reopened. This was either followed or even preceded by other US stock exchanges, indicating that the panic caused by the outbreak of war was over in that country by the end of 1914.[7] Similarly, the Shanghai Stock Exchange had reopened in November to counter a growing outside market, but only with minimum prices and no forward market. The Johannesburg Stock Exchange reopened in January 1915 in line with the London Stock Exchange, as both were major markets for gold mining securities. In the meantime a street market had developed.[8]

In Europe the situation was more complex as the cost and disruption of military conflict continued to create problems and uncertainties for the securities markets. As an active inter-bank market had long existed in Germany, the need to reopen the stock exchanges in order to bring some order and regulation to buying and selling was less urgent or even necessary there. The Berlin Stock Exchange did not reopen until October 1917 and not fully for stocks until 3 December of that year. Dealing in bonds was not restored until 1 September 1919, after the war was over. Elsewhere in Europe the need to reopen the stock exchanges was more urgent, due to growing competition from outside markets and the need to provide a market for government debt. Few countries other than Germany possessed a well-established inter-bank securities market or the ability to tap the public directly for funds through the savings banks that traditionally placed their money in government bonds.[9] Accordingly, both internal and external arrangements were made that allowed stock exchanges to reopen towards the end of 1914 or in the course of 1915, as with Paris in December 1914, London in January 1915, and Amsterdam in February. These were only partial reopenings, with operations severely restricted by government control or supervision over the conduct of business or by internally agreed restrictions. The particular securities to be traded and the type of business that could be undertaken were all monitored and controlled, whilst minimum prices were often introduced to provide a floor to the market. Term dealing and short selling were all restricted or prohibited for long periods, being regarded as highly speculative and likely to disrupt the financial system. This was as true of exchanges in the main belligerent countries of Britain, France, and Germany as of those on the fringes such Milan and Montreal. In many cases it was several years after the end of the war before such operations were again permitted. Paris saw a resumption of short selling on 2 January 1920, London on 22 May 1922 but Berlin not until 1 October 1925. In many cases the normal methods of trading in securities did not resume until the early or mid-1920s. Even when the Paris Bourse did reopen *rentes* could not be dealt with for time. Such restrictions even applied to the inter-bank market for securities in Germany, where forward transactions were also banned until 1925.[10]

Long before stock exchanges gradually reopened there was a recovery in the global securities market. Belligerent governments were quick to issue securities in order to tap the savings of their populations for use in the war effort. Between 1913 and 1919 the German national debt rose 20-fold from 4.9 billion marks to 92.8 billion, that of Britain rose tenfold from £0.7 billion to £7.5 billion, and that of France rose fivefold from 33 billion francs to 151.1 billion. In Italy, a late entrant to the war, the national debt rose fivefold from 15.1 billion lira to 74.5 billion, whilst in Japan, a marginal participant, it almost doubled from 2.7 to 4.1 billion yen. Even neutral nations experienced a rapid rise in their national debt as governments took advantage of the inflationary environment to borrow funds to finance increased expenditure caused by the war, such as the disruption to trade and resulting economic distress. The long-term debt of the Dutch government doubled from 1,140 guilders in 1914 to 2,183 in 1919. It was not only in Europe that government borrowing came to dominate the issue of securities, throughout the British Empire dominion governments sold securities to their own people in order to support the war effort in Europe.[11] The New Zealand government issued a loan for £2 million in 1915, which was absorbed by local investors.[12] Similarly, between 1915 and1918 the Canadian government raised $2.1 billion domestically.[13] Although the United States did not enter the war until 1917 the increase in its national debt was one of the most spectacular, reaching $25.5 billion in 1918 compared to $1.2 billion in 1914.[14]

The result was an enormous and rapid expansion in the supply of government bonds around the world. As most of these were issued and held domestically their existence contributed to the growth of national securities markets rather than the global market. However, trading in these national debts was relatively subdued as they were often bought and held by individual and institutional investors for patriotic reasons. Consequently, activity on many securities markets around the world remained low for most of the war years, even when the stock exchanges did reopen. In Canada there was little interest in mining and oil stocks, for example, as investors placed their savings in government debt.[15] Contributing to this low level of activity were the restrictions imposed by governments and the actions of the stock exchange authorities themselves. These were designed deliberately to reduce market volatility and in this they were successful, especially in stock exchanges in London and Paris, financial centres of two of the main countries at war. Here money that would previously have been lent out to those holding securities as collateral was now absorbed by governments. The French government made particularly heavy use of short-term treasury notes to finance the war.[16] Under these conditions banks either lent directly to governments or bought short-dated bonds, so depriving the securities markets of much of their traditional business. In contrast, many smaller securities markets in neutral countries or those only on the fringes of the war did experience prolonged speculative booms. Their economies benefited enormously both from purchases made by nations at war and from the removal of foreign competition. Italy enjoyed great prosperity due to the demand for war materials and the need to replace imports from belligerent nations. This fuelled much speculative activity based on abundant bank lending on easy terms.[17] A similar situation prevailed in Norway, where there was a stock market boom between 1915 and 1920, as banks lent liberally to customers using securities as collateral.[18] In Japan there was also a boom as investors borrowed heavily from banks at low rates of interest to subscribe to new issues in the hope of making large capital gains.[19]

Consequently there was a reordering of stock exchange business as the smaller and more peripheral securities markets benefited at the expense of the larger and more central. However, the greatest casualty of the war was the global securities market itself. In order to subscribe to the securities issues made by their own governments to finance the war, British, French, and German investors all sold international securities. Furthermore, western European governments then took control of what remained of these securities and disposed of them as they sought to obtain the foreign exchange, especially US dollars, required to wage a war. The German government persuaded, and then forced, German investors to surrender their foreign securities in exchange for mark-denominated government debt, leaving little still in their hands when the war ended. By the end of the war all foreign securities had disappeared from the lists of German stock exchanges.[20] Similarly, over the period of the First World War there was considerable liquidation of French holdings of foreign securities, though this was mainly due to repudiation of their debts by both the Russian and Ottoman governments. As the main external holders of these debts French investors experienced the total loss of these investments.[21] In Britain, it was largely sale not repudiation that accounted for the massive liquidation of the holdings of foreign securities. By the end of 1915 British government sales in New York of US$ securities, purchased from British investors, had reached $233 million. Eventually in May 1916 British investors were forced to surrender such securities to the government. Overall, by 6 April 1919 a total of 2,027 different securities with a value of £655 million had been purchased for resale by the UK government, whilst another £400 million US stocks and bonds were sold by UK investors themselves during the war.[22] This seriously undermined the status of both London and Paris in the global securities market as they lost the very securities that had been traded internationally. As the Netherlands was neutral throughout the war, Amsterdam benefited greatly from being conveniently located for investors in Germany, France, and Britain. The considerable inflow of funds in search of a safe haven helped to place the Amsterdam Stock Exchange, when it reopened, at the centre of an active international market in securities. There was an enormous increase in business on the Amsterdam Stock Exchange, which became the interface between the belligerent nations themselves and with the United States, which was neutral until 1917. By selling US$ securities on the Amsterdam Stock Exchange, which were then resold in New York, the German government gained access to the foreign exchange it required despite attempts by the Allies to prevent this happening.[23]

Nevertheless, even on the Amsterdam Stock Exchange domestic business became increasingly important as a result of the war. The number of foreign securities quoted on the Amsterdam Stock Exchange fell from 840 in 1914 to 746 in 1918 whilst issues of Dutch government debt and domestic industrials expanded rapidly. Much of the international securities business transacted on the Amsterdam Bourse had been underpinned by the *prolongatie* system of finance. However, this was frozen at the outbreak of war and the suspension of the market. Even when the Exchange reopened it was impossible to revive the *prolongatie* system because of the collapse of confidence. Instead, investors placed their savings with commercial banks and switched their investments to domestic securities, selling some of their holdings of US railroad stocks and bonds in the process.[24] The increasing repatriation of securities both contributed to the development of securities markets and gave them a strongly domestic focus. Swedish investors, especially the banks and insurance companies, repurchased all the country's external debt during the war and traded it domestically, boosting the local securities market. Other neutral nations in Europe such as Greece, Norway, and Switzerland did the same.[25] The Spanish case exemplifies the effects of this. Spain benefited from the war through supplying both France and Britain. This caused inflation and expansion, with a rapid increase in the number of banks and their lending. In the process Spanish investors were able to buy back securities held abroad, especially the government debt and railway stocks and bonds held in France. The Spanish national debt held abroad fell from 1,028 million pesetas in 1914 to 78 million in 1925. In addition, there were substantial re-purchases of Spanish railway securities held abroad. More than 1.5 million shares of the Compania del Norte flowed back to Spain, as did shares in various Spanish banks such as Banco Hipotecario and Banesto. The substantial German participation in the largest Spanish electrical firms was also liquidated. The Spanish government itself issued new public loans totalling around 3.8 billion pesetas. The result was a substantial increase of business on the Madrid Bolsa, rather than Barcelona, as that was where the government debt and railroad stocks and bonds were traded.[26]

Elsewhere in the world securities markets benefited from the activity produced by the trading in repatriated securities and the issues made by national governments and domestic businesses. Such was the increased volume of business in China that an additional stock exchange was established in Peking in 1917 to provide a domestic market for the bonds issued by the Chinese government.[27] Though Japan was involved in the war militarily, as an ally of France and Britain, the main theatre of activity was far away, and its economy benefited enormously from the removal of external competition in the Asia/Pacific region. The resulting economic and financial boom in Japan led to the repatriation of externally held securities and increased domestic issues, financed by greatly increased by credit.[28] Nevertheless, not all securities markets outside Europe benefited from the war. In neither Australia nor Canada was there much speculative activity in their tightly controlled stock exchanges, with available savings largely absorbed in financing their share of the imperial war effort. There was rather a greater domestic focus as their own governments increasingly sought to borrow domestically, now that access to London was either difficult or impossible. Trading in bonds on the Montreal and Toronto stock exchanges rose from $6.1 billion in 1913 to $132.1 billion in 1919. This favoured the major stock exchanges, giving an impetus towards the centralization of both the Canadian and Australian securities markets.[29]

However, the greatest beneficiary of distress sales of European holdings of foreign securities was the United States, as the largest pre-war debtor nation. On 1 July 1914 an estimated $5.4 billion in US securities were held abroad. By 31 December 1919 that amount had shrunk to $1.6 billion. Investors in the United States bought back almost $2 billion worth of securities in the first three years of the war, often at sizeable discounts, from sellers in Europe or from governments desperate for dollars. The British, the largest holders of US corporate stocks and bonds, were the major sellers. A total of $2.6 billion, or 70% of their holdings, had been sold by 1919. Railroad securities and those of major industrials like US Steel led the disposals. Business revived on the New York Stock Exchange, where the largest and most liquid of stocks were traded. Turnover rose from 48 million shares in 1914 to 213 million in 1916 before falling back slightly. Reviving again, it reached 313 million shares in 1919, propelled by a domestic investor boom due to the inflationary environment, easy bank credit, and rising confidence. This booming activity spread. The curb market in New York flourished during the war whilst turnover on the Boston Stock Exchange rose from 3.5 million shares in 1914 to 13 million in 1916 before falling back to 3.9 million in 1918 and then recovering to 9.2 million in 1919. Expansion in the securities market encouraged major US banks to extend their operations in that direction, not only through increased lending with stocks and bonds as collateral but also in issuing and trading. In 1916 National City Bank acquired the investment banking firm of N. W. Halsey. The boom in US securities was given a further boost in 1917 when the United States entered the war and government debt rose sharply. The number of US investors holding government bonds grew from 350,000 in

1917 to 11 million in 1919 due to patriotic subscriptions to war loan issues. These raised $21.5 billion between 1917 and 1919. The US bond market, which had been the poor relation of London and Paris before the war, was transformed. Turnover in bonds on the New York Stock Exchange rose from $469 million in 1914 to $1,052 million in 1917 and then to $3,772 million in 1919 due to US government borrowing. In addition, though there was no bond market of any significance outside New York, there was substantial trading between the major banks and via specialist bond houses. New York was now on a par with the major European financial centres.[30]

SECURITIES MARKETS AND THE LEGACY
OF THE FIRST WORLD WAR

The consequences of the First World War for the global securities markets were profound and permanent. A major shift had occurred in the location of the central players in this market, with the greatly increased importance of the United States being only one of the most obvious consequences. However, it took time for a new balance to emerge, reflecting the diminished importance of London, Paris, and Berlin and the increased importance of New York, Amsterdam, and Tokyo. This was not simply due to the repatriation of securities during the war but to a switch among borrowers, especially those in Canada and Latin America, away from European financial centres towards New York and wealthy US investors. By the end of the war the German securities market had lost its international orientation, and became wholly focused on domestic stocks and bonds.[31]

A period of instability was inevitable. The global securities market had lost most of those securities that had constituted an international currency, namely Russian and US stocks and bonds. Russian government debt and corporate securities had ceased to have value whilst US railroad and industrial stocks and bonds had flowed back to the United States and were now much more closely held at home. Between 1914 and 1918 foreign holdings of the common stock of the US Steel Company shrank from 1.3 million to 0.5 million, or from 25% to 10%, and then declined further after 1918, dropping to 0.2 million (4%) by 1923. As this had been a core arbitrage stock, widely held and actively traded across north America and Western Europe, its disappearance was a major blow to the global securities market.[32] New securities issued during the war were no real substitute as they were largely government debt held by national investors. Even where securities had been issued externally they tended to revert to national investors fairly quickly. The

French government had made four issues in London between November 1915 and November 1918 raising £54.5 million. However, these were denominated in francs and depreciated enormously in the early post-war years when the franc was devalued against the £, and were bought back at low prices by French investors.[33] Again, it took time for new securities to appear to replace those which had served as liquid stock before 1914.

The war therefore boosted national securities markets rather than the global market. However, four years of conflict had created a highly unstable financial position in numerous countries, and national markets themselves were affected. The belligerent nations had spent enormous sums of money, financing their expenditure not only by taxing and borrowing but also by printing money, creating an inflationary situation at home and abroad. Advances to the French government by the Bank of France rose from 6% of total assets in 1914 to 62% in 1918.[34] As this money had been spent in waging a war with no productive results for those involved, there were no income-generating assets to service the debts created or to match the vastly increased purchasing power of populations around the world. Once hostilities ended and government spending ceased, national banking systems found themselves vulnerable to a collapse in the value of the assets acquired during the war and in the brief flurry of post-war prosperity. No matter whether these assets were physical plant and machinery or stocks and bonds used as collateral; in many cases they no longer generated the income required to service the loan or possessed a redemption value. One measure of how wartime inflation had undermined the stability of national financial systems was the fact that in all major economies the ratio of bank reserves and capital to bank liabilities worsened between 1913 and 1920. The ratio fell from 10% to 7% in Britain, 20% to 12% in France, 39% to 4% in Germany, 53% to 29% in the Netherlands, 24% to 15% in Belgium, 31% to 15% in Denmark, and from 20% to 12% in the United States. Regardless of the different nature of these banking systems, all were left highly exposed in the immediate post-war years when the spending boom came to an end and inflation turned into deflation. This in turn had serious implications for the national securities markets.[35]

Finally, a long-term consequence of the First World War was to greatly enhance the level of government intervention in securities markets. The suspension of trading and the subsequent gradual resumption of business under conditions controlled, supervised, or permitted by governments had made central bankers and treasury officials aware of the power they possessed over organized stock exchanges. Even after the termination of hostilities government intervention continued, if only as a means of policing the abuses that had characterized the pre-war years, whether it was the perceived evil of speculation or the more warranted problems associated with fraud, insider dealing and market manipulation. However, self-interest was also at work as governments, faced with a volatile foreign exchange situation and the need to finance huge debt overhangs from the war years, saw control over the securities market as one of the tools available to them. Consequently, there was no rapid return to the pre-war situation of unsupervised self-regulation, where it had prevailed. In Britain the government exercised informal control over the London Stock Exchange well into the 1920s, as it tried to cope with the international weakness of the £ sterling and the domestic need to refinance short-term borrowings. Similarly in Canada, under government influence, the self-regulation of the securities market was considerably tightened. Only in the United States was intervention not attempted, with the Capital Issues Committee, only formed after the United States entered the conflict in 1917, being discontinued in August 1919. States had long been active in maintaining orderly markets in continental Europe, and this was often translated into further controls during and after the war. As early as 5 August 1914, the Spanish government legislated to give itself increased, direct control over the stock exchange, and this was reinforced with additional controls in 1918. In Denmark in 1919 the government acquired legal control over the Copenhagen Stock Exchange whilst in Belgium the government appointed a commissioner to oversee the stock exchanges. One result of this increase in government intervention was to restrict foreign access to national securities markets, desired by governments faced with crippling debts to finance during and after the war. In France the securities market was practically closed to foreign issues during the war and a law of 1916 banning foreign issues remained in force until the late 1920s. Similarly, in Spain in 1918 government controls restricted foreign access to its securities market, despite the growing popularity of Latin American issues among investors.[36]

Global securities had thrived when government intervention was minimal and the level of confidence among investors was high. The war itself shattered that confidence as those holding Russian securities lost everything whilst those holding Austrian, Bulgarian, and Turkish securities also suffered large losses. Post-war inflation in Germany and France then caused substantial further losses. The trust in international investment that had flourished in the decades prior to 1914 had been greatly undermined and would take years to rebuild. Compounding this lack of trust was an operational difficulty as the centres through which these financial flows took place had also been badly affected. Berlin had been destroyed as an international financial centre whilst Paris did not begin to recover its position until after the stabilization of the franc in 1927. This left London, though without much of the resources of the past, whilst New York was not immediately able to play a full role. The position of New York had always rested upon foreign interest in US securities not US interest in foreign securities, which left it with a rather passive role in the global securities market. Though this did change with the war, and New York's position was helped by the arrival of foreign bankers and brokers, a rapid reversal was not easy to achieve, given the preference among US investors for domestic assets. Within Europe financial centres in neutral countries had benefited from the war but none were in a position to occupy the place of either London and Paris, or even Berlin, in the global securities market. The Swiss were very domestically focused and made no attempt to develop an international presence. Dutch financiers focused on replacing London in terms of European trade finance rather than becoming an international centre for the trading of securities. Stockholm did become a more important component of the global securities market but only played a regional role for Scandinavia. With trust absent and operational efficiency impaired governments could have intervened to help restore confidence and repair the trading system but their actions only compounded the difficulties. Faced with more pressing domestic problems governments frequently intervened to hamper the international mobility of securities and payments. Einzig probably reflected the prevailing thinking of the post-First World War governments in observing that '[a]lthough the existence of a certain amount of securities that have free access to several markets is desirable, an excessive amount of such international counters may endanger international monetary stability'. Here was ample justification for control rather than freedom.[37]

The First World War thus caused a major disruption in the operation and structure of securities markets around the world and the domestic and international financial systems within which they operated. Its consequences were wide-reaching and long-standing. It totally transformed the basis upon which the global securities market had operated before 1914. The integration of national securities markets was now hindered by government intervention, often aimed at restricting external access or discouraging foreign investment. There was a shortage of internationally mobile securities, as these had been largely liquidated and replaced by inter-allied debts that did not possess active markets in numerous financial centre (see Table 6.1). Finally, there was now a high degree of fragility inherent in both national and international financial systems leaving them highly vulnerable to any economic difficulties. Even alone each of these problems would have been a serious blow to the global securities market. Together they threatened its entire existence if it was not given the time and the freedom to adjust to the fundamentally different circumstances.[38] Though unrecognized at the time the defaults on Russian securities and the reduction in US securities held abroad, from $5.4 billion to $1.6 billion, represented a major disaster for the world economy. It removed, at a stroke, the most mobile assets that had played such an

Table 6.1. Inter-allied war debts in 1919: Lending and borrowing
(£ million)

Borrower/Lender	UK	France	US	Total borrowed
UK	—	—	842	842
France	508	—	550	1,058
Russia	568	160	38	766
Italy	467	35	325	827
Others	197	160	135	492
Total lent	1,740	355	1,890	3,985

Source: Derived from C. P. Kindleberger, *A Financial History of Western Europe* (London, 1984), p. 307.

important role in maintaining international equilibrium at a time of fixed exchange rates, and replaced them with nationally held assets. Between 1913 and 1920 the nominal value of the National Debt quoted on the London Stock Exchange rose by £5.4 billion or from 9% of all quoted securities in 1913 to 33%. Also, capital markets became much more nationally orientated. At the institutional level stock exchanges now operated within a much more restricted environment whether imposed externally by governments or a product of the regulatory regime imposed during the war.

THE 1920s

The effects of the First World War extended far into the 1920s. Immediately after the end of the war there was a boom during which wartime shortages were filled. This, in turn, created a mood of optimism that underpinned both further lending by banks and speculative conditions in securities markets. Eventually, however, in the early 1920s there was a stock market collapse in the major European centres, Japan, and the United States.[39] As many banks had made loans with securities as collateral this stock market collapse endangered both them and the entire financial system. A greater proportion of bank assets than before the war were tied up in loans and investments that would be difficult to liquidate quickly, whilst a greater proportion of funds were deposits that could be easily withdrawn. Though a number of banks did collapse or were left with a portfolio of unsaleable assets it did encourage greater caution in making loans and a demand for more marketable securities as either investments or collateral. In some countries, especially Italy, the initial response to the stock market collapse was for banks to buy even more securities in order to support their value as investments and collateral. This prevented a widespread collapse in confidence, and thus averted a financial crisis, but it also left banks with large holdings of securities that could not be sold in the late 1920s.[40]

A more common response to these financial crises was government control of some kind. Rampant speculation and bank collapses were seen as linked and so governments took steps to prevent the latter by checking the former. In Sweden much bank lending during the war had been to companies with securities as collateral. When the market began to fall in 1918 the banks faced serious trouble as the loans could not be repaid, the securities could not be sold, and depositors started to withdraw their money. Faced with a looming crisis the government began to regulate the stock exchange as early as 1919, and again after a series of crises between 1920 and 1923. It intervened to forcibly separate deposit and investment banking, believing that to be the root cause of the problem. Similar developments unfolded elsewhere in Europe, such as Spain and Norway, as well as further afield. In Japan steps were taken to separate investment and commercial banking after a financial crisis in 1927, whilst in 1925 the British government in India started to exert some control over the Bombay Stock Exchange. The Mexican government and then the Turkish government placed their stock exchanges under government control in 1928 and 1929 respectively. One long-term consequence of the First World War was thus a readiness among governments to intervene in their domestic securities markets when they felt threatened by crises. They attempted to prevent speculation and to create a division between banking and the securities market. What concerned governments most was a collapse of the banking system, which would pose much more of a threat to economic and social stability than the rise and fall of speculation on the securities market.[41]

The national financial systems most endangered were in central Europe, particularly Germany and Austria, where the post-war financial legacy was made more difficult by rampant inflation. Currency in circulation in Germany rose from 6.3 billion marks in June 1914 to 33.1 billion in December 1918, or a fivefold increase during the war, but then grew to 17,393 billion by June 1923, an increase that was over 100 times greater. This inflation destroyed the value of fixed interest securities denominated in marks, including government debt, and much of what remained of banking capital. The major Berlin banks lost *c.*30% of their capital and *c.*40% of their reserves due to the 1920s' hyperinflation. This left these banks highly vulnerable to any failures among their major customers. In Austria many smaller banks either collapsed or merged as they no longer had the capital and reserves to survive defaults, having overextended themselves during the speculative boom on the Vienna bourse during 1923–4. Consequently, in both Germany and Austria banks were driven to operate on the basis of deposits rather than capital, leading them to develop branch banking. Between 1914 and 1924 the Diskonto-Gesellschaft took over thirty-six smaller banks whilst Deutsche Bank absorbed twenty-one others and Dresdner fourteen. By 1925 the seven leading Berlin banks were dominant but they still remained weak as they had been unable to rebuild their assets. Though they attempted to restrict long-term lending this proved particularly difficult given the established traditions within German and Austrian banking and the need for funds from their business customers in the aftermath of the rampant inflation of the early 1920s. The largest companies in these countries issued securities abroad in the 1920s, in both London and New York. However, that still left the great mass of smaller undertakings looking to banks for finance, which the banks provided by accepting deposits from both home and abroad. Increasingly in the 1920s German and also Austrian banks used short-term funds borrowed from foreign banks to finance local lending. The Frankfurt Borse became an important market for the issues of German chemical companies.[42] Though this lending was, nominally, short term it could not be liquidated quickly as neither businesses nor public authorities could repay at once the sums they had borrowed. Whilst the securities market was buoyant this strategy worked, as loans could be repaid through public issues. However, this was a much more dangerous situation than in the past when the Universal banks had compensated for a more illiquid lending and investment policy by employing a much higher level of capital.

By 1929 the ratio of capital to deposits in German banks was 1:11, around the British level, and German bankers were well aware of the risks they were running. During a British inquiry in 1929–31 into the relationship between finance and industry, the German banker Jacob Goldschmidt of the Darm-stadter und National Bank was asked whether 'the German banker, like the English banker, does not like to have his money tied up permanently in industry'. He replied emphatically, 'No, the German banker dislikes that as much as any banker anywhere else in the world'.[43]

With the stock exchange crisis in Germany on 13 May 1927 German bankers, faced with loans they could not recall, financed long-term loans out of short-term deposits, which could be easily withdrawn, whilst the weakness of the stock market made it impossible to sell portfolios of securities. On this occasion they were lucky as the market recovered but any prolonged collapse would have exposed the banking system's vulnerability.

In France and Britain the condition of the securities market was less precarious as their financial systems had been less damaged by the war and subsequent monetary turmoil and had firmer foundations. In France, after the loss of a large proportion of the outstanding international holdings during the war, there was an understandable reluctance to invest abroad. This was compounded by continuing government restrictions on overseas investment. Various taxes and laws biased the French market against foreign issues and prevented the revival of Paris as an international financial centre. Paris ceased to be a central component in the global securities market for most of the 1920s despite the rising prosperity of the French people after the economic difficulties of the early 1920s. Part of this wealth was absorbed by the French government, which issued bonds to the value of 16 billion francs in the 1920s. However, by the late 1920s French banks were awash with money and desperately looking for ways to employ deposits. Investment banks sought opportunities in commercial banking whilst commercial banks invaded the territory of the investment banks, such was the shortage of profitable openings in their traditional business. Advances against securities made by banks expanded enormously, peaking in 1929. One outlet was the stocks and bonds issued by a growing number of French joint-stock companies. The Coulisse, in particular, replaced foreign securities with the shares of French companies operating in such new sectors as cinema, photography, and automobile manufacture, generating a very large turnover. However, even the Parquet, which was dominated by activity in French government bonds, quoted 663 French companies in 1929 compared to 338 in 1921. The Coulisse quoted 334 compared to 139. In addition the provincial bourses in such cities as Lyons and Lille provided active markets for local industrial securities. There even developed in Paris an additional and unregulated curb market, the Marché Hors Côte, to cater for growing investor interest in such securities. By the late 1920s there was a limited recovery of the role played by Paris within the global securities market. Once again it became a market for government bonds with issues by Bulgaria, Hungary, Poland, Romania, and Turkey between 1927 and 1929. However, there remained a strong reluctance to become involved in external investment, apart from the repatriation of that part of the national debt held abroad. Consequently, despite the growing activity in domestic stocks and bonds, the overall importance of the securities market within the French economy roughly halved during the course of the First World War and the 1920s.[44]

Unlike Paris the London securities market remained a major international market in the 1920s. This was despite continuing intervention by the Treasury and the Bank of England to ensure its operations met the government's perceived national needs, especially in the early years after the war. A particular aim of government policy was to restrain investment abroad as this provided competition for its own financing requirements and put pressure on the £sterling. It was not until late 1922, eight years after the outbreak of war, that some semblance of normal trading practices were restored on the London Stock Exchange. However, there remained one major casualty in the London Stock Exchange's international business, which was now taking place at a much reduced level due to the long period of control and the disposal of so many foreign securities. In addition, increasing enforcement of the rules on minimum commission rates and the refusal to admit banks and foreign brokers as members meant that much of what remained of the international market in London in the 1920s was undertaken outside the London Stock Exchange. A growing band of American brokers opened London offices to provide direct contact to the New York market for the numerous British and foreign banks still in London. There was also a revival of interest among British investors in foreign securities despite government restrictions and taxes. Over the period 1920–9 securities worth £1.2billion were issued in London on behalf of overseas borrowers. However, this was noticeably lower than before 1914, both absolutely and as a proportion of the total. Whereas between 1910 and 1913 overseas loans had comprised 71% of all new issues, during the 1920s their share was only 37%. London now faced far greater competition for international business and was largely deserted both by overseas railway companies seeking new finance and by foreign governments. There remained colonial governments, whose securities found favour in London because of the imperial links, and companies involved in such activities as oil production, metal mining, and rubber plantations. In addition, central European enterprises turned to London as a means of rebuilding their capital after the financial and monetary turmoil of the early 1920s.

One factor undermining the attractions of the London market for foreign securities issues was the weakened links with the money market. It took time for lenders to recover sufficient confidence to begin lending extensively to those providing securities as collateral. Loans to members of the stock exchange, by British banks, for example, grew from only £18 million in 1921 to £48 million in 1928, whilst foreign and overseas banks were attracted to better rates in New York. This weakened relationship was due partly to the nature of the securities to be found in London. Though British investors did retain large foreign holdings in 1918, such as Argentinian and Indian railways, few commanded the international appeal of the pre-war American securities. A few north American securities still continued to be widely held and actively traded, as with US Steel and Canadian Pacific Railway. A small number of large mining companies, especially those involved in South African gold but including International Nickel of Canada, attracted worldwide interest, as did the Anglo-Dutch oil company, Shell. However, compared to the billions of dollars worth of securities traded in London before 1914, these were but little compensation. Though the growing interest of US investors in British corporate stocks, matched by the attractions of minor US industrials for

British investors, did boost the Anglo-American trade in securities, there was no longer the volume of business to support the really active markets that had previously been so attractive for the employment of short-term funds in London.

In contrast to the weakened position of foreign securities in the London market those issued by domestic borrowers grew enormously. The principal cause was the great growth of UK government borrowing in order to finance the war effort. The British government entered the war with debts of around £0.7 billion and finished it with £7.5 billion, of which over £6 billion had come from British savers. A large proportion of the British people had become investors for the first time through buying War Bonds. A 1918 estimate suggested that the number of investors stood at 13 million compared to 1 million at the outbreak of war. In the 1920s these investors were attracted to the stocks and bonds issued by prominent British industrial and financial companies. With many of these companies firmly entrenched in the domestic market, and dominating particular branches of the economy, they offered some immunity from the problems of the world economy that affected both foreign government bonds and British companies operating overseas, like Argentinian railways or Far Eastern rubber plantations. In 1926 the collective number of shareholders in seven of the largest British companies was 385,500. Clearly, a consequence of the First World War was to shift the London securities market towards a much more domestic focus leaving it with a rump of foreign stocks and bonds for which it was, largely, the sole market, namely the debt of imperial governments and Argentinian and Indian railway stocks and bonds. This was far removed from the position it had occupied before 1914.

At a national level much activity took place in the global securities market during the 1920s, despite the problems of financial instability at home and abroad (Table 6.2). Securities continued to be regarded as a cheap and convenient way of raising finance by both government and business across the world, with the exception of the Soviet Union where state ownership and self-reliance were now the preferred options. Elsewhere, securities markets continued to evolve, boosted by the repatriation of assets previously issued and held abroad. This was especially true for the various Latin American stock exchanges such as those in Asuncion, Buenos Ayres, Lima, Mexico City, Montevideo, Rio de Janeiro, Santiago, and Valparaiso, all of which had benefited from the acquisition by local residents of the securities once held by British investors of British companies operating there. In 1921, the transfer of ownership of Bolivian mining stocks from British to local investors generated a great deal of business on the local exchanges. Across the world there now existed a much larger basis for national securities markets as domestic investors held many securities that had previously been traded in

Table 6.2. Securities as a proportion of national assets, 1927–30

Country	Government debt (%)	Corporate bonds (%)	Corporate stocks (%)	Domestic securities (%)	Foreign assets (%)	Total (%)
Belgium	7.6	0.5	7.9	16.0	6.1	22.1
Denmark	3.0	0.4	13.0	16.4	−0.4	16.0
France	14.6	1.7	2.7	19.0	0.8	19.8
Germany	2.4	0.5	3.0	5.9	−1.3	4.6
India	3.4	0.6	0.6	4.6	−4.1	0.5
Italy	11.7	0.5	3.8	16.0		16.0
Mexico	0.2		6.4	6.8		6.8
Japan	5.0	1.7	6.8	13.5	1.0	14.5
Norway	7.4	0.6	4.7	12.7		12.7
Russia	0.6			0.6		0.6
South Africa	7.3	—	12.0	19.3	—	19.3
Switzerland	5.7	1.4	10.6	17.7	4.0	21.7
UK	18.3	2.6	15.7	36.6	10.8	47.4
USA	3.4	3.9	19.4	26.7	1.3	28.0

Source: R. W. Goldsmith, *Comparative National Balance Sheets* (Chicago, 1985), National Tables.

such centres as London and Paris, or Berlin and Vienna. The holdings of securities by Japanese commercial banks, which had already reached 0.8 billion Yen in 1918, grew to 3.3 billion in 1929, for example.

The result was growing activity on securities markets in Africa, Asia, and Latin America. The number of companies quoted on the Shanghai Stock Exchange rose from 97 in 1920 to 113, with most being either rubber plantations or involved in local manufacturing, especially in cotton textiles. This led to the formation of additional stock exchanges in new centres such as Beirut and Madras in 1920, Bogotá in 1928, and Casablanca in 1929. Also in 1929 brokers in Buenos Ayres acquired a dedicated trading floor within the mercantile exchange. However, there was no dramatic transformation of these national securities markets despite the transfer of some business from western Europe. The New Zealand securities market continued to be dominated by mining shares despite the fact that more of the New Zealand government's borrowing was done locally. It was often the smaller and less traded issues that were made in New Zealand, such as the Wellington City Council issue of 1929, and London remained an active market for the largest and most active New Zealand securities. Though there was a bigger securities market in Australia for its national debt the various stock exchanges continued to reflect local or regional specialities rather than national securities. Only slowly did a national market emerge through the trading of the national debt and the securities of companies either operating across the whole continent or attracting investors throughout the country. London continued to provide a deep and broad market for Australian securities whilst the market in Australia and

New Zealand remained fragmented between the different cities. This fragmentation was intensified by the stock exchanges themselves with their restrictions on sharing commission and the banning of dual membership, as these prevented the creation of nationwide firms and the centralization of trading. In Canada the securities market took time to recover from government controls that lasted until 1919. However, beginning with the main market in Montreal and then extending to Toronto and finally the mining exchanges in Calgary and Vancouver, there was a gradual revival in business culminating in a speculative boom in the late 1920s. This focused especially on mining and oil shares though there was a steady turnover in utility and industrial stocks. In addition there was a large market in government debt, which had risen to $2.6 billion in 1919 as a result of the war, but much of this was traded in an OTC market rather than on the stock exchanges.[45]

Regardless of the vitality of the global securities market at the national level in the 1920s, it possessed serious problems at its core. The war had considerably undermined the importance of the twin centres of the global securities market, London and Paris. Though London recovered much though not all of its previous role, Paris did not. Paris ceased to be important for global securities and instead turned inward to operate increasingly as a national securities market. Other centres that had been of major importance before 1914 also suffered. Both Berlin and Vienna lost their position through the direct effects of the war and the subsequent economic turmoil that hit their countries. Both cities now served a substantially diminished hinterland, as their empires had disintegrated, as well as being located in countries temporarily dependent on borrowings from abroad. Other financial centres rose to prominence such as Amsterdam and the Swiss stock exchanges. However, the Amsterdam Bourse never recovered the international position it had possessed before the First World War as the 1920s lacked the stable monetary and financial conditions within which it could flourish. It was impossible to recreate the *prolongatie* system whereby operations on the stock market were financed through short-term loans, especially after the financial crisis of 1921–3. Both individual investors and banks adopted a much more cautious lending policy, depriving the Amsterdam market of much of its pre-war vitality. Though German companies turned to Amsterdam in the 1920s as a source of finance it was much more domestically orientated than before the war. Similarly, though the Swiss exchanges did well in the 1920s, with Zurich achieving a record turnover in 1928, they did not play a central role in the global securities market. This left an opening for Luxembourg where the government attempted to create a central position in the global securities market itself with the establishment of a stock exchange in 1927. However, that was hardly operational by 1929.[46]

Consequently, the First World War and its repercussions had not only had a dramatic effect on the global securities market through the destruction and repatriation of international securities, it had also removed Paris, weakened London, and destroyed Berlin and Vienna. More generally, the once strong links which had existed between the global securities market and the global money market had now been undermined because of the greatly increased risks run by banks and individual investors. A League of Nations memorandum of 1931 noted that '[t]he risks involved in immobilising a large proportion of short-term funds in long-term credits became very patent during the difficult periods of shaken confidence through which most countries passed after the war.'[47] This warning was also applicable to lending with securities as collateral as it was now apparent that such collateral could either evaporate in value or become unrealizable. The outcome was to leave only one major financial centre where such confidence had not been shaken and where there existed an abundance of short- and long-term funds. That place was New York.

WALL STREET CRASH[48]

New York was the principal gainer from the financial tumult caused by the First World War as it was now the dominant market for all US$ securities. This position was sustained in the 1920s with a continuing liquidation of foreign holdings of US railroad securities. In turn the volume of US$ securities had been enormously boosted by the huge issue of government bonds to finance its war effort. Consequently, by 1918 the New York securities market was in a position to challenge London and Paris and had displaced Berlin. This position was further bolstered by subsequent events at home and abroad. Domestically, the First World War had made the United States a nation of investors. There had been an enormous increase in numbers of the investing public through the patriotic subscription to war bonds, creating a lasting legacy for the 1920s. Possibly as many as 20 million Americans had some involvement in the securities market in the 1920s compared to at most 2 million before 1914, though the number of serious investors was very much smaller at around 5 million. The buying and selling of securities became a mass activity as these investors were ready to invest in other types of securities. With the reduction of US government debt by almost $9 billion, from $25.5 billion in 1919 to $16.9 billion in 1929, investors sought alternative homes for their money. The stocks and bonds of major industrial and commercial companies, most of which had been closely held before 1914, became especially popular, offering attractive rates of return and the prospect of rapid capital gains. Between 1924 and 1930 the number of investors holding corporate bonds grew from 1.3 million to 6 million whilst those owning stocks increased from a maximum of 6 million in 1927 to 9 million in 1929 and then 11 million in 1930. Between 1910 and 1930 the number of shareholders in American Telephone and Telegraph rose from 35,823 to 469,801, in US Steel from 22,033 to 167,951, and in Pennsylvania Railroad from 65,283 to 196,119.

This enthusiasm for securities reflected the fact that bank deposits paid low rates of interest whilst stock prices were on a steadily rising trend. In turn this enthusiasm met a ready response from US business with the conversion of established firms into public companies and the issue of ever more stocks and bonds. The number of new stock issues grew from 1,822 in 1921 to 6,417 in 1929, by which time they comprised 62% of all securities being issued compared to 15% in 1921. The major US banks also played an active role. During the war they had become increasingly involved in selling Victory bonds to the public, with government support. Faced with a decline in lending in the 1920s the major New York banks sought alternative forms of business, one of which was selling bonds to the greatly enlarged investing public as well as lending extensively to those holding securities, whether financial intermediaries like brokers or individual investors. This function was officially sanctioned by the McFadden Act of 1927 which allowed national banks to issue bonds. A growing number of the largest commercial banks did just that either directly or through specialist subsidiaries. Altogether, in bonds alone a total of $50 billion were issued in the United States between 1921 and 1929, with 80% being domestic and 20% foreign, and by 1929 commercial banks handled 82% of the issues. At the same time loans with securities as collateral rose strongly during the 1920s. By 3 October 1928 such loans had reached $12.4 billion and then increased by almost another $5 billion in the following year, peaking at $17 billion on 4 October 1929. Much of this went directly to members of the New York Stock Exchange who were borrowing extensively to finance both their own speculative operations and also those of their clients, who numbered 1.4 million by 1929. Members' borrowings, with securities provided as collateral, grew from $1 billion on 1 January 1919 to $3.5 billion on 1 February 1926 and then to $8.5 billion on 1 October 1929. Inevitably, lending on this scale to support purchases of securities fostered a speculative boom, though the ratio of loans to the market value of securities remained constant between 1926 and 1929, indicating that it was speculative enthusiasm driven by constantly rising prices and easy money that lay behind the boom, rather than profligate credit from brokers. There was also a rapid increase of business on the Curb market in the 1920s driven by investor enthusiasm for US industrials and a developing market in foreign bonds, especially those issued in Europe and Latin America. Volume though not value of trading on the Curb even overtook that of the New York Stock Exchange, leading the Curb to rename itself the New York Curb Exchange in 1929.

Behind these easy money conditions lay a deliberate policy of the Federal Reserve Bank from 1924 onwards to maintain low interest rates in the United States in order to help the $/£ exchange rate. This encouraged an outflow of capital and credit and aimed to meet the dollar shortage of the 1920s, which resulted from the disruptive effects of war on the European export economies and the reversal of financial flows. A chronic financial imbalance between the United States and Europe lay at the heart of the world's economic problems. The solution adopted was not a fundamental realignment of economies to reflect post-war realities but the maintenance of easy borrowing conditions in New York. It was assumed that short-term dollar credits would suffice until stability could be restored through a return to the gold standard. However, the international financial system no longer possessed the fundamental equilibrium necessary to cope with the instability created by huge outflows and inflows of money in the absence of a large mass of securities capable of floating between highly integrated financial centres. The flows were too great and the means of cushioning them too small. Previously significant financial centres were no longer functioning adequately. Berlin and Vienna had been destroyed by war and hyperinflation. Paris had been crippled by war, defaults, and government restrictions and then contributed to undermining the international financial system as the instability of the franc drove short-term funds abroad in the early 1920s whilst its stabilization in the late 1920s attracted them back. London was weak throughout the 1920s due to the poor performance of the economy, the unrealistic valuation of sterling against the dollar, especially after the return to the gold standard in 1925, and the removal of the safety net provided by the vast holdings of dollar securities largely liquidated during the war. The result was a concentration of financial flows through New York in the 1920s as the only financial system capable of propping up the system. However, the US financial system could not do that alone. The Federal Reserve System had only come into being in 1913 and was less experienced in responding to periodic financial crises compared to the longer established European central banks. Even if it had been it is doubtful whether that would have made much difference given the magnitude of the crisis that began unfolding in 1929.

Until then the policy was successful because it did promote an outflow of dollars and placed New York at the very centre of the global securities market for the first time. Only the American investor could meet the needs of borrowers worldwide in the 1920s. Encouraged by low US interest rates foreign borrowers made extensive use of the New York market to raise funds, whether they were sovereign governments or major corporations. With Paris, Berlin, and Vienna no longer international capital markets, London favouring imperial countries, and Amsterdam and Madrid unwilling to come forward, New York was the only option for many borrowers, especially those from central Europe and Latin America. They met a ready response from US investors flush with savings generated in a booming economy but faced with a lack of attractive openings because of low interest rates. Excluding intergovernment debt US holdings of foreign securities had already reached $2.6 billion by 1919, grew to $4.6 in 1914, and then peaked at $7.8 in 1929, before falling back to $5.6 in 1935. It was estimated that American investors absorbed $3.6 billion in European securities between 1921 and 1926, split almost equally between those issued by governments, at all levels, and those issued by companies. In addition, foreign investors also flocked to New York to subscribe to the international issues that were no longer made in London and Paris because of explicit or implicit government controls. Currency instability in the early 1920s also added to the attractions of $-denominated stocks and bonds, especially for French and German investors. In the 1920s buying and selling of US securities on the New York market by foreigners averaged around $1 billion per annum. Though London did reclaim some standing this was largely within its own extensive empire. Liberal lending by US individual and institutional investors provided a partial replacement for London and Paris in the global securities market in the 1920s and so compensated for the absence of Paris, Berlin, and Vienna.

As long as this lending continued the world economy was provided with the dollars that now supported international trade and kept weakened banks in central Europe afloat. However, that outflow depended on the willingness of US investors to buy the foreign securities issued and US banks to make deposits abroad, and that was conditioned by the relative attractions of home versus foreign investment and lending. This relative attractiveness was endangered by the stock market boom in New York which provided an alternative use for the funds of US investors and banks as well as attracting in funds from abroad. The capital gains to be made in US industrial stocks, for example, attracted investors throughout the world but especially from Europe. Foreign holdings of US securities rose from $1.6 billion in 1919 to $1.9 billion in 1924 and then to $4.3 billion in 1929. Foreign banks with temporarily available balances found that they could employ them remuneratively in New York. The speculative boom in New York was sustained by absorbing ever more funds which drove up prices and so encouraged reinvestment rather than profit-taking. However, by absorbing funds that had previously flowed abroad, as well as sucking in foreign money, the speculative boom in New York was endangering the stability of the fragile post-war financial and monetary system. Without the funds flowing from New York many international borrowers would be unable to repay loans coming due, service existing loans, or sustain domestic lending policies. If that could not be done the conditions that had sustained economic recovery at national and international levels in the 1920s would unravel as defaults and bank collapses would create a worldwide crisis of confidence. A great deal rested upon the speculative boom in New York in the late 1920s, both for the United States and the world economy.

It was against this international background that the Wall Street boom and then crash took place. On 27 July 1927, with a speculative boom already underway, the Federal Reserve Bank signalled a further lowering of interest rates by reducing its discount rate from 4% to 3.5%. Rather than repel foreign lenders, this had the opposite effect on those with short-term funds to employ. As a report for the Bank for International Settlements in 1934 noted '[t]he boom on the American Stock Exchange had a special attraction for short-term foreign funds in the years 1927–9, not so much on account of the interest rates offered as on account of the prospect of profiting from the rise in the value of investments'. The attraction of the New York call market caused the Bank of England to raise its loan rate from 5.5% on 7 February 1929 to 6.5 % on 26 September 1929. As the BIS report stated: 'In the first three months of 1929 the boom continued, draining Europe of floating funds and making the American market for capital unavailable to many countries who wished to borrow'. Whereas the proportion of capital raised on foreign account in New York averaged around 17% of the total between 1920 and 1928 it fell to only 6.6% in 1929, having begun to fall away in 1928. A reaction was inevitable and began when the Federal Reserve Bank raised interest rates to 6% on 9 August 1929, worried about the domestic situation. 'The crash came on 19 October, about ten weeks after the New York bank rate had been raised to 6 (after remaining at 5 for well over a year).' 'When the boom on the New York Stock Exchange collapsed in October 1929, a back-flow of short-term foreign funds set in immediately, in spite of rising interest rates.' It was all too late by then.[49]

Compounding the problems experienced by the US securities market by the late 1920s, due to the position it now occupied globally, were fundamental structural weaknesses, especially the divisions that existed between its various components. These had mattered little in the past when New York operated in a subsidiary capacity to the large European stock exchanges but that was no longer the case. The US securities market was not fragmented geographically despite the existence of numerous stock exchanges across the United States.

There were numerous established stock exchanges that developed from origins in mining and oil shares to become markets for local specialities as with motion pictures and aircraft in the case of Los Angeles, whilst new ones continued to appear, such as Seattle in 1927.[50] However, the market value of the issues they quoted was tiny in comparison to New York. One indication of the relative importance of New York is the fact that in 1930, when the market value of corporate stocks quoted on the twenty-three major US stock exchanges came to $82 billion, 60% or $49 billion was listed on the New York Stock Exchange and another $20 billion (24%) on the New York Curb Exchange. That left only $14 billion (16%) for all other exchanges. For that same year 65% of all transactions in stocks in the United States took place on the New York Stock Exchange and another 18% on the New York Curb market suggesting an equal degree of dominance whether assessed by quoted stocks or volume of transactions. In bonds New York was totally dominant. This dominance of New York was supported by the nationwide operations of the major US brokerage houses, with membership of many local exchanges. In 1929, forty-five members of the Boston Stock Exchange also belonged to the New York Stock Exchange, acting as channels to the New York securities market.

Where fragmentation did exist was within New York itself, most obviously with the Curb market. This catered for a much wider variety of corporate stocks than the New York Stock Exchange, especially those issued by banks, insurance companies, and investment trusts as well as many public utility, railroad, and industrial concerns. Such was the success of the Curb market that it acquired its own building and moved indoors in 1921. Much less visible but actually more important was the OTC bond market. By 1929 the value on the bonds in circulation in the United States was $75 billion split roughly equally between government and corporate issues. This was close to the value of corporate stocks and though most were quoted on the various exchanges few were traded there, including the New York Stock Exchange which dealt with less than 10% of bonds. The level of fixed commission and the lack of dealers meant that US stock exchanges were poor markets for bonds, especially those issued by governments and public authorities. Instead, these bonds were largely traded directly between banks or specialist bond houses, where no commission was paid. This meant that there was no large and orderly market for bonds in the United States producing clear and unambiguous current prices. In consequence the speculative boom was focused heavily on the stocks traded on the New York Stock Exchange, and to a lesser extent those found on the Curb. These stocks possessed the most active organized market, with highly visible current prices via the ticker, and attracted those who operated on borrowed money, as their prices were always known and they could be easily sold if a loan was recalled.

Before the First World War US$ stocks, such as those issued by the railroads, possessed an international market. However, that was not the position in the 1920s. US$ stocks were largely held in the United States and few possessed an international market on the pre-war scale. Even when held abroad trading took place in New York, now the dominant market where trading was solely in US dollars. Whereas before 1914 the effects of any buying or selling surge were quickly dissipated among a number of different exchanges, so preserving a high degree of price stability, that no longer happened in the 1920s as the integration between markets had been destroyed by the massive decline in international securities during and after the war, compounded by the post-war restrictions imposed by governments. What foreign interest there was in US$ securities was focused on the industrial and commercial stocks traded on the New York Stock Exchange or on the rapidly growing Curb market.

During the 1920s domestic and foreign investors increasingly focused not on US railroad and utility stocks with relatively stable earnings, but on industrial and commercial corporations dependent on fluctuating sales in a competitive market and on the continuance of economic prosperity. This posed a risk to the market as stocks were much more volatile than bonds. Whereas the value of bonds was largely determined by prevailing interest rates, with an inverse relationship between the two, the price of stocks was a product of expectations about corporate performance. In a buoyant economy expectations regarding future dividend payments would be high, so pushing up the price of stocks, whereas the income generated by bonds would be static. In turn, rising stock prices would generate speculative activity which then developed a momentum of its own as the possible income to be generated from holding a stock became detached from its intrinsic value, which became a product of speculative supply and demand. Under these conditions stocks gained in value not because of the income they promised in the future but because they were expected to rise in price and could thus be sold for a profit.

As long as those expectations existed the price would rise, and so would the desire to buy rather than sell. However, a sudden change in these expectations would reverse the position, as falling prices would produce sales which further depressed prices and created more sales. With bonds there were floors and ceilings as the specific income was guaranteed unless there was a risk of default, and that also limited the risks being run by those who had borrowed money to finance their holdings. Even with the stocks of railroads and utilities such floors and ceilings existed for the level of demand for the services they provided was roughly constant. However, industrial and commercial stocks had no such guarantees as the current value was based on expectations about the future and that was unknown. Whilst there always existed buyers for bonds when their prospective yield was sufficiently attractive compared to alternative homes for savings, no such situation existed for stocks as their future yield could easily be negligible given the situation of the issuer or the general economic climate. All this was rather unfortunate for the United States because the continually rising market from 1923 onwards had led many to expect its indefinite continuance, with the result that banks had extended a vast amount of credit with securities, especially stocks, as collateral. This was a highly dangerous situation as a precipitate decline in prices would leave these banks highly exposed, holding securities as collateral that no longer covered the amount of the loan. There was a lack of awareness of how the situation had altered from that prevailing before the war. In 1914 call loans of $3.9 billion in New York were secured by stocks and bonds but those were stable securities that possessed large international markets in the main money market centres of Europe, especially London. In the 1920s the market on which the stocks and bonds used as collateral were traded was restricted to New York and the securities were very much more volatile in nature.

Consequently, a highly dangerous situation was building up in the United States in the 1920s and the longer the boom went on the more likely it was that the collapse would be sudden and steep, as it was based more and more on expectations that were becoming daily less and less realistic. In itself, that was not a problem as a correction in stock prices occurred regularly within any and all securities markets. The problem for the United States was the strong links between the securities market and the money market, through the extensive lending by banks with stocks as collateral. The call loan market had grown rapidly in the 1920s with money from the largest banks in the city who employed not only their own money but also the large balances maintained with them by correspondent banks from across the United States. One of the few outlets for such balances, upon which interest was paid, was to lend it out to those holding stocks as collateral, as the very volatility of the balances created a need for an active market where stocks could, if required, be immediately bought and sold. Though this had been taking place before 1914 the scale of the operation grew enormously in the course of the 1920s. By September 1929 a total of $6.5 billion was lent out to New York brokers and dealers of which only 16% came from banks based in New York City. The rest had been collected from throughout the United States and even abroad, attracted by the high rates of interest. In the past any crisis in New York could call upon resources from around the world, as in 1907, whereas now the responsibility rested with the US Federal Reserve Bank, which had no relevant experience. The situation was worsened by the instability of the US banking system due to legislative impediments to the creation of a nationwide branch banking system. Instead, there existed a vast number of individual banks that were aggressive in the pursuit of deposits and lending but lacked robustness in the face of financial difficulty. In any crisis it was inevitable that many of these banks would collapse, producing a contraction in the supply of credit and reversing any expansionary cycle.

Inevitably, the speculative boom came to an end as the cost of borrowing rose and the level of selling grew as investors sought to realize their gains. A knowledgeable insider like Charles Merrill, of Merrill Lynch, started to liquidate his personal holdings from late 1928 onwards, though he had difficulty in persuading his business partners to do likewise. During 1929, in response to a gradual tightening in the money market, the balance between investors seeking to realize gains began to outweigh those making new purchases. Faced with rampant speculation the Federal Reserve Bank began raising the interest rate charged on loans, and this was a signal to the market as a whole. Rising interest rates in London and elsewhere had already restrained the flow of funds to New York, reducing the wall of money that supported rising stock prices. Foreign deposits with Citibank in New York had risen from $105 million in 1921 to a peak of $256 million in 1927, fell back to $172 million in 1928, and then recovered to $214 million in 1929. Driven first by expectations of capital gain and then fear of capital loss, turnover on the New York Stock Exchange soared from 237 million shares in 1923 to 577 million in 1927, 921 million in 1928 and then to 1,125 million in 1929, before collapsing and reaching only 425 million in 1932. In contrast, turnover on the New York Stock Exchange in bonds was roughly constant over all these years. It rose from $2.8 billion in 1923 to $3.8 billion in 1924 and then ranged between $2.8 billion and $3.4 billion for the rest of the period. Stock prices peaked on 3 September 1929, when the Dow Jones Industrial Average reached 381. The inevitable fall prompted a build-up of sales as investors tried to realize their holdings. The Crash began on 24 October 1929 (Black Thursday) when sales reached almost 13 million on the day, with a sharp fall in prices. On 29 October (Black Tuesday) sales reached almost 16 million with another sharp fall in prices. Eventually the bottom of the market was reached in July 1932, when it was down 89% from the 1929 peak.

Many investors were left much poorer as their stocks collapsed in value. That would have been serious enough for the US economy for investors would have reigned in their spending to reflect the sudden downward adjustment to their wealth. Much more pervasive was the fact that banks were left holding both overvalued securities and loans with inadequate collateral and little prospect of repayment. Citibank alone had to accept losses of $100million. Even worse were the implications for thousands of weaker banks. The failure of the Bank of the United States in December 1930, with deposits of $200 million, was a major blow. Numerous small banks in the west and south were already in a fragile condition because of depressed agricultural conditions. A sequence of crises and banking collapses followed as depositors rushed to make withdrawals when the precarious situation of individual banks became known or rumoured. By the end of 1931 a total of 2,290 banks had failed in the United States with a further 1,450 in 1932. Savers were reluctant to trust banks. Banks restricted all types of investing and lending, concerned to ensure a high level of liquidity in order to meet sudden panic withdrawals. This severe credit contraction created temporary but serious difficulties both within the United States and abroad given the high dependency upon US funds. As each crisis came and went there was a slow unravelling of the complex web of financial links that had supported the international economy during the 1920s. Consequently, through the central role played by New York in the global securities market after the First World War, the Wall Street Crash had great significance not only for the US economy, through the domestic banking system, but also for the international economy as a whole. It was no longer possible to conceal the fundamental imbalances created by the war through temporary financial lows for these only worked in a situation of rough equilibrium, as had existed before 1914.[51]

SECURITIES MARKETS AND GOVERNMENTS
IN THE 1930S

Despite the dramatic nature of the Wall Street Crash its immediate consequences were not particularly serious for the global economy. The crash had little immediate impact on US regional markets such as Seattle.[52] Elsewhere in the world a number of stock markets had already peaked, and were already falling when New York collapsed and so experienced only limited repercussions. This was especially so as the volume of internationally held securities had been dramatically reduced as a result of the First World War and there was much less integration between national securities markets than before 1914. Even before the Wall Street Crash of October 1929 the London securities market was in difficulty, having experienced its own domestic crisis in September. The financier Charles Hatry had taken to creating additional securities on behalf of well-respected companies and public authorities whose issues he handled. This provided a simple and low-cost source of temporary finance. As long as he paid the interest and dividends due, this fraud escaped detection. The problem came when he could no longer do so because of investment losses. This began to happen in February 1929 when the Bank of England raised interest rates and the market started to weaken. When Hatry's fraud was exposed there was a sudden collapse of confidence in all securities, as there was no guarantee that this was not a widespread practice. Interestingly, the London Stock Exchange believed that the Wall Street Crash was due to revelations that came from the Hatry scandal, as it had 'caused great uneasiness in the United States, and the confidence, which the public had in the stability of the stock markets was rudely shaken'.[53] However, such was the fundamental and catastrophic nature of the Wall Street Crash that the Hatry scandal was unlikely to have had a much greater effect there than in Britain, to which his activities were confined, no matter what the level of British selling. Certainly, when the Wall Street Crash did come in October it had little direct impact on London where prices were already falling.

Nevertheless, there was a worldwide relapse in national securities markets around the world in 1929, some of which may have been due to the Wall Street Crash. The main stock exchanges in Belgium, Britain, Canada, China, France, Germany, Italy, Mexico, the Netherlands, New Zealand, Peru, South Africa, Spain, Sweden, and Switzerland were all affected. However, in most cases there were no collapses, certainly not on the scale experienced in New York, whilst in others the falls were very mild indeed. Canadian securities markets did suffer as there had been considerable American investment in its mining securities whilst there existed some inter-listed stocks with New York, namely Brazilian Traction and International Nickel. In Paris, like London, prices had begun falling in September and continued to do so until 1934. Despite the steepness of the decline, with the index of French stocks rising from 100 in 1922 to 426 in 1929 and then falling to 195 in 1935, there was no extended financial crisis. This was despite the fact that Paris had received substantial short-term money flows between 1926 and 1933, that left French banks awash with money, and that there had also been a speculative boom in industrial stocks from 1927 onwards. In contrast to the United States the French banking system was, like the British, much more securely based whilst lending had been focused on bonds as well as industrial stocks. Compared to the stock index, the index of French bonds had only risen from 100 in 1922 to 113 in 1929 and then only fell back to 111 in 1935. Similarly, in Spain banks had invested heavily in or lent upon public debt, which was much more marketable in a crisis than industrial stocks. This indicates that the Wall Street Crash was very much confined to the United States, certainly in terms of magnitude, due to the peculiar conditions of its securities market and the focus of short-term financial flows on its call money market. It also indicates that the ramifications of the Wall Street Crash for the United States was made much worse by the nature of its banking system and its dependence on a call loan market focused on lending with stocks as collateral rather than the full range of securities, especially bonds. It was only in countries where similar conditions prevailed that the consequences of a stock market collapse were as serious. One such case was Italy. In Italy during the stock market boom between 1922 and 1925 banks lent extensively on industrial securities and were brought to the verge of collapse when the boom ended. They only saved themselves by buying up stocks in order to stabilize prices, giving the appearance that their liabilities were matched by assets. However, when the market again collapsed between 1930 and 1932 that fiction was exposed and they were only saved by government intervention.[54]

Thus, the world did not experience an all pervasive stock market crash in 1929 beginning in New York and then circling the globe. Instead, it experienced one major crash in New York and a series of relatively mild declines elsewhere. However, not all banking systems were sufficiently robust to resist a substantial and prolonged stock market decline. In addition to Italy, the highly vulnerable financial systems of Germany and Austria suffered the most. Deprived of the supply of foreign credits and then the decline of the securities markets, German and Austrian banks were in serious trouble by the early 1930s. They were faced with loans that their customers had no prospect of repaying as the securities market was too weak to absorb new issues, whilst the decline in prices reduced the level of capital and reserves available, as much was invested in industrial stocks. Banks could no longer meet such losses and the decline of securities markets abroad meant that they could not tap those through new issues, as had happened in the 1920s. In fact the reverse was taking place, with foreign investors beginning to liquidate their holdings so driving down prices further and draining banks of deposits. However, the existence of exchange controls and other government-erected barriers limited the use to which asset arbitrage could be used as a means of settling imbalances between economies. The price of the same security traded in different stock exchanges now exhibited wide differences due to the compartmentalization of national markets which arbitrage was powerless to remove. Austrian bonds were traded in both Vienna and New York, and their prices shared an average gap of only 1% before May 1931. Subsequently the gap widened to 30% between October and December 1931, and then averaged 27% for the whole of 1932.[55]

Under these circumstances governments intervened to protect their financial systems against external instability. On 13 July 1931 the German government imposed exchange controls and closed the stock exchanges. Though these reopened briefly between 3 and 20 September it was not until 12 April 1932 that they finally resumed business. As during the war an inter-bank market developed in the meantime.

Government intervention in Germany enforced the acceptance of exchange controls that cut off the country from normal international financial transactions, including the operation of the global securities market. There was also a high level of direct intervention involving control over the entire financial system extending from banks to the securities market. Whilst banks could continue to lend, the securities market was largely reserved for financing government debt. Corporate issues were virtually excluded in 1934 through a ceiling imposed on the amount that could be paid out in dividends. As a result corporate share issues, which had been running at around 1.3 billion marks per annum in 1927–8, fell to a low of only 91 million in 1933, and then only recovered to 0.4 billion in 1936–7. The government's aim was to make bonds more attractive and easier to issue at low rates of interest. Bond issues fell from 2.9 billion in 1927–8 to 0.3 billion in 1934 and then reached a high of 7.8 billion in 1938. Also in December 1934 the number of stock exchanges was reduced from twenty one to nine so that the government was better able to control the securities market. Many stock exchanges merged: Dusseldorf, Cologne, and Essen in 1934, and Bremen, Hamburg, Kiel, and Lubeck in 1935. The supervision of remaining stock exchanges was taken away from the separate states and made the responsibility of central government. As a result all but the Berlin Stock Exchange were marginalized, leaving inter-bank transactions to constitute the main component of the securities market in Germany in the second-half of the 1930s. That system was extended to Austria in 1938 when that country was absorbed by Germany. The Austrian government had also been forced to intervene in the 1930s in order to save the financial system from collapse. Consequently, by the end of the 1930s both Germany and Austria had experienced an emasculation of their domestic securities market and the severing of its participation in the global securities market.[56]

The experience of the securities markets of central Europe was representative of what took place throughout the world in the 1930s. Signalling the end of attempts to restore the liberal international environment prevailing before 1914 was the departure of Britain from the gold standard in September 1931. Even before the Wall Street Crash of 1929 the £sterling was under pressure on international markets. This pressure was intensified by the problems in New York, the flow of funds to Paris, and Amsterdam, and then the financial crisis in Germany and Austria. It then became impossible to maintain the £ sterling on the gold standard at the prevailing exchange rates as the Bank of England simply did not have the gold and foreign exchange reserves necessary to support it against adverse speculation. Eventually on 20 September 1931 Britain left the gold standard. That event dealt a mortal blow to the stability of the international financial system and forced the closure of numerous European stock exchanges on 21 September, including London, Berlin,

Brussels, and Vienna, and more distantly Tokyo. However, New York and Paris stayed open, encouraging those which had closed to resume business as quickly as possible, many from the 22nd. The London Stock Exchange reopened on 24 September though only on 18 December did normal business resume.[57]

For the global securities market the collapse of the restored gold standard in September 1931 was a much greater blow than the Wall Street Crash. The Canadian stock exchanges were much more affected by the 1931 crisis despite their proximity to New York. The 1931 crisis undermined the confidence of bankers in the entire financial structure whilst the 1929 crash was something of an inevitable market correction. Unlike the United States the Canadian banking system was robust, based on large banks operating through a nationwide branch system. Though the Wall Street Crash registered strongly with the public, it was the demise of the gold standard that made the greatest impact financially, for in its wake came a decade of currency turmoil and the introduction of government restrictions that greatly interfered with the oper-ation of the global securities market. In particular, exchange controls of various forms proliferated around the world making it difficult to buy and sell securities internationally as delivery and payment could prove impossible, costly, or simply time consuming. The widespread introduction of exchange controls began with Iran and Turkey in 1930 and ran through to Poland and Venezuela in 1936. Many of these were deliberately aimed at curbing the international flow of capital in order to protect the value of domestic currency against fluctuations. Such controls were most extreme in countries where national financial systems were least robust, as in Latin America, and relatively mild where strong banks and markets existed, as in Britain and its empire. Even where formal controls were not rigorous, pressure was exerted by central banks, such as the Bank of England, to limit purchases of foreign securities. In place of a relatively open international economy, where money and assets could flow between countries in response to supply and demand in the market, came a series of interventions and *ad hoc* measures that created relatively closed national economies or, at best, regional or imperial groupings. At worst it led to the economic autarchy as practiced in Germany under Hitler. Within these new arrangements there was little room for the operation of a global securities market.[58]

SECURITIES MARKETS AND NATIONAL GOVERNMENTS

This decline in the global securities market occurred despite a continuing advance in telecommunications that permitted the creation of an ever more integrated market. The expansion of international telephony linked ever more distant centres. In 1927 the radio-telephone was introduced on the North Atlantic route, offering immediate communication. However, though cost was a problem with the wireless, the real difficulty was technical. Short-wave radio had limited capacity and was subject to fading, blackouts, and extensive interference. It was simply not possible to base a business requiring rapid, clear, and guaranteed contact, on the service it provided. Thus, until physical telephone lines were laid the global securities market remained dependent on the telegraph. Nevertheless, the international telephone network was being continuously extended between the wars, as with the cable between London and Johannesburg in the early 1930s. That eliminated a delay of ten minutes by constant and immediate contact, with a resulting great growth in business. This was possible as both markets were in the sterling area and thus free of controls. Elsewhere improvements in communications were negated by government-imposed barriers. These were not simply on external links, as with exchange controls. The Wall Street Crash and its aftermath had forced governments to become more closely involved with their national financial systems in order to prevent a wholesale banking collapse. This was then followed by the widespread introduction of legislation in the 1930s aimed at controlling, directing, or regulating national financial systems. In Germany, Austria, and Italy the government took control of the entire system and reorganized it. Both banks and the stock exchange became servants of the state rather than responsive to the financial needs of the market economy. This was mirrored to a greater or lesser extent throughout the world. Countries as diverse as Argentina, Belgium, Canada, Denmark, Finland, France, Mexico, Portugal, Spain, Sweden, Switzerland, and the United States all experienced degrees of government intervention in the operation of their financial systems.

Inevitably this government intervention was extended to securities markets as well as banks, given the widespread belief that speculative boom and collapse lay at the heart of the financial crises and economic depression. The precedent for such intervention already existed from the 1920s when a number of countries had acted to curb market exuberance after earlier crises. In particular, the problems associated with close links between banks and the securities markets had already been identified whilst the dangers of rampant speculation were well known. The Wall Street Crash created conditions where government intervention in financial systems was not only considered acceptable but was also demanded by the public and by politicians of all political persuasions. Such demands had long existed and at times had produced results, as with the limitations placed on the pre-1914 securities market in Germany. However, before 1914 there had been a general tendency to leave financial markets alone, especially as the adverse consequences of intervention were well documented. Such a policy of benign neglect ended with the Wall Street Crash. By the mid-1930s governments across the world were imposing increasing control over national securities markets, mostly through the organized stock exchanges.

In many cases the degree of government control was a direct consequence of the depth of the stock market crash and subsequent financial crisis. In Belgium the stock market collapse in the early 1930s endangered the entire financial system. Banks had lent extensively to those pledging securities as collateral, and as the crisis worsened their holdings of securities grew from 15% of assets in 1928 to 28% in 1933, bringing them to the verge of collapse. That was only averted by government intervention. The price was legislation to separate investment and commercial banking and to control the securities market. The commissioner overseeing the Belgian stock exchanges was given additional powers in 1934 leading to government control in 1935. In contrast, in the Netherlands, the financial crisis was relatively subdued, the degree of intervention relatively mild, and the securities market escaped government control. However, irrespective of the severity of the financial crisis governments took the opportunity to enact legislation covering the securities market, which usually took the form of the regulation and supervision of the stock exchange. A stock exchange law was adopted in Egypt in 1933, for example.

The result was a patchwork of legislation and control ranging from those countries where the stock exchanges were left to police themselves, though conscious of government monitoring, as in Britain and its empire, to those countries where the stock exchanges were subjected to a high degree of control, as in Mexico in 1933 and Argentina in 1937. Even where formal control was not imposed the activities taking place on their securities market were not ignored by national governments. In Canada, at both national and provincial levels, governments focused on preventing securities fraud, as that was the main public concern. Their efforts do not appear to have been particularly successful, apart from driving some business off the main stock exchanges, as a series of mining scams took place during the 1930s. Even though the London Stock Exchange escaped any form of legislative intervention, despite the Hatry scandal, there was a noticeable shift in attitude to the business it hosted. Increasingly the London Stock Exchange saw itself not simply as a market for securities but also as a guardian of quality. Though this conservative stance meant that the London Stock Exchange lost some of its vitality as a market it did mean that it escaped government intervention.[59]

Naturally enough the arena for the greatest hostility to the securities market was the United States, with the New York Stock Exchange being the prime focus. Both the US government and the American public blamed the banks and the stock exchange for the financial and monetary crisis which engulfed the country between 1929 and 1933. At the time it seemed much the most obvious explanation rather than the fundamental problems stemming from the conditions created during the war and the government policies followed thereafter. In a report on stock market control, published in 1934 in New York, the Twentieth Century Fund made the case for government intervention based on imperfections in the operation of the securities market.

[T]he unduly large volume of uncontrolled speculation, coupled with the frequent interference with the free play of supply and demand by manipulative activity, interferes with the performance of the proper functions of security exchanges and also has a serious disruptive effect on the national economy. . . public policy requires that speculative activities be brought under such control that they will add to and not detract from, the value of the functions which security exchanges are designed to perform; and so that such activities will no longer create credit disturbances and other maladjustments throughout our economic structure.[60]

It was easy to produce a catalogue of abuses that investors had been exposed to, stretching back to the First World War and beyond, and to suggest that the Wall Street Crash was simply part of an ongoing scandal that had to be tackled by the government.

Given the magnitude of the speculative boom and its collapse, the government had no alternative but to become involved despite attempts by members of the New York Stock Exchange, especially the president, Richard Whitney, to rebut the criticisms made.[61] The outcome was the Securities Exchange Act of 1933, followed by the establishment of the Securities and Exchange Commission (SEC) in 1934. These were designed to prevent market manipulation and to limit speculation by forcing all exchanges to register and to abide by a strict set of rules. Exchanges could be fined and their members suspended if any rules were broken. However, there were no measures to deal with the unorganized OTC market as its existence was largely ignored. There was also an acceptance that the long-term effect on the securities market as a whole was unknown, but such was the desire for some kind of control that this was regarded as of minor importance.[62] The result was a much more restrictive regime involving the separation of commercial and investment banking (Glass–Steagall Act, 1933) and the regulation of the stock exchange (SEC, 1934). These strictures were not just confined to New York and the New York Stock Exchange but applied nationwide. Though all US stock exchanges had operated on the rules and regulations of the New York Stock Exchange, as autonomous institutions they had been able to vary them as they wished, which they did regarding the securities they quoted, the members they admitted, and the charges they made. This ended with the acts of 1933 and 1934. As William Douglas, Chairman of the SEC, commented in 1937: 'Operating as private membership associations, exchanges have always administered their affairs in much the same manner as private clubs. For a business so vested with public interest, this traditional method has become archaic'.[63] A new order was now in place.

With the enactment of the Securities Exchange Act of 1934, on June 6, 1934, the 'New Deal' legislators finally brought all the country's stock exchanges under government supervision. This legislation marks the most important development in stock market practice in a century. It regulates not only the exchange as a body, but the practices of brokers and operators, and provides for the supervision of the broker–customer relationship.[64]

This represented a triumph for all those who had long regarded as unacceptable the operation of a securities market unregulated by the rule of law. This triumph was confirmed in the Securities Exchange Act of 1938. The US Congress specifically rejected self-regulation as inadequate protection for investors and insisted instead on public scrutiny of every stock exchange's rules and regulations and the overarching regulation of a government-appointed body. The self-regulated securities markets of the Anglo-American world were now converging with those of continental Europe where state regulation had long been important. This was a lasting legacy of the Wall Street Crash.

   A major consequence of these government controls on the operation of stock exchanges was to circumscribe the way they conducted business, and to reduce their attractions as markets. Securities markets, including stock exchanges, were continually evolving in response to change whilst the creation of fixed rules and regulations governing their conduct, embodied in law and enforced by a government appointed commission, made that change both slow and difficult. In contrast the unregulated OTC market could respond much more readily to the needs of both issuers of securities and investors as well as those who traded in stocks and bonds, and so increased its market share throughout the 1930s. By the end of the decade it was recognized that the cost of compliance with government-imposed stock market regulation was discouraging US companies from making new issues of securities, and to trade on the OTC market rather than on a formal stock exchange. Whereas in 1920 the OTC market commanded only 6% of all trading in corporate stocks, and 14% in 1929, this had reached 23% in 1939. This reflected the perennial problem that excessive intervention would both drive the securities market underground and discourage its use as a means of raising finance.[65] According to Cherrington, 'Unless the government is to assume responsibility for directing the flow of capital into industry, there are limits to what it ought to do for investors. It cannot safely act as their guardians; it cannot afford to become a bulwark of defense against all the hazards which exist in the securities markets'.[66] The outcome was both a reduction in trading and a diversion from the organized markets. In 1920 the estimated turnover in outstanding stocks was put at $39 billion and this had risen to $157 billion in 1929. In contrast the figure for 1935 was $17.5 billion, which fell even further to $14.8 billion in 1939. Similarly, business on the New York Curb was depressed throughout the 1930s.[67]

A further consequence of government regulation of the US securities market was to centralize trading in New York to an even greater degree. Whereas an institution the size and importance of the New York Stock Exchange could cope with the legal requirements placed upon it, even appointing a full-time chairman in 1938, most other exchanges could not, especially the smaller ones, without a significant rise in costs and charges. Given the decline in business and membership in the 1930s it was difficult for these smaller stock exchanges to generate additional revenue in any other way. Thus, of the transactions conducted on organized markets in 1938, 88% were done on the New York Stock Exchange with a further 7% on the New York Curb. This left a mere 5% for all other markets. Faced with a shortage of new issues because of the regulatory burden, and the competition from the OTC market for what there was, the US regional exchanges were an endangered species by the late 1930s. By 1938 some 80% of the trading taking place on the Boston Stock Exchange was in stocks that were also listed in New York. What saved the US securities market from being stifled by government regulation and supervision was the dynamic nature of the New York brokerage firms. Given the exclusion of commercial banks from securities brokerage, because they could not gain admission to stock exchanges, and from investment banking, with the Glass–Steagall Act, members of the New York Stock Exchange were free to develop their business in different ways. Some special-ized in investment banking where they could combine the issue of corporate stocks and bonds with the ability to make a market in the securities created either by selling directly to their clients or on the floor of the exchange. In contrast to that wholesale business others focused on the retail side by opening branches across the United States and becoming members of the various stock exchanges outside New York. They were able to offer a nationwide service for those investors still interested in stocks, and by generating a high turnover they could survive in an environment of fixed commission fees at a time of depressed prices. By 1940 Merrill Lynch had 50 offices staffed by 300 brokers. Overall, in 1936 the members of the New York Stock Exchange maintained a total of 1,185 branch offices, including sixty-eight overseas.[68]

Nevertheless, despite this prominence, the overall position of the New York Stock Exchange was in steady decline. In addition to the growing importance of the OTC market for the newer and smaller corporate issues, the Exchange was also losing its residual share of the bond market. The level of commission charged by New York brokers had long made them uncompetitive in transactions in government debt, and this grew substantially in the 1930s whilst overall corporate issues stagnated or declined. Federal government borrowing rose substantially in the 1930s, expanding from $16.2 billion in 1930 to $40.4 billion in 1939, as a result of New Deal spending.[69] This meant that the New York Stock Exchange was accounting for a falling share of the total securities market. Thus, it was less the market provided by the New York Stock Exchange that was the underlying strength of the US securities market, circumscribed by government imposed controls, but the operations of the major brokerage firms and the active OTC markets in smaller stocks and government bonds.

What happened in the United States was replicated worldwide. Stock exchanges which had thrived when they were able to respond efficiently to the needs of the securities market found that was less and less possible in the 1930s. This both reduced the overall volume of business and drove part of that which remained off the exchanges. Trading on the Mexico City Stock Exchange fell from 104,484 shares in 1933, when government controls were imposed, to 13,695 in 1938.[70] This decline in trading on the organized stock exchanges not only undermined their power to dominate and control national securities markets but also reduced the importance of securities markets within economies. The effect of government regulations was not distributed evenly across the business transacted on stock exchanges. Curbs were aimed at anything considered speculative, resulting in a tendency for the major stock exchanges in western Europe and north America to restrict themselves to trading the stocks and bonds of the largest and most established domestic companies, leaving the securities of smaller and newer industrial and commercial ventures to be traded on the OTC market, or to rely upon self-finance and the banks. New companies involved a high degree of risk because of the greater uncertainty regarding future returns. There could be a popular backlash if many investors lost money, and so risky securities were not provided with an organized market.

This also affected the shares of mining companies but they possessed alternative markets in the stock exchanges located where the exploration and production took place. The authorities in these regions or countries were inclined to view such markets favourably as contributing to the local economy, and so did not restrict their activities. Thus, business in speculative mining exchanges thrived in the 1930s, especially after 1931. As the gold standard collapsed so the price of the metal rose. One beneficiary was the Vancouver Stock Exchange, where turnover fell from 143 million shares in 1929 to 10 million in 1931 and then recovered due to speculation in the shares of Canadian gold mining companies, with 100 million being traded in 1936. When that bubble burst it was followed by one in the shares of Canadian oil companies. There was even sufficient business to support a curb market in Vancouver. Elsewhere in Canada, such were the attractions of mining and oil stocks that the Toronto Stock Exchange and its local rival, the Standard Stock Exchange, which specialized in such securities, merged in 1934. A similar situation occurred in Australia and New Zealand, where there was also significant gold production. As both these countries were part of the sterling area and mining stocks were widely held, along with government debt, the speculative boom in the mid-1930s helped promote the integration of the securities market in that region. However, it was in South Africa, the world's largest producer, that the greatest impact of the booming gold mining market was felt. After South Africa went off the gold standard in 1932 there was heavy external buying of local mining shares from London and Paris, producing a speculative boom between 1934 and 1937. The Johannesburg Stock Exchange was a crucial part of the international market for gold mining stocks with brokers maintaining direct telephone contact with London. The boom collapsed when a rumour, later denied, spread that the US government was no longer willing to pay a fixed price for gold. The Johannesburg Stock Exchange was hit by a wave of international selling that wiped £45 million from the price of shares and led to the failure of two members. Clearly there still existed a global market for gold mining stocks in the 1930s for those investors able to participate in it, which meant those in the £Sterling or US$ areas. For those outside these areas, exchange controls rendered buying and selling difficult.[71]

In the eyes of many the Wall Street Crash and related crises were a product of the way securities markets operated, especially the facility they gave to buy and sell both easily and for future delivery, and then reverse the deal before payment or delivery was required. This was seen as speculation rather than investment and when taken to excess was a destabilizing force within the entire financial system and a danger to the economy. The Wall Street Crash was considered to provide proof of this belief. However, within this there was no recognition that securities markets were as much part of the money market as the capital market and, in fact, provided an essential link between the two. The ability to buy and sell quickly was essential if operations were to take place upon borrowed money which could become available or be withdrawn at short notice. Banks, in particular, used loans to those operating in the securities markets as a means of employing their idle balances and upon this lending rested a large mass of long-term debt.[72] However, this connection and these operations were seen to lie at the heart of speculative bubbles and their damaging consequences for national economies, and thus governments sought to restrict or even outlaw them. Hence the enforced split found in many countries between investment banking and commercial banking, and the attempt to limit buying and selling for future payment and delivery. However, in combination with the instability that pervaded both securities markets and entire financial systems from the early 1930s onwards, this legislative intervention discouraged banks from lending to those providing securities as collateral, whether businesses looking for additional funds, investors seeking to finance their purchases, or market professionals using short-term loans to finance portfolios of liquid securities. To be able to lend huge sums of money on the basis of irredeemable stocks and bonds, and minimize the risks involved, required the combination of both deep and wide money and securities markets. This is what London, and to a lesser extent Paris, possessed before 1914, and what New York, and to a lesser extent London, possessed in the 1920s. In the 1930s no major financial centre was in quite the position of any of these because of the collapse in confidence and the imposition of restrictive controls domestically and internationally.

With the controls imposed from 1933 onwards New York lost its international position as the securities market in which transactions could be most easily and cheaply financed by short-term bank borrowing. Security loans in the United States fell from $13 billion on 31 December 1929 to $5.4 billion by 31 December 1930 and remained at that lower level. By 1937 brokers' loans were down to $1 billion and running at 1% or 2% of the market value of all listed stocks compared to 10% in the 1920s.[72] Meanwhile, London once again assumed the position as the securities market where short-term money was most abundant, though on a much reduced scale compared to before 1914. Loans to members of the London Stock Exchange by British banks fell from a peak of £48 million in 1928 to a low of £16 million in 1932 before starting to recover slowly. In France banks appeared even more reluctant to lend. Instead, in all three countries banks themselves started to hold securities directly, including government debt and corporate bonds, rather than lending to those that did. Bankers were now much more aware of the risks of using short-term funds to fund purchases of long-term securities. Also, with low interest rates the gap between long- and short-term interest rates left little scope for the market operator to profit from the differential. Thus, turnover on the major securities markets was hit by a reluctance of banks to lend with securities as collateral and a reluctance of brokers to borrow for such purposes because of the lack of potential profits. Turnover on the New York Stock Exchange fell from 1.1 billion shares in 1929 to 0.3 billion in 1939. That drove down the level of business further as it became more difficult to buy and sell in large amounts both quickly and at current prices, because the markets had become shallower. Whereas in 1930 the volume of turnover on the New York Stock Exchange was equivalent to 72% of the total number of shares listed, by 1939 it was a mere 18%.[73] As Aldrich, Chairman of the Chase Manhattan Bank, noted in 1937, '[t]he recent demonstration that the stock market has been greatly reduced in breadth and in activity presents a problem of first importance'.[74] Consequently, one of the great casualties of the financial crisis that gripped the world between 1929 and 1932 was the close connection that had long existed between the securities market and the money market in the main financial centres. This had marked them apart from securities markets elsewhere and it was this that instability and controls had conspired to destroy. Neither New York nor London was in the dominant position that they had once occupied.

More generally, internal and external government controls, combined with currency instability, drove securities markets around the world to become more domestically focused. In the Netherlands Dutch investors preferred securities issued by Dutch companies, including those which operated internationally such as Phillips, or the Anglo-Dutch companies Unilever and Royal Dutch Shell. By 1939 the Amsterdam Stock Exchange quoted 424 Dutch companies with a paid-up capital of 2.3 billion guilders whilst also providing a market for the greatly enlarged national debt. In Switzerland the securities market remained depressed due to government measures, until the attempt to defend the international value of the franc was abandoned on 26 September 1936. In France the strong network of investment and commercial banks, along with a state-controlled Paris Bourse, ensured that the 2–3 million French investors directed their savings towards the national debt and the securities issued by the major industrial and commercial companies, rather than into foreign securities. Only a few favoured foreign governments navigated the various levels of exchange control in order to raise loans in Paris, including Britain in 1931, 1933, and 1934, Belgium in 1932, Austria in 1933, and Czechoslovakia in 1937. Though the British securities market was much less isolationist in the 1930s, with a large empire to serve as well as the sterling area, its focus did become increasingly domestic. Not only did the government absorb much of the funds itself, as it refinanced short-term borrowings with long-term loans, but investors showed a marked preference for the shares of major domestic companies. The five largest British banks had attracted around 400,000 shareholders by the late 1930s. In contrast, the bonds of foreign governments lost their appeal and were shunned by British investors. Many other foreign corporate securities suffered similarly when a collapse in commodity prices or currency restrictions made it impossible to remit dividends to British investors. In consequence even the London Stock Exchange, still the largest international market for securities, gave a greater focus to domestic securities in the 1930s. By 1939 the nominal value of foreign securities quoted was down to 34% of the total, whilst in terms of market value the proportion was very much less, at around 20%, reflecting the greatly depreciated value of many foreign government issues.[75]

Investors in western Europe and north America had lost faith in foreign securities because of the frequent defaults of the early 1930s, as governments found it impossible to either service their debts or obtain the foreign exchange necessary to make payments to investors living abroad. Of the £1.2 billion of sterling securities issued by south American borrowers, and outstanding in 1934, a total of £708m, or 59%, was estimated to be in default. Faced with such circumstances investors naturally gave priority to safety rather than return, preferring securities issued by their own government or by their own corporations, even those operating internationally. Consequently governments and companies from less-developed regions and economies lost access to the cheap sources of finance through the securities market which had been so important in funding infrastructure development before 1914. States had to undertake that role instead. The result of the 1929 crash, the 1931 crisis, and subsequent government controls during the 1930s was to destroy the international movement of capital, and thus greatly diminish those markets that had serviced these capital flows.[76]

Nevertheless, at a national level certain securities markets continued to thrive, especially in Asia. In Japan the combination of bank loans and new stock issues continued to provide the largest industrial firms with a substantial part of their new funds. In India there was also considerable activity on the securities market with new stock exchanges being formed in Lahore in 1934 and Madras in 1937 as well as additional exchanges in Bombay and Calcutta during a speculative boom in the late 1930s focused on the issues of new manufacturing companies. There was even a growing integration of those stock exchanges into the local financial system. In 1929 the Shanghai Stock Exchange admitted its first Chinese member and by December 1941 over a third of the membership was foreign. New securities markets also appeared in the 1930s, though under somewhat unusual circumstances. In the British mandate of Palestine, though there was some limited trading in securities in the 1920s, no market developed because both companies and the government drew most of the funds they required from abroad. This changed in the 1930s with the arrival of Jewish immigrants from Germany, among whom were bankers and brokers as well as wealthy investors. A securities market developed between 1932 and 1939 as the stock of corporate securities rose from £P 3.4 million to £P 12 million, although the largest enterprises continued to tap the London market. Nevertheless, there was now sufficient domestic trading in securities to support the formation of an embryonic, though not particularly active, stock exchange in Tel Aviv in 1935. In contrast, in Europe, which had given birth to the global securities market, problems continued to mount that had serious effects on those stock exchanges still operating. Civil war in Spain, for example, between 1936 and 1939 led to the closure of the main stock exchanges until 1940, and then only after government reorganization.[77]

Despite all the difficulties it experienced the global market for securities was not totally destroyed in the course of the 1930s though the number of securities that could command an international market by the end of that decade was very limited (see Table 6.3). American interest in foreign securities evaporated in the early 1930s faced with a domestic financial crisis and the triple blow of defaults, falling prices and exchange losses as currencies were devalued against the dollar. Similarly, with the Wall Street Crash, foreign investors' confidence in speculative American securities largely disappeared. Though the recovery in US stock prices was slow in the 1930s there was some revival of foreign interest in US stocks and bonds towards the end of the decade, because of the attractions of dollar assets at a time of instability. However, this did not generate much international trading as orders flowed either directly to New York or via the overseas offices of north American brokers. By 1937 there were 25 branches of American and Canadian brokers in London. Instead, the lifeblood of the global securities market in the 1930s was the securities of a small number of companies held internationally either

Table 6.3. Securities as a proportion of national assets, 1937–40

Country	Government debt (%)	Corporate bonds (%)	Corporate stocks (%)	Domestic securities (%)	Foreign assets %	Total (%)
Belgium	10.1	1.0	3.5	14.6	7.5	22.1
Denmark	3.0	0.4	7.3	10.7	−1.8	8.9
Germany	4.1	0.4	2.5	7.0	0.9	7.9
India	3.7	0.8	0.8	5.3	−5.1	0.2
Italy	14.1	0.4	3.0	17.5		17.5
Japan	8.0	1.0	11.8	20.8	0.3	21.1
Mexico	1.0		11.9	12.9		12.9
Norway	5.1	0.6	3.5	9.2		9.2
Russia	3.5			3.5		3.5
South Africa	7.2	—	17.5	24.7	—	24.7
Switzerland	6.6	1.1	9.5	17.2	2.0	19.2
UK	16.5	2.5	17.6	36.6	9.0	45.6
USA	7.7	3.7	11.5	22.5	2.4	24.9

Source: R. W. Goldsmith, *Comparative National Balance Sheets* (Chicago, 1985), national tables.

because of their ownership structure or the appeal they had to investors worldwide. In the former category came such companies as the Anglo-Dutch concerns, Royal Dutch Shell, and Unilever, whilst in the latter included South African and Australian gold-mining companies. These were traded between stock exchanges in Amsterdam, Brussels, Johannesburg, London, Montreal, New York, and Paris.[78] However, this category of securities was relatively small and not growing compared to those that commanded a purely domestic market. Even when international dealings in securities did recover somewhat after the early 1930s business was fraught with complications, controls, and risks. Instead of being conducted openly on organized stock exchanges, it became increasingly a business pursued privately between banks as they could internalize operations and employ staff to either comply with or evade the supervision and restrictions of government. Currency instability and exchange controls had made the whole process of buying and selling securities between countries, and remitting payment, either difficult or impossible whilst one of the objectives of the close government supervision exercised over stock exchanges was to restrict their field of operation to the domestic economy. The ability to effect automatic adjustments between economies through the constant buying and selling of securities had almost ceased to exist in the 1930s, with serious consequences for the stability and equilibrium of the world economy.[79]

CONCLUSION

By 1914 the global securities market held an established position as the essential interface between money and capital markets both nationally and internationally. It facilitated the mobilization of the vast sums of money required for the financing the world's railway systems and contributed significantly to the stability of the world monetary system. All this began to crumble with the First World War, which not only removed the internationally held securities that were vital elements in integrating national markets into an international network, but also ushered in an era of control and instability. Stock exchanges were increasingly identified as the causes rather than the symptoms of financial and monetary instability, particularly with the Wall Street crash of 1929 and the world economic crisis of 1931. These events encouraged governments to police and restrict market operations, either driving the business they had once conducted into the hands of others or preventing it being done altogether. The core of the global securities market provided by London, Paris, and then New York was destroyed. Even though many national securities markets remained operational in the 1930s, with some playing an enhanced role within their national economies, the global market was hardly recognizable compared to the position it had once occupied.

Curiously, the declining importance of the global securities market occurred for the very same reasons which had led to its appearance and growth in the first place, namely war. Though the First World War did necessitate a huge increase in government borrowing it also radically altered the environment within which most securities markets operated. It brought in its wake a far greater degree of control by national governments whilst shattering the international links that had underpinned the global market before 1914. Such was the importance of securities within the financial systems of advanced economies, especially in the world's main financial centres, that these were very susceptible to war-related crises emanating from the money market. In turn, the close links between national securities markets meant that what happened in one centre had implications for all. This forced the temporary closure of all the world's major stock exchanges. When they reopened it was under conditions of government supervision or increased control, which greatly restricted their freedom to operate.

Nevertheless, the costs involved in waging a prolonged and extensive war did create a need by those governments most involved to raise funds by whatever means available. Though much of this was by way of taxation, printing money, and short-term borrowing, in many countries it also involved the issue of bonds. This immediately reversed the gradual decline in the relative importance of government debt as a proportion of the securities in circulation, and helped fuel activity in securities markets. Even in countries which remained neutral the war had profound implications for their financial systems. The wholesale disposal of foreign assets by the belligerent nations to raise funds, along with their huge purchases of vital war material, produced an inflationary environment around the world, encouraging investment and speculation on the securities markets. This was a temporary situation, lasting only as long as the fighting, but as that stretched into years the inevitable reaction, when the war ended and governments ceased to spend, was particularly acute. Many financial systems were left vulnerable to collapse on a grand scale. Thus, as a result of the First World War, the landscape occupied by securities markets was fundamentally altered both in the short and the long term, and both domestically and internationally. This necessitated not only the rebuilding of national securities markets in the post-war years but also the re-balancing of distorted relationships.

These problems were further compounded in the 1920s by continuing monetary and financial stability. This was particularly acute in some countries, amounting to a destruction of national currencies and the collapse of banking systems. The national stability characteristic of the years before the First World War proved impossible to recapture, forcing financial systems to be reorganized in view of the new circumstances. This was also true internationally with the return to the fixed exchange rates required by the return to the gold standard being impossible to sustain. National governments failed to recognize either the fundamentally altered economic relationship between countries resulting from the war or the necessity of a period of adjustment to allow markets to re-establish themselves. A series of unsatisfactory compromises ensued as governments and central bankers attempted in vain to re-establish a new international financial system after the fashion of the old. One crisis followed another until it became impossible for the international financial system to withstand the need for fundamental change. Twin crises finally destroyed the world within which the global securities market had operated so successfully before 1914. The first was the Wall Street Crash of October 1929. This destroyed the financial system of the world's leading economy, namely the United States, and enforced government intervention in order to stabilize the situation. The second was on the international front with the departure of the £sterling from the gold standard in September 1931. This destroyed post-war attempts to rebuild a stable international monetary system. Combined with other crises around the world before, during and after these events, the outcome was to put an end to the liberal economic era that had prevailed before 1914 and to the environment which had supported the operation of a global securities market.

This liberal economic environment was succeeded by an era of government controls, interventions, and restrictions in the 1930s. Exchange controls cut across international markets by preventing flows of money and capital, thus separating one country financially from the next. This had inevitable consequences for the global securities markets as it prevented the high degree of integration that had once existed. National governments sought to exert increasing control by operating a process of divide and rule which insulated their own financial system from that operating globally, and then exerting a degree of control over that system so that it delivered the results that they judged to be in the best interests of their national economy. Internally, the same situation prevailed as governments sought to limit the volatility of the market place, and the instability of banking systems, by placing ever more restrictions on their freedom to operate. By the 1930s, the trust in the power of the market that was so evident before 1914 had evaporated, to be replaced by trust in government. The most extreme examples of this were to be found in communist Russia and Nazi Germany but manifestations of it appeared across the world, including the New Deal in the United States.

The global securities market was reduced to a series of compartmentalized marketplaces only loosely linked to each other rather than the fully integrated system that was in full flow before 1914.

Unfortunately, as few people before or after 1914 recognized the contribution that the global securities market had made to world prosperity and stability, unlike the perceived benefits of the gold standard, there was little outside pressure to recreate and maintain what was being lost. In the eyes of many, securities markets were associated with speculative excesses and fraud and so were better suppressed than supported. Such views were reinforced between the wars, especially in the wake of the Wall Street Crash of 1929. This was blamed by many for the world depression of the 1930s and the misery that had created for millions of people around the world. Consequently, securities markets were seen as rather marginal appendages within financial systems with pride of place being given to the actions of governments and banks.

7

Suppression, Regulation, and Evasion: 1939–70

SECURITIES AND THE SECOND WORLD WAR

The era of economic liberalism that had existed before 1914, and within which the global securities market had flourished, finally ended with the outbreak of the Second World War. That event, following the crisis and depression of the 1930s, ushered in an era of government management and control over national economies that was also extended to the international arena. During the war the operation of the market was suppressed in the interests of national survival, involving both the direction of labour and capital and control over the production and use of goods and services at home and abroad. Such control was found in all combatant nations and even in many that remained neutral. By 1945 the conditions required to support a functioning global securities market had ceased to exist whilst many national markets were no longer operational. As many in government associated securities markets with speculation and fraud, their suppression was welcomed rather than regretted.

Unlike the First World War the coming of the Second was widely predicted long before it occurred. With the financial crisis that accompanied the First World War a recent memory for many, those operating in the securities market, limited their exposure to risk, afraid of being caught by a sudden change in the international political climate. Contracts to buy or sell at fixed prices in the future were avoided where possible, the amount of business financed by borrowed funds remained low, and international commitments were reined in. These negative steps were also accompanied in many cases, though not all, by discussions on appropriate action if war did break out. This often involved liaising with both governments and central banks to formulate a coordinated action plan. The contingency arrangements made by the London Stock Exchange in 1937 included how to cope with the new dangers associated with aerial bombing. In contrast, the Brussels Bourse had no such plan despite their greater proximity to any possible conflict. When war did break out in autumn 1939 it did not produce financial panic in the countries involved or create shockwaves that reverberated across the world. Instead, most stock exchanges stayed open or only closed briefly, before reopening on a wartime basis with cash transactions, no forward trading, minimum prices, and close cooperation with the national government. The London Stock Exchange closed on 1 September 1939 and reopened a week later. This smooth transition experienced by stock exchanges worldwide was greatly assisted not only by the limited business being transacted and the planning undertaken, but also by the reduced level of international commitments and the increased role that governments and central bankers already played in most countries by the late 1930s.[1]

According to the New York magazine *The Exchange*: 'When the news flashed that war in Europe was a reality, a heavy swell of orders flooded over the wires, precipitating a sudden and tremendous pressure upon the nation-wide facilities of the entire brokerage community—the full force of this pressure culminating finally upon the trading floor of the Exchange itself'.

However, that situation was fundamentally different from that in 1914: 'the news of the start of the world war [in 1914] came with the abruptness of a bombshell, whereas, the present war in Europe had been threatening for so long that the business and financial community had time to prepare for the emergency'. Turnover on the New York Stock Exchange had been falling steadily since the brief revival in 1936. By 1939 turnover as a proportion of the shares listed had fallen to 18.4%, compared to 71.9% in 1930 and never less than 50% for the entire period 1900–1930. Government legislation together with stock exchange rules and regulations had all combined to reduce the volume of turnover both absolutely and proportionately, so that it was already at a low ebb when war broke out.[2]

During the war national securities markets began to face serious problems as countries were occupied by enemy troops, buildings were destroyed by aerial and ground attack and financial and monetary systems collapsed. The Germans had already occupied Austria and Czechoslovakia before the Second World War broke out, and these were quickly followed by Belgium, Denmark, the Netherlands, Norway, Poland, and France. Successful invasion meant the closure of stock exchanges and often their reopening under German military control. In Belgium all four stock exchanges closed, though an unofficial market continued. Eventually the Brussels and Antwerp stock exchanges reopened under German supervision in September 1940, though there was no forward market or trading in foreign securities, and Jewish brokers had to be excluded. In the Netherlands the Amsterdam Stock Exchange closed in May 1940 but reopened in July. Where an existing mechanism for state control existed, as in Belgium, the occupying German authorities used this, as it gave them the required power over the securities market. Where it did not, as in the Netherlands, they created it. Under German occupation the Dutch stock exchanges were re-constituted in one single organization and placed under public control. As in Germany, this allowed for mobilization of savings for government use, control of speculation, and the exclusion of Jews. A centralized securities market developed in those countries under German control, boosting the position of the largest stock exchange where more than one existed, as in both Belgium and the Netherlands.[3]

However, such a pattern was not confined to those parts of Europe under Nazi control. When the Madrid Stock Exchange reopened in 1940 after the civil war, it did so under much greater government supervision, which curtailed the business it could do. In France the Paris Bourse, which had been closed between June 1940 and April 1941, reopened under the authority of the French Vichy government, and under much stricter control than in the 1930s. The *agents de change* were given additional powers and a Securities Commission was set up in 1942. These measures were designed to aid the Vichy government to implement its economic and monetary policies by isolating Paris as a financial centre from the international market. Contributing to the final destruction of Paris as a key component in the global securities market was the disposal of the remaining French-held foreign assets between 1944 and 1946, so as to release foreign exchange for imports.[4] Similarly, in Britain the London Stock Exchange became an executive arm of the state, as the government sought to control the securities market and mobilize all savings and foreign exchange for the war effort. In return for this loss of independence the London Stock Exchange sought, and to an extent received, government support against competitors in the securities market. Generally, governments needed stock exchanges to control the securities market and were willing to extend their influence.

As the course of the war turned against Germany the Nazi government took ever more extreme measures to control the securities market both in Germany and in occupied countries. This included freezing quoted prices in May 1942, so as to preserve an air of stability and confidence, and then making these prices legally enforceable for any transaction in September 1943. In consequence, between 1942 and the end of the war, trading on the German stock exchanges gradually descended into chaos, and they started to close. Enemy bombing was already rendering it very difficult to keep open certain German exchanges. Many, including Berlin, had been physically destroyed. The Dusseldorf Stock Exchange continued to trade despite the destruction of its building, whilst in Frankfurt brokers conducted business in the cellars after the main building was largely destroyed in 1944. Elsewhere in German-controlled Europe stock exchanges were also subjected to the same restrictive rules, which made trading very difficult and, along with the progress of the military conflict, resulted in gradual closure, as with Amsterdam in March 1944 and Vienna in March 1945. What little trading remained took place on the unofficial market until the stock exchanges were able to resume business once the war had ended.[5] Outside continental Europe the physical effects of the war were much less damaging. Despite pre-war worries about aerial bombing, the London Stock Exchange remained open throughout the war though staff shortages, air raids, and travel disruption led to a growth of inter-office trading via the telephone.

After the war many European stock exchanges that had closed gradually reopened or found an alternative venue if their buildings had been destroyed. The Vienna Stock Exchange resumed on 15 November 1945, providing a market for domestic securities. However, in many cases resumption of formal operations was delayed because of the need to make proper arrangements and problems over the disputed ownership of securities, as with Jewish-held stocks and bonds confiscated by the Nazis. The Amsterdam Stock Exchange reopened only in mid-1946, though a small unofficial market had operated in the interim. In Germany there was a relatively speedy resumption of trading, despite the immense difficulties to be overcome, because the US and British governments wished to restore some kind of normal financial structure. The British allowed the Hamburg Stock Exchange to reopen on 9 July 1945, whilst Munich and Frankfurt in the American zone resumed in August and September, respectively.[6]

However, in all cases government controls were maintained in some form irrespective of whether a country had been directly involved in the war, had remained neutral, or had been under German control. During the war national financial systems had become subservient to government, which circumscribed their operations with ever more elaborate and intrusive laws and regulations. Banks coped better with these controls than markets as they were large centrally run organizations with well-established administrative structures. Stock exchanges were much looser organizations which provided an orderly trading forum rather than actually conducting the business of buying and selling stocks and bonds. Also, unlike banks, which monopolized the provision of credit in advanced economies, a significant proportion of the trading in securities was undertaken outside the stock exchanges, so weakening their ability to police the market and exposing them to unregulated competition. Consequently, the long-term legacy of the Second World War for the European securities market was the far greater involvement of government in its operation and the universal use stock exchanges, whether state-owned state or independent, to make their control effective. This set the scene for at least the next twenty-five years.[7]

The European securities market had also lost most of its international dimension as those foreign securities that still commanded a value had been sold, if buyers could be found. These included all available dollar securities and any others that foreign investors would buy, such as those issued by Latin American utilities, South African gold mines, and Malayan rubber plantations. British disposals alone totalled £3.9 billion during the war, of which at least £1.1 billion were securities, and there were few compensating acquisitions. Overseas capital issues in London amounted to a mere £9.5 million for the 1940–5 period compared to £23.3 million for 1939 alone. Generally, the extensive control over capital flows adopted by most countries during the war ensured that investors had little opportunity to acquire foreign assets. This was also true for government debt. Funds were obtained at the intra-government level, as with the Anglo-American Lend/Lease programme or by accumulating foreign balances, rather than through the issue of formal loans. By 1945 much of the little international trade remaining in securities, mainly South African mining stocks, was in the hands of a few New York brokerage houses that still maintained London offices, notably Baker, Weeks & Harden; Carl M. Loeb; Rhoades & Co.; and White Weld & Co, as well as A. E. Ames & Co. of Toronto.

There was also limited domestic compensation in Europe for the collapse of the global securities market as war finance had relied heavily on taxation and the issue of paper currency rather than debt. Even where government debt was created much of it was short term and held by banks and other financial institutions until maturity, rather than traded on the securities market. Although the British National Debt tripled, rising from £7.1 billion in 1939 to £21.1 billion in 1945, much of this was either temporary or held by public and financial institutions as permanent investments. Though the London Stock Exchange still operated a market in government debt, this was severely constrained because all transactions were for cash and there were no facilities for dealing for time, so severing the link with the money market. Thus, even where a functioning securities market remained its contribution to government finance was limited because of the nature of the debt instruments used and the restrictions on trading methods.[8] As the ability of companies to issue stocks and bonds was curtailed during the war, the importance of these securities shrank. From 1941 to 1945 only £32.4 million of new non-government securities appeared on the London Stock Exchange.

One of the few countries to benefit from the war was a neutral nation like Switzerland. The Zurich Stock Exchange was seen by foreign investors as safe from the prying eyes and grasping hands of their own government. However, even there the growth of business was restrained because of the need to establish ownership of the securities being traded.[9]

The Second World War began as a purely European affair but did not remain one. In addition to the worldwide ramifications of British imperial involvement, the entry of Japan and the United States into the war at the beginning of 1942 made it a truly global affair. The Far East in particular experienced a similar level of military disruption and destruction to that which had occurred in Europe from late 1939, with the occupation of countries by foreign troops and the aerial bombing of major cities. With the capture of both Hong Kong and Shanghai by Japanese troops in 1942, the stock exchanges there closed and remained so for the rest of the war. In Jakarta the securities market ceased to operate after the capture of the Dutch East Indies (Indonesia) by the Japanese, also in 1942.[10] However, as the war turned against Japan, the Japanese securities market began to suffer. As early as 1941 the government had tried to limit speculative activity by imposing price controls on the Japanese stock exchanges. In March 1943 all eleven of Japan's stock exchanges were consolidated into one single organization, the Japan Securities Exchange. This gave the government effective control as the securities market was now run from a central base in Tokyo with the other stock exchanges operating as branches. Though the securities market continued to be used as a source of corporate finance, with new issues being made and traded, this was much less than in the 1930s, as government demands absorbed available savings. Eventually, with worsening air raids, the Japanese securities market suspended trading on 10 August 1945. On 26 September the Ministry of Finance announced the reopening of the stock exchanges but this was countermanded by the Supreme Commander for the Allied Powers, and they remained shut, leaving trading to the unofficial market.[11]

In the rest of Asia and in Africa and Latin America the Second World War proved to be something of a boon to the securities market. The absence of European supplies of manufactured goods, and the voracious appetites of the belligerent economies for essential food and raw materials, sparked a rising tide of prosperity in many countries. Benefiting from the savings generated and the repatriation of funds from Europe, both governments and companies turned to local investors for finance. In Latin America the Peruvian Stock Exchange in Lima boomed, whilst turnover on the Mexico City Stock Exchange jumped from 13,695 shares in 1938 to 278,067 in 1945. In British-administered Palestine (Israel) the securities market recovered quickly from a crisis in 1940 and then benefited increasingly from the inability of both the government and local companies to continue to issue securities in London. In 1944–5 new issues totalled £6.8 million, of which £5 million was on behalf of the government and the rest was corporate, especially industrial concerns. By 1945 a domestic market for securities was well established.[12]

In countries that were formal members of the British Empire it was only when a successful outcome to the war appeared likely that activity in their securities markets began to grow. In India the Calcutta Stock Exchange was closed for three months from 20 May 1940, with the government introducing minimum prices and other measures aimed at curbing speculation. However, from 1943 the Indian securities market began to boom. By 1946 there were 1,125 listed companies in India, the market value of whose paid-up capital was almost four times its value at the time of issue, indicating the height that speculative activity had reached. Many additional stock exchanges were formed, both in cities where one already existed, as in Bombay, and in new locations such as Delhi, Kanpur, Nagpur, Hyderabad, and Bangalore. In contrast, the South African securities market boomed from the outset, buoyed up by the security attached to the value of gold at a time of monetary and political uncertainty, and by its location far from either theatre of war. Not only did gold mining stocks enjoy great support both domestically and internationally but a growing number of other local companies issued securities in order to raise finance and in response to booming demand from local investors. The number of industrial companies quoted on the Johannesburg Stock Exchange grew from around 50 before the war to 178 by 1946.[13]

In India and South Africa the securities market benefited from both local conditions and the relative absence of government controls. In contrast, though similar local conditions prevailed in Australia and New Zealand the local securities market there did not experience the same boom. Governments imposed a high degree of control in order to curb speculation and direct savings towards the war effort. Speculation was tackled through minimum prices and the banning of forward trading and short selling, whilst additional measures were taken to restrict external access to the local market. In October 1939 the Australian government passed the National Securities Regulation Act prohibiting both the export of securities and dealing in foreign securities. This was adopted in New Zealand the following year. Following the Japanese bombing of the Australian town of Darwin in February 1942, the Australian government imposed further restrictions on local stock exchanges, which were only gradually eased from 1944 onwards. Combined with exchange control this gave the Australian and New Zealand governments effective control over the securities market during the war, and led to subdued trading, which reached a low point in 1942. They benefited by being able to raise large loans from their local population. The New Zealand government raised a War Loan for £10 million in 1941, a Liberty Loan for £35 million in 1943, and a further loan for £40 million in 1944. These measures promoted the integration of the securities markets within both Australia and New Zealand, where the trading of government debt became increasingly important. However, the external measures undermined existing pre-war regional integration, splitting the securities markets of the two countries and reducing participation in the global securities market as links with London became much less important.[14]

As in the First World War it might have been expected that the New York Stock Exchange would have benefited enormously from the disappearance of European competition in the global securities market. Certainly the United States did benefit from a flight of capital to its shores during the Second World War. However, most of this was placed on deposit with banks such as Citibank rather than invested in stocks and bonds. Whereas foreign purchases of US stocks and bonds exceeded sales between 1935 and 1939, during the war the reverse was true, as European governments disposed of $ securities in their desperate search for foreign exchange. It was not until the 1950s that foreign investors again became net purchasers of US securities. Though the Second World War greatly enhanced the position of New York as an international financial centre, the New York Stock Exchange was not a major beneficiary of this. Instead, it was the banks and the money markets that gained, largely at the expense of European centres.[15] Within the United States there was a huge increase in government borrowing, especially from 1942 onwards. The gross debt of the Federal government rose from $40.4 billion in 1939 to $258.7 billion in 1945 or over sevenfold. However, the securities market was largely bypassed. The issue of bonds was handled by the US Treasury and the Federal Reserve Bank, with direct sales to banks and the public, rather than taking place through the investment banking and brokerage community. Moreover, many of these bonds were held as long-term assets rather than traded. What trading there was in government bonds largely took place on the OTC market rather than the organized stock exchanges. Low as the commission rate was on transactions in government bonds at the New York Stock Exchange, it could not match the terms offered by the bond houses which traded on a net basis. Although the turnover in bonds on the New York Stock Exchange did rise from $1.7 billion in 1940 to $2.3 billion in 1945, this was mainly in railroad and industrial issues.[16]

Consequently, the New York Stock Exchange was left reliant upon trading corporate stocks and bonds. These exhibited only modest growth during the war, whilst the number of interested investors remained static. However, the eclipse of the New York Stock Exchange was not solely due to a diversion of investor interest into government debt and the activities of the government and central bank. It was also affected by the progressive undermining of its competitiveness within the securities market due to the actions of the SEC. Cumbersome regulations and restrictions on modes of operation rendered the issuing of new company securities progressively unattractive, and gradually deprived the corporate securities market of its lifeblood. The decline of the call money market further deprived members of the New York Stock Exchange of one of their main advantages, the ability to finance their own operations, and those of their clients easily and cheaply. The number of clients of New York Stock Exchange members operating on margin fell from 256,504 in 1939, which was less than half the 1929 peak, to 56,131 in 1946. Similarly, whereas in 1937 New York Stock Exchange members had borrowed $1.1 billion, equivalent to 2% of the market value of listed stocks, in 1948 the respective figures were $0.3 billion and 0.3%. Further, the New York Stock Exchange introduced an annual listing fee in 1939 in order to generate extra income. This replaced the once-and-for-all payment previously demanded, increasing the costs of maintaining a public market for a company's stocks and bonds. As a result over the 1940–8 period US corporations financed themselves mainly through retained earnings (61%) and borrowings (34%) and made only limited use of new stock issues (5%).[17]

Within what remained of the market for corporate stocks and bonds the New York Stock Exchange faced growing competition from regional exchanges, which were even more affected by the collapse of new business. The constant supply of new issues, allied to speculative trading in mining and oil companies, had provided much of the activity on local markets. Much of this business was lost because of the controls imposed by the SEC. Such was the growing effectiveness of US government actions against all types of speculative trading that part of the business, and those who conducted it, moved to Canada, which was easily accessible by telephone. Turnover on the Vancouver Stock Exchange, a speculative mining market, had fallen from 29.6 million shares in 1938 to a low of 3.5 million in 1942, but recovered to 27.6 million in 1945. Although the Canadian government came under heavy pressure from the US government to curb this speculative activity, only in December 1945 was an act passed modelled on the US legislation of 1933–4.[18] Faced with the loss of new and speculative business the US regional exchanges sought to capture some of that undertaken in New York, by listing stocks already quoted by the New York Stock Exchange. In response, as early as July 1940 the New York Stock Exchange tried to prevent this competition by prohibiting its members from buying or selling on any other exchange those stocks it listed.[19]

The combination of the SEC, competition from the OTC market and regional exchanges, and the monopolization of new issues by the government increasingly marginalized the New York Stock Exchange. In particular, the unregulated OTC market thrived at the expense of its regulated rival. This was the case not only in government bonds, where trading was virtually the preserve of the OTC market, but also increasingly in corporate stocks. In 1939 the estimated turnover in corporate stocks in the United States was estimated at $14.8 billion, which was split between the OTC market (23%) and the exchanges (77%) of which the New York Stock Exchange was dominant. By 1946 this turnover had doubled to $29.2 billion but now 36% was done on the OTC market and 64% on the exchanges, where New York Stock Exchange faced growing competition. The number of brokers, underwriters, and dealers on Wall Street fell from 5,855 in 1940 to 4,343 in 1947, whilst the price of a seat on the New York Stock Exchange, which had peaked at $625,000 in 1929, fell from a top price of $70,000 in 1939 to a high of $30,000 and a low of $17,000 in 1942, with only limited recovery by end of the war. Though the Second World War may have presented an obvious opportunity for the New York Stock Exchange to replace London as the pre-eminent international marketplace, in reality it had difficulty retaining command of its own domestic market, only just managing in the case of corporate stocks. Helping the New York Stock Exchange retain its position domestically were retail brokers like Merrill Lynch. Using the experience in supermarket retailing with Safeway in the 1930s, Charles Merrill had re-entered the securities business in 1940 and actively developed retail brokerage. By 1949 the firm had 100 offices and was channelling a growing volume of business to the New York Stock Exchange. Though abiding by the minimum commission rules Merrill Lynch undercut brokers located at some distance from New York who charged a premium to compensate for the cost of long-distance telephone calls. In contrast, Merrill Lynch only charged minimum commission and compensated for the lower rate through higher volumes and other efficiency gains, so attracting investors in such places as California. By 1945 they had 250,000 customers and were responsible for around 10% of the turnover on the New York Stock Exchange.[20]

The Second World War completed the destruction of the global marketplace. Foreign-held assets were liquidated without replacement, national governments exercised near universal control of national securities markets, and barriers were erected to prevent the international flow of securities. There was no expectation that such a market would ever re-appear. The Bretton Woods Agreement of 1944 created the International Monetary Fund (IMF) and the International Bank for Reconstruction and Development (World Bank) as replacements for the international financial markets that were seen to have failed between the wars. The post-war aim was not to rebuild a global securities market but to create a new basis for international financial relations which minimized the use of markets and maximized the role of national governments, inter-government organizations, and

Table 7.1. Securities as a proportion of national assets

Country	1947–55 (%)	1970–3(%)
Belgium	20.8	17.9
Denmark	10.4	4.7
France	11.1	11.0
Germany	4.4	6.7
Italy	11.5	13.5
Norway	8.7	9.7
Sweden	—	7.9
Switzerland	16.5	19.0
UK	33.3	17.8
Canada	—	10.1
USA	24.2	19.1
Australia	20.4	11.2
Mexico	16.8	10.6
South Africa	25.8	12.4
India	6.7	3.6
Israel	11.0	19.0
Japan	6.9	7.8
Average	15.2	11.9

Source: R. W. Goldsmith, *Comparative National Balance Sheets: A Study of Twenty Countries, 1688–1978* (Chicago, 1985), appendix tables.

state-controlled central banks. If a global securities market were to re-emerge after 1945 it would not simply be a matter of restoring what had been lost but also of replacing what had been put in its place,[21] (see Table 7.1).

US SECURITIES MARKETS, 1945–70

For some countries the end of the war allowed stock exchanges to reopen and the restoration of normal peacetime trading to begin. Others had to adjust to the ending of a wartime boom as the spending of the belligerent nations tailed away. Whatever the individual circumstances, the main challenge for both the global securities market and most of its national components was how to cope with the greatly enhanced importance of government. Unlike the years after the close of the First World War, governments had no intention of restoring the pre-1939 situation, considering how economically troubled were the 1930s. There was also no expectation that the pre-1914 situation could be restored, as attempts in that direction had failed in the 1920s. The Wall Street Crash of 1929 was seen as a prime cause, especially in American eyes, of the world economic collapse of the early 1930s and there was little prospect that securities markets would be left free to operate on their own terms. As the United States was now the dominant economic and political power this popular American belief extended worldwide. As the public had long been suspicious of the securities markets, any policy which offered to police their activities was likely to receive broad support. Consequently, nationally and internationally, there was little prospect that the global securities market would be given the freedom to operate that it had possessed before the First World War.[22]

In the United States the legislation of the 1930s and supervision by the SEC exercised a powerful influence over the domestic securities market. As New York was now the most important financial centre in the world, having replaced London in the course of the Second World War, the New York Stock Exchange was the leading institution within the global securities market, with the potential to be even more dominant than the London Stock Exchange had been before 1914. Then London had had to share its domestic role with numerous provincial exchanges and its international role not only with Paris but, to a lesser extent, with Berlin and Amsterdam. However, by 1945 the regional exchanges in the United States were already waning, undermined by constantly improving telecommunications, the growth of large-scale enterprise, and the nationwide reach of New York brokerage houses. Internationally, the impoverishment of western Europe had removed, temporarily at least, the competitive power of all their leading stock exchanges.

The changes wrought by the Second World War favoured a growing centralization of the US securities market, given the greatly enhanced role of the Federal government and its borrowing. By 1945 the size of the US government debt was $252 billion, from which it fell only moderately in the post-war years before rising again in the 1960s, reaching $301 billion in 1970. Wartime patriotism had swollen the size of the investing public, which was then maintained at a high level by continued post-war prosperity. In 1965 it was estimated that there were around 20 million US investors, rising to 30 million by 1970, though the number who regularly bought and sold securities was very much smaller. Given these conditions there was every expectation that the New York Stock Exchange would dominate the national securities market in the post-war years. However, the New York Stock Exchange had never been a particularly good market for government debt of any kind because of the level and inflexibility of the commission rate structure mandatory for all members. US government debt was not actively traded on the New York Stock Exchange, even during the war, and disappeared totally after 1950. Instead, the market in government debt was maintained by around twenty specialist dealers who bought and sold net of commission, surviving on the difference between the bid and sell price. It was a market without a physical floor which operated through telephone links between the trading rooms of the main participants, and generated a turnover of over $300 million a day in 1950. The result was a stable and highly liquid market ideal for the employment of the short-term money possessed by banks, other financial institutions, and even large corporations. It posed a direct threat to the market on the floor of the Stock Exchange for those wishing to invest temporarily available funds in easily saleable securities.

The New York Stock Exchange also failed to command the market for corporate bonds. As Irwin Friend observed in 1958, '[p]ractically all transactions in US Government, State, and municipal securities, the bulk of transactions in corporate bonds, and a very substantial proportion of the activity in preferred stock flow through these (OTC) markets.'[23] Institutional investors made heavy and increasing use of OTC markets to buy and sell not only the national debt but other bonds as well. Whereas the New York Stock Exchange failed to cater for the government bond market because of its imposition of rigid minimum commission rates, it was the cap on membership at 1,366 and its trading system that made it a poor market for less actively traded bonds, such as those issued by municipal authorities or smaller companies. Turnover in many bonds was insufficient to attract the interest of the members of the New York Stock Exchange in comparison to the business generated by more actively traded securities. Specialists who made the markets in quoted stocks were not willing to do so unless the volume of trading was sufficient to allow sales and purchases to be undone without undue risk of a corner or sharp price reversal. Consequently the New York Stock Exchange provided a market only for widely held and actively traded corporate bonds.

A similar position also prevailed in corporate stocks. Only those issued by large and established companies found a market on the New York Stock Exchange. The New York Curb Exchange catered for newer and smaller companies. Such was the volume of business generated from trading in the corporate stocks excluded by the New York Stock Exchange in the 1950s, that the curb market formally constituted itself in 1953 as the American Stock Exchange. Members of the New York Stock Exchange also extended their business to OTC stocks in the 1950s in order to retain the custom of investors. Outside New York the regional stock exchanges performed a similar role to the curb market, dealing in those stocks issued by companies that were too small or closely held to warrant quotation on the New York Stock Exchange. However, as these other stock exchanges followed the lead set by New York, in terms of commission rates and methods of business, they also did not cater for the bond market. This left the trading in bonds of whatever kind largely in the hands of the OTC market. An estimate for 1950 suggested that around 99% of the turnover in government bonds took place on an OTC basis as did 95% of that in corporate bonds. The only component of the US securities market that the organized exchanges, including the New York Curb, still commanded was that for corporate stocks. In the 1950s and 1960s the organized stock exchanges had between 60% and 75% of the market in corporate stocks compared to the OTC, which had between 25% and 40%, indicating a significant level of competition.

The OTC market thus provided serious competition even in stocks in the post-war years. It was also becoming more organized due to the Maloney Act of 1938, which attempted to extend the authority of the SEC beyond the recognized stock exchanges. This had led in 1939 to the formation of the National Association of Security Dealers (NASD), to provide self-regulation for brokers who were not members of stock exchanges. In 1940 NASD had a membership of 2,900, and after falling to 2,700 in 1950 it grew substantially to 4,470 by 1970, whilst the number of offices they operated from had increased to 6,990. Competition from these non-members was particularly acute in less widely held stocks which did not fit the organization and commission structure of the stock exchanges. Also, as such stocks had no active market, the benefit of a stock exchange quotation was somewhat marginal. By tailoring their charges and services to the needs of specific customers, whether issuers of securities or investors, brokers operating in the OTC market could take business away from members of the stock exchanges. As the New York Stock Exchange was home to the most widely held and actively traded stocks it suffered least from the OTC market in stocks. Such stocks were highly valued by the investing public because of their ready marketability at well publicized prices only available through a quotation on the New York Stock Exchange. Both the New York Curb and the local stock exchanges were more vulnerable as the stocks they traded tended to be the less popular ones. As a result, within the organized stock exchanges New York was dominant in the 1950s with around 85% of all trading, whilst the New York Curb Exchange had 7%, which left the regional exchanges with 8%. However, important as this trading on the organized exchanges was, it was totally overshadowed by the volume of business now undertaken on the OTC market. During the 1950s and 1960s the OTC market was responsible for around 90% of trading in securities, by value, in the United States compared to 10% on the organized stock exchanges. In 1958 turnover in the government bond market alone was put at $176 billion compared to $34 billion on the New York Stock Exchange. Though the public identified the securities market with the New York Stock Exchange it was merely a sideshow in comparison to the bond market and other OTC transactions.

US local exchanges did badly in the post-war years. The old curb market, the American Stock Exchange, established a niche for itself by continuing to market those stocks which were actively traded but which were too small or too insecure to be quoted on the New York Stock Exchange. If such stocks did gravitate to being quoted at the New York Stock Exchange they ceased to be traded on the Curb, so removing a potential source of friction between the two markets. There were even tentative, though abortive, merger discussions between these two exchanges. Membership of the New York Stock Exchange was too valuable to be diluted through the inclusion of members of the American Stock Exchange. The problem for regional exchanges was that they could neither hold onto their established stocks nor generate a sufficient level of new business to support their operational costs. By the late 1950s many had closed, merged, or become inactive. The Philadelphia Stock Exchange took over Baltimore in 1949 and Washington (DC) in 1953, whilst Chicago absorbed St Louis, Cleveland, and Minneapolis. As long as active local markets existed trading locally held stocks on behalf of local investors then these exchanges had a secure niche for themselves within the national securities market. However, that had ceased to be the case by the 1940s.

Over the long term, the integration of the US economy was destroying local markets and replacing them with national ones, and the securities market was in the forefront of such a process. However, this process was also driven by major changes in the investment environment from the 1940s onwards, especially in response to government action. The huge size of the national debt and its universal appeal to investors helped to create a single market for securities across the United States in the 1940s, and this was extended into stocks during the 1950s and 1960s. A combination of tax and government regulation after 1945 encouraged the institutionalization of investment, as characterized by the huge growth of pension funds. Prior to the Second World War, institutional ownership of stocks in the United States was limited and largely confined to insurance companies. Initially, institutional funds were largely invested in fixed interest securities which produced the stable income and guaranteed payment needed to match institutional liabilities. In 1951 the portfolio composition of US pension funds was 31% in government debt, 33% corporate bonds, and 12% common stock. However, with the gradual erosion of the real value of fixed–interest securities due to inflation there was a switch into stocks. In 1971 the portfolio of US pension funds contained only 2% government debt and 21% corporate bonds compared to 68% in common stock. Between 1949 and 1962 institutional holdings of stocks grew from $9.7 billion to $67.7 billion, with pension funds experiencing the greatest increase, rising from \$0.5 billion to \$18.2 billion. Stocks offered a return that would keep pace with inflation, as corporate earnings had the capacity to increase both through building up the business by a process of reinvestment and through the ability to pass on rising prices to customers. That in turn was reflected in the value of the business and the dividends paid, which would result in rising share prices. In contrast, the income of a bondholder was fixed, which meant a real decline at a time of rising prices.

As institutions preferred the most marketable of these stocks, because of their need to acquire and dispose of them readily, it was those quoted on the New York Stock Exchange that were the most popular. Institutions held 13% of all New York Stock Exchange listed stocks in 1949, 20% in 1962, and 28% in 1971. Local stock exchange markets were too small to cope with the scale of activity in individual stocks undertaken by financial institutions. Although institutions did purchase less marketable stocks where these offered both a higher yield and a greater prospect of capital gain, despite the greater risk, this did not help local stock exchanges as such stocks could be obtained via the OTC market. In the absence of a nationwide branch banking system the New York investment banks and brokerage houses became increasingly expert at packaging small corporate issues so as to appeal both to the business seeking to raise finance and the financial institution with funds to employ. As the regulations imposed by the SEC had made such issues both costly and cumbersome only these New York firms possessed the expertise necessary to handle the regulatory burden. Between 1946 and 1970 the number of such corporate issues rose from 6,900 to 38,944.

Also damaging the smaller stock exchanges in the west of the United States were the actions taken by the SEC to eliminate speculative stocks such as those issued by companies exploring for minerals and oil. Activity in stocks like these had given birth to numerous stock exchanges across the United States and helped to sustain them with a succession of new discoveries. Unfortunately, a number of these companies turned out to have bogus prospects whilst many of the genuine ones failed completely, as was the nature of the business. In the more regulatory climate, all activity associated with speculative mining companies tended to be seen as fraudulent and was thus suppressed. One consequence was to drive such activity across the border to Canada, where the government took a much more liberal view, and to deprive once thriving local securities markets of much of their essential business. What remained was simply too little to sustain the costs of running an organized market involving the maintenance of a building and the payment of staff. Such costs were not present in the OTC market, which was also not subject to the rigorous scrutiny and regulatory burden imposed on the stock exchanges.

Faced with extinction, local stock exchanges in the 1950s sought to capture some of the business that was now drifting away to New York. Membership of a local stock exchange was both easier and cheaper than purchasing a seat on the New York Stock Exchange and so was attractive to any aspiring broker, especially if it also gave access to the same market for securities. Consequently, these local stock exchanges increasingly quoted stocks already traded on the New York Stock Exchange, and amended their rules and practices so as allow them to compete with it. By operating on New York prices but offering greater flexibility on commission rates and trading practices, brokers on local stock exchanges could take business away from New York, aided by the very telephone system that previously encouraged centralization. As membership of these local stock exchanges was open to New York brokers it also meant that large firms who operated nationally could route orders through the most appropriate market and take business away from those who operated solely on the floor of the New York Stock Exchange, even though all abided by the same rules and regulations for sales and purchases completed there. Under these circumstances the number of separate members of the New York Stock Exchange fell steadily, dropping from 620 in 1950 to 570 in 1970, whilst the number of offices they operated correspondingly expanded, rising from 1,660 to 3,640. In 1969 one of the largest member firms was Francis Dupont and Company, which served 325,000 investors from 100 offices. Given the restrictions placed on US banks both in terms of the establishment of branches and links between investment and commercial operations, New York brokers were able to meet a demand for nationwide financial services. Recognizing the inevitable, the New York Stock Exchange allowed its members to incorporate as private companies in 1953, so giving them access to additional sources of capital. In 1970 the New York Stock Exchange recognized that some of its members, such as Merrill Lynch, had become major financial institutions in their own right and allowed them to become public companies.

An unwillingness to recognize developments in the securities market also characterized other actions taken by the New York Stock Exchange. To counter competition from the local exchanges, in 1955 the New York Stock Exchange tried to stop its members buying or selling the stocks it listed anywhere other than on its own trading floor. This was opposed by the SEC, which was determined to ensure that investors obtained the best possible price. In 1962 the New York Stock Exchange adopted a different tactic to achieve the same end, which was to try and prevent non-members trading on its prices. This was declared illegal. Consequently, the New York Stock Exchange was unable to use fully its dominant position as the market for the more actively traded stocks to destroy the competition it faced from the local stock exchanges, as the actions of the SEC prevented it doing so. In the 1960s the share of total turnover on the organized stock exchanges undertaken by the New York Stock Exchange was in decline, and fell to 79% by 1970, though this was within an enormous overall increase in business. Nevertheless, for the stocks it did quote the New York Stock Exchange remained totally dominant due to the depth and breadth of the market it provided compared to any alternative.

Underpinning the increasing business on all stock exchanges and OTC markets in the United States was the fact that individual investors were, once again, discovering the merits of stocks as investments. Turnover on all exchanges rose from $18.1 billion in 1945 to $22.8 in 1950, $46.9 in 1960, and then to $136.5 in 1970. During the 1950s individual investors had been content with government bonds but in the 1960s they began buying stocks, recognizing that the prices of these had risen steadily since 1945 whilst the SEC had removed many of the practices associated with the Wall Street Crash. The number of shareholders in the United States grew from 6.5 million in 1952 to 20 million in 1965. As with institutions, individual investors were also attracted to the stocks issued by the largest corporations as they were easy to buy and sell and offered the greatest security given the extent and even diversity of their operations. By 1970 45% of the market value of all quoted stocks was provided by only fifty companies, which were the focus of investor attention. Among the favourites were IBM, with a market value of $38 billion in 1971, and AT and T at $25 billion, for each dominated a particular sector of the economy, namely computing and telecommunications, respectively. The New York Stock Exchange benefited most from this investor preference as it dominated the market for such stocks. The turnover of shares on the New York Stock Exchange, which had reached 1.1 billion in 1929, and stood at 0.3 billion in 1939, 0.4 billion in 1945, 0.5 billion in 1950, and had only reached 0.8 billion in 1960, escalated to 2.9 billion shares by 1970.

Nevertheless, this did not mean that individuals once again dominated activity on the securities market. The trend towards institutional ownership was well established, supported by tax breaks and complex regulations. Whereas the market value of corporate stocks grew from $110 billion in 1946 to $859 billion in 1970, the proportion owned by individual investors fell from 93% to 79%. Furthermore, it was institutions that were the most active in the market. In 1952 25% of the stock trading on the New York Stock Exchange was for institutions and 57% for individual investors, with 18% between members. In 1969 42% was for institutions, 33% for individuals, and 24% between members. This had serious implications for the US securities market. As institutions were responsible for more of the buying and selling they became less willing to accept the rigid commission structure of the New York Stock Exchange. Financial institutions were used to trading on a net position on the government bond market and at negotiated commission rates on the OTC market. Such institutions began to demand a reduction in rates, especially for large volume business, but the New York Stock Exchange was unwilling to concede these. Nor could they be offered discounts or rebates even though members could trade between themselves at discounted rates. This was not allowed for non-members, and membership was denied to major financial institutions such as the big deposit banks, the insurance companies, and the trust companies, even though they generated so much of the business either from within or on behalf of their customers. In 1952 the Stock Exchange membership rejected a system of discounts. It was not until December 1968 that such a scheme was introduced and only then in a limited form. Consequently, the major financial institutions had every incentive to bypass the New York Stock Exchange wherever possible, developing in the 1960s a system of block trading involving the transfer of stocks directly between the major institutional investors.

With no statutory monopoly over the buying and selling of stocks, let alone the securities market as a whole, the New York Stock Exchange had to provide a trading forum that would attract investors and persuade them to pay the fees charged by the membership. With individual investors the New York Stock Exchange was in a semi-monopolistic position for it commanded the market in the most popular stocks. The nationwide coverage of its membership produced a constant stream of buying and selling orders from across the country. Also central to this commanding position was the role of specialists. With over 300 specialists ready to buy and sell quoted stocks on demand the New York Stock Exchange possessed the broadest and deepest market in these, whatever the competition from the local exchanges or the OTC market. However, action taken by the SEC undermined this. With a staff of over 1,100 in 1950, including numerous lawyers and accountants, and operating from a head office in Washington and ten regional offices, the SEC was in a position to effectively dictate to the New York Stock Exchange how it should operate. It was particularly concerned to stamp out those practices deemed responsible for the Wall Street Crash, such as short-selling and operating on borrowed money. Thus, there was only a limited recovery in the call loan market where the members of the New York Stock Exchange were concerned, whilst brokers' loans and margin trading were both restricted. Only for new issues was heavy reliance placed on borrowed funds to finance temporary positions, rather than the permanent use of such funds to support holdings of existing securities. This reduced the attractions of the market provided by the New York Stock Exchange, especially for those operating on temporarily idle funds. The US government bond market absorbed these whilst the OTC or Canadian markets attracted the speculator, as both escaped direct SEC control.

The New York Stock Exchange was left heavily reliant on the market for a particular group of stocks, namely those issued by the largest companies; on a particular group of investors, namely the financial institutions who increasingly owned them; and on a particular segment of the membership, namely the major investment bankers and retail brokers. Even before the 1970s this vulnerability was becoming apparent not only in the growth of block trades that bypassed the trading floor but also in attempts to create an alternative marketplace using the latest advances in technology. The idea of an alternative market existed as early as 1957 but made little progress, though the New York Stock Exchange itself made use of technological advances in 1966 to improve the dissemination of prices and in 1968 for the transfer of securities. However, this stopped short of a market that bypassed or replaced the physical trading floor staffed by market makers because only that could cope with a diversity of business in a diversity of securities from a diversity of investors, and do so with speed and certainty. Furthermore, until a technology was devised that provided the capacity and flexibility present on the trading floor then the New York Stock Exchange benefited from the increasing scale of business generated by financial institutions and the ability to attract sales and purchases from afar through the use of the telephone and the tentacles of its retail brokers.

However, important as quoted securities were becoming to investors in the 1950s and 1960s, their role within the economy was somewhat marginal. Although the market value of quoted stocks grew substantially in the 1950s and 1960s very little of it was the result of companies issuing securities to raise development finance. Between 1952 and 1968 new issues accounted for less than 3% of the total increase in the value of quoted stocks. Instead, the rise in value was due to a combination of an adjustment for inflation and a revaluation of existing stocks to reflect the enhanced earning capacity of the quoted companies. The financing of long-term development was left to reinvested earnings and bank loans rather than a steady stream of new issues, as had been the case with railroads before 1914. Any new issues went mainly through the OTC markets, to finance newer and smaller companies. The securities market became highly hierarchical. The OTC markets formed the base, where the greatest number of new issues was made and where finance was provided for business. The resulting securities possessed little by way of a public market, being traded between brokers and dealers, including members of the New York Stock Exchange. Above the OTC market was the American Stock Exchange and the regional stock exchanges which provided a market for

OTC stocks if and when they reached a stage of attracting growing investor interest, and therefore required a public market. Finally, there was the New York Stock Exchange providing a market for the most actively traded stocks of the increasing number of giant US national and international corporations. The American Stock Exchange was continuously losing stocks to the New York Stock Exchange and gaining them from the OTC market. In addition, there also existed a large bond market with two distinct components. On the one hand there was an OTC market for little traded bonds such as those issued by municipalities and companies, though a few were traded on the New York Stock Exchange. On the other hand there was the large and liquid government bond market where the US national debt was bought and sold between banks and brokers, bypassing the institutional arrangements of a stock exchange. This market provided ideal conditions for the employment of the short-term money in New York banks, generated either within their own operations or through their extensive network connections at home and abroad. Thus, the New York Stock Exchange only really mattered to investors, whether individual or institutional, rather than to borrowers. The link to the money market had also been broken.

There thus existed in the United States between 1945 and 1970 a strongly compartmentalized securities market, only part of which was really subject to SEC regulation. Its largest single component was the US government bond market which operated free of regulation and government control. Next in importance was the market in the major corporate stocks found largely on the floor of the New York Stock Exchange, with the American Stock Exchange and the local stock exchanges much less important. It had grown substantially during the 1960s and was heavily regulated both by the government through the SEC and by the stock exchanges themselves. Finally there also existed a vast and somewhat diffuse OTC market catering for a large number of separate issues of stocks and bonds. This was collectively very important but individually isolated, being maintained by a large number of individual brokers spread throughout the country as well as by direct trading arrangements between major institutional investors. It was almost totally unregulated. Overall this lack of regulation over the various OTC markets and the relative freedom enjoyed by the New York brokerage houses to expand nationwide underpinned the continued growth of the US domestic securities market. Most US stock exchanges other than New York were marginalized due to the intrusive regulation of the SEC and their own rules, and even the New York Stock Exchange only commanded the market in those stocks it quoted. As the SEC largely operated through the regulated stock exchanges, especially that of New York, this process gradually undermined its influence over the securities market as a whole.[24]

THE SECURITIES MARKET OUTSIDE THE
UNITED STATES, 1945–70

In the United States after 1945 a system was established for regulating and controlling the securities market focusing entirely on meeting domestic needs such as investor protection and national financial stability. Less important was the role of the securities market in mobilizing savings for investment or providing a link between the money and capital markets. Warranting even less consideration was the international role of securities markets. In consequence the role of the US securities markets diminished both in terms of its contribution to the domestic economy and to that economy's external financial relations. This meant an enhanced role for self-finance and bank lending, though a huge unregulated OTC market and the activities of large brokerage houses ensured that securities continued to occupy a prominent position within the US economy. However, viewed from an external perspective US developments appeared to be the triumph of government regulation over self-regulation as the market not only continued to function but also appeared more stable and less exposed to manipulation. Consequently, for many countries the United States appeared to provide a model to follow, offering a compromise between market capitalism and state control. There were a number of countries such as the Soviet Union and Eastern Europe generally which went to the other extreme and chose to operate without a securities market at all. In China the communist takeover in 1949 led to the closure of the stock exchanges, with all trading being ended in 1951.[25] Elsewhere the securities markets also decayed when the state took control of corporate assets and financed itself through taxation. In Egypt the securities market had prospered both during the Second World War and into the 1950s, but then experienced a severe decline in the 1960s due to a nationalization programme.[26] Similarly, in Indonesia the securities market revived after 1945 but nationalization in 1958 and then the departure of many of the Dutch expatriates who had generated much of the activity left only a small and informal market in the 1960s.[27]

Nevertheless, most countries which already possessed a securities market retained it after the Second World War, though modifying its organization and regulation to suit post-war conditions. In Latin America there were securities markets in all the major economies with Buenos Aires, Rio de Janeiro, and São Paulo among the most important. Most of these stock exchanges, and the regulations that covered them, were largely modelled on US practice adopted in the post-war years. The resulting system suffered increasingly from the competition of the unregulated OTC market, where banks, major investors, and large brokerage houses traded with each other free from the constraints of both government regulation and stock exchange rules. Throughout the 1960s the Lima Stock Exchange had difficulty retaining the business even of its own members. In Mexico in 1964 at least 80% of the total trading in listed stocks took place on the OTC market where banks and other financial institutions traded directly with each other. Only the occasional speculative boom, as with a mining discovery, could generate sufficient turnover to maintain an active market on the organized stock exchanges. Most securities tended to be closely held and little traded, making direct negotiation the easiest and cheapest method for arranging transfers.[28]

The post-war years also witnessed a host of new securities markets, especially in the numerous newly independent nations emerging from the ending of empires during the 1950s and 1960s. Stock exchanges were often formed on government initiative and modelled on those in the United States, though Britain, France, and even Germany continued to provide examples to be copied, especially when their own nationals were found in these exchanges. Stock exchanges appeared in such diverse countries as Kenya, the Philippines, South Korea, Taiwan, and Tunisia. The stock exchange formed in Venezuela in 1947 was modelled on the New York Stock Exchange, that in Casablanca in 1967 on the Paris Bourse, that in Lagos in 1960 on the London Stock Exchange, whilst Tel Aviv in 1953 copied German practice.[29] Nigeria typifies the pattern of development. In the 1950s a group of native Nigerians and British expatriates made moves to establish a stock exchange in cooperation with the government. However, there was a lack of active interest from local investors whilst both the government and companies still saw London as the best market for any stocks and bonds they wished to issue. Nevertheless, in 1960 the Lagos Stock Exchange was formed to provide a market for locally issued securities, such as those of the Nigerian Cement Company. In 1961 it commenced business basing its procedures on those of the London Stock Exchange and operating under an act passed by the Nigerian government.[30]

However, despite the appearance of these new stock exchanges, and government efforts to stimulate their use by both investors and borrowers, very little trading in securities developed in most of these countries, even in the 1960s. There remained a lack of locally available savings held by investors willing to purchase stocks and bonds, especially with the departures of so many expatriates after independence. Also, there were few local companies of sufficient size to warrant an issue of securities in the local market as most were too small, whilst the largest ones continued to be owned abroad. Combined with these fundamental problems was the fact that these stock exchanges usually operated under government supervision or control, which greatly restricted the type of business that could be done, especially the speculative activity which had assisted the development of local securities markets in the past. Though governments were keen to promote the formation of securities markets they were not willing to give them the freedom to operate that was necessary if they were to flourish. Even when flourishing markets did develop as in Beirut and Kuwait in the 1960s the resulting structures were either insufficiently robust to withstand the inevitable financial crisis following a speculative boom, or the countries suffered from political instability that undermined progress. One exception was Israel where the securities market began to prosper in the 1960s. However, as a heavily expatriate community containing many bankers, brokers, and experienced investors from Europe it was something of an exception among newly independent nations.[31]

Of all the countries establishing or re-establishing a securities market after the Second World War none was more influenced by the US experience than Japan, as it was under Allied, largely American, military rule from the end of the war until 1949. The securities market was entirely reorganized and stock exchanges not allowed to reopen until they had agreed to implement the changes. A Securities and Exchange Law, almost a literal translation of the US law of 1933–4, was passed in March 1947 and came into force a year later. The single securities exchange established by the Japanese government during the war was dissolved and replaced by individual exchanges in the major cities beginning with Tokyo, Osaka, and Nagoya in May 1949. Their operational rules and regulations were copied from the Pacific Stock exchange in San Francisco, as those of the New York Stock Exchange were deemed to complex even for Tokyo. These rules specifically controlled margin requirements and future trading in order to curtail the possibility of speculation. The combination of bank and securities houses was prohibited and the large trust companies, the Zaibatsu, were broken up with their holdings of corporate securities redistributed to individual investors between 1947 and 1950. As in the US model, the aim of the American military regime was not only to reduce the risks inherent in the securities market but also to limit its power.

After the departure of the American authorities in 1949 the Japanese government abandoned or reversed some of the measures that had been introduced and re-established some of the pre-war practices. During the 1950s the antitrust laws were relaxed whilst trading based on bank borrowing was reintroduced, helping to stimulate more market activity in the second-half of the decade. The controls introduced by the American authorities stifled the growth of the Japanese securities market in the post-war years even though it had been one of the most dynamic in Asia since the late nineteenth century. It was not until these controls were relaxed that the market started to recover, which it did towards the end of the 1950s. The number of Japanese investors rose from 2 million in 1952 to 6 million in 1969 whilst the value of securities in circulation rose from 1.8 billion yen to 298.5 billion, and from 26% to 48% of GNP, over the same period. As the government itself issued no new bonds between 1945 and 1965 corporate securities were one of the few investments readily available, especially with the need of Japanese business to raise finance for expansion. These changes were reflected in the securities market with trading on the Tokyo Stock Exchange growing from 1.3 million shares per day in 1949 to 70.9 million in 1959 and then to 130.4 million in 1963. These transactions were largely channelled to Tokyo by a small number of large brokerage houses operating on a nationwide basis. Even before the Second World War Japanese brokers, like Daiwa, Nikko, Nomura, and Yamaichi were already establishing branch networks to retail government and corporate bonds. This was expanded after 1949. Whereas the number of securities firms fell from 1,152 in 1949 to 255 in 1968, the number of offices remained the same, at around 1,800. By 1960 these four leading firms were responsible for 65% of stock transactions compared to 33% in 1953. The result was a gradual decline in the importance of the regional stock exchanges as Tokyo became ever more dominant. In 1970 Tokyo handled 72% of the total volume of trading, compared to 63% in 1960 whereas Osaka fell from 29% to 20% over the same period. Tokyo was already emerging as the premier financial centre in Japan in the post-war years as that was where the government was based and the major financial institutions were located. Considering the influence of government over the securities market in post-war Japan there was a gravitational pull in the direction of the centre in which it was located, Tokyo, and away from Yokohama, which had previously been of equal importance. Unlike administrative cities such as Washington, Ottawa, or Canberra, Tokyo was a large and established commercial and financial centre, and so capable of supporting an active securities market. Tokyo's importance in the securities market was also enhanced by the growing power of the Japanese financial institutions located there in the 1950s and 1960s, through their ownership of stocks and bonds. Institutions held 39% of listed stocks in 1950 but 57% in 1970.

An active OTC market did not develop in Japan due to a legal rule that all listed securities had to be traded on a recognized stock exchange. There had been an active OTC market in the years when the stock exchanges were closed after the Second World War, but that disappeared on their reopening. It then re-appeared with the revival of the securities market from the mid-1950s, when many unlisted securities appeared. However, knowing that they had a monopoly of listed securities, the Japanese stock exchanges opened separate sections from 1961 to cater for the less actively traded stocks and bonds. In1963 OTC turnover in Japan was only 0.2% of that of the Tokyo Stock

Exchange. However, this action did sap vitality from the Japanese securities market as all trading went through the organized markets with their high listing requirements, fixed commission charges, and bureaucratic methods of arranging sales and purchases. In the absence of an active OTC market the costs and regulations attached to the issue and subsequent trading of new issues in small or untried companies were raised to prohibitive levels in certain cases. Japanese business was therefore forced to rely heavily on bank finance. Banks themselves were major issuers of bonds, accounting for 18% of those in circulation in 1969. These provided them with a ready source of finance, which could then be lent to customers.

Prior to the mid-1960s corporate issues of stocks and bonds were of growing importance, so reducing the reliance upon bank finance and self-generated funds. However, the collapse of the corporate bond market in 1962 and of the Japanese stock market in 1965 led to a renewal of government controls to protect investors. The government itself also began to issue bonds in order to fund its growing expenditure. Domestic bonds in circulation, which had only risen from 241 billion yen in 1950 to 446 billion in 1960 and then escalated to 3.6 trillion in 1970. Though most of these bonds were traded directly between and within the banks and brokers, a market was established on the Tokyo Stock Exchange from 1966 onwards. Tightened regulations and the government's own borrowing limited the issue of securities by Japanese companies until after 1970, forcing them to rely more upon bank loans. No matter what the risks involved in making long-term loans to their corporate customers, banks were confident that the Japanese central bank, the Bank of Japan, would act as the lender of last resort in the event of any serious defaults on their loans. Consequently, the post-war development in Japan of strong bank/business links, and the risks attached to excessive long-term lending were an accidental by-product of the way the securities market was organized and regulated. The post-war American administration had tried to stop this happening. Unfortunately, the monopoly given to the organized stock exchanges and their use by the government as instruments for its supervision and regulation of the securities market did just that. Whereas securities market had been important sources of corporate finance in Japan before the war they ceased to be afterwards, having been replaced by retained earnings, bank loans, and corporate networks. This can be traced directly to the monopoly given to the organized stock exchanges and the costly and rigid government regulations.[32]

Given the geographical proximity of the two countries and the similarity in the structure of their stock exchanges, it might have been expected that US developments would exert a strong influence on the post-war Canadian securities market. However, the Canadian government was reluctant to introduce the elaborate regulatory regime found in the United States, deeming it largely unnecessary. Recognizing that the Canadian economy was much more dependent on resource-based companies than the United States, there was an unwillingness to discourage the speculative activity though which mineral and oil exploration and development were financed. Instead the securities market was left to police itself. The government bond market, which had grown because of issues made during the war, was supervised by the Investment Dealers Association. The market for listed stocks was regulated by the stock exchanges such as Toronto and Montreal, whilst responsibility for the OTC market, where the most speculative issues were found, lay with the Broker Dealers Association. There also existed government regulation at the provincial level, such as the Ontario Securities Commission.

On the whole this self-regulation worked relatively well, providing each market was provided with a regulatory system that fitted its requirements in terms of the participants involved, the securities traded, the way business was conducted, and the needs of the clients. During the 1950s the Toronto Stock Exchange became the leading market for mining and oil stocks in north America, helped by restrictions imposed in the United States compared to the relative freedom it enjoyed. Trading in such securities provided around 40% of the value of trading on the Toronto Stock Exchange in 1961, establishing it as the leading stock exchange in Canada rather than Montreal. Following public complaints after every speculative outburst and a number of fraudulent mining and financial companies, both the stock exchange and the government began to tighten control over the securities market in the 1960s. This was despite the fact that the greatest excesses were to be found in the unregulated OTC market. The Canadian government was also under pressure from the SEC in the United States to improve the supervision of its securities market. A number of dubious brokers from the United States had based their operations in Canada so as to escape the control imposed by the SEC.

What brought the issue to a head was the threat from some of the largest and most respectable Canadian mining and oil companies to list on the New York Stock Exchange. Major international companies such as INCO, Imperial Oil, and Noranda were concerned that association with the speculative mining stocks traded on the in-house curb market of the Toronto Stock Exchange would undermine their value in the eyes of investors. The Toronto Stock Exchange therefore closed its in-house curb market in 1962, and succeeded in remaining the principal market for the stocks and bonds issued by the largest Canadian companies, occupying a similar role in that country as the New York Stock Exchange did in the United States. The speculative market in mining and oil stocks survived by changing venue, and re-emerged in Vancouver. By buying seats on the Vancouver Stock Exchange major Canadian brokers could transact their clients' business there even though the stocks were no longer listed in Toronto. Turnover on the Vancouver Stock Exchange rose from 21.3 million shares in 1960, with a value of $40.5 million, to 755.7 million shares, and a value of $1.1 billion in 1969.

In Canada a single national securities market had emerged in the post-war years which allowed local exchanges like Vancouver to reinvent themselves as specialist markets catering for companies and investors from across the country. Increasingly, this process was not confined to Canada but extended to the whole of north America. The major US brokers did not see the border as a barrier and so extended their operations into that country both by opening offices and by buying seats on the various stock exchanges. Regarding this as a threat to their livelihood, Canadian brokers tried to resist the American tide by refusing to admit any more US firms as members after 1960. They also faced an internal threat from the Canadian financial institutions excluded from membership as they attempted to avoid or minimize the payment of commission fees. Pressure from these institutions forced the Canadian stock exchanges to agree a common scale of charges in 1967 as well as offer volume discounts. The Canadian government endorsed the anti-competitive measures of the stock exchanges as it was through them that it policed at least part of the domestic securities market, for the bond market and OTC trading remained unregulated.[33]

Though its economy was on the wane and its empire in decline Britain remained a major influence in the world, with the London Stock Exchange second only in importance to New York during the 1950s and 1960s. In Britain after 1945 an informal arrangement slowly emerged whereby the London Stock Exchange was entrusted with the management of the securities market within a framework set by the government. The more the London Stock Exchange complied with government demands the more it was allowed to restore market practices, because it was trusted to police their use and limit their abuse. Though this informal control might appear a more flexible arrangement than direct intervention, backed by the power of the law, it also had major disadvantages. Principally, it encouraged a high degree of caution. The merest hint of disapproval from the Bank of England, whether acting on its own or on behalf of the Treasury, was sufficient to discourage the London Stock Exchange from pressing ahead with any contemplated changes. The actual or perceived requirements of the government or the Bank of England were now all important. In return, the London Stock Exchange acquired a semi-monopolistic position within the British securities market. This was the other major disadvantage of this system of informal control, in that the London Stock Exchange exploited its position for the benefit of its members through the maintenance of a regime of fixed commission charges, barriers to entry, and restrictive regulations. In particular, it was able to delay the forces of change that were gradually transforming the British securities market in the 1950s and 1960s. However, informal control did have its benefits in that it provided a relatively successful means of policing the securities market and ensuring that the effects of financial crises were minimized. Both the devaluation of the £sterling in November 1967 and the gold crisis of March 1968 passed off with little more than a brief one-day closure.

However, the London Stock Exchange was not immune from competition, as it possessed no monopoly within the securities market. During the 1950s and 1960s the London Stock Exchange's control over various segments of the securities market was gradually eroded. The volume of business generated by financial institutions in the 1950s and 1960s was such that they sought to either trade at reduced commission rates or buy and sell on a net basis. As membership of the London Stock Exchange was only available to those operating solely as brokers and dealers, and then only to partnerships and not companies, financial institutions such as banks could not gain direct access to the dealers by joining. In consequence there was a leakage of business from the London Stock Exchange as large financial institutions dealt with each other both in government debt and in corporate securities. In addition, the provincial stock exchanges took advantage of the improvements in telecommunications to enhance their ability to compete with London, as they sought an alternative to the diminishing activity in local stocks for local investors. The London Stock Exchange could not prevent provincial brokers gaining access to its current prices via the telephone whilst the formation of regional stock exchanges in the mid-1960s, like the Scottish and the Northern, allowed them to trade easily between each other.

The trading-floor provided by the London Stock Exchange remained of major importance. Institutions often hesitated to deal directly with each other, because of what it revealed, whilst the telephone system lacked the capacity and the flexibility to cope with many users trying to contact each other at the same time in active markets. It best served the broker or investor trying to negotiate a particular deal. At the same time the practice of offering discounts and sharing commission was sufficient to persuade most large investors to channel their business through members of the London Stock Exchange as the ready market in major stocks maintained by the dealers was difficult to replicate. Consequently, the London Stock Exchange was relatively successful in retaining its domestic market. Unlike the US situation it did not face the invasive supervision of a SEC. In Britain power still remained with the central market located on the London Stock Exchange. This marked a fundamental divide in this period between the US securities market and those in Britain and many other countries, even though the fundamental forces at work were very similar, such as the rising importance of corporate stocks and the increasing ownership of securities by financial institutions. The result was a strong centralizing tendency in the post-war securities market in Britain, which even the restrictions imposed by the London Stock Exchange could not halt.

This tendency had consequences for the economy as a whole. As the London Stock Exchange was entrusted with weeding out any securities that might be worthless or fraudulent it became a market only for the stocks and bonds of established companies with a proven earnings record. There was also a reluctance to restore methods of trading that might be seen as speculation such as the use of options. Consequently, it was only slowly and partially that the London Stock Exchange restored those trading practices attractive to both speculative new companies and those operating on borrowed money. Self-finance, generated from reinvested profits, was the source of around 90% of the funds used even by quoted companies. Post-war nationalization of major sectors of the economy removed whole categories of securities from the London Stock Exchange, such as railways and utilities providing electricity, gas, and water. Members of the London Stock Exchange became ever more dependent on trading in UK government debt for their livelihood. An estimate for 1949 suggested that 85% of the turnover on the London Stock Exchange was in UK government debt. That position gradually changed in the 1950s and 1960s. With persistent and rising inflation, and a build-up of private savings looking for investment, there was growing resistance to holding only fixed interest securities. Both institutional and individual investors began to switch to corporate stocks as an alternative. In 1950 56% of the company securities issued were in the form of debt compared to 36% in ordinary shares. By 1955 the position had already been reversed, with 65% in ordinary shares. In response to this demand, rather than as a means of raising extra capital, a growing number of businesses in Britain converted themselves into public companies and sold shares to investors. As institutional investors in particular preferred large issues from large companies, because of their liquidity, this process created large national enterprises whose stocks were traded on the London Stock Exchange. In 1969, 85% of commission income was generated by the buying and selling of domestic corporate stocks.

Even in Australia which, like Canada, adopted many US stock exchange practices in the post-war years, there was no rapid move to introduce a SEC. Certainly wartime controls were only slowly relaxed with some not ending until the early 1950s, especially those relating to forward trading and bank lending, but the stock exchanges were then left to regulate themselves. The slow return to peacetime trading practices was thus only partly the responsibility of the government for the stock exchanges themselves were allowed to decide on such matters as methods of business. In this the Sydney Stock Exchange proved much more dynamic than Melbourne, where the membership wished to maintain the less risky wartime trading environment when such activities as forward trading and short selling were banned. The Sydney Stock Exchange reintroduced short-selling in 1953, combining it with a move to the US system of trading posts rather than the more cumbersome call-over. In contrast, the Melbourne Stock Exchange was slow to change, only abandoning the call-over in 1961–2 compared to 1953–4 in Sydney. Similarly, the Sydney Stock Exchange was quick to adopt advances in communication technology, and captured a growing share of the buying and selling of securities in Australia in the 1950s and 1960s. This included the speculative business in mining and oil stocks which came to dominate Australian securities trading in the late 1960s, compared to that in industrial stocks and government loans, which had been of prime importance after 1945 and through the 1950s.

The Sydney Stock Exchange's aggressive embrace of US practices and new technology gave it leadership of an increasingly integrated Australian securities market, largely at the expense of Melbourne. Competition between the various Australian stock exchanges forestalled the growth of a large and active OTC market despite the increasing power of financial institutions such as banks and insurance companies in the ownership of securities. On one or another of the Australian stock exchanges there was a response to the needs of both investors in and issuers of securities as no single one had a semi-monopoly reinforced by the power of the state. Instead there existed both cooperation between the stock exchanges, as with common listing rules in 1964, and competition as an all-Australian securities market developed. Securities continued to be important within the Australian financial system, both to investors and to companies seeking to raise finance. Between 1959 and 1967 Australian public companies drew 26% of their finance from new issues compared to 52% from internal sources and 22% from the likes of bank loans. This combination of British self-regulation and US trading and membership practices, within a competitive environment, appeared to ensure a continued importance for the securities market within Australia between 1950 and 1970.[34]

Similarly, in New Zealand the relaxation of wartime controls saw a gradual return to normal trading in the 1950s under a system of self-regulation. A combination of government borrowing at all levels, and the issue of corporate stocks and bonds, ensured an active securities market. A New Zealand government loan for £20 million in 1950 was taken up by 11,000 investors domestically, indicating the ability of the local market to absorb whatever securities were made available. Though London continued to be used for the very largest government issues, even these were now shared with the local market, so generating a considerable volume of activity.[35] In contrast, in South Africa an Act passed in 1947 gave the government legal control over the securities market through the stock exchange. As every broker had to be a member of a stock exchange, and the stock exchange was responsible for policing the market, from membership to listing, this Act gave the Johannesburg Stock Exchange a virtual monopoly of the South African securities market. Along with a turnover tax on securities introduced in 1948 this monopoly led to rather depressed trading conditions in the 1950s. Entrusted with the regulation of the entire securities market the Johannesburg Stock Exchange took a very cautious attitude to listing new stocks whilst it also took the opportunity to support its members' interests. A regime of fixed commission charges was policed and no corporate membership was allowed. Illustrative of the lack of change was the fact that the call-over system continued until 1969. As the gold-mining industry was experiencing difficulties in the 1950s because of low output prices and rising costs of production, these additional costs and burdens were sufficient to suppress investor interest. Nevertheless, in spite of these controls the Johannesburg Stock Exchange experienced boom conditions from the late 1950s and throughout the 1960s as demand for gold-mining stocks increased enormously due to monetary instability. As all South African brokers had to be members of a stock exchange there was no scope for the growth of an OTC market, and the Johannesburg Stock Exchange was able to maintain its control despite its charges, restrictions, and trading systems. There was little alternative to its market in South African securities, especially gold mining stocks, and investors had to accept its rules and regulations if they wanted to participate. During 1968–9 the market value of stocks quoted on the Johannesburg Stock Exchange doubled, suggesting that the charges and difficulties were worth accepting.[36]

The British model of self-regulation was also to be found throughout Asia. Though the newly independent Indian government appointed a commission in 1948 to investigate the securities market, only in 1957 did its recommendations became law. Principally, trading in securities could only be conducted through recognized stock exchanges. Otherwise the government left stock exchanges to police both themselves and the securities market. Although many which had flourished during the Second World War had withered away or become moribund during the difficult post-war years, this still left stock exchanges in Ahmedabad, Bombay, Calcutta, Delhi, Hyderabad, Indore, and Madras. Bangalore was added in 1963. Each operated under their own rules, which were similar to those of British stock exchanges, but they had to be approved by the government. The one exception to the monopoly exercised by the stock exchanges over the Indian securities market was trading in government bonds. These did not attract general investor interest, because of the low yield, and were held exclusively by banks and large financial institutions. These dealt directly with the Reserve Bank of India or through a small number of brokers in Bombay, Calcutta, and Madras. As the average size of each transaction was so large each was handled by direct negotiation between the parties concerned rather than through the normal market mechanism. This left the Indian stock exchanges to compete for business in corporate securities. Bombay was the most important as it traded securities of interest to investors across India whilst the others provided a market for local specialities, such as jute, tea, and mining companies in Calcutta. Even Bombay had a speciality, providing a forum for trading the stocks of Indian textile and steel companies. However, many corporate securities were closely held and little traded. Nevertheless, the relative freedom the Indian stock exchanges enjoyed compared to those in Pakistan contributed to the existence of an active securities market, with some 2 million investors by the early 1960s. In contrast, the Lahore stock exchange closed in the post-war trading slump and government restrictions prevented the Pakistan securities market from reviving in the 1950s and 1960s.[37]

The demise of the Shanghai Stock Exchange created an opportunity for those in Hong Kong. Although two had existed before the Second World War they reopened as one in 1946 and provided a market for the stocks of many of the leading companies once traded in Shanghai. Most members of this stock exchange were expatriates and they operated on the British self-regulatory pattern with very little control being exercised by the Hong Kong authorities. However, the Hong Kong Stock Exchange attracted very little business during the 1950s as the few existing stocks were held by a small number of wealthy investors. Only in the 1960s did the market begin to grow as Hong Kong's economy expanded, though the greatest advances were made in banking and foreign exchange trading not securities markets. Another stock exchange, the Far Eastern Exchange, was formed in 1969 to cater for those, mainly Hong Kong Chinese, excluded from the established market. This suggests that the Hong Kong Stock Exchange and its membership had done little to develop an active securities market beyond the expatriate population. Consequently, the Hong Kong securities market only began to make an impact at the end of the 1960s. In contrast, in another British colony, Malaysia, a relatively active securities market developed under government regulations. This market attracted sufficient interest from local investors to sustain trading floors in both Kuala Lumpur and Singapore. US trading practices, such as trading posts, also gradually replaced British ones.[38]

In most of continental Europe the state had long played a major role in the operation of the securities market including the supervision and even ownership of stock exchanges. Given the post-war emphasis on public accountability and national interest it was only to be expected that this situation would continue, with European governments intervening even more in the operation of their domestic securities markets. The Second World War had produced an enormous increase in state involvement in domestic securities markets and, once established, such controls were unlikely to be abandoned even with a change of government. In those Eastern European countries which fell under Soviet control securities markets ceased to operate even where they had survived the war.

However, Germany did see an end to the central control of the securities market that had begun with the Nazis in the 1930s. This reflected the desire among the Western allies to dismantle the power of the German state. It was even debated whether the German financial system required a centre at all given that Berlin was now deep in Soviet-controlled East Germany. With Berlin deemed unacceptable and a need to locate the central bank somewhere else, Hamburg was poised to become the new financial centre. It was favoured by the British, in whose zone it was located, and by the Germans, whilst it had a strong pedigree as a major commercial centre with an international orientation. The Reichsbank already had a regional office in Hamburg and the stock exchange there had been reopened shortly after the end of the war. However, Hamburg's major disadvantage was that it was not in the American zone. Frankfurt was, and accordingly became in 1948, the new location for the central bank and subsequently the financial centre of West Germany. This process took time. In the early 1950s Dusseldorf was a more important financial centre than Frankfurt because of its status in industrial finance. Only when German banks established their head offices in Frankfurt in the 1950s did the city began to establish itself as the financial centre of the country.

However, Frankfurt did not dominate the securities market. Control over the various stock exchanges was returned to the provincial authorities after 1945 rather than being placed with the government in Bonn or the central bank in Frankfurt. Each German stock exchange therefore enjoyed a great deal of autonomy in the post-war years and an integrated securities market developed only slowly. There was no attempt to recreate the various German stock exchanges in the American image or to impose a US-style SEC as in Japan. In any case, the German post-war securities market was slow to revive.

Though the Frankfurt Stock Exchange resumed business in September 1945, this was only on an informal basis and it was not until August 1948 that official trading began. Similarly, the Dusseldorf Stock Exchange did not reopen until 1949 and Berlin in 1952. The level of business remained very limited until a measure of financial and monetary stability returned to Germany in the mid-1950s. Only then had incomes recovered sufficiently for investors to contemplate buying, selling, and holding securities in any volume, given the destruction of savings during the war. In the meantime the government itself relied on foreign aid for reconstruction whilst German business financed itself from re-invested earnings. When recovery did begin to gather pace in the 1950s banks collected the growing savings and lent them to business. In contrast the stock exchanges were hampered both by external controls on their methods of operation and by a system of self-regulation that fragmented and depressed the securities market. The ban on the forward trading of shares, which had been in force since 1931, was not lifted until 1970 and then only partially. The absence of a strong and long-established financial centre, where a dominant stock exchange was located, compounded this problem as there was no natural focus for trading in stocks and bonds as was the case in Britain, France, and the United States. Instead there was a proliferation of stock exchanges each operating under their own regulations, and backed by regional governments, that also imposed further rules. Though there was trading between these stock exchanges their independence and regional support hampered the creation of a single integrated securities market.

Active trading on and between the various German stock exchanges became commonplace only in the 1960s. Even then the securities market remained weak. Its fragmented nature produced thin and volatile markets rather than the deep and broad ones favoured by institutional investors in particular. Under these circumstances banks dominated the German financial system, as they had in the past, with the large universal banks providing the whole range of services required by borrowers and savers alike. This included control over the securities market, where their membership of the stock exchanges allowed them to almost monopolize trading. Two-thirds of the investment finance utilized by corporate Germany came from internal sources between 1950 and 1969, with most of the rest provided by banks. Even in the 1960s there was a limited use of stocks and bonds by business with those issued being closely held by a few wealthy individuals, banks, and corporate networks. Only in a few of the very largest companies were shares widely held by individual investors, and they controlled only around one-third of the total in the 1960s. With continuing low inflation in Germany there was little pressure from investors for companies to issue stocks for purchase, as they were content with bank deposits and bonds.[39]

In contrast to Germany the French government not only retained but extended central control over the securities market during the 1950s and 1960s. In 1961 the Coulisse and Parquet were merged, so vesting all authority in the state-controlled Paris Bourse. In 1962 the Paris Bourse obtained a virtual monopoly over the entire French securities market as dual listing was banned. This had helped preserve business on regional exchanges faced with a declining trade in local securities for local investors, as they were able to provide a competing market in a number of nationally traded stocks. Deprived of the ability to do so, these local exchanges lost any significant role within the securities market. In 1966 a single organization was created under the control of the Paris Bourse, leaving the state in full charge of the entire national securities market. Consequently, in the post-war years the French government ensured that the securities market served purely national needs, especially those of the state itself. In 1963 60% of bond issues in Paris were on behalf of the government or major state-owned enterprises. The securities market was highly regulated, with every attempt made to eliminate those practices leading to speculation or deemed unacceptable. As many of these were also an integral part of a successful and efficient securities market the result was to reduce the attractions of securities either to raise finance or employ savings. Consequently, French business relied on reinvested profits and bank loans for its funding.[40]

What happened in France was fairly typical of the position across continental Europe, for everywhere experienced an enormous increase in the level of state involvement. This ranged from rigid regulation of stock exchanges, as in Belgium, to the position in Italy where brokers were made public officials in 1967. Inevitably the focus in securities markets turned upon trading government debt, so encouraging business to rely on self-finance, inter-company arrangements, and bank loans. Only in the 1960s, with growing investor interest in corporate stocks, did most national securities markets experience much of a recovery, and that was not universally so as high taxes and restrictive regulations continued to blunt the issue and purchase of corporate stocks.[41] The Amsterdam Stock Exchange exemplifies this transformation of European securities markets. From being one of those least affected by government controls before 1939, the wartime era of statutory control introduced under the Germans lasted until 1953, and only in 1954 were normal trading arrangements again in operation. Nationalization of the Nederlandische Bank in 1948 had given the government direct power over the entire financial system, ushering in a much more interventionist era. The government deliberately created barriers between short-term credit and long-term capital, and intervened in order to protect investors, prevent the evasion of taxes, safeguard exchange control, and ensure that its own ability to borrow was given priority. Between 1952 and 1970 the Dutch public debt rose from 8.4 billion guilders to 23.5 billion.

This undermined the ability of the securities market to operate as a channel between Dutch savers and corporate borrowers. Instead, primacy was given to trading the national debt whilst banks became much more central to the Dutch financial system. Internal financing also became a more prominent source of business finance. Only gradually, with rising inflation, did stocks experience rising popularity among both investors and companies, especially in the1960s. Between 1960 and 1970 turnover on the Amsterdam Stock Exchange, which had doubled in the 1950s, grew from1.9 billion guilders to 15.5 billion by which time two-thirds was in stocks and only one-third in bonds. As elsewhere, the growing importance of institutional investors and the increased size of stock-broking firms led to the progressive erosion of the power of the central market as more deals were matched internally or through private negotiation. As elsewhere, government attempts to regulate the market in the Netherlands had achieved the same object of undermining its importance. Only continued state borrowing, combined with inflation, which was also a product of government action, sustained the securities market.[42]

In the aftermath of the 1930s' depression and the Second World War financial markets were out of fashion, whilst governments were regarded as economic saviours. Where securities markets still functioned, governments had a mandate for control that went way beyond the eradication of market abuse and fraudulent practices. It extended to a system of supervision and intervention that both transformed stock exchanges into executive arms of the state and restricted their ability to fully respond to the needs of investors and borrowers. Inevitably, governments acted in their own self-interest when intervening in the securities markets, ensuring that their borrowing requirements were given precedence and that activities in the securities markets did not conflict with policy aims. Governments were not impartial bystanders ensuring fair play for investors and borrowers but active participants with a vested interest in the way securities markets operated. The same was true of stock exchanges, as the mechanism through which governments exercised control over the securities market. As distinct organizations, stock exchanges were also driven by a degree of self-interest, which in the past had been moderated by the threat of competition. However, with the additional power they now possessed either from specific legislation or through formal or informal government support, stock exchanges enhanced their position. This allowed them to adopt or maintain a wide range of restrictive practices justifiable on regulatory grounds, such as a fixed scale of charges, restricted access to the market, and risk-free modes of operation without fearing a loss of business or the appearance of rivals. Regulated securities market then lost out to the unregulated as controls, restrictions, and charges were avoided and minimized by those in a position to do so. This was a worldwide phenomenon after 1945.

An uneasy relationship had always existed between organized and unorganized components within the securities market. The former imposed both costs and discipline on its participants but, in return, provided a better market in terms of contact and certainty, which made it worth paying for and accepting the common rules and regulations. However, as participants in the market themselves grew in size and could impose their own discipline, as with financial institutions, the value of the organized market was eroded and the transaction charges not fully justified. The latter involved no costs or discipline and the market provided was inadequate and uncertain, being prone to both counter-party risk and opaque pricing. However, the growing importance of large financial institutions as buyers and sellers greatly reduced counter-party risk whilst office-to-office telecommunications provided an alternative means for transacting business and broadcasting prices. Here the absence of rules and regulations, including those relating to minimum commission charges, was an advantage as terms and conditions could be adjusted to suit the business being done. Such flexibility was further enhanced if the organized market was heavily regulated by the state whilst the unorganized one was not, as the burden of compliance could be avoided. Consequently, though an obvious solution to the problem of market supervision and control appeared to be through the use of the existing organized exchanges, as they already regulated the activities of their members, this was limited both in time and scope. If stock exchanges were given a monopoly of the market, the more they would use their position to advance the interests of their members through the exclusion of competitors and the increase in charges. If stock exchanges were not given a monopoly of the market, the less effective they would be in regulating it, as buyers and sellers of securities would seek to avoid its restrictions and charges. Somewhere between these two positions existed a compromise that met the needs of the market as a whole considering the diversity of securities, participants, and trades. Unfortunately, there is no evidence that these complexities were recognized in the post-war years when the response to any of the problems, fluctuations, and abuses in the securities market appeared to be control by the state to a greater or lesser degree.

More generally, in the long-run these actions by both government and the stock exchanges gradually undermined the operational efficiency of the securities market as a whole, encouraging those seeking to raise funds or employ savings to look elsewhere. Thus, in many countries securities markets were relatively quiescent in the 1950s and 1960s, such as in Chile and Turkey. Even where new stock exchanges were established the amount of trading taking place there was in most cases very limited, and more a symbol of national independence than the product of an active securities market. Hence there arose the importance of governments, banks, and large companies in the provision of finance in the post-war years. Instead of lessening over time the degree of intervention grew as state control became the preferred solution to either speculative surges or capital market imperfections. There was no recognition that the regimes under which securities markets were forced to operate constrained and distorted the entire financial system. The slow recovery in securities markets during the 1950s and 1960s owed most not to the needs of borrowers, whether government or corporate, but to the needs of investors, both institutional and individual, to diversify their savings into assets that could cope with the ravages of inflation. This produced a revival in many domestic securities markets during the 1960s as corporate stocks rose rapidly in value, being seen as inflation proof assets.[43]

THE INTERNATIONAL SECURITIES MARKET, 1945–70

Access to national securities markets was a privilege jealously guarded by governments in the post-war years. The importance given to stock exchanges by governments seeking to regulate their domestic securities markets turned their focus inward. Instead of attempting to promote the interests of their members by attracting business in securities from all over the world, their prime role was to supervise the domestic securities market and the actions of their own members within it. Preserving their own position within this securities market was now fundamental to their existence rather than providing an active and orderly securities market that was attractive to as many investors and issuers as possible. National securities markets served domestic investors and borrowers leaving others to cater for the international dimension, especially governments themselves, along with international agencies and multinational companies.

Reflecting this state of affairs was the widespread maintenance of exchange controls after 1945. These enabled governments to insulate their national economies from the rest of the world, and so escape the consequences of their own actions in the short run. Internal interest rates and the international value of a national currency were set by government, irrespective of comparative economic performance or the consequences of excessive borrowing and spending. Exchange controls were a necessity in the immediate aftermath of the war as individual countries tried to cope with the economic chaos left in its wake, and some balance was restored to the international value of currencies. Any attempt to relax controls at an unrealistic rate simply prompted a massive outflow of funds, as the British government discovered in 1947. Some stability in the relative value of the major currencies of the world was achieved only gradually, involving the devaluation of the franc in 1948 and the £ in 1949 as well as various inter-government agreements and interventions in the 1950s, such as the European Payments Union. It was not until 1958 that the major European countries agreed to make their currencies freely convertible into dollars.

Even then government control and intervention in the foreign exchange market remained, aimed especially at the international mobility of capital. Governments also employed devices other than foreign exchange to restrict outflows or inflows of funds. The German government banned the purchase of foreign securities until 1956, whilst in the 1960s both the United States and Switzerland, which possessed the two strongest currencies in the world, restricted external access to their financial markets in order to protect themselves from destabilizing financial flows. It was not until after 1970 that governments began to remove these controls over the international movement of money. Consequently, during the entire period from 1945 until the 1970s international financial relations were subjected to government control in a variety of ways. Naturally, such controls were not compatible with the operation of a global securities market. For much of the early post-war years the international flow of funds was achieved at the inter-government level rather than through the market, as seen in the Marshall Aid scheme whereby the US government provided war-torn economies with the funds essential both to rebuild and to make dollar purchases on the world market. Between 1948 and 1952 around $13 billion was distributed to western Europe and a further $1.2 billion to Japan. By 1953 total US aid to Japan amounted to $4.4 billion. Subsequent inter-government cooperation and the actions of such bodies as the World Bank and the IMF played an important role in managing and directing the flow of funds between countries. In business it was the financial decisions taken by the boards running the growing number of multinational companies that determined the allocation of capital around the world rather the actions of investors in the securities markets. Direct corporate investment replaced portfolio investment, with much of the expenditure financed out of reinvested earnings rather than the issue of new stocks and bonds that could then be traded on securities markets at home and abroad.[44]

Thus the post-1945 global securities market operated in an environment of intrusive government controls both domestically and internationally. It was also a time when the US government, and to a lesser extent the Canadian government, took responsibility for providing the world with the dollars it so desperately required. Consequently, New York emerged as the most important financial centre in the world but at a time when the role it might have been expected to play was both supplanted and constrained by the actions of government, especially that of the United States itself. Nevertheless, given the strength of the US economy, the prosperity of the American people and the international importance of the dollar, foreign borrowers turned to New York in search of funds which were not available on an intra-government basis. The first international bond issue after the Second World War was made in New York in 1947 on behalf of the World Bank. It took time for such issues to build up but between 1955 and 1962 new foreign securities totalling $4.2 billion were sold in New York. These securities were taken not just by US investors for European debt issued in New York but were also bought by European investors attracted by the denomination in $s, which was now displacing the £ as the universal currency. These bonds were then actively traded in New York on an OTC basis within a slowly re-emerging global securities market.

However, large as the amounts appear they were tiny in comparison to either past flows or inter-government aid. They also bordered on insignificance in comparison to domestic issues of securities in the United States, which over the same period totalled $126.5 billion, or a sum thirty times greater. Given the size and importance of the post-war US economy, the bankers and brokers of New York were little interested in overseas opportunities. This was especially so for the heavily regulated New York Stock Exchange. It was 1957 before the first overseas stocks were listed whilst foreigners were not accepted as members until 1967. Reflecting this lack of interest was the fact that transactions by foreign investors in US corporate stocks ranged from just 3% to 6% of the total between 1958 and 1968. Combined with the highly restrictive legislation imposed upon the US financial system, which imposed heavy costs upon foreigners issuing securities in New York, this removed both the incentive and the ability of those in New York who might have wished to exploit this international opportunity. With rising inflation the limits placed on the interest payable encouraged not only foreigners to place their money elsewhere but also encouraged US banks and companies to do so. Thus, even before the measures taken in the 1960s to protect the international value of the $, the ability of New York to operate as an international financial centre had been seriously undermined. That position was further worsened by the

Interest Equalisation Tax, introduced in 1963. This increased the cost of raising capital in the United States, forcing both foreign governments and companies to look elsewhere. Consequently, whether from the perspective of investors or issuers New York was not an especially attractive centre for the international securities market and became even less so during the 1960s.[45]

The only other major financial centre still operating in the international field was London, which retained a residual importance because of the imperial legacy and the existence of the sterling area. Even after the end of the Second World War British investors continued to sell foreign securities, which were then repatriated to such countries as Canada, Australia, New Zealand, and South Africa. Even where there were not domestic investors ready to purchase British holdings, as in much of Asia, Africa, and Latin America, US investors were often ready to acquire such securities, particularly those issued by South African gold mines, Malayan rubber plantations, and Latin American utilities. Nationalization was also common abroad with the Argentine government buying its own railway network in 1948 for £150 million. The sale of these foreign securities was not matched by the purchase of others, as foreign exchange controls made it impossible for investors to reinvest abroad. The overseas holdings of British investors fell by an estimated £1.2 billion over the 1938–46 period, and then by a further £0.4 billion by 1948. The exchange control regime also prevented the London Stock Exchange operating as an intermediary market between foreign investors and foreign securities as in the past. Instead of dealing through London in international securities, European investors bought and sold in New York instead. The London Stock Exchange itself became increasingly restrictive on what international business it permitted its members to transact as there was an increasing suspicion that this was responsible for a loss of business.

However, despite exchange controls there was a revival of interest among investors in the 1950s in overseas securities. Institutional investors were keen to diversify away from the heavy commitment to government debt that the Second World War, and post-war nationalizations, had created, with US$ stocks being found attractive because of their high yields and easy marketability. At the same time the presence in London of so many bankers and brokers from continental Europe, especially Jews from Germany, meant that there was a wealth of expertise and connections in London through which international business could be developed. For north American securities there was the long-standing presence of US and Canadian brokerage houses in London, who conducted much of the investment in dollar securities for British investors. However, the London Stock Exchange's own rules, more than exchange controls, continued to hamper the growth of this international business as it was seen to clash with the desire to monopolize the domestic market. Consequently such trading was increasingly conducted outside the stock exchange, including that in South African mining stocks. The admission of foreigners as members of the London Stock Exchange was rejected as late as 1969. International business was simply not regarded as being especially important. What little remained was because the London Stock Exchange was the market for a number of major multinational companies such as the Anglo-Dutch concerns of Unilever and Shell. It was estimated in 1966 that around 350,000 individual US investors had holdings in UK companies, and that was sufficient to support a market in New York in their securities repackaged as American Depository Receipts (ADRs).

These restrictions in London and New York were unfortunate, for the 1960s did see a revival in the international trading of securities, benefiting from the relaxation of exchange controls and continuing improvements in communications. Regular transatlantic flights and an efficient and reliable international telephone service allowed bankers and brokers to visit foreign financial centres whilst keeping in constant touch with home offices. An International Federation of Stock Exchanges was formed in 1962, reflecting these forces of globalization. There developed an entirely new international market in securities, though incorporating many of the features that had existed before the Second World War. Increasing restrictions on the use of the dollar led to a market in dollar-denominated bonds in London. By 1968 it was estimated that 60% of the trading in Euro-Currency Bonds was in London, totalling $15 million per day and handled by a growing number of European banks and US brokerage houses. Merrill Lynch established a London office in 1961, followed in 1963 by Weeden & Co., a New York firm of OTC brokers with an aggressive policy of undercutting existing commission rates.

Eurobonds began as a means of employing idle balances more remuneratively than in the New York, where the interest paid was capped. However, there was a continuing desire to hold such funds in US dollars as the most stable and widely used of the world's currencies. Hence the growth of the Eurodollar markets where banks offered dollar-denominated deposit accounts paying attractive rates of interest. As these had to be located somewhere other than the United States, London became the logical location because of its long-established international banking connections and the lack of control imposed over foreign dollar deposits. Though these rapidly growing funds could be employed in a variety of ways, including through London's traditional role of financing international trade, their existence created a demand for suitable investments such as high yielding but marketable securities. Consequently, in the wake of the Eurodollar market came the Eurobond market. These were bearer bonds denominated in dollars but issued outside the United States and not subject to tax. They were thus ideal investments for those institutions with large dollar-denominated deposits. Bonds of this kind had appeared in Europe in the post-war years to meet investors' needs. In 1949 the Dutch manufacturing firm of Phillips issued dollar bonds, whilst in 1957 the Belgian oil company, Petrofina, made a $5 million Eurobond issue. However, the first proper issue is usually considered to be that of the Italian highways operator Autostrade, made on 1 July 1963 by S. G. Warburg for $15 million. Though Eurobonds could be issued anywhere London emerged as a popular centre, because of the heavy concentration there of banks holding dollar deposits. The trading of these bonds also occurred in London, where the main holders were located even though the funds they used and the issues they bought came from across the world, whilst the transactions were cleared in Brussels and Luxembourg.

The Eurobond market grew rapidly in the 1960s propelled by the build-up of dollar deposits outside the United States and the restrictions placed on foreigners using the New York bond market. However, these early bonds lacked a proper market. Their natural home was the London Stock Exchange but it steadfastly refused to alter its charges and procedures to accommodate this new market, fearing to damage its core business in British corporate stocks and so disadvantage its own members. For much the same reasons no established stock exchange elsewhere in Europe would provide a home for these bonds. Governments did not want their national securities markets to play host to financial instruments designed to evade taxes and regulations. As a result the early Eurobonds were often held until maturity and possessed little by way of a market, so limiting their attractions as investments to financial institutions. Financial institutions wanted securities to buy and sell immediately at prevailing market prices in the quantities they required with minimal inconvenience and without creating any significant change in the market price. To achieve this Eurobonds needed to build up a market of their own as they could not get one through listing on an established stock exchange. This gradually happened during the 1960s as banks located in London increasingly traded these Eurobonds among themselves using the telephone links through which they already operated in the money and foreign exchange markets. Eventually in 1969 the participants formed the Association of International Bond Dealers but the Eurobond market had yet to reach the depth and breadth possessed by such domestic securities markets as that for government bonds or corporate stocks in the United States.[46]

By 1968 it was estimated that there were nineteen New York brokerage houses with branches in London actively competing for business. Their presence, along with the numerous foreign banks that maintained branches in London, meant that during the 1960s London re-emerged as the centre of the global securities market, attracting business from throughout the world including the oil-rich Middle East, the increasingly wealthy Germans, and the US investors constrained by domestic controls. It was these foreign banking and broking firms, with their branch networks, that were now responsible for putting London at the heart of a rapidly growing global securities market in the 1960s.

Restrictions in London had driven international borrowers and investors to New York in the 1950s, also attracted by the prospect of tapping the largest and most abundant supply of funds in the world. Restrictions in New York then drove these borrowers and investors back in the 1960s, as a residual international market still existed. Between 1955 and 1962, when foreign issues in Europe totalled $2.9 billion over a third, or 36%, were made in London despite the attractions of Zurich as a financial centre, with only 30% made there. From the 1960s onwards London re-established its position as the leading financial centre in Europe, particularly with regard to the global securities market. The number of foreign banks with branches in London grew from 53 in 1950 to 159 in 1970, principally during the 1960s. London was increasingly awash with short-term money available for lending or investing. At the very time the actions of the US government were driving financial business away from New York most European governments acted to repel the inflows, with London being the main beneficiary. In the 1960s both Americans and Germans began to conduct much of their international business through London.[47]

In contrast to London, previously important European financial centres like Paris, Amsterdam, and Brussels all turned inward after the Second World War, playing a greatly diminished role in the international securities market. As French investors had disposed of virtually all their foreign securities during and after the war, the securities market was very domestically focused. This continued throughout the 1950s and 1960s as government controls made it difficult for foreigners to access the Paris market, despite the fact that it was the centre of the franc currency zone. Unlike the sterling area this was very limited and included few countries with either idle balances to employ or governments and companies seeking to issue a large volume of securities. The instability of the French franc during the late 1940s and in the 1950s also made Paris unattractive as a financial centre whilst the continuance of capital controls during the more stable decade of the 1960s restricted the use of the franc as a currency for either borrowing or lending. The number of foreign securities quoted on the Paris Bourse fell throughout the period as few new ones appeared to replace those that had been paid off or defaulted on. Many of those quoted were little traded, with what business there was being confined to the stocks issued by a few South African gold mines, a number of European multinationals, like Royal Dutch Shell, and the largest US corporations, like AT & T None of these had their principal market in Paris.

Some attempt was made to develop international business in Paris after the currency conversion in 1958 but to little effect. The French government was reluctant to allow the Paris market to be used by foreigners to raise funds as this could jeopardize both its own ability to raise money cheaply whilst also threatening the stability of the currency. Thus, any relaxation on access was reversed when any crisis occurred, as after 1967. In turn, there was little trading in foreign securities with the situation made even worse by the reluctance of the Paris Bourse to quote foreign securities. The Paris Bourse refused to list the German bank, Commerzbank Bank, in 1962 whilst the London Stock Exchange did agree to do so. It was not until 1971 that it was listed on the Paris Bourse. The Paris Bourse was a poor market for foreign stocks and bonds throughout the 1950s and 1960s. No more than 10% of transactions were in foreign securities during these years, and normally the proportion was very much less.[48]

Both Amsterdam and Brussels also played a much more domestic role in the 1950s and 1960s.[49] In Germany, Frankfurt began to emerge as an international financial centre in the 1950s as the German government was slow to permit its own population to buy foreign securities whilst high interest rates and currency revaluation discouraged foreigners from issuing securities there. By the 1960s these problems had largely disappeared but the government itself acted to prevent Frankfurt becoming an international financial centre, worried by the domestic effects of destabilizing financial flows. In 1965 a tax was imposed on German bonds owned by non-Germans. In stocks it was not until the late 1960s that business in non-German securities became important on the Frankfurt Stock Exchange. These measures not only discouraged the issue of foreign securities in Frankfurt, but also encouraged German investors to use other financial centres, especially Luxembourg and London, when buying and selling securities. The Italian government took similar action in the 1960s, so preventing Milan developing as an international financial centre.[50] Only a few minor countries emerged as important financial centres in post-war continental Europe. Switzerland, in particular, emerged as an important location for the international securities market in the 1950s as it could combine financial sophistication, low taxation and confidential banking with relative openness, and a reasonably large and wealthy pool of domestic investors. The Luxembourg Stock Exchange, which hardly existed before 1939, and the Zurich Stock Exchange, experienced much activity during the 1950s and 1960s when they became important components of the global securities market. However, even the governments of these countries were wary of the risks that such a position created for their domestic economies. Due to a sudden deterioration in the country's external accounts in 1961 the Swiss authorities closed the market to foreign borrowers and, when faced with destabilizing financial flows they put pressure on banks not to accept foreign deposits.[51]

Elsewhere, Tokyo had the opportunity to develop as a major international financial centre in the 1950s and 1960s, given the dramatic growth of the Japanese economy and the demise of Shanghai as the major financial centre in Asia. However, it failed to exploit this opportunity. Not only did the way the Japanese securities market was organized mean that it was domestically focused but controls over capital flows remained even after the foreign exchange market was liberalized. This created opportunities for Hong Kong which increasingly acted as the interface between China and the west in terms of banking and foreign exchange, though much less in terms of the securities markets. In Asia as in Europe, there was a switch to a minor centre due to the controls and restrictions imposed by governments.[52] In fact, the Johannesburg Stock Exchange in South Africa played a more important international role in the global securities market. It was home to the largest concentration of gold mining stocks in the world, which were widely held in South Africa, Europe, and the United States as attractive investments at a time of rising inflation and currency instability. Such stocks were thus actively traded in Johannesburg on foreign orders as well as between major markets in London, Paris, and Brussels, and in north America. Illustrative of the world-wide appeal of these stocks was the fact that most stock exchanges did not open for trading on 15 March 1968 after the closure of the London gold and foreign exchange market, in the wake of the metal breaking through the $35 an ounce barrier.[53]

CONCLUSION

By the end of the Second World War securities markets had become rather marginal appendages within financial systems, with pride of place being given to the actions of governments and banks. Government intervention was seen as the solution to all types of economic problems, whether it was a domestic shortage of finance or the stability of the international monetary system. There was a general continuance of policies forged either during the war or in the depression years into the post-war years. Confidence in these policies was fostered by the fact that the post-1945 years witnessed rapid economic growth and rising prosperity, necessitating only a gradual dismantling of national barriers to international trade and finance. Governments continued to play a major role not only in framing the parameters within which financial systems operated both nationally and internationally but also in controlling their functioning at a quite detailed level. This control extended to the securities markets, which were subject to active government intervention both internationally, with the widespread use of exchange controls, and domestically, where stock exchanges were transformed into semi-official regulatory bodies.

Nevertheless, the barriers that fragmented markets were slowly being eroded in the face of technological advances and growing international liberalization, and this gradually undermined the effectiveness of control at the national level. At the same time the exercise of authority through the formal exchanges had the effect of limiting their command of the very markets they sought to control, so making them less and less effective in that role. When most governments turned stock exchanges into the regulatory arm of the state and introduced deliberate discrimination against foreign borrowers and lenders, it was inevitable that alternative financial markets would develop offering opportunities to evade the restrictions imposed. This had happened domestically with OTC markets, which came to dominate within the United States. Internationally the same phenomena began to appear from the late 1950s. The Eurobond market was a direct successor to the pre-1914 international securities market though it lacked the base it had had then within the organized stock exchanges, and this undermined its ability to compete with its national equivalents.

The systems established in the aftermath of the Second World War slowly unravelled after 1950, as they no longer fitted the changing needs of the global securities markets. In retrospect, the years between 1945 and 1970 represent the high water mark for the power exercised by governments over the global securities market. Such was the strength of that power that even the existence of such markets was outlawed in many countries whilst even those in operation were restricted and marginalized. Conversely, those years represented the modern low water mark for the global securities market for they no longer served a central function with national financial systems whilst internationally their role had been replaced by the actions of governments and bankers. The little remaining importance of the global securities market rested with the continuing need by governments to borrow in order to finance their expenditure and the growing interest among investors in assets that could cope with the destruction in real capital value and real income wrought by inflation.

8

A Transatlantic Revolution: 1970–90

The growth and development of the global securities market in the 1970s and 1980s were marked by two major turning points. The abolition of fixed commissions on the New York Stock Exchange in May 1975 was of crucial significance, putting pressure on other stock exchanges not just within the United States but also around the world. Big Bang in London in October 1986 not only transformed the British securities market but also intensified the pressure for change already experienced by other stock exchanges, especially in Europe. By 1990 the effects of these twin developments were clearly visible worldwide. Securities markets re-emerged as essential components of national financial systems whilst the global securities market once again became a key element in the financial flows that brought stability to the international monetary system. These major turning points at national level were accompanied by significant long-term developments internationally. One, symbolized by the gradual disappearance of exchange controls, was the decline of the barriers between countries imposed by national governments increasingly since 1914. This gave full force to national changes as domestic markets were increasingly exposed to external competition. A second force at work was the convergence of communications and computing technology as these undermined the authority of existing institutional arrangements. Electronic marketplaces provided a real alternative to the regulated stock exchanges as well as contributing to the growth of trading on a global basis. A third force, related to declining barriers and expanding contact, was the process of globalization at all levels. The growing integration of national economies produced a functioning global economy involving the movement of manufactured goods, commodities, services, labour, and capital worldwide in response to the price signals generated by international supply and demand.

This technological convergence in communications and computing permitted a far greater degree of integration than had ever been possible before. Combined with advances in corporate organization and management the communication revolution permitted the creation of financial businesses that treated the world economy as a single unit and operated at a multinational level, as was the case with Citibank, HSBC, and Merrill Lynch. No longer was globalization the preserve of transactions between national businesses and national markets for it now included internal transfers between components of the same company, so threatening the whole concept of sovereign authority and financial independence. This change was accompanied by the converse to globalization, which was the collapse of regionalism. Whereas at the beginning of the twentieth century the global securities market had a large, dynamic, and important local component, with specific stock exchanges catering for local companies and local investors, this ceased in the 1970s and 1980s. Instead, there were national stock exchanges catering for national investors and national securities. These included a small number that played a supranational role, especially those located in major financial centres catering for cross-border ownership and trading in securities. There also existed transnational markets like that in Eurobonds, which met the needs of international borrowers and investors, such as the multinational company and the inter-government organization. The power of these cross-border and transnational securities markets meant that even national stock exchanges found themselves threatened. The period 1970s to 1990 was therefore one of dramatic changes for the global securities market.

THE 1970S IN THE UNITED STATES: THE CAUSES AND CONSEQUENCES OF MAY DAY[1]

Though the Eurobond market was already changing the nature of the global securities market in the 1960s, this was not the most immediate threat to national markets in the 1970s. Rather, the evolution of these national markets since 1945, in response to government pressure, was rendering them highly unstable by the 1970s. This was especially so in the United States, though it was also becoming apparent across Western Europe and in Australia, Canada, India, Japan, New Zealand, and South Africa. Stock exchanges had been given important privileges by governments in return for performing a regulatory function, but had increasing difficulty in balancing the conflicting needs for order and freedom as markets evolved in the 1960s. By the early 1970s the US securities market had to respond to challenges from several different directions. As the largest securities market in the world, and the model from which many others took their lead, changes there had great significance far beyond that country's national boundaries.

Key to an understanding of the inherent tension that existed within the US securities market by the 1970s was the relationship that existed between the

SEC and the New York Stock Exchange. The further the SEC extended its remit beyond enforcing the general law of the land, as in preventing fraud, the more it constrained the operations of the New York Stock Exchange and thus its ability to control and command the US securities market. The more the New York Stock Exchange tried to protect or even further the interests of its members the more it came into conflict with the SEC as well as antagonizing its own customers. The outcome was a growing importance for the OTC markets as these operated outside the jurisdiction of the New York Stock Exchange and could also escape most of the controls imposed by the SEC. Whilst the OTC market could escape invasive SEC regulations, they had to conduct business without the ease and speed that a central marketplace delivered and without the elimination of counter-party risk, which membership of an organized stock exchange provided. This was acceptable in the bond market, as these were traded among major financial institutions by a small number of broker/dealers located in New York. In other types of securities the situation was less satisfactory. For less frequently traded stocks there were always problems in creating and maintaining an active, orderly market to ensure that prices were not manipulated and investors defrauded. The trade-off between regulation and certainty on the one hand and freedom and risk on the other gave an element of immunity to the New York Stock Exchange, which could provide a market that delivered the required speed and volume at a price users were willing to pay. It thus dominated the market for actively traded stocks despite the imposition of fixed commission charges and the exclusion of certain categories of member, including banks and financial institutions.

However, the formation of Institutional Networks (Instinet) in 1967 threatened this relative immunity from competition. In 1969 this company launched a computer-based trading system which provided the first electronic securities market. Though not considered a real threat to the New York Stock Exchange, because it catered more for less frequently traded stocks, it revealed the ability to link up physically separate brokers through a single trading platform. This was followed in February 1971 by the formation of National Association of Securities Dealers Automated Quotations (NASDAQ). This system delivered instantaneous quotes, provided by authorized market-makers, on OTC stocks allowing all participants to trade by telephone on the same basis, wherever located. It thus provided a means of trading for brokers and dealers who were not members of stock exchanges. Such brokers were numerous and, collectively, conducted a substantial business, but were scattered across the United States and had thus been unable to participate in a central market. In 1975 there were 2,890 members of the NASD, operating operated from 5,950 offices. With the opening of NASDAQ these

brokers could trade in a far more organized OTC market, posing a real challenge to the remaining regulated stock exchanges.

Although the New York Stock Exchange had already been trying to bolster
its defences against outside competition, the appearance of NASDAQ exposed
divisions within the institution. The market specialists on the floor of the
Stock Exchange exerted pressure to limit the dissemination of prices and to
try and force all members to operate exclusively through them, without
conducting any business in quoted securities in the OTC markets. The
specialists were well aware that much of the trading outside the New York
Stock Exchange, in stocks listed there, was based on the prices they quoted,
and they wanted to restrict access to these. They were also aware that the
quality of these prices, and their ability to balance sales and purchases, was
dependent on a constant flow of orders. If they lost those orders the prices
they quoted would be less in tune with supply and demand, and brokers
would look to deal somewhere else. Though brokers recognized the need to
buy on sell on the floor, because of the benefits they derived from exclusive
access to the market it provided, they also wanted the rapid dissemination of
prices to meet the needs of their customers both among the major financial
institutions and across the retail networks. Brokers also wanted to be able to
buy and sell in the best market as that satisfied their clients, from whom they
derived their commission. This was especially the case with the major
financial institutions who had the option of trying to complete a deal either
internally or between themselves, being concentrated and few in number,
whilst individual investors were numerous and widely diffused. Although
institutions did not hold the majority of stocks, they did own the stocks
issued by the largest corporations and these were the most actively traded.
Thus, a growing share of the buying and selling on the New York Stock
Exchange was driven by financial institutions which were increasingly
reluctant to pay the fixed commissions charged. By 1975 75% of trading on
the New York Stock Exchange was on behalf of institutions. Much of the rest
came via the extensive retail network maintained by a small number of large
brokers. Collectively, in 1975, the 490 members of the New York Stock
Exchange maintained 3,430 offices across the United States.

Mergers between members of the New York Stock Exchange created large
and efficient brokerage houses keen to break free from the straitjacket imposed
by minimum commissions. Competition for business did exist but was
restricted to such areas as the quality of service provided, research information, and incidental costs such as telephone charges. However, institutions
increasingly demanded more, especially concerning the commission charged
for buying and selling, but that concession was not in the gift of members of
the New York Stock Exchange. Certain members were more willing than others

to respond to pressure for more flexible charges, especially those who dealt predominantly with either the large financial institutions or who operated large and efficient retail brokerages. Such brokers recognized the competitive forces at work and the need to change whilst others did not. As a member-controlled organization the New York Stock Exchange required a majority decision for change and any move away from fixed commissions was of such fundamental importance that it would not be easily achieved. It had taken until 1970 for the New York Stock Exchange to permit its own members to incorporate and obtain a public quotation, with Merrill Lynch doing so in 1971. There was thus a division within the brokers, splitting the large broker/dealers with extensive institutional business or retail operations and nation-wide branch networks from the small brokers conducting business solely in New York City.

The result was an uneasy compromise between the interests of the two groups as all saw that their collective future was well served by the mainten-ance of rules and regulations that hampered access to their market by non-members. The exclusion of commercial banks from membership, and legal impediments restricting the ability of banks to both operate nationwide and engage in broking, had removed competition from that quarter, leaving members of the New York Stock Exchange with an entrenched position within the securities market. However, by the early 1970s this was threatened by the looming competition from electronic marketplaces and the growing power of the institutional investor. This competition was already affecting the American Stock Exchange, which was dependent on a constant stream of new companies seeking quotation so as to compensate for those it regularly lost to the New York Stock Exchange once they reached a size that made a listing there possible. By the early 1970s between 30 and 40 companies a year were transferring from the American to the New York Stock Exchange but few replacements appeared. So improved was the OTC market with NASDAQ that companies were choosing to remain there, especially as both institutional and individual investors became familiar with the service provided, including flexible commissions. This forced the American Stock Exchange to develop new products to trade. As 90% of the members of the American Stock Exchange were also members of the New York Stock Exchange they, at least, were aware of what was beginning to happen by the early 1970s, though the overall growth in the business of both exchanges masked the growing competition faced by the New York Stock Exchange and reduced the need for a radical response.

Despite its divisions, the New York Stock Exchange did try to use its power over the membership as a whole to bolster its position within the securities market. It tried to force onto its floor all the buying and selling in the securities it listed by insisting that members transacted all such business there. Here, however, it met opposition from the SEC which felt it had a duty to protect other stock exchanges from unfair competition. With the progressive improvement in telephone communications, the spread of nationwide brokerage firms, the institutional ownership of stocks, and the disappearance of large local companies through mergers, the role for US regional stock exchanges was declining. The continued suppression of speculative securities, such as those of mining companies, also removed a previously flourishing category of business. If the remaining regional exchanges were also to lose the business they had built up in those stocks listed on the New York Stock Exchange there would be no place left for them within the United States securities market. The SEC was unwilling to allow this, and intervened to prevent the New York Stock Exchange from restricting access to its prices and forcing its members to bring to it all business in listed stocks, or face expulsion. This enabled the remaining regional exchanges in the United States to survive. The cap on membership of the New York Stock Exchange and the huge differential in the costs of a seat also meant that amalgamation of all stock exchanges in the United States was not feasible, though this would have created a single organization controlling the securities market.

Whilst acting to protect the regional stock exchanges the SEC was unsuccessful in limiting the competition the New York Stock Exchange faced from the OTC markets. As a body appointed to protect the public interest it was justifiable for the SEC to prevent the New York Stock Exchange trying to abuse the power it possessed. Conversely, it was not justifiable for the SEC to bolster that power, attractive as it would have been to suppress the OTC markets in the interests of regulating the securities markets. Consequently, the SEC stopped supporting the New York Stock Exchange against the growing OTC competition. It had not only condoned but supported the fixed commission regime on the New York Stock Exchange as part of the price to be paid for the maintenance of an orderly and regulated securities market. However, by 1970 SEC support turned to opposition due to growing demands from major financial institutions for flexible rates and to competition from the OTC markets, where such a position already existed. There was also an element of self-interest in such a change of policy as the fixed commission rates maintained by the New York Stock Exchange were now counteracting the drawing appeal of its central market. If the New York Stock Exchange abandoned fixed commission rates it would be able to recover the business in stocks that it had lost, so restoring the SEC's authority over the whole securities market.

Thus, in September 1973, when the SEC approved the New York Stock Exchange's increased scale of minimum commissions it did so only on condition that these fixed charges would eventually be abolished. It was agreed that this would happen on 1 May 1975. The result of this May Day change was to promote the interests of the large and efficient members of the New York Stock Exchange, so encouraging further mergers among them. The largest brokerage houses could survive in a world of competitive commissions because of the volume of wholesale business they did for their institutional clients or the retail business serving numerous individual investors through large branch networks. They were also left free from outside competition as financial institutions were still excluded from the New York Stock Exchange and the prohibition on combined banking and broking operations continued.

Though the abolition of minimum commission rates helped to make the large brokerage firms more competitive it was an incomplete revolution. As an institution the New York Stock Exchange was slow to embrace the new trading technology or change the rules governing the conduct of the market or the admission of members. Whereas the Philadelphia Stock Exchange adopted a computer-based trading system for the most actively traded US stocks in 1975, to coincide with the abolition of minimum commissions, the New York Stock Exchange did not. This was despite the views of its own expert on computer dealing systems, Andy Hays, and of a number of its largest member firms, such as Salomon Brothers, who were convinced that floor trading could not survive indefinitely. The New York Stock Exchange was unwilling to undermine floor trading and so only used the new technology to enhance or supplement that process, such as price dissemination, clearing, and settlement. Transactions on the floor of the New York Stock Exchange remained central to its operations, though it was unable to restrict access by non-members to the current prices being generated. There had always been leakage via both the ticker tape and the fact that many brokers were members of more than one stock exchange. However, in 1975, under pressure from the SEC, the New York Stock Exchange was forced to accept the introduction of a consolidated ticker which collected and disseminated current prices throughout the country and made access to New York prices immediately available to all, wherever they were located. This was followed in 1978 by the introduction of the Inter-market Trading System linking all components of the US securities market together to allow orders to be matched wherever the best price could be obtained. Nevertheless, in the securities that it quoted the New York Stock Exchange remained the dominant market in the 1970s, because of the competitive advantages of the floor trading system. When in 1976 the American Stock Exchange stopped automatically delisting stocks that obtained a quotation on the New York Stock Exchange, it discovered that all buying and selling quickly gravitated there anyway.

May Day 1975 in New York helped make the US securities market as a whole far more efficient and competitive, enhanced the position of the largest broking firms, and even boosted the New York Stock Exchange as high fixed commission charges no longer discouraged use. Nevertheless, it was an incomplete revolution. US banks and other financial institutions were still denied direct participation in the securities business. Electronic communication networks did threaten to bypass physical trading floors for all categories of securities, though the technology was not yet there to support it. Pressure from the SEC, which had forced the abolition of the minimum commission rules, indicated that it could not be relied upon to support the New York Stock Exchange within the US securities market. However, these were all issues and problems of the future. The May Day reform unleashed the competitive power of the world's largest stock exchange and the world's most aggressive brokers. The result had implied consequences for global securities market but those consequences could only be felt if strongly entrenched national and international barriers were overcome.

INTERNATIONAL REPERCUSSIONS IN THE 1970s

Elsewhere in the world a combination of technological change, international liberalization, growing discontent among institutional investors, and government unwillingness to tolerate the abuse of monopoly power conspired to pose a serious threat to stock exchanges in the 1970s. The OECD even recommended major reform at national level before a more competitive forum for trading securities internationally could be established. Luckily for these national stock exchanges the precise combination that had forced the abolition of minimum commissions on the New York Stock Exchange in 1975 was absent elsewhere in the 1970s. Similar developments in technology were present as was the growth in importance of the institutional investor, but competititon was less and governments were either benign or supportive. Exchange controls continued to compartmentalize the global securities market and maintained national monopolies no matter how inefficient and expensive they were. The natural inertia of long-established institutions ensured that the pace of change was restricted. What developed in the 1970s was a national response to a global phenomenon as many national stock exchanges moved to consolidate their control over the domestic market, whilst leaving the growing international trade in bonds to global players.

The London Stock Exchange faced many of the same pressures as New York, but underwent very little reform in the 1970s and continued to monopolize the domestic market for stocks. Despite attempts to force through change, fixed minimum commissions remained, banks were still excluded, and the trading floor was sovereign. Nevertheless, it was becoming increasingly difficult for the London Stock Exchange to satisfy the interests of both government and its own members. The government was aware of growing complaints by the major banks and insurance companies about the charges made for buying and selling securities in Britain. Following the financial crisis of 1974, in which a number of members did fail, action was taken to eradicate trading practices that could be considered risky, but these made the market even more bureaucratic and cumbersome. More generally, there were complaints that the London Stock Exchange was failing to provide a market for small and dynamic companies. Certainly, with the object of both limiting the risks that its membership collectively ran and ensuring that speculative and fraudulent practices were minimized, the London Stock Exchange was reluctant to grant a quotation to other than the securities issued by governments and well-established companies. This fulfilled its regulatory function but made it a poorer securities market. Recognizing the problem as early as 1974, the London Stock Exchange began planning for an Unlisted Securities Market (USM) in 1978. However, in contrast to the United States, where a similar problem existed for a similar reason and a thriving OTC market developed as an alternative, the problem in Britain was more deep-seated than simply the power of the London Stock Exchange within the securities market.

Though the London Stock Exchange did maintain a regime of fixed commission rates in the 1970s it was conscious of the growing pressure for reform coming from the major financial institutions in the City of London. These firms were well aware of the changes taking place in New York, even before May 1975, and pressed London brokers to respond. In turn, those members with the largest institutional business urged the London Stock Exchange to amend or relax its minimum commission rules so that they would not lose the custom of these important clients. In contrast, the bulk of the membership bought and sold securities for private clients and wanted to retain and even increase the minimum commission rates. The compromise was an amended set of charges introduced in 1974 that permitted a substantial discount for volume business and, temporarily, satisfied most institutional customers. By responding to the needs of institutional investors the stock exchange not only quietened outside criticism and discouraged the growth of an OTC market, but also managed to preserve its fixed commission structure throughout the 1970s.

Along with fixed commissions, the other pillar of the London Stock Exchange structure was the strict separation of brokers and dealers. During the 1970s this separation was seen as a key element in the London Stock Exchange's ability to police the securities market. As all transactions had to be made through a dealer it was difficult, though not impossible, for brokers to manipulate prices in their favour as there was another party to the bargain. This worked well for active securities with a constant turnover which allowed dealers to reverse sales and purchases, but less well for inactive securities. However, that had always been the case and the market had developed procedures to cope with it. More worryingly for the London Stock Exchange, the largest financial institutions were now responsible for such a large proportion of sales and purchases that they wanted to establish direct contact with the dealers, so cutting out the brokers and their charges completely. By 1978 financial institutions owned 47% of all UK company shares. The largest dealers were keen to respond to this for they risked losing business to outside dealers such as European banks and north American brokerage houses. However, as privileged access to the dealers was one of the key benefits of London Stock Exchange membership, the brokers would not permit it. With no pressure equivalent to that of the SEC in the United States, the London Stock Exchange was able to deny non-members access to its dealers and restrict the dissemination of current prices. Fearing that competition from large and well-capitalized north American firms, if they were allowed to become members, would take business away from existing British brokers, the London Stock Exchange used its rules to exclude them in the same way as it excluded banks. Business was lost as a result, as in the Eurobond market, but in compensation the London Stock Exchange retained its virtual monopoly as the sole market for UK corporate stocks.

This monopoly was enhanced in March 1973 when the London Stock Exchange merged with all its regional rivals, including the Dublin Stock Exchange in the independent Irish Republic. Prior to this merger regional exchanges had tried to ensure their own survival by trading London-quoted securities as the local shares held by local investors, or even specialities like coal, textiles, and shipping companies progressively disappeared. With the merger the ability of the London Stock Exchange to monopolise the British securities market was greatly reinforced. Again there was no SEC to intervene on anti-competitive grounds. The open access that all brokers now had to London dealers boosted the efficiency of the market as the great volume of business passing through London could justify keener prices and easier matching of bargains. The merger also discouraged the creation of large nationwide broking firms. British branch banking had always acted as a feeder to the London Stock Exchange and its membership. With virtually all brokers in the country as members there was even less opportunity for London firms to try and compete with well-established local firms.

However, even as one threat to the London Stock Exchange's control of the domestic securities market was receding another was growing. By the mid-1970s the London Stock Exchange was fully aware of the challenge posed by computerized dealing systems and the amount of business conducted over the telephone between different brokers. There had been a considerable investment in dealing rooms located within the offices of its own members. Mergers among its membership were producing ever larger broking and dealing firms that could afford the investment required to establish expensive dealing rooms within which it was possible to match internally the orders received from investors, as these firms handled a increasingly large share of the buying and selling taking place. Inevitably an electronic rival soon appeared in Britain, supported by the major banks and financial institutions. Unlike the United States the ability of the London Stock Exchange to restrict access to current prices in quoted stocks, and the lack of unquoted ones, made it difficult for non-members to generate sufficient business to support an alternative trading system in domestic securities, especially after the merger with the provincial stock exchanges. As a result the electronic market for British stocks failed to erode the London Stock Exchange's control of the market.

Nevertheless, the ability of the London Stock Exchange to provide the market required by investors was declining in the 1970s. Rules on access to outside capital restricted the finance available to dealers, so that they were not able to provide the ready market that institutions, or even the large brokers, required as the size of transactions grew. That business flowed instead to New York investment houses or European banks, as in Eurobonds, where it was necessary to finance large holdings of securities in order to supply the market when opportunity arose. There remained an almost total control of the domestic securities market, including the market in the UK national debt. However, this was only achieved by operating at low commission rates or even commission free if undertaken on behalf of the government. This element of the London securities market continued to be driven by money market considerations as financial institutions, and the government, employed or obtained short-term funds through continuous buying and selling operations in the most liquid securities. In contrast, the commission charged on the transactions in stocks was far greater, whether undertaken for individuals or institutions, with the result that this business preoccupied the membership of the London Stock Exchange and was central to what they wanted to preserve from competition. Hence the merger with the provincial stock exchanges, whose role in this area had always been of major importance.

The London Stock Exchange was able to resist the pressure for change and to preserve its position within the domestic securities market because the government was much more supportive than in the United States. As the Bank of England and successive governments continued to rely on the London Stock Exchange as the main mechanism for policing the domestic securities market there was considerable reluctance to undermine its effectiveness by challenging the way it conducted business. In the absence of an equivalent to the SEC, with its remit to protect investors and promote competition, the London Stock Exchange was able to eliminate domestic competition by merging with the provincial exchanges and by restricting access to its market-makers and the current prices they generated. Consequently it was difficult to establish an alternative market despite the possibilities offered by electronic networks or the competition of large and well-capitalized rivals, whether north American banks and brokerage firms or British financial institutions. The London Stock Exchange also contributed to its own success by its willingness to compromise over commission charges with banks and other major financial institutions, thereby blunting opposition to its restrictive practices. However, by the late 1970s the London Stock Exchange was facing growing challenges to its regime of fixed commission charges from such bodies as the Restrictive Practices Court and the Monopolies and Mergers Commission. The ending of exchange controls in late 1979 suddenly exposed the London Stock Exchange to the full force of foreign competition, especially from New York.

Generally the 1970s was not a period of significant change within national securities market apart from the United States.[2] The influence of national governments combined with the institutional control exercised by stock exchanges ensured that little changed. The British pattern, where the London Stock Exchange was totally dominant within the domestic securities market, was much more typical than the US model, where the New York Stock Exchange was under attack and forced to make concessions. Even in Canada the competitive pressures from the United States after the ending of fixed commissions were largely thwarted. This occurred despite the fact that 185 of the most actively traded Canadian stocks were also listed on US stock exchanges, especially New York, and these accounted for 25% of the volume and 43% of the value of trading on the Toronto Stock Exchange in 1975. With the backing of the Canadian regulatory authorities a revised set of minimum commission rates was agreed in 1977, applying not only to the Toronto Stock Exchange but also to Montreal and Vancouver. With no competition between the stock exchanges, and the dissemination of prices limited, it was difficult to establish a market for Canadian stocks outside that provided by the stock exchanges. Furthermore, a new Securities Act in 1974 capped at 25% the level of foreign ownership permitted in a Canadian stock-broking firm. This prevented US brokers from taking control of their northern neighbours and integrating the Canadian securities market into their own operations. However, there was a steady drift of business to New York after 1975, prompting the Toronto Stock Exchange to embrace the new electronic technology in order to retain the business of its own members. In 1977 the Toronto Stock Exchange became the first established institution to embrace computerized trading, when it introduced Computer Assisted Trading System (CATS).[3]

Japan, like Canada, experienced a very limited degree of change despite its heavy post-war American influence. The Japanese securities market was highly regulated by the state through the established stock exchanges. However, unlike the US or even Britain, stock exchanges had a statutory monopoly of trading in all quoted securities which made them impervious to outside competition. With growing institutional ownership of stocks, reflecting their increased popularity in an inflationary period, buying and selling increasingly centred on the Tokyo Stock Exchange. Also, unlike the United States, broking activity was dominated by a few large firms that were highly regulated by the state and little exposed to competition, especially as banks were restricted from operating in this field. In 1970 the four largest brokerage firms handled 48% of the transactions in stocks and 66% in bonds, channelling most of this to the Tokyo Stock Exchange, so further increasing its already dominant position. Consequently, neither the government nor the main participants in the securities market had any desire to create a more competitive environment through abandoning fixed commissions and promoting deregulation. The Japanese securities market emerged little altered in the course of the 1970s.[4]

In continental Europe state dominance over the securities market, whether at central, regional, or local level, continued. In Portugal the government closed down the Lisbon Stock Exchange in 1974 and did not allow it to reopen fully until 1977. Where allowed to operate, stock exchanges acted as official or unofficial regulatory arms of the state, which rendered them able to withstand most pressures for change. In France the Paris Bourse had already acquired control over the securities market in the 1960s, exercising this under government authority and with immunity from competition. A similar situation existed in Belgium, which was largely modelled on the French example. In Germany, although numerous separate and independent stock exchanges remained there was no competition as these were locally regulated and dominated by their banking members. Banks had little desire to see securities market becoming serious competitors for the business they conducted, and were little interested in stock exchange reform. Even in the Netherlands, where the state was much less involved, the Amsterdam Stock Exchange changed little in the 1970s as it was able to monopolize its own domestic market. In 1972 it opened up membership to all brokers in the Netherlands with the result that rival stock exchanges ceased to exist by 1974. This removal of competition allowed the Amsterdam Stock Exchange to preserve its fixed commission structure by restricting direct access to its market and current prices. In 1974 member firms were required to dismantle the private networks they had installed to distribute prices from the floor of the exchange to their offices, and thence to clients such as the major institutional investors.

In continental Europe a single stock exchange increasingly dominated all trading in each national securities market and with the active or passive support of government was able to resist all force for change. Thus, despite the lack of innovation in trading technology and a proliferation of restrictive practices, high charges, and administrative barriers, national stock exchanges remained dominant within the securities market of their own countries. By the late 1970s the Paris Bourse was responsible for some 98% of all trading in French securities, Milan undertook around 75% of transactions in Italian securities, and even in the more fragmented German market the Frankfurt Stock Exchange handled around half the total. In all these countries previously thriving local exchanges had either closed or were in decline in the face of financial and regulatory centralization. Inevitably, this diminished the role played by the securities market within the financial system, giving ample opportunity for banks to dominate. Only the growing interest in stocks at a time of rising inflation surmounted the inadequacies of such securities market and drove up the volume of trading undertaken. However, where possible major financial institutions internalized the buying and selling of securities or resorted to telephone trading with each other.[5]

The European pattern was replicated around the world. In countries as diverse as Australia, South Africa, India, and Peru trading increasingly converged on a single stock exchange and fixed commissions remained in use, often coordinated among the stock exchanges of each country where more than one existed. This was either condoned or encouraged by national governments as an easy solution to the problem of ensuring that the national securities market was orderly and relatively free of excesses and scandals. In Australia in the 1970s 90% of trading in the securities market was undertaken on the Melbourne and Sydney stock exchanges. In 1976 these exchanges agreed to formally cooperate, in response to greatly increased government regulation in the wake of the abuses revealed by the collapse of the mining boom in the early 1970s. Centralization and increased regulation were also experienced in South Africa. The collapse of two large stock-broking firms because of fraud led to greater government scrutiny whilst the decline of business outside Johannesburg led to the closure of the other stock exchanges in Cape Town and Durban in the mid-1970s. Where new securities markets were established a high degree of government involvement was frequently present from the very outset. In Nigeria a stock exchange was established in Lagos in 1977 followed by a branch in Kaduna in 1978. Though based on British practice, and preceded by developments by British expatriates, this stock exchange was under the authority of an SEC, indicating that the US securities market was now the model being copied, especially in newly independent countries. Government control was further strengthened in 1979, following a series of scandals and frauds.[6]

Lost in this ambition of governments to control the securities market was any desire to ensure that it was both competitive and dynamic. The securities market was not seen as a central part of the financial system compared to the role played by banks and the activities of the government itself, with its power to tax and spend. Intent on preserving their fixed charges and other restrictive practices, the regulated stock exchanges were willing to accept a gradual seepage of business away from their market, as with trading in government debt between the banks and other major financial institutions. This seemed a small price to pay for the control they could exercise over a booming domestic market in corporate stocks, fuelled by the worldwide inflation of the 1970s. Among the stock exchanges formed in newly independent countries in this decade there was little evidence that much trading activity was generated, as the state continued to control large sections of the economy and place impediments in the way of private business and individual wealth. In countries where communist regimes were still in power, there remained no need for a securities market of any kind.[7]

Only in those few countries where government control was absent or lax did newly formed securities markets, whether organized through stock exchanges or not, appear to flourish. In Kuwait, rising oil prices produced a flurry of speculative activity in the rapidly expanding unofficial market, the Al-Manakh. Similarly, a dynamic securities market appeared in Beirut but was destroyed during the civil war that engulfed Lebanon in the mid-1970s.[8] One location where the securities market did become both firmly established and flourished in the 1970s was Hong Kong. Driven by inflation, rising prosperity, and monetary instability the Hong Kong securities market boomed in the early 1970s, leading to the formation of two more stock exchanges, in addition to the two already in existence. After the collapse of the speculative boom in December 1973 the government attempted to regulate this rapidly expanding market, due to concerns about investor protection and financial stability. However, in the downturn of business that followed the end of the

speculative boom these four stock exchanges, with collectively 1,000 members, actively competed for business and were little interested in either
investor protection or financial stability. The survival of both the institution
and its members was paramount. The government of Hong Kong gradually
discovered this in the late 1970s but was unable to arrange its preferred
solution, the merger of all the stock exchanges into one, because of the intense
rivalry between them and their members. Thus, the Hong Kong securities
market was largely left to fend for itself by the British authorities that ruled the
colony in the 1970s.[9]

   Consequently, apart from the United States and Hong Kong, national
securities markets marked time in the 1970s. As a result of the actions of
the SEC, the dominant stock exchange in the United States, New York, was
forced to drop or relax several anti-competitive practices, the most significant
being the abolition of minimum commission rates. As a result of the absence
of government controls by the British in Hong Kong, the securities market
there flourished in a highly competitive environment. These two examples
reveal the inadequacy of the situation in most other parts of the world where
the regulation of national securities markets was left to the dominant stock
exchange with little or no attempt by government to limit the power it thus
possessed. Only where a stock exchange had a near monopoly over all or part
of the securities market, was it able and willing to regulate that market. This
produced problems of anti-competitive behaviour which restricted both
innovation and growth in the securities market, unless moderated by the
active intervention of a body such as the SEC. In contrast, where a stock
exchange did not have a monopoly, as in Hong Kong, it had to be very
competitive and thus policed the market inadequately. In between were
numerous domestic securities markets that operated not only in a compartmentalized world but also in one where they received the explicit or implicit
support of their governments and were bolstered by the institutional power
exercised by the dominant stock exchange. This kept the forces for change
at bay, whilst marginalizing the role played by securities markets within
financial systems. Only the desire by investors to purchase corporate stocks
as a hedge against inflation, and the attractions this had for corporate
managements both in terms of raising finance and increasing business
through mergers and acquisitions, generated real activity in these regulated
securities markets. Even then, institutional investors tried to bypass regulated
markets, as in the OTC market in the United States. Under such conditions
banks were able to establish a commanding position within the financial
system, extending far beyond the collection of savings and provision of credit
to finance business of all kinds and in all ways, as was the case across
continental Europe.

THE GLOBAL MARKET IN THE 1970s

Both government regulation and institutional controls at national level continued to impede the development of an international trade in securities during the 1970s. Trading was also rendered more difficult by a combination of exchange controls and restrictions on capital mobility. External business of any kind was of minor importance within national securities markets, where the focus remained on trading national securities for national investors. The level of activity generated by either trading in foreign securities on behalf of domestic investors or in domestic securities on behalf of foreign investors was tiny on the London Stock Exchange and almost non-existent on the Paris Bourse. The London Stock Exchange had an international presence because of the multinational companies listed and because the South African gold-mining stocks owned by British investors were actively traded between London and Johannesburg. Similarly, the New York Stock Exchange attracted an international business because it was home to the greatest number of multinational companies, especially in oil and motor manufacturing, and the stocks they issued were held by institutional investors outside the United States. Nevertheless, even though the New York Stock Exchange was located in the largest financial centre in the world, the level of business generated on foreign account was miniscule. It was not until 1976 that the New York Stock Exchange began to accept foreign securities for trading and 1977 before foreign brokers were acceptable as members.

Instead, the international business attracted to New York was largely focused on the market for US government bonds. The liquidity its depth and breadth gave this market attracted institutional investors not only from the United States but throughout the world. Banks, in particular, had huge amounts of temporarily idle funds to employ remuneratively, and the US Treasury Bond market was ideal for this purpose, especially as the currency involved was the US$. Consequently, the principal component of the international buying and selling of securities mainly comprised the direction of orders to the national markets where the most liquid government bonds and multinational corporate stocks were traded. Holdings outside these markets were simply too small to generate much of a local market in foreign stocks, leading to arbitrage transactions across national boundaries. One of the few exceptions was the development of a small market in New York in the shares of a few of the largest British multinational companies, where they were traded as ADRs. Consequently, the world economy continued to operate without the benefit of a mobile class of assets whose ownership could easily and quickly switch between countries, so helping to maintain international equilibrium. Instead, this role was left to governments and banks, including central banks, who found it increasingly difficult, sometimes impossible, to cope with the national imbalances that were apparent in the world economy by the early 1970s.

Conversely, what continued to happen in the 1970s was the emergence of a small number of financial institutions possessing the expertise and the staff capable of arranging and handling the buying and selling of securities between different monetary and regulatory zones. Most of these financial institutions were banks but certain New York brokers also made the jump to global status, based upon the nationwide operations they had built up in the United States and the restrictions placed on US banks entering broking. In 1972 the New York brokerage house of Merrill Lynch had forty-eight overseas offices, which generated 10% of the company's income, and the ending of fixed commissions in 1975 provided a further incentive to expand into less competitive markets. Though competitive pressure was much less in evidence in both Canada and Japan, the existence there of large US-style brokers also led them to expand internationally in the 1970s, especially as a number of their largest institutional clients and corporate customers also operated overseas. Nomura had branches in the United States whilst Canadian brokers were found in London.

In contrast, the continuing regime of fixed commissions along with other restrictive practices, removed both the incentive and the ability of British stock-broking firms to expand internationally. Those London brokers who wished to do so in the 1970s faced considerable opposition from the stock exchange as their mode of operation was seen to threaten both minimum commission rates and the broker/dealer division. Also, the exclusion of banks from membership of the London Stock Exchange gave them little interest in broking and no desire to develop internationally that which they did not do domestically. Conversely, banks in continental Europe had traditionally combined investment banking and stock-broking activities with deposit-taking and lending, and were ideally placed to expand internationally. Crédit Suisse (Zürich), Algemene Bank (Amsterdam), Commerzbank (Frankfurt), and Crédit Lyonnais (Paris) were all members of US stock exchanges in the 1970s. These international networks of banks and brokers constituted a new element in the global securities market, and allowed the controls and restrictions imposed by governments and stock exchanges to be evaded. As these financial institutions grew in scale and reach they began to internalize trading within their own organization or between each other rather than operate through organized securities markets. This was especially true for bonds, which were largely an institutional market, and so trading in these continued to migrate from the floors of stock exchanges.

As investors' horizons increasingly extended beyond national boundaries in the 1970s, those banks and brokers with a global presence were well positioned to benefit from it. Although these were mainly North American and continental European, London was often the fulcrum of their activities given the restrictions imposed by their own governments in contrast to the freedom they enjoyed there. Though the British government retained exchange controls until late 1979, and even reinforced them during the decade, these did not apply to a business conducted in US dollars in London by foreign banks and brokers. Similarly, though the London Stock Exchange would not admit banks and foreign brokers as members, and forced a separation between broking and dealing, that was no barrier to them establishing a base in London, from where they could adopt any combination of financial activities desired. There were no British laws enforcing a separation between banking and broking as with the Glass–Steagall Act in the US. The attractions of a London location to US banks and brokers, and to European banks, was manifest. The number of foreign banks in London more than doubled in the 1970s, reaching 351 in 1980 with those from Europe experiencing the most rapid growth.[10]

The attractions of a London location and an international business were greatly enhanced in the 1970s as the rigid control exercised by governments and central banks broke down and financial markets began to revive. Between 1971 and 1973 the system of fixed but adjustable exchange rates, which had been operated by central bankers through the 1950s and 1960s, fell apart, with March 1973 being seen as the end of the post-war Bretton Woods System. Due to weakening confidence in the dollar, despite all attempts by the US government to support it, there was a growing conversion of dollars into gold at an artificially low official price, in the expectation that adjustment was inevitable. Under these circumstances, the US government suspended the convertibility of the dollar into gold in 1971. This further weakened international confidence in the dollar and undermined even more the ability of governments to maintain currency equilibrium. The dollar was at the fulcrum of the post-war international monetary system, having become the dominant currency for trade and finance, and there were no real alternatives available. Sterling was weak and neither the Swiss, German, nor Japanese governments wanted to see their currencies extensively used externally, because of the instability this might have for domestic economies. Thus, with the demise of the dollar the international monetary system was, increasingly, left to find its own solution to problems caused by imbalances that were both temporary, as with the huge financial flows to petroleum producers because of the rising price of oil, and permanent, as with the enhanced economic position of Germany and Japan compared to the United

States and the UK. Most countries opted to suspend the convertibility of their currencies into gold, in order to halt a potential outflow. There could be no return to the gold standard, given the highly unequal distribution of holdings and the power that would be given to producers like South Africa and the Soviet Union. Instead, most countries opted for floating exchange rates accompanied by official intervention by national central banks in order to smooth the fluctuations. Between May 1970 and January 1974 most major currencies were floated.[11]

One of the tools employed by governments and central banks in order to achieve some level of stability in exchange rates was control over capital flows. This further impeded the external use of national securities markets whilst encouraging business to flow though banking and broking networks, to the detriment of New York and to the advantage of London as financial centres. Consequently, one of the most rapidly growing markets in the 1970s was the Eurobond market, which operated outside the bounds of government or stock exchange control. Though quoted on stock exchanges, often for legal reasons, Eurobonds were little traded there. Instead they were bought and sold on a telephone market involving inter-dealer brokers or directly between banks. By using the US dollar it was possible to create a single market for bonds outside the United States that overcame the divisions created by separate currencies and separate institutional and legal practices and procedures. The result was a market that could begin to match the depth of the US bond market. It not only attracted European institutions with funds to invest but also US borrowers seeking to tap cheaper sources of foreign finance. Recognizing the challenge now facing the New York market for Treasury bonds, in 1974 the US government repealed the Interest Equalisation Tax. This reopened the New York bond market for international borrowers, but as other restrictions remained in place, such as the withholding tax on interest paid by US issuers to non-resident investors, the downturn in the Eurobond market was only temporary and it quickly revived to reach new heights in the late 1970s. Turnover grew more than tenfold during the 1970s to reach $240 billion a year in 1980.

This still left the Eurobond market with problems, which were only slowly addressed during the 1970s. One problem was that Eurobonds were issued in far smaller amounts and with unique characteristics compared to the government debt of the largest economies. Eurobonds were much less easily bought and sold at prevailing market prices as they did not possess a highly liquid secondary market. However, that was gradually addressed as the size of issue grew, though German, Japanese, and, especially, the US government bond issues remained far more liquid. The secondary market grew simultaneously in size, sophistication, and reliability as various problems associated with transfers and counter-party risk were addressed. By the early 1970s not only were there two clearing houses in existence, namely Euroclear (1968) and Cedel (1970), but those involved in the market had formed in 1969 the Association of International Bond Dealers. This was a self-regulatory body for the Eurobond market largely consisting of banks from around the world. Though the head office of this organization was in Zurich, and the clearing took place in continental Europe, the main trading was in London where the greatest number of banks and brokers were located. Nevertheless, it took time for market discipline to reach the level prevailing on either the main organized stock exchanges or government debt markets. However, the Eurobond market was generating some truly international firms, reflecting the nature of the business taking place. One such was Credit Suisse First Boston. The New York brokers White Weld had opened a London office in the 1960s, to evade US government restrictions. This then played a leading role in the development of the Eurobond market, merging the London office in 1974 with the London office of Credit Suisse to create a transnational operation, Credit Suisse White Weld. In 1978, when Merrill Lynch took over White Weld in New York, Credit Suisse First Boston emerged in London.

The London-centred Eurobond market marked both a new response to the problems faced in a disintegrating international monetary system in the 1970s and the beginning of the revival of the global securities market. Until the expansion of the Eurobond markets international capital markets were not deep or liquid enough to cope with the flows created by balance of payments imbalances. Even then the maintenance of tight controls on capital flows by governments limited the role the Eurobond market could play. Until 1980 Japanese investors were not able to buy foreign securities. Instead of recognizing that a global securities market provided some kind of equilibrium through facilitating international financial flows, governments continued to associate their trading with volatility, and so sought to achieve currency stability through intervention and controls. Throughout the 1970s there remained government reluctance to trust market-based solutions to the problems of disequilibria that had built up over the post-war years. Instead, the collapse of the Bretton Woods System was seen as a temporary occurrence to be rectified at a later date by the return to fixed exchange rates and central bank authority. In the meantime barriers erected by governments created isolated capital markets lacking the capacity or speed to equalize imbalances through countervailing financial flows.[12] Though changes were taking place in the global securities market both domestically and internationally in the 1970s they did not yet amount to a profound transformation in the way business was conducted or a major revival in the fortunes of that market. A partial revolution had taken place but it did not yet extend beyond the ending of minimum commissions on the New York Stock Exchange and the growth of the Eurobond market in London.

LONDON IN THE 1980s: BIG BANG AND ITS CONSEQUENCES

The impediments to international financial flows began to be dismantled from the late 1970s onwards. In 1979–80 Japan, Britain and the US simultaneously, but without coordination, removed key barriers to capital flows. The US authorities abandoned interest rate ceilings, the UK government abandoned exchange controls and the Japanese government abandoned controls over capital outflows. As these countries were all major components of the world economy, the result was a vast increase in international capital flows. A major beneficiary was the London-based Eurobond market which was truly international and so attractive to financial institutions from around the world. Its use was driven by a combination of the restrictive regimes still governing domestic securities markets and the absence in many parts of the world of financial centres of sufficient size and sophistication to support a securities market where temporary funds could be employed. Thus the Eurobond market attracted savings from Japan because of domestic restrictions, and from the Middle East because of the lack of a major financial centre in that region. Even though governments did liberalize their bond markets in the 1980s, as with the ending of the withholding tax in both Germany and the United States in 1984, the Eurobond market continued to thrive, as it was now driven by fundamentals in an increasingly global world. In particular, a succession of defaults and financial crises in the 1980s made banks recognize the risks they were running when making long-term loans to both sovereign and corporate borrowers. This encouraged a switch to lending in the form of long-term bonds rather than short-term paper, as these could be sold on the secondary market if circumstances changed for either borrower or lender.

By the 1980s the Eurobond market had also established a size and infrastructure that meant it could service an increasing number of investors and borrowers. Eurobond issues rose from 321 for $19.8 billion in 1980 to 1,692 for $221.7 billion in 1989 with an increasing variety to suit all purposes, such as those offering a fixed rate of interest, a floating rate, or convertible from one to the other. In turn, the secondary market also grew. Turnover rose from $240 billion in 1980 to $8,833 billion in 1991. Though there remained a proliferation of smaller corporate issues with widely different structures, where trading was limited and difficult, there also grew in importance those bonds that were widely quoted by a large number of market-makers at competitive rates or narrow spreads, so creating a liquid market. These were especially the issues of sovereign borrowers and multinational corporations. Sovereign borrowers with strong economies and large domestic bond markets relied on their domestic market, as with Britain, France, Germany, Japan, and the United States but those with small economies and small markets were large users of the Eurobond market, such as Sweden and Denmark, finding it both cheaper and more flexible.

London remained the centre of the Eurobond market, with ever more banks opening offices there so as to participate. By 1990 there were 521 foreign banks with offices in London, and the offices of the world's largest brokers such as Merrill Lynch and Goldman Sachs from New York and Nomura from Tokyo, and a host of other types of financial institutions such as insurance companies and fund managers. As London contained more branches of financial institutions and intermediaries from around the world compared to any other financial centre, and was home to the world's money and foreign currency markets, it was the obvious place for Eurobond trading. The banks had money they needed to employ and the foreign exchange market gave them the confidence to do so in London as it minimized the risk of imbalances in the currency in which assets and liabilities existed, with the US$ as the vehicle currency for holdings and transactions. Not only in London but also in New York and Tokyo there was constant interaction between the markets for foreign exchange, bank deposits, and securities as internal and external barriers broke down. Trading also took place between these centres as rapid developments in communications made such links possible on a global basis.[13]

However, London was not only at the centre of a rapidly growing international bond market but also a catalyst for change elsewhere in securities. The abolition of British exchange controls in October 1979 was an essential link in the chain reaction that led to the transformation of the global securities towards the end of the twentieth century. The British securities market was now fully exposed to the competition coming both from New York for stocks and from within London itself for bonds. As New York was already home to a growing market in UK shares, because of growing US ownership, the trading facilities it could offer were very attractive to British institutional investors. Access to this market was greatly eased by the presence in London of branches of the largest New York brokerage firms. At the same time, the existence in London of the Eurobond market meant that the members of the London Stock Exchange faced strong competition on their own doorstep, as traders there were perfectly capable of switching to the domestic securities market once exchange controls disappeared. Although many of the members undertaking a private client business did not realize it, the ending of exchange controls meant that it was no longer possible for the London Stock Exchange to monopolize the domestic securities market and impose its own rules, regulations, and charges. In contrast, those in the larger firms doing institutional business recognized that their situation was now unsustainable, as did those running the London Stock Exchange. Accordingly, the strategy after 1979 was one of managing the transition to a more competitive world, despite the continuing opposition of many of the members.

The trigger for change came in an agreement with the government in 1983 under which the restrictive practices case would be dropped but only on condition that minimum commissions would be ended. This was scheduled to take place in October 1986 and became known as Big Bang. What was to be enacted in London was a replica of what had happened in New York ten years before. Although important, the latter had meant only limited changes for the domestic securities market and had created few fundamental changes world-wide. The London Big Bang had much greater repercussions as it both built upon what had already happened in New York and introduced major new features. The situation in London was different from that in New York whilst the global securities market had moved on in terms of both trading and technology. What took place in London involved an entirely new relationship between the London Stock Exchange and the UK government. The Bank of England, on behalf of the British government, had regulated the domestic securities market through the London Stock Exchange, condoning and even supporting the growing body of rules, regulations, and restrictive practices required to achieve that end. Shorn of the power to impose a minimum commission regime on its members, the London Stock Exchange was in no position to enforce many of the rules that lay at the heart of the regulated market it provided, such as the division between broker and dealer and the separation between banks and the securities market. To maintain these would put its own members at a competitive disadvantage compared to non-members. The more competitive the securities market was the less able was a single institution like the London Stock Exchange to police it. In 1985 there appeared in Britain an equivalent to the SEC in the shape of the Securities and Investment Board (SIB), indicating the triumph of the US regulatory model for securities markets. Under the supervision of the SIB the London Stock Exchange tried to establish a monopoly for itself by becoming the sole recognized exchange for all securities traded in Britain. This failed as there now existed in London the major securities market in Eurobonds, which did not want to accept the authority of the London Stock Exchange. Turnover in Eurobonds had reached 20%–30% of that of London Stock Exchange by the mid-1980s, largely in the hands of 120 European banks and US brokers. They were happy to police their own market and negotiate directly with the SIB.

Not only in relations with the government was Big Bang in London fundamentally different from May Day in New York. The nature of the British securities market was unlike that in the United States. Britain possessed neither a statutory barrier between broking and banking nor the large broking firms with a nationwide presence able to channel business to and from New York. In 1983 Merrill Lynch had assets of $1.3 billion whilst those of one of the largest London brokers, Hoare Govett, was a mere £30 million and that of the largest dealers, Akroyd and Smithers, was £40 million. This made Merrill Lynch ten times bigger than the two of these combined. Instead, members of the London Stock Exchange operated through British banking firms and their extensive branch networks for their retailing operations whilst the financial community had customary divisions between broking, dealing, investment banking, and commercial banking. With the ending of minimum commissions in London at a time when the institutional investor had become dominant, when an electronic marketplace had been proved feasible, and when a thriving international market was in existence, it was not possible to drop one component of the London Stock Exchange's restrictive practices and leave the rest unchanged. A far more fundamental change was required if the London Stock Exchange was to survive the ending of both exchange controls and minimum commissions. Otherwise, the market would drift into the hands of the major US brokerage firms such as Goldman Sachs and Merrill Lynch, and the large integrated European banks, like Deutsche Bank and Société Générale, which already conducted substantial operations in London and were eager to participate more fully in the domestic market. These US brokers were already handling transactions in such British multinational companies as BP, Shell, Unilever, and Rio Tinto. Faced with the impossibility of resisting such rivals, the London Stock Exchange had no option but to include them. This meant the admission of not only foreign members but also corporate members, including banks, because of their dominant position in the Eurobond market. The transformation of the London Stock Exchange thus included not only the ending of fixed commissions and the broker/dealer division but also the admission of foreign and domestic financial institutions as members and the creation of an entirely new trading system.

The London Stock Exchange rejected the trading system used by the New York Stock Exchange. Although this represented the easiest option, it was apparent that the New York Stock Exchange was losing market share and almost 40% of the stock exchange's own turnover bypassed the specialists by the early 1980s. Instead, a computerized trading network (SEAQ) was introduced, with that used by NASDAQ being preferred to the Toronto Stock Exchange's CATS system. Consequently, with Big Bang the London Stock Exchange not only liberalized its rules and regulations but also moved into the electronic age. This was no easy step as the introduction of the new system on the day of Big Bang (27 October 1986) was the culmination of nine parallel IT projects launched in 1983. Indicating that success was by no means guaranteed was the fact that a parallel attempt to create a computerized system for settling transactions in equities, codenamed Taurus, ended in failure in 1993 after a number of false starts and expenditure of over £80 million by the London Stock Exchange.[14] The costs, complexities, and risks involved in moving to an electronic marketplace, along with opposition from many members of the London Stock Exchange, explain why the New York Stock Exchange persevered with its floor-trading model throughout the 1980s, despite advances in technology and the growing competition it faced.

In terms of membership, the London Stock Exchange also faced an easier task than New York where numbers were capped and admission possible only through the purchase of an expensive seat. The London Stock Exchange could expand membership and set a low price. With the most restrictive regulations being withdrawn membership of the London Stock Exchange became attractive to British and foreign banks as well as overseas brokers. In March 1986 Merrill Lynch and Nomura were both granted membership. In addition numerous large banks and foreign brokerage firms purchased existing members of the London Stock Exchange, so gaining an established position in both broking and dealing. By 1989 there were 391 corporate members of the London Stock Exchange, of whom 248 were British whilst the remainder were foreign, including 52 from the US, 17 from France, and 14 from Japan. Many of these were owned by larger groups engaged in a wide variety of financial activities, both in Britain and abroad. The London Stock Exchange thereby became an international marketplace welcoming the major players in the global securities market irrespective of their nationality or structure.

Big Bang in Britain in October 1986 thus created a new securities market in London. This was a market dominated by large banks and brokers drawn from throughout the world, freed from rules and regulations covering the conduct of business, and able to trade by telephone from well-equipped offices using current prices instantly available on screen. Nevertheless, it still operated under the guise of the London Stock Exchange and under the authority of a statutory regulatory body, the SIB, which gave it a credibility denied to OTC trading. The securities market in London had been simultaneously de-materialized and internationalized making it highly competitive. The New York Stock Exchange had failed to achieve this in the 1970s. Domestically, the London Stock Exchange was left virtually unchallenged.

It had retained the market in government debt though only nominally as trading was now conducted through a group of recognized dealers answerable to the Bank of England. The creation of a USM in 1981 also allowed the London Stock Exchange to forestall most of the emerging competition from OTC trading as there was now a market for the shares issued by new or smaller companies. By September 1986, 508 companies had floated on the USM raising £1 billion in the process.[15] In addition, the government's privatization programme of large state industries had greatly expanded the number of UK investors. By 1986 there were 5 million investors compared to 3 million in 1980 and this rose again to 11 million in 1991. Nevertheless, the influence of institutions continued to grow with the share of equities they owned rising from 71.8% in 1981 to 78.7% in 1989, in the face of heavy buying from the pension funds.

Internationally, developments in London in the 1980s had major implications for the global securities market. Securities markets either had to copy London or face the gradual loss of business. This was especially true in Europe for as Britain was a full member of the European Union (EU) members of the London Stock Exchange were able to transact business there for clients across the continent, whatever the restrictions and charges imposed by their national governments and domestic stock exchanges. As London was one of the most important financial centres in the world it already possessed the offices of the major banks and financial institutions that were most engaged in the buying and selling of securities ranging from Eurobonds to corporate stocks and bonds. There were 104 foreign securities houses operating in London 1980 but 158 by 1989. The biggest increases were among those from other than the United States (43 rising to 55), with those from Japan (21 to 42) and Europe (13 to 24) doubling. With Big Bang the London Stock Exchange provided the main trading forum for these firms. By 1990 the London Stock Exchange quoted foreign corporate stocks with a market value of £1.3 trillion, alone constituting 61% of the value of all quoted securities. By 1989 foreign equity turnover in London had reached £40 billion per annum, or one-third that of UK equities, with that in French, Swedish, and Japanese securities being especially important. In contrast, bond trading, whether government or corporate, flowed through other channels even though largely conducted by many of the banks and brokerage houses who were members of the London Stock Exchange.

Not only could foreign banks and brokers join the London Stock Exchange, bringing their international business with them, but all members could now operate more competitively. In the gilt-edged market by the end of 1987 over half of all transactions now bypassed brokers, as institutional investors dealt directly with market-makers, whilst 90% of total business involved no commission payment. Similarly in equities, whether domestic or foreign, large institutions dealt either directly with market-makers, cutting out the brokers, or paid a much smaller commission fee. One estimate for February 1987 suggested that commissions paid by institutions had fallen by around 50% as a result of Big Bang. The stamp duty charged by the government was now a much heavier cost than commission rates for those buying and selling securities. These lower charges, added to the London market's strength in terms of liquidity, meant that it was now very competitive, able not only to retain business in UK equities but also attract that in major non-British stocks. This had implications for the securities markets elsewhere in the world.

As long as national securities markets existed in a world partly closed to outside competition through exchange controls, they could maintain practices like fixed commissions and divisions between banking and broking. Once the abolition of exchange controls opened up that world, practices that hampered significantly the competitive power of the membership could not be sustained for long. In the 1980s there was a simultaneous dismantling of barriers at both national and international levels resulting in an enormous expansion of the global trading in securities, which increasingly extended beyond the Eurobond market and into corporate stocks. Financial institutions worldwide needed a hedge against inflation after the ravages of the 1970s and corporate stocks proved especially attractive. By September 1989 cross-border equity holdings totalled $640 billion, or 6.4% of all equity holdings, compared to a negligible proportion ten years before. This worked its way through into the secondary market with cross-border equity trading increasing from $73.1 billion in 1979 to $1.6 trillion in 1989. Of these cross-border transactions around 60% passed through London as banks, brokers, and institutional investors sought to avoid the restrictions and costs imposed upon domestic markets elsewhere. As with the Eurobond market in the 1960s and 1970s, much of the international business in corporate stocks that flowed to London from the mid-1980s was driven not by the emergence of a truly global marketplace but to escape domestic restrictions.

THE SCOPE AND LIMITS OF GLOBAL CHANGE IN THE 1980s

Although the most important changes in the global securities market took place in London this was by no means an isolated occurrence. However, most of these passed the New York Stock Exchange by. Having been at the forefront of deregulation in the 1970s, with the abolition of minimum commissions, and an important catalyst for changes in London in the 1980s, the New York Stock Exchange altered very little during that decade. Continuing command of the market for the corporate securities it quoted, which were mainly the most actively traded in the United States and thus in the world, cushioned the New York Stock Exchange from competitive forces. Sales rose from $108 billion in 1970 to $398 billion in 1980 and then to $1.6 trillion by 1989. The New York Stock Exchange was in an entirely different league among other stock exchanges within the United States, despite a growth of business everywhere. The nearest contender, the American Stock Exchange, was fighting a losing battle as the New York Stock Exchange increasingly took the market in its most actively traded stocks. The New York Stock Exchange listed 3,030 stocks and 1,412 bonds in 1989 compared to 636 stocks and 113 bonds in 1970. Sales on the American Stock Exchange did grow from $15 billion in 1970 to $47 billion in 1980 and $80 billion in 1989 but this represented a fall from 14% to 5% of the New York total. Markets in Chicago, San Francisco, and Philadelphia fared a little better, having some major local stocks to rely on, as well as a vibrant investor population, but collectively total sales reached only $215 billion in 1989 compared to $13 billion in 1970 or a rise from 12% to 14% of New York's over the period. By investing extensively in trading floor technology, as well as other areas of the market, the New York Stock Exchange was able to greatly increase capacity after the ending of minimum commissions, and maintained its position compared to other regulated exchanges.[16]

Where the New York Stock Exchange failed to compete was in the market for newer and smaller companies, especially in the rapidly emerging high technology sector. Here the NASDAQ market was dominant, achieving official recognition in 1979 from the SEC. Sales on NASDAQ rose from $68.7 billion in 1980 to $431.4 billion in 1989 or from 17% to 27% of New York's total. Contributing to NASDAQ's success was the growing importance of fully electronic integrated communication and trading networks. Instead of a system whereby dealers posted prices on electronic screens and then responded to telephone orders from brokers, these new trading networks allowed all authorized users to buy and sell online with computers automatically matching deals. By 1987 one of the leading trading platforms for stocks, Instinet, provided an automated trading network based in New York that connected 300 brokers dealing in over 8,000 US stocks via computer terminals. The competition from NASDAQ and the electronic trading systems meant that from 1982 onwards that the SEC was gradually forced to relax some of the rules it imposed upon regulated stock exchanges. Despite SEC attempts to bring the OTC market under its control in the 1980s, it remained largely unregulated compared to the stock exchanges.

The New York Stock Exchange did make some concessions to the challenge posed by electronic trading in the 1980s. One of the most important took place in 1986 when the rules forbidding links between brokers and specialists were relaxed. In an increasingly competitive environment, in which commission fees were shrinking, firms like Merrill Lynch, Goldman Sachs, Paine Webber, and Salomon Brothers increasingly traded commission free for the major institutional investors, expecting to make a profit from the spread between the buying and selling prices. This required access to large amounts of capital, whether generated internally or borrowed externally, and the ability to assemble or resell securities quickly, through an extensive investor network. Inevitably, this undermined the operations of the market markers on the floor of the New York Stock Exchange, who were increasingly absorbed into the activities of the largest brokers, so allowing them to become active broker/ dealers. Merging the wholesale and retail operations of brokers produced firms that did both. By acquiring White Weld in 1978 Merrill Lynch welded onto its extensive retail operations one of Wall Street's major investment houses, creating an integrated broking and investment banking operation. No longer could brokers rely on a steady flow of commission income for their earnings, whether generated from the financial institutions, such as those managing the mushrooming mutual funds, or from individual investors, with over 50 million in existence by the end of the 1980s. Instead, brokers had to become more responsive to the needs of fund mangers and more imaginative in maintaining the interest of individuals, which required different strategies from different firms in the pursuit of success. However, with banks still excluded from the securities business in the 1980s, brokerage firms had the business to themselves, though they operated in a highly competitive world.

Domestic competition encouraged the largest firms of US brokers to expand overseas in the 1980s, in pursuit of additional and less volatile earnings. However, outside the United States these brokers faced barriers to entry or strong competition. In Canada there were restrictions on the foreign ownership of local brokers whilst in Japan the entrenched position of a few large firms made it difficult for US brokers to build up a business. Elsewhere banks were important players in the securities business and had unrivalled access to investors, especially if they possessed an extensive branch network. With retail broking rarely an option the largest US brokers targeted the world's major investors, namely the financial institutions, and the largest borrowers, namely governments and multinational corporations, providing them with a range of services, including trading in world securities markets. In this they were increasingly successful, especially where market liberalization allowed them to join domestic exchanges and purchase domestic brokers, as happened in London as a result of Big Bang.

Thus, in the 1980s New York played an increasingly important role in the global securities market in two distinct ways. It was home to three of the largest securities markets in existence, not only catering for domestic investors but also attracting many from abroad. The market in US government bonds, the most liquid in the world, was used extensively as a temporary home for idle funds accumulating in banks. The New York Stock Exchange provided an unrivalled market in corporate stocks, including those issued by many of the world's biggest companies whose very reach made them attractive to investors far beyond the United States. Finally, the rapidly developing NASDAQ trading system provided a growing market for new and smaller companies, which were also attractive to investors because of the prospects for rapid capital gains. The combination of these three separate markets kept New York at the centre of the global securities market, even though the main international developments were taking place in London. In addition to its strengths in markets New York was also home to a number of firms with increasingly global operations, including the largest brokers and investment bankers such as Merrill Lynch and Goldman Sachs and the largest banks like Citibank. Freed from the restrictions of the Glass–Steagall Act when operating outside the United States, these US banks combined banking and broking, employing the vast resources of their deposit base to issue and trade securities. This combination was especially important in dealing with institutional investors when securities had to be bought outright and then resold with the return coming from the difference in price, not the commission paid, as had been the case previously. Hence, the importance of a London location for these US banks and brokers where they could operate as they chose, unlike in New York.[17]

Outside the United States and Britain, the pressure for fundamental change in national securities markets was limited in the 1980s unless driven by growing competition and government intervention. Such a combination was found mainly in those countries with financial systems similar to and influenced by those of the United States and Britain. By the early 1980s the Canadian securities market was finding it difficult to compete with the aggressive competition for business from US brokers, able to buy and sell at lower rates of commission or no commission at all, especially on behalf of Canadian institutional investors or in the stocks of the largest Canadian companies. The regime of fixed commissions was ended in 1982 whilst in 1987 Canadian financial institutions were allowed to operate as brokers and dealers. The Toronto Dominion Bank built up its own securities operation as a result but most acquired existing firms, with the Canadian Imperial Bank of Commerce absorbing Wood Grundy, the Royal Bank of Canada taking Dominion Securities, the Bank of Montreal taking Nesbitt Burns, and the

Bank of Nova Scotia buying Macleod Young Weir. The nationwide retail network of Canada's branch banks joined with a broking capacity largely centred on Toronto. As foreign ownership was still restricted Canadian banks were able to achieve this position with limited opposition from the United States, where banks were still prevented from operating nationally and entering broking. This freedom of operation also helped the Vancouver Stock Exchange emerge as a global centre for mining securities.[18]

Australia was in a similar position in the 1980s, with the domestic securities market challenged by both the government and external competition. In 1981 the Australian Trade Practices Commission began investigating restrictive practices on the Australian stock exchanges, noting similar actions in the United States and Britain. The following year's report required the ending of fixed commissions within 3 years. It took until April 1984 for the stock exchanges to agree to this, by which time London, the principal alternative market for Australian mining stocks, was already committed to moving in that direction. The ending of minimum commissions in Australia also brought a fundamental reform to the whole securities market, with the abandonment of the seat system and acceptance of corporate ownership of brokers, including foreign firms. In 1987 all Australian stock exchanges merged to create one organization covering the entire market.[19] Similar developments occurred in New Zealand, though at a slower pace. The Sydney Stock Exchange had abandoned the call-over trading system in 1953, when it adopted post-trading, but it was not until 1962 that same process began in New Zealand. Similarly, the deregulation of the New Zealand securities market lagged behind that of Australia in the 1980s. A Securities Commission was established in 1978 and exchange controls abandoned in 1984 but it was the loss of trading in major New Zealand companies, as they were listed in London or Australia, that forced the pace of change. Between 1984 and 1986 the New Zealand securities market was transformed by the amalgamation of all separate stock exchanges, the expansion of stock-broking firms through branches and links with financial institutions, and the ending of fixed commissions.[20]

Elsewhere the pace of change was both slow and modest, including countries like South Africa and India, despite their strong links to London and their high awareness of developments there and in New York. A general relaxation of the rules on the Johannesburg Stock Exchange in the 1980s did not extend to such radical steps as the abolition of minimum commissions. A market for smaller companies was set up in 1984 but generally the Johannesburg Stock Exchange remained immune from internal and external competition, with its monopoly within South Africa and the continuance of exchange controls, and there was no government pressure for reform.[21]

Similarly in India the stock exchanges remained self-governing institutions with a statutory monopoly over the market for corporate stocks. Minimum commissions remained and banks were excluded. Any expansion of membership was resisted by the stock exchanges in order to preserve the available business for themselves. The result was a proliferation of stock exchanges and thus a fragmentation of the Indian securities market, though Bombay remained the largest single centre for trading. Nevertheless, India did possess an active and growing securities market focusing on corporate stocks. In the mid-1980s there were some 1,400 brokers servicing approximately 10 million investors and the issues of around 4,000 companies. Though many of these remained closely held and generated little buying and selling there were others that attracted a wide investing public and were extensively traded. One such was Reliance Industries with 700,000 shareholders. Consequently, the issue of securities was a significant source of funding in India.[22]

Securities markets elsewhere continued to grow slowly, and new stock exchanges did appear, but the amount of business remained low, often stifled by government antagonism towards corporate enterprise, excessive bureaucratic control over the marketplace, and resistance to change within the organization itself. Many stock exchanges remained under the management of the state, as in Peru, or heavily regulated by governments, as was the case across Africa. In Kuwait the government intervened to control the rapidly expanding unofficial market after a crisis in 1982. When prices collapsed many of those involved reneged on their deals and the informal nature of the market meant that no mechanisms were in place to cope with such a situation. In the absence of a formal self-regulating stock exchange, government intervention became inevitable. Successful securities markets were emerging in other centres, often in response to the willingness of governments to relax the prohibitions and restrictions of the past. Prior to 1987 the Jakarta Stock Exchange operated under a highly restrictive regime imposed by the government with the aim of preventing fraud. This stifled the securities market with only thirteen stocks listed in 1982. Following reforms which removed these controls and restrictions, the securities market suddenly expanded, attracting domestic and foreign investors as well as domestic companies looking for financial support. The result was a frenzy of speculation in 1989 that left 100 quoted companies, capitalized at $19.2 billion, and substantial foreign investment. By then a second stock exchange had been formed, along with a flourishing OTC market, and the Indonesian securities market was being served by both local and foreign banks and brokers.

Even communist regimes were coming to recognize the role played by stocks and bonds in financing both the state and private enterprise. The Chinese government began issuing bonds in 1981 and in 1987 joint-stock companies appeared. A market for the securities issued then followed with bond trading becoming well established in Shanghai and Shenyang by 1986. Formal stock exchanges were formed in 1990 in Shanghai and Shenzhen. Nevertheless, these developments still left China, the world's most populous country, with a far smaller and less important securities market than the neighbouring island state of Hong Kong. There a single stock exchange had appeared in 1986, after years of government pressure, and was left to regulate the securities market there with fairly minimal government supervision. However, the stock market crash of 1987 exposed the inadequacies of the newly created stock exchange to simultaneously police the activities of its own membership and to maintain an orderly market. A government inquiry led to the formation in 1989 of a Securities Commission to oversee the market. Such an arrangement became standard practice across the developed securities markets of the world by the end of 1980s.[23]

Surprisingly, there were two parts of the world, both with advanced capitalist economies and highly sophisticated financial systems, where the securities market proved highly resistant to change. One was continental western Europe and the other was Japan. Across continental Europe the degree of change remained limited in the 1980s, despite the challenges posed by developments in London. Big Bang made the London Stock Exchange a very competitive marketplace for the stocks of the largest European companies, attracting orders from the major European banks and financial institutions already accustomed to use it for trading in Eurobonds. By the end of the 1980s an active market in the shares of some of Germany's largest companies, such as Siemens and Deutsche Bank, was to be found in London as they were extensively held by financial institutions operating there. Paris also lost out to London in the second-half of the 1980s. The response among the stock exchanges of continental Europe to developments in London was usually tardy and limited. Commission rates were reduced and restrictions modified. These stock exchanges were much more willing to create additional markets catering for small and new companies, as in Amsterdam in 1982 and Frankfurt in 1986, than to radically reform the way they operated and the charges they made. Similarly, new technology was introduced but only to enhance the display and dissemination of information rather than to provide an alternative to traditional methods of buying and selling stocks.

Changes were being forced upon these stock exchanges as their major users, namely the banks, started to develop electronic computer networks which replicated the markets that stock exchanges provided and allowed floor trading to be bypassed completely. The Paris Bourse replaced its open outcry trading with an electronic auction system in 1986 whilst in the Netherlands an electronic trading system was gradually rolled out on the Amsterdam Stock Exchange from 1988 onwards. German banks developed an alternative onscreen trading system, IBIS, in 1989 so providing a direct challenge to the stock exchanges. However, where a stock exchange enjoyed a monopoly of its domestic market and had government backing, as was the case with Milan and Paris, it was able to continue resisting the forces pressing for fundamental change, despite these technological developments. The Paris Bourse placed an ever greater reliance upon its ability to dominate the domestic market for government debt and corporate stocks and bonds whilst French trading in foreign securities and foreign trading in French securities took place in London. As long as the government remained supportive and activity in domestic stocks for domestic investors continued to grow the Paris Bourse prospered in an unreformed state.[24]

By the end of the 1980s the Japanese securities market was one of the largest in the world, with the Tokyo and New York stock exchanges having almost identical capitalizations at $2.7/2.8 trillion in 1990. They were both markets largely for corporate stocks, and to a lesser extent bonds, with the huge government debts of each country being almost entirely traded on the OTC market. Only in the 1960s had domestic bond issues by the government begun to be important, rising from a mere 446.8 billion yen in 1960 to 3.6 trillion in 1970, but thereafter they escalated to very large proportions, reaching 71.9 trillion in 1980 and then 168.5 trillion in 1990.[25] There were also other similarities between the Japanese and US securities markets, notably the exclusion of banks from operating as brokers. Like their US equivalents, the largest Japanese brokers had branches throughout their domestic market and had expanded abroad, including into neighbouring Asian countries, the United States, and Western Europe. Nomura had fifty-one offices in twenty-three countries in 1990. Finally, control over the securities market rested with a Securities Commission in both countries with everyday authority devolved to the dominant stock exchange. However, there the parallel ended, as there was almost no OTC market in Japanese stocks. In Japan stock exchanges continued to enjoy a statutory monopoly of trading in quoted stocks, which in turn gave the Securities Commission there the authority that the SEC in the US lacked, because of its inability to control OTC trading.

This arrangement eased the regulation of the Japanese securities market, protected the position of the Tokyo Stock Exchange and enhanced the power of the largest brokers. In Japan the problem of unregulated trading was solved as there were no markets outside the stock exchanges, apart from government bonds. As bonds were largely traded between the banks, insurance companies and other financial institutions, which were deemed sufficiently aware of the risks involved, such a situation was considered acceptable. This arrangement also solved the 'free-rider' problem whereby the non-members of stock exchanges traded on the prices generated by those who bore the costs and obeyed the rules of the markets. Additionally, as business gravitated towards the broadest and deepest market the Tokyo Stock Exchange benefited and its share of total trading continued to grow in the 1980s. In 1990 turnover on the Tokyo Stock Exchange was 84% of the national total with the OTC share being negligible. Thus, by regulating the Tokyo Stock Exchange the government was able to regulate the entire market for stocks though at the cost of giving that institution a virtual monopoly. In turn, that monopoly even extended to the brokers as four firms continued to dominate the market for both stocks and bonds. Whereas Nomura alone undertook 30% of all trading on the Tokyo Stock Exchange, foreign firms had only a 5% share by the late 1980s, having had to wait until 1986 for admission. Consequently, in the interests of achieving effective control over the Japanese securities market the government entrusted monopoly power to the Tokyo Stock Exchange and a small number of its largest member firms.

This monopoly provided little incentive to modernize the Japanese securities market, especially as the volume of business grew rapidly. A second section to the market opened in 1961 to cope with the extra companies seeking a quotation added greatly to capacity without the need to change. Trading volume per day rose from 90 million shares in 1960 to 144 million in 1970, 359 million in 1980, and then to 500 million in 1990, having peaked in 1988. By 1990 the Tokyo Stock Exchange provided a market for 1,627 companies with a market value of 379.2 trillion yen compared to 1,280 companies with a market value of 16.2 billion in 1970. There was no incentive to dispense with minimum commission rates, reform the way trading was conducted, or introduce any of the other changes taking place elsewhere. What continued to drive change on the Tokyo Stock Exchange was the need to further expand capacity if it was to retain its domestic monopoly by quoting all the stocks issued by Japanese companies. This forced the Tokyo Stock Exchange to devise ways of coping with the large block trades of the financial institutions and the small retail orders of individual investors. That led to both the introduction of new technology and the relaxation of certain rules. Computerized trading was introduced in 1982 whilst markets were created for particular groups of stocks.

This failure to modernize the Japanese securities market had implications for the entire financial system. In 1990, whereas individuals owned 21% of the market value of Japanese companies, and foreigners a mere 4%, the holdings of insurance companies were 16%, banks 21%, and other companies 30%. Insurance company holdings reflected the move towards stocks at a time of inflation, but those of both banks and other companies were a product of the interlocking nature of Japanese business. Driven by inefficiencies and costs in the Japanese securities market, due to over-regulation and the power of the Tokyo Stock Exchange, companies and banks internalized financial arrangements. Corporate stocks and bonds were not issued, held, or traded on the open market but locked away in the treasuries of specific banks and allied enterprises, creating a network of linked businesses covering both finance and manufacturing. This produced a steady flow of funds to favoured areas, assisting Japanese industrial development, but also creating problems as the securities issued lacked a deep and active market and could not be sold if the returns did not materialize or a financial crisis required banks to liquidate assets. This classic paradox faced by all banks in trying to balance assets and liabilities was the reason that securities markets had become so important. The ability to buy, hold, and sell securities was an essential ingredient in any successful financial system, providing the flexibility necessary if risk and return were to be balanced and survival over time achieved.

Failure to respond to the needs of Japanese corporate borrowers and Japanese investors encouraged them to use overseas securities markets to circumvent domestic costs and rigidities. In the early 1980s the Japanese government relaxed controls over inward and outward capital flows, producing a rapid internationalization of both investment and borrowing. Offshore bond issues by Japanese companies rose from 562 billion yen in 1978 to 11,831 billion in 1989. In 1989 between 60% and 70% of the Eurobonds issued by Japanese companies were bought by Japanese investors, and there was an active market in dollar bonds in Japan. This helped to make the issue of stocks and bonds a more important source of finance for Japanese companies, rising from 5% of funds in the first-half of the decade to 11% in the second-half. However, it did not internationalize the Japanese securities market, which remained heavily focused on the trading of Japanese investors in the stocks of Japanese companies and the bonds issued by the Japanese government.[26]

THE GLOBAL MARKET IN THE 1980s

Generally in the 1980s there was a huge increase in the trading volumes experienced by stock markets around the world, with equity turnover in New York rising almost fourfold, Tokyo ninefold, and London 17-fold. This removed much of the incentive for change among stock exchanges supported by their national governments and not exposed to an erosion of business from either OTC trading at home or alternative markets abroad. Nevertheless, there was a gradual freeing of domestic financial markets during the decade, as governments recognized the limits of their power and sought to regulate rather than control. Governments also recognized their inability to control international financial flows and sought instead to moderate their impact. The world within which domestic securities markets operated became a much more competitive environment, especially given the revolution in communications and trading technology. Business in securities markets flowed ever more strongly to the largest and most liquid markets. This happened nationally with Frankfurt, London, Milan, New York, Paris, Sydney, and Tokyo dominant within their domestic securities markets. It also happened internationally with London in particular stealing a march over all others. As a result of Big Bang London combined an already strong position in bonds with one in stocks. Nevertheless, the broadest and deepest markets remained at the national level with New York in the supreme position of possessing three of the most important.

The relaxation of government controls produced a slow but growing convergence among securities markets worldwide in the 1980s. Increasingly the relationship between the securities market and the state was conducted through an independent statutory body rather than either directly by the government or devolved to the main stock exchange. Those bodies were more aware of the inefficiencies and distortions created by the restrictive practices inherent in any stock exchange, and several acted to improve the level of competition. Finally, trading methods relied more and more upon electronic networks and the telephone rather than in person on the stock exchange floor. Significant differences remained but by 1990 it was evident that no country could resist the pressure for change, even those that possessed centralized economies and rigid external controls.[27]

Despite increasing liberalization most domestic securities markets remained biased towards domestic investors trading domestic securities. Only slowly were foreign securities quoted, foreign firms admitted to the stock exchange, and foreign investors catered for. London remained a rare exception. Though there was a growing recognition among governments that restrictive laws governing the securities markets hampered their efficiency and competitiveness, there remained a general reluctance to force through fundamental change. Each country regulated its securities market in its own way to suit its own needs and circumstances. Most securities markets focused on domestic requirements to the neglect of the international market, creating important differences in their national markets and their participation in the international market. This can be seen in the differences between countries in pension provision, for managers of such funds played an increasingly important role within the securities market, being responsible for the investment of vast sums of money. Pension fund investment was relatively more important in the United States and the UK than in continental Europe or Japan, where state provision financed from taxation and government borrowing was more common.[28]

Given the diversity in aims and attitudes between countries and governments, harmonization of national securities markets was almost impossible to achieve. The institutional arrangements of the markets themselves created major differences. This was especially true of corporate stocks for the more international bond market was driven by institutional investors and served by banks and brokers who increasingly operated from offices located in the major financial centres. Nevertheless, even here domestic bond markets tended to favour domestic issuers and borrowers, with the self-interest of governments well to the fore, as they were major issuers of debt. By 1990 governments were still treating their domestic securities markets as isolated from the global market. Nevertheless, the waning power of governments can be seen in the case of Sweden. In 1979 the Swedish government abolished the tax on securities transactions but it was then reintroduced in 1984 and doubled in 1986. However, with the ending of currency controls in 1989 the market in the stocks of the major Swedish companies moved abroad, mainly to London, forcing the government to abandon the tax in 1991. A country with a small and rather marginal securities market could not afford the luxury of a tax on transactions, no matter how attractive it was for revenue purposes, if the result was to drive trading abroad, along with the employment and other activities linked to the buying and selling of stocks and bonds.[29]

Government intervention in the securities market, however well intentioned, tried to satisfy too many divergent and incompatible ends, most of which were driven by national rather than global considerations and included many political and social objectives as well as wider economic ones. Even among the financial aims many were in conflict, such as attempts to correct perceived market failures, protect investors against fraud and default, minimize the risk to the entire financial system of failures, and ensure a level playing field for all participants. It was impossible to achieve all these goals simultaneously whilst at the same time permitting the market to function efficiently and satisfy the needs of all participants, namely the investors, the borrowers, and the intermediaries, for these also had different requirements. Governments and regulatory bodies often attempted to impose a uniform, standard mode of operation and behaviour on the entire securities market with the result that large numbers of investors, borrowers, and intermediaries functioned under a sub-optimal system. This encouraged increased use of alternatives to the regulated securities market and the proliferation of OTC solutions. With the advent of computerized trading systems operating outside the formal exchanges there were increased opportunities to evade regulations. A consequence of regulation was often the splintering of securities trading across many different markets and intermediaries, resulting in less liquidity than if all trading had been centralized. This occurred even at a time when communications and computing capacity permitted increasing centralization of trading activity, though it was also due to the need to tailor markets to suit the needs of the securities traded, and those who traded them.[30]

Continued fragmentation of the global securities market meant that the world continued to lack the large and liquid markets now essential, in the absence of inter-government cooperation and controls, to prevent the shocks and imbalances of the past. Such markets were required for banks and financial institutions to employ productively the huge sums of money that they only held on a temporary basis. This required securities that could be easily and quickly bought and sold without causing much variation of price, and only a few markets possessed that capability. Government bond markets in New York, Frankfurt, and Tokyo did offer this but these were not freely or equally available to all. Instead, the Eurobond market increasingly played this role, offering international securities held by international investors and traded by international firms in an international market.

However, the Eurobond market was but one component of the rapidly developing global securities market of the 1980s, for that also involved links between national markets, aided by the ending of exchange controls in many countries and the easing of domestic restrictions. This can be seen from the growing volume of US transactions involving the United States, centring on New York. In 1980 US transactions in foreign securities totalled $53.1 billion with around 70% being in bonds. In the same year foreign transactions in US securities amounted to $198 billion of which some 50% was in Treasury bonds. Altogether that meant an ebb and flow of securities through New York totalling $250 billion. By 1989 the magnitude of these transactions had been totally transformed. In that year US transactions in foreign securities reached $706.9 billion, though still split roughly 70%/30% in favour of bonds. Foreign transactions in US securities were far greater, amounting to $4.8 trillion, of which almost 90% was in US Treasury bonds. Overall, this meant that the ebb and flow of international transactions in securities through New York had reached $5.5 trillion or a twenty twofold increase in the course of that single decade.[31]

A similar phenomenon took place in Japan, with Tokyo, the world's second largest financial centre, at the centre of activity. There was a growing two-way traffic in securities as Japanese institutions bought foreign bonds and foreign institutions bought Japanese stocks. Japanese investors sought more attractive returns than were available domestically whilst foreign investors sought to participate in the rapid growth of the Japanese economy. The relaxation of controls over US interest rates in 1979 made US assets attractive to the Japanese whilst British abandonment of exchange controls in the same year opened up sterling securities. This produced a continuous movement of both stocks and bonds to and from Japan. In 1990 the two-way pull in stocks generated a turnover of $414 billion whilst that in bonds was $3,085 billion or over seven times greater.[32]

More generally an estimate for trading in stocks for the United States and Japan shows a total transformation in the volume of international activity in the 1980s. In 1977 gross overseas activity in domestic stocks was $25.6 trillion for the United States and $1.8 trillion for Japan whilst in 1989 the equivalent amount was $416.7 trillion for the United States and $55.2 trillion for Japan. From the reverse angle of gross domestic activity in overseas stocks, the figure for 1977 for the United States was $4.9 trillion and a mere $60 billion for Japan. In contrast, by 1989 the total was $232.4 trillion for the United States and $22.9 trillion for Japan.[33] Along with the operation of an international market for stocks and bonds in London, these transactions involving New York and Tokyo indicated that the global securities market was once again effective in transferring assets around the world in response to constant fluctuations in supply and demand. The international bond market regained its position as one of the stabilizing forces in the global economy, providing banks and other financial institutions with the means of employing temporarily idle funds productively, moving money around the world easily, and constantly adjusting assets and liabilities so as to avoid a catastrophic crisis that would endanger their survival. In 1987–90 financial institutions held 60% of long-term government bonds in the United States, 82% in Japan, 67% in the UK, 55% in Germany, 65% in France, and 40% in Italy.[34]

During the 1980s the contribution that the global securities market could make to both the mobility of finance and the stability of financial systems was gradually recognized. Financial crises continued to occur, largely due to the actions of governments as they borrowed and spent without regard for the domestic and international consequences of their actions. However, these could now be absorbed within an international financial system that possessed the ability to respond by moving and liquidating assets, and avoiding both a widespread collapse and the need for government intervention. However, the contribution being made by the global securities market to the stability of the international financial system still went unrecognized by the majority, who believed that they were witnessing speculative surges around the world, contributing to currency instability. Rather there was a financial system capable of adjusting to the problems occurring in one country by diffusing and absorbing its impact around the world, so lessening the seriousness of what had taken place, and therefore the permanent damage caused. The global securities market allowed the easy transfer of assets to allow those in a weaker financial situation to liquidate investments and repay creditors on an international basis. Increasingly banks conducted their lending and borrowing through stocks and bonds possessing liquid markets, so that they were always in the position of being able to liquidate assets, when required and even at a loss, so lessening the risk of collapse.

This can be seen in the stock market crash of October 1987, which was truly international in scope, including not only the main financial centres of London, New York, and Tokyo but also much smaller markets such as Singapore and New Zealand. The crash was sparked by fears about the weakness of the US dollar, in the face of rising interest rates, combined with over-expansion in those markets where de-regulation had gone furthest in the 1980s, such as London. Those operating in these newly liberalized securities markets took time to adjust their ways of operating to produce a balance between risk taking and prudence, as that required practical experience and received wisdom as well as mathematical knowledge and programmed trading. The former came through time whilst the latter could be quickly learnt. However, the crisis did not only affect stock markets but also extended to bonds, with the Eurobond market experiencing a downturn in 1987–8. The progressive de-regulation of national securities markets and the internationalization of trading with the likes of the Eurobond had rendered governments unable to control what was taking place and to isolate their domestic market from a worldwide contagion. However, recovery from the stock market crash of 1987 was fairly rapid. The worst consequences were not experienced by New York, Tokyo, and London, because these financial centres had broad and deep markets but by those that were shallow and narrow. Three weeks after the collapse the New York market was down 15.5%, Tokyo 18.3%, and London 28.5%. In contrast, Australia was down 41.6% and New Zealand 37.4%. The 1987 crash indicated the resilience now possessed by global financial centres, rather than their exposure to crisis and the risk of systemic collapse. Booms and slumps were an inevitable part of any active and dynamic financial system which was why it was important to have a fully functioning global securities market to spread the activity and cushion the effects. What was experienced in 1987 were the problems associated with the transition from a system highly reliant upon government control and central bank intervention to one based on the operation of open and independent markets and the constant ebb and flow of money and securities between countries.[35]

CONCLUSION

By the end of the 1960s the financial and monetary systems set up after the Second World War were already disintegrating. Internationally, the Bretton Woods System proved far too rigid to cope with a rapidly changing world economy where the $ and the £ were no longer totally dominant. New and more flexible arrangements were desperately needed. Rigid control by central banks and inter-government agreements no longer sufficed for a world where international financial flows were growing rapidly in amount and variety. Domestically, the controls placed over the securities market had stifled development, supported anti-competitive practices and encouraged evasion. In a world where OTC markets operated both within countries and internationally the power of regulated markets was steadily undermined. It was also clear to a number of governments that the solution was no longer to be found in bolstering the authority of the stock exchanges for this led to the abuse of a monopoly position. Finally, the ability to combine advances in communications with the processing power of the computer was creating the ability to bypass physical trading floors completely by establishing an interactive network linking buyers and sellers directly. As yet this did not extend much beyond the extensive use of the telephone to create a market outside the stock exchange but some already saw where this was leading.

To writers at the time and subsequently, what was happening to international financial flows and the integration of national stock and bond markets into a global securities market in the 1970s and 1980s appeared totally novel. Prior to that time there was the widespread belief that national capital markets had remained well insulated and isolated from each other for hundreds of years, thanks to regulatory restrictions and communication/transaction difficulties. The historical role of securities markets had been extinguished from memory during the twentieth century, given the prominence of banks and governments. It thus seemed natural to suggest that the transformation was due to the revolution in technology. 'With the rapid developments in communications technology, the international opportunities suddenly made available to national investors appeared to be almost infinite when the regulatory barriers were lifted in the late 1970s and early 1980s.'[36] In reality it was the removal of these internal and external barriers that reversed the trends in place since the First World War, and especially since 1945. Once these barriers started to fall, the forces of globalization, greatly accentuated by the enormous advances in telecommunications and data processing, destroyed the independence of national markets, forcing governments to change the way these markets were regulated. Thus divisions between banks and brokerage houses were unsustainable if the combination of the two produced the most competitive business in the global securities market.

However, by 1990 the progress of these changes was largely confined to the world dominated by an Anglo-American style of financial system, namely the United States, Britain, Australia, Canada, and New Zealand. Even countries such as Japan, India or South Africa, which had been heavily influenced by the Anglo-American model remained unreformed though some changes were beginning to take place. Across most of the world, and especially in Europe, securities markets remained tightly regulated and rather marginal, with governments and banks dominating. Even internationally, fixed exchange rates and managed currencies still existed in many countries, as well as a degree of central bank intervention in most others. Capital movements had not yet been freed from the controls that had long prevented the full integration of national securities markets despite the enormous advances made in communications. The process of transformation had begun in the course of the 1970s and 1980s but was a long way from completion, not least because politicians and government officials were reluctant to give up the power they had come to possess. In this they were supported not only by the population at large, who associated activity in the securities market with fraud and speculation, but also by numerous academic economists wedded to a belief that the intervention of government and the direction of bankers was required for the successful management of the economy. The belief in the power of markets that came with Adam Smith in the eighteenth century had been destroyed in the twentieth and had yet to be fully recovered even in the 1980s, with the contribution made by the constant buying and selling of stocks and bonds being the last to experience any kind of rehabilitation.

9

A Worldwide Revolution: Securities Markets From 1990[1]

Towards the end of the twentieth century the global securities market reached and probably surpassed the position it had occupied at the beginning. Securities markets had once again become essential components of national financial systems and provided a key element in the financial flows that redistributed savings around the world, bringing stability to the international monetary system. Nevertheless, this did not mean a return to the conditions prevailing before the First World War. The world that existed around 2000 was very different from that of a hundred years previously. Governments possessed much greater influence even though they had retreated from the excessive centralization, control, and ownership that had characterized much of the intervening period. Regulation at national level, supranational organizations, and intergovernment agencies and agreements conditioned much of what took place in financial markets whereas around 1900 the level of government intervention was almost minimal in comparison. Another major difference was the degree of integration made possible by technological change in communications and computing. Though the telegraph and the telephone had already transformed the global securities market by 1900, the speed and capacity available through electronic trading networks, at low cost, revolutionized both wholesale and retail operations by 2000. Finally, the enormous advances made in corporate organization and management allowed the creation of global financial businesses on a scale which had not existed previously. No longer was the global securities market just the product of transactions between national businesses and national markets. It now included internal transfers between components of the same company.

The operations of global banks and brokers and access to the same marketplace no matter where the physical location of the participant changed the whole nature of the global securities market. This death of distance was an entirely new feature with far reaching consequences. Informal networks became managed organizations with power to challenge governments in a way that markets never could. However, it would be a mistake to exaggerate the differences with the past for even global enterprises were run from particular locations and operated under specific jurisdictions, which imbued them with distinctive, and often national, characteristics. Similarly, for all the importance of a single global securities market, often this still meant just the ability to access a particular trading environment from a distance. The ownership of securities continued to exhibit a heavy national bias with few, if any, of the stocks and bonds in existence commanding a truly global following. In that sense the global securities market around 2000 continued to possess many of the elements found in that of a hundred years before.

THE TRIUMPH OF SECURITIES

In the late twentieth century the forces of supply and demand led to an inexorable growth in the importance of securities. Whether from the perspective of those issuing stocks and bonds, such as governments and business, or from those buying them, including individuals and financial institutions, securities were seen increasingly as either a cheap and convenient means to raise finance or as attractive assets in terms of returns and flexibility. This was despite financial crises involving sovereign borrowers such as Russia and Argentina, speculative bubbles like the dot.com boom, or even corporate scandals as in the case of Enron and Parmalat. Important as these were their overall effect in the use of securities worldwide was both limited and temporary. Most governments did not default and most companies serviced their bonds and increased their earnings. In 1990 the market value of all securities in circulation was around $21.2 trillion, split almost equally between stocks ($10.8 trillion) and bonds ($10.4 trillion). By 1997 the figure had doubled to around $40 trillion, again split equally between stocks and bonds. Growth by 2005 was even more rapid, with the amount reaching $95 trillion, or more than double the 1997 figure and almost five times that of fifteen years before. With the collapse of numerous high-technology companies and a rash of corporate scandals, especially in the United States in the early years of the twenty-first century, bonds became relatively more important. By 2005 the market value of bonds was $58.4 trillion compared to stocks at $36.6 trillion.[2]

This absolute growth in the value of securities in circulation was reflected in their rising importance within the world economy. Between 1990 and 2004 the ratio of bonds alone to world GDP doubled from around 60% to 117%, as they occupied an ever more prominent position in the financing of governments and business and in the assets of investors.[3] A similar development took place in stocks. During the 1990s the ratio of quoted stocks to world GDP rose from 57% to 99%. Though as always the issue of stocks for business funding remained low compared to reinvested earnings and bank loans, their importance to management and investors was high, as was the contribution they made to particular sectors and situations.[4] Though the dot.com boom left many investors nursing large losses it represented a very large investment in a high-risk area with enormous potential for economic growth. By 2000, securities had clearly acquired a major position within the world's economy.

Governments actively contributed to the triumph of securities by the process of privatization. After the British government disposed of state assets through public sales of shares in the 1980s, the rest of the world followed suit in the 1990s. From Western Europe, through Eastern Europe and Turkey to Asia and Latin America, governments were attracted by the possibility of selling poorly performing enterprises and receiving an immediate influx of funds and enhanced revenue through the taxation of corporate profits. Between 1990 and 1999 a total of $850 billion in state assets around the world was transferred from public to private hands. More than 40% of the total was in Europe, including the previously communist countries of Eastern Europe and the Soviet Union. Many privatized assets belonged to state enterprises such as those providing telecommunications and electricity, operating banks and airlines, and producing or distributing oil, gas, and minerals. Their stocks and bonds were of immediate appeal to investors at home and abroad, especially when sold at a generous discount in order to stimulate interest. The result was the sudden appearance of a large investing public, both individuals and institutions, owning highly liquid securities in numerous countries. Even in Western Europe, with its long tradition of major joint-stock companies, 70% of the most liquid stocks by 2000 were privatization issues. Among these was Deutsche Telecom, privatized in 1996 when DM 20 billion in stocks was issued to the German public. This transformed their enthusiasm for securities, helping to fuel their active participation in the dot.com boom, especially through online trading.[5]

Despite the amount raised from privatization, governments also continued to borrow heavily, and were able to do so fairly easily as most took care to service their debts or renegotiate terms if difficulty arose. With no major conflict between the leading countries this borrowing was largely undertaken to meet an annual shortfall between the revenue from taxation and the rising expenditure incurred in such areas as improved provision for health and education, major infrastructure like roads and housing, and the escalating costs of pension provision for a population with increasing life expectancy. As always, governments found it much easier to spend, which was popular with the electorate, than to tax, which was not, and so chose the former over the latter. The Japanese national debt tripled between 1990 and 2002, reaching over 600 trillion yen, the largest in the world. It overtook that of the United States, which itself grew from $2.2 trillion in 1990 to $3.6 trillion in 2003.[6] As most of this government debt was in bonds the amount in circulation rose enormously. Between 1990 and 2005 the total rose from $5.8 trillion to $21.7 trillion, or fourfold.[7]

This, combined with privatization, produced an enormous expansion in the stock of securities. Business also continued to issue stocks and bonds, whether to finance the development of new products, processes, and markets, as with the high-technology companies, or to acquire other companies in allied fields to expand the company being managed. Increasingly the corporate form of enterprise was favoured throughout the world because of the appeal of their stocks and bonds to all categories of investor and the flexibility of operation provided to management. By 2005 the world's 500 largest companies had a market capitalization of $18.9 trillion, or equivalent to 20% of the total value of stocks and bonds in circulation. Though over 40% of these companies had their head office in the United States, and most of the others in Western Europe and Japan, a growing number were emerging from Australia, Brazil, China, India, Russia, Saudi Arabia, Singapore, South Africa, South Korea, and Taiwan. These companies ranged from huge multinationals with operations spread across the globe, like the oil companies ExxonMobil, BP, and Royal Dutch Shell, to national champions producing specialized products for the world market, such as in mobile telephones with Nokia of Finland. Almost all areas of economic activity were now undertaken by joint-stock companies, giving investors a wide choice.[8]

There was an enormous expansion both in the value of securities in circulation and also in the variety on offer. Government bonds were packaged in innumerable ways to appeal to all types of investors, through the use of different currencies, maturity dates, or fixed versus variable interest rates. Companies issued both stocks and bonds, again appealing to different type of investors depending on the prospects of the business and the degree of risk involved. Those concerned by inflation, which had destroyed the value of fixed-interest investment in many countries in the post-war years, favoured shares, which offered the prospect of capital gain as well as a revenue stream. In contrast, those with fixed future commitments favoured bonds as both the annual income and the date of repayment were known. This flexibility was one of the reasons why securities were so popular among all types of investors.

Banks were less willing to make loans to business and government because of the risks involved. A series of crises in the 1970s and 1980s had made banks increasingly aware that their survival was threatened if large borrowers failed to service their loans or repay on the due date. Previously, national governments and central banks had provided support but in an era of globalization and international competition such certainties no longer existed. Instead banks in the 1990s had to operate within a complex, competitive and changing environment if they were to survive and prosper. The old assumptions of the highly regulated post-war era had disappeared leaving banks to make judgements about balancing risk and return. Here securities made a major contribution by allowing banks to better match assets and liabilities. They could either invest directly in securities or lend to those who did. This could be done both in the short term, as with the simultaneous purchase and resale agreements in the highly liquid government bond markets, or in the long term by holding corporate bonds rather than making loans, as these could be sold if required in a financial crisis. Such operations could also be conducted through an intermediary like a mutual or hedge fund, which supplemented the capital raised from investors by employing short-term funds borrowed from banks at low interest to buy, sell, and hold securities of all kinds.

By holding highly marketable assets, by re-packaging loans in the form of bonds, and by lending to those operating in the securities markets, banks were able simultaneously to reduce their risks and increase their returns whilst still meeting the needs of those requiring finance or a home for their savings. This meant a greatly enhanced role for securities within the financial system. Although many saw this as contributing to the risks of collapse, because of the volatility of prices in securities markets, the result was quite the reverse, providing banks with an environment within which they could operate safely and profitably. It did not produce a financial system without crises but one that was sufficiently robust not to collapse when they did occur and with the ability to limit the damage and recover quickly. The dramatic East Asian crisis of 1997 did not have the damaging consequences of the Latin American financial crisis of the early 1980s, because so much lending was now in the form of securities tradable both between institutions and across borders. Similarly, the dot.com or TMT speculative boom and collapse did not lead to financial crisis though many individual and institutional investors lost heavily as a result. If these governments and companies had been directly financed through bank loans, the consequences for the financial system would have been disastrous through the usual sequence of a collapse in confidence, depositor withdrawals, and bank failures. However, these did not occur to any great extent, indicating the resilience that securities gave to the financial system.

The investing public also expanded enormously. This was not simply a product of growing affluence and a willingness to diversify beyond bank deposits and property. The privatization programmes had stimulated investor interest in such countries as Germany as well as in former communist economies where private property had hardly existed. In Britain the number of individual investors reached 16 million by 2000, largely as a result of privatization. However, important as was the enormous expansion in the number of individual investors, with the dot.com speculative bubble being one of the results, much more marked was the continuing growth of the institutional investor. Collective investment vehicles were especially popular whether of the more traditional form, such as mutual funds that had long been popular in the United States, or the new variant, the hedge fund. By 2005 mutual funds worldwide controlled assets of between $30 and $40 trillion with the rapidly emerging hedge funds having $1 trillion at their disposal. Not all of this comprised stocks and bonds but hedge funds, in particular, were very active traders in securities, responsible for between a third and a half of daily turnover in London and New York by 2005. Dwarfing all types of collective investments were occupational pension funds, which covered many of those in employment in the most developed, and thus most affluent, economies. These either possessed their own managements or had their funds handled by banks, brokers, or specialist fund managers. Pension funds were major holders of stocks and bonds, controlling much of that outstanding in countries like the United States and Britain. Elsewhere their importance was much less as the state accepted greater responsibility for pension provision. In 1999 pension fund assets totalled $1,241 billion in Britain but only $286 billion in Germany, $195 billion in Italy, and $95 billion in France.

Irrespective of these national variations the outcome was to return securities to centre stage. The great events of the twentieth century, such as the two world wars, the rise and fall of Fascism, and the triumph and decline of Communism had left no permanent legacy on the global securities market, apart from the fact that it had delayed and distorted its development. However, they had left a permanent legacy in the greatly enhanced power of governments and an antagonism towards global forces. The pre-1914 era was one of relative economic liberalism, in which governments interfered little in the operation of economies whether internally or externally, and one of relative openness encouraged by the existence of empires both within Europe and across the world. The ruling philosophies of liberalism and imperialism counteracted the ever-present forces of interventionism and nationalism. Although the latter triumphed after each of the two world wars, liberalism and internationalism slowly recovered the dominant position which they had once occupied, and which was conducive to the successful operation of a global securities market.

GLOBALIZATION AND GOVERNMENT

From the 1980s global forces of supply and demand supplanted those operating within national or even supranational economies. The problem with government intervention in financial activities was that it was driven by short-term national interest and so played scant regard to long-term external considerations. Globalization began to regain its momentum in the 1950s, but then slowed down and was even reversed in part in the 1960s and 1970s because of national and international monetary, financial, and economic turbulence. However, it then became unstoppable during the 1980s and 1990s, given the inability of national governments to erect and then maintain effective barriers against the free movement of goods and capital. Governments did not lose their appetite for intervention but they increasingly recognized the limitations to the power they possessed, the ineffectiveness of the measures they could take, and the benefits to be gained from an increased exposure to the global marketplace. Nevertheless, considerable barriers to worldwide economic integration still existed, being especially acute in the international mobility of labour, the world market for services, and the international trade in agricultural produce.

However, these remaining barriers and the degree of government intervention were now at a much lower level than before, increasingly so in the field of finance. The 1990s witnessed a gathering momentum to exchange rate liberalization around the world, accompanied by the ending of restrictions on financial flows. Whereas previously governments had sought to restrict or impede financial inflows and outflows, in order to bolster the control they exercised over the national economy, this gradually ceased from the 1990s onwards. In consequence national securities markets were simultaneously exposed to external competition and integrated into the global market. However, some government control remained. Almost universally governments either enhanced existing supervisory authorities or established them to ensure that national securities markets remained responsive to the wishes of national governments. What had changed was the aim, which was much less that of control and direction and more to ensure that abuses were eliminated, the exercise of monopoly power restrained, and any risks to the financial system minimized. Nevertheless, combined with other government actions covering such areas as taxation, investment, corporate governance, and pension provision, the result was to foster national characteristics within national securities markets.[9] The universal problem faced by the securities market was the distrust found among many in government and their advisors. Constant price fluctuations, and the large and continuous financial flows, were seen as both random and valueless, being driven by speculation. Even worse they were regarded as destabilizing, posing a serious threat to national financial systems. The basic philosophy of those in government was akin to that of those running a railway line in which access and exit were controlled, the movement of people and freight was carefully directed and managed, and there was an overall authority in place. In contrast, the world of the market was like a road network in which individuals of all types and sizes pursued their own objectives in their own way though using common facilities and obeying general rules, to a degree. Under these circumstances the best that the securities market could expect from those in government was a level of toleration rather than a positive endorsement. Where that toleration did exist the global securities market was able to develop in response to the needs of borrowers and investors, which was increasingly the case worldwide by around 2000.

Despite the differences created by this nationally driven intervention in securities markets, a high degree of global integration existed, as indicated by the convergence in the prices of bonds traded in the world's leading financial centres. At the same time considerable competition existed between different components of the global securities markets, as in their attempts to lure both those issuing securities and investing in them to use the trading facilities they provided.[10] Essentially, the internal and external barriers imposed by governments to the free flow of money had been broken down allowing the global securities market to respond to the competing forces of supply and demand on a worldwide basis. National securities markets were no longer isolated elements immune from global forces. Instead, they existed in a highly competitive environment in which business could and did flow to the location that offered not only the cheapest cost of transaction but was also easily accessible and delivered a constant, reliable, and fast service, in terms of price and volume, for those securities in which investors wished to trade.

National governments then sought to respond to national concerns by imposing costs and controls over those using their national securities markets that were not present elsewhere. The transfer tax levied on transactions in the British securities market acted as a disincentive for buying and selling there, and encouraged the use of avoidance tactics, such as trading in contracts for price difference rather than the underlying stocks. Similarly, the US Sarbanes-Oxley Act of 2002, designed to improve corporate governance in the wake of the Enron and other scandals, made New York a much less attractive market for foreign companies to have their stocks listed. The cost of compliance was too large compared to the benefits obtained. The result was a switch to London, as with Russian companies, though proposed EU legislation on corporate governance in the wake of the Parmalat frauds could have the same effect there, so encouraging a switch to yet another market. Regulatory regimes were designed to meet national requirements, creating a unique set of regulations which could only be fully satisfied by those operating within a particular country. Nevertheless, important as these legislative barriers were they were much less harmful than those which had prevented the free flow of money and capital and prevented access to foreign securities markets.

This new situation was recognized by governments, and the lawyers and economists who advised them, in terms of a quest for some kind of supranational body to supervise the global securities market. A level of government intervention was required nationally in order to ensure that no financial collapse took place and to protect investors. However, the degree and nature of that intervention had to be carefully judged so as not to drive business away or to undermine the securities market as a whole. The global nature of the market by the beginning of the twenty-first century made this balance difficult to achieve. National regulatory systems were less and less effective but there was no desire to return to the compartmentalized world of the past. Instead, a new regulatory body was required, as self-regulation led to both abuses and crises. This view was very much influenced by the Wall Street Crash of 1929 which had led to the establishment of the SEC in the United States. However, that reflected a particular set of circumstances, being a combination of the restrictions placed on branch banking in the United States, the fractured nature of the securities market, and the unstable conditions stemming from the financial and economic impact of the First World War. In contrast, the longer history of the British securities market, and its much greater global involvement, suggested that self-regulation, though by no means perfect, was perfectly adequate. The successful development of the Eurobond market from the 1960s suggested that the global securities market continued to possess a sufficient capacity for self-regulation.

By 2000, much of the trading that took place was in the hands of either very large global banks such as Barclays, Citibank, Deutsche, Morgan Chase, and UBS, or international brokerage houses like Goldman Sachs, Merrill Lynch, Morgan Stanley, and Nomura. By the mid-1990s Merrill Lynch operated a network of 475 branches in the United States and had offices in forty-five countries. These included London, where they became the largest dealer in quoted stocks after buying Smith New Court in 1995, and Tokyo, where they had bought most of the assets of Japan's fourth largest broker, Yamaichi, after its failure in 1997. From a network of offices located in the world's main financial centres, including New York, Tokyo, Frankfurt, Hong Kong, Singapore, and Sydney, these banks and brokers operated a 24-hour market spanning the globe. They traded a bewildering variety of financial products on a large number of separate markets. As part of integrated banking and broking operations their activities were driven by the internal requirements of their own business as well as their clients' interests as they sought to employ money at their disposal safely and remuneratively. As large, highly capitalized companies they had their own procedures to minimize risk, safeguard stability, enforce market discipline, and protect their clients whilst operating within a highly competitive world. Banks and brokers of this size and diversification, both sectoral and spatial, possessed the resources and reputation to guarantee payment and delivery. As such they added an entirely new dimension to the global securities market. Informal networks did not possess the collective responsibility and central management that these global banks and brokers enjoyed, and from which they drew their strength and stability.[11]

The revolution in communications from the 1950s onwards transformed the whole landscape of operations by the 1990s, as can be seen in the cost of transatlantic communication. Whereas the cost of a three-minute telephone call between London and New York, at 1966 prices, was £487 in 1927, and then fell from £63 in 1945 to £12 in 1970, and by the mid-1990s was only 50 pence. Capacity constraints had been eliminated through the laying of fibre optic cables capable of handling millions of simultaneous messages, as well as satellite transmitters providing truly global reach. Developments in electronic computing added an entirely new factor, displaying information instantaneously on screens around the world and providing the capacity to match buying and selling orders automatically.

Electronic communication networks operated at both the retail and the wholesale level. At the retail level they provided a means for brokers to communicate directly with numerous investors, so extending the contact that had long existed over the telephone with the large financial institutions. By the late 1990s, online brokerage services challenged the entrenched operations of retail brokers in the United States and Japan and banks in continental Europe. Through the power of the internet the biggest US online broker, Charles Swab, was able to offer investors instant access to a low commission dealing service and so compete with the long-established branch networks of the major New York firms and subsequently to expand in Europe and Asia. At the wholesale level the development of computerized order-matching systems allowed the creation of automatic markets which eliminated the need for either a physical trading floor or telephone trading. The screen that provided information could now be used interactively to buy and sell securities. During the 1990s such systems were developed for both stocks and bonds, often financed by New York investment banks seeking a cheaper and faster alternative to that offered by established stock exchanges. Morgan Stanley Dean Witter funded a number of different electronic trading

systems in both Europe and the United States whilst one of the most successful US trading platforms, Archipelago, launched in 1997, was heavily
supported by Goldman Sachs.

Much of the retail and wholesale trading in securities therefore gravitated
to electronic platforms. In 2003 Edward Nicoll, the chief executive of one such
platform, Instinet, claimed that '[w]e have technology that allows people to
trade directly with each other, so we can now have a completely open and
transparent market-place where everyone can have access'.[12] The *Financial
Times* was similarly enthusiastic, observing in 2000 that 'almost all financial
markets now exist only on computer screens' and noting for the global
securities market that

Alternative trading systems and electronic communications networks are flourishing
in the US, providing competing pools of liquidity in stocks listed on the New York
Stock Exchange and NASDAQ. Rival trading systems are now emerging in Europe,
such as Tradepoint, an electronic stock exchange, and Jiway, a proposed market for
retail online investors.[13]

Though this was a rather optimistic assessment written at the height of the
dot.com euphoria, it did indicate the speed and extent of the transformation
in progress. Essentially, the global securities market had undergone a
technological revolution during the 1990s, which eliminated geography as a
factor supporting separate securities markets.

However, this did not lead to the creation of a single securities market
either nationally or globally because of the enormous differences remaining
in securities themselves, in those who issued them and in those who bought
them. At the most basic there were stocks versus bonds, for each had very
different characteristics making different demands upon the market in which
they were traded. Even within stocks and bonds the market required by large
and actively traded issues was not the same as that for small and little traded
ones. Added to that were the issues made by governments versus companies,
for each had to be catered for in a particular way as did the stocks of large
established companies with a proven earnings record compared to small
speculative concerns offering little more than promise. Finally, there existed
both individual investors and financial institutions, for each had their
distinctive preferences and way of operating. What the revolution in trading
and communications technology did was allow the development of new
solutions to the way securities were traded without prejudging the outcome,
given the flexibility and capacity of the systems that evolved. The development of a global securities market in the late twentieth century did not mean
the appearance of one market serving the entire world for that was neither
necessary nor desirable, given the fact that securities were far from being

homogenous as were the motives of those who issued and bought them. Instead, what it meant then, as it had in the past, was a series of markets operating at different levels and serving different interests but interconnected so as to form an integrated unit. The key to a successful global securities market was not a single exchange supervised by a single authority but a multitude of different trading environments that were open and accessible and operated within a competitive environment. Herein lay the importance of institutional change for, deprived of many of the barriers imposed by governments, the rules and regulations operated by individual stock exchanges now constituted a formidable obstacle to the creation of an integrated global marketplace.

THE GLOBAL BOND MARKET

Before 1914 the global securities market was conducted largely through numerous self-regulated stock exchanges subject to light regulation by the state or none at all; Germany and Austria were the main exceptions to this. Where restrictive practices did exist, as in New York and Paris, active and organized OTC markets had developed but these mainly catered for stocks rather than bonds. In the mid-twentieth century stock exchanges were still at the heart of the global securities market but were now either heavily regulated by the state or imposed onerous rules upon their membership. Bolstered by state support, these stock exchanges often monopolized dealings in securities, including both stocks and bonds, though New York was something of an exception as there government debt was largely traded on the OTC market. By 2000, in the absence of any international financial authority with sufficient power to command adherence to a common set of rules and regulations, self-regulation had again become of major importance, though subject to the oversight of national statutory agencies. However, there now existed a wider variety of markets, with stock exchanges largely confined to trading corporate stocks. Even there they faced strong competition from the OTC market in many countries. The bond market, especially those issued by governments, was largely an OTC market and had even generated its own organizational structure in some cases, in order to provide some order to the trading process. The global securities market had thus fractured into stocks and bonds in terms of its organization though, often, it was the same banks and brokers that handled trading in both for the major institutional investors who were large holders of both.

Organized markets delivered both a trading platform, whether an electronic network or a physical floor, and also the guarantee that each and every transaction would be completed with respect to time, type, amount, price, and condition. These were the hallmarks of any organized market making the cost of the transaction secondary in many cases. This was especially the case in securities trading as both payment and delivery were often contingent on numerous large and ongoing deals, particularly when involving global financial companies dealing in global securities on behalf of global investors. A failure in any part of the trading process could have disastrous consequences for all concerned leaving them unable to make a payment or deliver securities, and so destroying their business. Unlike transactions in other assets, such as the buying and selling of property, dealing in securities was an almost instantaneous process leaving no time for inspection and guarantees at the time or legal recourse and the intervention of a supervisory authority if a problem arose. For a modern securities market to operate successfully and provide a continuous interface between money and capital domestically and internationally, a high degree of trust between the participants was essential, as every transaction involved promises about the future, which could not be immediately verified.

Given the highly institutional nature of the holding of bonds, and the strong links between the buying and selling of bonds and money market activity by banks, counter-party risk was at its highest in the bond market. Any failure to pay or deliver could have very serious consequences for the entire financial system as so many transactions rested upon the employment of either temporarily idle funds for short periods of time, or the lending of securities for equally short periods. Such actions where only possible if an absolute guarantee existed that the funds would be repaid and the securities returned as agreed. To that end those operating in the bond market, either on their own account or on behalf of clients, needed to be absolutely certain that those with whom they did business could be trusted to deliver their part of a deal when required to do so. When such dealing took place on the floor of a stock exchange, there was always the sanction that any default would result in expulsion from the market, forcing a strong commitment from all parties to pay and deliver. However, by the 1990s OTC markets had come to dominate bond trading. Instead of the stock exchange, with its rules and regulations, standing behind every transaction it was now the nature of the participants that guaranteed payment and delivery. As the major dealers in bonds were large financial institutions in their own right, whether banks or fund managers, it was their credit worthiness that was all important rather than the brokers through which they dealt or the trading platform they used. These financial institutions had too much at stake, because of their size and standing, to be in a position where they failed to complete a deal for such an event would permanently destroy their reputation. Consequently, OTC markets in bonds were largely confined to the major banks and other financial institutions trading with each other on a basis of mutual trust, and employing whatever means suited their purpose whether through the telephone or electronic order-matching networks.

During the 1990s the largest component of the global securities market was the trading in bonds. Whereas turnover in corporate stocks was around $41 trillion a year by 2004–5, which for bonds was around $300 trillion, representing an enormous increase since 1990. Trading in US Treasury securities, of all kinds, stood at $111.2 billion a day in 1990 and reached $733.8 billion by 2003. This expansion was not confined to the United States but was a worldwide phenomenon being especially marked in Europe and Japan. Trading in international bonds had risen from $6 trillion a year in 1994 to $50 trillion in 2004, with 70% of the total taking place in London.[14] There was also a great increase in cross-border trading in bonds as the secure yields and liquid markets that many possessed proved especially attractive to institutional investors. Japanese financial institutions traded not only in their own government and corporate bonds in Tokyo but were major participants in the New York market for US government bonds. Similarly, even before the advent of the single European currency in 1999 the German and French government debt markets, located in the financial centres of Frankfurt and Paris respectively, were not only favoured by domestic investors but also attracted foreign investors because of the depth of the market and the attractive yields on offer. Foreign holdings of German government bonds rose from 38% of the total in 1991 to 46% in 1996, whilst some two-thirds of French bonds were held by non-residents by the mid-1990s.

In the major financial centres of the world, where the largest banks had head offices or branches, the local bond market was an attractive place in which to employ temporarily idle balances in bonds originating from around the world. New York was the most attractive as its bond market was by far the most liquid in the world, and thus ideal for those wishing to place funds on a short-term basis. New York was followed by London, not for its local bond market as that was relatively small, but because it was home to the international or Eurobond market. Though only generating around 16% of total turnover in bonds by 2004–5 this was an increasingly active and important market as the size of individual issues grew and fewer were bought and then held until maturity. The Eurobond market was especially useful for those wishing to issue bonds or invest funds on a temporary basis, but lacking a liquid domestic market. Governments, companies, banks, and institutional investors from the Nordic countries made extensive use of it. In consequence, a growing proportion of all bonds were issued or held on an international basis generating an increased volume of cross-border trading. Nevertheless, most bonds continued to be issued, bought and sold on a domestic basis, making such financial centres as New York and Tokyo central to the global bond market, rather than London, whose position rested on the international issues and cross-border trading.

However, following European monetary union in 1998 a pan-European bond market emerged to challenge both the domestic markets of New York and Tokyo and the London-based international market. This new market was based on that for Italian government bonds. By 1992 the Italian bond market was the third largest in the world due to the rapid rise in Italian government borrowing over the previous fifteen years. The total amount in circulation had reached $850 billion. In order to facilitate trading in these bonds an electronic trading platform was developed from 1988 onwards, the MTS (Mercato dei Titolodi Stato). In 1998 MTS was chosen as the electronic platform for trading Eurozone government bonds on a bank-to-bank basis. The creation of a single currency in 1999 unified the market for the government debt of Italy, France, and Germany. The result in 2000 was a large and liquid bond market that could begin to challenge those in New York and Tokyo for the employment of short-term funds. By 2004–5 turnover on the various MTS platforms had reached $85 billion a day which was considerably larger than that for British government debt at $20 billion though still well adrift of the US market with its $500 billion. Although Britain did not join the Euro, the Euro MTS bond market was based in London as the European centre with the greatest concentration of banks and institutional investors most likely to buy and sell bonds.

By 2000 trading in bonds was increasingly taking place using electronic platforms such as MTS, which in 2005 even extended its operations to Israel. Though telephone contact remained important, especially for sales and purchase of less traded bonds or large and small deals, the electronic platforms increasingly dominated. By 2004 MTS handled 70% of the transactions in Eurozone government debt. The same pattern was emerging in the United States where inter-dealer brokers like Cantor Fitzgerald and ICAP operated their own electronic trading networks to handle the sales and purchases of government and corporate bonds on behalf of their clients, namely the world's largest banks. In 2004 Broker Tec, owned by ICAP, handled a trading volume that varied between $200 and $300 billion a day. Cantor Fitzgerald even abandoned voice broking in favour of their electronic platform E-Speed, when their trading floor was destroyed in the September 11th terrorist attack on the Twin Towers. There were also additional electronic systems, such as Trade Web and Market Access, which specialized in providing a trading platform linking banks to institutional investors rather than a forum for bank-to-bank trading. Such systems were ideal for the bond market as both banks and institutional investors were able to make their own judgements about the risks they were running and accept the consequences for any mistakes made and losses incurred. To qualify for inclusion in the MTS system individual bond houses had to have 5 billion euros freely available, have five market-makers operating, and be able to continuously trade all securities at tight bid-offer spreads. Only the subsidiaries of the largest banks were in a position to do this and thus participate in such a market. Though the British regulator, the Financial Services Authority, did have supervisory role and could levy fines where it felt appropriate, EuroMTS basically policed itself as all participants realized that its existence was for their mutual benefit. In addition, in 1992 the major participants in the global bond market had formed the International Securities Market Association (ISMA), which was both a trade association and self-regulatory body. By 1998 ISMA had about 800 members from fifty countries, being major banks and finance houses. As a result the global bond market handled a volume of business approaching a trillion dollars every working day at waver thin margins and with almost no problems, and all without much in the way of either governmental or institutional supervision or intervention.[15]

THE GLOBAL STOCK MARKET

The global stock market was both smaller and more complicated that that for bonds. There was a great similarity among bonds as they bore a fixed rate of return and were usually guaranteed by stable governments or the largest corporations. Defaults did occur but were usually confined to the governments of countries with poorly developed financial systems or companies that had grown quickly through merger and acquisition. Both these categories attracted a risk premium though at times creative accounting created an illusion that mislead investors, especially those seeking high returns or rapid capital gain. By the 1990s most governments could be relied upon to service their debts and most companies paid interest on their bonds, whatever happened to the dividends paid to shareholders. In contrast, the value of stocks was much more the product of individual circumstances as it depended on the quality of the management, the state of the economy, the business being pursued, and the location of operations. The result was that stocks generated a far greater volatility than bonds, whatever the general economic conditions being experienced, with the smaller the company the greater the volatility.[16]

Given these unique characteristics and volatility, stocks attracted a much wider spectrum of issuers and investors than the bond market. At one extreme were the stocks of large companies providing gas, electricity, and fixed line communications or those whose business was in the diversified provision of products and services with a stable pattern of demand, such as alcohol, tobacco, and certain branches of retailing and finance. These offered a relatively safe return in dividends, and so appealed to cautious investors. These were both individuals looking to safeguard their capital and, especially, the major financial institutions with responsibility for the savings of millions and the commitment to make future payments through insurance policies or pension funds. In contrast there were the stocks of those smaller companies operating in such fields as the development of new technology or exploring for oil and minerals. These appealed to the speculator seeking spectacular capital gains, and these were mainly individual investors though a number of specialist collective funds were also involved. In between existed the stocks issued by a wide range of companies operating in numerous diverse fields. Stocks had something to offer all types of investors and the market in which they were traded needed to reflect this variety.[17]

With the great expansion in the amount of stocks in circulation around the world, especially in the wake of the privatization programmes, new markets rapidly appeared. Despite the growing internationalization of investment in stocks most tended to be owned by investors resident in the country where the business was based and operated.[18] This created a need for a national market where the stocks of national companies held by national investors could be traded. Even when there was considerable foreign interest in particular stocks, a market was required where the trading of all investors could be centred, and thus was often best located within the country where the company was based, where the single greatest concentration existed. The result was a rash of new exchanges, especially in those countries where none had existed either because they had been communist states or because the level of economic development had been too low to support one in the past. In Eastern Europe stock exchanges appeared in Budapest in 1990, Warsaw in 1991, and Prague in 1992, often though the efforts of local financial institutions and with the participation of foreign banks and brokers like Citibank from the United States, ABN-Amro from the Netherlands, Credit Suisse from Switzerland, and Nomura from Japan. A stock exchange was established in Botswana in 1994, Palestine in 1997, and Saudi Arabia in 2001 whilst two appeared in Dubai in 2005. However, not all these emerging markets were successful. Government controls continued to hinder their development, stock exchanges failed to enforce orderly rules for trading, and privatized companies were acquired by foreign corporations. Latin America continued to be a region where the development of securities markets was relatively weak because of continuing state intervention. Many companies remained largely privately owned, with their stock being little traded, whilst others were easy prey for foreign companies, especially Spanish. Among the largest Latin American companies many preferred to seek a listing in New York because of the poorly developed state of their own national securities market. A similar situation existed in Russia, where the securities market remained small and chaotic, being prone to price manipulation and corporate fraud as well as government intervention. This encouraged the largest Russian companies to list in London. Nevertheless, from 1990 onwards organized markets for corporate stocks spread to almost every country in the world irrespective of their size, level of economic development, or political regime.

Even within those countries where stock markets had been long established new markets appeared to cater for particular segments of the market. Most evident were those catering for the speculative enthusiasm of investors during the worldwide dot.com bubble in the late 1990s. A number of countries, like Australia, Britain, Canada, New Zealand, and the United States, had long had numerous individual investors. By 2000 there were an estimated 85 million Americans holding stocks, either directly or collectively, and this was around 45% of the population. A similar percentage occurred in Australia, where there were around 5.5 million holders of stocks. Given the right conditions these investors always had a tendency to become over enthused by particular stocks that appeared to offer incalculable gains, especially in such areas as new technology or mineral discoveries. However, by the 1990s they were joined by numerous investors in the privatization programmes who were only familiar with the rather certain gains to be made from the purchase of the deeply discounted issues of state companies or the free shares that came with the conversion of mutually owned enterprises into joint-stock companies. In Germany, for example, a very small proportion of the population owned stocks until the flotation of Deutsche Telecom in 1996. Such was the success of that issue that an enthusiasm for stocks was born throughout the German population, with the proportion of the population owning stocks rising from 5% to 20% as a result, reaching 12 million by 2001. This was typical of what happened after privatization in countries across the world. Combined with this newly expanded and empowered investing public was a period of low inflation and cheap and abundant credit. Financial crises in 1997–8 in East Asia and Russia temporarily discouraged further lending to these areas from the United States and Western Europe. Banks were left with ample funds at their disposal which meant both low rates of interest and a willingness to lend extensively to their personal customers. At the same government action had brought under control the ravages of inflation that had plagued the 1970s and 1980s, and so produced a climate of confidence in future investment returns among individual investors.

The focus of these investors turned increasingly to the new developments springing from the convergence of computing and communications technology, beginning in the United States in 1996. The flotation of Netscape in that year, and the rapid rise in the price of its stock, sparked a growing investor enthusiasm that spread to any sector of the US economy that could possibly benefit from the advent of the internet and mobile telephony. These were companies that produced the equipment required, supplied the services that used it, or were expected to benefit from its use. Such was the enthusiasm for these stocks that at the height of the US boom in 2000 the technology sector comprised one-third of all quoted stocks, by market value. One company alone, Microsoft, had a market value ten times greater than that of all quoted mining companies from around the world. With so many technology companies including Microsoft traded on NASDAQ rather than the New York Stock Exchange, that market became the largest in the world in 2000, before experiencing a precipitate collapse when the bubble burst in that year. By then the whole world had begun to participate in the dot.com mania, with investors in Europe being especially enthusiastic. A rash of new securities markets opened in Europe to replicate the facilities provided by NASDAQ, considered vital if the needs of high technology companies and those who invested in them were to be met.

The most successful at the time was the Neuer Markt in Germany as investors there were particularly attracted to the sector after their experience with Deutsche Telecom. Most of these new European markets were offshoots of the established stock exchanges in Frankfurt, Paris, London, Amsterdam, Milan, and Brussels. However, it did include one entirely independent exchange, EASDAQ, which tried to do for Europe what NASDAQ had done for the United States. NASDAQ itself tried to capitalize on the worldwide dot.com boom by expanding internationally, setting up operations in both Europe and Japan. There was even press speculation that NASDAQ would merge with the London Stock Exchange to provide a global stock market. However, the valuations of the stock issued by these dot.com companies were increasingly driven not by realistic estimates of future earnings but by the expectation of buying and selling at a profit many times over. The lure of investing in another Microsoft encouraged more and more investors. Inevitably, the bubble burst in the middle of 2000 with disastrous consequences not only for many individual investors but also for the specialist markets created. The Neuer Markt was closed down by Deutsche Borse whilst NASDAQ was forced to abandon its global ambitions, closing down both its Japanese and European operations. Nevertheless, NASDAQ did survive and had recovered partially by 2005, continuing to provide a market for both those companies that survived the dot.com bubble, such as Microsoft, and new entrants, like the search engine Google. In Europe, the London Stock Exchange's market for smaller companies, AIM, emerged as the leading exchange in Europe for speculative issues, benefiting from the established strength of the main market.

What the dot.com bubble indicated was that by the late 1990s an integrated global stock market existed, though operated through a variety of exchanges and trading platforms. It also indicated the difficulty any new market had in becoming established once the speculative interest that had given rise to it faded away. It was difficult to dislodge established exchanges from the position they occupied either geographically, sectorally, or both. Given the continuing national preferences of investors most stock exchanges provided a market in national stocks for national markets, and commanded the largest pools of liquidity in these securities. In the United States in 2000, whereas foreigners accounted for 5% of the Treasury bond market, and 20% of the corporate bond market, the figure for stocks was only 7%. Generally, as many domestic markets remained the largest pools of liquidity for the stocks that they quoted orders continued to flow to them from around the world, so reinforcing rather than weakening their position. Even NASDAQ, which was very much a specialist market for high-technology stocks, largely catered for US companies and US investors. Of total equity turnover in the world in 2004–5 only $5 trillion, or 12% involved the buying and selling of stocks outside their domestic market compared to $36 trillion, or 88% traded domestically. Most of what took place happened in London, with 60% of the total, split between the London Stock Exchange (45%) and the Swiss Stock Exchange Virt X (15%) which had relocated there. Apart from London the only other financial centre that hosted a market in foreign stocks was New York with 32%, split between the New York Stock Exchange (20%) and NASDAQ (12%).[19] Thus, though there had been enormous advances in economic integration and communication technology, the global stock market still consisted of a series of spatially dominant stock exchanges. Each contained the stocks issued by distinctive national companies, and investors turned to these markets if they wanted to buy or sell these stocks, even if they were large institutional investors using the services of banks and brokers with global operations.

Judged by the market value of these domestic companies this made the US securities market the largest in the world in 1990, with a value of $3,059 billion, just ahead of Japan with $2,918 billion. Most other stock markets were relatively small. The third largest was that of Britain with $849 billion followed by Germany ($355 billion), France ($314 billion), Canada ($242 billion), Switzerland ($160 billion), Italy ($149 billion), and the Netherlands ($120 billion). In 1990 the global stock market remained firmly in the grip of north America, Western Europe, and Japan. By 2003 some change had taken place in that the market value of quoted stocks had grown enormously whilst a number of countries elsewhere now possessed sizeable stock markets, having overtaken some of the smaller economies in Western Europe. The US stock market was in a league of its own with a market value of $14,266.3 billion, even after the bursting of the dot.com bubble. In contrast, after a decade of economic stagnation the Japanese stock market had not kept pace, at $3,040.7 billion being hardly much larger than in 1990. Britain had almost caught up with Japan, at $2,412.4 billion whilst France ($1,355.6 billion), Germany ($1,079 billion), Canada ($894 billion), and Switzerland ($726.7 billion) had all expanded. More spectacular was the growth of the Hong Kong stock market, which at $714.6 billion was now larger than that of Italy ($614.8 billion), whilst China ($681.2 billion) and Australia ($585.5 billion) were both larger than the Netherlands ($488.6 billion). A comparison of trading volumes shows a similar but not identical pattern. Between 1990 and 2003 the market value of stocks traded in the United States grew from $1,751.3 billion to $15,547.4 billion. In 1990 the US market was closely challenged by Japan, with a turnover of $1,602 billion but by 2003 Japan's was only $2,273 billion, even though it remained the second largest. By then turnover in the third largest market, that of the UK, had reached $2,150.8 billion, up from $278.7 billion in 1990. By 2003 turnover in some of the newer stock markets such as South Korea, Taiwan and China had also risen rapidly. This reflected the results of privatization and an emerging equity culture that attracted investors to stock markets and business to the joint-stock form because of its financial and managerial flexibility.[20]

Though the national preferences of investors gave national stock exchanges a high degree of protection this did not make them immune from competition. The removal of exchange controls and other barriers to the flow of funds and securities allowed investors to evade domestic costs and restrictions by routing their orders elsewhere. There was a considerable loss of business for those national stock still maintaining fixed rates of commission, limitations on membership, and restrictions on methods of trading. Combined with a growing interest in cross-border investment in stocks, especially those issued by major international companies, this encouraged the creation of alternative markets beyond the jurisdiction of national governments and national stock exchanges. No longer did the national stock exchange enjoy an automatic monopoly when providing a market for national securities and national investors. This threatened the very existence of highly regulated stock exchanges, whatever the wishes of their national governments. No longer did the survival of national stock exchanges depend on national needs and the wishes of national governments but instead upon the place they could command in the global securities market. This was especially the case as banks and brokers increasingly operated across national boundaries and were more than willing to direct the buying and selling of their customers to the market that offered the lowest charges and the best service.

However, this decline in the immunity from competition was not wholly or universally evident. The greater the size and maturity of the domestic securities market the less it was exposed to the forces of change. This was especially the case for the United States, which had by far the most numerous investing public, the most well-endowed pension funds, and the largest corporate sector, including 212 of the world's 500 largest companies such as Citigroup, Exxon Mobil, General Electric, IBM, Microsoft, Procter and Gamble, and Wal-Mart.[21] Change in the US securities market was driven by the interaction between US companies and US investors, competition between the New York Stock Exchange and NASDAQ, rivalry between the large brokerage houses, and the interventions of the SEC, and other arms of the US government. This competition put New York at the forefront of innovation in the securities market when it came to the design of financial instruments and the development of trading strategies. Most of the new products and trading methods developed in the global stock market from the 1990s emanated from New York. Conversely, the ability of the New York Stock Exchange to totally dominate trading in the stocks it quoted, also meant that certain aspects of market development in the United States remained somewhat arrested, despite the arrival of electronic trading networks.

During the 1990s the New York Stock Exchange had invested over $1 billion in improving the ability of its trading floor to cope with greatly increased turnover and to ensure that the prices offered by the specialists were highly competitive. In addition, actions taken by the SEC to ensure a competitive marketplace for the individual investor actually benefited the New York Stock Exchange. The specialists on its floor were legally required to offer the best price whilst the SEC's 'trade-through' rule required that all transactions were done at the best available price. This channelled all business to the New York Stock Exchange as it offered the best price 90% of the time. It therefore handled around 80% of all trading in the stocks it quoted even though many of the institutional investors, and many of the members, would have preferred to deal elsewhere as price was not the only consideration. Of equal or even greater consideration in many cases were such elements as speed, timing, and certainty as well as the costs involved. On the London Stock Exchange, where no such rules applied, around 35% of all trading in the stocks quoted took place through direct negotiation between institutional investors or internally within the major banks and brokers. Though the trading floor maintained by the New York Stock Exchange was highly efficient and did serve many of the stocks quoted well it was not the ideal means for conducting all transactions, and relied on SEC regulations for part of its command of the market.[22]

Increasingly, sophisticated electronic trading systems captured more and more of the market for corporate stocks. No longer did companies switch their listing to the New York Stock Exchange once they reached an appropriate size. Instead, many retained their listing on NASDAQ especially if they operated in the field of high technology, for which that market was noted. Two of the leading US high-technology companies, Microsoft and Intel, which were respectively ranked third and fifteenth largest in the world in 2005, continued to be listed on NASDAQ. Thus, important as the New York Stock Exchange was, with the largest turnover of any stock exchange in the world in 2004–5, its command of the US market was slipping. NASDAQ was once again challenging it with a turnover of $8 trillion in domestic stocks compared to the New York Stock Exchange's $10.5 trillion. However, even NASDAQ was facing growing competition. The combination of screens displaying prices from dealers with telephone buying and selling, which lay at the heart of NASDAQ, was increasingly outdated in comparison to the fully electronic market places like Instinet and Archipelago. Unlike the New York Stock Exchange the stocks quoted on NASDAQ were not protected by SEC rules as it was not a recognized exchange, only a market. Hence the ability of Instinet and Archipelago to compete with NASDAQ's own trading platform in the stocks it quoted. By 2005 around half of all trading in NASDAQ stocks was channelled through these electronic platforms, because of their ability to match sales and purchases instantly and at low cost.

Nor was the New York stock Exchange immune from the competition from electronic markets, despite the protection due to ECN rules. In 2005 Archipelago's purchase of the Pacific Stock Exchange circumvented all the difficulties involved in gaining authorization from the SEC to operate as a stock exchange in its own right rather than simply as an electronic broker. Also, as a stock exchange, it could now provide a market for stocks quoted in New York, in competition with the specialists operating on the trading floor of the New York Stock Exchange. Both the telephone trading system of NASDAQ and the floor trading system of the New York Stock Exchange were under serious threat by 2005 from the electronic platforms operated by Archipelago and Instinet. NASDAQ's response was to agree a merger with Instinet, whilst the New York Exchange decided to merge with Archipelago. Both would gain access to an advanced electronic trading platform allowing each to control a particular component of the US market for corporate stocks. This move was also designed to convert both into joint-stock companies rather than mutually owned organizations, a move which was already underway at NASDAQ but resisted by many of the 1,366 members of the New York Stock Exchange.

However, such radical change was difficult to achieve, being blocked by those whose business would not benefit or would actually be harmed by the proposals. Hence the long-standing commitment to specialists and the physical trading floor by the New York Stock Exchange, and to the posting of prices on screens by market-makers on NASDAQ. By switching to the publicly owned corporate form, both the New York Stock Exchange and NASDAQ would acquire the means to finance the development of computer-based trading platforms, the flexibility to merge with other companies operating exchanges at home and abroad, and the incentive to remain competitive through the need to generate profits. However, the regulatory systems within the United States restricted their freedom to respond to challenges and exploit opportunities.

Certainly since the Wall Street Crash, and to some extent predating it with the Money Trust investigations before 1914, there had existed a widespread distrust of the activities of many of those operating in the securities market within the United States. One of the principal aims of the SEC was therefore the protection of the interests of the individual investor, whether from direct fraud or from exposure to an unfair marketplace. The New York Stock Exchange acted as the principal regulatory arm of the SEC, which in turn condoned the rules that forced almost all the buying and selling conducted by its members in the stocks it quoted onto its trading floor. Such a concentration of securities trading produced a much better market as those operating there had an oversight of all current business, so enabling them to trade at the finest prices and in the greatest volume. It was also easier for the SEC to monitor market behaviour and thus fulfil its remit of investor protection.

The growth of NASDAQ, a market rather than a regulatory stock exchange, had already eroded this position. However, any transformation of the New York Stock Exchange into a competitive profit-maximizing company would be incompatible with its status as a regulatory arm of the state, and would give it an unfair advantage over its rivals through the powers it possessed to protect and enhance its position in the US securities market. This created a dilemma for the US government, for the conversion of the New York Stock Exchange into a company had to be approved by its own membership and a new arrangement for supervising and regulating the securities market had to be devised. One obvious problem was the fact that both the New York Stock Exchange and NASDAQ, as companies, would be close to possessing a near monopoly in the trading of the stocks they quoted. Such a position was acceptable when both existed as not-for-profit organizations but once converted into companies, that restraint would be replaced by the need to deliver returns to investors rather than to meet the needs of their users. These difficulties facing the organizational, institutional and regulatory structure of the US securities market, and the specific role to be played by the state, renouned to be resolved.

A complete overhaul of the entire US stock market was required. This was certainly overdue because the momentous event of May Day 1975, when fixed commissions were abandoned, had not been followed by the progressive transformation of the market in the light of subsequent internal and external developments. Change was long overdue given the transformation of the US securities market through the growing power of the institutional investors, and the growth of the large investment banking/broking firms which challenged the authority of the markets within which they operated. Firms like Goldman Sachs, Merrill Lynch, and Salomon Brothers now conducted so much of the trading that they could match bargains internally or through direct negotiation with the major institutional investors, whether within the United States or internationally, especially in London and Tokyo. The collapse of the Glass–Steagall Act was slowly changing the nature of financial services in the United States, creating the possibility of banks operating through a single nationwide branch network and covering both the collection of deposits and the making of loans, to the management of collective funds and the issuing and trading of securities. It was no longer possible to maintain a system which drove the trading of its members onto a physical floor or which continued to see a division between banking and broking at home and abroad. Neither reflected reality by the early twenty-first century, though the timing, form, and outcome of change remained unclear.

A similar situation existed in Britain in the 1990s. The changes ushered in with Big Bang, fundamental and far-reaching as they were, were only a partial response to the rapidly changing securities market. During the 1980s the major British banks had secured an unrivalled position in that country's retail securities market by combining an extensive branch network with a broking and dealing facility. Only the development of online broking provided an opportunity for others to enter the retail side of the securities market, with the largest US firm, Charles Swab, establishing a foothold in the late 1990s at the time of the dot.com boom. In the wholesale market the position was different, with strong competition for the business of large institutional investors. Major banks and brokers, including many from abroad, were willing to buy and sell at very low rates of commission or for free, expecting to profit from the difference between the buying and selling price. Institutional business was concentrated in the hands of a small number of financial firms as only they had the extensive resources and connections necessary. Some of these were British but most were not. The largest London dealers, Smith New Court, became part of Merrill Lynch, whilst the most prestigious brokers, Casenoves, allied itself to J. P. Morgan Chase. By 1999 membership of the London Stock Exchange was down to 298, with 80% of all trading being done by only sixty large banks and brokers. The level of concentration was even greater by 2005 when ten firms did 50% of the trading.

By then the London Stock Exchange had become a suite of markets catering for distinct groups of investors and served by banks and brokers from home and abroad. At one level was the Alternative Investment Market (AIM), established in 1995, which traded the issues of new and small companies. These were riskier investments involving fewer safeguards to protect investors, with many of the stocks traded being issued by companies operating in such fields as new technology, pharmaceuticals, mining, and oil exploration. By the early 2000s AIM had established itself as one of the world's most successful junior markets, attracting listings from numerous companies from outside Britain. At the next level was the main market catering for the stocks and bonds of a variety of established British companies of all sizes, but especially the largest. As these included a number of major multinationals such as BAT (tobacco), BP (oil), Diageo (drink), Glaxo (pharmaceuticals), HSBC (banking), Rio Tinto (mining), and Vodafone (Telecoms) this market was also very international. In 2000 an estimated 20% of UK equities was held by international investors. The main market of the London Stock Exchange also attracted a number of foreign companies whose domestic market lacked the depth, breadth, and sophistication required for companies of their size, especially if their shares were extensively held by British institutional investors, as was often the case. These included such mining giants as Anglo-American and BHP Billiton. Finally, the London Stock Exchange also provided a market for foreign companies that attracted the interest of the international investment community such as a succession of Russian enterprises operating in a variety of sectors. The London Stock Exchange was no longer exclusively identified with British companies and British investors.

Crucial to the success of the London Stock Exchange as a securities market were the facilities it provided through which securities could be easily and cheaply traded. Due to Big Bang the London Stock Exchange had made the successful transition from a floor-based trading system to a screen/telephone-based one. However, many of the vestiges of the old restrictive practices remained and further progress was slow. Until 1995 there were attempts to monopolize trading by limiting access to the prices generated by market-makers. It was not until 1997 that a fully electronic market place was introduced where trading could take place on-screen and a central computer automatically match orders in terms of securities, amounts, and prices. This delay allowed other exchanges to catch up with developments in

London and recover some of the business lost in the 1980s. Similarly, it was not until 2000 that the London Stock Exchange was converted from a member-owned institution into a company, so giving it the flexibility to compete internationally. Accompanying this change in status was the final abandonment by the London Stock Exchange of the wider regulatory powers it had acquired during and after the Second World War such as control over the dissemination of price sensitive information and policing broker–client relationships. Instead, the London Stock Exchange became subject to the Financial Services Authority, which had been set up in 1997 to oversee the entire British financial system, including the international activities taking place in London. Thus, the London stock Exchange was no different from any of the other securities markets operating out of London, whether it was the Swiss Stock Exchange, Virt X, the government bond trading platform Euro MTS, or the international organization supervising the Eurobond market.

The organization of the London Stock Exchange as a company, the use it made of an electronic trading platform, the use made of it by global brokers and dealers, and the relationship it had with the national regulatory authorities had become increasingly commonplace among stock exchanges around the world by the start of the twenty-first century. What remained of exchange and capital controls were finally dismantled in the 1990s whilst governments removed controls and restrictions that had protected their national stock exchanges from competition. As business ebbed away to more competitive markets, stock exchanges around the world were forced to abandon fixed commissions, liberalize rules and regulations, and introduce electronic trading in order to retain control over their own domestic markets. A chain reaction occurred as changes in one country forced others to respond, eventually forcing further changes so as to remain competitive. The situation was particularly acute in Western Europe. Change occurring on the Paris Bourse and the Madrid Bolsa in 1989 then rolled on throughout Europe, including Milan in 1991. Reforms led to the repatriation of much of the business that had migrated to London in the wake of Big Bang as it was these national stock exchanges that possessed the deepest and broadest markets in national securities. By 1998 the Amsterdam Stock Exchange was handling two-thirds of the transactions in Dutch stocks, having reclaimed the business from London. With the introduction of electronic trading platforms and remote membership during the 1990s, European stock exchanges attracted the buying and selling of London-based global bankers and brokers. In the final analysis trading in securities gravitated to the most liquid market unless prevented by barriers, restrictions, and charges. During the 1990s these impediments to access were removed and business flowed to those national markets where national securities were traded.[23]

The extent and speed of the advances made can be seen in the German securities market from the early 1990s onwards. In 1991 the government repealed the longstanding turnover tax in 1991 whilst during 1992–3 a single organization was created, Deutsche Börse. Though local floors remained, the result was an increasing concentration of trading in Frankfurt. At the same time as the internal and external barriers imposed by the government were being removed there was a progressive deregulation within the Deutsche Börse itself. In1991 the Frankfurt Borse had become a company rather than a division of the Chamber of Commerce. Instead of operating as a public service it adopted a more competitive and aggressive stance, responding to the rapid changes in the securities market and embracing the new developments in technology. The screen-based trading system developed by the banks was taken over in 1992 and this became a fully electronic trading platform when Xetra was introduced in 1997. Also in that year a market for small- and medium-sized companies was refined and expanded, modelled on NASDAQ. Within one decade the German securities market had moved from being fragmented and backward to being concentrated and advanced. This allowed it to repatriate trading in German securities from London and gave it the confidence to plan an alliance with the London Stock Exchange in 1998. In May 2000 a merger between the London Stock Exchange and Deutsche Börse was agreed but foundered due to opposition from financial intermediaries in both countries because of the complexity of the trading arrangements and the currency risks involved. Not to be thwarted the Deutsche Borse tried to takeover the London Stock Exchange in 2005, only to be defeated once again by an unwillingness of its own shareholders to finance an acquisition with such uncertain benefits.[24] This left both London and Frankfurt as independent stock exchanges, with London being in the stronger position because of the extensive international business generated there.

The actions of the Deutsche Borse indicated the increasingly competitive world occupied by stock exchanges in Europe. Though they could retain the market for national companies owned by national investors, many did not possess either the depth or breadth to survive on their own, deprived of government support, and the protection provided by distance and artificial barriers. This was especially true of the stock exchanges of smaller European countries. Though these provided a market for a variety of securities of interest to national investors, most activity was concentrated in the securities issued by one or two major companies. Though Vodafone accounted for 13.4% of the capitalization of the London securities market in February 2000, Ericsson had reached 44.3% of the Swedish securities market. Increasingly it was the stocks of a small number of companies that dominated trading on the various European stock exchanges, being the very stocks that were attractive to the large financial institutions, including many from outside the country, because of the combination of yield and marketability. Where the home exchange for these stocks was in London, Frankfurt or Paris then it possessed the depth of trading required to retain the market. However, the smaller stock exchanges such as Amsterdam, Brussels, and Stockholm did not possess deep markets and so found it difficult to monopolize the trading in their most active stocks. The combination of liberalization and communications permitted the buying and selling of securities to flow both from and to London, depending on those who were conducting the business required. Recognizing the difficulty in holding on to the market for such Swiss multinationals as Nestle, Novartis, Roche, and UBS in Zurich the Swiss Stock Exchange, under pressure from the major banks and institutional investors, took the bold step of relocating its main market to London, in the shape of Virt-X in the course of 2000–1. It was even hoped that Virt-X would become the core of a pan-European stock market based on its trading of over $2 billion a day in the major Swiss-based multinationals.

Another response from smaller stock exchanges was to merge so as to provide a larger and more attractive market for both investors and companies. This was made possible not only by the disappearance of barriers in an expanding EU but also the conversion of stock exchanges from mutual organizations into profit-maximizing companies. That change greatly facilitated cross-border mergers and alliances whilst the ability to create a single electronic trading platform destroyed geographic barriers. A number of different combinations resulted. One of the most successful was Euronext, led by the Paris Bourse, which had become increasingly concerned about losing out to London and Frankfurt. Euronext was formed in March 2000 as an alliance between the Paris, Amsterdam, and Brussels stock exchanges, and later extended to Lisbon. By 2004–5 Euronext had become the second largest stock market in Europe with a turnover of $2.3 trillion compared to the London Stock Exchange at $2.8 trillion, and far ahead of the Deutsche Borse at $1.1 trillion. Another development was led by Sweden's O and M group. Having developed a highly efficient trading technology, this company took over the Stockholm Stock Exchange and proceded to create a single securities market covering Scandinavia and the Baltic states. Finally, the Vienna Bourse took the lead in trying to form an alliance of central European stock exchanges, acquiring a stake in the Budapest Stock Exchange in June 2005. Nevertheless, there still remained a number of major stock exchanges in Europe still independent, such as Madrid and Milan, whilst some of the smaller ones like Warsaw and Prague were undecided about which combination to join or whether to merge at all. A single securities market was gradually emerging in Europe, with increasingly few operators as stock exchanges merged. As the EU failed in the 1990s to harmonize the rules and regulations governing national stock exchanges, and so create an integrated pan-European securities market, the process was left in the hands of the companies that increasingly owned and ran that market. By the early 2000s there was a patchwork of trading platforms which, though competing with each other, were also accessible to all through remote membership. The result was, collectively, the deep and broad market that companies and investors required, with only the costs and complexities of settlement and clearing restricting its further development.

Not only in Europe did a fundamental transformation of the securities market take place from the 1990s. Though the development of an electronic trading system was well to the fore in Japan the organizational structure of the market for stocks changed little, as long as the stock exchanges retained a monopoly over the buying and selling of listed stocks. Pressure for change gradually mounted, coming especially from the institutional investors. By 1995 financial institutions owned 41% of Japanese stocks whilst pension funds had assets of $1.6 trillion and were familiar with the lower costs and better service provided by markets abroad. Also, foreign brokers gained membership of the Tokyo Stock Exchange and were responsible for a growing volume of business transacted. In 1990 the foreign firms that were members of the Tokyo Stock Exchange conducted 6% of the trading but this had grown to 30% by 1997. Eventually, in 1998 the monopoly of stock exchanges over trading in securities was ended, as was the minimum commission rate on high-volume business. The following year the Tokyo Stock Exchange trading floor closed, the limit on the number of members and fixed commission rates both ended, the embargo on the combination of banking and broking was lifted, and a market for small and emerging companies set up. In 2000 the Tokyo Stock Exchange consolidated its grip over the domestic securities market by absorbing the Hiroshima and Niigata stock exchanges and in 2001 converted itself into a company. This brought the Japanese securities market much more into line with developments elsewhere, though the pace and degree of change remained slower and more limited than in north America and Europe. As a result Tokyo failed to develop into a major international market for stocks as had happened in London and, to a lesser degree, New York. Instead there was strong competition from Hong Kong, Singapore, and Sydney for any cross-border trading of stocks in the Asia-Pacific region.[25]

There was a convergence of trading and organizational patterns in the 1990s and beyond as changes and innovations spread from one country to another. The process of demutualization really began with the Australian Stock Exchange in 1998 and was rapidly taken up elsewhere, especially in

Europe. It became commonplace for securities markets to be run by companies for profit, so making them far more responsive to the needs of their users than had the member-only clubs of the past. Generally, existing stock exchanges either liberalized their rules and regulations and replaced floor-based markets with electronic systems or faced growing outside competition if they did not. In India the failure to modernize of the dominant Bombay Stock Exchange resulted in the creation of an electronic platform, the National Stock Exchange, which rapidly emerged as the largest trading forum. Even where no alternative stock exchange existed, as in South Africa, it was impossible to resist the need for change. Faced with a loss of business, especially to London, floor trading was ended on the Johannesburg Stock Exchange in 1996 with the introduction of computer trading. The model initially followed was that of NASDAQ, with prices displayed on screens and buying and selling on the telephone, as with Hong Kong's market for smaller companies in the late 1990s. However, there was also a fairly rapid introduction of fully electronic trading platforms. On the newly formed stock exchanges an electronic platform was often used from the outset, with those developed for Paris, Frankfurt, or Stockholm being especially popular. The electronic trading systems introduced on the Lima Stock Exchange in 1995 and on the Tunis Stock Exchange in 1997 both used the technology developed for the Paris Bourse. The overall supervision of these electronic securities markets, whether stock exchanges or OTC trading platforms, was increasingly placed in the hands of statutory authorities. Though self-regulation did continue to play a role in ensuring an orderly market the state now possessed ultimate authority in ensuring both a competitive and efficient market and one free from abuses and manipulation. It became standard practice to establish such a body as securities markets grew in importance. When the Lima Stock Exchange was freed from state control in 1991 it was put under the supervision of a National Securities Commission, whilst in 1993 the Chinese government introduced national securities regulations to police its emerging securities regulation.[26]

The result for the world was a global stock market which possessed neither central direction nor a single organization. At its foundation were numerous national markets that provided pools of liquidity for the particular stocks that they quoted, largely those issued by national companies and owned mainly by national investors. Thus New York was the market for the stocks of US companies, London for British companies, Tokyo for Japanese companies, Frankfurt for German companies, and so on, through smaller and smaller financial centres in smaller and smaller economies. However, unless there was a particular group of companies capable of sustaining an active market, as with mining stocks in Canada, some of these stock exchanges were not large enough to provide the depth of market required. This led to the creation of regional exchanges, as in parts of Europe, and attempts to do so elsewhere in the world. In 2003 there were plans for a pan-African stock exchange that would be led by the Johannesburg Stock Exchange but include those in Ghana, Namibia, Zimbabwe, and Zambia.

In the absence of such moves there was a steady drift of business to those few markets with a truly international business, especially London but also New York and NASDAQ. These stock exchanges also attracted trading in those stocks where domestic restrictions were such as to stunt the growth of a domestic securities market. In addition, there was always a residual amount of international business attracted by these stock exchanges because London and New York were home to such a large number of banks, brokers, fund mangers, and other financial institutions from around the world. Between 1981 and 1997, the ratio of foreign share transactions to total transactions fell from 59% to 13% for Brussels, from 29% to 2% for Paris and from 12% to 5% for Frankfurt, as they lost control of the buying and selling activities that their national investors conducted in non-national securities. In contrast the ratio in London reached 58% in 1997, as it attracted this very business, especially from the rest of Europe. The same was happening in New York which played a similar role for the Americas. In contrast, Tokyo failed to establish that position, even after the changes between 1998 and 2000. However, this international market in stocks remained small in comparison to the trading in and between these domestic markets, though that was increasingly in the hands of a small number of international banks and brokers. Essentially, even by 2005 the global stock market remained an amalgam of national markets with a small amount of international and cross-border trading. However, the internal and external barriers had largely disappeared, so opening up these domestic markets to international forces of supply and demand. The outcome was a merging of these national markets into a single global market and so creating opportunities to global providers.[27]

THE NEW GLOBAL SECURITIES MARKET

The turn of the twenty-first century was characterized by an evolving compromise between the desire of national governments to control and regulate the markets they hosted and the desire of these markets to escape such strictures and respond to the limitless opportunities now existing in a world with few artificial boundaries and where technology offered instant-aneous contact regardless of distance. An entirely new global securities market gradually came into being. It could not be a recreation of what had existed before the First World War because so much had changed in the meantime, especially the expectation and ability of governments to intervene in the marketplace and the greatly increased level of economic integration both within countries and internationally. This new global securities market was the product of three separate forces. The first was the return to something similar to the importance and operations that had been prevalent before 1914. The second was the conditions that had prevailed since the Wall Street Crash of 1929, which had then been reinforced by the experience of the 1930s and the Second World War. The third and last were the conditions peculiar to the late twentieth century onwards, especially the fusion of communications and computing to produce markets that were truly global in scope and could function without the need for any physical location. Though the basic design of that market was clear by then, and its implications for national and international financial systems, many other components were not yet established, such as the institutional structure of stock exchanges, the relationship between markets and banks, and the role to be played by national governments in a global age. All these remained to be resolved.

National monopolies had largely been broken down, forcing stock exchanges to become competitive marketplaces rather than regulatory organizations. Mutuality worked well in static situations where it was important to satisfy the interests of all participants through a compromise solution, but it did not work well in rapidly changing environments, which demanded quick responses and involved both winners and losers. In contrast, the switch to a corporate structure for stock exchanges placed the power firmly in the hands of the major banks and brokers, as they could exert the greatest influence over an exchange's future direction as they had the funds to become major shareholders. This had long been the case in OTC markets where the user not the provider was sovereign. A corporate structure also allowed stock exchanges to develop a strategy independent from the country in which they were located. The ability to convince shareholders not governments became the overriding consideration as stock exchanges competed for business in an increasingly global market, so encouraging them to adopt the transnational structure that had already proved so successful for the corporate enterprise. Electronic trading networks had replaced floor trading in almost all cases, widening the market, lowering transaction costs, and eroding the power of incumbent institutions and intermediaries so that only the efficient survived.

Unless prevented by legislation there was also a convergence of banking and broking as each had invaded the territory of the other. The large banks with extensive retail networks and the wholesale investment banks emerged as the clear leaders. Such was the size of these financial intermediaries and their increasingly global networks that they rivalled the markets they used and threatened the authority of national governments. So many market activities were now internalized within large financial firms. Banks, in particular, were able to employ temporarily idle funds through their own brokers, allowing them to purchase outright a portfolio of securities on offer or deliver what was wanted from their own holdings. This allowed banks to operate directly in the market rather than through subsidiaries or independent brokers and dealers. National governments had been forced to recognize the power and integration of banks and financial markets and so limit their intervention to the realm of supervision and regulation rather than control and manipulation. Nevertheless, national governments like that of the US or supranational bodies such as the EU continued to operate as if their sovereign actions were free of implications beyond their own borders, which made them the sole remaining threat to the final fulfilment of a truly global market in corporate stocks.

There was also little recognition that behind the volatility of the marketplace was a constant process of adjustment that not only met the needs of a dynamic economy but also reduced the possibility of highly damaging financial crises and diffused the consequences when they did occur. It was not the rise or fall of stock and bond prices or the movement of money around the world that endangered the health of financial systems but the existence of banks with overextended loans and the interventions of governments in the pursuance of policy objectives. Nevertheless, strident cries for intervention were to be heard after any financial crisis. These came from such luminaries as the New York investment banker, Henry Kaufman, in 1997 and the World Bank economist, Joseph Stiglitz, in 1998.[28] They noted the contrast between national financial systems, where securities markets were highly regulated and the central bank acted as lender of last resort, and the global situation where no such supervision or support existed. So conditioned had the world become to a situation which had evolved during the nineteenth century in Britain, with the Bank of England, and during the twentieth century in the United States, with the SEC, that no other alternative could be envisaged. Without a world central bank and a regulatory authority for the global securities market, the only solution was one of restrictions and controls until such institutions could be agreed upon.[29]

The abiding fear was a repetition of the events of 1929 and 1931, which only the coordinated actions of central bankers and other regulators had prevented since the end of the Second World War. Forgotten was the part played by governments in those events and their responsibility for the crises that continued to plague the post-war world, whether it was excessive international borrowing, misguided currency pegs, politically motivated monetary unification, or inflationary domestic policies. In contrast, the global financial system in existence before 1914 had worked reasonably well without any central direction and management, as had the Eurocurrency markets that had developed since the 1960s. Central to both these was the existence of a global securities markets for that provided the flexibility and mobility necessary to employ, release, and transfer funds as required by banks. The problem after 1914 until the 1990s was the existence of barriers to the international mobility of capital and the inadequate volume of securities capable of being bought and sold in and between national markets, as that was the mechanism through which equilibrium was achieved. Foreign-held capital fell from 18% of world GDP in 1914 to a low of 5% by 1945, recovered to 25% in 1980, and then reached 62% in 1995, when it stood at $15.5 trillion. By then much was again in the form of stocks and bonds that were actively traded on securities markets.

In 2003 US holdings of foreign stocks and bonds stood at $2.5 trillion whilst foreign holdings of US securities totalled $4.9 trillion. Much of this was in highly liquid government and corporate bonds along with the stocks issued by many of the world's largest companies. Indicative of the volume of international transactions was the fact that US transactions in foreign securities grew from $907 billion in 1990 to $7.1 trillion in 2003, whilst foreign transactions in US stocks and bonds rose from $4.2 trillion in 1990 to $30.7 trillion in 2003. This growth was despite the rise and fall of the dot.com boom, showing that international transactions were driven by far more than speculative surges. The constant ebb and flow of funds in and out of New York, amounting to $38 trillion by 2003, demonstrated the ability of the global securities market to maintain international equilibrium in the absence of rigid controls by national governments, the active intervention of central bankers, or some powerful supranational body with the oversight of the global financial system and the power to enforce market discipline. The world had rediscovered the mechanism that had produced stability before 1914. This was not adherence to fixed exchange rates under the gold standard, but the operations of the global securities market.[30] Rather than threatening financial stability the explosive growth in international capital flows, when accompanied by the development of broad and deep markets at the national level, provided a means of coping with crises.[31]

CONCLUSION

By 2005 a global securities market was in full operation. It involved a degree of integration and interaction never before achieved, being the culmination of technological and organizational advances during the twentieth century. It had also overcome the governmental and institutional barriers that had previously restricted its development. This market allowed governments to obtain the funds they wanted at low rates of interest, as long as they abided by the basic rule of servicing their debts and repaying when and where promised. It also met the needs of those managing business to organize and finance their activities to suit all circumstances, as long as they maintained certain accepted standards of corporate behaviour. Though transgressions occurred by both governments and managements, procedures existed to deal with these and to cope with the consequences. However, it would be a mistake to see this global securities market simply in terms of those who used it to issue stocks and bonds. Of even more importance were those who bought, held, and traded these securities whether operating alone or collectively. Their actions mobilized idle or under-utilized savings for productive use, if only to release the funds of another. Their constant trading contributed to the equilibrium of the world economy by redistributing money and capital across the globe in response to supply and demand. The banks and brokers that conducted so much of this trading were engaged in a process central to the functioning of the global financial system, though few recognized the wider implications of what they were doing. Similarly, most onlookers regarded their activities as little more than valueless speculation driven by greed and of no value in the real economy. As a result securities markets remained very vulnerable to government control or taxation as neither was felt to have serious consequences for either the national or global economy. The lesson of the twentieth century was that the consequences were both extensive and prolonged.

Conclusion

GENERAL

The history of the global securities market is both the history of a market and the institutions which made it work. On the one hand it traces the growing importance of transferable government debt and corporate stocks and bonds and the role they played in economic and political affairs of the world. On the other hand, it recognizes the need to devise methods of trading and organizational systems that allowed these securities to become an integral part of national and international financial systems. There is a strong tendency to see the development of the global securities market solely from the perspective of those who raised money through the issue of stocks and bonds. However, of equal or even greater importance was the position of those who bought, held, and traded these securities. In many ways the driving force behind the growth of the global securities market has not been the needs of governments and business, because their financial requirements could be met in a variety of different ways, but the desire by investors for an asset that was easily divisible, mobile, and flexible in terms of space and time, as well as delivering a return either through income or capital appreciation. Securities became that asset and the securities market grew and thrived over the centuries despite all the setbacks it suffered and the attempts made by governments to curb or even destroy it. Securities were like money itself, an essential element within the fabric of life, and this made the global securities market an integral component of the modern world economy.

This history of the global securities market divides into six distinct periods. The first begins in the twelfth century and culminates in 1720. In this early period securities markets emerged as a distinct entity within the financial system of many European countries, trading mainly government debt. However, even in Amsterdam, the leading financial centre by 1700, this trading lacked an organized forum being but one component of a general market for commodities, bills of exchange, and other financial instruments. The second period from 1720 lasted until the end of the Napoleonic wars in 1815. During most of the eighteenth century securities markets made many advances in terms of organization and importance, with Paris leading the former and

Amsterdam the latter, though London was gaining rapidly on both fronts. Securities markets also developed outside Europe in the newly independent United States. However, in the era of revolution and warfare that plagued Europe between 1789 and 1815 most of these gains were lost, with London being almost the sole beneficiary. The third period covers the years from the end of one major European war in 1815 to the beginning of the next in 1914. This century witnessed the arrival of the global securities market on the centre stage of financial systems, playing an important role within an ever expanding number of countries around the world as well as in the international economy. The global securities market not only facilitated the mobilization of long-term capital for both national and world economic development but it also imparted liquidity and mobility to the monetary systems of the world. An integrated global economy resulted with the railway and the stock exchange as symbols of the age. The fourth period covered the years from the outbreak of the First World War in 1914 to that of the Second in 1939, with the virtual collapse of the international economy in between. Within those 25 years, the achievement of the past century was largely lost or reversed. Inflation and defaults played havoc with the value of securities whilst government controls at home and abroad restricted the freedom of markets to operate. The Wall Street Crash in 1929 and the European financial and monetary crises of 1931 were turning points in the history of the global securities market, ushering in an era of regulation and even suppression. In the fifth period, from 1945 until 1970, the global securities market was in retreat both domestically and internationally, with many countries dispensing with stock exchanges entirely. Such was the degree of control exercised by governments that a stateless international market appeared in the shape of the Eurobond market. The final period from 1970 onwards saw a revival in the fortunes of the global securities market. On the domestic front the attack on restrictive practices, beginning in New York in the 1970s, followed by a general move towards regulation rather than control, saw securities markets revive as important components of national financial systems. Internationally, the relaxation and then abandonment of controls on financial flows saw the re-emergence of the global securities market as a key element within an increasingly integrated world economy.

The development of the global securities market has experienced both advances and reversals. On the eve of the First World War there seemed nothing that could stop the market's onward march. In the aftermath of the Second World War it was doubtful if a global securities market even existed, and its presence at national level was in jeopardy. The fact that the global securities market did recover indicates its fundamental importance within the world's financial system whilst recognizing that it could only prosper under conditions of trust and stability. The purchase of a transferable security was itself an act of faith in the existence of a guaranteed future income and/or the ability to resell as and when required. It took years to build up confidence in the safety and marketability of securities, to a level where they could be used as temporary homes for the profitable employment of short-term money. Confidence was also required to underpin the ownership of assets in one country by investors from another, whether on a long-or short-term basis. It was this confidence that was most affected by the First World War, and subsequent events, such as hyperinflation in Germany, the Wall Street Crash, the collapse of monetary and financial systems worldwide, the imposition of exchange controls, and the repudiation of sovereign debts. Thus, after the Second World War much of the trust and confidence that had underpinned the growing use of transferable securities and the free operation of markets had gone. Instead the power of government to direct, regulate, manage, and control had now become the central belief, to a greater or lesser extent, all round the world. Within this new climate stock exchanges, as the central institutions of the securities market, were converted into government-sponsored regulatory organizations, becoming in consequence restrictive and reactionary rather than dynamic and progressive. Much of the trading in securities gradually moved away from the stock exchanges unless channeled there through restrictive practices and the actions of national governments, whilst securities markets were marginalized within financial systems compared to governments and banks. Only when these practices were banned and governments ceased to be supportive were stock exchanges forced to change. Many did not at a time when markets were becoming both electronic and global but even unregulated markets discovered the need for rules of behaviour and methods of enforcement if they were to operate successfully. Thus, though in a different form, order and importance returned to the global securities market by 2000.

Behind the many changes experienced by the securities market were short- and long-term forces, both economic and political. These can be seen in the revolution in communications with the telegraph and the telephone, the transformation of business with the development of the joint-stock company, the actions of governments both in creating the market through the issue of securities and in destroying its operation through controls and suppression, and the continuous rise and fall of trading in response to the varying interest of investors, leading at times to the unbridled euphoria of speculative outbursts. Without the global securities market both national and international financial systems lacked the flexibility of operation that facilitated the mobilization and transfer of savings and the maintenance of equilibrium. Only securities markets had the ability to deliver both within a dynamic and changing world, making them an integral part of any financial system, complementing rather than competing with banks. However, the role played by securities markets has never been universally recognized. Instead, credit is given to governments and business for raising and using finance or to the financial intermediaries, such as the banks, that helped collect and employ savings. In contrast, there is limited understanding of how the existence of transferable securities and an organized market blurred the distinctions between the short- and long-term use of funds, and their contribution to international stability. Throughout its history the prime function of the global securities market has been downplayed because of its association with speculation. Instead of trying to investigate the causes and consequences of this constant buying and selling, the assumption is made that, because it is rooted in the individual's desire to sell rather than produce for a profit, it does not perform a function within the wider economy. Consequently, the existence of the global securities market can only be justified by attributing it to the activities of others, such as those issuing securities and the use government and business made of the finance so obtained.

Equally, there is a tendency to ignore the ability of the global securities market to regulate itself, developing rules and regulations that not only permitted orderly trading within the nation state but also internationally, with the minimum of barriers and the maximum of freedom. Instead, the impression given is that everything that preceded statutory regulation was inadequate and ineffective, and that only the state had the ability to police the global securities market. However, until recently markets neither operated autonomously nor were regulated by governments. Instead, they operated largely under rules and regulations of their own devising and did so relatively successfully. The very development of stock exchanges testified to the need for organization and regulation, and the ready response from those directly involved. The era before 1939 was one not so much of *laissez-faire* but self-regulation. In increasingly complex and interdependent economies the forces of supply and demand present in the global securities market had to be modified so as to ensure the speedy completion of transactions. This was not simply a process of price determination but one that included amount, timing, type, place, and condition if any sale or purchase was to constitute a good delivery. As one deal was dependent on the next in a rapidly moving marketplace, and involved attendant connections to other components of the financial system as well as risks to those involved, all this required a great deal of trust between the participants. It was this that stock exchanges delivered long before the involvement of government and which the securities market had to continue to deliver whatever the requirements of the law.

SPECIFIC

The problem with sophisticated securities markets was that they involved inherent conflicts of interest. Barriers to contact between buyers and sellers had to be at a minimum so that all interested could participate when and where they wanted. Conversely, confidence in agreed delivery or payment had to be at a maximum, in order to both facilitate and encourage sales and purchases, and this required strict controls on the admission and conduct of those permitted to participate. The number of participants had to be sufficiently small so as to permit the greatest contact between those with the most business to transact, and there had to be a high degree of trust between those participants so that every bid to buy or offer for sale was equally acceptable, and only price determined the counter-party to a deal. Conversely, the number of participants had to be as large as possible so as to ensure that the prices at which business was done fully reflected the forces of supply and demand. There was also the question of cost. The provision of a sophisticated securities market was expensive in terms of facilities and staff, and that cost had to be borne by the users. In return, those who paid to use a stock exchange expected certain privileges compared to those who did not. Membership of a stock exchange gave immediate access to others involved in the buying and selling of securities as well as the confidence that action would be taken against those who failed to honour any commitments made. Thus, a stock exchange both created a climate of confidence and a forum for trading, both of which contribute greatly to the development of an active securities market. Conversely, by restricting membership of the stock exchange competition could be curtailed and charges could be maintained or increased. Consequently, a compromise had to be devised between the requirements of an open market and those of a closed one. The nature of this compromise changed constantly as economic and financial circumstances altered.

This conflict between an open and closed securities market can be highlighted by looking at access to the prices at which securities were traded. One of the privileges of access was knowledge of current prices, which was denied to non-members, though a level of dissemination was essential. It was important for investors to be aware of general trends when they made decisions on whether to buy or sell particular securities whilst those lending money with securities as collateral needed to know the current value of the assets provided. The very fact that prices were constantly in flux, and that this was publicized, encouraged those who wished to buy for a rise or sell for a fall, so generating business for the members of a stock exchange. Also, as activity on each exchange responded to that taking place elsewhere, either because of the existence of the same or similar securities, it was essential that current prices were widely circulated, to encourage arbitrage operations. Stock exchanges were therefore keen to disseminate price information. However, too rapid a dissemination of prices would remove one of the essential privileges of membership as it would allow those who were excluded, or who did not choose to join, to trade at current prices. As such people could charge less, not having to meet the cost of membership, and operate more freely, as they were not bound by the rules, they would be at a competitive advantage. As long as stock exchanges offered additional benefits of membership, such as minimizing counter-party risk or maximizing contact with potential buyers and sellers, then the need to control access to current prices was of limited importance. However, if privileged access to prices became one of only a few benefits to membership it could easily become outweighed by the costs and restrictions involved. Trading would then move away from the exchange and the market would fragment. Conversely, restricting access to current prices was a way of limiting the competition experienced by members of stock exchanges, so allowing them to charge higher fees to those wishing to buy or sell securities than otherwise would be possible. One solution to this conflict of interest was government intervention. On the one hand a government could outlaw restrictions on access to current prices as an anti-competitive practice working against the interests of an improved marketplace and lower charges. On the other hand it could levy a fee on those handling the buying and selling of securities, so ensuring that all who benefited from the market paid for its operation. Furthermore, governments could always ensure that the rules and regulations required for an orderly market would be complied with. Unfortunately, though this legalistic solution appealed to many, in itself it created further conflicts of interest. At no stage were governments ever totally neutral. Whilst being large borrowers themselves, they were also frequently tempted to manipulate the market for their own ends in the interests of specific policy objectives or in response to public concerns about perceived abuse or fraudulent practice. Even if power was devolved to an independent body, tensions would arise between those who had a very legalistic interpretation of the way a securities market should operate and those who had a practical experience of how it actually did work. The outcome could very well be the imposition of restrictions that raised the market's costs and reduced its efficiency to such an extent that it was bypassed by those it was designed for.[1]

Hence, though it was the supply and demand for securities that created the market, the form that market took was by no means pre-ordained but reflected a complex interaction of economic and non-economic forces conditioned by changing circumstances. Out of that arose a variety of securities markets across the world differing from each other in many substantial ways, such as the number and nature of the membership, the organization of the marketplace, the securities traded, the charges made to customers, and the relationship with other powerful institutions, such as governments and banks, or other markets, like those dealing in money and commodities. This diversity also meant that the place of the securities market within any national economy also differed enormously from one country to another. There was no single model which every country copied, whilst extensive variations of practice also appeared over time, modified to suit local conditions. Rules were drawn up and frequently changed by the membership of these stock exchanges in order to protect their own interests and facilitate the business to be done by creating an orderly and regulated marketplace. The varying nature of this demand was also a major force in determining the type of stock exchange that was formed and the way it developed.

Stock exchanges also differed from each other in significant respects reflecting the way they had evolved, the relative power of groups within the membership, and the degree of government intervention. One illustration of the differences was their attitude to membership. Some stock exchanges permitted banks to become full members whilst others regarded banks, with their large capital and client bases, as major competitors, and tried to exclude them. Combined with differing attitudes to a fixed scale of charges to customers, willingness to quote new or different securities, and hostile or permissive government legislation, the consequence was that the role of the stock exchange was not the same in all countries. This had implications for the way financial and business systems were organized, which in turn had implications for the growth and operation of the economy. For too long the institutions that provided the markets through which supply and demand operated were taken for granted and given no role in the success or otherwise of the markets they controlled. Stock exchanges as institutions grew out of the securities markets, which itself indicates the need for them. Their very existence then conditioned the way these markets developed. However, eventually out of this diversity came uniformity as the forces of globalization re-emerged from the shadows in the late twentieth century. Though differences between securities markets remained, often reflecting differences in size, function, and financial sophistication, the individuality of the past quickly faded. Almost universally the oversight of the securities market lay with a statutory securities commission ultimately answerable to national government. This was a product of the response in the United States to the Wall Street Crash and the subsequent financial crisis. Increasingly common was also the separation of the ownership of a stock exchange from access to the market it provided. Stock exchanges were increasingly run for profit by joint-stock companies whilst their users were charged a fee, whether those whose securities were traded or those who undertook the trading. This reflected the structure of the London Stock Exchange which had prevailed from 1801 until 1947, and constituted the world's most successful securities market for much of that period. The direct participation of banks in these stock exchanges also became increasingly commonplace as the resistance of specialist brokers and dealers was broken down. Such a position had long prevailed in Germany and elsewhere in central Europe. The modern securities market was very much an amalgam of different elements from around the world, containing features from both the Anglo-American tradition and that of continental Europe, and was the product of the forces of globalization that transformed the world economy in the second-half of the twentieth century.

Notes

INTRODUCTION

1. J. P. Raines, *Economists and the Stock Market: Speculative Theories of Stock Market Fluctuations* (Cheltenham, 2000), p. 1; cf. pp. 1–2, 23, 28, 45, 54–7, 69, 73, 92–3, 99, 106, 109, 111, 149.
2. P. J. Drake, *Money, Finance and Development* (Oxford, 1980), pp. 34–6, 192–3, 215.
3. N. Dimsdale and M. Prevezer (eds.), *Capital Markets and Corporate Governance* (Oxford, 1994), pp. 14, 71–2, 80, 179–83, 191, 295–9; F. Allen and D. Gate, Comparing Financial systems (Cambridge Mass. 2000) p. 50.
4. R. J. Schiller, *Irrational Exuberance* (New York, 2001), pp. 9, 12, 35, 38, 60–1, 182, 188–9, 193, 195, 228, 233, 246.
5. J. Kay, *The Truth About Markets* (London, 2004), pp. 10, 223, 249, 268, 335, 337, 339, 353, 357–8, 362–3, 370, 373.
6. For example R. Levine and S. Zervos, 'Stock Markets, Banks, and Economic Growth' and T. G. Rajan and L. Zingales, 'Financial Dependence and Growth', *American Economic Review*, 88 (1988); and P. L. Rousseaux and R. Sylla, 'Financial Systems, Economic Growth, and Globalization', in M. D. Bordo, A. M. Taylor, and J. G. Williamson (eds.), *Globalization in Historical Perspective* (Chicago, 2003).
7. N. Ferguson, *The Cash Nexus: Money and Power in the Modern World, 1700–2000* (London, 2001), pp. 166, 310; V. Tanzi and L. Schuknecht, public spending in the 20th century (Cambridge 2000) pp. 64–6. For the effects on stocks and bonds over the course of the 20th century and in different countries see E. Dimson, P. Marsh and M. Slanton, Triumph of the optimists: 101 years of Global Invesment Returns (Princeton 2002) pp. 229, 313.
8. For a recent overview of the importance of globalization see Bordo, Taylor, and Williamson (eds.), *Globalization in Historical Perspective*. This includes a number of chapters specifically on financial systems.
9. H. C. Reed, *The Pre-Eminence of International Financial Centres* (New York, 1981), pp. 18–19, 28–9, 93, 131–9.
10. R. Roberts (ed.), *International Financial Centres* (Aldershot, 1994), vol. 2, pp. 146–7, 173.
11. For a general history of stock markets see L. Neal, 'On the historical Development of Stock Markets', in H. Brezinski and M. Fritsch (eds.), *The Emergence and Evolution of Markets* (Cheltenham, 1997).
12. L. Oxelheim, *Financial Markets in Transition: Globalization, Investment and Economic Growth* (London, 1996), p. 417.

CHAPTER 1

1. For the medieval developments see C. P. Kindleberger, *A Financial History of Western Europe* (London, 1984), pp. 34, 39, 184; J. Bernard, 'Trade and Finance in

the Middle Ages, 900–1500', and E. Miller, 'Government Economic Policies and Public Finance, 1000–1500' in C. M. Cipolla (ed.), *The Fontana Economic History of Europe: The Middle Ages* (London, 1972,) pp. 293–5, 550; S. Homer and R. Sylla, *A History of Interest Rates* (New Brunswick, 1996), pp. 74, 92, 96, 101, 108, 110, 135; P. Spufford, *Money and Its Use in Medieval Europe* (Cambridge, 1988), pp. 254, 338; R. C. Mueller, 'Foreign Investment in Venetian Government Bonds and the Case of Paolo Guinigi, Lord Lucca, early Fifteenth Century', in H. Diedericks and D. Reeder (eds.), *Cities of Finance* (Amsterdam, 1996), pp. 71, 75–6, 84; R. A. Goldthwaite, *Private Wealth in Renaissance Florence: A Study of Four Families* (Princeton, 1968), pp. 37, 43, 53, 58–73, 112, 165, 204–5, 219, 244–8; Center for Medieval and Renaissance Studies, *The Dawn of Modern Banking* (Los Angeles, 1979), pp. 16, 55, 69, 70–5, 77–9, 89, 93–7, 102–8, 132, 153, 172, 214–15, 261–2, 267–8, 270–1; J. D. Tracy, *A Financial Revolution in the Hapsburg Netherlands: Renten and Renteniers in the County of Holland, 1516–1565* (Berkeley, 1985), pp. 9–20; J. B. Baskin and P. J. Miranti, *A History of Corporate Finance* (Cambridge, 1997), pp. 33, 50–2, 60.

2. For Bruges, as well as generally, see R. de Roover, *Money, Banking and Credit in Medieval Bruges* (Cambridge, MA., 1948), pp. 3, 11–12, 17, 29–30, 42, 48, 53–5, 61–6, 77–8, 83–4, 88–91, 203, 209, 237, 247, 250, 279–80, 292–4, 303–4, 310–11, 314, 318, 349–53.

3. For Antwerp see H. Van der Wee, *The Growth of the Antwerp Market and the European Economy* (The Hague, 1963), pp. 18, 110–11, 130, 140–14, 178, 199, 206, 220, 263, 280, 339–40, 349, 352–5, 362–4, 366–8. See also Tracy, *Financial Revolution*, pp. 24, 109, 131, 138, 164.

4. R. Ehrenberg, *Capital and Finance in the Age of the Renaissance* (1938, repr. in New York, 1963), pp. 33–4, 40, 44, 53–8, 237, 244–5, 248–50, 262, 280–3, 293, 299, 309–10, 314, 324–5, 327–8, 330, 334; G. Parker, 'The Emergence of Modern Finance in Europe', in C. M. Cipolla (ed.), *The Fontana Economic History of Europe: The Sixteenth and Seventeenth Centuries* (London, 1974), pp. 531, 541, 548, 551, 554–60, 567; Homer and Sylla, *History of Interest Rates*, pp. 112–13, 115–18, 135–8.

5. M. Hart, J. Jonker, and J. l. Van Zanden, *A Financial History of the Netherlands* (Cambridge, 1997), pp. 5, 12, 18, 20; J. I. Israel, *Dutch Primacy in World Trade, 1585–1740* (Oxford, 1989), pp. 28–9, 35–7, 42, 46, 48, 51–2, 54–5, 73–9; J. de Vries and A. Van der Werde, *The First Modern Economy: Success, Failure, and Perseverance of the Dutch Economy, 1500–1815* (Cambridge, 1997), pp. 120, 130–4, 137–8, 151, 365, 368–9, 498, 667–8; O. Gederblom and J. Jonker, 'Completing a Financial Revolution: The Finance of the Dutch East India Trade and the Rise of the Amsterdam Capital Market, 1595–1612' (unpublished paper), p. 117; Ehrenberg, *Capital and Finance*, pp. 350–2, 357–67; Homer and Sylla, *History of Interest Rates*, pp. 122–6, 135, 174–5, 513–14; Parker, 'Emergence of Modern Finance', pp. 556–9; Baskin and Miranti, *Corporate Finance*, p. 58.

6. Joseph de la Vega, *Confusion de Confusiones* (Amsterdam, 1688; in English with an introduction by Herman Kellenbenz, 1957; repr. in Wiley Investment Classics: New York, 1996). See pp. 134–45 for the introduction and pp. 147–79 for the text. See also J. Israel, 'The Amsterdam Stock Exchange and the English Revolution of 1688', *Tijdschrift voor Geschiedenis* 103 (1990), pp. 412–18; Tracy, *Financial Revolution*, pp. *206, 211, 222.*

7. B. G. Carruthers, *City of Capital: Politics and Markets in the English Financial Revolution* (Princeton, 1996), pp. 13–14, 23, 55, 60, 62–4, 67–8, 123, 138, 146; A. M. Carlos, J. Key, and J. L. Dupree, 'Learning and the Creation of Stock-Market Institutions: Evidence From the Royal African and Hudson's Bay Companies, 1670–1700', *Journal of Economic History*, 58 (1998), pp. 341–2.

8. Carruthers, *City of Capital*, pp. 76–80, 82–5, 103–5, 108, 150, 155–8; K. G. Davies, 'Joint-Stock Investment in the Later 17th Century', *Economic History Review*, 4 (1951–2), pp. 288–96.

9. S. Banner, *Anglo-American Securities Regulation: Cultural and Political Roots, 1690–1860* (Cambridge, 1998), pp. 20–2, 28, 39; W. R. Scott, *The Constitution and Finance of English, Scottish and Irish Joint-Stock Companies to 1720* (Cambridge, 1912), vol. I, pp. 44, 155, 161, 345, 443, 460; Carruthers, *City of Capital*, pp. 162–84, 193–4, 201–4.

10. M. Potter, *Corps and Clienteles: Public Finance and Political Change in France, 1688–1715* (Aldershot, 2003), pp. 138–40, 161, 179–83; W. C. Scoville, *The Persecution of Huguenots and French Economic Development, 1680–1720* (Berkeley, 1960), pp. 5, 261–4, 274, 289–99; Ehrenberg, *Capital and Finance*, p. 363.

11. D. Stasavage, *Public Debt and the Birth of the Democratic Sate: France and Great Britain, 1688–1789* (Cambridge, 2003), pp. 78, 83, 91.

12. A. E. Murphy, *John Law: Economic Theorist and Policy-Maker* (Oxford, 1997), pp. 159–67, 188–95, 201–2, 206–10, 227–9, 238, 241, 244, 250–7, 265–6, 304–5, 310, 325, 329; Parker, 'Emergence of Modern Finance in Europe', pp. 581–2.

13. J. Carswell, *The South Sea Bubble* (revised edn., London, 1993), pp. 69–71, 77–9, 85, 87, 122, 129–31, 133–6, 140, 147, 164, 202; Parker, 'Emergence of Modern Finance in Europe', pp. 583–4.

14. Ehrenberg, *Capital and Finance*, pp. 370–1; F. C. Spooner, *Risks at Sea: Amsterdam Insurance and Maritime Europe, 1766–1780* (Cambridge, 1983), pp. 24, 45; Parker, 'Emergence of Modern Finance in Europe', pp. 585–6.

15. Parker, 'Emergence of Modern Finance in Europe', pp. 586–9; Stasavage, *Public Debt*, p. 92; Baskin and Miranti, *Corporate Finance*, p. 123.

16. For an alternative view that places the actions of government in a more positive light, see H. L. Root, *The Fountain of Privilege: Political Foundations of Markets in Old Regime France and England* (Berkeley, 1994), pp. 3–4, 165, 171–2, 175, 179, 181, 186, 209, 242.

CHAPTER 2

1. C. Mackay, *Extraordinary Popular Delusions and the Madness of Crowds* (London, 1841; repr. in Wiley Investment Classics: New York, 1996), pp. 36–7, 76–9; R. Ehrenberg, *Capital and finance in the age of the Renaissance* (1938, repr. in New York, 1963), pp. 369–70.

2. G. V. Taylor, 'The Paris Bourse on the Eve of the Revolution, 1781–1789', *American Historical Review*, 67 (1962), pp. 951–70; S. Homer and R. Sylla, *A History of Interest Rates* (New Brunswick, 1996), p. 168; D. Stasavage, *Public Debt*

and the Birth of the Democratic State: France and Great Britain, 1688–1789 (Cambridge, 2003), pp. 93–7.

3. H. L. Root, *The Fountain of Privilege: Political Foundations of Markets in Old Regime France and England* (Berkeley, 1994), pp. 175–86; C. P. Kindleberger, *A Financial History of Western Europe* (London, 1984), p. 207.
4. Ehrenberg, *Capital and Finance*, pp. 371–3.
5. Stasavage, *Public Debt*, pp. 93, 97.
6. W. Fairman, *The Stocks Examined and Compared* (3rd edn.) (London, 1798), p. 2.
7. P. G. M. Dickson, *The Financial Revolution in England: A Study in the Development of Public Credit, 1688–1756* (London, 1967), pp. 489, 514.
8. D. Hancock, *Citizens of the World: London Merchants and the Integration of the British Atlantic Community, 1735–1785* (Cambridge, 1995), pp. 258–72.
9. S. Banner, *Anglo-American Securities Regulation: Cultural and Political Roots, 1690–1860* (Cambridge, 1998), pp. 78–111.
10. M. Hart, J. Jonker, and J. L. Van Zanden, *A Financial History of the Netherlands* (Cambridge, 1997), pp. 55–62; J. de Vries and A. Van der Werde, *The First Modern Economy: Success, Failure and Perseverance, 1500–1815* (Cambridge, 1997), pp. 12, 124, 129, 141–4, 154–5, 683; F. C. Spooner, *Risks at Sea: Amsterdam Insurance and Maritime Europe, 1766–1780* (Cambridge, 1983), pp. 66–75; Kindleberger, *Financial History*, pp. 214–17; J. C. Riley, *International Government Finance and the Amsterdam Capital Market, 1740–1815* (Cambridge, 1980), pp. 7–8, 19, 45, 50, 61–5, 77, 84–5, 105, 114, 123–7, 174, 178, 183–6, 194, 281; C. Wilson, *Anglo-Dutch Commerce and Finance in the 18th Century* (Cambridge, 1941), pp. 79–83, 97, 111, 116–17, 191, 195; B. Stancke, *The Danish Stock Market, 1750–1840* (Copenhagen, 1971), pp. 11–12, 16, 20–2, 110.
11. A. Elon, *Founder: Meyer Amschel Rothschild and his Time* (London, 1996), pp. 30, 84, 106.
12. G. Yogev, *Diamonds and Coral: Anglo-Dutch Jews and the Eighteenth Century Trade* (Leicester, 1978), pp. 202, 213, 242–5.
13. L. Neal, *The Rise of Financial Capitalism: International Capital Markets in the Age of Reason* (Cambridge, 1990), pp. 27, 45, 169; Ehrenberg, *Capital and Finance*, pp. 370–5; Banner, *Anglo-American Securities Regulation*, pp. 130–3; J. Jonker, *Fingers in the Dike, Fingers in the Pie: the Position of the Amsterdam Stock Exchange on the Dutch Capital Market, 1800–1940* (unpublished paper 1994), p. 3.
14. B. Stancke, *The Danish Stock Market, 1750–1840* (Copenhagen, 1971), pp. 12–13.
15. *A Summary Chronicle of the Zurich Stock Exchange* (Zurich, 1977), p. 297.
16. E. J. Perkins, *American Public Finance and Financial Services, 1700–1815* (Columbus, 1994), pp. 200, 226, 230–1, 235, 310, 312–15; R. Sylla, A. Tilly, and G. Tortella (eds.), *The State, the Financial System and Economic Modernization* (Cambridge, 1999), pp. 251–63; Banner, *Anglo-American Securities Regulation*, pp. 130–50.
17. Riley, *International Government Finance*, pp. 201–16, 243–7; M. D. Bordo and E. N. White, 'British and French Finance During the Napoleonic Wars', in M. D. Bordo and F. Capie (eds.), *Monetary Regimes in Transition* (Cambridge, 1994),

pp. 264; R. E. Cameron, *France and the Economic Development of Europe, 1800–1914* (Princeton, 1961), p. 29; Kindleberger, *Financial History*, p. 207; Ehrenberg, *Capital and Finance*, p. 375; S. R. Cope, *Walter Boyd: a Merchant Banker in the Age of Napoleon* (Gloucester, 1983), pp. 3, 8, 10, 25–9, Sylla, Tilly, and Tortella (eds.), *The State, the Financial System and Economic Modernization*, p. 47.

18. Elon, *Meyer Amschel Rothschild*, p. 89; A. Teichova, G. Kurgan-Van Hentenryk, and D. Zeigler (eds.) *Banking, Trade and Industry: Europe, America and Asia from the 13th to the 20th Century* (Cambridge, 1997), pp. 162–3; L. Neal and L. Davis, 'The Evolution of the Rules and Regulations of the First Emerging Markets: the London, New York and Paris Stock Exchanges, 1792–1914', *Quarterly Review of Economics and Finance*, 45 (2005), pp. 304–6.

19. Hart, Jonker, and Van Zanden, *Financial History of the Netherlands*, pp. 51, 64, 92; J. Jonker, *Merchants, Bankers, Middlemen: The Amsterdam Money Market During the First Half of the 19th Century, 1814–1863* (Cambridge, 1996), pp. 22–3, 30, 61, 69, 91, 98, 126, 137, 189–90, 236, 242, 301, 312.

20. Homer and Sylla, *History of Interest Rates*, pp. 198–9.

21. Perkins, *American Public Finance*, pp. 305, 310–17, 328, 336, 356, 362–75; Banner, *Anglo-American Securities Regulation*, pp. 133–40, 150, 161, 251, 267, 271; R. Sylla, J. W. Wilson, and R. E. Wright, 'America's First Securities Markets, 1790–1830: Emergence, Development and Integration' (unpublished paper), pp. 4–15; C. R. Geisst, *Wall Street: A History* (Oxford, 1997), pp. 10–21; W. Werner and S. T. Smith, *Wall Street* (New York, 1991), pp. 3, 13, 17–18, 43; J. E. Hedges, *Commercial Banking and the Stock Market before 1863* (Baltimore, 1938), pp. 17–18, 29–30; R. E. Wright, *The Wealth of Nations Rediscovered: Integration and Expansion in American Financial Markets, 1780–1850* (Cambridge, 2002), pp. 83, 88–91, 94.

22. Perkins, *American Public Finance*, pp. 336, 368.

23. Riley, *International Government Finance*, p. 100.

24. Riley, *International Government Finance*, pp. 205–16, 243.

CHAPTER 3

1. M. Wilkins, *The History of Foreign Investment in the United States to 1914* (Cambridge, MA, 1989), pp. 35–9.

2. J. Jonker, *Merchants, Bankers, Middlemen: The Amsterdam Money Market During the First Half of the 19th Century, 1814–1863* (Cambridge, 1996), pp. 79, 110–11, 126–9, 189–91, 199, 242–4; M. Hart, J. Jonker, and J. I. Van Zanden, *A Financial History of the Netherlands* (Cambridge, 1997), pp. 69, 92, 105–6.

3. D. C. M. Platt, *Foreign Finance in Continental Europe and the United States, 1815–1870: Quantities, Origins, Functions and Distribution* (London, 1984), p. 10; D. Weatherall, *David Ricardo: A Biography* (The Hague, 1976), p. 131; Jonker, *Merchants, Bankers, Middlemen*, p. 283; C. E. Freedman, 'The growth of

the French Securities Market, 1815–1870', in C. K. Warner (ed.), *From the Ancien Regime to the Popular Front* (New York, 1969), pp. 76, 84; C. P. Kindleberger, *A Financial History of Western Europe* (London, 1984), p. 207.

4. W. Werner and S. T. Smith, *Wall Street* (New York, 1991), pp. 26–9, 37–8, 86, 158–9, 162, 172; J. E. Hedges, *Commercial Banking and the Stock Market Before 1863* (Baltimore, 1938), pp. 17–8, 29–30, 38; J. K. Medbery, *Men and Mysteries of Wall Street* (New York, 1870), pp. 3, 5, 288; R. E. Wright, *The Wealth of Nations Rediscovered: Integration and Expansion in American Financial Markets, 1780–1850* (Cambridge, 2002), pp. 74, 103–18, 121, 136, 167, 196–200.

5. This is a revision of a view that I have previously expressed. Such is the benefit of the comparative perspective!

6. Freedeman, 'French Securities Market', 84; R. E. Cameron, *France and the Economic Development of Europe, 1800–1914* (Princeton, 1961), p. 83; G. P. Palmade, *French Capitalism in the Nineteenth Century* (Newton Abbott, 1972), pp. 59, 72, 88, 91.

7. See F. G. Dawson, *The First Latin American Debt Crisis: the City of London and the 1822–25 Loan Bubble* (New Haven, 1990); Corporation of Foreign Bondholders, *The Principal Foreign Loans* (London, 1877), listed by year; M. P. Costeloe, *Bonds and Bondholders: British Investors and Mexico's Foreign Debt, 1814–1888* (Westport, CT, 2003), pp. xiii–xv, 1, 269.

8. Freedeman, 'French Securities Market', 84.

9. Wilkins, *Foreign Investment in the United States,* pp. 35, 54, 68.

10. Jonker, *Merchants, Bankers, Middlemen,* pp. 167, 185–6, 191–2, 199, 255, 283; Hart, Jonker, and Van Zanden, *Financial History of the Netherlands* pp. 69, 92; J. Jonker, 'Fingers in the Dike, Fingers in the Pie: The Position of the Amsterdam Stock Exchange on the Dutch Capital Market, 1800–1940' (unpublished paper 1994), pp. 6, 23–4.

11. J. A. Torrente Fortuno, *Historia de la Bolsa de Madrid* (Madrid, 1974), vol. 1, pp. 313–15.

12. Kindleberger, *Financial History of Europe,* pp. 229–30; *The German Stock Exchanges: A History of Many Regions* (Germany's Almanac, 1985–6), pp. 41–2; C-L. Holtfrerich, *Frankfurt as a Financial Centre: From Medieval Trade Fair to European Banking Centre* (Munich, 1999,) pp. 144, 147–8; G. R. Gibson, *The Vienna Bourse* (New York, 1892), p. 7; R. E. Wright, 'Early US Financial Development in Comparative Perspective: New Data, Old Comparisons' (unpublished paper, 2003), p. 13.

13. Cameron, *France and Economic Development,* p. 83.

14. E. Vidal, *The History and Methods of the Paris Bourse* (Washington, 1910), pp. 181–3; C. E. Freedeman, *Joint-Stock Enterprise in France, 1807–1867* (Chapel Hill, 1979), pp. 22–34, 50–6, 67–8; G. Palmade, *French Capitalism,* pp. 88, 91–2, 101; R. Cameron (ed.), *Banking in the Early Stages of Industrialization* (New York, 1967), pp. 106, 111–12, 130–5, 145, 154; Cameron, *France and Economic Development,* pp. 82–3; Freedeman, 'French Securities Market', pp. 82–5; Kindleberger, *Financial history of Europe,* pp. 206–7, 210–11, 267; H. Kiehling, 'Efficiency of Early German Stock Markets, 1835–1848' (unpublished paper, Vienna, 2005), p. 4.

15. Werner and Smith, *Wall Street,* pp. 4–5, 60, 80–4, 119, 134, 158–9, 172, 184; Hedges, *Commercial Banking,* pp. 29, 34, 35–7; Wright, 'Early US Financial Development', pp. 15–19.

16. R. Tilly, *Financial Institutions and Industrialization in the Rhineland, 1815–1870* (Maddison, 1966), pp. 117–18; Holtfrerich, *Frankfurt,* pp. 161–3.

17. Cameron, *Banking in the Early Stages of Industrialization,* p. 130.

18. J. A. Torrente Fortuno, *Historia de la Bolsa de Madrid,* vol. 1, pp. 315–17; vol. 2, pp. 657–9.

19. Homer and Sylla, *History of Interest Rates,* p. 218.

20. Werner and Smith, *Wall Street,* p. 30; Hedges, *Commercial banking,* p. 75; S. Banner, *Anglo-American Securities Regulation: Cultural and Political Roots, 1690–1860* (Cambridge, 1998), pp. 194, 254–5.

21. R. W. Goldsmith, *Comparative National Balance Sheets* (Chicago, 1985), pp. 216, 232, 297, and Appendix A.

22. Wilkins, *Foreign Investment in the United States,* pp. 70–8; W. B. English, 'Understanding the Costs of Sovereign Default: American State Debts in the 1840s', *American Economic Review,* 86 (1996), pp. 259–61, 268.

23. Freedeman, 'French Securities Market', pp. 77, 80, 85–8; A. Liesse, *Evolution of Credit and Banks in France: From the Founding of the Bank of France to the Present* (Washington, 1909), pp. 54, 73–5, 129; Vidal, *The Paris Bourse,* pp. 177–83; Freedeman, *Joint-Stock Enterprise in France,* pp. 69–80, 102–4; Palmade, *French Capitalism,* pp. 111, 139; Cameron, *Banking in the Early Stages of Industrialization,* pp. 106, 111, 143–5, 156, 164–80.

24. Jonkers, *Merchants, Bankers, Middlemen,* pp. 192–3, 199; Torrente Fortuno, *Historia de la Bolsa de Madrid,* vol.1, pp. 661–5; Holtfrerich, *Frankfurt,* pp. 161–3.

25. Werner and Smith, *Wall Street,* pp. 44–5, 60; Hedges, *Commercial Banking,* pp. 32, 36, 47, 55–69, 75–7; Banner, *Anglo-American Securities Regulation,* pp. 174, 193, 222, 227, 250–71; See Wright, 'Early US financial development'.

26. S. Salsbury and K. Sweeney, *The Bull, the Bear and the Kangaroo: The History of the Sydney Stock Exchange* (Sydney, 1988), pp. 7–14; A. R. Hall, *The Stock Exchange of Melbourne and the Victorian Economy, 1852–1900* (Canberra, 1968), pp. 3–6.

27. R. S. Rungta, *Rise of Business Corporations in India, 1851–1900* (Cambridge, 1970), pp. 23, 25, 28–9, 31, 56.

28. See Wright, 'Early US Financial Development'.

29. Cameron, *Banking in the Early Stages of Industrialization,* pp. 106, 111, 143–5, 156, 164–80; Jonkers, *Merchants, Bankers, Middlemen,* p. 199.

CHAPTER 4

1. M. G. Myers, *Paris as a Financial Centre* (London, 1936), p. 136.

2. H. D. Jencken, 'On Some Points of Difference Between the English System of Law and that Prevailing on the Continent Regarding Negotiable Securities', *Journal of the Institute of Bankers* I (1880), p. 430; A. G. Webb, *The New Dictionary*

of Statistics (London, 1911), p. 81; cf. M. A. Neymarck, *Le Statistique Internationale des Valeurs Mobilières* (Institut International de Statistique: La Haye, 1911), p. 3.

3. For this data see M. G. Mulhall, *The Progress of the World* (London, 1880), p. 32; M. G. Mulhall, *Industries and Wealth of Nations* (London, 1896), p. 54.
4. P-C. Hautcoeur and P. Verley, 'Le marche financier français' (unpublished paper, 1994), p. 7.
5. C. Goodhart, 'Monetary Policy and Debt Management in the United Kingdom: Some Historical Viewpoints', in K. A. Chrystal (ed.), *Government Debt Structure and Monetary Conditions* (London, 1999), p. 96.
6. M. Hart, J. Jonker, and J. L. Van Zanden, *A Financial History of the Netherlands* (Cambridge, 1997), p. 69.
7. On Ottoman borrowing see C. Clay, *Gold for the Sultan: Western Bankers and Ottoman Finance, 1856–1881* (London, 2000).
8. *Historical Statistics of the United States: Colonial Times to 1970* (Washington, 1975), p. 1118; T. Conway, *Investment and Speculation* (New York, 1911), pp. 155, 167–8.
9. T. Eeda, 'The Role of the Securities Market in Industrialization in Japan' (unpublished paper, 1994), p. 15.
10. For Japan see T. Suzuki, *Japanese Government Loan Issues on the London Capital Market, 1870–1913* (London, 1994), pp. 69–71.
11. Mulhall, *Industries and Wealth*, p. 54.
12. R. L. Nash, *A Short Inquiry into the Profitable Nature of Our Investments* (London, 1881), p. 3.
13. S. Homer and R. Sylla, *A History of Interest Rates* (New Brunswick, 1996), p. 192, Table 76; C. P. Kindleberger, *A Financial History of Western Europe* (London, 1984), p. 327.
14. This data is taken from the public debt, gdp, and exchange rate tables in M. Flandreau and F. Zumer, *The Making of Global Finance, 1880–1913* (Paris, 2004). The data for the United States is taken from *Historical Statistics of the United States*.
15. Data calculated from the country tables in B. R. Mitchell, *International Historical Statistics* (London, 1998), vol. 3, table F1.
16. Mulhall, *Industries and Wealth*, p. 46, cf. p. 390.
17. British data from B. R. Mitchell, *British Historical Statistics* (Cambridge, 1989); US data from *Historical Statistics of the United States*.
18. Calculated using data from Mitchell, *International Historical Statistics*; *Historical Statistics of the United States*; Mitchell, *British Historical Statistics*. The figure would be even higher if the costs of the British railway network were used. These reflect the greater expense of land purchase in Britain and the much higher quality of track. However, such a figure would only be appropriate for the heavily populated countries of Western Europe. In contrast the pattern of railway construction and operation adopted in the United States reflects more accurately the position prevailing across the world where whole continents were provided with railway systems rather than small countries.

19. F. Caron, 'France' in P. O'Brien (ed.), *Railways and the Economic Development of Western Europe, 1830–1914* (New York, 1983), p. 30; see also chapter on Europe.
20. Hart, Jonker, and Van Zanden, *A Financial History of the Netherlands*, p. 112.
21. Hautcoeur and Verley, 'Le marche financier français' p. 3.
22. C. E. Freedeman, *Joint-Stock Enterprise in France, 1807–1867* (Chapel Hill, 1979), p. 144.
23. Mulhall, *Industries and Wealth*, pp. 48–9.
24. See *The Russian Journal of Financial Statistics* (St Petersburg, 1899 and 1900).
25. Eeda, 'The Role of the Securities Market in Industrialization in Japan', pp. 3, 6–8, 15–16.
26. R. S. Rungta, *Rise of Business Corporations in India, 1851–1900* (Cambridge, 1970), pp. 54–9, 61, 75, 76–7, 90, 94–6, 103–8, 113–14, 119, 150, 158–9.
27. See R. Cameron and V. I. Bovykin (eds.), *International Banking, 1870–1914* (New York, 1991): on Belgium, pp. 118, 129; Russia, pp. 143–4, Sweden, p. 194; Italy, p. 350; Canada, p. 202; Japan, p. 226; Brazil, pp. 356–9; Middle East, pp. 414, 418–19; L. E. Davies and R. J. Cull, *International Capital Markets and American Economic Growth, 1820–1914* (Cambridge, 1994), pp. 2, 8, 44, 111–12.
28. George Gregory and Company, *Gregory's Hints to Speculators and Investors in Stocks and Shares* (London, 1895), p. 317.
29. M. Petit-Konczyk, 'Emergence of a French Regional Exchange: Lille Stock Exchange in the 19th Century', Working Paper Lille 2 University, 2004 (no pagination).
30. Hautcoeur and Verley, 'Le Marche Financier Français' p. 16; Myers, *Paris*, p. 137; R. Cameron, *France and the Economic Development of Europe, 1800–1914* (Princeton, 1961), pp. 266, 283, 412–13, 418–20, 424, 508; W. Parker, *The Paris Bourse and French Finance* (New York, 1920), pp. 27–9; L. Neal and L. Davis, 'The Evolution of the Rules and Regulations of the First Emerging Markets: the London, New York and Paris Stock Exchanges, 1792–1914', *Quarterly Review of Economics and Finance*, 45 (2005), p. 307.
31. J. A. Torrente Fortuno, *Historia de La Bolsa de Madrid* (Madrid, 1974), vol. 2, pp. 671–7; vol. 3, p. 645; X. Tafunel and L. Castaneda, 'La Bolsa de Barcelona entre 1849 y 1913' (unpublished paper, 1994), p. 20; see A. Hoyo, 'La evolution del Mercado de Valores en Espana: La Bolsa de Madrid 1831–1874 (unpublished paper, 1994).
32. (Zurich) *A Summary Chronicle of the Zurich Stock Exchange* (Zurich, 1977), pp. 298–9.
33. J. Hermans, *ICT in Information Services: Use and Deployment of ICT in the Dutch Securities Trade, 1860–1970* (Rotterdam, 2004), pp. 18, 47, 50–3; Hart et al., *Financial History*, pp. 102, 111–12; J. Jonker, 'Fingers in the Dike, Fingers in the Pie: the Position of the Amsterdam Stock Exchange on the Dutch Capital Market, 1800–1940' (unpublished paper, 1994), pp. 8–9, 19, 23–4; *A Century of Stocks and Shares: a Historical Sketch of the Vereniging voor de Effectenhandel and the Amsterdam Stock Exchange* (Amsterdam, no date), pp. 5–11.
34. C-L. Holfrerich, *Frankfurt as a Financial Centre* (Munich, 1999), pp. 133, 147–8, 172, 176, 199, 201, 210; R. Gommel, 'The Modern Stock Market in Germany'

(unpublished paper, 1994), pp. 3–8, 15–16, 19–25; J. C.Baker, *The German Stock Market: Its Operations, Problems and Prospects* (New York, 1970), pp. 4–8, 36–53; G. R. Gibson, *The Berlin Bourse* (New York, 1890), pp. 3, 6–9; R. Sylla, R. Tilly, and G. Tortella (eds.), *The State, the Financial System and Economic Modernisation* (Cambridge, 1999), pp. 140–1.

35. R. Cameron (ed.), *Banking and Economic Development* (New York, 1972), pp. 34–41.

36. Gommel, 'Modern Stock Market in Germany', pp. 9–17, 19; Myers, *Paris*, p. 137; R. H. Tilly, 'German Banking, 1850–1914: Development Assistance for the Strong', *Journal of European Economic History*, 15 (1986), pp. 126, 148–50; Holtfrerich, *Frankfurt*, pp. 207–8; Lazonick and O'Sullivan, 'Finance and Industrial Development', pp. 127–9.

37. L. Conte, G. Toniolo, and G. Vecchi, 'Lessons from Italy's Monetary Unification (1862–1880) for the Euro and Europe's Single Market', in P. A. David and M. Thomas (eds.), *The Economic Future in Historical Perspective* (Oxford, 2003), pp. 325–34.

38. E. Chaboz, *Vade-Mecum des Bourses de Bale, Zurich, Genève, 1907–1908* (Zurich, 1907), pp. 11–12.

39. R. Cameron (ed.), *Banking in the Early Stages of Industrialization* (New York, 1967), pp. 234; Sylla, Tilly, and Tortella, *The State, the Financial System*, p. 215; A. Teichova, G. Kurgan-Van Hentenryk, and D. Ziegler (eds.), *Banking, Trade and Industry* (Cambridge, 1997), pp. 206; *Oslo Stock Exchange: Facts and Figures* (1986).

40. 'The German Stock Exchanges: A History of Many Regions', *Germany's Almanac 1985/6*, pp. 25–42; *Summary Chronicle of the Zurich Stock Exchange*, pp. 297–9; S. Salsbury and K. Sweeney, *The Bull, the Bear and the Kangaroo: The History of the Sydney Stock Exchange* (Sydney, 1988), pp. 38–44, 55; J. A. Torrente Fortûno, *Historia de la Bolsa de Madrid* (Madrid, 1974), vol. 1, pp. 309–19; C. Westheimer, 'The Durable Cincinnati Stock Exchange', *Queen City Heritage: Journal of the Cincinnati Historical Society*, 49 (1991), pp. 40–3; *Los Angeles Stock Exchange* (Los Angeles, 1939), pp. 3–4.

41. T. Suzuki, *Japanese Government Loan Issues on the London Capital Market, 1870–1913* (London, 1994,) pp. 19, 41.

42. D. C. North, 'International Capital Movements in Historical Perspective' in R. C. Michie (ed.), *Financial and Commercial Services* (Oxford, 1994), p. 24; M. Wilkins, *The History of Foreign Investment in the United States to 1914* (Cambridge, MA, 1989), p. 197; Suzuki, *Japanese Government Loan Issues*, pp. 19, 41.

43. Davis and Gallman, *Evolving Financial Markets*, pp. 599, 626, 694, 722.

44. *The Boston Stock Exchange* (Boston, 1930), pp. 13–15; C. Westheimer, 'The Durable Cincinnati Stock Exchange', *Queen City Heritage: Journal of the Cincinnati Historical Society*, 49 (1991), pp. 40–1; *The Los Angeles Stock Exchange*, pp. 3–8.

45. M. H. Smith, *Twenty Years Among the Bulls and Bears of Wall Street* (Harford, 1870), p. 83.

46. W. Werner and S. T. Smith, *Wall Street* (New York, 1991), pp. 136–40; J. E. Hedges, *Commercial Banking and the Stock Market Before 1863* (Baltimore, 1938), pp. 77, 98, 116; L. E. Davis and R. J. Cull, *International Capital Markets and American Economic Growth, 1820–1914* (Cambridge, 1984), pp. 65–9.

47. S. Banner, *Anglo-American Securities Regulation: Cultural and Political Roots, 1690–1860* (Cambridge, 1998), p. 250, cf. pp. 270–1, 280–4.

48. H. Clews, *Fifty Years in Wall Street* (New York, 1908), p. 956, cf. 91, 913–16.

49. A. R. Hall, *The Stock Exchange of Melbourne and the Victorian Economy, 1852–1900* (Canberra, 1968), pp. 3, 7, 12, 20, 22, 37, 39, 41, 57–9, 62, 67, 69, 72, 90, 95, 98, 101–4, 107, 111–12, 122–4, 134, 137–9, 146, 149, 153, 168, 186–9, 197, 204, 208–9, 214, 217, 220–1, 226–7, 232–3, 238; S. Salsbury and K. Sweeney, *The Bull, the Bear and the Kangaroo: the History of the Sydney Stock Exchange* (Sydney, 1988), pp. 7–10, 14, 19, 38, 42–6, 55, 72–4, 79, 82, 86–7, 91, 100, 104–5, 113–15, 122–31, 139, 143, 151, 158, 170–6, 189–90, 196; K. Merrett, *The Brisbane Stock Exchange, 1884–1984* (Brisbane, 1984), pp. 10–13, 16, 19, 21–4, 27, 34, 36–7, 39, 41–8, 57–8; A. Lougheed, 'The London Stock Exchange Boom in Kalgoorlie Shares, 1895–1901', *Australian Economic History Review*, 35 (1995), pp. 87–92; N. G. Butlin, *Australian Domestic Product, Investment and Foreign Borrowing, 1861–1938/9* (Cambridge, 1962), pp. 422–4.

50. D. Grant, *Bulls, Bears and Elephants: A History of the New Zealand Stock Exchange* (Wellington, 1997), pp. 21–2, 26–7, 35–7, 40–2, 45, 49, 59, 95–8, 128.

51. M. Bryan, *Taking Stock: Johannesburg Stock Exchange—the first 100 Years* (Johannesburg, 1987), pp. 1, 5, 10, 13–16, 21–7; *The Story of the Johannesburg Stock Exchange, 1887–1947* (Johannesburg, 1948) pp. 8–17, 19, 22–4, 26, 29–34, 41–6, 49.

52. D. K. Eiteman, *Stock Exchanges in Latin America* (Ann Arbor, 1966), pp. 1–2, 14, 33–4, 66–7; C. M. Snader, *A General Analysis of the Mexico City Stock Exchange: Its Limitations as a Free Market* (Mexico City, 1965), pp. 1–3; M. Giesecke, *La Bolsa de valores de Lima: 140 Anos de Historia* (Lima, 1997), pp. 42, 48, 51, 59, 71, 79, 87, 93.

53. Rungta, *Rise of Business Corporations in India, 1851–1900*, pp. 28–33, 47, 54, 54–6, 61, 75–7, 90, 94, 108, 144–7, 206–8, 226–7, 260: K. L. Garg, *Stock Exchanges in India* (Calcutta, 1950), pp. 22–4, 107; D. E. Wacha, *A Financial Chapter in the History of Bombay City* (Bombay, 1910), pp. 6–7, 24–5, 31, 34–7, 144, 214.

54. W. A. Thomas, *Western Capitalism in China: A History of the Shanghai Stock Exchange* (Aldershot, 2001), pp. 36–7, 64–5, 68, 79, 83, 86, 90–2, 131

55. Eeda, 'Role of the Securities Market in Industrialization in Japan', pp. 8, 15–18; Suzuki, *Japanese Government Loan Issues*, p. 64.

56. A. S. F. Abdul-Hadi, *Stock Markets of the Arab World: Trends, Problems and Prospects for Integration* (London, 1988), p. 84.

57. H. C. Emery, *Speculation on the Stock and Produce Exchanges of the United States* (New York, 1896), pp. 13, cf. 13–15.

58. Twentieth Century Fund, *The Security Markets* (New York, 1935), pp. 527–54.

59. Conte, Toniolo, and Vecchi, 'Lessons from Italy's monetary unification', pp. 325–34.

60. Hermans, *ICT*, pp. 5, 46, 141–4.
61. J. A. Torrente Fortuno, *Historia de La Bolsa de Madrid*, vol. 3, pp. 30, 651.
62. D. C. M. Platt, *Foreign Finance in Continental Europe and the United States, 1815–1870* (London, 1984), pp. 14, 17, 33, 49, 57, 61–6, 74, 84–7, 92, 127–33, 151–6, 172.
63. J. Veenendaal, *Slow Train to Paradise: How Dutch Investment Helped Build American Railroads* (Stanford CA, 1996), p. 55.
64. Royal Institute of International Affairs, *The Problem of International Investment* (Oxford, 1973), pp. 153–5, 166; M. Wilkins, *The History of Foreign Investment in the United States to 1914* (Cambridge, MA, 1989), pp. 159, 197; A. J. Veenendaal, Jr., *Slow Train to Paradise*, (Stanford CA, 1996) pp. 55, 174.
65. G. R. Gibson, *The Vienna Bourse* (New York, 1892), pp. 30–2.
66. L. E. Davis and R. E. Gallman, *Evolving Financial Markets and International Capital Flows: Britain, the Americas, and Australia, 1865–1914* (Cambridge, 2001), pp. 102–3, 126, 266, 276, 373, 565, 666, 674.
67. Sir Robert Giffen, *Statistics* (London, 1913), pp. 286–7.
68. J. Edward and S. Ogilvie, 'Universal Banks and German Industrialization: A Reappraisal', *Economic History Review*, XLIX (1996), pp. 427–9.

CHAPTER 5

1. W. C. Van Antwerp, *The Stock Exchange From Within* (New York, 1913), p. 387. For a critical view that appeared in the same year, see Charles A. Lindberg, *Banking and Currency and the Money Trust* (New York, 1913).
2. Calculated from the national tables in R. W. Goldsmith, *Comparative National Balance Sheets: A Study of Twenty Countries, 1688–1978* (Chicago, 1985).
3. Goldsmith, *Comparative National Balance Sheets* (national sections); V. Tanzi and L. Schuknecht, *Public Spending in the 20th Century* (Cambridge, 2000), p. 65; M. C. Urquhart and K. A. Buckley (eds.), *Historical Statistics of Canada* (Toronto, 1965), p. 203; *Historical Statistics of Japan*: National Debt Tables.
4. L. G. Chiozza Money, *Money's Fiscal Dictionary* (London, 1910), p. 219.
5. F. W. Hirst, *The Credit of Nations* (Washington, 1910), p. 9.
6. R. Cameron (ed.), *Banking in the Early Stages of Industrialization* (New York, 1967), p. 270; T. Suzuki, *Japanese Government Loan Issues on the London Capital Market, 1870–1913* (London, 1994), p. 84, 102–23.
7. The Sources are B. R. Mitchell, *International Historical Statistics* (London, 2004); Mitchell, *British Historical Statistics* (Cambridge, 1988); U.S. Department of Commerce/Bureau of the Census, *Historical Statistics of the United States* (Washington, 1975).
8. C. J. Schmitz, *The Growth of Big Business in the United States and Western Europe, 1850–1939* (Cambridge, 1993), p. 22; C. R. Geisst, *Wall Street: A History* (Oxford, 1997), chapter 4.
9. E. J. Perkins, *Wall Street to Main Street: Charles Merrill and Middle-Class Investors* (Cambridge, 1999), p. 128.

10. Cameron (ed.), *Banking in the Early Stages of Industrialization*, pp. 184–6, 191–5.

11. L. E. Davis and R. E. Gallman, *Evolving Financial Markets and International Capital Flows: Britain, the Americas, and Australia, 1865–1914* (Cambridge, 2001), pp. 694, 722.

12. G. H. Le Maistre, *The Investor's India Year-Book* (Calcutta, 1911), pp. 63–4, 68, 105–6, 208, 213.

13. See *China Stock and Share Handbook* (Shanghai, 1914).

14. R. Cameron (ed.), *Banking and Economic Development* (New York, 1972), pp. 172–97; R. Cameron and V. I. Bovykin (eds.), *International Banking, 1870–1914* (New York, 1991), pp. 226–7; Cameron (ed.), *Banking in the Early Stages of Industrialization*, pp. 274–83; Goldsmith, *Comparative National Balance Sheets: National Chapters*.

15. Cameron (ed.), *Banking and Economic Development*, pp. 41–57, 72–4, 80–3, 150.

16. F. Capie and A. Webber, A *Monetary History of the United Kingdom, 1870–1982* (London, 1985), pp. 516–17; *Historical Statistics of the United States: Colonial Times to 1970* (Washington, 1976), p. 1037; B. R. Mitchell, *European Historical Statistics* (London, 1980), tables H2 and 3.

17. Cameron and Bovykin (eds.), *International Banking*, pp. 118–19, 121, 127, 144; L.Gall, et al., *The Deutsche Bank, 1870–1995* (London, 1995), pp. 20, 28 ; H. Van B. Cleveland and T. F. Huertas, *Citibank, 1812–1970* (Cambridge, MA, 1985); P. L. Cottrell, A. Teichova, and T. Yuzawa (eds.), *Finance in the Age of the Corporate Economy* (Aldershot, 1997), pp. 81–3, 100; E. Paulet, *The Role of Banks in Monitoring Firms: The Case of the Credit Mobilier* (London, 1999), pp. 16, 19, 33, 74, 90, 108, 125, 130–3.

18. E. Wicker, *Banking Panics of the Gilded Age* (Cambridge, 2000), pp. 32–5, 47, 82, 113, 116, 120, 137, 147; D. K. Sheppard, *The Growth and Role of UK Financial Institutions, 1880–1962* (London, 1985), p. 130; Cleveland and Huertas, *Citibank*, pp. 28, 49, 52; J. Edward and S. Ogilvie, 'Universal Banks and German Industrialization: A Reappraisal', *Economic History Review*, XLIX (1996), pp. 427–9.

19. Cameron (ed.), *Banking and Economic Development*, pp. 41–57, 72–4, 80–3, 150.

20. R. H. Tilly, 'German Banking, 1850–1914: Development Assistance for the Strong', *Journal of European Economic History*, 15 (1986), pp. 140, 150.

21. T. Balderston, 'Universal Banks', in *New Palgrave Dictionary of Money and Finance*, pp. 732–3.

22. For these calculations see R. C. Michie, 'Banks and Securities Markets, 1870–1914', in D. J. Forsyth and D. Verdier (eds.), *The Origins of National Financial Systems* (London, 2003), p. 57.

23. Y. Cassis, G. D. Feldman, and U. Olsson (eds.), *The Evolution of Financial Institutions and Markets in Twentieth Century Europe* (Aldershot, 1995), pp. 124–5; P. L. Cottrell, A. Teichova, and T. Yuzawa (eds.), *Finance in the Age of the Corporate Economy* (Aldershot, 1997), p. 100; Cameron and Bovykin (eds.), *International Banking*, p. 185; W. Lazonick and M. O'Sullivan, 'Finance and

Industrial Development: Evolution to Market Control; Japan and Germany' *Financial History Review*, 4 (1997), pp. 119–20.

24. Gall et al. *Deutsche Bank,* pp. 29, 156; Cleveland and Heurtas, *Citibank,* pp. 47–9, 57.

25. Cassis et al. (eds.), *Evolution of Financial Institutions,* pp. 255–6, 264, 272–5; G. Caprio and D. Vitas (eds), *Reforming Financial Systems: Historical Implications for Policy* (Cambridge, 1997), pp. 18, 71, 118, 145–7, 170–2, 201.

26. J. A. Torrente Fortuno, *Historia de la Bolsa de Madrid* (Madrid, 1974), vol. 3, pp. 28–30, 123, 189, 645–51; X. Tafunell and L. Castaned, 'La Bolsa de Barcelona entre 1849 y 1913' (unpublished paper) (Milan, 1994), p. 20.

27. S. S. Huebner, 'The Scope and Functions of the Stock Market', in *Annals of the American Academy of Political and Social Science,* 35 (1910), p. 20, cf. Conway, *Investment and Speculation,* p. 54.

28. S. A. Nelson, *The ABC of Options and Arbitrage* (New York 1904), pp. 15, 50, 53, 58, 70.

29. For this see A. Britton, *Monetary Regimes of the Twentieth Century* (Cambridge, 2001), chapter 1; D. H. Aldcroft and M. J. Oliver, *Exchange Rate Regimes in the Twentieth Century* (Cheltenham, 1998), p. 35; F. Capie, *Capital Controls: A 'Cure' Worse Than the Problem* (London, 2002), pp. 33–7; M. Flandreau and F. Zumer, *The Making of Global Finance, 1880–1913* (Paris, 2004), p. 21.

30. Flandreau and Zumer, *Making of Global Finance,* pp. 21, 125; G. P. Palmade, *French Capitalism in the Nineteenth Century* (Newton Abbot, 1972), pp. 195–6.

31. D. C. North, 'International Capital Movements in Historical Perspective' in R. C. Michie (ed.), *Financial and Commercial Services* (Oxford, 1994), p. 24; M. Wilkins, *The History of Foreign Investment in the United States to 1914* (Cambridge, MA, 1989), pp. 145, 197, 262; T. Suzuki, *Japanese Government Loan Issues on the London Capital Market, 1870–1913* (London, 1994), p. 120; M. G. Myers, *Paris as a Financial Centre* (London, 1936), p. 13; Cassis, Feldman, and Olsson (eds.), *Evolution of Financial Institutions,* p. 80; A. Teichova, T. Gourvish, and A. Poyany (eds.), *Universal Banking in the Twentieth Century* (Aldershot, 1994), p. 14; L. E. Davis and R. J. Cull, *International Capital Markets and American Economic Growth, 1820–1914* (Cambridge, 1994), p. 112.

32. The Nomura Shoten, *Handbook of Japanese Securities* (Osaka, 1910), preface.

33. Royal Institute of International Affairs, *The Problem of International Investment* (Oxford, 1973), pp. 153–5, 166; A. J. Veenendaal, *Slow Train to Paradise: How Dutch Investment Helped Build American Railroads* (Stanford, CA, 1996), pp. 55, 174.

34. A. Neymarck, *French Savings and Their Influence Upon the Bank of France and Upon French Banks* (Washington, 1910), pp. 168–77.

35. League of Nations, *Memorandum on Commercial Banks, 1913–1929* (Geneva, 1913), pp. 14, 138, 149, 192–9, 269, 342, 407, 411–24; S. Flink, *The German Reichsbank and Economic Germany* (1930; repr. New York, 1969), pp. 34–5; Cameron, *Banking and Economic Development,* pp. 256–7.

36. F. W. Hirst, *The Credit of Nations* (Washington, 1910), p. 4.

37. Huebner, 'Scope and Functions of the Stock Market', p. 5.

38. W. J. Greenwood, *American and Foreign Stock Exchange Practice, Stock and Bond Trading and the Business Corporation Laws of all Nations* (New York, 1921), pp. 259, 273, 629, 640, 657, 661, 754, 783, 823, 907, 916, 923, 926–7, 953; J. A. Torrente Fortuno, *Historia de la Bolsa de Madrid,* vol. 3, pp. 28–30, 123, 189, 645–51; Tafunell and Castaned, 'La Bolsa de Barcelona entre 1849 y 1913' (unpublished paper, Milan, 1994), p. 20.

39. Sylla, Tilly, and Tortella, *The State, the Financial System,* pp. 206, 208; S. L. N. Simha, *The Capital Market of India* (Bombay, 1960), p. 218.

40. D. Cruise and A. Griffiths, *Fleecing the Lamb: The Inside Story of the Vancouver Stock Exchange* (Vancouver, 1987), pp. 4, 13, 262; Cameron and Bovykin (eds.), *International Banking,* pp. 202, 205.

41. D. K. Eiteman, *Stock Exchanges in Latin America* (Ann Arbor, 1966), pp. 1–2; C. M. Snader, *A General Analysis of the Mexico City Stock Exchange: Its Limitations as a Free Market* (Mexico City, 1965), p. 8.

42. D. Grant, *Bulls, Bears and Elephants: A History of the New Zealand Stock Exchange* (Wellington, 1997), pp. 95, 128.

43. G. L. Leffler, *The Stock Market* (New York, 1951), p. 75.

44. Zurich Stock Exchange, *A Summary Chronicle of the Zurich Stock Exchange* (Zurich, 1977), p. 298.

45. Cameron (ed.), *Banking in the Early Stages of Industrialization,* pp. 209–10, 221, 226, 228, 234; Sylla, Tilly, and Tortella (eds.), *The State, the Financial System,* pp. 214–15; A. Teichova, G. Kurgan-Van Henteryk, and D. Ziegler (eds.), *Banking, Trade and Industry: Europe, America and Asia From the 13th to the 20th Century* (Cambridge, 1997), p. 283.

46. R. Benson, *State Credit and Banking: During the War and After* (London, 1918), p. 29. See Correspondence of H.M. Embassy at Berlin, 1912—Stock Exchange Gambling (National Archives).

47. D. Waldenstrom, *A Century of Securities Transaction Taxes: Origins and Effects* (Stockholm, 2000), pp. 1–2.

48. M. G. Myers, *Paris as a Financial Centre* (London, 1936), p. 137.

49. W. Parker, *The Paris Bourse and French Finance* (New York, 1920), pp. 59, 63; C. T. Hallinan, *American Investments in Europe* (London, 1927), pp. 15, 38–9; Cassis et al. (eds.), *Evolution of Financial Institutions,* pp. 84–5, 187–90; M. Bordo and R. Sylla (eds.), *Anglo-American Financial System: Institutions and Markets in the Twentieth Century* (New York, 1995), pp. 395–400; O. Checkland and S. Nishimura (eds.), *Pacific Banking, 1859–1959: East Meets West* (London, 1994), pp. 68–70; Cameron and Bovykin, *International Banking,* pp. 414–19; *A Century of Stocks and Shares: A Historical Sketch of the Vereniging Voor de Effectenhandel and the Amsterdam Stock Exchange* (Amsterdam n.d.), pp. 5, 11; Y. Cassis (ed.), *Finance and Financiers in European History, 1880–1960* (Cambridge, 1992), pp. 68, 72–3; Veenendaal, *Slow Train to Paradise,* p. 172.

50. E. Vidal, *The History and Methods of the Paris Bourse* (Washington, 1910), p. 25, cf. 28, 85, 181, 188.

51. Van Antwerp, *Stock Exchange from within*, p. 407.
52. Parker, *The Paris Bourse*, p. 21.
53. Cassis et al., *Evolution of Financial Institutions*, pp. 124–8; Cameron and Bovykin (eds.), *International Banking* (New York, 1991), p. 184.
54. See H. W. Wildschut, *General Methods in Vogue With Dealings on the Amsterdam Stock Exchange* (Amsterdam, 1912).
55. Myers, *Paris*, pp. 52, 61, 100–12, 122–4 134–7, 146–52; Cassis et al., *Evolution of Financial Institutions*, pp. 124–8.
56. J. Moody, *The Art of Wall Street Investing* (New York, 1906), pp. 141–2.
57. W. A. Thomas, *Western Capitalism in China: A History of the Shanghai Stock Exchange* (Aldershot, 2001), pp. 36–7, 92, 104. See *China Stock and Share Handbook* (Shanghai 1914).
58. Teichova et al. (eds.), *Universal Banking*, pp. 80–93.
59. Cameron (ed.), *Banking in the Early Stages of Industrialization*, pp. 209–10, 221, 226, 228, 234; Sylla, Tilly, and Tortella, *The State, the Financial System*, pp. 214–15; Teichova et al. (eds.), *Banking, Trade and Industry*, p. 283.
60. See C. Armstrong, *Blue Skies and Boiler Rooms: Buying and Selling Securities in Canada, 1870–1940* (Toronto, 1997), chapters 1–4.
61. S. Salsbury and K. Sweeney, *The Bull, the Bear and the Kangaroo: The History of the Sydney Stock Exchange* (Sydney, 1988), pp. 176, 189–90, 205, 215; K. Merrett, *The Brisbane Stock Exchange, 1884–1984* (Brisbane, 1984), pp. 70, 78–81; A. R. Hall, *The Stock Exchange of Melbourne and the Victorian Economy, 1852–1900* (Canberra, 1968), p. 238; Davis and Gallman, *Evolving Financial Markets*, pp. 599, 641.
62. M. Bryan, *Taking Stock: The Johannesburg Stock Exchange, the First 100 Years* (Johannesburg, 1987), p. 26; *The Story of the Johannesburg Stock Exchange, 1887–1947* (Johannesburg, 1948), pp. 59–60, 70, 73.
63. Thomas, *Western Capitalism in China*, pp. 36–7, 92, 104.
64. Cameron and Bovykin (eds.), *International Banking*, pp. 80, 257, 332.
65. E. de Saugy (ed.), *Vade-mecum des Bourses de Bale, Zurich, Genève, 1913/14* (Zurich, 1913), pp. 3–5; Cameron and Bovykin, *International Banking*, pp. 482–3; Zurich Stock Exchange, *A Summary Chronicle of the Zurich Stock Exchange* (Zurich, 1977), p. 300.
66. Cameron and Bovykin (eds.), *International Banking*, p. 124.
67. Torrente Fortuno, *Historia de la Bolsa de Madrid*, vol. 3, pp. 28–30, 123, 189, 645–51; Tafunell and Castaned, 'La Bolsa de Barcelona entre 1849 y 1913', p. 20.
68. A. E. Davies, *The Money, and the Stock and Share Markets* (London, 1920), p. 70.
69. General Securities Corporation, *The Investor's Handy Book of Active Stocks and Shares* (London, 1910), p. xx, cf. pp. xvi–xxiii; Cameron and Bovykin, *International Banking*, pp. 453–61; M. C. Urquhart and K. A. H. Buckley (eds.), *Historical Statistics of Canada* (Toronto, 1965), p. 279; Suzuki, *Japanese Government Loans*, pp. 9, 12, 19, 41.
70. Parker, *Paris Bourse*, pp. 72–3; Cameron and Bovykin (eds.), *International Banking*, pp. 80, 257, 332.

71. Vidal, *Paris Bourse*, p. 192.
72. Parker, *Paris Bourse*, pp. 59, 63; Hallinan, *American Investments in Europe*, p. 15, 38–9 ; Cassis et al. (eds.), *Evolution of Financial Institutions*, pp. 84–5, 187–90; Bordo and Sylla (eds.), *Anglo-American Financial System*, pp. 395–400; Checkland and Nishimura (eds.), *Pacific Banking*, pp. 68–70; Cameron and Bovykin, *International Banking*, pp. 414–19; *A Century of Stocks and Shares: A Historical Sketch of the vereniging voor de effectenhandel and the Amsterdam Stock Exchange* (Amsterdam n.d.), pp. 5, 11; Cassis (ed.), *Finance and Financiers*, pp. 68, 72–3; Veenendaal, *Slow Train to Paradise*, p. 172.
73. Y. Cassis and E. Bussiere (ed.), *London and Paris as International Financial Centres in the Twentieth Century* (Oxford, 2005), pp. 43–5, 49, 89, 91, 93, 95, 97, 114–15, 122, 143, 147.
74. M. Hart, J. Jonker, and J. L. Van Zanden, *A Financial History of the Netherlands* (Cambridge, 1997), pp. 113–14; J. Jonker, 'Fingers in the Dike, Fingers in the Pie: the Position of the Amsterdam Stock Exchange on the Dutch Capital Market, 1800–1940' (unpublished paper 1994), pp. 11–14, 17–20, 23–4; J. Hermans, *ICT in Information Services: Use and Deployment of ICT in the Dutch Securities Trade, 1860–1970* (Rotterdam 2004), pp. 49, 54–6, 61, 78, 84, 87, 145–6, 170, 181, 196.
75. C-L. Holtfrerich, *Frankfurt as a Financial Centre: From Medieval Trade Fair to European Banking Centre* (Munich, 1999), p. 210; Cameron and Bovykin (eds.), *International Banking*, pp. 95, 108, 257, 332, 340, 475; Sylla, Tilly, and Tortella (eds.), *The State, the Financial System*, p. 154; R. Gommel, 'The Modern Stock Market in Germany' (unpublished paper, 1994), pp. 9–10, 14–17; W. Lazonick and M. O'Sullivan, 'Finance and Industrial Development: Evolution to Market Control—Japan and Germany', *Financial History Review*, 4 (1997), p. 127–9; P-C. Hautcoeur and P. Verley, 'Le marche financier français', p. 16; Gommel, *Modern Stock Market in Germany*, pp. 13–17; Myers, *Paris*, p. 137; Tilly, 'German Banking, 1850–1914', *Journal of European Economic History*, 15 (1986), pp. 126, 148–50.
76. C. Lewis, *America's Stake in International Investments* (Washington, 1938), pp. 337–8; Suzuki, *Japanese Government Bonds*, pp. 121–9.
77. Lewis, *America's Stake*, pp. 73, 77.
78. R. W. Goldsmith (ed.), *Institutional Investors and Corporate Stock* (NBER, 1973), pp. 38, 40.
79. J. E. Meeker, *The Work of the Stock exchange* (New York, 1930), p. 110; Cameron and Bovykin (eds.), *International Banking*, pp. 55, 60, 67, 238–40.
80. US Bureau of the Census, *Historical Statistics of the United States* (Washington, 1975), p. 1007; Huebner, 'Scope and Functions of the Stock Market', p. 3.
81. T. Conway, *Investment and Speculation* (New York, 1911), pp. 9–11.
82. S. Bruchey, *Modernization of the American Stock Exchange, 1971–1989* (New York, 1991), pp. 12–14, 18.
83. M. Giesecke, *La Bolsa de valores de Lima: 140 anos de historia* (Lima, 1997).
84. A. S. F. Abdul-Hadi, *Stock Markets of the Arab World: Trends, Problems and Prospects for Integration* (London, 1988), p. 84.
85. Cameron (ed.), *Banking in the Early Stages of Industrialization*, p. 234.

86. Sylla, Tilly, and Tortella (eds.), *The State, the Financial System*, p. 146.
87. M. Patron, *The Bank of France in its Relation to National and International Credit* (Washington, 1910), p. 66.
88. E. Vidal, *Paris Bourse*, p. 76.

CHAPTER 6

1. F. Capie and E. Wood (eds.), *Financial Crises and the World Banking System* (London, 1986), pp. 85–7.
2. W. S. Schwabe, *Effect of War on Stock Exchange Transactions* (London, 1915), p. 69.
3. W. S. Schwabe, *Effect of War*, p. 1.
4. Reprinted in R. C. Michie, *The London Stock Exchange: A History* (Oxford, 1999), p. 144.
5. H. G. S. Noble, *The New York Stock Exchange in the Crisis of 1914* (New York, 1915), pp. 9, 12–13, 30, 33.
6. J. E. Meeker, *Short Selling* (New York, 1932), pp. 107, 112–16, 216; M. Bryan, *Taking Stock: The Johannesburg Stock Exchange—the First 100 Years* (Johannesburg, 1987), p. 33.
7. Noble, *New York Stock Exchange*, pp. 24, 38, 46, 82.
8. W. A. Thomas, *Western Capitalism in China: A History of the Shanghai Stock Exchange* (Aldershot, 2001), pp. 191, 195, 243–8; Bryan, *Taking Stock*, p. 33.
9. Meeker, *Short Selling*, pp. 112, 216; C. P. Kindleberger, *A Financial History of Western Europe* (London, 1984), pp. 290, 294.
10. Meeker, *Short Selling*, pp. 216–17; D. Cruise and A. Griffiths, *Fleecing the Lamb: the Inside Story of the Vancouver Stock Exchange* (Vancouver, 1987), pp. 14–15, 31–3; Meeker, *The Work of the Stock Exchange* (New York, 1930), p. 606; Noble, *New York Stock Exchange*, p. 9; M. G. Myers, *Paris as a Financial Centre* (London, 1936), pp. 138, 149; C-L. Holtfrerich, *Frankfurt as a Financial Centre: From Medieval Trade Fair to European Banking Centre* (Munich, 1999), pp. 211–12, 215; *The German Stock Exchanges: A History of Many Regions* (Germany's Almanac, 1985/6), p. 42.
11. Kindleberger, *Financial History*, p. 296.
12. D. Grant, *Bulls, Bears and Elephants: A History of the New Zealand Stock Exchange* (Wellington, 1997), p. 119.
13. C. Armstrong, *Blue Skies and Boiler Rooms: Buying and Selling Securities in Canada, 1870–1940* (Toronto, 1997), chapter 5.
14. I. O. Scott, *Government Securities Market* (New York, 1965), pp. 11–13.
15. Cruise and Griffiths, *Fleecing the Lamb*, pp. 14–15, 31–3.
16. Myers, *Paris*, p. 150.
17. H. James, H. Lindgren, and A. Teichova (eds.), *The Role of Banks in the Interwar Economy* (Cambridge and Paris, 1991), pp. 185–8.
18. G. Feldman, U. Olssen, M. Bordo, and Y. Cassis (eds.), *The Evolution of Modern Financial Institutions in the Twentieth Century* (Milan, 1994), pp. 53–4, 85–9, 96.

19. P. L. Cottrell, A. Teichova, and T. Yuzawa (eds.), *Finance in the Age of the Corporate Economy* (Aldershot, 1997), pp. 100–1, 120; A. Alletzhauser, *The House of Nomura* (London, 1990), p. 56; O. Checkland, S. Nishimura, and N. Tamaki (eds.), *Pacific Banking, 1859–1959: East Meets West* (London, 1994), p. 179.

20. Holtfrerich, *Frankfurt*, pp. 211–12, 215; *The German Stock Exchanges: A History of Many Regions* (Germany's Almanac, 1985–6), p. 42.

21. P. C. Hautcoeur and P. Verley, 'Le marche financier français' (unpublished paper, 1994), pp. 27–8.

22. E. E. Spicer, *The Money Market in Relation to Trade and Commerce* (4th edn.), (London, 1924), pp. 183, 196–7, 202–3; C. T. Hallinan, *American Investments in Europe* (London, 1927), p. 12.

23. M. Hart, J. Jonker, and J. L. Van Zanden, *A Financial History of the Netherlands* (Cambridge, 1997), pp. 124, 130, 136–7, 141–2; J. Hermans, *ICT in Information Services: Use and Deployment of ICT in the Dutch Securities Trade, 1860–1970* (Rotterdam, 2004), pp. 49, 79, 167, 170, 188; *A Century of Stocks and Shares: A Historical Sketch of the Vereniging voor de Efeecten Handle and the Amsterdam Stock Exchange* (Amsterdam Stock Exchange), pp. 11, 14.

24. Hart et al. *Financial History of the Netherlands*, pp. 124, 130, 136–7, 141–2; Hermans, *ICT in Information Services*, pp. 49, 79, 167, 170, 188; *A Century of Stocks and Shares*, pp. 11, 14; A. J. Veenendaal, *Slow Train to Paradise: How Dutch Investment Helped Build American Railroads* (Stanford, 1996), pp. 147, 174.

25. James et al. (eds.), *Role of Banks*, p. 208; G. Feldman, U. Olssen, M. Bordo, and Y. Cassis (eds.), *The Evolution of Modern Financial Institutions in the Twentieth Century* (Milan, 1994), pp. 53–4, 85–9, 96, 125–6; Y. Cassis, G. D. Feldman, and U. Ollson (eds.), *The Evolution of Financial Institutions and Markets in Twentieth-Century Europe* (Aldershot, 1995), p. 67; Zurich Stock Exchange, *A Summary Chronicle of the Zurich Stock Exchange* (Zurich, 1977), p. 300; A. Teichova, T. Gourvish, and A. Poyany (eds.), *Universal Banking in the Twentieth Century* (Aldershot, 1994), p. 5.

26. G. Tortella and J. Palafox, 'Banking and Industry in Spain, 1918–1936', *Journal of European Economic History*, 13 (1984), p. 83; J. A. Torrente Fortuno, *Historia de la Bolsa de Madrid* (Madrid, 1974), vol. 3, pp. 189, 651–9.

27. Thomas, *Western Capitalism in China*, pp. 191, 195, 243–8.

28. James et al. (eds.), *Role of Banks*, p. 253.

29. Armstrong, *Blue Skies*, chapter 5; Salsbury and Sweeney, *The Bull, the Bear and the Kangaroo*, p. 176, 242; A. L. Lougheed, *The Brisbane Stock Exchange, 1884–1984* (Brisbane, 1984), p. 81; D. T. Merret, 'Capital Markets and Capital Formation in Australia, 1890–1945', *Australian Economic History Review*, 37 (1997), p. 192–3.

30. Twentieth Century Fund, *The Security Markets* (New York, 1935), p. 749; C. Lewis, *America's Stake in International Investments* (Washington, 1938), pp. 114–23, 375, 445–7, 455, 544, 652; *The Boston Stock Exchange* (Boston, 1930), p. 23; C. R. Geisst, *Wall Street: A History* (Oxford, 1997), pp. 147–50; Geisst, *Visionary*

Capitalism: Financial Markets and the American Dream in the Twentieth Century
(New York, 1990), pp. 3–4; S. Bruchey, *Modernization of the American Stock
Exchange, 1971–1989* (New York, 1991), p. 21.

31. Noble, New York Stock Exchange, pp. 24, 38, 46, 82; H. van B. Cleveland and T. F.
Huertas, *Citibank, 1812–1970* (Cambridge, MA, 1985), pp. 74, 86; Y. Cassis (ed.),
Finance and Financiers in European History, 1880–1960 (Cambridge, 1992), p. 362;
Holtfrerich, Frankfurt, pp. 211–12, 215; *The German Stock Exchanges: A History of
Many Regions*, p. 42.

32. Meeker, *Work of the Stock Exchange*, p. 110; M. Wilkins, *The History of Foreign
Investment in the United States, 1914–1945* (Cambridge, MA, 2004), pp. 36, 72.

33. A. Turner, 'British Holdings of French War Bonds: An Aspect of Anglo-French
Relations During the 1920s', *Financial History Review*, 3 (1996), pp. 154–5.

34. J. Bouvier, 'The French Banks, Inflation and the Economic Crisis, 1919–1939',
Journal of European Economic History, 13 (1984), pp. 36, 43, 59.

35. Hart et al., *Financial History of the Netherlands*, pp. 125, 143.

36. The Economist, *Directory of World Stock Exchanges* (London, 1988), p. 105;
H. D. Wynne-Bennett, *Investment and Speculation* (London, 1924), p. 31; H. V.
Cherrington, *The Investor and the Securities Act* (Washington, 1942), p. 41; Myers,
Paris, p. 138; Cruise and Griffiths, *Fleecing the Lamb*, pp. 14–15, 31–3.

37. P. Einzig, *The Fight for Financial Supremacy* (London, 1931), p. 92; cf. pp. 16, 43,
50, 53, 58–9, 62, 65, 73, 75, 79–81, 91–2, 96, 101, 120–1, 133–6, 139–41, 143, 145.

38. Kindleberger, *Financial History*, p. 284.

39. Cassis, Feldman, and Olsson (eds.), *Evolution of Financial Institutions*, pp. 85–9,
125–9; M. D. Bordo and R. Sylla (eds.), *Anglo-American Financial Systems:
Institutions and Markets in the Twentieth Century* (New York, 1995), p. 20;
James et al. (eds.), *Role of Banks*, pp. 8, 85–9, 92, 96, 107–8, 114, 188, 194–5,
253, 260; C. P. Kindleberger, 'Banking and Industry Between Two World Wars: An
International Comparison', *Journal of European Economic History*, 13 (1984), p. 13;
Tortella and Palafax, 'Banking and Industry in Spain, 1918–1936', pp. 83–9;
P. Ciocca and G. Tiniolo, 'Industry and Finance in Italy, 1918–1940', *Journal of
European Economic History*, 13 (1984), p. 122; R. Nötel, 'Money, Banks and
Industry in Interwar Austria and Hungary', *Journal of European Economic History*
13 (1984), pp. 142–3.

40. J. Jonker and J. L. Van Zanden, 'Method in the Madness? Banking Crisis Between
the Wars: An International Comparison', in C. Feinstein (ed.), *Banking, Currency
and Finance in Europe Between the Wars* (Oxford, 1995), pp. 84–5, 88. Cassis et al.,
Evolution of Financial Institutions, p. 325; James et al., *Role of Banks*, pp. 188,
194–5, 260; Kindleberger, 'Banking and Industry', p. 13; Ciocca and Toniolo
'Industry and Finance', p. 122; Cleveland and Huertas, *Citibank*, p. 104; Feinstein,
Banking, Currency and Finance, Italy, p. 301, France, p. 321, Norway, p. 444.

41. Torrente Fortuno, *Historia de la Bolsa de Madrid*, vol. 3, pp. 659, 661, 667, 671;
G. Caprio and D. Vittas (eds.), *Reforming Financial Systems: Historical Implica-
tions for Policy* (Cambridge, 1997), pp. 20–30; James et al., pp. 135–6, 260; C. M.
Snader, *A General Analysis of the Mexico City Stock Exchange: Its Limitations as a*

Free Market (Mexico City, 1965), p. 10; S. L. Simha, *The Capital Market of India* (Bombay, 1960), pp. 218–20; Cassis, Feldman and Olsson (eds.), *Evolution of Financial Institutions*, pp. 95, 128–9.

42. Cassis et al., *Evolution of Financial Institutions*, pp. 259–60; James et al., *Role of Banks*, pp. 21–2, pp. 55, 75–6; Nötel, 'Money, Banks & Industry', pp. 142–3, 158. Hardach, 'Banking and Industry', pp. 214–15; Gall et al., *Deutsche Bank*, pp. 199–200; A. Schubert, *The Credit-Anstalt Crisis of 1931* (Cambridge, 1991), pp. 33–4, 39–46; Balderston, *German Banking*, pp. 554, 568–9, 572–2; Feinstein, *Banking, Currency and Finance*, pp. 281–4, 344–5, J. C. Baker, *The German Stock Market: Its Operations, Problems, and Prospects* (New York, 1970) p. 53; *The German Stock Exchanges: A History of Many Regions* (Germany's Almanac, 1985/6), p. 73; Balderson, *Universal Banks*, pp. 10, 14, 21, 27; Holtfrerich, *Frankfurt*, p. 215; A. Teichova, G. Kurgan-Van Hentenryk, and D. Ziegler (eds.), *Banking, Trade and Industry: Europe, America and Asia from the 13th to the 20th Century* (Cambridge, 1997), p. 222; Kindleberger, *Financial History*, pp. 312–20.

43. Committee into Finance and Industry, *Minutes of Evidence* (London, 1931), Q. 7285.

44. Hautcoeur and Verley, 'Le marche financier français' (unpublished paper, 1994), pp. 25–9; Wynne-Bennett, *Investment and Speculation*, pp. 27–9; Myers, *Paris*, pp. 105–7, 137, 142, 149–58; Cassis (ed.), *Finance and Financiers*, p. 49; Y. Cassis and E. Bussiere, *London and Paris as Financial Centres in the 20th Century* (Oxford, 2005), pp. 47–8, 183, 231, 313.

45. W. J. Greenwood, *American and Foreign Stock Exchange Practice, Stock and Bond Trading and the Business Corporation Laws of all Nations* (New York, 1921), pp. 935–43, 973, 981, 987, 1012; Grant, *Bulls, Bears and Elephants*, pp. 95, 134; Salsbury and Sweeney, *The Bull, the Bear and the Kangaroo*, pp. 243, 251–4, 261, 313, 319; Merret, *Brisbane Stock Exchange*, p. 100; Armstrong, *Blue Skies*, pp. 73, 90, 114–23; Cruise and Griffiths, *Fleecing the Lamb*, pp. 37, 246; A. S. F. Abdul-Hadi, *Stock Markets of the Arab World: Trends, Problems and Prospects for Integration* (London, 1988), p. 76; M. Xia, J. H. Lin, and P. D. Grubb, *The Re-emerging Securities Market in China* (Westport, 1992), p. 2.

46. Hart et al., *Financial History of the Netherlands*, pp. 124–33, 143; Zurich Stock Exchange, *Summary Chronicle*, p. 300.

47. League of Nations, *Memorandum on Commercial Banks, 1913–1929* (Geneva, 1931), p. 14.

48. For New York at this time see the following: Twentieth Century Fund, *The Security Markets* (New York, 1935), pp. 38–43, 48, 50, 55, 102, 104, 113–14, 129, 155, 209, 219–22, 240, 250, 254, 257, 264, 749, 767; R. Sylla, R. Tilly, and G. Tortella (eds.), *The State, the Financial System and Economic Modernization* (Cambridge, 1999), pp. 276–82; Lewis, *America's Stake*, pp. 134, 148, 375, 450–4; Wynne-Bennett, *Investment and Speculation*, p. 24; D. F. Jordan, *Investments* (New York, 1924), p. 336; C. A. Dice, *The Stock Market* (Chicago/New York, 1926), pp. 10, 508, 515–16; Hallinan, *American Investments in Europe*, pp. 13, 17, 24–5, 39, 47; Cassis (ed.), *Finance and Financiers*, p. 364; Cleveland and Huertas, *Citibank*, pp. 114,

127–8, 139–40; Myers, *Paris*, p. 138; Meeker, *Work of the Stock Exchange*, pp. 516, 587; Geisst, *Visionary Capitalism*, pp. 2–4; W. R. Burgess, *The Reserve Banks and the Money Market* (New York, 1927, rev. edn. 1946), pp. 144–7; K. Dowd and M. K. Lewis (eds.), *Current Issues in Financial and Monetary Economics* (New York, 1992), pp. 59–62, 68; I. Walter (ed.), *Deregulating Wall Street: Commercial Bank Penetration of the Corporate Securities Market* (New York, 1985), pp. 44, 67–8, 72–3; Scott, *Government Securities Market*, pp. 11–13; Leffler, *The Stock Market*, pp. 6, 61–4, 92, 244, 269, 275; J. B. Baskin and P. J. Miranti, *A History of Corporate Finance* (Cambridge, 1997), pp. 177, 181–2, 232; E. J. Perkins, *Wall Street to Main Street: Charles Merrill and Middle-Class Investors* (Cambridge, 1999), pp. 86, 88, 104, 129; Bruchey, Modernization, pp. 20–3; Wilkins, *History of Foreign Investment in the US*, pp. 72, 85, 184, 187, 202. See also B. A. Wigmore, *The Crash and its Aftermath: A History of Securities Markets in the United States, 1929–1933* (Westport, Connecticut 1985).

49. See Bank for International Settlements, 'Capital Movements to and From London', pp. 18–25; 'International Movements of Capital and Prices' pp. 6–10; 'Reasons for the Movement of Capital to Paris in 1926–1928', pp. 4, 11; 'Movements of Capital in France From 1929 to 1933', p. 29 (May 1934).

50. *Seattle Stock Exchange, Report of the President* (Seattle, 1929–30), pp. 5–6, 11–15; *Boston Stock Exchange* (Boston, 1930), pp. 17, 19, 23; *Los Angeles Stock Exchange* (Los Angeles, 1939), p. 5.

51. H. Bierman, *The Causes of the 1929 Stock Market Crash: A Speculative Orgy or a New Era* (Westport, 1998), pp. 2–3, 27, 133–5, 151; Cleveland and Huertas, *Citibank*, pp. 114, 127–30, 139–40, 207; Myers, *Paris*, p. 138; Meeker, *Work of the Stock Exchange*, p. 587; Geisst, *Visionary Capitalism*, pp. 2–4; Burgess, *Reserve Banks*, pp. 144–7; Walter (ed.), *Deregulating Wall Street*, pp. 43–52, 80.

52. *Seattle Stock Exchange, Report of the President*, p. 6.

53. *London Stock Exchange, Minutes of the Meeting for General Purposes, 15 May 1930*. On this point see W. C. Brooks, *How the Stock Market Really Works* (London, 1930), p. 121.

54. Armstrong, *Blue Skies*, p. 145; Grant, *Bulls, Bears and Elephants*, p. 138; Thomas, *Western Capitalism in China*, p. 204; Snader, *Mexico City Stock Exchange*, p. 10; Bryan, *Taking Stock*, p. 38; Myers, *Paris*, p. 144; Bouvier, 'French Banks', p. 32, 43, 55–7, 62–4; Kindleberger, 'Banking and Industry', p. 17; Torrente Fortuno, *Historia de la Bolsa de Madrid*, vol. 3, pp. 667, 671; Tortella and Palafox, 'Banking and Industry in Spain', pp. 92. 105–7; Ciocca and Toniolo, 'Industry and Finance', pp. 122, 130–3; Hardach, 'Banking and Industry', p. 219.

55. A. Schubert, *The Credit-Anstalt Crisis of 1931* (Cambridge, 1991), p. 93.

56. Balderston, *German Banking*, pp. 29–32; J. C. Baker, *The German Stock Market: Its Operations, Problems, and Prospects* (New York, 1970), pp. 12, 33; L. Gall, G. D. Feldman, H. James, C-L. Holfrerich, and H. E. Buschgen, *The Deutsche Bank, 1870–1995* (London, 1995), pp. 286, 290; *The German Stock Exchanges: A History of Many Regions* (Germany's Almanac, 1985/6), pp. 43, 56, 67, 73; C. Kopper, 'Banking in National Socialist Germany, 1933–39', *Financial History Review*, 5

(1998), pp. 51–3; Holtfrerich, Frankfurt, pp. 216–18; James et al., *Role of Banks*, pp. 21–4; Hart et al., *Financial History of the Netherlands*, p. 148; A. Teichova, G. Kurgan-Van Hentenryk, and D. Ziegler (eds.), *Banking, Trade and Industry: Europe, America and Asia from the 13th to the 20th Century* (Cambridge, 1997), pp. 200–5; The Economist, *Directory of World Stock Exchanges* (London, 1988), p. 20.

57. Meeker, *Short Selling*, pp. 133, 241, 247–8.

58. F. Capie, *Capital Controls: A 'Cure' Worse Than a Problem* (London, 2002), pp. 45–6, 60–1; P. A. David and M. Thomas (eds.), *The Economic Future in Historical Perspective* (Oxford, 2003), pp. 352–8; K. H. O'Rourke and J. G. Williamson, *Globalization and History: The Evolution of a Nineteenth Century Atlantic Economy* (Cambridge, MA, 1999), p. 27; Zurich Stock Exchange, *Summary Chronicle*, p. 300; Armstrong, *Blue Skies*, chapters 8 and 9.

59. James et al., *Role of Banks*, pp. 8, 33, 85–92, 96, 110–11, 114, 179, 181, 188, 194–5, 199, 208, 213, 225, 227, 248; Ciocca and Toniolo, 'Industry and Finance', pp. 130–3; S. Cassese, 'The Long-Life of the Financial Institutions Set up in the Thirties', *Journal of European Economic History*, 13 (1984), p. 276; Schubert, *Credit-Anstalt*, pp. 33, 173; Feinstein (ed.), *Banking, Currency and Finance*, p. 284; D. K. Eiteman, *Stock Exchanges in Latin America* (Ann Arbor, 1966), pp. 21, 41–2; Armstrong, *Blue Skies*, chapters 11–13; Abdul-Hadi, *Stock Markets of the Arab World*, p. 84.

60. Twentieth Century Fund, *Stock Market Control*, pp. 163–4.

61. See C. R. Gay, *Stock Market Controls* (New York, 1935), and *Wall Street in a Time of Change* (New York, 1936); R. Whitney, *Economic Freedom* (Chicago, 1934); R. Whitney, *Public Opinion and the Stock Market* (Boston, 1931); Whitney Radio Broadcasts: 'Industry and Securities Markets' (1935); 'Security Markets and the People' (1935); 'The New York Stock Exchange' (1932); 'Short selling' (1931); 'Short Selling and Liquidation' (1931); and Whitney, 'Statement to the Banking and Currency Committee' (932). In the late 1930s Whitney was disgraced and imprisoned for embezzlement, which did not help the image of the New York Stock Exchange.

62. C. H. Meyer, *The Securities Exchange Act of 1934: Analyzed and Explained* (New York, 1934), pp. 11–12, 15–16, 19, 22, 25; Cherrington, *The Investor and the Securities Act*, pp. 1–36, 41, 58, 101.

63. Quoted in Leffler, *Stock Market*, p. 94, cf. pp. 95–6.

64. R. I. Warshow, *Understanding the New Stock Market* (New York, 1934), p. viii.

65. I. Friend, G. W. Hoffman, W. J. Winn, M. Hansburg, and S. Schlat, *Securities Markets* (New York, 1958), pp. 169–70; Bordo and Sylla (eds.), *Anglo-American Financial System*, pp. 127, 130; Leffler, *Stock Market*, pp. 68–9; H. V. Cherrington, *Understanding the Securities Act*, pp. 24, 298; Bruchey, *Modernization*, p. 27.

66. Cherrington, *The Investor and the Securities Act*, p. 246, cf. pp. 244–5.

67. I. Friend et al., *The Over-the-Counter Securities Market* (New York, 1958), pp. 25, 107–10.

68. P. F. Wendt, *The Classification and Financial Experience of the Customers of a Typical New York Stock Exchange Firm, 1933 to 1938* (Maryville, Tennessee, 1941), pp. 15, 17, 23, 219, 222; Leffler, *Stock Market*, pp. 72–3, 95, 435–7; Perkins, *Wall Street*, p. 145, 151, 161.

69. Scott, *Government Securities Market*, pp. 11–13, 16.

70. C. Westheimer, 'The Durable Cincinnati Stock Exchange', *Queen City Heritage: Journal of the Cincinnati Historical Society*, 49 (1991), pp. 41–3.

71. Snader, *Mexico City Stock Exchange*, p. 19; Cruise and Griffiths, *Fleecing the Lamb*, pp. 39, 41, 45, 50, 53; Merret, *Brisbane Stock Exchange*, pp. 97, 109; Bryan, *Taking Stock*, pp. 35, 40, 42; Grant, *Bulls, Bears and Elephants*, pp. 138–9, 166.

72. Twentieth Century Fund, *Security Markets*, p. 113; Leffler, *Stock Market*, pp. 244, 251, 261, 266, 269.

73. Cleveland and Huertas, *Citibank*, pp. 160, 172, 198; Geisst, *Visionary Capitalism*, pp. 18, 21, 28, 31; F. Capie and M. Collins, *Have the Banks Failed British Industry* (London, 1992), p. 54; Feinstein (ed.), *Banking, Currency and Finance*, p. 330; Myers, *Paris*, pp. 107–9, 124, 135–6; *The Exchange*, vol. I (December 1939), p. 16 and (March 1940), p. 6.

74. Winthrop W. Aldrich, *The Stock Market From the Viewpoint of a Commercial Banker* (New York, 1937), p. 4.

75. Hart et al., *Financial History of the Netherlands*, pp. 133–4, 136–7, 151, 168; J. Jonker, 'Fingers in the Dike, Fingers in the Pie: The Position of the Amsterdam Stock Exchange on the Dutch Capital Market, 1800–1940' (unpublished paper, 1994), pp. 20, 23–4; Myers, *Paris*, pp. 107–9, 124, 135–6; Cassis and Bussiere (eds.), *London and Paris*, pp. 194–5.

76. L. E. Davis and R. E. Gallman, *Evolving Financial Markets and International Capital Flows: Britain, the Americas, and Australia, 1865–1914* (Cambridge, 2001), pp. 857–60; Royal Institute of International Affairs, *The Problem of International Investment*, p. 23.

77. M. Sarnat, *The Development of the Securities Market in Israel* (Tübingen, 1966), pp. 11–20; M. Sarnat, 'The Emergence of Israel's Security Market: A Note', *Journal of Economic History*, 49 (1989), pp. 693–6; Torrente Fortuno, *Historia de la Bolsa de Madrid*, vol. 3, p. 677; Krishan, *Industrial Securities Market in India*, pp. 175–6.

78. R. M. Kindersley, 'British Foreign Investments in 1930', *Economic Journal*, 42 (1932), p. 193 and subsequent issues 44 (1934), p. 373; 47 (1937), p. 650; 48 (1938), p. 623; 49 (1939), p. 689.

79. B. Eichengreen, *Golden Fetters: The Gold Standard and the Great Depression, 1919–1939* (New York, 1992), pp. 83, 201–3, 220, 390–1, 398; L. Officer, *Between the Dollar–Sterling Gold Points* (Cambridge, 1996), p. 275; B. Eichengreen, *Elusive Stability: Essays in the History of International Finance, 1919–1939* (Cambridge, 1990), p. 152, 271; B. Eichengreen, *The Gold Standard in Theory and History* (New York, 1985), p. 18; K. Burk, 'Money and Power: The Shift From Great Britain to the United States', in Cassis (ed.), *Finance and Financiers*, p. 36; Royal Institute of International Affairs, *The Problem of International Investment*, pp. 23, 50, 73, 76–7, 79, 107–8, 130, 155; Merret, 'Capital Markets and Capital

Formation in Australia, 1890–1945', *Australian Economic History Review*, 37 (1997), pp. 192–8.

CHAPTER 7

1. S. Homer and R. Sylla, *A History of Interest Rates* (New Brunswick, 1996), pp. 439–40.
2. *The Exchange*, December 1939, p. 11, cf. p. 16. See also *The Exchange*, March 1940, p. 6.
3. M. Hart, J. Jonker, and J. L. Van Zanden, *A Financial History of the Netherlands* (Cambridge, 1997), p. 170; J. Hermans, *ICT in Information Services: Use and Deployment of ICT in the Dutch Securities Trade, 1860–1970* (Rotterdam, 2004), pp. 49, 64; Y. Cassis, G. D. Feldman, and U. Olsson (eds.), *The Evolution of Financial Institutions and Markets in 20th Century Europe* (Aldershot, 1995), p. 99.
4. Y. Cassis and E. Bussiere (eds.), *London and Paris as International Financial Centres in the Twentieth Century* (Oxford, 2005), pp. 189, 200, 236–8; J. A. Torrente Fortuno, *Historia de La Bolsa de Madrid* (Madrid, 1974), vol. 3, pp. 677, 681; A. Brown, *The Flight of International Capital: A Contemporary History* (London, 1988), p. 149.
5. F. Pick, *Common Stocks Versus Gold* (New York, 1963), pp. 21, 31, 70, 129, 171, 193, 209; *The German Stock Exchanges: A History of Many Regions* (Germany's Almanac, 1985/6), p. 68; J. C. Baker, *The German Stock Market: Its Operations, Problems, and Prospects* (New York, 1970), pp. 41–2, 54.
6. *The Economist, Directory of World Stock Exchanges* (London, 1988), p. 20; Pick, *Common Stocks Versus Gold*, p. 21; C-L. Holtfrerich, *Frankfurt as a Financial Centre: From Medieval Trade Fair to European Banking Centre* (Munich, 1999), pp. 218, 261–2; Hart et al., *Financial History of the Netherlands*, p. 193.
7. G. D Feldman, U. Olssen, M. Bordo, and Y. Cassis (eds.), *The Evolution of Modern Financial Institutions in the Twentieth Century* (Milan, 1994), pp. 57–61.
8. Y. Cassis and E. Bussiere (eds.), *London and Paris as International Financial Centres in the Twentieth Century* (Oxford, 2005), pp. 189, 200, 236–8; S. Homer and R. Sylla, *A History of Interest Rates* (New Brunswick, 1996), p. 440; L. E. Davis and R. E. Gallman, *Evolving Financial Markets and International Capital Flows: Britain, the Americas, and Australia, 1865–1914* (Cambridge, 2001), p. 862; Kindleberger, *Financial History*, pp. 405, 409, 425; Amsterdam Stock Exchange, *A Century of Stocks and Shares: A Historical Sketch of the Vereniging voor de Effectenhandel and the Amsterdam Stock Exchange* (Amsterdam, n.d.), pp. 5, 11, 16; Hart et al., *Financial History of the Netherlands*, pp. 153, 168 ; F. Capie, *Capital Controls: A 'Cure' Worse Than the Problem* (London, 2002), pp. 65, 68, 101.
9. Y. Cassis (ed.), *Finance and Financiers in European History* (Cambridge, 1992), p. 300; Zurich Stock Exchange, *A Summary Chronicle of the Zurich Stock Exchange* (Zurich 1977), p. 301.

10. W. A. Thomas, *Western Capitalism in China: A History of the Shanghai Stock Exchange* (Aldershot, 2001), pp. 224, 232–3, 264; R. Chia et al., *Globalization of the Jakarta Stock Exchange* (Singapore, 1992), pp. 15–16.

11. S. Takagi (ed.), *Japanese Capital Markets: New Developments in Regulations and Institutions* (Oxford, 1993), pp. 519–20; *The Economist, Directory of World Stock Exchanges* (London, 1988), p. 203; R. G. Rajan and L. Zingales, *The Great Reversals: The Politics of Financial Development in the 20th Century* (Paris, 2000), pp. 30–1.

12. M. Giesecke, *La Bolsa de Valores de Lima: 140 Anos de Historia* (Lima, 1997), pp. 182–8; C. M. Snader, *A General Analysis of the Mexico City Stock Exchange: Its Limitations as a Free Market* (Mexico City, 1965), p. 11; M. Sarnat, The Development of the Securities Market in Israel (Tubingen, 1966), pp. 22–4; M. Sarnat, 'The Emergence of Israel's Security Market: A note', *Journal of Economic History*, 49 (1989), pp. 697–8.

13. B. Krishan, *Industrial Securities Market in India* (New Delhi, 1989), pp. 176–9, 280; M. Bryan, *Taking Stock: Johannesburg Stock Exchange—the First 100 Years* (Johannesburg, 1987), pp. 42, 51–2.

14. D. Grant, *Bulls, Bears and Elephants: A History of the New Zealand Stock Exchange* (Wellington, 1997), pp. 168–70; S. Salsbury and K. Sweeney, *The Bull, the Bear and the Kangaroo: The History of the Sydney Stock Exchange* (Sydney, 1988), p. 305; A. L. Lougheed, *The Brisbane Stock Exchange, 1884–1984* (Brisbane, 1984), pp. 116–17, 121.

15. R. Roberts (ed.), *Global Financial Centres* (Aldershot, 1994), pp. 289, 299; H. Van B. Cleveland and T. F. Huertas, *Citibank,1812–1970* (Cambridge, MA, 1985), p. 225.

16. G. L. Leffler, *The Stock Market* (New York, 1951), pp. 6, 11, 435–41; I. O. Scott, *Government Securities Market* (New York, 1965), pp. 11–13, 16; R. O. Wright, *Chronology of the Stock Market* (Jefferson, North Carolina, 2002), pp. 45–6.

17. Leffler, *Stock Market*, pp. 244, 264–9, 427, 560.

18. Leffler, *Stock Market*, p. 74.

19. Leffler, *Stock Market*, p. 74.

20. I. Friend et al., *The Over-the-Counter Market* (New York, 1958), pp. 109–11; J. S. Gordon, *The Great Game: The Emergence of Wall Street as a World Power, 1653–2000* (New York, 1999), p. 250; Leffler, *Stock Market*, p. 104; E. J. Perkins, *Wall Street to Main Street: Charles Merrill and Middle-Class Investors* (Cambridge, 1999), pp. 151, 161, 165, 168, 177, 194.

21. Rajan and Zingales, *The Great Reversals*, pp. 14–15, 36; J. J. Kaplan and G. Schleiminger, *The European Payments Union: Financial Diplomacy in the 1950s* (Oxford, 1989), pp. 9–12.

22. Kindleberger, *Financial History*, p. 435.

23. I. Friend et al., *Securities Markets*, p. 7.

24. Leffler, *Stock Market*, pp. 5–6, 96, 104, 111, 155, 195, 244, 251, 261, 266, 269, 341, 436–52, 553; I. Friend et al., *Securities Markets*, pp. 21, 45, 77, 106, 109, 116, 235, 255, 411–13, 435; I. Friend et al., *Over-the-Counter Securities Market*, pp. 7, 24–6, 411–12, 415, 435; New York Stock Exchange, *Institutional Share-Ownership: A Report on Financial Institutions and the Stock Market* (New York, 1964), pp. 11,

13–14, 39, 46; US Department of Commerce, *Historical Statistics of the United States* (Bureau of the Census, Washington, 1975), pp. 973, 987, 1007; J. H. Lorie and M. T. Hamilton, *The Stock Market: Theories and Evidence* (Homewood, 1973), pp. 4–6; R. W. Goldsmith (ed.), *Institutional Investors and Corporate Stock: A Background Study* (NBER, 1973), pp. 74–8, 84, 144, 148, 151, 164, 202; S. Homer, *The Great American Bond Market: Selected Speeches* (New York, 1978), pp. 18, 22, 287–93, 297–8, 301; A. C. Sobel, *Domestic Choices, International Markets: Dismantling National Barriers and Liberalising Securities Markets* (Ann Arbor, 1994), pp. 27, 50; A. Benn, *The Unseen Wall Street of 1969–1975* (Westport, 2000), pp. 2, 136–7, 132; Gordon, *The Great Game*, pp. 275–7; C. R. Geisst, *Visionary Capitalism: Financial Markets and the American Dream in the 20th Century* (New York, 1990), pp. 28, 36, 310; I. O. Scott, *Government Securities Market* (New York, 1965), pp. 27, 48, 77, 110, 172; Wright, *Chronology*, pp. 47–8, 52–3, 79; J. E. Walter, *The Role of Regional Security Exchanges* (Berkeley, 1957), pp. 2, 8, 11, 16, 18, 21–2, 27, 34, 70, 79, 105; C. R. Geisst, *Wall Street: A History* (Oxford, 1997), pp. 281, 298, 301; M. D. Bordo and R. Sylla (ed.), *Anglo-American Financial System: Institutions and Markets in the Twentieth Century* (New York, 1995), pp. 107, 127–30, 132–5, 201; M. E. Blume, J. J. Siegel, and D. Rottenberg, *Revolution on Wall Street: The Rise and Decline of the New York Stock Exchange* (New York, 1993), pp. 105, 109, 113, 133; M. Keenan, *Profile of the New York Based Security Industry* (New York, 1977), pp. 12, 18, 23, 55; Perkins, *Wall Street to Main Street*, pp. 212, 219, 230, 232, 258; Bruchey, *American Stock Exchange*, pp. 27–8, 34, 38, 44–5; J. B. Baskin and P. J. Miranti, *A History of Corporate Finance* (Cambridge, 1997), pp. 232–3, 323.

25. Thomas, *Western Capitalism*, pp. 233, 236.

26. A. S. F. Abdul-Hadi, *Stock Markets of the Arab World: Trends, Problems and Prospects for Integration* (London, 1988), pp. 84–5.

27. Chia *et al.*, *Jakarta Stock Exchange*, pp. 14–16.

28. D. K. Eiteman, *Stock Exchanges in Latin America* (Ann Arbor, 1966), pp. 2–7, 14–21, 33–7, 54–7, 69; Snader, *Mexico City*, pp. 11, 26–8, 32, 36, 43; Giesecke, *Bolsa de Valores de Lima*, pp. 190, 199, 233–5, 238–41, 270.

29. Eiteman, *Stock Exchanges in Latin America*, p. 54; Abdul-Hadi, *Stock Markets of the Arab World*, pp. 20, 76, 84–5, 101; R. A. Clark, *Africa's Emerging Securities Markets: Developments in Financial Infrastructure* (Westport, 1998), pp. 55, 58, 85, 134, 177, 206.

30. R. B. Areago, *Nigerian Stock Exchange: Genesis, Organisation and Operations* (Ibadan, 1984), pp. 3–10, 21, 41; G. O. Nwankwo, *The Nigerian Financial System* (London, 1980), pp. 132, 137, 142, 147.

31. Sarnat, *Securities Market in Israel*, pp. 27, 32, 59, 109.

32. S. Takagi (ed.), *Japanese Capital Markets: New Developments in Regulations and Institutions* (Oxford, 1993), pp. 108, 164–7, 181–2, 197, 217, 242, 305–6, 308, 311–13, 453–6, 517–22; J. Isaacs and T. Ejiri, *Japanese Securities Market* (London, 1990), pp. 1–4, 35, 85; L. Pressnell, *Money and Banking in Japan* (London, 1973), pp. 427–9, 436–9; W. F. Monroe, *Japan: Financial Markets and the World Economy* (New York, 1973), pp. 121–2; W. Lazonick and M. O'Sullivan, 'Finance and

Industrial Development: Evolution to Market Control', *Financial History Review*, 4 (1997), pp. 125–7; R. Roberts (ed.), *Global Financial Centres* (Aldershot, 1994), pp. 27, 32, 34, 76, 90; F. Allen and D. Gale, *Comparing Financial Systems* (Cambridge, MA, 2000), p. 39.

33. C. Armstrong, *Moose Pastures and Mergers: The Ontario Securities Commission and the Regulation of Share Markets in Canada, 1940–1980* (Toronto, 2001), pp. 64, 71, 74, 81–4, 119, 257, 266, 285–7, 325; Cruise and Griffiths, *Fleecing the Lamb*, pp. 55–6, 68, 71–2, 128–9, 262.

34. Salsbury and Sweeney, *The Bull, the Bear and the Kangaroo*, pp. 305, 320, 324–31, 340–1, 355, 368, 484–5; Merrett, *Brisbane Stock Exchange*, pp. 121, 123–4, 134, 137, 145–7, 149, 160, 165.

35. Grant, *Bulls, Bears and Elephants*, pp. 172–6.

36. Bryan, *Taking Stock*, pp. 45–8, 56, 62–8, 88, 97–100, 104, 126, 174.

37. Krishan, *Industrial Securities Market in India*, pp. 180, 197, 280, 283, 315, 335; K. L. Garg, *Stock Exchanges in India* (Calcutta, 1950), pp. 61, 113, 124; S. L. N. Simha, *The Capital Market of India* (Bombay, 1960), pp. 19–22, 219–23, 233–4; K. D. Doodha, *Stock Exchanges in a Developing Country* (Bombay, 1962), pp. 1, 61, 153; M. S. Khan, *The Securities Market in Pakistan* (Karachi, 1993), pp. 4, 8, 26, 38.

38. Thomas, *Western Capitalism*, p. 234; M. J. Cascales and M. Ho, *The Stock Exchange of Hong Kong: Past, Present and Future* (Hong Kong, 2000), p. 2; C. R. Shenk, 'Regulatory Reform in an Emerging Stock Market: The case of Hong Kong, 1945–1986', *Financial History Review*, 11 (2004), pp. 142–7; *The Economist, Directory of World Stock Exchanges*, pp. 241, 307.

39. Baker, *German Stock Market*, pp. 12, 24–5, 42, 54, 130–2; *German Stock Exchanges*, p. 68; J. Edwards and K. Fischer, *Banks, Finance and Investment in Germany* (Cambridge, 1994), pp. 55, 182; Holtfrerich, *Frankfurt*, pp. 221–5, 236, 245–8, 250, 261–2, 263–4, 268–70.

40. Cassis and Bussiere (eds.), *London and Paris*, pp. 6, 81–2, 314–5; P. Stonham, *Major Stock Markets of Europe* (Aldershot, 1982), pp. 70–1; *The Economist, Directory of World Stock Exchanges*, pp. 119–29.

41. Stonham, *Major Stock Markets*, pp. 22–4, 142–9, 168, 330; Cassis et al., *Evolution of Financial Institutions*, pp. 10, 132.

42. Hart et al., *Financial History of the Netherlands*, pp. 168–9, 171, 187–9; Amsterdam Stock Exchange, *Century of Stocks and Shares*, pp. 17, 19, 21–2, 26; Hermans, *ICT in Information Services*, pp. 54, 81.

43. L. Oxelheim, *Financial Markets in Transition: Globalization, Investment and Economic Growth* (London, 1996), p. 108; Rajan and Zingales, *Great Reversals*, pp. 33, 35; Davis and Gallman, *Evolving Financial Markets*, pp. 863, 873.

44. A. Britton, *Monetary Regimes of the 20th Century* (Cambridge, 2001), pp. 137–40; D. H. Aldcroft and M. J. Oliver, *Exchange Rate Regimes in the 20th Century* (Cheltenham, 1998), pp. 95, 100, 103; Kaplan and Schleiminger, *European Payments Union*, pp. 51, 57, 200, 207, 235, 272, 319–32; Capie, *Capital Controls*, pp. 67, 70; K. Dowd and M. K. Lewis (eds.), *Current Issues in Financial and Monetary*

Economics (New York), pp. 67–8; S. Takagi (ed.), *Japanese Capital Markets: New Developments in Regulations and Institutions* (Oxford, 1993), pp. 108.

45. Davis and Gallman, *Evolving Financial Markets*, pp. 863, 873; S. Battilossi and Y. Cassis (eds.), *European Banks and the American Challenge: Competition and Co-operation in International Banking under Bretton Woods* (Oxford, 2002), pp. 8, 12, 14, 54–5, 57–61, 63–4, 69, 80, 85; Goldsmith (ed.), *Institutional Investors and Corporate Stock*, p. 157; Sobel, *Domestic Choices, International Markets*, p. 27; Cleveland and Huertas, *Citibank*, pp. 253, 255, 267, 295; Kindleberger, *Financial history*, p. 449.

46. G. Dosoo, *The Eurobond Market* (London, 1992), pp. 7–21, 26, 30–3, 176, 206–8; Kindleberger, *Financial History*, pp. 449–55; Walter (ed.), *Deregulating Wall Street*, pp. 256–8, 268; Battilossi and Cassis (eds.), *European Banks and the American Challenge*, pp. 210, 213.

47. Cassis and Bussiere (eds.), *London and Paris*, pp. 250–4, 261–2, 276; Battilossi and Cassis (eds.), *European Banks and the American Challenge*, pp. 12–13, 26, 38, 57–62, 63–4, 69, 75, 85–7, 91–2, 94, 106–12, 187; Geisst, *Wall Street*, p. 276.

48. Cassis and Bussiere (eds.), *London and Paris*, pp.189–90, 195, 201, 213, 216, 229, 231, 236, 238, 240, 273–7, 315; Battilossi and Cassis (eds.), *European Banks and the American Challenge*, pp. 12, 92, 178.

49. Stonham, *Major Stock Markets*, pp. 19, 22–4.

50. Holtfrerich, *Frankfurt*, pp. 263–4, 269–70.

51. *The Economist, Directory of World Stock Exchanges*, p. 232, 366 ; Cassis et al., *Evolution of Financial Institutions*, p. 71; Battilossi and Cassis (eds.), *European Banks and the American Challenge*, pp. 12, 87–9.

52. Takagi (ed.), *Japanese Capital Markets*, pp. 453–6; Isaacs and Ejiri, *Japanese Securities Market*, pp. 1–4, 35, 85; Roberts (ed.), *Global Financial Centres*, pp. 27, 32, 34, 76, 90.

53. Bryan, *Taking Stock*, pp. 64–8, 88, 97–100.

CHAPTER 8

1. For developments in the United States in the 1970s see D. P. McCaffrey and D. W. Hart, *Wall Street Polices Itself: How Securities Firms Manage the Legal Hazards of Competitive Pressures* (New York, 1998), pp. 3, 6–7; R. O. Wright, *Chronology of the Stock Market* (Jefferson, N.C.), pp. 54, 58; S. Homer, *The Great American Bond Market: Selected Speeches* (New York, 1978), p. 10; C. R. Geisst, *Visionary Capitalism: Financial Markets and the American Dream in the Twentieth Century* (New York, 1990), pp. 37–9; A. W. Lo (ed.), *The Industrial Organization and Regulation of the Securities Industry* (Chicago, 1996), pp. 63, 209, 318; J. S. Gordon, *The Great Game: The Emergence of Wall Street as a World Power, 1653–2000* (New York, 1999), pp. 274, 280; A. Benn, *The Unseen Wall Street of 1969–1975* (Westport, 2000), p. 132; M. E. Blume, J. J. Siegel, and D. Rottenberg, *Revolution on Wall Street: The Rise and Decline of the New York Stock Exchange*

370 *Notes to pp. 254–267*

(New York, 1993), pp. 105, 134, 139; R. A. Schwartz, *The Electronic Call Auction: Market Mechanism and Trading—Building a Better Stock Market* (Boston, 2001), pp. 5, 9, 30, 46; M. Keenan, *Profile of the New York Based Security Industry* (New York), p. 12; J. O. Mathews, *Struggle and Survival on Wall Street* (New York, 1994), pp. 25–6, 87, 106; C. R. Geisst, *Wall Street: A History* (Oxford, 1997), pp. 305–8; M. Bordo and R. Sylla (eds.), *Anglo-American Financial System: Institutions and Markets in the Twentieth Century* (New York, 1995), pp. 122–4, 133–5; E. J. Perkins, *Wall Street to Main Street: Charles Merrill and Middle-Class Investors* (Cambridge, 1999), pp. 232, 263–4; S. Bruchey, *Modernization of the American Stock Exchange, 1971–1989* (New York, 1991), pp. 38, 44–5, 53, 58, 60–70, 120, 170; J. B. Baskin and P. J. Miranti, *A History of Corporate Finance* (Cambridge, 1997), pp. 232–3, 323.

2. Some authors do see the 1970s as period of dramatic change that came to fruition in the 1980s. However, that view is largely based on US experience and ignores the absence of fundamental change elsewhere in the world during that decade. See A. C. Sobel, *Domestic Choices, International Markets: Dismantling National Barriers and Liberalising Securities Markets* (Ann Arbor, 1994), pp. 27, 31, 50; K. J. Cohen et al., *The Microstructure of Securities Markets* (Englewood Cliffs, 1986), p. 1.

3. C. Armstrong, *Moose Pastures and Mergers: The Ontario Securities Commission and the Regulation of Share Markets in Canada, 1940–1980* (Toronto, 2001), pp. 278, 289, 294–7, 329–33, 337–8.

4. S. Takagi (ed.), *Japanese Capital Markets: New Developments in Regulations and Institutions* (Oxford, 1993), pp. 171–82, 192.

5. P. Stonham, *Major Stock Markets of Europe* (Aldershot, 1982), pp. 22–8, 31, 41–2, 60, 64–5, 70–2, 76, 79, 90, 99, 101, 103, 108, 114–15, 121, 126, 142, 149, 165, 168, 182–3, 186; I. Walter (ed.), *Deregulating Wall Street: Commercial Bank Penetration of the Corporate Securities Market* (New York, 1985), p. 281; J. Edwards and K. Fischer, *Banks, Finance and Investment in Germany* (Cambridge, 1994), pp. 66, 120; Amsterdam Stock Exchange, *A Century of Stocks and Shares* (Amsterdam n.d.), pp. 19, 22, 26; M. Hart, J. Jonker, and J. L. Van Zanden, *A Financial History of the Netherlands* (Cambridge, 1997), p. 169; J. Hermans, *ICT in Information Services: Use and Deployment of ICT in the Dutch Securities Trade, 1860–1970* (Rotterdam, 2004), pp. 68, 159; Y. Cassis and E. Bussiere (eds.), *London and Paris as International Financial Centres in the Twentieth Century* (Oxford, 2005), pp. 233, 316.

6. R. B. Areago, *Nigerian Stock Exchange: Genesis, Organisation and Operations* (Ibadan, 1984), p. 26.

7. S. Salsbury and K. Sweeney, *The Bull, the Bear and the Kangaroo: The History of the Sydney Stock Exchange* (Sydney, 1988), pp. 395–6, 399, 402, 423–4; M. Bryan, *Taking Stock: Johannesburg Stock Exchange—the First 100 Years* (Johannesburg, 1987), pp. 116, 125, 140, 143, 177–8; G. O. Nwankwo, *The Nigerian Financial System* (London, 1980), pp. 132, 137, 142, 145–6; Areago, *Nigerian Stock Exchange*, pp. 18–19, 41, 68, 87.

8. A. S. F. Abdul-Hadi, *Stock Markets of the Arab World: Trends, Problems and Prospects for Integration* (London, 1988), pp. 20, 25, 77, 84.

9. C. R. Shenk, 'Regulatory Reform in an Emerging Stock Market: The Case of Hong Kong, 1945–1986', *Financial History Review*, 11 (2004), pp. 147, 149, 154; M. J. Cascales and M. Ho, *The Stock Exchange of Hong Kong: Past, Present and Future* (Hong Kong, 2000), pp. 2–11.

10. J. O. Mathews, *Struggle and Survival on Wall Street* (New York, 1994), pp. 214; Wright, *Chronology of the Stock Market*, pp. 60–1; P. Moore, *Autostrade to the Superhighway: The Future of Global Debt Markets* (London, 2001), p. 22.

11. D. H. Aldcroft and M. J. Oliver, *Exchange Rate Regimes in the Twentieth Century* (Cheltenham, 1998), pp. 103, 115, 142, 164–6; A. Britton, *Monetary Regimes of the Twentieth Century* (Cambridge, 2001), pp. 148, 159, 177.

12. G. Dosoo, *The Eurobond Market* (London, 1992), pp. 15–16, 18, 20–1, 30–1, 33–6, 42, 113, 116–18, 176, 206–8, 215, 233–7; Walter (ed.), *Deregulating Wall Street*, pp. 266–8, 276–9; Cassis and Bussiere (eds.), *London and Paris*, pp. 66–9, 103, 192, 210, 216, 250; Keenan, *Profile of the New York Based Security Industry*, pp. 23, 55; Geisst, *Wall Street*, pp. 303, 331; Takagi (ed.), *Japanese Capital Markets*, p. 82.

13. Dosoo, *Eurobond Market*, pp. 42–3, 48, 52–4, 69–72, 80–1, 83–5, 95, 99, 111, 116–18, 123–5, 130, 136–7, 206–8, 215, 233–7, 272–3, 277; Moore, *Autostrade to the Superhighway*, pp. 45, 48; Walter (ed.), *Deregulating Wall Street*, p. 264; Abdul-Hadi, *Stock Markets of the Arab world*, pp. 46–9, 54, 104, 125, 133, 136; Cassis and Bussiere (eds.), *London and Paris*, pp. 236, 250, 306–9; Takagi (ed.), *Japanese Capital Markets*, p. 80.

14. H. Drummond, *Escalation in Decision-Making* (Oxford, 1996), pp. 51, 62, 66, 94, 158, 177, 182, 196–7, 199.

15. C. Londsdale, *The UK Equity Gap: The Failure of Government Policy* (Aldershot, 1997), pp. 124, 129, 144, 150.

16. Bruchey, *American Stock Exchange*, pp. 120,170; Data from *Statistical Abstract of the United States, 1991* (Washington, 1991), pp. 514–17.

17. Mathews, *Struggle and Survival on Wall Street*, pp. 25–6, 106, 214–16, 223; Lo (ed.), *Industrial Organization and Regulation*, pp. 5, 63, 93–6, 114, 177, 182–3; McCaffrey and Hart, *Wall Street Polices Itself*, p. 3; Geisst, *Wall Street*, pp. 331–4, 356, 367.

18. Armstrong, *Moose Pastures and Mergers*: pp. 343–4; D. Cruise and A. Griffiths, *Fleecing the Lamb: The Inside Story of the Vancouver Stock Exchange* (Vancouver, 1987), pp. 208, 237, 242–6, 256.

19. Salsbury and Sweeney, *The Bull, the Bear and the Kangaroo*, pp. 432, 436–9, 441, 447, 451; A. L. Lougheed, *The Brisbane Stock Exchange, 1884–1984* (Brisbane, 1984), pp. 169, 174–5; *The Economist, Directory of World Stock Exchanges* (London, 1988), pp. 10–11.

20. D. Grant, *Bulls, Bears and Elephants: A History of the New Zealand Stock Exchange* (Wellington, 1997), pp. 194, 196, 212–14, 222, 224, 245–9, 250–2, 259, 261, 271–80.

21. Bryan, *Taking Stock*, pp. 148, 152, 161, 174, 177–8, 181.
22. B. Krishan, *Industrial Securities Market in India* (New Delhi, 1989), pp. 196–8, 207, 280, 285, 289, 297, 300, 315, 317, 328–9, 335.
23. M. S. Khan, *The Securities Market in Pakistan* (Karachi, 1993), pp. 8, 26, 38; M. Giesecke, *La Bolsa de Valroes de Lima: 140 anos de historia* (Lima, 1997), pp. 270–2, 282, 338; R. A. Clark, *Africa's Emerging Securities Markets: Developments in Financial Infrastructure* (Westport, 1998), pp. 69, 98, 167, 188; Abdul-Hadi, *Stock Markets of the Arab World*, pp. 20, 25, 29, 44; R. Chia, M. Usman, S. Gondokuaumo, and W. Cheong, *Globalization of the Jakarta Stock Exchange* (Singapore, 1992), pp. 13–14, 23, 33–6, 40–1, 60–70, 92, 157, 170; M. Xia, J. H. Lin, and P. D. Grubb, *The Re-emerging Securities Market in China* (Westport, 1992), pp. 59, 64, 105, 112; W. A. Thomas, *Western Capitalism in China: A History of the Shanghai Stock Exchange* (Aldershot, 2001), pp. 275–9, 287; Shenk, 'Regulatory Reform', pp. 147, 149, 154, 157–8, 160–2; Cascales and Ho, *Stock Exchange of Hong Kong*, pp. 2–11.
24. C-L. Holtfrerich, *Frankfurt as a Financial Centre: From Medieval Trade Fair to European Banking Centre* (Munich, 1999), pp. 277, 291–6; Amsterdam Stock Exchange, *A Century of Stock and Shares* (Amsterdam n.d.), pp. 24–5; M. Hart, J. Jonker, and J. L. Van Zanden, *A Financial History of the Netherlands* (Cambridge, 1997), p. 169; J. Hermans, *ICT in Information Services: Use and Deployment of ICT in the Dutch Securities Trade, 1860–1970* (Rotterdam, 2004), pp. 160–2; Cassis and Bussiere (eds.), *London and Paris*, pp. 233, 316–22; *The Economist, Directory of World Stock Exchanges* (London, 1988), pp. 10–11, 129, 180; Schwartz, *Electronic Call Auction*, p. 133.
25. *Historical Statistics of Japan*.
26. Lo (ed.), *Industrial Organization and Regulation*, pp. 1, 8, 10, 12, 51, 79–80, 257; Takagi (ed.), *Japanese Capital Markets*, pp. 57, 82–6, 127, 137, 143, 172–3, 145, 150–1, 172–3, 176–9, 182, 192, 234–7, 275, 277–8, 303–5, 309, 311–4; J. Isaacs and T. Ejiri, *Japanese Securities Market* (London, 1990), pp. 2–7, 27–9, 32–4, 43, 63, 71, 85; Schwartz, *Electronic Call Auction*, p. 125; P. A. David and M. Thomas (eds.), *The Economic Future in Historical Perspective* (Oxford, 2003), pp. 221–2.
27. Sobel, *Domestic Choices, International Markets*, p. 53; Cohen et al., *Microstructure of Securities Markets*, pp. 16, 25, 38–40, 44, 51–2, 57, 66–7, 83; Britton, *Monetary Regimes*, pp. 187, 196, 206, 214–16.
28. V. Conti, R. Hamaui, and H. M. Scobie (eds.), *Bond Markets, Treasury and Debt Management: The Italian Case* (London, 1994), pp. 225, 237; Geisst, *Wall Street*, pp. 349, 351; Dosoo, *Eurobond Market*, pp. 48, 52–4, 68.
29. D. Waldenstrom, *Why Are Securities Transactions Taxed?* (Stockholm, 2000), pp. 2, 21, 24, 28, 30–1.
30. Lo (ed.), *Industrial Organization and Regulation*, pp. 1–4, 10–11, 35, 94, 231–44.
31. *Statistical Abstract of the United States*, 1991 (Washington, 1991), pp. 514–15.
32. Lo (ed.), *Industrial Organization and Regulation*, pp. 1, 8, 10, 12, 51, 79–80, 257; Takagi (ed.), *Japanese Capital Markets*, pp. 57, 172–3, 145, 150–1, 172–3, 176–9, 182, 192, 234–7, 275, 277–8, 312–14.

33. Sobel, *Domestic Choices, International Markets*, p. 52.

34. Conti, Hamaui, and Scobie (eds.), *Bond Markets, Treasury and Debt Management*, pp. 225, 237; Geisst, *Wall Street*, pp. 349, 351; Dosoo, *Eurobond Market*, pp. 48, 52–4, 68.

35. Grant, *Bulls, Bears and Elephants*, pp. 328–9, 331, 352.

36. R. C. Koo in Takagi (ed.), *Japanese Capital Markets*, pp. 81, 239–41.

CHAPTER 9

1. Much of the information in this chapter has been culled from a daily reading of the *Financial Times*. Specific references are given, where appropriate, especially for direct quotation or in citing the views of others.

2. *Financial Times* 14 September 1990, 24 April 1997; International Financial Services (IFS), 'Securities Dealing', 5 July 2005.

3. IFS, 'Securities Dealing'.

4. R. C. Rajan and L. Zingales, *The Great Reversals: The Politics of Financial Development in the 20th Century* (OECD, 2000), p. 36.

5. *Financial Times*, 'Europe Reinvented' (London, 2001), part 2.

6. *Historical Statistics of Japan*: National Debt Tables; *Statistical Abstract of the United States, 2004/5* (Washington, 2004), p. 750.

7. IFS, 'Securities dealing'.

8. *Financial Times*, 'The FT global 500', 11 June 2005.

9. L. Oxelheim, *Financial Markets in Transition: Globalization, Investment and Economic Growth* (London, 1996), pp. 21–3, 45–6, 50–1, 135, 182, 188, 147, 166, 191; D. H. Aldcroft and M. J. Oliver, *Exchange Rate Regimes in the Twentieth Century* (Cheltenham, 1998), pp. 164–6; A. Britton, *Monetary Regimes of the Twentieth Century* (Cambridge, 2001), pp. 197, 206, 214, 216.

10. S. Homer and R. Sylla, *A History of Interest Rates* (New Brunswick, 1996), pp. 651–3; Rajan and Zingales, *The Great Reversals*, pp. 38–9.

11. J. O. Mathews, *Struggle and Survival on Wall Street* (New York, 1994), pp. 94–6, 114; R. A. Schwartz, *The Electronic Call Auction: Market Mechanism and Trading—Building a Better Stock Market* (Boston, 2001), pp. 215–16, 223; R. O. Wright, *Chronology of the Stock Market* (Jefferson, N.C.), p. 85; E. J. Perkins, *Wall Street to Main Street: Charles Merrill and Middle-Class Investors* (Cambridge, 1999), pp. 232, 258, 262.

12. Quoted in *Financial Times*, 12 May 2003.

13. *Financial Times*, 6 April 2000.

14. Extrapolated from the data in IFS, 'Securities Dealing'. Trading in the US bond market was estimated to be $125 trillion ($0.5 trillion a day over 250 working days) and US bonds comprised 40% of the domestic total outstanding, but they were also the most actively traded. Turnover in international bonds was stated to

be $50 trillion a year. Thus, $300 trillion appears a reasonable estimate. See also *Statistical Abstract of the United States, 2004/5*, p. 750.

15. P. Moore, *Autostrade to the Superhighway: The Future of Global Debt Markets* (London, 2001), pp. 16, 29, 48, 157; C-L. Holtfrerich, *Frankfurt as a Financial Centre: From Medieval Trade Fair to European Banking Centre* (Munich, 1999), p. 282; Y. Cassis and E. Bussiere (eds.), *London and Paris as International Financial centres in the Twentieth Century* (Oxford, 2005), pp. 320–3; V. Conti, R. Hamaui, and H. M. Scobie (eds.), *Bond Markets, Treasury and Debt Management: The Italian Case* (London, 1994), pp. 1, 6, 9–10; Oxelheim, *Financial Markets in Transition*, pp. 259–61, 283, 309–12, 318, 416–17.

16. *Financial Times*, 'Mastering Investment' (London, 2001), part 7, pp. 6–7.

17. J. A. Frankel (ed.), *The Internationalization of Equity Markets* (Chicago, 1994), pp. 1–3, 11–15.

18. *Financial Times*, 'Mastering Investment' (London, 2001), part 7, pp. 14–15; part 8, p. 14; part 9, p. 7.

19. IFS, 'Securities Dealing'.

20. *Statistical Abstract of the United States, 2004/5*, p. 872.

21. *Financial Times*, 11 June 2005.

22. M. E. Blume, J. J. Siegel, and D. Rottenberg, *Revolution on Wall Street: The Rise and Decline of the New York Stock Exchange* (New York, 1993); A. W. Lo (ed.), *The Industrial Organization and Regulation of the Securities Industry* (Chicago, 1996).

23. J. Hermans, *ICT in Information Services: Use and Deployment of ICT in the Dutch Securities Trade, 1860–1970* (Rotterdam, 2004), pp. 1, 55, 160–2.

24. Holtfrerich, *Frankfurt*, pp. 277, 282.

25. A. W. Lo (ed.), *The Industrial Organization and Regulation of the Securities Industry* (Chicago, 1996), pp. 275–7, 311.

26. R. A. Schwartz, *The Electronic Call Auction: Market Mechanism and Trading—building A Better Stock Market* (Boston, 2001), pp. 87, 125, 133; M. J. Cascales and M. Ho, *The Stock Exchange of Hong Kong: Past, Present and Future* (Hong Kong, 2000), pp. 2–12, 18; M. Giesecke, *La Bolsa de Valores de Lima: 140 Anos de Historia* (Lima, 1997), pp. 324, 328; R. A. Clark, *Africa's Emerging Securities Markets: Developments in Financial Infrastructure* (Westport, 1998), pp. 149, 177; W. A. Thomas, *Western Capitalism in China: A History of the Shanghai Stock Exchange* (Aldershot, 2001), pp. 275–9, 287.

27. Schwartz, *Electronic Call Auction*, p. 126; Y. Cassis and E. Bussiere (eds.), *London and Paris*, pp. 5, 231, 236, 319–23, 320–3; Cascales and Ho, *Stock Exchange of Hong Kong*, p. 11.

28. *Financial Times*, July 1997, 25 March 1998.

29. *Financial Times*, 'Mastering Finance' (London, 1997), part 11, p. 13.

30. *Statistical Abstract of the United States, 2004/5*, pp. 752, 753.

31. M. D. Bordo, A. M. Taylor, and J. G. Williamson (eds.), *Globalization in Historical Perspective* (NBER/Chicago 2003), pp. 121–2, 133, 141–4, 173–5, 218, 233, 283, 331, 356, 424–5, 461–3, 473, 488, 492, 497, 502–6, 511, 531–5, 539–40.

CONCLUSION

1. A. Crockett, T. Harris, F. S. Miskin, and E. N. White, *Conflicts of interest in the Financial Services Industry: What Should We Do About Them* (Geneva, 2004), p. 3, 56; R. Lee, *The Ownership of Price and Quote Information: Law, Regulation, Economics and Business* (Oxford, 1995), pp. 16–17, 21, 24–5, 54, 75, 184; R. Lee, *What is an Exchange? The Automation, Management, and Regulation of Financial Markets* (Oxford, 1998), pp. 1–3, 8, 11, 13, 15–16, 26, 29–30, 35–6, 42, 51, 55–9, 63, 99–101, 187, 192–3, 253.

Bibliography

A Century of Stocks and Shares: A Historical Sketch of the Vereniging voor de effecten-handel and the Amsterdam Stock Exchange (Amsterdam, n.d.).

Abdul-Hadi, A. S. F., *Stock Markets of the Arab World: Trends, Problems and Prospects for Integration* (London, 1988).

Aldcroft, D. H. and Oliver, M. J., *Exchange Rate Regimes in the Twentieth Century* (Cheltenham, UK, 1998).

Aldrich, W. W., *The Stock Market From the Viewpoint of a Commercial Banker* (New York, 1937).

Allen, F. and Gale, D., *Comparing Financial Systems* (Cambridge, MA, 2000).

Alletzhauser, A., *The House of Nomura* (London, 1990).

Areago, R. B., *Nigerian Stock Exchange: Genesis, Organisation and Operations* (Ibadan, 1984).

Armstrong, C., *Blue Skies and Boiler Rooms: Buying and Selling Securities in Canada, 1870–1940* (Toronto, 1997).

—— *Moose Pastures and Mergers: The Ontario Securities Commission and the Regulation of Share Markets in Canada, 1940–1980* (Toronto, 2001).

Baker, J. C., *The German Stock Market: Its Operations, Problems and Prospects* (New York, 1970).

Balderston, T. S., 'Universal Banks', in *New Palgrave Dictionary of Money and Finance* (London, 1992).

Balderston, 'German Banking 1913–1939' University of Manchester: Working papers in Economic and Social History no. 2 (1990).

Bank for International Settlements, 'Capital movements to and from London', pp. 18–25; 'International Movements of Capital and Prices', pp. 6–10; 'Reasons for the Movement of Capital to Paris in 1926–1928', pp. 4, 11; 'Movements of Capital in France From 1929 to 1933', p. 29 (May 1934).

Banner, S., *Anglo-American Securities Regulation: Cultural and Political Roots, 1690–1860* (Cambridge, 1998).

Baskin, J. B. and Miranti, P. J., *A History of Corporate Finance* (Cambridge, 1997).

Battilossi, S. and Cassis, Y. (eds.), *European Banks and the American Challenge: Competition and Co-operation in International Banking Under Bretton Woods* (Oxford, 2002).

Benn, A., *The Unseen Wall Street of 1969–1975* (Westport, CT, 2000).

Benson, R., *State Credit and Banking: During the War and After* (London, 1918).

Bernard, J., 'Trade and Finance in the Middle Ages, 900–1500', in C. M. Cipolla (ed.), *The Fontana Economic History of Europe: The Middle Ages* (London, 1972).

Bierman, H., *The Causes of the 1929 Stock Market Crash: A Speculative Orgy or A New Era* (Westport, CT, 1998).

Blume, M. E., Siegel, J. J., and Rottenberg, D., *Revolution on Wall Street: The Rise and Decline of the New York Stock Exchange* (New York, 1993).

Bordo, M. D. and Sylla, R. (eds.), *Anglo-American Financial System: Institutions and Markets in the Twentieth Century* (New York, 1995).

—— Taylor, A. M., and Williamson, J. G. (eds.), *Globalization in Historical Perspective* (Chicago, IL, 2003).

—— and White, E. N., 'British and French Finance During the Napoleonic Wars', in M. D Bordo and F. Capie (eds.), *Monetary Regimes in Transition* (Cambridge, 1994).

(Boston) *The Boston Stock Exchange* (Boston, MA, 1930).

Bouvier, J., 'The French Banks, Inflation and the Economic Crisis, 1919–1939', *Journal of European Economic History*, 13 (1984).

Britton, A., *Monetary Regimes of the Twentieth Century* (Cambridge, 2001).

Brooks, W. C., *How the Stock Market Really Works* (London, 1930).

Brown, A., *The Flight of International Capital: A Contemporary History* (London, 1988).

Bruchey, S., *Modernization of the American Stock Exchange, 1971–1989* (New York, 1991).

Bryan, M., *Taking Stock: Johannesburg Stock Exchange—the First 100 Years* (Johannesburg, 1987).

Burgess, W. R., *The Reserve Banks and the Money Market* (New York, 1927, revised edn. 1946).

Burk, K., 'Money and Power: The Shift From Great Britain to the United States', in Y. Cassis (ed.), *Finance and Financiers* (Cambridge, 1992).

Butlin, N. G., *Australian Domestic Product, Investment and Foreign Borrowing, 1861–1938/9* (Cambridge, 1962).

Cameron, R. (ed.), *Banking in the Early Stages of Industrialization* (New York, 1967).

Cameron, R. E., *France and the Economic Development of Europe, 1800–1914* (Princeton, NJ, 1961).

Cameron, R. and Bovykin, V. I. (eds.), *International Banking, 1870–1914* (New York, 1991).

Capie, F., *Capital Controls: A 'Cure' Worse Than the Problem* (London, 2002).

—— and Collins, M., *Have the Banks Failed British Industry* (London, 1992).

—— and Webber, A., *A Monetary History of the United Kingdom, 1870–1982* (London, 1985), pp. 516–77.

—— and Wood, E. (eds.), *Financial Crises and the World Banking System* (London, 1986).

Caprio, G. and Vitas, D. (eds.), *Reforming Financial Systems: Historical Implications for Policy* (Cambridge, 1997).

Carlos, A. M., Key, J., and Dupree, J. L., 'Learning and the Creation of Stock-Market Institutions: Evidence From the Royal African and Hudson's Bay Companies, 1670–1700', *Journal of Economic History*, 58 (1998).

Caron, F., 'France' in P. O'Brien (ed.), *Railways and the Economic Development of Western Europe, 1830–1914* (New York, 1983).

Carruthers, B. G., *City of Capital: Politics and Markets in the English Financial Revolution* (Princeton, NJ, 1996).

Carswell, J., *The South Sea Bubble* (revised edn.) (London, 1993).

Cascales, M. J. and Ho, M., *The Stock Exchange of Hong Kong: Past, Present and Future* (Hong Kong, 2000).

Cassesse, S., 'The Long-Life of the Financial Institutions Set Up in the Thirties', *Journal of European Economic History*, 13 (1984).

Cassis, Y. (ed.), *Finance and Financiers in European History, 1880–1960* (Cambridge, 1992).

—— and Bussière, E. (ed.), *London and Paris as International Financial Centres in the Twentieth Century* (Oxford, 2005).

—— Feldman, G. D., and Olsson, U. (eds.), *The Evolution of Financial Institutions and Markets in Twentieth Century Europe* (Aldershot, UK, 1995).

Center for Medieval and Renaissance Studies, *The Dawn of Modern Banking* (Los Angeles, CA, 1979).

Chaboz, E., *Vade-Mecum des Bourses de Bale, Zurich, Genève, 1907–1908* (Zurich, 1907).

Checkland, O. and Nishimura, S. (eds.), *Pacific Banking, 1859–1959: East Meets West* (London, 1994).

Cherrington, H. V., *The Investor and the Securities Act* (Washington, DC, 1942).

Chia, R., Usman, M., Gondokuaumo, S., and Cheong, W., *Globalization of the Jakarta Stock Exchange* (Singapore, 1992).

China Stock and Share Handbook (Shanghai, 1914).

Chiozza Money, L. G., *Money's Fiscal Dictionary* (London, 1910).

Ciocca, P. and Tiniolo, G., 'Industry and Finance in Italy, 1918–1940', *Journal of European Economic History*, 13 (1984).

Clark, R. A., *Africa's Emerging Securities Markets: Developments in Financial Infrastructure* (Westport, CT, 1998).

Clay, C., *Gold for the Sultan: Western Bankers and Ottoman Finance, 1856–1881* (London, 2000).

Cleveland, H. Van B. and Huertas, T. F., *Citibank, 1812–1970* (Cambridge, MA, 1985).

Clews, H., *Fifty years in Wall Street* (New York, 1908).

Cohen, K. J. et al., *The Microstructure of Securities Markets* (Englewood Cliffs, 1986).

Committee into Finance and Industry, *Minutes of Evidence* (London, 1931).

Conte, L., Toniolo, G., and Vecchi, G., 'Lessons from Italy's Monetary Unification (1862–1880) for the Euro and Europe's Single Market', in P. A. David and M. Thomas (eds.), *The Economic Future in Historical Perspective* (Oxford, 2003).

Conti, V., Hamaui, R., and Scobie, H. M., (eds.), *Bond Markets, Treasury and Debt Management: The Italian Case* (London, 1994).

Conway, T., *Investment and Speculation* (New York, 1911).

Cope, S. R., *Walter Boyd: A Merchant Banker in the Age of Napoleon* (Gloucester, 1983).

Correspondence of H. M. Embassy at Berlin, 1912—Stock Exchange Gambling (National Archives).

Corporation of Foreign Bondholders, *The Principal Foreign Loans* (London, 1877).

Costeloe, M. P., *Bonds and Bondholders: British Investors and Mexico's Foreign Debt, 1814–1888* (Westport, CT, 2003).

Cottrell, P. L., Teichova, A., and Yuzawa, T. (eds.), *Finance in the Age of the Corporate Economy* (Aldershot, UK, 1997).

Crockett, A., Harris, T., Miskin, F. S., and White, E. N., *Conflicts of Interest in the Financial Services Industry: What Should We Do About Them* (Geneva, 2004).

Cruise, D. and Griffiths, A., *Fleecing the Lamb: The Inside Story of The Vancouver Stock Exchange* (Vancouver, 1987).

David, P. A. and Thomas, M. (eds.), *The Economic Future in Historical Perspective* (Oxford, 2003).

Davies, A. E., *The Money, and the Stock and Share Markets* (London, 1920).

Davies, K. G., 'Joint-Stock Investment in the Later 17th Century', *Economic History Review*, 4 (1951–2).

Davies, L. E. and Cull, R. J., *International Capital Markets and American Economic Growth, 1820–1914* (Cambridge, 1994).

—— and Gallman, R. E., *Evolving Financial Markets and International Capital Flows: Britain, the Americas, and Australia, 1865–1914* (Cambridge, 2001).

Dawson, F. G., *The First Latin American Debt Crisis: The City of London and the 1822–25 Loan Bubble* (New Haven, CT, 1990).

Dice, C. A., *The Stock Market* (Chicago/New York, 1926).

Dickson, P. G. M., *The Financial Revolution in England: A Study in the Development of Public Credit, 1688–1756* (London, 1967).

Diedericks, H. and Reeder, D. (eds.), *Cities of Finance* (Amsterdam, 1996).

Dimsdale, N. and Prevezer, M. (eds.), *Capital Markets and Corporate Governance* (Oxford, 1994).

Doodha, K. D., *Stock Exchanges in a Developing Country* (Bombay, India, 1962).

Dosoo, G., *The Eurobond Market* (London, 1992).

Dowd, K. and Lewis, M. K. (eds.), *Current Issues in Financial and Monetary Economics* (New York, 1992).

Drake, P. J., *Money, Finance and Development* (Oxford, 1980).

Drummond, H., *Escalation in Decision-Making* (Oxford, 1996).

The Economist, *Directory of World Stock Exchanges* (London, 1988).

Edwards, J. and Ogilvie, S., 'Universal Banks and German Industrialization: A Reappraisal', *Economic History Review*, XLIX (1996).

—— and Fischer, K., *Banks, Finance and Investment in Germany* (Cambridge, 1994).

Eeda, T., 'The Role of the Securities Market in Industrialization in Japan' (unpublished paper 1994).

Ehrenberg, R., *Capital and Finance in the Age of the Renaissance* (1938; repr. New York, 1963).

Eichengreen, B., *Elusive Stability: Essays in the History of International Finance, 1919–1939* (Cambridge, 1990).

—— *The Gold Standard in Theory and History* (New York, 1985).

—— *Golden Fetters: The Gold Standard and the Great Depression, 1919–1939* (New York, 1992).

Einzig, P., *The Fight for Financial Supremacy* (London, 1931).

Eiteman, D. K., *Stock Exchanges in Latin America* (Ann Arbor, MI 1966).

Elon, A., *Founder: Meyer Amschel Rothschild and his Time* (London, 1996).

Emery, H. C., *Speculation on the Stock and Produce Exchanges of the United States* (New York, 1896).

English, W. B., 'Understanding the Costs of Sovereign Default: American State Debts in the 1840s', *American Economic Review*, 86 (1996).

The Exchange, Vol. I (December 1939) and (March 1940).

Fairman, W., *The Stocks Examined and Compared* (3rd edn.) (London, 1798).

Feinstein, C. H. (ed.), *Banking, Currency and Finance in Europe Between the Wars* (Oxford, 1995).

Feldman, G., Olssen, U., Bordo, M., and Cassis, Y. (eds.), *The Evolution of Modern Financial Institutions in the Twentieth Century* (Milan, 1994).

Ferguson, N., *The Cash Nexus: Money and Power in the Modern World, 1700–2000* (London 2001).

Financial Times 1980–2005.

Flandreau, M. and Zumer, F., *The Making of Global Finance, 1880–1913* (Paris, 2004).

Flink, S., *The German Reichsbank and Economic Germany* (1930; repr. New York, 1969).

Frankel, J. A. (ed.), *The Internationalization of Equity Markets* (Chicago, IL 1994).

Freedeman, C. E., 'The Growth of the French Securities Market, 1815–1870', in C. K. Warner (ed.), *From the Ancien Regime to the Popular Front* (New York, 1969).

—— *Joint-Stock Enterprise in France, 1807–1867* (Chapel Hill, NC 1979).

Friend, I., Hoffman, G. W., Winn, W. J., Hansburg, M., and Schlat, S., *Securities Markets* (New York, 1958).

—— *et al.*, *The Over-The-Counter Securities Market* (New York, 1958).

Gall, L., Feldman, G. D., James, H., Holfrerich, C-L., and Buschgen, H. E., *The Deutsche Bank, 1870–1995* (London, 1995).

Garg, K. L., *Stock Exchanges in India* (Calcutta, India 1950).

Gay, C. R., *Stock Market Controls* (New York, 1935).

—— *Wall Street in a Time of Change* (New York, 1936).

Gederblom, O. and Jonker, J., 'Completing a Financial Revolution: The Finance of the Dutch East India Trade and the Rise of the Amsterdam Capital Market, 1595–1612' (unpublished paper).

Geisst, C. R., *Visionary Capitalism: Financial Markets and the American Dream in the Twentieth Century* (New York 1990).

—— *Wall Street: A History* (Oxford, 1997).

General Securities Corporation, *The Investor's Handy Book of Active Stocks and Shares* (London, 1910).

George Gregory and Company, *Gregory's Hints to Speculators and Investors in Stocks and Shares* (London, 1895).

[Germany] 'The German Stock Exchanges: A History of Many Regions', *Germany's Almanac, 1985–6.*

Gibson, G. R., *The Berlin Bourse* (New York, 1890).
—— *The Vienna Bourse* (New York, 1892).
Giesecke, M., *La Bolsa de valores de Lima: 140 anos de historia* (Lima, 1997).
Giffen, Sir Robert, *Statistics* (London, 1913).
Goldsmith, R. W., *Comparative National Balance Sheets* (Chicago, IL, 1985).
—— (ed.), *Institutional Investors and Corporate Stock* (NBER, 1973).
Goldthwaite, R. A., *Private Wealth in Renaissance Florence: A Study of Four Families* (Princeton, NJ, 1968).
Gommel, R., 'The Modern Stock Market in Germany' (unpublished paper 1994).
Goodhart, C., 'Monetary Policy and Debt Management in the United Kingdom: Some Historical Viewpoints', in K. A. Chrystal (ed.), *Government Debt Structure and Monetary Conditions* (London, 1999).
Gordon, J. S., *The Great Game: The Emergence of Wall Street as a World Power, 1653–2000* (New York, 1999).
Grant, D., *Bulls, Bears and Elephants: A History of the New Zealand Stock Exchange* (Wellington, 1997).
Greenwood, W. J., *American and Foreign Stock Exchange Practice, Stock and Bond Trading and The Business Corporation Laws of All Nations* (New York, 1921).
Hall, A. R., *The Stock Exchange of Melbourne and the Victorian Economy, 1852–1900* (Canberra, 1968).
Hallinan, C. T., *American Investments in Europe* (London, 1927.
Hancock, D., *Citizens of the World: London Merchants and the Integration of the British Atlantic Community, 1735–1785* (Cambridge, 1995).
Hardach, G., 'Banking and Industry' *Journal of European Economic History*, 13 (1984).
Hart, M., Jonker, J., and Van Zanden, J. I., *A Financial History of the Netherlands* (Cambridge, 1997).
Hautcoeur, P.-C. and Verley, P., 'Le marche financier français' (unpublished paper 1994).
Hedges, J. E., *Commercial Banking and The Stock Market Before 1863* (Baltimore, MD, 1938).
Hermans, J., *ICT in Information Services: Use and Deployment of ICT in the Dutch Securities Trade, 1860–1970* (Rotterdam, The Netherlands, 2004).
Huebner, S. S. 'The Scope and Functions of the Stock Market', in *Annals of the American Academy of Political and Social Science*, 35 (1910).
Holtfrerich, C-L., *Frankfurt as a Financial Centre: From Medieval Trade Fair to European Banking Centre* (Munich, 1999).
Homer, S., *The Great American Bond Market: Selected Speeches* (New York, 1978).
—— and Sylla, R., *A History of Interest Rates* (New Brunswick, NJ, 1996).
Hoyo, A., 'La evolution del mercado de valores en Espana: La Bolsa de Madrid 1831–1874 (unpublished paper 1994).
International Financial Services, 'Securities Dealing' (London, 5 July 2005).
Isaacs, J. and Ejiri, T., *Japanese Securities Market* (London, 1990).
Israel, J. I., *Dutch Primacy in World Trade, 1585–1740* (Oxford, 1989).
—— 'The Amsterdam Stock Exchange and the English revolution of 1688', *Tijdschrift voor Geschiedenis*, 103 (1990).

James, H., Lindgren, H., and Teichova, A. (eds.), *The Role of Banks in the Interwar Economy* (Cambridge and Paris, 1991).

(Japan) *Historical Statistics of Japan.*

Jencken, H. D., 'On Some Points of Difference Between the English System of Law and That Prevailing on the Continent Regarding Negotiable Securities', *Journal of the Institute of Bankers,* I (1880).

Jonker, J., 'Fingers in the Dike, Fingers in the Pie: The Position of the Amsterdam Stock Exchange on the Dutch Capital Market, 1800–1940' (unpublished paper 1994).

—— *Merchants, Bankers, Middlemen, The Amsterdam Money Market during the First Half of the 19th Century, 1814–1863* (Cambridge, 1996).

—— and Van Zanden, J. L., 'Method in the Madness? Banking Crisis Between the Wars: An International Comparison', in C. H. Feinstein (ed.), *Banking, Currency and Finance.*

Jordan, D. F., *Investments* (New York, 1924).

Kaplan, J. J. and Schleiminger, G., *The European Payments Union: Financial Diplomacy in the 1950s* (Oxford, 1989).

Kay, J., *The Truth About Markets* (London, 2004).

Keenan, M., *Profile of the New York Based Security Industry* (New York, 1977).

Khan, M. S., *The Securities Market in Pakistan* (Karachi, 1993).

Kiehling, H., 'Efficiency of Early German Stock Markets, 1835–1848' (unpublished paper, Vienna, 2005).

Kindersley, R. M., 'British Foreign Investments in 1930', *Economic Journal,* 42 (1932); 44 (1934); 47 (1937); 48 (1938); 49 (1939).

Kindleberger, C. P., *A Financial History of Western Europe* (London, 1984).

—— 'Banking and Industry Between Two World Wars: An International Comparison', *Journal of European Economic History,* 13 (1984).

Kopper, C., 'Banking in National Socialist Germany, 1933–39', *Financial History Review,* 5 (1998).

Krishan,B., *Industrial Securities Market in India* (New Delhi, 1989).

Lazonick, W. and O'Sullivan, M., 'Finance and Industrial Development: Evolution to Market Control; Japan and Germany' *Financial History Review,* 4 (1997).

League of Nations, *Memorandum on Commercial Banks, 1913–1929* (Geneva, 1913).

Lee, R., *The Ownership of Price and Quote Information: Law, Regulation, Economics and Business* (Oxford, 1995).

—— *What is an Exchange? The Automation, Management, and Regulation of Financial Markets* (Oxford, 1998).

Leffler, G. L., *The Stock Market* (New York, 1951).

Le Maistre, G. H., *The Investor's India Year-Book* (Calcutta, India, 1911).

Levine, R. and Zervos, S., 'Stock Markets, Banks, and Economic Growth' *American Economic Review,* 88 (1988).

Lewis, C., *America's Stake in International Investments* (Washington, DC, 1938).

Liesse, A., *Evolution of Credit and Banks in France: From the Founding of the Bank of France to the Present* (Washington, DC, 1909).

Lindberg, C. A., *Banking and Currency and the Money Trust* (New York, 1913).

Lo, A. W. (ed.), *The Industrial Organization and Regulation of the Securities Industry* (Chicago, IL, 1996).

(London), *London Stock Exchange, Minutes of the Meeting for General Purposes, 15 May 1930.*

Londsdale, C., *The UK Equity Gap: The Failure of Government Policy* (Aldershot, UK, 1997).

Lorie, J. H. and Hamilton, M. T., *The Stock Market: Theories and Evidence* (Homewood, AL, 1973).

(Los Angeles), *Los Angeles Stock Exchange* (Los Angeles, 1939).

Lougheed, A. L., *The Brisbane Stock Exchange, 1884–1984* (Brisbane, 1984).

—— 'The London Stock Exchange boom in Kalgoorlie Shares, 1895–1901', *Australian Economic History Review*, 35 (1995).

Lowenfeld, H., 'The World's Stock Markets', *Financial Review of Reviews* (October, 1907).

McCaffrey, D. P. and Hart, D. W., *Wall Street Polices Itself: How Securities Firms Manage the Legal Hazards of Competitive Pressures* (New York, 1998).

Mackay, C., *Extraordinary Popular Delusions and The Madness of Crowds* (London, 1841; repr. in Wiley Investment Classics, New York, 1996).

Mathews, J. O., *Struggle and Survival on Wall Street* (New York, 1994).

Medbery, J. K., *Men and Mysteries of Wall Street* (New York, 1870).

Meeker, J. E., *Short Selling* (New York, 1932).

—— *The Work of the Stock Exchange* (New York, 1930).

Merret, D. T., 'Capital Markets and Capital Formation in Australia, 1890–1945', *Australian Economic History Review*, 37 (1997).

Meyer, C. H., *The Securities Exchange Act of 1934: Analyzed and Explained* (New York, 1934).

Michie, R. C., 'Banks and Securities Markets, 1870–1914', in D. J. Forsyth and D. Verdier (eds.), *The Origins of National Financial Systems* (London, 2003).

—— *The London Stock Exchange: A History* (Oxford, 1999).

Miller, E., 'Government Economic Policies and Public Finance, 1000–1500', in C. M. Cipolla (ed.), *The Fontana Economic History of Europe: The Middle Ages* (London, 1972).

Mitchell, B. R., *International Historical Statistics* (London, 1998), vol. 1–3.

—— *British Historical Statistics* (Cambridge, 1989).

Monroe, W. F., *Japan: Financial Markets and the World Economy* (New York, 1973).

Moody, J., *The Art of Wall Street Investing* (New York, 1906).

Moore, P., *Autostrade to the Superhighway: The Future of Global Debt Markets* (London, 2001).

Mueller, R. C., 'Foreign Investment in Venetian Government Bonds and the Case of Paolo Guinigi, Lord Lucca, Early Fifteenth Century', in Diedericks and Reeder (eds.), *Cities of Finance.*

Mulhall, M. G., *Industries and Wealth of Nations* (London, 1896).

—— *The Progress of the World* (London, 1880).

Murphy, A. E., *John Law: Economic Theorist and Policy-Maker* (Oxford, 1997).

Myers, M. G., *Paris as a Financial Centre* (London, 1936).

Nash, R. L., *A Short Inquiry into the Profitable Nature of Our Investments* (London, 1881).

Neal, L., 'On the Historical Development of Stock Markets', in H. Brezinski and M. Fritsch (eds.), *The Emergence and Evolution of Markets* (Cheltenham, UK, 1997).

—— *The Rise of Financial Capitalism: International Capital Markets in the Age of Reason* (Cambridge, 1990).

—— and Davis, L., 'The Evolution of the Rules and Regulations of the First Emerging Markets: The London, New York and Paris Stock Exchanges, 1792–1914', *Quarterly Review of Economics and Finance*, 45 (2005).

Nelson, S. A., *The ABC of Options and Arbitrage* (New York, 1904).

New York Stock Exchange, *Institutional Share-Ownership: A Report on Financial Institutions and the Stock Market* (New York, 1964).

Neymarck, M. A., *Le Statistique Internationale Des Valeurs Mobilières* (Institut International de Statistique, La Haye, 1911).

Noble, H. G. S., *The New York Stock Exchange in the Crisis of 1914* (New York, 1915).

Nomura Shoten, *Handbook of Japanese Securities* (Osaka, 1910).

North, D. C., 'International Capital Movements in Historical Perspective', in R. C. Michie (ed.), *Financial and Commercial Services* (Oxford, 1994).

Nötel, R., 'Money, Banks and Industry in Interwar Austria and Hungary', *Journal of European Economic History*, 13 (1984).

Nwankwo, G. O., *The Nigerian Financial System* (London, 1980).

O'Rourke, K. H. and Williamson, J. G., *Globalization and History: The Evolution of a Nineteenth Century Atlantic Economy* (Cambridge, MA, 1999).

Officer, L., Between *the Dollar–Sterling Gold Points* (Cambridge, 1996).

(Oslo), *Oslo Stock Exchange: Facts and Figures* (Oslo, 1986).

Oxelheim, L., *Financial Markets in Transition: Globalization, Investment and Economic Growth* (London, 1996).

Palmade, G. P., *French Capitalism in the Nineteenth Century* (Newton Abbott, 1972).

Parker, G., 'The Emergence of Modern Finance in Europe', in C. M. Cipolla (ed.), *The Fontana Economic History of Europe: The Sixteenth and Seventeenth Centuries* (London, 1974).

Parker, W., *The Paris Bourse and French Finance* (New York, 1920).

Patron, M., *The Bank of France in its Relation to National and International Credit* (Washington, DC, 1910).

Paulet, E., *The Role of Banks in Monitoring Firms: The Case of the Credit Mobilier* (London, 1999).

Perkins, E. J., *American Public Finance and Financial Services, 1700–1815* (Columbus, 1994).

—— *Wall Street to Main Street: Charles Merrill and Middle-Class Investors* (Cambridge, 1999).

Petit-Konczyk, M., 'Emergence of a French Regional Exchange: Lille Stock Exchange in the 19th Century' (working paper, Lille 2 University 2004).

Pick, F., *Common Stocks Versus Gold* (New York, 1963).

Platt, D. C. M., *Foreign Finance in Continental Europe and the United States, 1815–1870: Quantities, Origins, Functions and Distribution* (London, 1984).

Potter, M., *Corps and Clienteles: Public Finance and Political Change in France, 1688–1715* (Aldershot, UK, 2003).

Pressnell, L., *Money and Banking in Japan* (London, 1973).

Raines, J. P., *Economists and the Stock Market: Speculative Theories of Stock Market Fluctuations* (Cheltenham, UK, 2000).

Rajan, R. G. and Zingales, L., 'Financial Dependence and Growth', *American Economic Review* 88 (1988).

—— and —— *The Great Reversals: The Politics of Financial Development in the 20th Century* (Paris, 2000).

Reed, H. C., *The Pre-Eminence of International Financial Centres* (New York, 1981).

Riley, J. C., *International Government Finance and the Amsterdam Capital Market, 1740–1815* (Cambridge, 1980).

Roberts, R. (ed.), *International Financial Centres* (Aldershot, UK, 1994).

Root, H. L., *The Fountain of Privilege: Political Foundations of Markets in Old Regime France and England* (Berkeley, CA, 1994).

Roover, R. de, *Money, Banking and Credit in Medieval Bruges* (Cambridge, MA, 1948).

Rousseaux, P. L. and Sylla, R., 'Financial Systems, Economic Growth, and Globalization', in M. D. Bordo, A. M. Taylor, and J. G. Williamson (eds.), *Globalization in Historical Perspective* (Chicago, IL, 2003).

Royal Institute of International Affairs, *The Problem of International Investment* (Oxford, 1973).

Rungta, R. S., *Rise of Business Corporations in India, 1851–1900* (Cambridge, 1970).

Russian Journal of Financial Statistics (St Petersburg, 1899, 1900).

Salsbury, S. and Sweeney, K., *The Bull, the Bear and the Kangaroo: The History of the Sydney Stock Exchange* (Sydney, 1988).

Sarnat, M., 'The Emergence of Israel's Security Market: A Note', *Journal of Economic History*, 49 (1989).

—— *The Development of the Securities Market in Israel* (Tubingen, 1966).

Saugy, E. de (ed.), *Vade-mecum des Bourses de Bale, Zurich, Genève, 1913/14* (Zurich, 1913).

Schiller, R. J., *Irrational Exuberance* (New York, 2001).

Schmitz, C. J., *The Growth of Big Business in the United Sates and Western Europe, 1850–1939* (Cambridge, 1993).

Schubert, A., *The Credit-Anstalt Crisis of 1931* (Cambridge, 1991).

Schwabe, W. S., *Effect of War on Stock Exchange Transactions* (London, 1915).

Schwartz, R. A., *The Electronic Call Auction: Market Mechanism and Trading—Building a Better Stock Market* (Boston, MA, 2001).

Scott, I. O., *Government Securities Market* (New York, 1965).

Scott, W. R., *The Constitution and Finance of English, Scottish and Irish joint-Stock Companies to 1720* (Cambridge, 1912).

Scoville, W. C., *The Persecution of Huguenots and French Economic Development, 1680–1720* (Berkeley, CA, 1960).

(Seattle), *Seattle Stock Exchange, Report of the President* (Seattle, 1929–30).

Shenk, C. R., 'Regulatory Reform in an Emerging Stock Market: The Case of Hong Kong, 1945–1986', *Financial History Review*, 11 (2004).

Sheppard, D. K., *The Growth and Role of UK Financial Institutions, 1880–1962* (London, 1985).

Simha, S. L. N., *The Capital Market of India* (Bombay, India, 1960).

Smith, M. H., *Twenty Years Among the Bulls and Bears of Wall Street* (Harford, MD, 1870).

Snader, C. M., *A General Analysis of the Mexico City Stock Exchange: Its Limitations as a Free Market* (Mexico City, 1965).

Sobel, A. C., *Domestic Choices, International Markets: Dismantling National Barriers and Liberalising Securities Markets* (Ann Arbor, MI, 1994).

Spicer, E. E., *The Money Market in Relation to Trade and Commerce* (4th edn.) (London, 1924).

Spooner, F. C., *Risks at Sea: Amsterdam Insurance and Maritime Europe, 1766–1780* (Cambridge, 1983).

Spufford, P., *Money and its Use in Medieval Europe* (Cambridge, 1988).

Stancke, B., *The Danish Stock Market, 1750–1840* (Copenhagen, 1971).

Stasavage, D., *Public Debt and the Birth of the Democratic Sate: France and Great Britain, 1688–1789* (Cambridge, 2003).

Statistical Abstract of the United States, 2004/5.

Stonham, P., *Major Stock Markets of Europe* (Aldershot, UK, 1982).

The Story of the Johannesburg Stock Exchange, 1887–1947. (Johannesburg, 1948).

Suzuki, T., *Japanese Government Loan Issues on the London Capital Market, 1870–1913* (London, 1994).

Sylla, R., Tilly, A., and Tortella, G. (eds.), *The State, the Financial System and Economic Modernization* (Cambridge, 1999).

—— Wilson, J. W., and Wright, R. E., 'America's First Securities Markets, 1790–1830: Emergence, Development and Integration' (unpublished paper).

Tafunel, X. and Castaneda, L. 'La Bolsa de Barcelona entre 1849 y 1913' (unpublished paper 1994).

Takagi, S. (ed.), *Japanese Capital Markets: New Developments in Regulations and Institutions* (Oxford, 1993).

Tanzi, V. and Schuknecht, L., *Public Spending in the 20th Century* (Cambridge, 2000).

Taylor, G. V., 'The Paris Bourse on the Eve of the Revolution, 1781–1789', *American Historical Review*, 67 (1962).

Teichova, A., Gourvish, T., and Poyany, A. (eds.), *Universal Banking in the Twentieth Century* (Aldershot, UK, 1994).

—— Kurgan-Van Hentenryk, G., and Zeigler, D. (eds.), *Banking, Trade and Industry: Europe, America and Asia From the 13th to the 20th Century* (Cambridge, 1997).

Thomas, W. A., *Western Capitalism in China: A History of the Shanghai Stock Exchange* (Aldershot, UK, 2001).

Tilly, R. H., *Financial Institutions and Industrialization in the Rhineland, 1815–1870* (Maddison, UK, 1966).

Tilly, R. H., 'German Banking, 1850–1914: Development Assistance for the Strong', *Journal of European Economic History*, 15 (1986).

Torrente Fortuno, J. A., *Historia de la Bolsa de Madrid* (Madrid, 1974), vol. 1–3.

Tortella, G. and Palafox, J., 'Banking and Industry in Spain, 1918–1936', *Journal of European Economic History*, 13 (1984).

Tracy, J. D., *A Financial Revolution in the Hapsburg Netherlands: Renten and Renteniers in the County of Holland, 1516–1565* (Berkeley, CA, 1985).

Turner, A., 'British Holdings of French War Bonds: An Aspect of Anglo-French Relations during the 1920s', *Financial History Review*, 3 (1996).

Twentieth Century Fund, *The Security Markets* (New York, 1935).

Urquhart, M. C. and Buckley, K. A. (eds.), *Historical Statistics of Canada* (Toronto, 1965).

(United States) US Department of Commerce, *Historical Statistics of the United States: Colonial Times to 1970* (Washington, DC, 1975).

(United States) *Statistical Abstract of the United States, 2004/5* (Washington, DC, 2004).

Van Antwerp, W. C., *The Stock Exchange From Within* (New York, 1913).

Van der Wee, H., *The Growth of the Antwerp Market and the European Economy* (The Hague, 1963).

Veenendaal, A. J., *Slow Train to Paradise: How Dutch Investment Helped Build American Railroads* (Stanford, 1996).

Vega, Joseph de la, *Confusion de Confusiones* (Amsterdam, 1688; in English with an introduction by Herman Kellenbenz, 1957; repr. in Wiley Investment Classics, New York, 1996).

Vidal, E., *The History and Methods of the Paris Bourse* (Washington, DC, 1910).

Vries, J. de and Van der Woude, A., *The First Modern Economy: Success, Failure, and Perseverance of the Dutch Economy, 1500–1815* (Cambridge, 1997).

Wacha, D. E., *A Financial Chapter in the History of Bombay City* (Bombay, 1910).

Waldenstrom, D., *A Century of Securities Transaction Taxes: Origins and Effects* (Stockholm, 2000).

Waldenstrom, D., *Why are Securities Transactions Taxed?* (Stockholm, 2000).

Walter, I. (ed.), *Deregulating Wall Street: Commercial Bank Penetration of the Corporate Securities Market* (New York, 1985).

Walter, J. E., *The Role of Regional Security Exchanges* (Berkeley, CA, 1957).

Warshow, R. I., *Understanding the New Stock Market* (New York, 1934).

Weatherall, D., *David Ricardo: A Biography* (The Hague, 1976).

Webb, A. G., *The New Dictionary of Statistics* (London, 1911).

Wendt, P. F., *The Classification and Financial Experience of the Customers of a Typical New York Stock Exchange Firm, 1933 to 1938* (Maryville, TN, 1941).

Werner, W. and Smith, S. T., *Wall Street* (New York, 1991).

Westheimer, C., 'The Durable Cincinnati Stock Exchange', *Queen City Heritage: Journal of the Cincinnati Historical Society*, 49 (1991).

Whitney, R., *Economic Freedom* (Chicago, IL, 1934).

—— *Public Opinion and the Stock Market* (Boston, MA, 1931).

—— 'Statement to the Banking and Currency Committee' (1932).

—— radio broadcasts: 'Industry and Securities Markets' (1935), 'Security Markets and the People' (1935), 'The New York Stock Exchange' (1932), 'Short Selling' (1931), 'Short Selling and Liquidation' (1931).

Wicker, E., *Banking Panics of the Gilded Age* (Cambridge, 2000).

Wigmore, B. A., *The Crash and its Aftermath: A History of Securities Markets in the United States, 1929–1933* (Westport, CT, 1985).

Wildschut, H. W., *General Methods in Vogue with Dealings on the Amsterdam Stock Exchange* (Amsterdam, 1912).

Wilkins, M., *The History of Foreign Investment in the United States to 1914* (Cambridge, MA, 1989).

Wilson, C., *Anglo-Dutch Commerce and Finance in the 18th Century* (Cambridge, 1941).

Wright, R. E., 'Early US Financial Development in Comparative Perspective: New Data, Old Comparisons' (unpublished paper 2003).

—— *The Wealth of Nations Rediscovered: Integration and Expansion in American Financial Markets, 1780–1850* (Cambridge, 2002).

Wright, R. O., *Chronology of the Stock Market* (Jefferson, NC, 2002).

Wynne-Bennett, H. D., *Investment and Speculation* (London, 1924).

Xia, M., Lin, J. H., and Grubb, P. D., *The Re-emerging Securities Market in China* (Westport, CT, 1992).

Yogev, G., *Diamonds and Coral: Anglo-Dutch Jews and the Eighteenth Century Trade* (Leicester, UK, 1978).

(Zurich) *A Summary Chronicle of the Zurich Stock Exchange* (Zurich, 1977).

Index

The letter t indicates a table.

ADRs (American Depository Receipts) 248
AIM (Alternative Investment Market) 323
AT and T 223
Adelaide 106
agents-de-change 39, 51, 63, 94, 139, 140, 147, 208
alternative markets 105, 323
American Civil War 103
American Depository Receipts *see* ADRs
American Stock Exchange 220, 282
Amsterdam 9, 24–5, 34, 38, 46–9, 52–3, 56–7, 60, 61, 67, 68, 71, 77, 96, 112–13, 140, 148, 165, 176, 324
  Bank of Amsterdam (Wisselbank) 24, 27, 48
  Stock Exchange *see* stock exchanges: Amsterdam
Antwerp 22, 23, 24, 71
arbitrage 11
arbritageurs 114, 116, 135
Archipelago 308, 320
assets 5, 89–90t
Association of International Bond Dealers 249, 274
Australia 80, 164, 175–6, 285
  stock exchanges *see* stock exchanges: Australia; Brisbane; Melbourne; Sydney
Austria 77, 98, 170–1
  banks 128, 188
  national debt 41, 51, 134
  see also Vienna

backwardation 44
Bank Charter Act (1844) 75

Bank for International Settlements 181
bank notes 31
Bank of Amsterdam (Wisselbank) 24, 27, 48
Bank of England 29, 36, 42, 233, 277
  and South Sea Bubble 34, 35
Bank of Japan 231
Bank of the United States 55, 186
bankers: and speculation 36 *see also* merchant bankers
banks 1, 8, 15, 197–8, 267, 271, 278, 279, 283, 295, 330–2
  Austria 128, 188
  Bank for International Settlements 181
  Bank of Amsterdam (Wisselbank) 24, 27, 48
  Bank of Bombay 80
  Bank of England 29, 36, 42, 233, 277
  Bank of Japan 231
  Bank of the United States 55, 186
  Banque de Belgique 77
  Banque de France 51
  Britain 198 *see also* Bank of England
  Caisse des Depots et Consignations 62
  Caisse d'Escompte 41
  Canada 284–5
  central 4, 331
  Citibank 129, 130, 185
  collapse 169
  commercial 116, 129–30, 141
  and competition 301–2
  and credit 134
  Credit Mobilier 127–8
  Federal Reserve Bank 179, 181, 184, 185, 213

banks (*cont.*)
  France 41, 51, 62, 70, 127–8, 146–7,
      171–2, 187
  General Bank (later Royal Bank) 31, 32
  Germany 140, 171, 188, 240
  global 306–7
  and governments 191
  Italy 18, 187–8, 188
  Japan 231
  London 45, 116, 140, 198, 250 *see also*
      Bank of England
  Mexico 145
  Nederlandische Bank 241
  New York 116, 128, 164, 178
  nineteenth century 91
  Paris 140–1 *see also* Banque de
      France
  and railway investment 75–6
  Reichsbank 97
  Royal Bank (formerly General
      Bank) 32, 33, 34
  Second Bank of the United States 70
  Second World War 209
  Spain 187, 188
  and stock exchanges 140
  United States 55, 185, 127–8, 130,
      131, 179, 181, 184–5, 186, 187–8,
      213, 284
  universal 125–6
  World Bank 215, 245
Banque de France 51
Barnard's Act (1734) 45
Beirut 268
Belgium
  banks 77, 192
  railways 77
  stock exchanges *see* stock exchanges:
      Belgium; Bruges; Bruges
Berlin 77, 115, 148–9, 160, 176
  stock exchanges *see* stock exchanges:
      Berlin
Big Bang (London) 275–81, 322
bills of exchange 57
  Amsterdam 24

Antwerp 22–3
  Italy 18–19
  Vienna 41
bonds 6, 7, 75, 119–20, 147, 148, 308,
      311–13
  company 301
  Eurobonds 248–9
  France 94, 147
  Germany 189
  government 10, 60–1, 161, 293, 301
  international 246
  Italy 8–9, 17–18, 19, 21, 312
  Japan 230, 231, 288–9, 290, 293–4
  railway 87–8
  ratio to world GDP 299–301
  transferable 26
  United States 55, 68, 73, 151, 152, 164,
      165, 178, 182, 183, 213, 214, 218,
      270, 273, 292, 298, 317, 331
booms 80, 107, 108–9, 110, 180–1
  see also bubbles; Wall Street Crash
borrowers 10, 62 *see also* investors
bourses *see* stock exchanges
Brazil 109
Bretton Woods Agreement (1944) 215,
      274, 296
Britain
  banks 126, 127, 128
  First World War 156–7, 162
  national debts 43, 48, 53, 63, 65
  railways 74–6, 77, 78, 87, 88
British Government
  and borrowing 28, 42, 43
  and bubbles 31, 33, 34, 36, 37
Broken Hill Proprietary Mining
      Company 106
Broker Tec 312
brokers 278
  Canada 233, 283
  commission 72–3, 257–8, 262, 264,
      267
  communication 131
  eighteenth century 57
  international 306–7

Japan 283
London Stock Exchange 30, 262–3, 280–1
Netherlands 27, 49
regulations 64, 103
United States 283
see also Goldman Sachs; Merrill Lynch; Paine Webber; White Weld
Bubble Act (1720) 43
bubbles 2, 31–5, 36, 75–6, 198, 316
business rules: United States 55–6, 64

CATS (Computer Assisted Trading System) 266, 279
Caisse d'Escompte 41
Caisse des Depots et Consignations 62
call-over 236
Canada 176, 231–33
banks 11
First World War 164
stock exchanges *see* stock exchanges: Canada; Toronto
see also north America
canals 43–4, 45, 53, 74
Cantor Fitzgerald 312
capital flows 275
capital mobility 270
Charles Swab 307, 322
Chile 109
China 109, 110, 124–5, 141, 163–4, 227, 286–7
see also stock exchanges: China; Shanghai
Citibank 129, 130, 185
closed markets: London 54–5
codes of conduct
Amsterdam 49
London 45, 54
stock exchanges 11, 138
see also regulations
commission: brokers 72–3, 257–8, 261, 278, 285, 286, 287, 289
communication technology 296

communications 11, 83, 112–18, 130–1, 153, 248, 254, 291, 298–9, 307, 329, 336
see also telecommunications; telegraph systems
communist regimes 14, 268, 286
Compagnie des Indes *see* Mississippi Company
companies: and stocks 313–14
multinational 301, 324
see also firms
competition
stock exchanges 291, 309, 318–19, 339
Japan 266
London 280
Netherlands 267
New York 269
Computer Assisted Trading System *see* CATS
computer-based trading systems 256
computing technology 254, 287, 307–8, 316, 330
consols 44, 53, 66
continuation 44
Copenhagen 49, 99
corporate enterprise 301
corporate securities 81
sixteenth century 24
nineteenth century 70, 76, 91, 94
twentieth century 123, 125
corporate stocks 241, 244, 284
Britain 235, 263
Japan 290
United States 150, 151–2, 218, 269
costs 338
Coulisse (Paris) 1–5, 139, 172, 241
counter-party risk 62, 243, 310
Courts (Emergency Powers) Act (1915) 156
crashes *see* Wall Street Crash
credit 33, 57, 134
Credit Mobilier 127–8
Credit Suisse 274

curb markets 153, 159, 178, 182, 218, 220
currencies 131, 132, 248
  dollars (United States) 228, 272
  Eurodollars 248
  flotation 273
  francs (France) 250–1
  paper 51
  single European 311
  sterling 189

dealers: London 30, 44, 263 *see also*
    NASD
debts
  governments 38, 40, 51, 68, 69
    Italy 8–9, 18
    Netherlands 25
  see also global public debts; national
    debts
Denmark 49, 52, 99 *see also* Copenhagen
deposit banking 18
Deutsche Börse 325
Deutsche Telecom 300, 315, 316
discipline: London Stock Exchange
    54–5, 55
dividends: General Bank 31
dollars (United States) 246, 248, 272,
    273, 295
dot.com boom 3, 300, 302, 303, 316
Dutch East India Company 25
Dutch West India Company 26

E-Speed 312
East India Company (Britain) 28, 29,
    34, 42
economies 3
  global 12, 130–5, 179
  growth 5, 7
  integration 304
  Italy 18
electronic revolution 14
electronic securities market 256, 278,
    279, 320
electronic trading systems 287–8, 308,
    312, 323–4, 330

Ericsson (firm) 325
Eurobonds 248–9, 253, 255, 273,
    274–6, 280, 281, 287, 293,
    294, 306, 311
Eurodollars 248
EuroMTS 313
Euronext 326
euros *see* single European currency
exchange controls 204, 244–5, 247, 254,
    261, 270, 276, 280–1

FSA (Financial Services Authority) 313,
    324
Federal Reserve Bank 179, 181, 184, 185,
    213
Federal Reserve System 154, 179
financial centres 6
financial institutions *see* banks
financial systems 5–6, 7
firms 325–6 *see also* companies
First World War 156–69, 202, 203, 204,
    335, 336
Florence 17, 21
Foreign Funds market 67
foreign investment 246
forward trading 236
fragmentation 293
France 30, 84, 102, 140–1, 199
  banks 41, 51, 62, 70, 127–8, 146–7,
    171–2, 187
  bubbles 31, 33
  international investment 134, 250–1
  national debt 27, 34–5, 39, 41, 51, 62,
    63, 65, 84–5, 87, 114
  railways 77, 88
  taxation 139
  see also Paris
Frankfurt 52, 67, 68, 71, 78, 97,
    112, 239
  Stock Exchange *see* stock exchanges:
    Frankfurt
French East India Company 30
French Revolution 50–1,
    52, 56

General Bank (later Royal Bank)
31, 32
Germany 13, 48, 52, 69, 70, 96–8, 125,
126, 127, 130, 138–9, 148–9, 266,
288, 325
banks 128–9
impact of First World War 160, 162,
170–1
impact of Second World War
208, 209
investors 315
railways 77
stock exchanges *see* stock exchanges:
Berlin; Frankfurt; Germany
telecom companies 316
Glass–Steagall Act (1933) 5, 13, 193, 194,
322
global economy 130–6
global marketplace 15
global public debts 84
globalization 248, 254, 255, 296–7,
298–9, 304–9
gold 107, 108, 113, 134, 143, 196–7, 237,
272, 273
gold standard 13, 114, 131, 134, 179,
189, 205, 272
Goldman Sachs 283, 284, 306, 308, 322
governments 9, 24, 26, 28, 186–9, 204,
241–2
and control 5, 6, 7, 8, 12, 13, 14, 98,
111, 138–9, 216, 239, 240, 241,
242, 244, 246, 252–3, 264, 268,
272, 277, 286, 291, 292–3, 294,
295, 296, 297, 329, 335, 339
and debt *see* national debts
and global economy 131
and globalization 304–9
post First World War 165–7

Hatry, Charles 186–7
Hays, Andy 260
hedge funds 303
Hudson's Bay Company 28
Huguenots 31, 44, 52

IBM 223
ICAP 312
IMF (International Monetary
Fund) 215, 245
ISMA (International Securities Market
Association) 313
idle balances 45
immigrants 124
India 50, 80, 109–10, 111, 124, 200, 237
stock exchanges *see* stock exchanges:
India
inflation 41, 165, 170, 235, 335 *see also*
bubbles
informal markets 14
infrastrucure developments 73–4
Inglis, Sir R. W. 157
Instinet (Institutional Networks) 256,
282, 308, 320
insurance *see* marine insurance
insurance companies: nineteenth
century 91
Inter-Market Trading System 260
Interest Equalisation Tax (1963) 247,
273
interest rates: pre World War I 134
intermediaries *see* arbritageurs
International Bank for Reconstruction
and Development *see* World Bank
international bonds 246
International Federation of Stock
Exchanges 248
international investment
portfolios 12
pre World War I 132, 133
post-war 5
International Monetary Fund *see* IMF
international monetary system
272–3
international portfolio investment 12
International Securities Market
Association *see* ISMA
internationally mobile securities
167
internet 307, 316

investment
  foreign 246
  international portfolio 5, 12,
    132, 133
  pension fund 220–1, 291–2,
    303
investors 10, 36, 113, 308
  Middle Ages 18, 19–20
  seventeenth century 29
  eighteenth century 43–4, 46–8, 57
  nineteenth century 3–5, 63–4, 69,
    101–2, 106, 117
  twentieth century 124, 142, 174,
    177–8, 179–80, 200, 228, 230,
    300, 246, 302–3, 314, 315
Italy
  banks 169–70
  communications 112
  medieval 8–9, 17–21
  nineteenth century 98, 99

Japan 110, 111, 125, 329
  banks 129, 200
  nineteenth century 86, 92, 109
  First World War 162, 164
  Second World War 211
  post Second World War 229–31, 252,
    266, 288–90
  stock exchanges *see* stock exchanges:
    Japan; Tokyo
Jews: eighteenth century 44, 48
jobbers 30
joint-stock banks 70
joint-stock enterprises 10–11, 31–2, 34,
    38, 88, 105
  Middle Ages 20
  sixteenth century 23
  seventeenth century 28
  eighteenth century 38, 41, 43, 52
  nineteenth century 60, 67–8, 70,
    74–5, 80, 91, 101, 105,
    107, 117
  twentieth century 121, 122, 123, 124,
    128, 142, 301, 336

kings: and borrowing 20, 22, 23, 24,
    26–7, 28
Kuwait 268, 286

Latin America 124, 227–8
  stock exchanges *see* stock exchanges:
    Latin America
Law, John 31, 32, 33, 39
loans: Second World War 212
local securities markets, France
    77–8
London
  Big Bang 275–81
  as securities market 29–30, 44–5, 52,
    53, 54–5, 61, 65–6, 165, 172, 179,
    186–7
    domestic 174
    foreign 173–4, 247, 249–50, 272,
      291, 329
  Stock Exchange *see* stock exchanges:
    London
London Assurance 44

MTS (Mercato dei Titodoli Stato) 312,
    313
McFadden Act (1927) 178
Malaya 2
Maloney Act (1938)
    219
manufacturing: twentieth century 122
marine insurance 18, 24–5
Market Access 312
markets *see* alternative markets; national
    securities markets; OTC ("over-
    the-counter")markets; organized
    markets; stock markets;
    transnational markets
Marshall Aid 245
May Day change: New York Stock
    Exchange 260–1
Mercato dei Titodoli Stato *see* MTS
merchant bankers 19, 52
merchant banks 66
merchants 18–19, 36

mergers
  London Stock Exchange 263–4
  New York Stock Exchange 261
Merrill, Charles 185
Merrill Lynch 194, 215, 248, 258, 271,
    278, 279, 283, 284, 306–7, 322
Mexico *see* stock exchanges: Mexico
Microsoft 316, 320
mining 92, 100, 105, 106, 107, 108, 109,
    110, 113, 122–3, 143, 174, 196,
    232–3, 221
Mississippi Company 32–3, 35
mobile securities 168
mobile telephones 316
monetary integration: eighteenth
    century 57
monopolies
  agents-de-change 51
  India 237–8, 286
  stock exchanges 67, 237, 241, 243,
      261, 263, 289, 296,
      318, 330
  see also Mississippi Company
Monopolies and Mergers
    Commission 264
Morgan Stanley Dean Witter 307–8
multinational companies 301, 324
mutuality: stock exchanges 330

NASD (National Association of Security
    Dealers) 219, 256
NASDAQ (National Association of
    Security Dealers Automated
    Quotations) 256–7, 282, 284,
    316–17, 320–1
national assets 89–90t, 201t, 216t
National City Bank of New York 128,
    164
national debts
  eighteenth century 57
    Britain 43, 48, 53
    France 34–5
  nineteenth century 86–7, 114
    Britain 63, 65, 76, 85

France 62, 65, 84–5, 87, 114
Netherlands 61, 62
Ottoman Empire 85
Russia 85
United States 56, 61, 64–5, 70, 85,
    103, 104
twentieth century 120–1, 132–3,
    160–1, 164–5, 169, 210, 213,
    300–1
  Canada 176
  Japan 149
  Netherlands 242
  Russia 153–4, 165
  United States 154, 177, 194, 217
national economies 121–30
national governments 190–202, 204
national securities markets 244, 292
National Securities Regulation Act
    (1939) 212
nationalization: railways 121, 247
nationalized industries 13, 14
Nederlandische Bank 241
Netherlands 23, 168, 192, 199
  national debt 51–2, 61, 62, 85
  see also Amsterdam
Neuer Markt (Germany) 316
New Deal 204
New York 12, 55–6, 64, 79, 165, 168,
    177–8, 246, 284
  Stock Exchange *see* stock exchanges:
    New York
  and SEC 256
New York Curb Market 179, 182, 195,
    218, 219
New Zealand 175–6
  stock exchanges *see* stock exchanges:
    New Zealand
Nomura 279, 288
north America 11, 12 *see also* Canada;
    United States
Norway
  First World War 162
  stock exchanges *see* stock exchanges:
    Oslo

OTC ("over-the-counter") markets 104, 150, 153, 182, 193, 194–5, 196, 213, 214–15, 218–19, 221, 225–6, 227–8, 230, 253, 256, 257, 258, 269, 282, 293, 309–10
occupational pension funds 303
oil 145, 268, 273
"Open Board" (New York) 103
organized markets 309–10

Paine Webber 283
Pakistan 238
Palestine 200–1
Paris
Bourse *see* stock exchanges: Paris
Coulisse 94–5, 139, 172, 241
as securities market 62, 65–6, 67, 68, 165, 179, 251
pension fund investment 220–1, 291–2, 303
Peru 109
Philadelphia 55, 56, 64
Stock Exchange *see* stock exchanges: Philadelphia
Philip II, King of Spain 22
Postponement of Payments Act (1915) 156
prices 338
privatization 280, 300, 303

railways 74–6, 77, 78–9, 80, 82, 86, 101–2, 121–2, 125
stocks and bonds 87–8, 114, 144, 146, 148, 164, 174
regulations 270, 291–2, 305, 309, 324, 335, 337, 340
stock exchanges 327
London 71–2, 103, 234, 275, 277
New York 103, 141, 193–4, 321
see also codes of conduct; self-regulation
Reichsbank 97
Reliance Industries 286
rentes 63, 65, 69, 94, 114, 139

restrictive practices: stock exchanges 105, 242, 268, 277, 291, 309
Restrictive Practices Court 265
risk 206
counter-party 62, 243, 310
Royal Bank (formerly General Bank) 32, 33, 34
rubber 143–4
Russia 91–2, 99, 116, 123, 138, 142, 165, 227

SEC (Securities and Exchange Commission) 192, 213, 214, 217, 219, 221, 222, 224, 232–3, 256, 259–60, 261, 321
SIB (Securities and Investment Board) 277, 278, 279
Sabanes-Oxley Act (2002) 305
Salomon Brothers 260, 283, 322
Second Bank of the United States 70
Second World War 206–16, 335, 336
securities
corporate 81
sixteenth century 24
nineteenth century 70, 76, 91, 94
twentieth century 123, 125
and national economies 84–93
transferable 19, 25, 55, 337
Securities and Exchange Commission *see* SEC
Securities and Investment Board *see* SIB
Securities Exchange Act (1933) 192, 194
self-regulation 232, 240 *see also* regulations
shares 330
Dutch East India Company 25–6
General Bank 31
Mississippi Company 32
nineteenth century 91
railways 75
South Sea Company 33
and speculation 35
short-selling 236

short-term funds 57
single European currency 311
socialism 13
South Sea Bubble 31–5, 36, 42
South Sea Company 29, 33–4, 35, 42
Soviet Union *see* Russia
Spain 145
  communications 113
  national debt 23, 27
  railways 77
  stock exchanges *see* stock exchanges:
    Spain
  see also Philip II, King of Spain
speculation: canals 43–4 *see also* bubbles
state control *see* governments: and
    control
sterling 189
stock exchanges 7, 9, 10–15, 22, 23, 71,
    73, 83, 94, 100–11, 119–20,
    135–54, 136t
  Amsterdam 96, 112–13, 115, 140, 148,
    162–3, 176, 199, 241, 242, 266–7,
    324
  Australia 105–7, 108, 197, 212, 236,
    267, 285, 327–8
  Belgium 111, 145, 167, 192, 266
  Berlin 77, 97, 112, 115, 148, 160, 165,
    167, 176, 239
  Boston 102, 151, 164, 182, 194
  Brazil 109
  Brisbane 106, 107
  Brussels 71, 115, 145
  Bruges 22
  Cairo 153
  Calcutta 109, 110
  Canada 103, 105, 112, 138, 142, 164,
    190, 214, 232, 233, 265–6
  centralization 267
  Chile 109
  China 328
  Cincinnati 102
  communications 112–18
  Dublin 53–4, 55, 76
  Düsseldorf 239, 240

Eastern Europe 314
Egypt 111–12, 153, 192
Europe 93–9, 189, 239, 287, 324
Far Eastern Exchange 238
First World War 15–64
France 135
Frankfurt 97, 240, 251, 325
Geneva 138
Germany 34, 97, 112, 135, 138–9,
    148–9, 160, 176, 188, 189, 208,
    239–41, 266, 325
Glasgow 146
Hamburg 34, 97, 112, 239
Hong Kong 238, 268–9, 328
India 109–10, 170, 200, 212, 237–8,
    285, 286, 328
Jakarta 286
Japan 110, 229, 288, 327
Johannesburg 108, 143, 197, 237, 252,
    285, 328
Latin America 109, 174, 314–15
Lille 95
Lima 153, 210, 227, 327
Lisbon 265
London 45–6, 54, 59, 63, 64, 67, 71,
    76, 84, 92, 98–9, 100, 105, 115,
    123, 130–1, 145, 167, 189–90,
    192, 198, 200, 317, 341
  First World War 157
  Second World War 207, 208, 209
  post Second World War 233–5,
    247–8, 262–5, 270, 277–80, 319,
    323
Los Angeles 102–3
Luxembourg 176, 251
Madrid 71, 96, 113, 115, 160, 162, 208
Malaysia 238–9
Melbourne 105, 106, 107, 236
membership 339, 340
Mexico 108–9, 138, 145, 196,
    211, 228
Middle East 314
Milan 251, 267
Montreal 105, 112, 164, 265

stock exchanges (*cont.*)
  national 255, 261
  Netherlands 111, 266–7
  New York 64, 70–1, 73, 102, 103, 115,
      123, 130, 131, 149–50, 182, 192,
      194, 198–9, 255–61, 269, 317,
      319–20
    collapse 181
    First World War 157–8
    Second World War 207, 213–15
    post Second World War 217–18,
      256–61, 270, 278–9, 283
  New Zealand 107, 137, 197, 212,
      236–7, 285
  Nigeria 228, 268
  Osaka 110
  Oslo 99, 142
  Pakistan 238
  Paris 9, 11, 23, 39–40, 51, 52, 63, 68,
      69, 71, 77, 94–5, 115, 139, 147,
      160, 172, 208, 241, 251, 266, 270,
      288
  Peking 163–4
  Philadelphia 102, 260, 282
  post First World War 175
  post Second World War 227–37
  provincial 72, 76, 95, 102–3, 140, 149,
      150, 234, 263, 264
  reforms 261
  restrictive practices 105, 242
  Second World War 209
  St Petersburg 116, 138
  Shanghai 110, 141, 143–4, 159, 175,
      200, 211, 238, 287
  South Africa 10, 108, 143, 159, 197,
      212, 237, 267, 284, 328
  Spain 71, 96, 113, 115, 135, 163, 167,
      201
  Spokane 149, 151
  Sydney 106, 107, 108, 236
  Taranaki (New Zealand) 138
  Tel Aviv 200–1
  Toronto 105, 112, 164, 197, 232, 265,
      266

  United States 102–5, 138, 149, 167,
      195, 214, 220, 221–2, 259, 282
  Vancouver 214
  Vienna 41–2, 77, 97, 115, 209, 326
  Zurich 96, 144, 176, 251
stock markets
  collapse (1920s) 169
  crash (October 1987) 295
  global 313–29
stockbrokers *see* brokers
Stockholm 99, 168
stocks 6, 7, 68, 119–20, 308, 329
  corporate 241, 244, 284
  France 94
  Italy 8–9, 20
  Japan 230, 231, 293–4
  railways 75, 87–8, 148
  ratio to world GDP 299–300
  South Sea Company 33
  United States 150, 183–6, 213, 214,
      220–1, 223, 256, 293–4, 331
Swab, Charles *see* Charles Swab
Sweden 99, 129, 140, 168, 170, 292
Switzerland 49–50, 96, 99, 138, 144, 168,
      199, 210, 251–2

TMT (Technology, Media and
      Telecommunications) 3, 302
taxes 139, 292, 305
technology 282, 291, 308
telecommunications 190–1, 234, 243
telegraph systems 80–1, 82, 98, 107,
      112–13, 130–1, 336
telephones 112, 130, 191, 307, 336
  mobile 316
ticker tape 260
time bargains 45, 79
Tokyo
  as securities market 165, 252
  Stock Exchange *see* stock exchanges:
      Tokyo
trade
  Dutch East India Company 25
  medieval Italy 19

trade barriers 304, 305, 329, 338
Trade Web 312
trading 30, 334
trading networks 282
transferable bonds: Netherlands 26
transferable securities
    medieval Italy 19, 337
    sixteenth century 23, 25
    United States 55
transnational markets 255
transport 93 *see also* railways
Treasury bonds 273
trust networks 65

US Steel 150, 151, 165
USM (Unlisted Securities Market) 280
United States 9, 38, 50, 55–6, 84, 216–26
    banks 70, 116, 126–7, 129, 130, 178,
        179, 181, 184–185, 186, 187–8,
        213, 284
    joint-stock companies 70
    May Day 255–61
    national debt 56, 61, 64–5, 70, 85,
        103, 104
    railroads 78–9, 88
    stock exchanges *see* stock exchanges:
        Boston; Cincinnati; Los Angeles;
        New York; Philadelphia; Spokane;
        United States
Unlisted Securities Market *see* USM
unregulated trading 288, 336

Venice 17, 18, 21
Verenigde Oostindische Compagnie
    (VOC)
    see Dutch East India Company
Vienna 69
    Bourse *see* stock exchanges: Vienna
Virt-X 324, 326
Vodafone 325

Wall Street Crash 12–13, 176–87, 191,
    204, 216, 306, 335, 340
War Bonds: First World War
        174
wars
    effects of 50, 51, 52, 60, 61, 84–5, 102,
        201, 335–6
        First World War 156–69, 202, 203,
        204
        Second World War 206–16
    funds for
        United States 50, 57
        Venice 17, 18
Weeden & Co. 248
White Weld 274
William III, King 28–9
Wisselbank *see* Bank of Amsterdam
World Bank 215, 245
world economy 12
world monetary system: collapse 13
World Wars: cost of 5, 12, 13 *see also*
        wars: effects of